Ninth Edition

The Urban World

J. John Palen

Paradigm Publishers
Boulder • London

For Madeleine, Jack,
Conor, and Emmett who are growing
up in an urban world

First edition copyright © 1975 by The McGraw-Hill Companies, Inc.
Sixth edition copyright © 2001 by The McGraw-Hill Companies, Inc.
Seventh edition copyright © 2005 by The McGraw-Hill Companies, Inc.
Eighth edition copyright © 2008 by Paradigm Publishers
Ninth edition copyright © 2012 by Paradigm Publishers

Published in the United States by Paradigm Publishers, 2845 Wilderness Lane, Boulder, CO 80301 USA.

Paradigm Publishers is the trade name of Birkenkamp & Company, LLC,
Dean Birkenkamp, President and Publisher.

Library of Congress Cataloging-in-Publications Data
Palen, J. John.
    The urban world / J. John Palen. — 9th ed.
        p.   cm.
    Includes bibliographical references and index.
    ISBN 978-1-61205-043-0 (pbk. : alk. paper)
1. Cities and towns.   2. Cities and towns—United States.   3. Urbanization—Developing countries.   I. Title.

    HT151.P283 2012
    307.76—dc23

                                                                    2011017729

Printed and bound in the United States of America on acid-free paper that meets the standards of the American National Standard for Permanence of Paper for Printed Library Materials.

Designed and Typeset by Mulberry Tree Enterprises.

16   15   14   13   12   1   2   3   4   5

Brief Contents

Part I Focus and Development

1 The Urban World   2
2 The Emergence of Cities   19

Part II American Urbanization

3 The Rise of Urban America   50
4 Ecology and Political Economy
   Perspectives   72
5 Metro and Edge City Growth   90
6 The Suburban Era   115

Part III Metropolitan Life

7 Urban Culture and Lifestyles   148
8 The Social Environment of Metro
   Areas: Strangers, Crowding,
   Homelessness, and Crime   167
9 Diversity: Women, Ethnics, and
   African Americans   188
10 Diversity: Hispanics, Asians, and
    Native Americans   210

Part IV Metro Issues, Housing, Sprawl, and Planning

11 Cities and Change   230
12 Housing Policies, Sprawl, and
    Smart Growth   247
13 Planning, New Towns, and
    New Urbanism   266

Part V Worldwide Urbanization

14 Developing Countries   294
15 Asian Urban Patterns   309
16 African and Latin American
    Urbanization   330
17 Conclusion: Toward the
    Urban Future   353

Name Index   373
Subject Index   377
About the Author   386

Contents

List of Boxes   x
Preface   xi
New to This Edition   xi
Pedagogical Aids   xiv
Acknowledgments   xiv

Part I Focus and Development

1 The Urban World   2

Introduction   2
The Process of Urbanization   3
Urban Growth   3
Megacities   4
The Urban Explosion   6
Defining Urban Areas   7
Urbanization and Urbanism   8
   Urbanization   8
   Urbanism   9
Organizing the Study of
  Urban Life   10
Concepts of the City   11
   Urban Change and Confusion   11
   Rural Simplicity versus Urban
     Complexity   12
Early Social Theories and Urban Change   12
   European Theorists   12
   The Chicago School   15
Summary   16
Review Questions   17

2 The Emergence of Cities   19

Introduction   19
The Ecological Complex   20
Political Economy Models   21

First Settlements   22
   Agricultural Revolution   22
   Population Expansion   23
   Mesoamerica   24
Interactions of Population, Organization,
  Environment, and Technology   25
City Populations   26
Evolution in Social Organization   26
   Division of Labor   27
   Kingship and Social Class   28
Technological and Social Evolution   28
Urban Revolution   29
Survival of the City   29
The Hellenic City   30
   Social Invention   30
   Physical Design and Planning   31
   Population   31
   Diffusion of People and Ideas   32
Rome   32
   Size and Number of Cities   33
   Housing and Planning   33
   Transportation   34
   Life and Leisure   34
European Urbanization until the
  Industrial City   35
   The Medieval Feudal System   36
   Town Revival   36
   Characteristics of Towns   37
   Plague   38
   Renaissance Cities   39
Industrial Cities   43
   Technological Improvements and
    the Industrial Revolution   43
   The Second Urban Revolution   43
Summary   45
Review Questions   46

Part II American Urbanization

3 The Rise of Urban America 50

Introduction 50
Colonists as Town Builders 50
Major Settlements 52
    New England 52
    The Middle Colonies 53
    The South 53
    Canada 54
Colonial Urban Influence 54
Cities of the New Nation 1790–1860 54
    Rapid Growth 56
    Marketplace Centers 57
The Industrial City: 1860–1950 58
    Technological Developments 58
    Spatial Concentration 59
    Twentieth-Century Dispersion 60
Political Life 63
    Corruption and Urban Services 63
    Political Bosses 63
    Immigrants' Problems 64
    Reform Movements 65
Urban Imagery 65
    Ambivalence 65
    Myth of Rural Virtue 68
Summary 69
Review Questions 69

4 Ecology and Political Economy Perspectives 72

Introduction 72
Development of Urban Ecology 73
    Invasion and Succession 74
    Criticisms of Ecology 74
    Role of Culture 75
Burgess's Growth Hypothesis 75
    Concentric Zones 77
    Limitations 79
Sector and Multiple-Nuclei Models 79
Urban Growth Outside North
    America 80
The Postmodern City: The Los Angeles
    School 82
Political Economy Models 82
Political Economy Assumptions 84
Examples of the Political Economy
    Approach 85
    The Baltimore Study 85

Urban Growth Machines 85
World Systems Theory and
    Globalization 86
    Challenges 86
Summary 87
Review Questions 88

5 Metro and Edge City Growth 90

Introduction 90
Metropolitan Growth 91
    In-Movement: 1900 to 1950 93
    Out-Movement: 1950 into the
        21st Century 95
Commuting and Communication 95
Canadian Urban Regions 97
Postindustrial Central Cities 97
Edge Cities 99
    Edgeless and Private Edge Cities 99
    Boomburgs 100
    Suburban Business Growth 100
    Malling of the Land 102
    Malls and "Street Safety" 103
Nonmetropolitan Growth 105
    Diffuse Growth 105
    National Society 105
The Rise of the Sunbelt 106
    Population and Economic
        Shifts 106
    Regional Consequences 108
    Sunbelt Problems 109
Movement to the Coasts 110
Summary 111
Review Questions 112

6 The Suburban Era 115

Introduction 115
Suburban Dominance 116
Emergence of Suburbs 116
    The 19th Century 117
    Electric Streetcar Era: 1890–1920 117
    Annexation 118
    Automobile Suburbs:
        1920–1950 118
    Mass Suburbanization:
        1950–1990 120
    Metro Sprawl: 1990–2010 121
Causes of Suburban Growth 123
    Postwar Exodus 123
    Non-Reasons 125

Contemporary Suburbia   126
Categories of Suburbs   127
   Persistence of Characteristics?   127
   Ethnic and Religious Variation   128
   High-Income Suburbs   128
   Gated Communities   130
   Common-Interest
     Developments   130
   Working-Class Suburbs   131
   Commercial Definitions   132
Exurbs   133
Rurban Areas   133
Characteristics of Suburbanites   134
Suburban Poverty   134
The Myth of Suburbia   135
Minority Suburbanization   137
   Suburban Diversity   137
   Black Flight   140
   Integration or Resegregation?   141
Latino Suburbanization   141
Asian Suburbanites   142
Summary   142
Review Questions   144

Part III Metropolitan Life

7 Urban Culture and Lifestyles   148

Introduction   148
Social Psychology of Urban Life   149
   Early Formulations   149
   The Chicago School   150
   "Urbanism as a Way of Life"   151
Reevaluation of Urbanism and Social
   Disorganization   152
   Determinist Theory   152
   Compositional Theory   153
   Subcultural Theory   154
Characteristics of Urban Populations   154
   Age   154
   Gender   155
   Race, Ethnicity, and Religion   155
   Socioeconomic Status   155
Urban Lifestyles   157
   Cosmopolites   157
   Unmarried or Childless   157
   Gay Households   157
   Ethnic Villagers   158
   Neighborhood Characteristics   160

Deprived or Trapped   162
A Final Note of Caution   163
Summary   164
Review Questions   165

8 The Social Environment of Metro
Areas: Strangers, Crowding, Homelessness,
and Crime   167

Introduction   167
Dealing with Strangers   168
Codes of Urban Behavior   169
   Neighboring   169
   Neighbors and Just Neighbors   170
Defining Community   170
Categories of Local Communities   171
Density and Crowding   172
   Crowding Research   173
   Practical Implications   175
Homelessness   175
   Characteristics of the Homeless   176
   Social Problems   177
   Disappearing SRO Housing   178
Urban Crime   178
   Crime and Perceptions of Crime   178
   Broken Windows Theory   179
   Crime and City Size   180
   Crime and Male Youth   181
   Crime and Race   181
   Crime Variations within Cities   183
   Crime in the Suburbs   183
Summary   184
Review Questions   184

9 Diversity: Women, Ethnics, and
African Americans   188

Introduction   188
Women in Metropolitan Life   189
   Female Domesticity   189
   Gendered Organization of
     Residential Space   190
   Feminist Housing Preferences   191
   Cohousing and Downsizing   191
   Current Housing Choices   192
   Gendered Public Spaces   193
   Workplace Changes   193
White Ethnic Groups   194
   Immigration   194
   First-Wave Immigrants   194
   Second-Wave Immigrants   195

Third-Wave Immigrants   195
"Racial Inferiority" and
Immigration   197
African Americans   198
Historical Patterns   198
Population Changes   199
Slavery in Cities   199
"Free Persons of Color"   200
Jim Crow Laws   200
"The Great Migration"   200
Moving South   201
Urban Segregation Patterns   201
Extent of Segregation   201
Housing Discrimination   202
21st-Century Diversity   203
The Economically Successful   203
The Disadvantaged   204
Summary   205
Review Questions   206

10   Diversity: Hispanics, Asians, and
Native Americans   210

Introduction   210
Fourth-Wave Immigrants   211
Recent Immigration Impact
on Cities   211
Melting Pot or Cultural
Pluralism   212
Latino Population   213
Legal Status   214
Growth   214
Diversity   215
Mexican Americans   216
Mexican Diversity   216
Education   217
Urbanization   217
Housing and Other Patterns   218
Political Involvement   218
Puerto Ricans   219
Asian Americans   219
A "Model Minority"?   220
Asian Residential Segregation   221
The Case of Japanese Americans   222
The Internment Camps   222
Japanese Americans Today   223
Native Americans   224
Nonurban Orientation   224
Movement to Cities   225
Summary   226
Review Questions   226

**Part IV   Metro Issues, Housing,
Sprawl, and Planning**

11   Cities and Change   230

Introduction   230
The Urban Crisis: Thesis   230
Urban Revival: Antithesis   231
A Political Economy Look at the
Urban Crisis   231
21st-Century City Developments   233
New Patterns   233
Central Business Districts   234
Mismatch Hypothesis   235
Downtown Housing   235
Fiscal Health   236
Crumbling Infrastructure   237
Neighborhood Revival   237
Gentrification   239
Government and Revitalization   240
Who Is Gentrifying?   240
Why Is Gentrification Taking
Place?   240
Displacement of the Poor   242
Decline of Middle-Income
Neighborhoods   242
Successful Working-Class Revival   243
Summary   243
Review Questions   245

12   Housing Policies, Sprawl, and
Smart Growth   247

Introduction   247
Housing in the 21st Century   248
Mobility   248
Housing Costs   248
Changing Households   249
Changing Federal Role   249
Federal Housing Administration
(FHA) Programs   250
Subsidizing Segregation   251
Upper- and Middle-Class
Housing Subsidies   251
Urban Redevelopment Policies   251
Critique of Urban Renewal   252
Phasing Out Public Housing   253
Urban Homesteading   254
Rent Vouchers: Section 8   255
HOPE VI Projects   255
Tax Credits   257

Designing for Safety   257
Growth Control   258
Suburban Sprawl   259
 Auto-Driven Sprawl   259
 Amount of Sprawl   259
 Costs and Consequences   260
Smart Growth   261
 Advantages   261
 Legislation   262
Summary   263
Review Questions   264

13 Planning, New Towns, and
New Urbanism   266

Introduction   266
 Ancient Greece and Rome   267
 Renaissance and Later
  Developments   267
American Planning   268
 Washington, D.C.   269
 19th-Century Towns   269
 Early Planned Communities   270
 Parks   270
 The City Beautiful Movement   271
 Tenement Reform   273
20th-Century Patterns   273
 The City Efficient   273
 Zoning and Beyond   274
 Master Plans to Equity
  Planning   275
 Crime Prevention through
  Environmental Design   275
European Planning   277
 Planning and Control
  of Land   278
 Housing Priorities   278
 Transportation   279
 Urban Growth Policies   279
 The Dutch Approach   280
New Towns   280
 British New Towns   280
 New Towns in Europe   283
American New Towns   284
 Public-Built New Towns   284
 Federal Support for
  New Towns   284
 Private New Towns: Reston,
  Columbia, and Irving   285
 Research Parks   286

New Urbanism or Traditional
 Neighborhood Developments   286
 Celebration   287
 Creating Community   287
 Limitations   288
Summary   288
Review Questions   289

Part V Worldwide Urbanization

14 Developing Countries   294

Introduction: The Urban Explosion   294
 Megacities   295
 Plan of Organization   295
 Common or Divergent Paths?   295
Developing-Country Increases   297
Rich Countries and Poor Countries   299
Global Cities   300
Characteristics of Third World
 Cities   300
 Youthful Age Structure   300
 Multinationals   301
 The Informal Economy   301
 Squatter Settlements   303
 Primate Cities   303
 Overurbanization?   305
The 21st Century   305
Summary   306
Review Questions   307

15 Asian Urban Patterns   309

Introduction   309
 Asian Cities   310
 Indigenous Cities   310
 Colonial Background Cities   310
India   312
 Mumbai (Bombay)   312
 Kolkata (Calcutta)   314
 Prognosis   315
China   316
 Treaty Ports   316
 Urbanization Policies   317
 Forced Movement from Cities   317
 Rural to Urban Migration   317
 Economic Boom   318
 Shanghai   318
 Beijing   320
 Hong Kong   321

Japan   321
    Extent of Urbanization   322
    Current Patterns   323
    Tokyo   323
    Planning   325
    Planned New Towns   325
    Suburbanization   325
Southeast Asia   325
    General Patterns   325
    Singapore   326
    Other Cities   327
Summary   328
Review Questions   328

16 African and Latin American
    Urbanization   330

Introduction   330
Africa   330
    Challenges   331
    Responses   332
    Regional Variations   333
Urban Development   333
    Early Cities   333
    Colonial Period   334
    Indigenous African Cities   335
    Contemporary Patterns   335
    Social Composition of African Cities   336
    Ethnic and Tribal Bonds   338
    Status of Women   338
    Differences from the Western
        Pattern   339
Latin America: An Urban Continent   340
Spanish Colonial Cities   340
    Colonial Organization   341
    Physical Structure   341
Recent Developments   343
    Urban Growth   343
    Economic Change   345
    Urban Characteristics   345
    Crime   345

Shantytowns   346
Future of Settlements   346
Maquiladoras   348
Myth of Marginality   348
A Success Story   349
Summary   349
Review Questions   350

17 Conclusion: Toward the
    Urban Future   353

Recapitulation   353
    Urban Concentration   353
    Deconcentration   354
Issues and Challenges   355
    Urban Funding   355
    People versus Places   356
    Changing Metropolitan
        Population   356
    Suburban Development   357
Social Planning Approaches   358
    Three Approaches to Social
        Planning   358
    Social Planning and
        Technology   359
Planning for the Future City   360
    Planned Utopias   360
    Las Vegas   363
    Quality-of-Life Planning   363
    Smart Cities   364
    Planning Metropolitan Political
        Systems   365
    A Working City   367
Toward a Metropolitan Future   368
Summary   369
Review Questions   370

Name Index   373
Subject Index   377
About the Author   386

List of Boxes

2.1 The Spanish on First Viewing
      Mexico City   24

2.2 Preindustrial and Industrial Cities:
      A Comparison   41

2.3 Engels on Industrial Slums   44

3.1 A Note on Urban Pollution   61

3.2 Carl Sandburg's Chicago   67

4.1 Ecology of the City: The Barbary
      Coast of San Francisco   78

4.2 A Note on Urbanization and
      Environment   81

5.1 Defining Metropolitan Areas   94

5.2 The Ultimate Malls   104

6.1 The Suburbs in Song   135

6.2 Case Study: Levittown   136

7.1 Montreal and the "Quiet
      Revolution"   156

7.2 Brain-Gain Cities   158

8.1 Street Etiquette   182

11.1 New Orleans: An American Tragedy   234

11.2 Harlam Uneasily Confronts
       Gentrification   238

12.1 Sprawl versus a Suburban Mother   262

13.1 Jane Jacobs: A Prophet in Her Time   276

15.1 Density and Economic
       Development   322

16.1 A Case Study of an Indigenous
       City   337

16.2 Mexico City   347

17.1 New Planned Capitals   362

Preface

This is the ninth edition of *The Urban World*. Since the last edition was written just a handful of years ago, urban life has experienced some major changes. Probably the factor having the greatest impact has been the economic consequences of the Great Recession. Recent years have seen the deepest economic and housing recession since the Depression of the 1930s. Today's urban change often comes with remarkable speed. For example, in 2007 Las Vegas seemed a charmed boomtown, the nation's fastest growing city. Only three years later Las Vegas was notable for being in severe recession and having the highest home foreclosure rate in the country. We live in a time of major urban change.

To give students some perspective on the fast pace of urban change it is worth noting that almost all of us reading this book grew up in cities or suburbs. And we assume that most of the world's population shared our experiences. However, the fact is that every one of us reading this book was born into a world that was predominately rural. Not until the early twenty-first century did more than half the world's people actually live in urban rather than rural places.

My goal has been to convey to students some of my own excitement over all the changes taking place in the urban environment. The world of the future will be an urban world, so it is important that we try to understand urban change and how urbanism as a way of life affects our lives and behavior. *The Urban World* is written to give students a coherent overview of the contemporary urban scene. To accomplish this it draws upon a wide body of research—including demographic, sociological, geographic, and urban studies—to provide up-to-date information on urbanization and the nature of urban life.

LOW PRICE

Both students and instructors will be happy to see that in an academic world where textbook prices constantly move ever higher, *The Urban World* is an exception. The ninth edition increases the text's strengths while holding down the text's price. *The Urban World* now is published in a quality paperback format with an affordable price. This means the instructor, if she or he chooses, can assign additional materials while keeping the total student cost reasonable.

NEW TO THIS EDITION

The Urban World is the most adopted urban text, and the ninth edition seeks to be readable, comprehensive, balanced, and up-to-date. This edition is designed to expose students to both an understanding of past urban trends and to the emerging twenty-first-century urban patterns. The text is organized into seventeen chapters, with chapters written in a self-contained manner that permits instructors to restructure topics to best suit their unique course interests and needs. A refreshed design includes updated figures and new photos. A large test bank file is also available for instructors' use.

A good textbook should provide a strong base, while also reflecting contemporary developments. Thus, the ninth edition contains updated data and reflects new developments such as:

- The impact of the Great Recession and the virtual collapse of the housing market.
- The hidden growth of suburban poverty.
- The continued growth of Latinos as the largest U.S. minority, and the demographic and social consequences of this change.
- Latest census findings from the United States and Canada and discussion of how the metro areas of both nations are changing. The political effect of reapportionment based on the 2010 census is discussed and illustrated.

  A NOTE ON 2010 CENSUS DATA: Results from the 2010 census continue to be released throughout 2011, 2012, and beyond. Results available as of press time for the ninth edition are included throughout the text.
- The rebirth of central cities and its causes and consequences (such as whether Vancouver—site of the 2010 Winter Olympics—has been too successful in having people move back into downtown).
- The post-recession future of North American cities.
- The dramatic changes taking place in the cities of the world's two largest nations, India and China.
- The future of urban developments such as smart growth, new urbanism, and the "greening" of cities (e.g., Chicago's turn-

ing the roof of City Hall into a garden of grass, plants, and trees).
- New worldwide urban developments such as Dubai having the tallest building in the world as of 2010 and Abu Dhabi's building a whole new city of the future.

The text seeks to continue its clear writing style with strong student appeal. What also hasn't changed are enduring features such as strong academic content and instructor-friendly organization. *The Urban World* is in its ninth edition because it successfully works as a text.

ORGANIZATION

Part One: Focus and Development begins by examining the dramatic changes caused by urbanization and the impact of the worldwide urban explosion. Concepts of the city and early theories of urban change are presented in Chapter 1. Chapter 2 looks at how and why cities emerged and at urban places from the earliest settlements up to the Industrial Revolution. The use of Ecological Complex and Political Economic Models is also discussed.

Part Two: American Urbanization switches the focus to North America. Chapter 3 discusses the rise of urban America and the importance of urban technology, immigrants, political bosses, and reform movements to contemporary cities. The impact of the American ambivalence about cities and our myth of rural virtue are also discussed. Chapter 4 presents competing models for understanding urban spatial patterns. Ecological and Political Economy models are presented and there is a discussion of the new Los Angeles School and the postmodern city. Chapter 5 looks at metropolitan out-movement and edge city growth. The unique characteristics of edge cities, the malling of the land, and the future of the Sunbelt are all covered. The ramifications of political reapportionment favoring the South and West based on the 2010 census are examined. Chapter 6 provides extensive discussion of the development of suburban dominance. Suburbs are seen moving from fringe settlements to the demographic and economic centers of the nation. The causes of suburbanization and categories of suburbs are discussed, as is the myth of suburbia. Data on the recession-based increase in suburban poverty are included. The latest census and other data are provided on African American, Latino, and Asian suburbanites.

Part Three: Metropolitan Life shifts from a macro focus on metro areas to the micro level of how urbanism affects the lives and lifestyles of those within the metro area. Chapter 7 explores urban lifestyles and the social psychology of urban life. The Chicago School, Compositional, and Subcultural theories of urban life are examined. Chapter 8 continues the discussion of urban life with an examination of how we deal with strangers, the codes of urban behavior, and the effects of density and crowding. The changing situation and characteristics of homeless people are examined. Urban crime variations and the Broken Window theory are discussed. Chapter 9 presents a discussion of urban diversity, focusing on the experiences of women, white ethnics, and African Americans. Issues such as the gendering of public spaces, changing immigration patterns, and urban segregation patterns are covered. The black "Great Migration" from the South to northern cities is discussed, as is the current movement of African Americans toward Southern urban areas. Chapter 10 continues the focus on urban diversity. Detailed discussion is provided on Latino, Asian American, and Native American patterns of urbanization. New data on the continued growth and diversity of Latino populations are discussed. The growth of Asian populations and the problem of being a "model minority" are covered as is the movement of Native Americans to metro areas.

Part Four: Metro Issues: Housing, Sprawl, and Planning moves the focus to contemporary issues over how to plan and design the city.

Chapter 11 discusses the impact of the housing recession. Also discussed are the urban crisis and urban revival theses and current issues such as downtown revitalization and neighborhood gentrification. What is the future of the urban core? Chapter 12 discusses the effects of the housing market downturn. It also contains material on the changing federal role from FHA loans to urban redevelopment policies to HOPE VI projects, to programs to prevent homes from foreclosures. Moving beyond the more immediate economic downturn there is also a discussion of the growing problems of commuting, suburban sprawl, and the development of Smart Growth policies. Chapter 13 extends the discussion of how to use urban space by examining planning policies in the United States and Europe. New Towns in both Europe and America are examined, and the growth of Traditional Neighborhood Developments and New Urbanism communities is discussed.

Part Five: Worldwide Urbanization takes us beyond North America and Western Europe to look at new and changing urbanization patterns in Asia, Africa, and Latin America. Chapter 14 provides new data on the rapid changes in developing countries. Chapter 15 looks at the cities of Asia and especially at the dramatic developments in the world's two largest nations of India and China. Chapter 16 discusses the social consequences of urbanization trends in both Africa and Latin America and the growing power of Brazil. The influence of colonial patterns is examined as is the effect of ethnic differences. The impact of the city on the status of women is discussed as is the role played by shantytowns and the myth of marginality. Issues covered include AIDS, crime, and squatter settlements.

Chapter 17, the Conclusion, looks toward the urban future. The Conclusion adds material on new developments from the ecological planting on the roof of Chicago's City Hall with grass and trees, to encouraging the use of bikes, to the building of whole cities of the future in Abu Dhabi and other Gulf States.

ENDURING FEATURES

The Urban World is the only American text to provide Canadian content throughout the text in order to provide a comparative North American context. *The Urban World* also remains the only urban text to devote two full chapters to minorities in metro areas. Specific discussion is given to emerging topics such as the increasing presence of minorities in suburbs. Chapter 9 discusses women, ethnic minorities, and African Americans while Chapter 10 covers the experiences of minority groups newer to the American city: Latinos, Asians, and Native Americans.

PEDAGOGICAL AIDS

The ninth edition of *The Urban World* provides a chapter OUTLINE at the beginning of each chapter and a SUMMARY at the chapter end. Additionally, to help answer the age-old student question, "What do we need to know?" each chapter concludes with REVIEW QUESTIONS prepared by the author. A student who can satisfactorily answer these questions knows the text material. Also available to the instructor is an extremely large and comprehensive test bank.

ACKNOWLEDGMENTS

For this ninth edition, it has been my good fortune to be able to work with a fine set of professionals at Paradigm Publishers, an independent press devoted to student-friendly texts and professor-friendly publishing. Special thanks go to Jennifer Knerr as Vice President and Executive Editor, Dean Birkenkamp as Publisher, Terra Dunham as College Marketing Associate, and Carol Smith as Director of Editorial Production. Legions of reviewers, instructors, and stu-

dent users of the text have improved it over the years. Here, to name only a few, are some of the people who have made this text possible:

Anna Bounds, Queens College
Obie Clayton, Morehouse College
George H. Conklin, North Carolina Central University
Sachi G. Dastidar, SUNY–Old Westbury
Kirk D. Fasshauer, Florida Southern College
Daniel Fischer, Mercer University
Karl Flaming, University of Colorado, Denver
Kate H. Fletcher, University of Florida
Joseph Galaskiewicz, University of Arizona
Joan M. Gibran, Tennessee State University
Janell Gibson, Keiser University
Katherine Johnson, Niagara County Community College
Marilyn C. Krogh, Loyola University, Chicago
Yvonne McDonald, Winston-Salem State University
Richard Mordi, Keiser University
James Mulvihill, California State University, San Bernardino
Charles Perabeau, Olivet Nazarene University
Dorothy Remy, University of the District of Columbia
Robert Ross, Clark University
David S. Surrey, St. Peters College
Karen Tejada, University of Hartford
Joshua Tetteh, Missouri Valley College
Frederick E. S. Wagg, Virginia Commonwealth University
Rachael Woldoff, West Virginia University

My thanks for your efforts.

—*J. John Palen*

Part I

FOCUS AND DEVELOPMENT

CHAPTER 1

The Urban World

A city is a collective body of persons sufficient in themselves for all purposes of life.
Aristotle, Politics

OUTLINE

Introduction
The Process of Urbanization
Urban Growth
Megacities
The Urban Explosion
Defining Urban Areas
Urbanization and Urbanism
    Urbanization
    Urbanism
Organizing the Study of Urban Life
Concepts of the City
    Urban Change and Confusion
    Rural Simplicity versus Urban Complexity
Early Social Theories and Urban Change
    European Theorists
    The Chicago School
Summary

INTRODUCTION

The second decade of the 21st century is witnessing major urban changes. The last decade saw the globe change from a predominantly rural world to one where the majority of us live in urban places. For the first time in history we now live in an urban world. The United Nations estimates that *all* worldwide growth in the next 30 years will be in urban areas.

Closer to home in North America, the United States population passed 308 million in 2010, and four out of five Americans now live in metropolitan areas. The situation is similar for Canada's 34 million people.

This text explores and explains the patterns of urban life in the second decade of the 21st century. Its goal is to help us better understand the cities and suburbs where most of us live, and to give us some awareness of the major urban changes taking place elsewhere on the globe. To do this, we begin at the beginning, since without knowing how we got here it is difficult to make sense of what is happening, both in North America and in the developing world where the great bulk of urban growth is now taking place. As you read the following chapters, keep in mind that the one constant in urban areas is change. Metropolitan areas are not museums but are constantly undergoing physical and social change.

THE PROCESS OF URBANIZATION

Cities, it turns out, are a relatively new idea. Archaeologists tell us that the human species has been on the globe several million years. However, for the overwhelming number of these millennia our ancestors lived in a world without cities. Cities and urban places, in spite of our acceptance of them as an inevitable consequence of human life, are in the eyes of history hardly even a blink. Not until the end of the last ice age around 11,000 years ago did the first villages emerge. Cities are a comparatively recent social invention, having existed at most 7,000 to 10,000 years. Their period of social, economic, and cultural dominance is even shorter.

Nonetheless, the era of cities encompasses the totality of the period we label "civilization." The story of human social and cultural development—and regression—is in major part the tale of the cities that have been built and the lives that have been lived within them. The saga of wars, architecture, and art—almost the whole of what we know of human triumphs and tragedies—is encompassed within the period of cities. The very terms *civilization* and *civilized* come from the Latin *civis*, which refers to a citizen living in a city. The city was civilization; those outside were barbarians. Among the ancient Greeks the greatest punishment was to be ostracized (banned) from the city. In Roman times *civitas* referred to the political and moral nature of community, while the term *urbs*, from which we get the term *urban*, referred more to the built form of the city.

The vital and occasionally magnificent cities of the past, however, existed as small islands in an overwhelmingly rural sea. Just over 200 years ago, in the year 1800, the population of the world was still 97 percent rural.[1] In 1900 the world was still 86 percent rural. A hundred years ago the proportion of the world's population living in cities of 100,000 or more was only 5.5 percent, and only 13.6 percent lived in places of 5,000 or more. While cities were growing very rapidly, most people still lived in the countryside or small villages. Today we live in a world that for the first time numbers more urban than rural residents. Demographically, the 21st century is the world's first urban century (Figure 1.1).[2]

URBAN GROWTH

The rapidity of the change from rural to urban life is at least as important as the amount of urbanization. A hundred and twenty-five years ago not a single nation was as urban as the world is today. The urban transformation initially took place in Europe and countries largely settled by Europeans, such as the United States, during the 19th century and the first half of the 20th century. These were the places that first developed modern agricultural, transportation, and industrial technologies. England, the first country to enter the industrial age, was also the first country to undergo the urban transformation. A century ago England became the world's only predominantly urban country.[3] Not until 1920 did half the population of the United States reside in urban places, and not until 1931 was this true of Canada. Figures 1.1 and 1.2 dramatically indicate how the urban population of the world has increased over the last century and will continue to expand. This rapid growth of cities during the 19th and 20th centuries is sometimes referred to as the *urban revolution*.

We take large cities for granted. Almost everyone reading this book has spent at least part of their lives living in a central city or suburb, so it is difficult for us to conceive of a world without large cities. However, 100 years ago only 12 cities housed a million or more inhabitants.

The rapidity and extent of the urban revolution can perhaps be understood if one reflects that if San Antonio, with a year 2010 population of 1.4 million, had had the same population two centuries ago, it would have

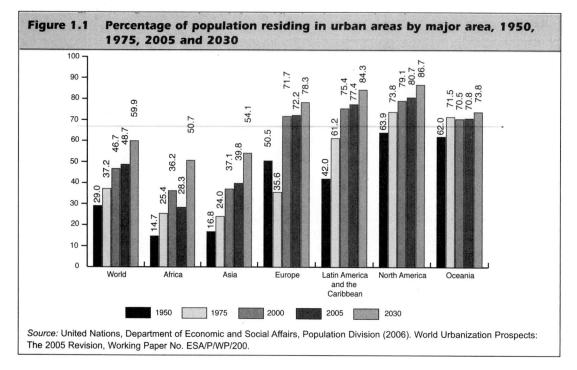

Figure 1.1 **Percentage of population residing in urban areas by major area, 1950, 1975, 2005 and 2030**

Legend: ■ 1950 □ 1975 ▨ 2000 ▨ 2005 □ 2030

Source: United Nations, Department of Economic and Social Affairs, Population Division (2006). World Urbanization Prospects: The 2005 Revision, Working Paper No. ESA/P/WP/200.

been the largest urban place.[4] By 2030—less than two decades from now—some 60 percent of the world's people will live in urban places.

By contrast, the United Nations estimates that as of 2005 some 414 cities had over a million inhabitants. More than a third of these cities first reached the million mark in the last 15 years. We now live in an urban world of mega-metropolises; Tokyo–Yokohama has a population of 36 million and greater Mexico City has 20 million. Within the United States the 2010 census reported the New York–New Jersey–Long Island metro area at 20 million and Los Angeles–Riverside–Orange County (California) at 16 million. Chicago–Gary (Indiana)–Kenosha (Wisconsin) was third largest at 9 million. Metro Toronto in Canada has 5 million.

MEGACITIES

Today, 95 percent of all urban growth is taking place not in Europe or North America, but in rapidly growing cities in the developing world. Some of this change is breathtakingly fast. In Beijing, China, the equivalent of three Manhattans were added to its skyline just for the 2008 Olympics. Twenty-first century world urbanization patterns are different from those of the twentieth century. Today developed Western nations are experiencing little urban growth. Of the 414 previously noted cities of over a million inhabitants, some two-thirds are in developing countries. Few of us could name more than a few dozen of such million-plus developing world cities. The United Nations uses the term *megacities* to designate places of over 10 million inhabitants. As recently as 1950 only New York and Tokyo had megacity status. By contrast, the World Bank estimates that there are now 26 megacities. Of these 26 megacities, 21 are found in developing countries. Mumbai (previously designated Bombay), India, for example, even with falling growth rates is still adding half a million new city residents each year. It is difficult for us to keep up either intellectually or emotionally with these changes.

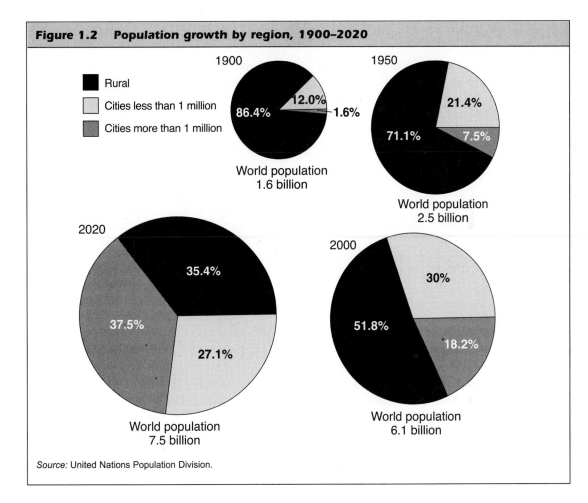

Figure 1.2   Population growth by region, 1900–2020

1900

■ Rural
□ Cities less than 1 million
▨ Cities more than 1 million

86.4%   12.0%   1.6%

World population
1.6 billion

1950

71.1%   21.4%   7.5%

World population
2.5 billion

2020

35.4%   37.5%   27.1%

World population
7.5 billion

2000

51.8%   30%   18.2%

World population
6.1 billion

Source: United Nations Population Division.

The United Nations estimates that 15 new megacities will be added to the globe between 2000 and 2015, all of them in the developing world. As of 2010, the United Nations estimated a population of 19.4 million for the megacity of Mexico City; 23 million for metropolitan São Paulo, Brazil; 23 million for Mumbai; and 16.5 million for Shanghai. Some demographers, such as this author, think these estimates are high by several millions, but by any measure these megacities dwarf anything the world has ever experienced. The United Nations estimates that by 2020, nine cities—Delhi, Dhaka, Jakarta, Lagos, Mexico City, Mumbai, New York, São Paulo, and Tokyo—will have more than 20 million inhabitants.[5]

Some of our difficulty in understanding or coping with urban patterns and problems can be attributed to the newness of the emergence of this urban world with its huge megacities. Living as we do in developed, Western, urban-oriented places, it is easy for us to forget three important facts:

First, even in the industrialized West, massive urbanization is a very recent phenomenon. This rapid transformation from a basically rural to a heavily urbanized world, and the development of urbanism as a way of life, have been far more dramatic and spectacular than the much better known population explosion. Today, the number of people living in cities of the developing world outnumbers the entire population of the world only 100 years ago.

Second, over 95 percent of future urban growth will occur in cities of the developing world. The population explosion is, in reality, a third world urban explosion.

Third, about half the urban residents in developing countries live in slums. There are currently some 1 billion slum dwellers, and this will rise to 2 billion slum dwellers by 2030.[6]

THE URBAN EXPLOSION

Urban growth first accelerated cumulatively during the 19th and 20th centuries. By 1800, London, the largest city on earth, reached almost 1 million, Paris exceeded 500,000, and Vienna and St. Petersburg had each reached 200,000. A century later, as the 20th century began, 10 cities had reached or exceeded 1 million: London, Paris, Vienna, Moscow, St. Petersburg, Calcutta, Tokyo, New York, Chicago, and Philadelphia. This urban explosion, which will be discussed in greater detail later, began over 200 years ago in the more developed nations of Europe. Among the more important reasons for this spurt in European population were (1) declining death rates, (2) the beginning of scientific management of agriculture, (3) improved transportation and communication systems, (4) stable political governments, and (5) the development of the Industrial Revolution. While details differ from country to country, the pattern for Western nations is similar. Improvements in agriculture raised the surplus above previous subsistence levels. Then, in rather short order, entrepreneurs, and later governments, transferred this extra margin into the manufacturing sector. The result was urban expansion and growth fed by a demand from the burgeoning manufacturing, commercial, and service sectors for a concentrated labor force. Today the developed world is over three-quarters urban. By contrast, only 41 percent of those in developing countries live in urban areas.

Heavy urbanization in the developing world is largely a post–World War II phenomenon (see Chapter 14: Developing Countries). The pace of urbanization in developing countries has been far more rapid than that found during the 19th century in Europe or North America. Note in Table 1.1 the dramatic projection of African, and especially Asian, urban growth over the next half century. At the same time the United Nations anticipates a declining population in Europe.

Whether we are delighted by the variety and excitement of urban life or horrified by the anonymity and occasional brutality of

Table 1.1	Percentage Urban by Major Area, Selected Periods, 1950–2030						
	Percentage urban					Rate of urbanization (percentage)	
	1950	**1975**	**2000**	**2005**	**2030**	**1950–2005**	**2005–2030**
World	29.0	37.2	46.7	48.7	59.9	0.94	0.83
Africa	14.7	25.4	36.2	38.3	50.7	1.75	1.12
Asia	16.8	24.0	37.1	39.8	54.1	1.57	1.23
Europe	50.5	65.6	71.7	72.2	78.3	0.65	0.33
Latin America and the Caribbean	42.0	61.2	75.4	77.4	84.3	1.11	0.34
Northern America	63.9	73.8	79.1	80.7	86.7	0.42	0.29
Oceania	62.0	71.5	70.5	70.8	73.8	0.24	0.17

Source: United Nations, Department of Economic and Social Affairs, Population Division, 2006. World Urbanization Prospects: The 2005 Revision, Working Paper No. ESA/P/WP/2000.

cities, population concentration—that is, urbanization—is becoming the way of life in developing as well as developed nations. Attempts to return to a supposedly simpler rural past must be viewed as futile escapism. Longings for a pastoral utopia where all exist in rural bliss have no chance of becoming reality. We live in an urban world; and for all our complaints about it, few would reverse the clock.

DEFINING URBAN AREAS

Before proceeding further, it is necessary to define some of the terms we will be using. This is not altogether as simple as it might seem, since countries differ in how they define a place as *urban*. About thirty definitions of *urban population* are currently in use, none of them totally satisfactory. Urban settlements have been defined on the basis of an urban culture (a cultural definition), administrative functions (a political definition), the percentage of people in nonagricultural occupations (an economic definition), and the size of the population (a demographic definition). In the United States, we define places as urban by using population criteria along with some geographical and political elements. In actual practice the various criteria tend to overlap and be reinforcing. Let us look briefly at some of the criteria that can be used. In terms of cultural criteria, a city is "a state of mind, a body of customs and traditions."[7] The city thus is the place, as sociologists put it, where relations are *gesellschaft* (larger-scale "societal" or formal role relationships) rather than *gemeinschaft* (more intimate-scale "community" or primary relationships) and forms of social organization are organic rather than mechanical (see p. 14). In short, the city is large, culturally heterogeneous, and socially diverse. It is the antithesis of "folk society." The problem with the cultural definitions of an urban place is the difficulty of measurement; for example, if a city is a state of mind, who can ever say where the boundaries of the urban area lie?

The United Nations has urban data for some 228 countries and accepts each nation's definition of what it considers urban. This makes cross-nation comparisons difficult. Economic activity is used in defining what is urban in 39 countries. In terms of economic criteria, a country has sometimes been described as urban if less than half its workers are engaged in agriculture. Here *urban* and *nonagricultural* are taken to be synonymous. This distinction, of course, tells us nothing about the degree of urbanization or its pattern of spatial distribution within the country. Distinctions have also been made between the town as the center for processing and service functions and the countryside as the area for producing raw materials. However, while in the past these distinctions may have had utility, today it is difficult to distinguish among areas by means of such criteria. How far out do the producing and service functions of a New York or a Los Angeles extend?

Politically or administratively a national government may define its urban areas in terms of functions. Roughly half the nations for which the United Nations has data use administrative criteria.[8] The difficulty is that there is no agreement internationally on what the political or administrative criteria should be. Often those residing in the capital of a country or a province are designated as urban. In some countries such as Kenya and Thailand, all incorporated places are urban, regardless of size. In Canada until 1971 all incorporated places were automatically urban.

Finally, some 51 countries use size of population as the criterion in deciding what is urban and what is not. Demographically, a place is defined as being urban because a certain number of people live in it, a certain density of people is within it, or both. Measurement and comparison of rural and urban populations within a country can be relatively simple when demographic criteria are used, although the problem of making comparisons among nations still remains. Only 250 persons are necessary to qualify an area as urban in Denmark, and only 1,000 in Canada, while

Democratic uprisings occurred throughout Egypt in the spring of 2011, but they were centralized in urban areas like Cairo and (as pictured here) Alexandria. The protesters were overwhelmingly young, urban, and well connected to social media, including Facebook and Twitter. Even in the context of predominantly rural countries like Egypt, both urbanism and urbanization are forces at work in effecting sociopolitical change. © Mohamed Hanno/Dreamstime.com

10,000 are needed in Greece. According to the definition used by the United States Bureau of the Census for the 2010 census, the official urban population of the United States comprises all persons living in urbanized areas, all persons outside of urbanized areas who live in places of 2,500 or more, and all persons living in unincorporated settlements of fewer than 2,500 persons living in "urbanized zones" on the fringes of metropolitan areas. By this definition, three-quarters of the United States population is urban.

Worldwide, the percentage of the population living in urban places varies from 10 percent in Burundi to 100 percent in Qatar, Singapore, and Hong Kong.[9] (Table 1.1 shows the percent of urbanization by world regions.)

URBANIZATION AND URBANISM

In this work we will distinguish between *urbanization*, which is the number of people in urban places, and *urbanism*, which is the sociocultural consequences of living in urban places, the human culture side of urbanization. As we will see in Part Five: Worldwide Urbanization, cities in the developing world are the largest and the fastest growing in the world. Nevertheless, it must be kept in mind that the growth of cities and a high level of national urbanization are not the same thing; in the Western world both happened at the same time, but it is possible to find extremely large cities in overwhelmingly rural countries. Some of the world's largest cities—for example, Shanghai, Mumbai, and Cairo—exist in nations that are still largely rural. Having extremely large cities does not necessarily indicate an urban nation.

Urbanization

Urbanization not only refers to the changes in the proportion of the population of a nation living in urban areas but also to the process of people moving to cities or other densely settled areas. The term is also used to describe the changes in social organization that occur as a consequence of population concentration. Urbanization is thus a process—the process by which rural areas become transformed into urban areas. In demographic terms, urbanization is an increase in population concentration (numbers and density); organizationally, it is an alteration in structure and patterns of organization. Demographically, urbanization involves two elements: the multiplication of points of concentration and the increase in the size of individual concentrations.[10]

Urbanization, described demographically as the percentage of a nation's total population living in urban areas, is a process that clearly has a beginning and an end. Four-fifths of the United States population of more than 300 million is now urban; the maximum level of urbanization is probably somewhere around 90 percent. (Nations that comprise only one city, such as Singapore, can be 100 percent urban.) Even after a nation achieves a high level of urbanization, its cities and metropolitan areas can continue to grow. While there is a limit to the percentage of urbanization possible, the practical limit for the size of cities or metropolitan areas is not yet known.

Urbanism

While urbanization has to do with metropolitan growth, *urbanism* refers to the social patterns and behaviors associated with living in cities. Urbanism, with its changes in the values, mores, customs, and behaviors of a population, is often seen as one of the consequences of urbanization.[11] Urbanism is a social and behavioral response to living in certain places.

Under the conceptual label "urbanism" is found research concerning the social psychological aspects of urban life, urban personality patterns, and the behavioral adaptations required by city life. Urbanism as a way of life receives detailed treatment in Chapter 6: The Suburban Era, Chapter 7: Urban Lifestyles,

and Chapter 8: Social Environment of Metro Areas.

It should be noted that it is possible to live in an area with a high degree of urbanization (population concentration) and a low level of urbanism (urban behaviors) or—less commonly—a low level of urbanization and a high level of urbanism. Examples of the former can be found in the large cities of the developing world, where the city is filled with immigrants who now reside in an urban place but remain basically rural in outlook.

Cairo, for example, is typical of developing cities in that over one-third of its residents were born outside the city. Many of these newcomers are urban in residence but remain rural in outlook and behavior. On the other hand, if the urbanization process in the United States becomes one of population decentralization, the United States might have some decline in levels of urbanization, while urban lifestyles become even more universal.[12]

The explicit belief in most older sociological writings—and an implicit premise in much of what is written about cities today—is that cities produce a characteristic way of life known as "urbanism." Moreover, urbanism as a way of life, while often successful economically, is said to produce personal alienation, social disorganization, and the whole range of ills falling under the cliché "the crisis of the cities."

A classic statement of the effects of urbanization on urban behavior patterns is Louis Wirth's article "Urbanism as a Way of Life."[13] According to Wirth, "For sociological purposes a city may be defined as a relatively large, dense, permanent settlement of socially heterogeneous individuals."[14] Wirth further suggested that these components of urbanization—size, density, and heterogeneity— are the independent variables that create a distinct way of life called "urbanism." Urbanism, with its emphasis on competition, achievement, specialization, superficiality, anonymity, independence, and tangential relationships, is often compared— at least implicitly—with a simpler and less competitive idealized rural past. (The adequacy of this approach is addressed in detail in Chapter 7: Urban Lifestyles.)

Today urbanism as a way of life is virtually universal in nations with high levels of urbanization such as the United States, with their elaborate media and communications networks. Even the attitudes, behaviors, and cultural patterns of rural areas in the United States are dominated by urban values and lifestyles. Rural wheat farmers, cattle ranchers, and dairy farmers—with their accountants, professional lobbies, and government subsidies—are all part of a complex and highly integrated agribusiness enterprise. They are hardly innocent country bumpkins, preyed upon by city slickers. By comparison, urban consumers often appear naive regarding contemporary rural life.

The degree to which even 50 years ago urbanism already had permeated every aspect of American culture was documented in Vidich and Bensman's study of an upstate New York hamlet with a population of 1,700. Their book, which they titled *Small Town in Mass Society,* presented a detailed and careful picture of how industrialization and bureaucratization totally dominated the rural village.[15] Everything—from 4H clubs and Girl Scout troops, through the American Legion and national churches, to university agriculture agents, the Social Security Administration, and marketing organizations to raise the price supports for milk—influenced how the village residents thought, acted, and lived. The town was totally dependent on outside political and economic institutions for its survival.

The small-towners, though, had an entirely different conception of themselves and their hamlet. They saw themselves as rugged individualists living in a town that, in contrast to city life, prided itself on friendliness, neighborliness, grassroots democracy, and independence. Their town was small, self-reliant, and friendly, while the city was large, coldly impersonal, and full of welfare loafers. In spite of the absence of a viable local culture, and the clear division of

the town by socioeconomic class differences, the myth of a unique rural lifestyle and social equality persisted.

Contemporary small-town America is totally enmeshed in an urban economic and social system despite its pride in its independence of the city and cosmopolitan ways. The small town even relies on the mass media to help reaffirm its own fading self image. Even the most isolated rural area in Montana has access to 200 channels of satellite TV, web access, e-mail, Twitter, and Facebook. Distances have shrunk. You can view American news on CNN in Indonesian villages, while the Internet provides an international information superhighway.

Today in North America, young people in both rural and urban areas follow the same rap, rock, and concert stars. Partially excepting separatist religious groups such as the Amish, there no longer is a unique rural culture independent of urban influence.

ORGANIZING THE STUDY OF URBAN LIFE

Over the years scholars have studied cities in many different ways. Academics in a variety of disciplines have concerned themselves with a wide variety of questions such as why cities are located at particular places and not others; what the growth patterns of cities are; who lives in cities; how different ethnic and racial groups arrange themselves therein; how living in cities affects social relationships; how cities govern themselves; and whether city living produces certain behaviors and social problems.

If these and numerous other questions addressed in this book are to have meaning for the student, the questions have to be more than an ad hoc list of interesting topics. The material has to be related and organized in some general fashion in order to provide a common understanding and body of knowledge.

The material that follows is organized—with an occasional bit of squeezing—under the previously mentioned headings of *urbanization* and *urbanism.* Under the more abstract heading of urbanization are included those questions and issues dealing with the city as a spatial, economic, and political entity. This traditionally has been referred to by sociologists as the *human ecological* approach since it is broadly concerned with how the ecology of the city developed, particularly the interrelationship and interdependence of organisms and their environment.

In recent decades an alternative approach called *political economy* has become widely used by urban scholars. Those taking a political economy perspective are less likely to give weight to ecological factors. Rather, in explaining the decline of the central city, suburbanization, edge cities, and the explosion of third world cities, they look to the explicit political and economic decisions made by multinationals and political institutions.[16] Those advocating a political economy approach are concerned with how economic forces shape urban patterns. Research, for example, might be done on how property values are manipulated to encourage gentrification. (Political economy and other conflict approaches are discussed in detail in Chapter 4, Ecology and Political Economy Perspectives.)

What both ecological and political economy approaches have in common is that they both focus on the larger macro-level urban units and social and economic questions. The urbanization, ecological, or political economy focus is generally on the big picture. They use cities—or, at their most micro-level, neighborhoods—as the unit of analysis. A human ecologist, for example, might research the predictable pattern of neighborhood change over time, while a political economy advocate might look at how major economic institutions decide growth patterns. Such macro-level approaches are heavily used in Part I: Focus and Development and Part II: American Urbanization.

Urbanism as a way of life, on the other hand, is far more micro-level oriented. It focuses on the impact of the city on small groups or individuals. This *cultural, sociocultural,* or *social psychological* approach focuses on how the experience of living in cities affects people's so-

cial relationships and personalities. The concern of this approach is primarily with the psychological, cultural, and social ramifications of city life. For example, one of the questions regarding the social psychological impact of city life that we will examine in some detail is whether living in a city, suburb, or rural area produces differences in personalities, socialization patterns, or even levels of pathology. To put it in oversimplified form, are city dwellers different? While human ecology focuses on how social and spatial patterns are maintained, and political economy focuses on economic systems, the social psychological or cultural approach is concerned with human effects.

Historically, urbanization scholars and urban social psychologists have gone their own way, while largely ignoring their opposite numbers. Some textbooks also perpetuate the division by all but ignoring alternative approaches, or by treating alternative explanations as discredited straw men. This is unfortunate, for the different perspectives complement each other in the same way that the social science disciplines of political science, economics, and sociology provide alternative focuses and approaches. This book, written by one trained in the urban ecology tradition who finds much of value in the political economy model, makes a conscious effort to present all positions fairly as a means of better understanding the patterns of metropolitan areas and of the lives of those of us living within them. I believe it is necessary to have an understanding both of urbanization and of urbanism as a way of life, or if you prefer an alternate terminology, of urban ecology and urban political economy on one hand, and of urban culture and urban social psychology on the other.

CONCEPTS OF THE CITY

Urban Change and Confusion

The scientific study of urbanism and urbanization is a relative newcomer to the academic scene. Systematic empirical examination of cities and city life only began during the first half of the 20th century, a period in which American cities were experiencing considerable transformation in terms of both industrialization and a massive influx of immigrants from the rural areas of Europe and the American South. To many observers of the time, the city, with its emphasis on efficiency, technology, and division of labor, was undermining simpler rural forms of social organization. The social consequences were disorganization, depersonalization, and the breakdown of traditional norms and values. Classic early 20th century social protest novels such as Upton Sinclair's *The Jungle* (1906) and Theodore Dreiser's *Sister Carrie* (1900) reflect this breakdown. An anonymous poem of 1916, called "While the City Sleeps," mirrors this negative view of urban life:

> Stand in your window and scan the sights,
> On Broadway with its bright white lights.
> Its dashing cabs and cabarets,
> Its painted women and fast cafes.
> That's when you really see New York.
> Vulgar of manner, overfed,
> Overdressed and underbred.
> Heartless and Godless, Hell's delight,
> Rude by day and lewd by night.

Rural Simplicity versus Urban Complexity

In the usual description of the transition from simple to complex forms of social organization, there is, at least implicitly, a time frame in which rural areas represent the past and traditional values, and the city represents the future with its emphasis on technology, division of labor, and emergence of new values. Early movies reinforced this view. In silent movies the villain invariably was the city banker, while the hero was a simple farm boy. Similarly, in cowboy movies the villain invariably lived in town, while the hero rode in from the open country. The picture of a fast-paced, alienating, stimulating, and anonymous city life, along with the contrasting romanticized picture of the warm, personal, and well-adjusted rural life is, of course, a stereotype. Such stereotypes affect not only social behavior but also social policy—even if they are poor reflectors of reality. For example, in spite of the emphasis on the isolation, anonymity, and mental stress of the city, there are indications that city residents are actually happier and better adjusted than their rural cousins.

With the exception of the largest cities, Claude E. Fischer found, for example, that on a worldwide scale there is greater evidence of rural as opposed to urban dissatisfaction, unhappiness, despair, and melancholy.[17] Also, research by Palen and Johnson on the relationship between urbanization and health status in 19th- and 20th-century American cities found that inhabitants of large cities were consistently healthier than inhabitants of rural areas or small towns.[18] Contrary to the stereotype, mental health is probably superior in the city.[19]

EARLY SOCIAL THEORIES AND URBAN CHANGE

The cleavage between the city and the countryside is, of course, not a uniquely American idea. The great European social theorists of the 19th century described the social changes that were then taking place in terms of a shift from a warm, supportive community based on kinship in which common aims are shared to a larger, more impersonal society in which ties are based not on kinship but on interlocking economic, political, and other interests. These views had, and continue to have, profound impact on sociological thought.[20]

European Theorists

Many of the core ideas of the classical (so-called) Chicago School writings of the 1920s and 1930s were based implicitly on the

In China, rapid urbanization and change run directly up against older settlements and country ways in cities like Guangzhou (formerly Canton), pictured here. © Kheng Ho Toh/Dreamstime.com

thoughts of late 19th and early 20th-century European social theorists. Of these, the most influential were the Germans Ferdinand Tönnies (1855–1936), Karl Marx (1818–1883), Max Weber (1864–1920), and Georg Simmel (1858–1918), and the Frenchman Émile Durkheim (1858–1917). These theorists sought to explain the twin changes of industrialization and urbanization that were undermining the small-scale, traditional, rural-based communities of Europe. All about, they saw the crumbling of old economic patterns, social customs, and family organization. The growth of urbanization was bringing in its wake new urban ways of life. They sought to theoretically explain these changes.

Typologies. Commonly, changes were presented by theorists in terms of typologies, which sociologists refer to as *ideal types*. The term *ideal type* doesn't mean "perfect;" rather, an ideal type is a *model*. An ideal type doesn't represent a specific reality; it is, instead, a logical construct. One ideal-type model was rural society; its opposite was urban society.

Probably the most important 19th-century European social theorist was Karl Marx, who was born in 1818 in Trier into an agrarian Germany that had yet to undergo the Industrial Revolution. Yet Marx spent most of his adult life in an industrializing London where factories, and exploitation of the new class of wage workers, were part of daily life. In the booming cities, a few industrialists enjoyed a level of wealth and comfort more luxurious than that of kings of old, while workers slaved 12 hours a day, 6 days a week, for subsistence wages and lived in unspeakable tenements and slums (see insert "Engels on Industrial Slums," in Chapter 2).

Not surprisingly, Marx saw economic structure as the infrastructural foundation of society. It therefore follows that change in society is through conflict over resources and the means of production. Ultimately, the final struggle of mature urban industrial capitalism would be between the capitalists, who owned factories and the means of production, and the urban proletariat, who provided the underpaid labor. However, for Marx, before this could occur, there first had to be a shift from agrarian feudal society to the new, urban, property-owning bourgeoisie. (Since a bourg, or burg, is a town, a bourgeois is by definition a town dweller.) According to Marx:

> The greatest division of material and mental labour is the separation of town and country. The antagonism between town and country begins with the transition from barbarism to civilization, from tribe to State, from locality to nation, and runs through the whole history of civilization to the present day. . . . Here first became the division of the population into two great classes, which is directly based on the division of labour and on the instruments of production.[21]

In early-20th-century urban sociology, Ferdinand Tönnies had great impact with his elaborate discussions of the shift from *gemeinschaft*— a smaller country or village community based on ties of blood (family) and kinship—to *gesellschaft*— a larger more complex urban society or association based on economic, political, or other interests.[22] In rural gemeinschaft, people were bound together by common values and by family and kinship ties, and they worked together for the common goal. At the gesellschaft pole of the typology, on the other hand, personal relationships count for little, with money and contract replacing sentiment. City people were individualistic and selfishly out for themselves. For Tönnies this change from common good to private advantage arose as a consequence of the growth of money-based capitalism. Further, he saw this evolutionary change as inevitable, but not desirable. Tönnies mourned the increasing loss of community. A century later his idea of the warm local town in contrast to the impersonal city still continues to influence popular views of urban life.

Others were more positive regarding urban life. The great French sociologist Émile Durkheim similarly saw societies moving from a commonality of tasks and outlook to a complex division of labor. Societies based on shared sentiments and tasks were said to possess "mechanical solidarity," while those based on integrating different but complementary economic and social functions were said to possess "organic solidarity."[23] In Durkheim's view, the collective conscience of rural society is replaced by a complex division of labor in urban society. The latter is both far more productive economically and far more socially liberating. Durkheim was more positive about urban life than Tönnies; while Durkheim saw the division of labor undermining traditional life, he also saw cities creating new forms of mutual interdependence.

Expanding his theory beyond the European city, the German sociologist Max Weber made an ideal type distinction between "traditional society" based upon ascription and "rational society" based on the "technical superiority" of formalized and impersonal bureaucracy.[24] Weber saw that with the rise of the nation state the autonomous city of the medieval period was no more.

All the above theorists looked at the city from a macro-level. More psychologically oriented was Georg Simmel, whose famous essay "The Metropolis and Mental Life" concentrated on how urbanization increases individuals' alienation and mental isolation.[25] Simmel's concern was on how the individual could survive the city's intense social interaction and still maintain her or his personality. Simmel saw the city as a place of intense stimuli that stimulated freedom but also forced the city dweller to become blasé and calculating in order to survive. Simmel's ideas were very important in influencing America's first urban sociologists and are the base of much of the work of the so-called Chicago School of sociologists. The influence of Simmel's ideas is fully discussed in Part Three: Metropolitan Life. Finally, a 20th-century anthropology version of the dichotomy between rural and urban places is the distinction made by the anthropologist Robert Redfield between what he characterized as "folk" and "urban" societies. He described folk peasant societies as:

> . . . small, isolated, non-literate, and homogeneous, with a strong sense of group solidarity. The ways of living are conventionalized into that coherent system which we call "a culture." Behavior is traditional, spontaneous, uncritical, and personal; there is no legislation, or habit of experiment and reflection for intellectual ends. Kinship, its relationships and institutions, are the type categories of experience and the familial group is the unit of action. The sacred prevails over the secular; the economy is one of status rather than market.[26]

Interestingly, Redfield never did define "urban life," simply saying that it was the opposite of folk society.

Assumptions. The theoretical frameworks described above all contain three general assumptions: (1) The evolutionary movement from simple rural to complex urban is unilinear (that is, it goes only in one direction: from simple to complex); (2) modern urban life stresses achievement over ascription (that is, what you do is more important than your parentage); and (3) the supposed characteristics of city life apply not just to specific groups or neighborhoods but to urban areas as a whole. As you read through this text, note whether these assumptions are supported or rejected.

All these models have at least an implicit evolutionary framework: Societies follow a unilinear path of development from simple rural to complex urban. Rural areas and ways of life typify the past, while the city is the mirror to the future. This change is assumed to be both inevitable and irreversible. A subset of this belief is that the city fosters goal oriented, formal, secondary-group relationships—rather than face-to-face primary-group relationships.

Unspoken but often implicit in this is the value judgment that the old ways were better, or at least more humane. The city is presented as more efficient, but the inevitable price of efficiency is the breakdown of meaningful social relationships. The countryside exemplifies stable rules, roles, and relationships, while the city is characterized by innovation, experimentation, flexibility, and disorganization. In cultural terms the small town represents continuity, conformity, and stability, while the big city stands for heterogeneity, variety, and originality. In terms of personality, country folk are supposed to be neighborly people who help one another—they lack the sophistication of city slickers but also lack the city dweller's guile. In short, country folk are "real," while city people are artificial and impersonal.

Fortunately, the newly emerging discipline of urban sociology did not calcify into explaining supposed differences between the rural and the urban, but rather began to examine the urban scene empirically and systematically. Eventually the original rural–urban dichotomy was abandoned, and hypotheses began to be developed on the basis of empirical research. This emphasis on the importance of actual studies and research data is one of the characteristics of urban sociology. The Chicago School of sociology set this pattern.

The Chicago School

Urban research (and in fact virtually all sociological research) until World War II is largely associated with a remarkable group of scholars connected with the University of Chicago during the 1920s and 1930s. The "Chicago School" found sociology a loose collection of untested theories, interesting facts, social work, and social reform. It converted sociology into an established academic discipline and an emerging science.[27] Foremost among the Chicago School pioneers was Robert Park (1864–1944), who emphasized not moral preachments about the sins of the city but detailed empirical observation. Park had held a variety of jobs, including newspaper reporter and personal secretary to national black leader Booker T. Washington. He was constantly fascinated by studying the city and passed his enthusiasm on to several generations of graduate students. He was also most interested in how the supposed chaos of the city actually was underlaid by a pattern of systematic social and spatial organization.[28]

Early empirical sociologists, studying under Park, described the effects of urbanization on immigrant and rural newcomers to the city, and the emergence of "urbanization as a way of life." Works such as *The Polish Peasant in Europe and America, The Ghetto, The Jack Roller,* and *The Gold Coast and the Slum* are minor classics describing the effects of urbanization.[29]

However, it remained for Louis Wirth (1897–1952), a student of Park, to consolidate and expressly formulate how the size, density, and heterogeneous nature of cities produce a unique urban way of life. Wirth's essay "Urbanism as a Way of Life," although much challenged, remains the most influential essay in urban studies.[30] Wirth suggested that large cities inevitably produce a host of changes that, although economically productive, are destructive of family life and close social interaction. Wirth's ideas are examined in detail in Chapter 7: Urban Lifestyles.

For now, however, let us temporarily put aside the questions of the social psychology of city living and focus our primary attention on the spatial and social organization of urban places. We will begin our discussion of the urbanization process by examining how and why cities have come into existence.

SUMMARY

As the 21st century progresses, the world is changing from one that always has been mostly rural to one that is majority urban. Cities have only existed for 7,000 to 10,000 years, but what we call "civilization" is the record of that period. At the beginning of the 20th century, 86 percent of the globe's inhabitants were rural. Today most are urban. We are now in a period of explosive urban growth, with the globe having 414 cities of at least a million inhabitants. Dramatic urban growth in the developing world is largely a postwar phenomenon, but today over nine-tenths of the world's urban growth is in developing countries, much of it in megacities.

Urban places can be defined on the basis of having an urban culture (a cultural definition), administrative function (a political definition), the percentage of the population in nonagricultural occupations (an economic definition), or on the basis of population size and concentration (a demographic definition). The latter is most commonly used and indicates that the percentage of urban population varies from a low of 5 percent in Rwanda to 100 percent in Kuwait and Singapore.

The term *urbanization* refers to the proportion of persons living in urban places, while *urbanism* refers to the social-psychological aspects or ways of life found in cities. Urbanism as a way of life has permeated even the most rural areas of North America. Social theorists of the late 19th and early 20th century focused on how moving from rural to urban places changes people's economic behavior, social customs, and family organization.

These changes, as discussed by theorists such as Ferdinand Tönnies, Karl Marx, Max Weber, Émile Durkheim, and Georg Simmel, were commonly presented as dichotomous models called *ideal types*. The ideal types commonly contrasted a simpler and more personal rural past with a complex and impersonal urban future.

Urban research (and most sociological research) prior to World War II is associated with urban sociologists at the University of Chicago known collectively as the "Chicago School." Their research was wide ranging but had at its core the study of the impact of urbanization on urban newcomers and the development of an urban social culture or urbanism as a way of life.

REVIEW QUESTIONS

1. How have urban growth patterns changed over the last two centuries?

2. How has the proportion of the world's population living in cities changed over the last century?

3. Where on the globe is virtually all contemporary urban growth (the so-called Urban Explosion) taking place?

4. Where did most urban growth occur a century ago?

5. What criteria do different countries use to define urban areas?

6. What is the difference between *urbanization* and *urbanism*?

7. Ecological and political economy models or approaches both focus on what level of analysis and questions?

8. Urbanism as a way of life focuses on what level of analysis and questions?

9. Who were some of the major European social theorists of the late 19th and early 20th century and how did their typologies explain urban change?

10. What was the focus of the Chicago School scholars, and how did they change urban sociology?

NOTES

1. As of 1800, only 1.7 percent of the world's population resided in places of 100,000 people or more, 2.4 percent in places of 20,000 or more, and 3 percent in communities of 5,000 or more. Philip Hauser and Leo Schnore (eds.), *The Study of Urbanization*, New York, 1965, p. 7.

2. *2010 World Population Data Sheet,* Population Reference Bureau, Washington, D.C., 2010.

3. Adna Ferrin Weber, *The Growth of Cities in the Nineteenth Century,* Cornell University Press, Ithaca, N.Y., 1899, Table 3.

4. For data for cities in earlier eras see, Tertius Chandler and Gerald Fox, *3,000 Years of Urban Growth,* Academic Press, New York, 1974.

5. United Nations, *World Urbanization Prospects: The 2009 Revisions.* United Nations, New York, 2010.

6. *2006 World Population Data Sheet,* Population Reference Bureau, Washington, D.C., 2006.

7. Robert E. Park, "The City: Suggestions for the Investigation of Human Behavior in the Urban Environment," in Robert E. Park, E.W. Burgess, and Roderick D. McKenzie (eds.), *The City,* University of Chicago Press, Chicago, 1925.

8. Martin P. Brockerhoff, "An Urbanizing World," *Population Bulletin,* Population Reference Bureau, Washington, D.C., September 2000, p. 6.

9. *2010 World Population Data Sheet,* Population Reference Bureau, Washington, D.C., 2010.

10. Hope Tisdale Eldridge, "The Process of Urbanization," in J. J. Spengler and O. D. Duncan (eds.), *Demographic Analysis,* Free Press, Glencoe, Ill., 1956, pp. 338–43.

11. Leo Schnore, "Urbanization and Economic Development: The Demographic Contribution," *American Journal of Economics and Sociology* 23:37–48, 1964.

12. Brian J. L. Berry, "The Counterurbanization Process: Urban America since 1970," in *Urbanization and Counterurbanization,* Vol. II: *Urban Affairs Annual Reviews,* Sage, Beverly Hills, Calif., 1976, pp. 17–39.

13. Louis Wirth, "Urbanism as a Way of Life," *American Journal of Sociology* 44:1–24, July 1938.

14. Ibid., p. 8.

15. Arthur J. Vidich and Joseph Bensman, *Small Town in Mass Society,* Princeton University Press, Princeton, N.J., 1958.

16. Mark Gottdiener and Joe Feagin, "The Paradigm Shift in Urban Sociology," *Urban Affairs Quarterly* (2412): 163–187, 1988; Ray Hutchinson, "The Crisis in Urban Sociology," in Ray Hutchinson (ed.), *Research in Urban Sociology,* JAI Press, Greenwich, Conn., 1993, p. 3–26; David A. Smith, "The New Urban Sociology Meets the Old: Rereading Some Classical Human Ecology," *Urban Affairs Review* 30(3):432–457, 1995.

17. Claude S. Fischer, "Urban Malaise," *Social Forces* 52(2):221, December 1973.

18. J. John Palen and Daniel Johnson, "Urbanization and Health Status," in Ann and Scott Greer (eds.), *Cities and Sickness,* Sage, Beverly Hills, Calif., 1983, pp. 25–34.

19. Leo Srole, "Mental Health in New York," *The Sciences,* 20:16–29, 1980.

20. Michael Peter Smith, *Transitional Urbanism: Locating Globalization,* Blackwell, London, 2001.

21. Karl Marx and Friedrich Engels, *The German Ideology,* R. Pascal (trans.), International Publishers, New York, 1947, pp. 68–69.

22. Ferdinand Tönnies, *Community and Society,* Charles P. Loomis (trans.), Harper & Row, New York, 1963.

23. Émile Durkheim, *The Division of Labor in Society,* George Simpson (trans.), Free Press, Glencoe, Ill., 1960.

24, H. H. Gerth and C. Wright Mills (trans. and ed.), *Max Weber: Essays in Sociology,* Oxford University Press, New York, 1966.

25. Georg Simmel, "The Metropolis and Mental Life," *The Sociology of Georg Simmel,* Kurt Wolff (trans.), Free Press, New York, 1964.

26. Robert Redfield, "The Folk Society," *American Journal of Sociology* 52:53–73, 1947.

27. For an evaluation of the Chicago legacy, see Lyn H. Lofland, "Understanding Urban Life: The Chicago Legacy," *Urban Life* 11:491–511, 1983.

28. Robert E. Park, "The City: Suggestions for the Investigation of Human Behavior in the Urban Environment," in Robert Park, E.W. Burgess, and Roderick McKenzie (eds.), *The City,* University of Chicago Press, Chicago, 1925.

29. William I. Thomas and Florian Znaniecki, *The Polish Peasant in Europe and America,* 5 vols., University of Chicago Press, Chicago, 1918–1920; Louis Wirth, *The Ghetto,* University of Chicago Press, Chicago, 1928; Clifford R. Shaw, *The Jack Roller,* University of Chicago Press, Chicago, 1930; and Harvey W. Zorbaugh, *The Gold Coast and the Slum,* University of Chicago Press, Chicago, 1929.

30. Louis Wirth, "Urbanism as a Way of Life," *American Journal of Sociology,* 44:1–24, July 1938.

CHAPTER 2

The Emergence of Cities

The past is prologue.
Shakespeare

OUTLINE

Introduction
The Ecological Complex
Political Economy Models
First Settlements
    Agricultural Revolution
    Population Expansion
    Mesoamerica
Interactions of Population, Organization,
    Environment, and Technology
City Populations
Evolution in Social Organization
    Division of Labor
    Kingship and Social Class
Technological and Social Evolution
Urban Revolution
Survival of the City
The Hellenic City
    Social Invention
    Physical Design and Planning
    Population
    Diffusion of People and Ideas
Rome
    Size and Number of Cities
    Housing and Planning

Transportation
Life and Leisure
European Urbanization until the Industrial
    City
    The Medieval Feudal System
    Town Revival
    Characteristics of Towns
    Plague
    Renaissance Cities
Industrial Cities
    Technological Improvements and the
        Industrial Revolution
    The Second Urban Revolution
Summary

INTRODUCTION

This chapter begins at the beginning of urban life. It outlines the dramatic growth from the first tentative agricultural villages to the massive industrial cities of the last century. In brief, what is being discussed is the rise of civilization. Our goal is not to memorize a series of dates and places, but rather to develop some understanding of the process of urban development—that

19

is, how and why cities developed. Thus, read this chapter to better understand patterns rather than to remember specific facts. We start with archaeological, anthropological, and historical material, not because there is anything sacred about beginnings as such, but because having some understanding of the origin and function of cities helps us to better understand contemporary cities and how and why they got to be what they are today.

THE ECOLOGICAL COMPLEX

One model that helps us to understand change is the ecological complex. The ecological complex is an ecosystem framework used to explain broad urban change. An *ecosystem* is defined as a natural unit in which there is an interaction of an environmental and a biotic system—that is, a community together with its habitat. At the upper extreme, the whole earth is a world ecosystem. The ecological framework has been criticized by political economy scholars for not giving sufficient attention to deliberate changes planned by economic and political elites.[1] This is a valid criticism when discussing industrial and postindustrial cities. However, for viewing early pre-industrial cities, an ecological framework is a useful tool.

In basic terms, the ecological complex identifies the relationship between four concepts or classes of variables: population, organization, environment, and technology. (Some add a fifth category of "social.") These variables are frequently referred to by the acronym "POET."

Population refers not only to the number of people but also to growth or contraction through either migration or natural increase. An example of the first is the growth of Houston from 1975 to the present through in-migration from frostbelt cities. Population also refers to the composition of the population by variables such as age, sex, and race.

Organization, or social structure, is the way urban populations are organized according to social stratification, the political system, and the economic system. For example, one might want to examine the effect of Las Vegas's pro-growth political system and related tax system in encouraging population growth through in-migration.

Environment refers to the natural environment (e.g., Houston's absence of snow, or Vancouver's mild maritime climate) and the built environment of streets, parks, and buildings.

Technology refers to tools, inventions, ideas, and techniques that directly impact urban growth and form. Examples in Dallas's case are the private automobile and air conditioning. Air conditioning made the sunbelt not only prosperous but possible. Without air conditioning the states of Nevada, Arizona, Florida, and Texas would still be the relative economic backwaters they were 60 years ago. Humid Houston, the control center for the world's gas and oil industry, would be unthinkable without air conditioning. Similarly, Dallas would never have emerged as a business center, and Austin's rise as a computer technology center would have been impossible. (Microchip manufacturing requires a constant 72 degrees and 35 percent humidity.) It should be kept in mind that how technology is used, and who has access to it, has social and political ramifications.

The ecological complex is not a theory, but it does provide a simplified way of reminding us of the interrelated properties of urban settings and how each class of variables is related to and has implications for the others.[2] Each of the four variables is causally interdependent; depending on the way a problem is stated, each may serve either as an independent (or thing-explaining) or a dependent (thing-to-be-explained) variable. In sociological research, organization is commonly viewed as the dependent variable to be influenced by the other three independent variables, but a more sophisticated view of organization sees it as reciprocally related to the other elements of the ecological complex.

For example, if we are looking at the destruction of the Brazilian rain forests, we can view rapid population growth and availability of modern technology as "causing" massive environmental degradation and destruction of the earth's ozone layer. On the other hand, one could view the environmental variable as "causing" the social organizational response of the international environmental movement.

A major advantage of the ecological complex as a conceptual scheme is its simplicity, since economy of explanation is a basic scientific goal. For example, using the example of smog in Los Angeles, one can see that as transportation technology changed, the environment, organization, and population of the city also changed. In Los Angeles a favorable natural environment led to large-scale increases in population, which resulted in organizational problems (civic and governmental) and technological changes (freeways and factories). These in turn led to environmental changes (smog), which resulted in organizational changes (new pollution laws), which in turn resulted in technological changes (antipollution devices on automobiles and an expensive subway system).

This example illustrates how sociologists can use the conceptual scheme of the ecological complex to clarify significant sets of variables when studying urban growth patterns. This can be of considerable help in enlightening policy options. Note, for example, the dominant importance of environmental factors in the first cities and how this, in time, is modified by technological and social inventions. The role of technology, for instance, becomes increasingly important in the 19th century (railroads, telephones, elevators, and high-rise buildings).

A problem with the ecological complex is that the categories themselves are somewhat arbitrary, and the boundaries between them are not always precise. The ecological complex is best seen as simply a tool to help us better understand the interaction patterns within urban systems. It is not intended to be a fully developed theory of urbanization.

Perhaps the greatest limitation of the original ecological complex is that it subsumes cultural values under the variable of organization. A strong case can be made that "culture" should be a separate reference variable in its own right. Thus as previously noted, some would add an "S" for social to make the acronym POETS. Another limitation is that the ecological complex as such does not explain how, when, to what degree, or under what circumstances the categories of variables interact. Nonetheless, the ecological complex remains a useful explanatory tool for organizing large bodies of material and showing relationships. It is less useful when addressing specific questions requiring conceptual precision.

POLITICAL ECONOMY MODELS

The ecological model has been challenged by a variety of political economy models. Conflict-based paradigms or models are commonly referred to as political economy models. Originally these were neo-Marxist in nature, but some contemporary models have moved beyond Marxism.[3] Today, both ecological and political economy models are undergoing considerable change. (Political-economic conflict theories are discussed in detail in Chapter 4: Ecology and Political Economy Perspectives.)

Political economy models differ in specifics, but they all stress that urban growth is largely a consequence of capitalist economic systems of capital accumulation, conflict between classes, and economic exploitation of the powerless by the rich and powerful. The capitalist mode of production and capital accumulation are seen as being manipulated by real estate speculators and business elites for their private profit. The assumption is that "societal interaction is dominated by antagonistic social relationships," "social development is unstable in societies with antagonistic owner relationships," and "power inequality is a basic element in societal relationships."[4]

Critical theorists criticize ecological models as being ahistorical and mechanistic, and stress that social conflict is an inevitable consequence of capitalistic political economies. Thus, they discount the ecological model's reliance on transportation and communication technologies in explaining urban–suburban development. Rather, they place greater emphasis on the deliberate and conscious manipulation by real estate and government interests in order to promote growth and profits. Suburbanization, for example, is not viewed as resulting from individual choices made possible by access to outer land by streetcar and automobile, but rather as the deliberate decision of economic elites to disinvest in the city and manipulate suburban real estate markets.[5]

The strength of political economy models is their attention to the influence of the economic elites on political decision making and the role played by real estate speculators. The weakness is the assumption that local government acts largely at the bidding of economic elites, and thus citizens' wishes have little impact on growth patterns or on local government. Both ecological and political economy models will be used throughout this text.

FIRST SETTLEMENTS

Our knowledge of the origin and development of the first human settlements, and our understanding of the goals, hopes, and fears of those who lived within them, must forever remain tentative. Because the first towns emerged before the invention of writing about 7500 B.C.E., we must depend for our knowledge on the research of archaeologists. Understand-

ably, historians, sociologists, and other scholars sometimes differ in their interpretations of the limited archaeological and historical data. Lewis Mumford has stated the problem aptly:

> Five thousand years of urban history and perhaps as many of proto-urban history are spread over a few score of only partly exposed sites. The great urban landmarks Ur, Nippur, Uruk, Thebes, Heliopolis, Assur, Nineveh, Babylon, cover a span of three thousand years whose vast emptiness we cannot hope to fill with a handful of monuments and a few hundred pages of written records.[6]

This chapter, which outlines the growth of urban settlements, must necessarily be based in part on scholarly speculation as to what happened before the historical era. Fortunately, our interest is not so much in an exact chronology of historical events as in the patterns and process of development.

Agricultural Revolution

Hunting-and-Gathering Societies. It is generally believed that before the urban revolution's first settlements could take place, an agricultural revolution was necessary.[7] Nomadic hunting- and-gathering bands could not accumulate, store, and transport more goods than they could carry with them. Hunting-and-gathering groups were small, ranging from 25 to at most 50 persons. Hunting-and-gathering societies were equalitarian, lacked private property, and had no fixed leadership. Since the group was mobile, parents could pass on little in goods to their children. However, there was not a total absence of culture. The hunter-gatherers of Japan's Jomon culture produced pottery with a cord pattern in the 10th millennium B.C.E.[8]

Settled Agriculture. Settled agriculture changed everything. Some groups gained enough knowledge of the seasons and the cycle of growth to forsake constant nomadic life in favor of permanent settlement in one location. The Neolithic period is characterized by this change from gathering food to producing it. There is fairly clear evidence that a transformation from a specialized food-collecting culture to a culture where grains were cultivated occurred in the Middle East around 8000 B.C.E. The population of the world at this dawn of agriculture was something on the order of 5 million.[9]

Only when the agricultural system became capable of producing a surplus was it possible to withdraw some labor from food production and apply it to the production of other goods.[10] A permanent place of settlement led to both population growth and rudimentary social stratification since not all land was equal. However, while a surplus was essential to the emergence of towns, it was not essential that the surplus come from agriculture. Early hamlets from India to the Baltic area based their cultures on the use of shellfish and fish. Within these Mesolithic hamlets possibly were seen the earliest domestic animals, such as pigs, ducks, geese, and our oldest companion, the dog. Mumford suggests that the practice of reproducing food plants through plant cuttings—as with the date palm, the olive, the fig, and the grape—probably derives from Mesolithic culture.[11]

Early settlements had only a rudimentary division of labor. The existence of some form of permanent social organization, more than just numbers of persons, is what separates more informally organized villages from formally organized towns. Jericho—which some argue was the first "city," with some 600 people as early as 8000 B.C.E.—had a fairly complex architectural construction.[12] This suggests the inhabitants had sufficient civic organization and division of labor to build defensive walls and towers in a period when they had barely begun to domesticate grains. Inside the town walls they built round houses of sun-dried bricks. Further north in what is now Turkey,

permanent villages emerged about the same time. However, the first true cities are generally thought to have begun in the "Fertile Crescent" of Mesopotamia around 4000 B.C.E.

Population Expansion

The first population explosion—an increase in tribe size to the point where hunting and gathering could no longer provide adequate food—further encouraged fixed settlements. This was most likely to occur in fertile locations where land, water, and climate favored intensive cultivation of food. Archaeologists suggest that population growth, in fact, forced the invention of agriculture.[13] Hunting, gathering, and primitive plant cultivation simply could not support the growing population.

Since the plow did not yet exist—it was not invented until sometime in the 6th century B.C.E.—farmers of this period used a form of slash-and-burn agriculture.[14] This method required cutting down what you could and burning off the rest before planting—an inefficient form of farming, but one with a long history. It was even used by the American pioneers who first crossed the Appalachian Mountains into the new lands of Kentucky and Ohio. It was still being used in isolated areas of the Appalachians in the first decades of the 20th century. The first farmers in ancient times soon discovered that slash-and-burn farming quickly depleted the soil and forced them to migrate—and probably spread their knowledge by means of cultural diffusion.

The consequences of these developments were momentous: with grain cultivation, a surplus could be accumulated and people could plan for the future. One of the early permanent neolithic farming communities—Jarmo, in the Kurdistan area of Iraq—was inhabited between 7000 and 6500 B.C.E. It has been calculated that approximately 150 people lived in Jarmo, and archaeological evidence indicates a population density of 27 people per square mile (about the same as the population density today in that area).[15] Soil erosion, deforestation, and 10,000 years of human warfare have offset the technological advantages of the intervening centuries.

Village farming communities like Jarmo had stabilized by about 5500 B.C.E. and spread over alluvial plains of river valleys like that of the Tigris- Euphrates. A similar process took place in the great river valleys of the Nile, the Indus, and the Yellow. The invention of agriculture was quite possibly an independent development in China and was certainly independent in the New World.

Although China's cities evolved somewhat after those of the Middle East, the latest archaeological evidence suggests the concept of the city probably was not borrowed from Mesopotamia but developed independently.[16] Certainly by the time of the Shang dynasty (1600–1100 B.C.E.) China had cities that apparently were laid out according to a plan, complete with ceremonial buildings and palaces, as well as dwellings.

Mesoamerica

The civilizations of Mesoamerica were physically isolated from those of the Middle East and Asia and thus had to invent independently. In pre-Mayan Mesoamerica, elaborate systems for irrigating and raising corn were developed.

The 15th-century high-Andean Inca City of Machu Picchu had an extensive canal system channeling fresh water to 16 fountains, as well as a well-thought-out drainage system.

In Mesoamerica, cities were not a product of cultural diffusion, but rather a separate invention. Mayan cities in Central America developed somewhat later than those in Mesopotamia or China. New research confirms that the city of Caral in Peru existed in 2600 B.C.E., a thousand years earlier than cities in the Americas were thought to exist.[17]

The Mayans had a major civilization and large cities dating from roughly 500 B.C.E. Since these cities had no walls, it was thought until roughly 20 years ago that the Mayans were peaceful. They weren't. Decoding of Mayan writing indicates that Mayan religious rituals and wars were remarkably bloody. There is dispute as to whether the Central American Mayan sites were true cities with resident populations or rather huge ceremonial sites. Most contemporary scholars incline toward seeing them as true cities. In 2000, one of the richest Mayan cities and royal palaces yet discovered was found buried deep and virtually intact in a neglected part of the Guatemalan rain forest.[18] The city, named Cancuen, or "place of serpents," after the name of its dynasty, rose to power about 300 C.E. and continued beyond 600 C.E. Because of constant warfare, none of the other Mayan dynasties lasted so long. The

---

Box 2.1   The Spanish on First Viewing Mexico City

The plunder-seeking Spanish conquistadors under the command of Cortez were overcome by the magnificence of Mexico City. It was the legendary City of Gold they had sought—and that Columbus and others had failed to find. The city was conquered in 1521 by a combination of guile and dishonesty—combined with the fact that most of the city's population was seriously ill or dying from European-introduced disease. The following excerpt is from *The True History of the*

Conquest of New Spain written in 1568 by Bernal Diaz del Castillo: *Gazing on such wonderful sights, we did not know what to say or whether what appeared before us was real, for on one side of the land there were great cities and in the lake ever so many more, and the lake itself was crowded with canoes, and in the causeway there were many bridges at intervals, and we did not even number four hundred soldiers.*

Mayan era of greatest city building was between 600 and 800 C.E.

Between 800 and 900, most of the great cities of Central America were abandoned, for reasons that are still debated and unclear.[19] It appears that populations increased while resources declined due to overfarming and drought. Cities were abandoned and taken over by the jungle. Population growth combined with constant warfare may have brought environmental collapse.[20]

At its peak, Teotihuacan, in central Mexico, built by the Mayans, numbered perhaps 150,000 persons or more. By the time the Spanish invaders arrived in 1521, both Mayan society and its cities had collapsed. However, their successors, the Aztecs, had built the city of Tenochtitlán (Mexico City), which dazzled Cortez and his Spanish troops. No such cities existed north of the Rio Grande.

INTERACTIONS OF POPULATION, ORGANIZATION, ENVIRONMENT, AND TECHNOLOGY

The relationships among population, organization, environment, and technology are clearer in their consequences than in their timing. The creation of an agricultural surplus made permanent settlements possible. Agricultural villages could support up to twenty-five persons per square mile, a dramatic improvement over the maximum of three to five persons per square mile found in hunting-and-gathering societies. Technology had spurred population growth. Stable yields meant that larger numbers of people could be sustained in a relatively compact space.

The establishment of sedentary agricultural villages with growing populations increased the pressure for more intensive agriculture and complex patterns of organization. Agriculture in the river valleys required at least small-scale irrigation systems, something not necessary in the highlands. Rudimentary social organization and specialization began to develop; periodic flooding made it necessary for village farmers to band together to create a system of irrigation canals and repair damage done by floods. The existence of irrigation systems also led to the development of systems of control and the emergence of more detailed social stratification within the permanent settlements.

Relatively permanent settlements in one place also allowed the structure of the family itself to change. In a hunting-and-gathering society, the only legacy parents could pass on to their progeny was their physical strength and knowledge of basic skills. Agriculturalists, though, can also pass on land to their children, and all land is not equal. Social stratification emerged over generations, with some children born into prosperity and others into poverty.

Extended family forms can also more easily emerge under sedentary conditions. Patriarchal family systems, such as those found in the Bible, can have major economic as well as sexual advantages for those in charge, since extra wives mean extra hands to tend animals and cultivate fields. More importantly, many wives meant many sons—sons to work the fields, help protect what one has from the raiding of others, provide for one in old age, make offerings to the gods at one's grave, and carry one's lineage forward. The last was particularly important in many early societies. For example, in the Old Testament the greatest gift God could bestow on Abraham was not wealth or fame or everlasting life, but that his descendants would number more than the stars in the sky and grains of sand.

Environmentally, those located on rivers had advantages not only in terms of soil fertility, but also for transportation and trade. Particularly environmentally blessed were those settlements in Mesopotamia and the Nile River valley that could exploit the rich soil of the alluvial riverbeds. The very name "Mesopotamia," which refers to the land between the Tigris and Euphrates Rivers in what is now Iraq, means "land between rivers."

By the middle of the fourth millennium B.C.E. the economy of the Nile valley in Egypt had shifted once and for all from a combination of farming and food gathering to a reliance on agriculture. In this great river valley, two and sometimes three crops a year were possible because the annual floods brought rich silt to replace the exhausted soil. (The Aswan Dam now blocks the annual floods.) To the dependable crops of wheat and barley was added the cultivation of the date palm. This was a great improvement since the palm provided more than simple food; from it were obtained wood, roofing, matting, wine, and fiber for rope. Grapes were also first crushed and fermented in the Middle East about 3000 B.C.E.

The use of rivers for transportation further encouraged the aggregation of population, for now it was relatively easy to gather food at a few centers. Thus, in the valleys of the Nile, the Tigris–Euphrates, the Indus, and the Yellow a population surplus developed, which in turn permitted the rise of the first cities (see Figure 2.1). By the third century B.C.E., Egyptian peasants from the fertile river floodplain could produce approximately three times the food they needed. The city served as a "central place" where goods and services could be exchanged.

CITY POPULATIONS

By contemporary standards, the largest early cities were little more than small towns. However, in their own day they must have been looked upon with the same awe with which 19th-century immigrants viewed New York, for these first cities were 10 times the size of the Neolithic villages that had previously been the largest settlements. Babylon, with its hanging gardens, one of the wonders of the ancient world, embraced a physical area of, roughly, only 3.2 square miles. The city of Ur, located at the confluence of the Tigris and Euphrates Rivers, was the largest city in Mesopotamia. With all its canals, temples, and harbors, it occupied only 220 acres.[21] Ur was estimated to have contained 24,000 persons; other towns ranged in population from 2,000 to 20,000 inhabitants.[22] Such cities, however, remained urban islands in the midst of rural seas.

Hawley estimates that although these cities were large for their time, they probably represented no more than 3 or 4 percent of all the people within the various localities.[23] Even Athens at its peak had only 612 acres within its walls—an area smaller than 1 square mile; ancient Antioch was roughly half this size. Carthage at its peak was 712 acres. Of all the ancient cities, only imperial Rome exceeded an area of 5 square miles. Even the biggest places before the Roman period could scarcely have exceeded 200,000 inhabitants, since from 50 to 90 farmers were required to support one person in a city.[24] In an agricultural world, the size of cities was limited by how much surplus could be produced and what technology was available to transport it.

EVOLUTION IN SOCIAL ORGANIZATION

Early cities were important, not because of their size, but because they encouraged innovations in social organization. Even though few in number, the urban elite were the principal carriers of the all-important cultural and intellectual values of the civilization. Needless to say, the city also held economic and political sway over the more numerous country dwellers. The Arab philosopher–sociologist Ibn Khaldun, writing in the 14th century, pointed out that the concentration of economic power and the proceeds of taxation in the cities led to a profound difference between the economic pattern of the city and that of the country. The concentration of governmental and educa-

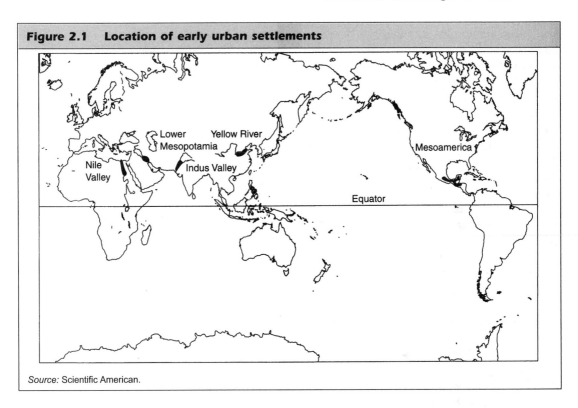

Figure 2.1   Location of early urban settlements

Source: Scientific American.

tional functions in the city also stimulated new demands that affected the patterns of production and supply.

Division of Labor

The earliest cities began to evolve a social organization immensely more complex than that found in the Neolithic village. The slight surplus of food permitted the emergence of a rudimentary division of labor. The city thus differed from a large village not only because it had more people but also because they did different things. The consequence was hierarchy and stratification. Surplus permitted inequality.[25] The early city was also an administrative religious center.

Archaeological records indicate that the earliest public buildings were temples, suggesting that specialized priests were the first to be released from direct subsistence functions. Early

Sumerian cities were basically theocracies—that is, they were ruled by priests. That the priests also assumed the role of economic administrators is indicated by ration or wage lists found in places where temples were located.[26] In Egypt the temples were near the granaries for the community surplus. This surplus could be used to carry a community through a period of famine.

The biblical story of Joseph—who was sold by his jealous brothers into slavery in Egypt, only to become advisor to the Pharaoh and to predict seven good years of harvest followed by seven lean years of famine—points out the relative control the advanced Egyptians had over their environment. Even if the nomadic Israelites had received Joseph's warning, they would have been unable to profit from it—they lacked the transportation and storage technology of the more urban Egyptians. Using granaries the Egyptians had learned how to move a surplus through time as well as through space. Long-term planning—whether to avoid famines, construct temples, or build pyramids—was possible only where a surplus was ensured and storage was available.

Kingship and Social Class

Warrior-leaders originally served only during times of external threat. Eventually, those chosen as short-term leaders during periods of war came to be retained even during periods of peace. As the process evolved in China in the fifth century B.C.E.:

> Perhaps whole settlements sometimes found it was easier to set up as warriors, and let the people around them work for them, than to labor in the fields. The chiefs and their groups of warriors, no doubt, provided the farmers with "protection" whether they wanted it or not, and in return for that service they took a share of the peasant's crop.[27]

It is hardly necessary to add that the size of the warrior's share of the peasant's crop was fixed by the warrior, not the peasant. The growth of military establishments did contribute, though, to technological innovations—metallurgy for weapons, chariots for battle, and more efficient ships.

It was but a step from a warrior class to kingship and the founding of dynasties with permanent hereditary royalty. The gradual shifting of the central focus from temple to palace was accompanied by the growth of social and economic stratification. Artists working in precious metals became regular attachments to palace life. Records of sales of land indicate that even among farmers there were considerable inequalities in the ownership of productive land. As a result, social differences grew. Some few members of each new generation were born with marked social and economic advantages over the others. If they couldn't afford the luxuries of palace life, they nonetheless lived in considerable comfort.

In China, specialization led to the replacement of hereditary lords with centrally appointed mandarins selected by examination. This bureaucratic system of social organization survived more than 3,000 years until its abolishment in 1905.

Archaeologically, the emergence of urban social classes can be seen clearly in the increasing disparity in the richness of grave offerings.[28] The tombs of royalty are richly furnished with ornaments and weapons of gold and precious metals; those of others, with copper vessels; while the majority have only pottery vessels or nothing at all. The building of burial pyramids was the ultimate case of monumental graves.

TECHNOLOGICAL AND SOCIAL EVOLUTION

In early cities, technology was spurred on by necessity. We are just discovering the elaborate water collection and distribution systems of the ancient Mayan culture of Central America. The system allowed the Mayan elite to develop large cities in areas that had long dry spells. The failure to maintain the water system may have led to the civilization's collapse about 900 C.E.[29]

Cities created new technological demands. The military required armor, weapons, and chariots, and the court demanded ever more ornaments and other luxuries. This demand created a constant market for nonagricultural commodities, and the result was the establishment of a class of full-time artisans and craft workers. The near-isolation of earlier periods was now replaced with trade over long distances, which brought not only new goods but also new ideas.

The first city was far more than an enlarged village—it was a clear break with the past, a whole new social system. It was a social revolution involving the evolution of a whole new set of social institutions. Unlike the agricultural revolution that preceded it, this urban revolution was far more than a basic change in subsistence. It was "preeminently a social process, an expression more of change in man's interaction with his fellows than in his interaction with his environment."[30]

The urban revolution created its own environment. Inventions that have made large settlements possible have been due to the city itself—for example, writing, accounting, bronze, the solar calendar, bureaucracy, and the beginning of science. Ever since Mesopotamia, the city as a social institution has been shaping human life.[31]

URBAN REVOLUTION

A number of years ago V. Gordon Childe listed 10 features that, he said, define the "urban revolution"— that is, features that set cities apart from earlier forms of human settlement. The features are:

1. Permanent settlement in dense aggregations,
2. Non-agriculturalists engaging in specialized functions,
3. Taxation and capital accumulation,
4. Monumental public buildings,
5. A ruling class,
6. The technique of writing,
7. The acquisition of predictive sciences— arithmetic, geometry, and astronomy,
8. Artistic expression,
9. Trade for vital materials,
10. The replacement of kinship by residence as the basis for membership in the community.[32]

We now know that all 10 are not necessary for cities. For example, monumental urban places developed in Mesoamerica without the wheel, the raising of animals, the plow, or the use of metals. (Actually, the Mayan civilization did have the wheel, but for some reason used it only on children's toys.) They did, however,

have other advantages; probably the most significant was the knowledge of how to use irrigation to cultivate large surpluses of domesticated maize (corn). The Mayans also had made major discoveries in mathematics, including the separate invention of the concept of zero. They were accurate astronomers and had an exact calendar; both skills were used for religious purposes but had secular consequences (e.g., indicating when to plant). Social organizations, culture, and technology were interrelated. Lists, such as Childe's, are most useful in indicating what we have come to accept as the general characteristics of cities.

SURVIVAL OF THE CITY

The stable location of the city was not an unmixed blessing. Cities had to be equipped to withstand a siege, since the earliest cities were vulnerable to periodic attacks.[33] The Bible, for instance, devotes considerable attention to the successes of the nomadic Israelites in taking and pillaging the cities of their more advanced enemies. The Biblical description of the fall of the Canaanite city of Jericho tells us that:

> The People went out into the city, every man straight before him, and they took the city. And they utterly destroyed all that was in the city, both man and woman, young and old, and ox and sheep and ass, with the edge of the sword— and they burnt the city with fire and all that was therein. (Joshua 2:20–24).

That "Joshua 'fit' the battle of Jericho . . . and the walls came tumbling down" is known to all those who have heard the stirring spiritual, even if they have not read the Old Testament. While the walls Joshua is said to have miraculously brought down with trumpet blasts about 1500 B.C.E. have not been located, the remains of other walls dating back to 8000 B.C.E. have been excavated. As with some other long-inhabited ancient sites, the walls had been breached many times—sometimes by invaders, sometimes fires, sometimes earthquakes. Actually, Joshua's destroying everything and everyone in the city was shortsighted. By Solomon's time a more complex social organization had evolved in which subjugated peoples were taxed yearly rather than destroyed.

Within the city walls there also were other threats to the inhabitants, the most dangerous being fires and epidemic diseases. Plagues spread easily in cities. City life was more exciting, but it was not necessarily more secure or healthful than life in the countryside.

THE HELLENIC CITY

Environmental factors played a decisive role in early cities. In fact, the history of the city can be considered the story of human attempts, through the use of technology and social organization, to lessen the impact of environmental factors. An example is Athens, widely regarded as the apex of ancient Western urbanism. Not

only was the Greek soil thin and rocky and of marginal fertility, but the mountainous hinterland made inland transportation and communication almost impossible. It is estimated that the cost of transporting goods 10 miles from Athens was more than 40 percent of the value of the goods.[34]

But Greece was blessed with fine harbors. Consequently, Athens turned to the sea. A Greek ship could carry 7,000 pounds of grain 65 nautical miles a day, and do it at one-tenth the cost of land transportation. (Storms at sea and pirates, however, often made this an ideal rather than a reality.) There were also technological contributions to Greek prosperity: the use of the lodestone as a basic nautical compass and the development of more seaworthy ships.

Social Invention

The greatest achievement of the Greeks was not in technology but in social organization.

Ancient Greece was in its day a model of social and political organization. Today, Greece is reeling from economic crises that reverberate throughout the European Union and the world. Here, a banner hanging from the Finance Ministry building in Athens protests harsh austerity measures and calls for demonstrations against the government. Urban settings are the norm for such demonstrations and many of the economic impetuses and impacts of the recession are centered in cities. © Louisa Gouliamaki/AFP/Getty Images

The social invention of the *polis,* or "city-state," enabled families, *phratries* (groups of clans), and tribes to organize for mutual aid and protection as citizens of a common state. Because they acknowledged a common mythical ancestry among the gods, different families were able to come together in larger bodies. Citizens were those who could trace their mythical ancestry back to the god or gods responsible for the city and thus could participate in public religious worship. Citizenship and religion were two sides of the same coin.

An Athenian citizen was one who had the right to worship at the temple of Athena, the protector of the city-state of Athens. Citizenship was at its basis a religious status.[35] Socrates' questioning the existence of the gods thus was considered a grave offense because, by threatening established religion, he was undermining the very basis of citizenship in the city-state. His crime was not heresy but treason. As punishment for such a subversive act, he was forced to drink poison hemlock. The Greeks never devised a system for extending citizenship beyond the city-state to all Greeks. This was to be the achievement of the Romans.

Being a citizen of the city was of supreme importance to the Greeks. When Aristotle wished to characterize humans as social animals, he said that man is by nature a citizen of the city. Thus, to the Greeks, being ostracized—that is, being forbidden to enter into the city—was an extremely severe punishment. To be placed beyond the city walls was to be cast out of civilized life. The terms *pagan* and *heathen* originally referred to those beyond the city walls; the contemporary adjective *urban* and the nouns *citizen* and *politics* are derived from the Latin terms for the city. As previously noted, the English terms *city* and *civilization* are both derived from the Latin *civis.*

Physical Design and Planning

Physically, the Greek cities were of fairly similar design, a phenomenon that is not surprising given the amount of social borrowing that took place among the various city-states, and the fact that the cities were built with military defense in mind. The major city walls were built around a fortified hill called an *acropolis.* Major temples were also placed upon the acropolis. The nearby *agora,* or open space, served as both a meeting place and, in time, a marketplace. All major buildings were located within the city walls. Housing, except for the most privileged, was outside but huddled as close to the protective walls as possible.

In describing the Greek *polis,* there is a strong tendency to focus on the image of the Athenian Acropolis harmoniously crowned by the perfectly proportioned Parthenon. Separated by seas and centuries, it is perhaps natural for us to accept Pericles's praise of his fellow Athenians as "lovers of beauty without extravagance and lovers of wisdom without unmanliness."

Yet it is easy to forget that the "classic" white stone of the Parthenon was originally painted garish colors. Traces of red paint can still be seen millennia later. Below the inner order and harmony of the Parthenon was a sprawling, jumbled town in which streets were no more than dirty, winding, narrow lanes and unburied refuse rotted in the sun. Housing for the masses was squalid and cramped. Although the town planner Hippodamus designed a grid street pattern for Piraeus, the port city of Athens, Athens itself had no such ordered arrangement. Athens was the center of an empire, but little of its genius was given to municipal management.

Population

During its peak, the city of Athens achieved a population of possibly 250,000 including slaves and non-citizens (slaves constituted perhaps one-third of the population). The great sociologist Max Weber put the Greek city-states in perspective when he wrote, "The full urbanite of antiquity was a semi-peasant."[36]

Expansion of Greek cities was limited not only by agricultural technology. There is an advantage in having a population low enough to live off the local food supply.[37] Also, the ancient Greeks preferred smaller cities. Both Plato and Aristotle believed that good government was directly related to the size of the city. Plato specified that the ideal republic should have exactly 5,040 citizens, since that number would "furnish numbers for war and peace, and for all contracts and dealings, including taxes and divisions of the land."[38] Adding non-citizens such as children, slaves, and foreigners into the calculation raises the total population of the city-state to approximately 30,000, or about the size chosen later by Leonardo da Vinci and Ebenezer Howard for their ideal cities. Aristotle informs us that Hippodamus envisioned a city of 10,000 citizens divided into three parts: one of artisans, one of farmers, and one of warriors. The land was likewise to be divided into three parts: one to support the gods, one public to support the warriors defending the state, and one private to support the farm owners.[39] This illustrates the classic Greek interest in balance.

Aristotle's views on the ideal size of the city are less specific, although he believed there needed to be limits so inhabitants could know each other's character and thus properly govern. Aristotle did not think justice should be blind. As he stated it:

> A state then only begins to exist when it has attained a population sufficient for a good life in the political community; it may somewhat exceed this number, but as I was saying there must be a limit. What should be the limit will be easily ascertained by experience.—If the citizens of a state are to judge and distribute offices according to merit, then they must know each other's characters: where they do not possess this knowledge, both the election to offices and the decisions of lawsuits will go wrong.— Clearly then the best limit of the population of a state is the largest number which suffices for

the purposes of life and can be taken at a single view.[40]

Diffusion of People and Ideas

Greek city-states kept growth under control by the policy of creating colonies. When a city began growing too large a colony city was established. Between 479 and 431 B.C.E., over 10,000 families migrated from established cities to newer Greek colonial settlements. Colonization both met the needs of empire and provided a safety valve for a chronic population problem. This diffusion of population led in turn to a spread of Greek culture and ideas of government far beyond the Peloponnesus. The military campaigns of Alexander the Great (356–323 B.C.E.) also spread Greek culture and led to the establishment of new cities to control the conquered territory (e.g., Alexandria in Egypt).

ROME

If Greece represented philosophy and the arts, Rome represented power and technology. The city as a physical entity reached a high point under the Roman Caesars. Not until the 19th century was Europe again to see cities as large as those found within the Roman Empire. Rome itself may have contained 1 million inhabitants at its peak, although an analysis of density figures would make an estimate two-thirds that number seem more reasonable; scholarly estimates vary from a low of 250,000 to a high of 1.6 million. These wide variations are a result of different interpretations of inadequate data. The number given in the total Roman census, for example, jumped from 900,000 in 69 B.C.E. to over 4 million in 28 B.C.E. No one is quite sure what this increase indicates—probably an extension of citizenship, perhaps the counting of women and children, perhaps something else.[41]

Readers should remind themselves that all figures on the size of cities before the 19th century should be taken as estimates rather than empirical census counts. At their most accurate, such figures are formed by multiplying the supposed number of dwelling units in a city at a given period, and then by estimating average family size.

Size and Number of Cities

Expertise in the areas of technology and social organization enabled the Romans to organize, administer, and govern an empire containing several cities of more than 200,000 inhabitants. The population of the Roman Empire exceeded that of all but the largest 20th-century superpowers. According to the historian Edward Gibbon, "We are informed that when the emperor Claudius [41 to 54 C.E.] exercised the office of censor, he took account of six million nine hundred and forty-five thousand Roman citizens, who with women and children, must have amounted to about twenty million souls." He concludes that there were "about twice as many provincials as there were citizens, of either sex and of every age; and that the slaves were at least equal in number to the free inhabitants of the Roman world. The total amount of this imperfect calculation would rise to about one hundred and twenty million."[42] The total world population at this time was roughly 250-300 million, so Rome controlled over a third of the world's population.

Italy was said to contain 1,197 cities—however defined—and Spain, according to Pliny, had 360 cities.[43] (Most of these we would consider towns.) North Africa had hundreds of cities, and north of the Alps major cities rose from Vienna to Bordeaux. Even in far-off Britain there were major cities at York, Bath, and London. What made all this possible for hundreds of years was a technology of considerable sophistication and—most importantly—Roman social organization. Wherever the legions conquered, they not only built roads, but also brought Roman law and Roman concepts of government. Rome's domination resulted in centuries of urban imperialism.

Housing and Planning

"Rome, Goddess of the earth and of its people, without a peer or a second" remains the wonder of the ancient world. Yet despite the emperor Augustus's proud claim that he found a city of brick and left one of marble, much of the city centuries later was still composed of buildings with wood frames and wood roofs on narrow crowded alleys. Fire was a constant worry, and the disastrous fires of 64 C.E. that some say Nero started left only 4 of the city's 14 districts intact.

Wealthy Romans lived on Palatine Hill, where the imperial palaces overlooked the Forum with its temples and public buildings and the Coliseum. However, as was the case in Athens, Roman municipal planning was definitely limited in scope. Magnificent though it was, it did not extend beyond the center of the municipality. Once one branched off the main thoroughfare leading to the city gates, there was only a maze of narrow, crooked lanes winding through the squalid tenements that housed the great bulk of the population. Magnificent public squares and public baths were built with public taxes for the more affluent Romans. In time even the Forum became crowded and congested, as the ruins still standing amply testify.

The city was supplied with fresh water through an extensive system of aqueducts. The most important of these, which brought water from the Sabine Hills, was completed in 144 B.C.E. Parts of the aqueducts still stand—testament to the excellence of the engineering and skill of their builders. (However, use of lead pipes in running water into homes gradually poisoned the wealthy with running water.) Rome even had an elaborate sewer system, at least in the better residential areas. It is an unfortunate comment on progress to note that present-day Rome still dumps sewage in the Tiber River. (The beautiful North American city of Victoria similarly dumps its raw sewage into the Pacific.)

In many ways provincial western Roman cities such as Paris, Vienna, Cologne, Mainz, and London exhibited greater civic planning than Rome itself. These cities grew out of semi-permanent military encampments and thus took the gridiron shape of the standard Roman camp (the pattern can be seen today on football fields and also is the origin of the city block). The encampments and later the cities were laid out on a rectangular grid pattern with a gate on each side. The center was reserved for the forum, the coliseum, and municipal buildings such as public baths.

In the conquered lands to the east, where there were already Egyptian, Hellenic, and other cities, the Romans simply took them over under Roman jurisdiction. Thus, while eastern cities differed from each other physically as well as politically, the provincial Roman cities of western Europe because of their commonality of origin, were remarkably similar. (for more detail on Hellenic and Roman planning, see Chapter 13: Planning, New Towns, and New Urbanism). The differences between the older eastern and newer western segments of the empire were never resolved, and the empire eventually split into eastern (Byzantine) and western (Roman) sections.

Transportation

Rome was an exporter not only of goods but also of ideas—such as Roman law, government, and engineering—which enabled Rome to control its hinterland. Rome was an importer of necessary goods and, therefore, depended on the hinterland not only for tribute and slaves but for its very life. The city of Rome could feed its population and also import vast quantities of goods other than food because of

an unrivaled road network and peaceful routes of sea trade. (The roads were built and the galleys powered largely by slaves.) Some 52,000 miles of well-maintained roads facilitated rapid movement of goods and people. Parts of some of the original roads are still in use today, and the quality of their construction surpasses that of most contemporary highways.

With the elimination of Carthage as a rival, the Mediterranean truly became "Interium," or a local sea. Foodstuffs for both the civilian population and the legions could be transported easily and inexpensively from the commercial farming areas of Iberia and North Africa. Rome declined when the African grain-producing areas were lost to the Vandals, and barbarians in Germany, Gaul, and England pressed the empire, disrupting vital transportation routes. Without easy transit the decline of Rome was inevitable since Rome lived off its hinterland.

Life and Leisure

The prosperity of the Roman Empire during its peak and the leisure it afforded the residents of the capital were imperial indeed. By the second century after Christ, between one-third and one-half of the population were on the dole, and even those who worked (including the third of the population who were slaves) rarely spent more than six hours at their jobs. Moreover, by that period, religious and other holidays had been multiplied by the emperors until the ratio of holidays to workdays was one to one.[44]

To amuse the population and keep their minds off uprisings against the emperor, chariot races and gladiatorial combats were staged. The scene of the races was the colossal Circus Maximus, which seated 260,000 persons, and gladiatorial fights were staged at the smaller Coliseum. When the emperor Titus inaugurated the Coliseum in 80 C.E., he imported 5,000 lions, elephants, deer, and other animals to be slaughtered in a single day to excite the spectators.

An aerial view of the old sections of Dubrovnik, Croatia, with its medieval town walls. © Jonathan Blair/Corbis

The role Christians came to play in these amusements is well known. Our contemporary beliefs about proper civic amusements were not necessarily shared by earlier eras of urbanites.

EUROPEAN URBANIZATION UNTIL THE INDUSTRIAL CITY

The dissolution of the Roman Empire in 476 C.E. marked the effective decay of cities in western Europe for a period of 700 years. This is not the place to detail why Rome fell; it is sufficient to note that under the combined impact of the barbarian invasion and internal decay, the empire disintegrated and commerce shrank to a bare minimum. Once proud Roman provincial centers disappeared or declined to the point of insignificance. By the end of the sixth century, war, devastation, plague, and starvation had destroyed the glory that once was Rome.

The city was reduced to a collection of separate villages whose population had taken shelter in the ruins of ancient grandeur and had dug wells to replace the aqueducts. The small population was supported by the pope, rather than by the emperor, from the produce of the papal territory.[45] Nonetheless, while the social and physical city withered and decayed into ruins, the idea and myth of Rome and a Roman Empire remained alive even in the darkest medieval periods, and led eventually in the Renaissance to a new burst of urban activity.

The throttling of Mediterranean trade by the advance of Islam in the seventh century, and the pillaging raids of the Norsemen in the ninth century, did further damage to what remained of European commercial life. In the east, however, cities continued to prosper.

Constantinople, built by the emperor Constantine between 324 and 330 C.E., survived as the capital of the Byzantine Empire until its conquest by the Turks in 1453. It was renamed Istanbul.

The Medieval Feudal System

The preceding pages discussed the development of the Western city through the Roman period. Here particular emphasis is placed on the reemergence of European urban places after the decline of Rome, and on how such cities laid the basis for the cities with which we are all so familiar.

The fall of Rome meant that each locality was isolated from every other and thus had to become self-sufficient in order to survive. Local lords offered peasants in the region protection from outside raiders in return for the virtual slavery—called *serfdom*—of the peasants. Removed from outside influences, local social structures congealed into hereditary hierarchies, with the local lord at the top of the pyramid of social stratification and the serfs at the bottom.[46]

It is important to note that the economic and political base of the feudal system, unlike that of the Roman period, was rural, not urban. Its center was not a city but the rural manor or castle from which the local peasantry could be controlled. Long-range trade all but vanished. The economy was a subsistence agriculture based solely on what was produced in the local area; transportation of goods from one area to another was extremely difficult. Lack of communication, the virtual absence of a commonly accepted currency, and the land-tenure system that bound serfs to the soil all contributed to a narrow inward-looking localism.

By the time of Charlemagne (9th century) the cities—or towns—had lost most of their urban functions:

> The Carolingians used the ancient cities as places of habitation, as fortified settlements

from which to dominate the surrounding countryside. The surviving physical apparatus of the old town the walls, and buildings, served because it already existed, a convenient legacy of an earlier age.[47]

However, in the few provincial cities that managed to survive with sharply reduced populations Catholic bishops often became the rulers. The Catholic church had based its diocesan boundaries on those of the old Roman cities, and as the empire faded and then collapsed, the bishops came to exercise secular as well as religious power. By the 9th century, *civitas* had come to be synonymous with these "episcopal cities."[48] The "episcopal cities" were cities in name only, for they more clearly resembled medieval fortresses than true cities. They had a maximum of 2,000 or 3,000 persons and were frequently smaller.[49]

Town Revival

Cities began to revive, very slowly, in the 11th century. According to Pirenne, most of these new towns were not continuations of ancient cities but new social entities. Originally they were formed as a by-product of the merchant caravans that stopped to trade outside the walls of the medieval "episcopal cities" such as Amiens, Tours, and Cologne. Under the influence of trade the old Roman cities took on new life and slowly became repopulated, while new towns were established. Also, trading groups formed around the military burgs, along seacoasts, on riverbanks, and at the junctions of the natural routes of trade and communication.[50]

Over time the seasonal fairs came to take on a more or less permanent year-round character. By the 13th century merchants had an important role in the growing medieval towns. Revitalized city life was most prominent in Italy when city-states such as Venice established extensive commercial ties with the Byzantine and even the Arab empires. Trade with Constantinople enabled the Venetians to prosper and in time create a mini-empire of their own based upon the skills of their sea captains and the size of their fleets.

Two external factors during the Middle Ages also greatly contributed to the growth of towns elsewhere in Europe: (1) the Crusaders and (2) the overall population growth. A great impetus for the revival of trade came from the medieval religious crusades. The Crusaders returned from the urban Byzantine Empire with newly developed tastes for the consumer goods and luxuries of the east. The crusading movement provided an excellent opportunity for the town entrepreneurs to put their commercial instincts into practice.[51] Sociologically, the marketplace made merchants negotiators responding to market conditions.

Trading activities and increased political stability led to a more constant food supply, which in turn resulted in lower death rates and improvement in the rate of natural increase of the population. Technological innovations also contributed to population growth. The moldboard plow, which had been used in Roman times, was rediscovered. This heavier plow could turn the tight soils of northern Europe, and it came to be commonly used. The substitution of three-field rotation for the two-field system also allowed three plantings a year rather than two. The effect of these agricultural improvements was to double production and permit stable growth.

England in the time of William the Conqueror (1066) had a population of approximately 1.8 million. Three hundred years later the population had increased to roughly 2.7 million. Some of this increased population migrated to the small but growing towns. Without such increases, the growth of towns would hardly have been possible.

While the feudal order was basically rural, certain elements of the medieval legal and social system indirectly encouraged the growth of towns. Feudal lords were forbidden by custom to sell their lands, but lords badly in need of new funds could sell charters for new towns within

their lands. Also, by encouraging the growth of older towns, such lords could increase their annual rents. Towns were frequently able to purchase or bargain for various rights, such as the right to hold a regular market, the right to coin money and establish weights and measures, the right of citizens to be tried in their own courts, and—most importantly—the right to bear arms.[52]

Over time cities became more or less autonomous and self-governing. City charters, in fact, bestowed the right of citizenship upon those living within the urban walls. As a result, medieval cities attracted the more skilled and the more ambitious of the rural population. In a sense the towns did not grow out of the feudal social order but in opposition to it. English common law developed in this way.

Characteristics of Towns

Medieval cities were quite small by contemporary standards, having hardly more inhabitants than present-day towns (Table 2.1). Even during the Renaissance, cities of considerable prominence often had only 10,000 to 30,000 inhabitants.[53] Only Paris, Florence, Venice, and Milan are thought possibly to have reached populations of 100,000.[54] These figures are of course scholarly estimates of past size, rather than counts taken at the time. Thick walls enclosed the medieval city; watchtowers and sometimes even external moats added to its military defense. The main thoroughfares led directly from the outer gates to the source of protection and power—the cathedral or the feudal castle. The religious cathedral dominated the medieval skyline as the skyscraper dominates the contemporary urban skyline.

The magnificent ring boulevards of Vienna and Paris are reminders of the medieval origins of these cities. When the city walls were finally demolished in the later part of the 19th century, the resulting open space was used to construct the now-famous boulevards.

Table 2.1	Estimated Populations and Areas of Selected Medieval Cities		
City	Year	Population	Land area, acres
Venice	1363	77,700	8,100
Paris	1192	59,200	945
Florence	1381	54,747	268
Milan	1300	52,000	415
Genoa	1500	37,788	732
Rome	1198	35,000	3,450
London	1377	34,971	720
Bologna	1371	32,000	507
Barcelona	1359	27,056	650
Naples	1278	22,000	300
Hamburg	1250	22,000	510
Brussels	1496	19,058	650
Siena	1385	16,700	412
Antwerp	1437	13,760	880
Pisa	1228	13,000	285
Frankfurt	1410	9,844	320
Liège	1470	8,000	200
Amsterdam	1470	7,476	195
Zurich	1357	7,399	175
Berlin	1450	6,000	218
Geneva	1404	4,204	75
Vienna	1391	3,836	90
Dresden	1396	3,745	140
Leipzig	1474	2,076	106

Source: J. C. Russell, *Late Ancient and Medieval Population,* American Philosophical Society, Philadelphia, 1958, pp. 60–62.

Within the medieval towns or burgs could be found a new social class of artisans, weavers, innkeepers, money changers, and metal smiths known as the *bourgeoisie.* This new class of merchants was in many ways the antithesis of the feudal nobility. They were organized into guilds, and their way of life was characterized by trade and functionally specialized production, not by the ownership of land. The rise of the medieval bourgeoisie undermined the traditional system and prepared the way for further changes, for, as a German phrase put it, *"Stadtluft macht frei"* ("City air makes one free").[55]

What eventually developed was a distinct form, a full urban community. Such communi-

ties, as defined by the German sociologist Max Weber, were economically based on trading and commercial relations. Each exhibited the following features: (1) a fortification; (2) a market, a court of its own, and at least partial autonomous law; (3) a related form of association; and (4) at least partial political autonomy and self-governance.[56] Weber argues convincingly that such a self-governing urban community could emerge only in the West, where cities had political autonomy and urban residents shared common patterns of association and social status. By the 14th century the growth of town-based commerce was turning Europe toward an urban-centered, profit-oriented economy.

Plague

Urban development, however, received a major blow from the physical environment in the 14th century with the outbreak of the plague. The plague was spread from the east by fleas carried by rats on ships. However, even the devastation of the plague could not reverse the long-term growth of cities, although in the short run it wrought havoc to a degree that is difficult to exaggerate. In its first three years alone, from 1348 through 1350, the plague, or "black death," wiped out at least one-fourth of the population of Europe. Before the year 1400, mortality due to the plague rose to more than one-third of the population of Europe, or 35 million deaths. One scholar of the plague simply says that "it undoubtedly was the worst disaster that has ever befallen mankind."[57]

Cities, with their congestion, were especially vulnerable. Over half the population of most cities was wiped out. Florence went from 90,000 to 45,000 inhabitants and Siena from 42,000 to 15,000, and Hamburg lost almost two-thirds of its inhabitants.[58] As put by the traditional nursery rhyme:

Ring around a rosie,
Pocket full of posies.
Ashes, ashes we all fall down.

(Rosies were the pox marks the plague made on a victim, and posies were supposed to ward off the plague.) Overall some 35 million Europeans died of the plague.

Since the path of the black death—it began in India and spread to the Middle East and then Europe—followed the major trade routes, the effects were most pronounced in seaports and caravan centers.[59] The blow to the cities was severe, but the effect of the plague on the rural manorial system was fatal. The feudal social structure never really recovered. Those peasants who were not killed by the plague fled to the towns, thus depriving the manors of their essential labor force. Serfs fleeing the plague often found that labor shortages had turned them into contract laborers or even town artisans. Population declines changed the economic structure.

The structure of basic social institutions such as the Catholic church was also dramatically altered by the black death. Many of the senior and most learned clergy perished; those who survived were often more concerned with taking care of themselves than their flocks. While some clergy did far more than their duties, others deserted their parishes when plague threatened. Their participation in the general loose living and immorality of the time contributed to the religious upheavals that swept Europe for the next two centuries and culminated in the Protestant Reformation.

Since the plagues were considered to be the result of the wrath and vengeance of God, some people became fanatically religious, while the majority embraced the philosophy of "Live, drink, and be merry, for tomorrow we may die." In the words of one scholar, "Charity grew cold, workers grew arrogant, revenues of Church and State dropped, people everywhere were more self-indulgent and frivolous than ever."[60] Chroniclers stress the lawlessness, depravity, and dissolute behavior of the time. In London, "In one house you might hear them roaring under the pangs of death, in the next tippling, whoring and

belching out blasphemies against God."[61] The plague had given the rural-based feudal system a blow from which it never recovered. From this point onward the history of Western civilization was again to be the history of cities and city inhabitants.

Renaissance Cities

By the 16th century, Europe had fully recovered from the plague, and numerous cities, particularly the Italian city-states, had a wealthy patrician class that had the interest, resources, and time to devote to the development and beautification of their cities. Renaissance cities such as Florence embarked on major building programs.

The revival of interest in the classical style and in classical symmetry, perspective, and proportion had a profound effect on the design of both public and private structures. The artistic talents of artists such as Michelangelo and Leonardo da Vinci were used to beautify the cities; Leonardo also developed proposals for urban planning. Rather than simply building at random, the prosperous city-states hired architects to make planned changes.

The classical effect can be seen in the use of straight streets and regular squares, and particularly in the use of perspective. The early medieval city with its semi-rural nature had aptly symbolized that age. A 16th and 17th-century Renaissance city, such as Florence, symbolized the humanistic ideology of the age and proudly proclaimed its secular urban culture.[62] While the Renaissance city gained ever greater economic and cultural domination over rural areas, it also marked the beginning of the end of the city as a self-governing unit independent of the larger nation-state. During the medieval period, kings and city dwellers had been natural allies, since both wished to subdue the power of the local nobility. In order to cast off the last fetters of feudal restraint, the city burghers supplied the monarch with men and—most importantly—money to fight wars;

the monarch in turn granted ever-larger charter powers to the towns.

Once the monarchs had subdued the rural lords, however, they turned their attention to the prosperous towns. Gradually the independent powers of the cities were reduced as they became part of nations in fact as well as in name. The structure of social organization in Europe was changing to the larger geographical unit: the nation-state. The loss of political independence, however, was compensated for by the economic advantages of being part of a nation-state rather than a collection of semi-independent feudal states and chartered cities. National government usually meant better and safer roads and, therefore, easier and cheaper transport of goods and a larger potential market area. Merchants also had the advantages of reasonably unified laws, a common coinage, and standardized measures of weight and volume—all of which today we take for granted. Emergent business classes prospered from the certainty and stability provided by the king's national government. The capitalist city was coming into existence.

Influences of Technology.   The technological developments of gunpowder and the cannon changed the nature of the walled city. The traditional defenses of rampart, bastion, and moat were of limited utility in stopping cannon fire. Cities that hoped to resist the armies of a king had to shift their attention from interior architecture and urban planning to the engineering of fortifications. Only elaborate defensive outworks could stop cannon fire, and so the city unwittingly became the captive of its own defenses. (See the photo of Palma Nova on p. 268.) While one can certainly question the urbanologist Lewis Mumford's view that the decline of the city as a place of comfortable habitation began with the end of the Middle Ages, it is certainly true that the city of the 17th century was changing.

Unable to grow outward, cities began to expand vertically and fill in open spaces within the city walls. The increased crowding that resulted had a bad effect on both the quality and the length of life. For example, extending the second floor of houses over the street decreased sunlight below; this led to vitamin D deficiency, which caused rickets in children. Filthy living conditions, combined with minimal sanitation and an absence of any knowledge of public health practices, resulted in the rapid spread of contagious diseases and consequently high death rates. As John Graunt's pioneer research on the London Bills of Mortality demonstrated, 17th-century London actually recorded more deaths than births. Only heavy in-migration from the countryside allowed the city to grow in population rather than decline. As late as 1790 the city of London had three deaths for every two births.[63] Well into the 19th century mortality rates in the city still exceeded those in rural districts.[64] European cities only grew when the possibility of jobs attracted rural in-migrants.

Demographic Transition.   Urban growth was closely tied to the growth of the population as a whole, and until about the middle of the 17th century, the population of the world had been growing at a very slow rate: 0.4 percent a year. As a result, by the beginning of the 18th century the world population was roughly 500 million, or double that at the time of Christ. Then momentous changes occurred that resulted in what we call the *demographic transition* or the *demographic revolution*. Population growth suddenly spurted in the latter part of the 18th century, not through increases in the birthrate—it was already high—but through declines in the death rate.

Population increases continued into the 20th century. The term *demographic transition* refers to this transition from a time of high birthrates matched by almost equally high death rates, through a period of declining death rates, to a period where birthrates also begin to decline, and eventually to a period where population stability is reestablished—

this time through low birthrates matched by equally low death rates.

Changes in Agriculture. Much of the decline in death rates can be attributed to technological changes in agriculture that ensured both a better and a more reliable food supply. Without such increases in food supply, cities could not grow and expand. As late as the beginning of the 19th century, the produce of nine farms was still required to support one urban family. (Today each American farmer supports approximately 75 other persons.)

At the beginning of the 18th century English agriculture was still primitive. One-quarter of the farmland was left fallow and thus unproductive each year. Pasturelands and water rights were held in common, as were the woods that provided hunting and firewood. Then, within the span of half a century, English agriculture

was revolutionized. Jethro Tull published the results of 30 years of research on his estates, and the new ideas were quickly adopted by much of the landed aristocracy. Tull advocated planting certain crops on fallow land to restore nutrients to the earth, thus radically increasing the usable acreage. (Today, we still use the expression "being in clover" to indicate prosperity.) He also recommended deep plowing and a system for foddering animals through the winter. Seeds were now planted in rows rather than through broadcasting into the air.

At the same time it was being discovered that selective breeding of animals was far superior to letting nature take its course. Previously it had been believed that animals could only grow larger by eating more. Striking changes can be seen by comparing the weight of animals at the Smithfield Fair in 1710 and 1795; the average weight of oxen went from 370

Box 2.2 *Preindustrial and Industrial Cities: A Comparison*

A comparison of the social structures of preindustrial and industrial cities helps us understand how the cities we live in differ from preindustrial cities and from some cities of the developing nations of the third world. The industrial and preindustrial cities here described are "ideal types"—that is, they do not exist in reality but are rather abstractions or constructs obtained by carrying certain characteristics of each type of city to their logical extremes. Such ideal types can never exist in reality, but they are most useful in accentuating characteristics for the purposes of comparative historical research.

In his much-quoted article "Urbanism as a Way of Life," Louis Wirth gives a number of characteristics that he suggests are common to cities, and in particular to industrial cities.* For Wirth, a city is a permanent settlement possessing the following characteristics: (1) size, (2) density, (3) heterogeneity. The city is the place where large numbers of persons are crowded together in a limited space—persons who have different skills, interests, and cultural backgrounds. The result is the independence, anonymity, and cultural heterogeneity of city dwellers.

Modern industrial cities, he says, are characterized by (1) an extensive division of labor, (2) emphasis on innovation and achievement, (3) lack of primary ties to a localized neighborhood, (4) breakdown of primary groups, leading to social disorganization, (5) reliance on secondary forms of social control, such as the police, (6) interaction with others as players of specific roles rather than as total personalities, (7) destruction of close family life and a transfer of its functions to specialized agencies outside the home, (8) a diversity permitted in values and religious beliefs, (9) encouragement of social mobility and working one's way up, and (10) universal rules applicable to all, such as the same legal system, standardized weights and measures, and common prices. The industrial city thus is achievement oriented and prizes a rationally oriented economic system. It is predominantly a middle-class city. In brief, urbanism as a way of life prizes rationality, secularism, diversity, innovation, and progress. It is change-oriented. According to Wirth, "The larger, the more densely populated, the more heterogeneous the community, the more accentuated the characteristics associated with urban-

continues

Box 2.2   *(concluded)*

ism will be."** (Wirth's views are discussed in detail in Chapter 7: Urban Lifestyles.)

Gideon Sjoberg paints a different picture for preindustrial cities.† He suggests that a number of factors we associate with cities are generic only to industrial cities. In contrast to Wirth he suggests that preindustrial cities serve primarily as governmental or religious centers and only secondarily as commercial hubs. Specialization of work is limited, and the production of goods depends on animate (human or animal) power. There is little division of labor; the artisan participates in every phase of manufacture. Home and workplace are not separate as in the industrial city; an artisan or merchant lives in back of or above the workplace. Justice is based not on what you do but on who you are. Standardization is not of major importance. Different people pay different prices for the same goods, and there is no universal system of weights and measures. In brief, the preindustrial city stresses particularism over universalism. Class and kinship systems are relatively inflexible; education is the prerogative of the rich. A small elite maintains a privileged status over the disadvantaged masses.

Emphasis is on traditional ways of doing things; the guild system discourages innovation. Ascription rather than achievement is the norm; a worker is expected to do the job he or she was born into. A person lives and works in a particular quarter of the city and rarely moves beyond this area. Social control is the responsibility of the primary group rather than secondary groups; persons are subject to strict kinship control. Formal police forces are unnecessary. Family influence is strong, with the traditional extended family accepted as the ideal. Children, and especially sons, are valued. There is great similarity in values, and little diversity in religion is tolerated. Opportunity for social mobility is severely restricted by a caste system or rigid class system. There is little or no middle class; one is either rich or poor.

The preindustrial city lacks what the great French sociologist Émile Durkheim called "moral density," or what we today call "social integration." By contemporary standards the preindustrial city is neither socially nor economically integrated. The walled quarters of the preindustrial city are largely independent units; their physical proximity to one another does not lead to social interaction. The city as a whole may possess heterogeneity, but actual social contacts rarely extend beyond one's own group.

Of course no real city conforms exactly either to the industrial model or to the preindustrial model. Models are best used as aids that sharpen our comparative understanding of differences; they should never be mistaken for actual places.

*Louis Wirth, "Urbanism as a Way of Life," *American Journal of Sociology* 44:1–24, July 1938.

**Ibid., p. 9.

†Gideon Sjoberg, *The Preindustrial City: Past and Present,* Free Press, New York, 1960.

pounds to 800 pounds, that of calves from 50 to 150 pounds, and that of sheep from 38 to 80 pounds.

Accompanying these agricultural improvements in England were the notorious Enclosure Acts, which took the village commons from joint ownership and gave them to the lord enjoying ancient title to the land. While disastrous for the local yeomen, the larger enclosures could be worked more efficiently by the lords who were using the new agricultural knowledge. The result was an increase in both the quality and the quantity of the food supply.

Death rates began to go down, and populations expanded rapidly.

The abandonment of traditional subsistence agriculture and the orientation to a market economy meant that rationality was replacing tradition, and contract was taking the place of custom. The calculation implicit in the land enclosure acts destroyed small peasant landholders but made it possible for London and other cities to be ensured foodstuffs and thus to grow as manufacturing and commercial centers. The movement of agriculture surpluses was facilitated greatly by the construction of new toll roads, which were built in great numbers after 1745.

INDUSTRIAL CITIES

Technological Improvements and the Industrial Revolution

Roughly at the same time that agricultural improvements were both increasing yields and releasing workers, inventions were being made that would allow for the growth of whole new industries. Eighteenth-century inventions in the manufacture of cloth, such as the flying shuttle and the spinning jenny, were capped in 1767 by James Watt's invention of a usable steam engine. The steam engine provided a new and bountiful inanimate source of energy. The cotton industry boomed, and it was soon

followed by other industries. The machines, rather than eliminating the need for workers, rapidly increased the demand for an urban workforce.[65] A factory system began to emerge based on specialization and mechanization. As a consequence, new forms of occupational structure and a more complex stratification system began to develop. In the mechanized, capital-intensive industries, urban bondage replaced rural bondage for poor laborers.

The Second Urban Revolution

The first urban revolution was the emergence of cities, and the second was the 18th-century changes that for the first time made it possible for more than 10 percent of the population to live in urban places. This new urban revolution started in Europe. Without population growth and the release of workers from the land, it is

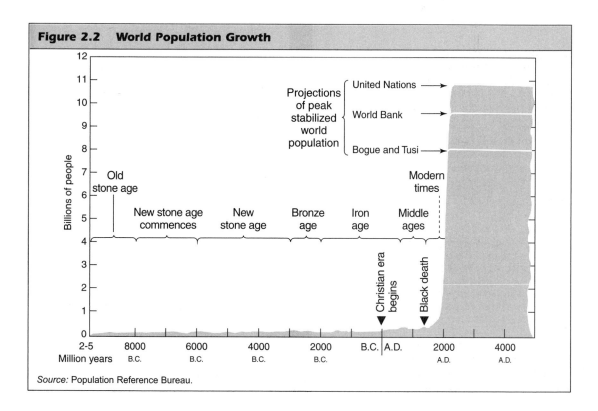

Figure 2.2   World Population Growth

Source: Population Reference Bureau.

hard to see how the early industrial cities could have grown at all for, as noted earlier, unhealthful living conditions in cities meant that they were not able to maintain, much less increase, their population without in-migration from rural areas.

Rapid expansion of population (Figure 2.2) and national economic expansion did not, however, translate into healthful living conditions in the bulging European towns that were turning into cities. Eighteenth-century London was a model of filth, crowding, and disease. The early stages of industrialism hardly did much to improve the situation. While rural mortality decreased, urban mortality was kept high by unbelievably poor sanitary conditions. The novels of Charles Dickens, such as *Oliver Twist* (1838), give an accurate portrayal of life in such cities. Cholera and other epidemics were common until the middle of the 19th century, and until the 1840s many of London's sewers emptied into the Thames just a short

---

Box 2.3   Engels on Industrial Slums

Friedrich Engels (1820–1895), Karl Marx's close associate and collaborator, was an acute observer of the social horrors of 19th-century urban industrialization. He likewise was a fine writer with a mastery of detail and mood rivaling that of Dickens. Note his description of the horror of life in the industrial slums of Manchester.*

> The view from this bridge—mercifully concealed from smaller mortals by a parapet as high as man— is quite characteristic of the entire district. At the bottom the Irk flows, or rather stagnates. It is a narrow, coal-black stinking river full of filth and garbage which it deposits on the lower-lying bank. In dry weather, an extended series of the most revolting blackish green pools of slime remain standing on this bank, out of whose depths bubbles of miasmatic gases constantly rise and give forth a stench that is unbearable even on the bridge forty or fifty feet above the level of the water. . . . Above Ducie Bridge there are tall tannery buildings, and further up are dye-works, bone mills, and gasworks. The total entirety of the liquid wastes and solid offscourings of these works finds its way into the River Irk, which receives as well the contents of the adjacent sewers and privies. One can therefore imagine what kind of residues the stream deposits. Below Ducie Bridge, on the left, one looks into piles of rubbish, the refuse, filth and decaying matter of the courts on the steep left bank of the river. Here one house is packed very closely upon another, and because of the steep pitch of the bank a part of every house is visible. All of them are blackened with smoke, crumbling, old, with broken window panes and window frames. The background is formed by old factory buildings, which resemble barracks. On the right, low-lying bank stands a long row of houses and factories. The second house is a roofless ruin, filled with rubble, and the third stands in such a low situation that the ground floor is uninhabitable and is as a result without windows and doors. The background here is formed by the paupers' cemetery and the stations of the railways to Liverpool and Leeds. Behind these is the workhouse, Manchester's "Poor Law Bastille." It is built on a hill, like a citadel, and from behind its high walls and battlements looks down threateningly upon the working-class quarter that lies below. . . . Passing along a rough path on the river bank, in between posts and washing fines, one penetrates into this chaos of little one-storied, one-roomed huts. Most of them have earth floors, cooking, living and sleeping all take place in one room. In such a hole, barely six feet long and five feet wide, I saw two beds—and what beds and bedding—that filled the room, except for the doorstep and fireplace in several others I found absolutely nothing, although the door was wide open and the inhabitants were leaning against it. Everywhere in front of the doors were rubbish and refuse, it was impossible to see whether any sort of pavement lay under this, but here and there I felt it out with my feet. This whole pile of cattlesheds inhabited by human beings was surrounded on two sides by houses and a factory and on a third side by the river. . . . [A] narrow gateway led out of it into an almost equally miserably-built and miserably-kept labyrinth of dwellings.

*Friedrich Engels, *The Condition of the Working Class in England in 1844* (first published in 1845), Publishers Moscow, 1973.

distance above the ducts that drew drinking water from the river. It was fortunate that the fascination and opportunities of the city continued to attract rural migrants, since without migration the cities would not have grown but died. Until the latter part of the 19th century, the old English observation: "The city is the graveyard of countrymen," was all too accurate.

SUMMARY

This chapter provides an overview of the emergence of urban places and discusses how and why cities developed. An ecosystem model, the ecological complex using the variables of population, organization, environment, and technology (POET), reminds us of the interrelationships of variables in the emergence of cities. For early social groups and emerging cities, environment played a crucial role. For understanding contemporary changes many sociologists prefer political economy models that stress the importance of the capitalistic economic system in shaping urban places and life.

The emergence of permanent settlements was dependent on the invention of agriculture with its promise of agricultural surplus to feed city dwellers. Cities encouraged innovation not only in technology but also in social organization. Kingship, nonagricultural specialists, and a division of labor emerged. Some suggest that Jericho with 600 people around 8000 B.C.E. was an early city. China's cities evolved somewhat after those in the Middle East, and cities in Mesoamerica were not a result of cultural diffusion but of separate invention. By 500 B.C.E. the Mayans had created large settlements. Their successors, the Aztecs, had a city of 200,000 at Tenochtitlán (Mexico City) when the Spanish arrived in 1512.

The major contribution of the Greeks was in the area of social organization, the social invention of the *polis* or city-state. Athenians thus were those who shared a common mythical ancestry from the gods and therefore could worship at the temple of Athena, goddess of the city. The Greeks believed in controlling city size and sent surplus population to establish colonies. This spread both Greek culture and Greek ideas of government. The Roman strength was in technology. They built aqueducts, coliseums, public baths, and 52,000 miles of public roads linking their cities.

The collapse of Rome led to the decay and virtual disappearance of large cities. Medieval society was organized around self-sufficient fortified manors. When burgs began again to grow in the 10th century, they often did so in opposition to the rural-based medieval order. Great plagues, beginning in 1351, were particularly virulent in cities, wiping out one-third of Europe's urban population. Renaissance cities of the 15th and 16th centuries were often self-governing and embarked on major building programs. However, the technologies of cannons and gunpowder meant the city walls were vulnerable and could be breached by a king's army.

Major technological improvements in agriculture beginning in the late 16th century produced greater surpluses, which allowed cities to grow larger than a tenth of the population. A *demographic transition*—from a time of high birthrates and high death rates, through a period of declining death rates, to an era in which birthrates also declined—led to dramatic population increases. Manufacturing inventions (especially for making cloth) and the development of the steam engine in the late 18th century led to industrialization and urban-based factories. Population increases, due to agricultural improvements that increased yields with fewer workers, provided a surplus population to staff the new urban factories. The crowded and growing cities were poor places to live, or even to survive. Death rates were higher than birthrates. Cities grew only because of massive rural in-migration.

Nineteenth-century factory workers living in developing industrial cities such as Manchester, England, suffered from poverty, poor health, and horrible living conditions.

REVIEW QUESTIONS

1. What is the ecological complex and what are its four concepts or categories of variables?

2. What are the strengths and weaknesses of the ecological complex?

3. What role did agriculture play in the development of the first urban settlements?

4. How were the cities and social organization of Athens and Rome similar and how did they differ?

5. How was the medieval city spatially organized and how did its organization change during the Renaissance?

6. How did the 14th-century plague, the black death, change the social organization in Europe?

7. What are the crucial differences in the ideal type social structure of preindustrial and industrial cities as listed by Gidion Sjoberg and Louis Wirth?

8. What is the demographic transition and how did it affect city growth?

9. What was the second urban revolution and what were its consequences?

10. What were the effects of the 19th-century Industrial Revolution on life in cities?

NOTES

1. Manuel Castells, *The Urban Question: A Marxist Approach*, Alan Sheridan (trans.), M.I.T. Press, Cambridge, Mass., 1977.

2. Otis Dudley Duncan, "From Social System to Ecosystem," *Sociological Inquiry* 31:145, 1961.

3. See the discussion by John Logan, Robert Beauregard, and Herbert Gans in *Community and Urban Sociology*, Section Newsletter, American Sociological Association, Summer 1995, pp. 6–7.

4. Mark Gottdiener and Joe Feagin, "The Paradigm Shift in Urban Sociology," *Urban Affairs Quarterly* 24, 174, 1988.

5. Joe Feagan and Robert Parker, *Building American Cities: The Real Estate Game*, Prentice-Hall, Englewood Cliffs, N.J., 1990.

6. Lewis Mumford, *The City in History: Its Origins, Its Transformations and Its Prospects*, Harcourt, Brace, and World, New York, 1961, p. 55.

7. Not everyone agrees with an implicit evolutionary typology such as the one used in this chapter. Bruce Trigger, for instance, strongly argues against an evolutionary approach in explaining the emergence and growth of cities, and he states that "what seems to be required is a more piecemeal and institutional approach to complex societies." Bruce Trigger, "Determinants of Urban Growth in Pre-Industrial Societies," in Peter Ucko, Ruth Tringham, and G. W. Dimbleby (eds.), *Man, Settlement, and Urbanism*, Schenkman, Cambridge, Mass., 1972, p. 576.

8. "Voices of the World," *National Geographic Society*, Washington, D.C., August 1999.

9. J. Carl Haub, "How Many People Have Ever Lived on Earth?" *Population Today*, Nov./Dec., 2002, p 1.

10. Jane Jacobs reverses the order presented here, suggesting that intensive agriculture was the result rather than the cause of cities. This theory suggests that population growth forced agricultural improvements. See Jane Jacobs, *The Economy of Cities*, Random House, New York, 1969.

11. Mumford, op. cit., p. 10.

12. Kathleen Mary Kenyon, *Archeology in the Holy Land*, 3rd ed., Praeger, New York, 1970; 4th ed., Methuen, London, 1985.

13. Kent J. Flannery, "The Origins of Agriculture," *Annual Review of Anthropology*, 2:271–310, 1973.

14. E. Cecil Curwen and Gudmund Hatt, *Plough and Pasture: The Early History of Farming*, Collier Books, New York, 1961, p. 64.

15. Robert Braidwood, "The Agricultural Revolution," *Scientific American*, September 1960, p. 7.

16. Ray Huang, *China: A Macro History*, M. E. Sharpe, London, 1988.

17. John F. Ross, "First City in the New World?" *Smithsonian,* August, 2002, pp. 56–64.

18. Robert Cooke, "Palace Found in Rain Forest," *Los Angeles Times/Washington Post* News Service, September 8, 2000.

19. Colin Woodard, "Wrestling Prizes of the Maya from the Yucatan Jungle," *Chronicle of Higher Education,* October 20, 2000, p. A22.

20. Guy Gugliotta, "The Mayan Glory and Ruin," *National Geographic,* August 2007, pp. 66–109.

21. V. Gordon Childe, *What Happened in History,* rev. ed., Penguin Books, New York, 1964, p. 87.

22. Ibid., p. 86.

23. Amos H. Hawley, *Urban Society,* Rowald Press, New York, 1981, pp. 32—33.

24. Kingsley Davis, "The Origin and Growth of Urbanization in the World," *American Journal of Sociology,* 60:430, March 1955.

25. Gerhard E. Lenski and Jean Lenski, *Human Society: An Introduction to Macrosociology,* McGraw-Hill, New York, 1987.

26. Robert M. Adams, "The Origins of Cities," *Scientific American,* September 1960, p. 7.

27. Herrlee Glessner Creel, *The Birth of China: A Study of the Formative Period of Chinese Civilization,* Reynal and Hitchcock, New York, 1937, p. 279.

28. Adams, op. cit., p. 9.

29. "Did Maya Tap Water for Power?" *Washington Post,* Feb. 18, 1991, p. A3.

30. Creel, op. cit., p. 279.

31. Adams, op. cit., p. 9.

32. V. Gordon Childe, "The Urban Revolution," *Town Planning Review,* 21:4–7, 1950.

33. Stuart Piggot, "The Role of the City in Ancient Civilization," in Robert Moor Fisher (ed.), *The Metropolis in Modern Life,* Russel and Russel, New York, 1955.

34. Gustave Glotz, *Ancient Greece at Work: An Economic History of Greece from the Homeric Period to the Roman Conquest,* M. R. Dobie (trans.), Norton, New York, 1967, pp. 291–93.

35. Numa Denis Fustel de Coulanges, *The Ancient City: A Study on the Religion, Laws and Institutions of Greece and Rome,* Doubleday, Garden City, N.Y., 1956 (first published 1865), p. 134.

36. Max Weber, *The City,* Don Martindale and Gertrud Neuwirth (trans.), Free Press, New York, 1958.

37. Mumford, op. cit., p. 180.

38. Plato, *The Laws, Book V,* Prometheus Books, Cincinnati, 2000.

39. Aristotle, *Politics, Book VII,* Richard Kraut (trans.), Oxford University Press, New York, 1998.

40. Aristotle, *Politics, Book VII,* op. cit.

41. William Petersen, *Population,* Macmillan, New York, 1969, p. 369.

42. All these are basically guesstimates.

43. Ibid., pp. 54–55.

44. Jerome Carcopino, *Daily Life in Ancient Rome: The People and the City at the Height of the Empire,* E. O. Lorimer (trans.), Yale University Press, New Haven, Conn., 1940.

45. Mason Hammond, *The City in the Ancient World,* Harvard University Press, Cambridge, Mass., 1972, p. 324.

46. Henri Pirenne, *Medieval Cities: Their Origins and the Revival of Trade,* Frank D. Halsey (trans.), Princeton University Press, Princeton, N.J., 1939, particularly pp. 84–85. For an excellent discussion of the Byzantine Empire, Islam, India, Japan, and Southeast Asia, see S. N. Eisenstadt and A. Shachar, *Society, Culture, and Urbanization,* Sage, Newbury Park, Calif., 1987.

47. Howard Saalman, *Medieval Cities,* Braziller, New York, 1968, p. 15

48. Weber, op. cit., p. 49.

49. Pirenne, op. cit., p. 76.

50. Fritz Rörig, *The Medieval Town,* University of California Press, Berkeley, 1967, p. 15.

51. For a superb analysis of the importance of trade to the development of Europe, see Fernand Braudel, *The Mediterranean and the Mediterranean World in the Age of Philip II,* Sian Reynolds (trans.), Harper & Row, New York, 1973.

52. Mumford, op. cit., p. 263.

53. Frederick Hiorns, *Town Building in History,* George Harrap, London, 1956, p. 110.

54. Henri Pirenne, *Economic and Social History of Medieval Europe,* I. E. Clegg (trans.), Harcourt, New York, 1956, p. 173.

55. In its precise sense, the phrase refers to the medieval practice of recognizing the freedom of any serf who could manage to remain within the walls of the city for a year and a day.

56. Weber, op. cit., p. 81.

57. William L. Langer, "The Black Death," in Kingsley Davis, *Cities, Their Origin, Growth, and*

Human Impact: Readings from Scientific American, Freeman, San Francisco, 1973, p. 106.

58. Ibid., pp. 106–107.

59. Andre Siegfried, *Routes of Contagion,* Harcourt, Brace and World, New York, 1965.

60. George Deauz, *The Black Death,* Weybright and Talley, New York, 1969, p. 145.

61. Langer, op. cit., p. 109.

62. For an excellent discussion of European urbanization, see Jan de Vries, *European Urbanization 1500–1800,* Harvard University Press, Cambridge, Mass., 1984; and Paul M. Hohenberg and Lynn Hollen Lees, *The Making of Urban Europe 1000–1950,* Harvard University Press, Cambridge, Mass., 1985.

63. Mary Dorothy George, *London Life in the Eighteenth Century,* Harper Torchbooks, New York, 1964, p. 25.

64. Eric Lampara, "The Urbanizing World," in H.J. Dyds and Michael Wolfe (eds.), *The Victorian World,* Routledge & Kegan Paul, London, 1976.

65. Colin Chant and David Goodman, *European Cities and Technologies,* Routledge, London, 2000.

Part II

AMERICAN URBANIZATION

CHAPTER 3

The Rise of Urban America

Thy alabaster cities gleam, undimmed by human tears.
"America, the Beautiful"

OUTLINE

Introduction
Colonists as Town Builders
Major Settlements
    New England
    The Middle Colonies
    The South
    Canada
Colonial Urban Influence
Cities of the New Nation:
    1790–1860
        Rapid Growth
        Marketplace Centers
The Industrial City:
    1860–1950
        Technological Developments
        Spatial Concentration
        Twentieth-Century Dispersion
Political Life
    Corruption and Urban Services
    Political Bosses
    Immigrants' Problems
    Reform Movements
Urban Imagery
    Ambivalence
    Myth of Rural Virtue
Summary

INTRODUCTION

In this chapter we cross the ocean to the wilderness of North America and trace the coming of age of the North American city. As you read through the following pages, note the major role played by environmental factors during the colonial period. (All the major early cities were seaports.) During the 19th century, by contrast, technology changes, particularly the railroad, came to have a far more important—if not dominant—impact. Dramatic population growth through immigration and changes in urban governance and organization also played a major role in the growth and development of cities. This chapter, then, takes us from Jamestown up to the contemporary era.

COLONISTS AS TOWN BUILDERS

We are rather new at being an urban continent. The first European colonists to arrive in North America found a land without indigenous cities. By contrast, Mayan societies in Central America had built major city-based civilizations 1,000 years before Europeans arrived. However, unlike the Spanish colonists, the first English settlers found no existing urban civilizations. At Mesa Verde in southwest Colorado the "ancient ones" had built cliff dwellings, but they had been abandoned before the first Spanish explorers arrived.

By and large, the North American Indian population was nomadic or lived in agricultural villages such as Taos in the Southwest. The farming and trade center Cahokia, located in the Mississippi River valley of southern Illinois, probably was the most populous pre-Columbian settlement north of Mexico, thriving from about 900 to 1400 C.E. The Native American population of North America numbered perhaps a couple million at the time of the first English settlement at Jamestown (1607).[1] (The French established Quebec City in 1608, and the Spanish long had settlements in Florida.)

From the first, the town-building orientation of the English colonists contrasted with Indian ways. North American Indians lived in nature rather than building upon it. They viewed themselves as part of the ecology, part of the physical world. Their goal was not to master nature but to identify their niche and their relationship with the world around them.[2] The Europeans came, on the contrary, not to fit into the environment but to dominate and reshape it. The Puritans, for example, believed themselves to be God's chosen people. Moreover, the Europeans brought a land-tenure system based on private ownership of land—something quite alien to the Native American way of life. Native Americans used the land but didn't think they owned it any more than they owned the waters or the sky.

The colonists' emphasis on conquering nature was fatal for the Indians since the colonists, seeing them as a part of the environment, treated them as just another environmental problem that had to be mastered before civilization could be introduced. The

implication for the future was clear. There was no niche for the Native Americans in the town-oriented civilization of the colonists. What has just been said is, of course, an overgeneralization, but the important point is that the concept of the city came to North America with the European colonists. This concept, with all the special technology, social organizations, and attitudes it entailed, was an importation from post-Renaissance Europe. This meant, among other things, that North American cities had no feudal period.[3]

The plans of the various companies that settled the English colonies in North America called for the establishment of tight little villages and commercial centers. The first successful settlements at Jamestown and Plymouth Colony were in fact small towns. Thus, early English settlers were town dwellers arriving with town expectations. In fact, the initially limited number of farmers was a problem. Jamestown nearly perished from an excess of adventurers and a dearth of skilled artisans and farmers. As John Smith wrote back to the English sponsors of the Jamestown colony,

> When you send againe I intreat you rather send but thirty Carpenters, husbandmen, gardners, fisher men, blacksmiths, masons, and diggers up of trees, roots, well provided; then a tousand of such as we haus: for except we be able both to loge them, and feed them the most will consume with what of necessaries before they can be made good for anything.[4]

To the colonists the wilderness of the new world appeared strange and hostile, and they sorely missed their English towns. William Bradford movingly describes the world of the Pilgrims of 1620:

> They had now no friends to wellcome them nor inns to entertaine or refresh their weatherbeaten bodys, no houses or much less townes to repaire too, to seeke for succoure. . . . Besids, what could they see but a hidious and desolate wilderness, full of wild beasts and wild men? and what multituds ther might be of them they knew not.[5]

MAJOR SETTLEMENTS

The following pages note the role played by population, organization, environment, and technology (POET) in shaping the cities of North America. Five seaports spearheaded the 17th-century English colonies. The northernmost was Boston on New England's "stern and rockbound coast;" the southernmost was the newer (1680) and much smaller settlement of Charles Town (Charleston) in South Carolina.[6]

Barely making an indentation in the 1,100 miles of wilderness separating these two were Newport, in the Providence Plantations of Rhode Island; New Amsterdam, which in 1664 became New York; and William Penn's Philadelphia on the Delaware River at the mouth of the Schuylkill River.

Environment played a heavy role in the early development of these first five cities. All five were seaports, either on the Atlantic or, as in the case of Philadelphia, with access to the sea. Later towns such as Baltimore had similar environmental advantages. As seaports they became commercial centers funneling trade between Europe and the colonies. In terms of social structure all were Protestant and against the established church, except for the ruling class of Charleston and (partially) New York. The social structure of these towns was fashioned by a background of relatively common political institutions; and the economic and cultural roots, whether English or Dutch, lay for the most part in the rising middle class of the old world.[7]

In Canada, by contrast, settlements were not populated by settlers, but rather were government and trade outposts. Quebec City (1608) and Montreal (1642) were garrisons from which fur traders and missionaries ventured into Indian lands.

The five important English urban settlements had certain similar characteristics. First, all had favorable sites. As noted, all were coastal seaports or, in the case of Philadelphia, were on a navigable river with access to the sea. Second, all were commercial cities emphasizing trade and commerce. Third, all had hinterlands or back country to develop, although Newport would find its hinterland increasingly cut off by Boston in the 18th century. Fourth, all were small, both in population and size. Finally, all these cities were fundamentally British. Even New York, which was more cosmopolitan than many European cities, was controlled by a British upper stratum.

New England

The story of New England is the story of its towns, for New England from the very beginning was town oriented. The Puritan religious dissenters who settled New England, starting with their landing at Plymouth Rock in 1620 came heavily from the towns and cities of England. They numbered in their midst many tradesmen, mechanics, and artisans. In the New World these religious dissenters sought to create tight urban communal utopias rather than spreading themselves widely over the landscape. Massachusetts Bay, according to John Winthrop, was to be "as a City upon a Hill." In the colony there existed a social system of a nature unknown outside New England. The cordial union between the clergy, the bench, the bar, and respectable society formed a tight, self-reinforcing social elite.

Boston outstripped its rivals early in both population size and economic influence and kept its lead for a century. Boston had barely 300 residents in the 1630s, but by 1650 there were over 2,000, and a visitor could report—with some exaggeration, perhaps—that it was a sumptuous "city" and "Center Towne and Metropolis of this Wildernesse."[8] By 1742, Boston had a population of 16,000.

The barrenness of Boston's hinterland inclined Bostonians to look to the sea, and the town grew to prosperity on trade and shipbuilding. Before Boston was a generation old, it had "begun to extend its control into the back country, and to develop a metropolitan form of economy that was essentially modern."[9]

Newport, the second New England city down the coast, was founded in 1639 by victims of religious bigotry in Massachusetts. Newport's growth was steady but far from spectacular; in a hundred years the population grew from 96 to 6,200. However, although Newport remained small, its growing commerce and well-ordered community life gave it a significant place in emerging urban America. In Newport, as in Boston, education was encouraged; in addition, Newport, due to the influence of religious leaders such as Anne Hutchinson, had religious toleration.

The Middle Colonies

Manhattan from the beginning had the most cosmopolitan population of the colonial cities, a fact reflected in the diversity of languages spoken there. Father Isaac Jogues recorded that as early as 1643 there were already "men of 18 different languages." Partially because of this mixture of national and religious backgrounds (Dutch Calvinists, Anglicans, Quakers, Baptists, Huguenots, Lutherans, Presbyterians, and even a sprinkling of Jews [Congregation Shearith Israel was organized in 1706]), New York was by far the liveliest of the towns, a position many people maintain it still holds. Interestingly enough, by 1720 a third of New York's population was black. By 1746 half of all New York households owned slaves.[10] After the War for Independence slavery was gradually abandoned in the north—largely for economic reasons. As a result the proportion of blacks in northern cities declined substantially .

New York also had decisive environmental advantages that contributed heavily to its eventual emergence as "the American city." First, Manhattan had a magnificent deepwater natural harbor. Second, New York was blessed with a fertile soil. Third, the city had easy access to

the interior hinterland by way of the Hudson River. The New England towns, by contrast, found their economic growth greatly hindered by the lack of an accessible, fertile hinterland.

Philadelphia, William Penn's "City of Brotherly Love," laid out in 1692, was the youngest of the colonial cities. This was in many ways an advantage, for by the time the city was organized, the Indians had departed and the land was already being settled. A policy of religious toleration and an extremely rich and fertile hinterland allowed rapid growth. By the time Philadelphia was six years old it had 4,000 inhabitants; by 1720 the number had risen to 10,000.[11] Accounts of the day noted the regularity of the town's gridiron pattern with its central square, and most frequently the substantial nature of its buildings.

> A City, and Towns were raised then,
> Wherein we might abide.
> Planters also, and Husband-men,
> Had Land enough beside.
> The best of Houses then was known,
> To be of Wood and Clay,
> But now we build of Brick and Stone,
> Which is a better way.[12]

The South

The southernmost of the colonial cities was Charles Town (Charleston), founded in 1680 on a spit of land between the mouths of the Ashley and Cooper Rivers. The town grew slowly; two decades after its founding it had only 1,100 inhabitants and had "not yet produced any Commodities fit for ye markett or Europe, but a few skins—and a little cedar."[13] For decades rice, indigo, and skins formed the basis of its commerce. Far more than the northern cities, Charleston retained a negative trade balance with Great Britain.

Charleston's social organization and structure were unique among the major cities. The major difference was that the middle-class artisans and shopkeepers who were the backbone of the northern cities were caught in Charleston between the aristocratic pretensions of the large landowners and the increasing skills of the trained slaves. The result was civic atrophy, the major local event being the opening of the horseracing season. Charleston had few municipal services and could not claim even a single tax-supported school.

Canada

To the north of the English colonies the French established Quebec in French Canada as early as 1608, and Montreal, which would develop into a cosmopolitan world city, in 1642. However, unlike the English colonies, the early French Canadian towns were not really major points of settlement or manufacture. Rather, they were garrisons and trading posts specializing in trading for furs with native peoples.[14] From the towns missionaries were also sent out to convert the Indian tribes. Canada had only 70,000 Europeans in 1765 when it became a British possession.

In 1791 Canada was divided into Upper-Canada, which was English, and Lower-Canada, which was French ("Upper" meant farther up— or west—on the St. Lawrence River). Upper-Canada's initial European population was largely composed of Loyalists fleeing the new American republic to the south. Not until the mid-19th century would Canadian cities become manufacturing and economic centers. Until the 1970s Canada's economic and social power remained largely in the hands of descendants of Loyalists.

COLONIAL URBAN INFLUENCE

The relatively small population sizes of the cities and towns of colonial North America should not distract us from their seminal importance. Politically and economically they dominated colonial life. In addition to their commercial function, they also served as the places where new ideas and forms of social organization could be developed. Because the colonial cities had to meet uniquely urban problems, such as paving streets, removing garbage, and caring for the poor, collective efforts developed.

As a result of the town-based settlement pattern, by 1690 almost 10 percent of the colonial population was urban, possibly a higher percentage than that found in England itself at the same time. With the subduing of the Indians and the opening up of the hinterland for cultivation, the percentage (not, of course, the actual number) of urban dwellers decreased between 1690 and 1790. The opening up of frontier hinterlands permitted greater population dispersal than had previously been possible. Not until 1830 was the urban percentage of the total population as high as it had been at the close of the 17th century.[15]

The cities set the political as well as the social tone. And the merchant classes became increasingly dissatisfied with British policy, especially new British tax measures. Boston, a center of opposition, was called "the metropolis of sedition." This was not surprising, since Britain's revenue policy had struck deeply at urban prosperity. Business and commercial leaders were determined to resist the Crown rather than suffer financial reverses on top of restraints of liberty. This helps to explain the middle-class and upper-class nature of much of the support for the American Revolution. As Lord Howe, commander of the British forces at the time of the American Revolution, noted, "Almost all of the People of Parts and Spirit were in the Rebellion."[16] Urban-based merchants, rather than frontier farmers, were the most upset by "taxation without representation."

CITIES OF THE NEW NATION: 1790–1860

The first United States census, taken in 1790, revealed that only 5 percent of the new nation's 4 million people lived in places of 2,500 or more.

America's population was overwhelmingly rural, but this demographic dominance was not reflected in the distribution of power or the composition of the leadership groups. The urban population had an influence on government, finance, and society far out of proportion to its size. The Federalist Party, which elected John Adams as the second president, was largely an urban-based party representing commercial and banking, rather than agrarian interests.

Although three-quarters of the national population still lived within 50 miles of the Atlantic Ocean, and only 5 percent of the population lived west of the Allegheny Mountains, there were already clear and widening differences between townspeople and rural dwellers. The farmers' orientation was toward the expanding western frontier, while the townspeople were still oriented toward Europe. Because of their status as ocean ports, the American coastal cities frequently had more in common with the Old World, and certainly better communication with it, than with their own hinterlands. Traveling from Washington to New York took eight days by horse or coach in 1790.

The census of 1790 showed that the largest city in the young nation was New York, with 33,000 inhabitants. Philadelphia was the second-largest city, with a population of 28,000 (see table 3.1). Twenty years later New York had over 100,000 persons. Such rapid growth of the cities after the Revolutionary War was not only the result of foreign and rural immigration; an exceptionally high rate of natural replacement also played a large part. Precise data are lacking, but it is estimated that each married woman in 1790 bore an average of almost eight children. One result of the high birthrate and the immigration from Europe of young adults was a national median age of only 16 years. (By comparison, the median age for the white population in 2010 was 39 years.) Between 1790 and 1860 the population would increase dramatically, doubling every 23 years—a rate equivalent to that in some developing countries today.

Table 3.1	Great Cities of America, 1790, 1870 (post–Civil War), 2010*	
1790	**1870**	**2010**
New York, NY	New York, NY	New York, NY
Philadelphia, PA	Philadelphia, PA	Los Angeles, CA
Boston, MA	Brooklyn, NY	Chicago, IL
Charleston, SC	St. Louis, MO	Houston, TX
Baltimore, MD	Chicago, IL	Phoenix, AZ
Salem, MA	Baltimore, MD	Philadelphia, PA
Newport, RI	Boston, MA	San Antonio, TX
Providence, RI	Cincinnati, OH	San Diego, CA
Gloucester, MA	New Orleans, LA	Dallas, TX
Newburyport, MA	San Francisco, CA	San Jose, CA

*City population only, not total metropolitan area population.

Source: U.S. Census Bureau and *Statistical Abstract of the United States,* 2010.

The sheer abundance of land and the almost unlimited possibilities for fee-simple tenure meant freedom from Europe's lingering feudal constraints.[17] As put by a European visitor, "It does not seem difficult to find out the reasons why people multiply faster here than in Europe. . . . There is such an amount of good land yet uncultivated that a newly married man can get a spot of ground where he may comfortably subsist with his wife and children."[18]

As table 3.2 indicates, the percentage of the population that is urban has grown every

Table 3.2	Percent of Population Urban, United States, 1790–2010		
1790	5.1	1910	45.7
1800	6.1	1920	51.2
1810	7.3	1930	56.2
1820	7.2	1940	56.5
1830	8.8	1950 (new def.)	64.0
1840	10.8	1960	69.9
1850	15.3	1970	73.5
1860	19.8	1980	73.7
1870	25.7	1990	73.9
1880	28.2	2000	74.5
1890	35.1	2010	79.0
1900	39.7		

Source: U.S. Bureau of the Census and *Statistical Abstract of the United States*, 2010.

Wall Street, New York City, 1790. The two men in the foreground are Governor Phillip Schuller and Alexander Hamilton. Walking toward them are Aaron Burr and his daughter, Theodosia. Burr would kill Hamilton in a duel in 1804. Reproduction after painting by Jennie Brownscombe. Museum of the City of New York, The J. Clarence Davies Collection

decade except 1810–1820. The decline in that decade was chiefly due to the destruction of American commerce resulting from the Embargo Acts and the War of 1812. That war came close to destroying the coastal cities; and partially as a result of isolation from English manufacturers and products, the American cities began developing manufacturing interests. Even Thomas Jefferson, previously an ardent opponent of cities, was forced to concede:

> He, therefore, who is now against domestic manufacture, must be for reducing us either to dependence on that foreign nation or to be clothed in skins and to live like wild beasts in dens and caverns. I am not one of them; experience has taught me that manufacturers are now as necessary to our independence as to our comfort.[19]

Rapid Growth

The period before the Civil War saw a rapid expansion of existing cities and the founding of many new ones. The invention of the railroad played a major role in this growth. During the period from 1820 to 1860, cities grew at a more rapid rate than at any other time before or since in American history.[20] Cincinnati, Pittsburgh, Louisville, Detroit, Chicago, Denver, San Francisco, Portland, and Seattle are all early- and mid-19th-century cities. In the far West, the discovery of gold and then silver did much to spur town building. Some settlements later became ghost towns, but San Francisco prospered as *the* major city of the West.

The influence of environmental factors on the growth of 19th-century cities can be seen from the fact that of the nine cities that by 1860 had passed the 100,000 mark, eight were ports. The one exception really wasn't an exception; it was the then-independent city of Brooklyn, which shared the benefits of the country's greatest harbor.[21]

By the eve of the Civil War (1861–1865) the first city of the nation was clearly New York. It had both a magnificent harbor and a large hinterland to sustain growth, and relatively flat terrain westward from the Hudson River. Nonetheless, what ensured New York its dominance was the willingness to speculate on the technologies of first the Erie Canal and then the railroad. Mayor DeWitt Clinton at the canal opening prophesied that it would "create the greatest inland trade ever witnessed" and allow New York to "become the granary of the world, the emporium of commerce, the seat of manufactures, the focus of moneyed operations." He was right. The completion of the canal from Albany to Buffalo in 1825 meant goods could move by water from the Great Lakes to New York City. It gave New York an economic supremacy that has yet to be surpassed. New York's quick acceptance of railroads as a technological breakthrough, and the possibilities thus presented, further solidified the city's dominant position.

By the time of the Civil War not only was New York the most important American city; it also had become a major world metropolis. New York grew from just over 60,000 in 1800 to over 1 million in 1860. Of the world's cities, only London and Paris were larger. By 1860, in addition to serving as the nation's financial center, New York also handled one-third of the country's exports and a full two-thirds of the imports. New York's increase in size was matched by the increasing heterogeneity of its inhabitants, with their different tastes, aspirations, and needs—all of which could be best satisfied only in the large city.

Land speculation spurred the growth of cities. Fueled by a stream of immigrants and a greed for profits, cities went through periods of wild land speculation and building mania, only to be followed eventually by economic collapse and depression. Cincinnati, the "Queen City of the West," for example, experienced a boom during the 1820s, and during that decade its population expanded rapidly as a result of the development and use of steamboats. In other cities the technology of the railroad played a similar role in spurring growth.

Only in the deep South, where cotton was king and slavery remained, did the building of cities languish. In the plantation owners' view, cotton fields came before manufacturing and commerce. The dominance of agriculture can be seen in the development—or, more correctly, the lack of development—of Charleston. At the beginning of the 19th century Charleston was the fifth-largest American city; by 1860 it had slipped to 26th place.[22] As a consequence of the Civil War, a devastating earthquake, and economic stagnation, Charleston was not numbered among even the 50 largest cities in 1900. The city had lost its economic reason for existing. The post–Civil War stagnation of Charleston is reflected in the saying that Charleston was "too poor to paint and too proud to whitewash."

Marketplace Centers

Before the Civil War, American cities, while undergoing tremendous growth, still retained many preindustrial characteristics. The urban economy was still in a commercial rather than an industrial stage. Businesspeople were primarily merchants who intermittently took on subsidiary functions such as manufacturing, banking, and speculating. In 1850, 85 percent of the population was still classified as rural; 64 percent was engaged in agriculture. Physically, the city prior to the Civil War was compact enough to walk around, with a radius extending not more than 3 miles. The separation of workplace and residence so common in contemporary American cities was limited. Local transportation technology was limited and relatively expensive. Omnibuses (an urban horse-drawn stagecoach first operated in 1827) were slow, uncomfortable, and relatively expensive. Residences, businesses, and public buildings were intermixed with little specialization by area: "The first floor was given over to commerce, the second and third reserved for the family and clerks, and the fourth perhaps for storage. People lived and worked in the same house or at least in the same neighborhood."[23]

The separation that did occur was the obverse of the pattern of wealthy in the suburbs and poor in the city that we have come to accept as the American norm. (See Chapters 4 and 5 for discussion of contemporary urban growth.) In early American cities, the well-to-do tended to live, not on the periphery, but near the center. In an era of slow, uncomfortable, and inadequate transportation, the poor were more often relegated to the less accessible areas on the periphery.[24]

THE INDUSTRIAL CITY: 1860–1950

The Civil War accelerated the shift from a mercantile or trade economy to an industrial one. Aided by new protective tariffs and inflated profits stimulated by the war, northern industrialists began producing steel, coal, and woolen goods, most of which had previously been imported. The wartime closing of the Mississippi was a boon to Chicago and the east–west railroads.

At its hundred-year anniversary (1880), the American nation had grown to 50 million and stretched from coast to coast. The lands of the Louisiana Purchase and the Northwest Cession were already settled, while the western prairie was being peopled and plowed. However, in retrospect, this was the end, not the beginning, of the age of agriculture. The census of 1880 for the first time indicated that less than half the employable population worked in agriculture. Meanwhile, foreign immigration was swelling the cities, and urban areas held 28 percent of the population.

The year 1900 showed a census count of 76 million persons. (Today, we have 305 million people.) In 1890, New York was the nation's largest city with 1.5 million (Brooklyn, then separate, had 800,000 more people).[25] The other cities with over a million persons were Chicago and Philadelphia. By 1900, 4 out of 10 Americans lived in cities.[26]

During the first quarter of the 20th century, urbanism became the controlling factor in national life. Capital-intensive industrialism

had changed America from a rural to an urban continent. The extent of this change can be seen in table 3.3.

While the American image was of the frontier, the bulk of the nation's actual growth during the 19th century took place in cities. (The classic statement on the significance of the West was Frederick J. Turner's famous 1893 paper, "The Frontier in American History." A major urban response did not come until almost half a century later, with Arthur M. Schlesinger's "The City in American History."[27])

By the opening of the 20th century, 50 cities had populations of over 100,000; the most notable of these new cities was the prairie metropolis of Chicago, which had bet heavily on the technology of the railroad. Chicago mushroomed from 4,100 at the time of its incorporation in 1833 to 1 million in 1890 and 2 million in 1910. Between 1850 and 1890 Chicago doubled its population every decade. Nationally, in the 100 years between 1790 and 1890 the total population grew 16-fold, while the urban population grew 139-fold.

Technological Developments

Urban technology opened the frontier and overcame the environment. This was particu-

Table 3.3	Number of Urban Places, by Population Size: Selected Years, 1850–2000			
Size of Place	1850	1900	1950	2000
1,000,000 or more	—	3	5	9
500,000 to 1,000,000	1	3	13	17
250,000 to 500,000	—	9	23	41
100,000 to 250,000	5	23	65	151
50,000 to 100,000	4	40	126	354
25,000 to 50,000	16	82	252	622
10,000 to 25,000	36	280	778	1,384

Source: U.S. Census Bureau, U.S. Census of Population 1950, vol. II; 1980, vol. I, table 23, and Statistical Abstract of the United States, 2000.

larly true west of the Mississippi, where the technology of the railroad had reversed earlier patterns of settlement. Josiah Strong, writing in 1885, noted:

> In the Middle States the farms were the first taken, then the town sprang up to supply its wants, and at length the railway connected it with the world, but in the West the order is reversed—first the railroad, then the towns, then the farms. Settlement is, consequently, much more rapid, and the city stamps the country, instead of the country stamping the city. It is the cities and towns which will frame state constitutions, make laws, create public opinion, establish social usages, and fix standards of morals in the West.[28]

The railroad was crucial in the development of the West. During the second half of the 19th century, the railroads expanded from 9,000 to 193,000 miles—much of it built with federal loans and land grants. The railroads literally opened the West. The building of the Canadian Pacific in Canada had a similar effect. Both Calgary and Vancouver boomed in response to the railroad. In the American South new railroad-based cities such as Atlanta and industrial Birmingham were growing in size and power.

At the same time, changes in farming technology were converting the self-sufficient yeoman into an entrepreneur raising cash crops for market. Horse-drawn mechanical McCormick reapers, steel plows, and mechanical threshers heralded the shift from self-sufficient to commercial farming.

Within cities technology was making massive changes. In the brief 12-year period between 1877 and 1889, inventions such as steel-frame buildings, the light bulb, electric power lines, electric streetcars, electric elevators, the telephone, subways, and the internal combustion engine were introduced.[29] Such inventions spurred the growth of cities.

The compact trade- and commerce-oriented central business districts of northern industrial and commercial cities reflected the needs of the 19th century. Before the widespread use of the automobile and telephone, it was necessary that business offices be close to one another so that information could be transmitted by means of messengers. High central-city land values were an inevitable result of the common business demand for a central location. Nineteenth-century inventions such as a practical steam elevator and steel-girded buildings enabled the core area to become even more densely inhabited. Prior to the late 1880s office buildings were supported by massive outer walls and about 10 stories was the maximum size. (The Washington Monument reflects this construction method—the stone blocks at the base are 15 feet wide while those at the top are 18 inches wide.) However, steel-girded buildings no longer had to be supported by massive outer walls; now the walls were literally hung from a building's steel frame. Offices and businesses could be stacked vertically upon one another as high as foundations, local ordinances, and economics would allow.

The fact that New York, Chicago, Philadelphia, and San Francisco, to name only a few, are essentially cities built before the 20th century, and before the automobile, is a problem we have to cope with today. Any attempt to deal with present-day transportation or pollution problems has to take into account the fact that most American cities were planned and built in the 19th century. We still live largely in cities designed, at best, for the age of steam and the horse-drawn streetcar.

Incidentally, a quick way of determining the earlier boundaries of a city is to note the location of older cemeteries. Since cemeteries were traditionally placed on the outskirts, large cemeteries within present city boundaries effectively show earlier extent of urban growth.

Spatial Concentration

The great cities of the East and Midwest, with their multitude of immigrants, frantic pace,

This Currier & Ives print, "Westward the Course of Empire Takes Its Way" expresses
19th-century America's belief in "Manifest Destiny." The print suggests that as the
frontier recedes, the railroad brings settlement, civilization (schools), and prosperity.
Library of Congress

municipal corruption, and industrial productivity, built much of their present physical plant
in the era of steam, which stretched from the
1880s to the depression of the 1930s. It is important to remember that the late-19th-century
city was a city of *concentration and centralization*
accentuated by industrialization.

Industrialization encouraged centripetal
rather than centrifugal forces. Since steam is
most cheaply generated in large quantities and
must be used close to where it is produced,
steam power fostered a compact city, and encouraged the close proximity of factory and
power supply. Manufacturing was concentrated
in a core area that surrounded the central business district and had access to rail and often
water transportation. This in turn concentrated
managerial and wholesale distributing activities.

Low worker pay and the limited transportation technology meant that workers had to live
near the factories; this in turn gave rise to row
upon row of densely packed tenements. The
separation of place of residence and place of
work was a luxury only the very wealthy in com-

muting suburbs could afford. Surrounding the
factories, slumlords built jaw-to-jaw tenements
on every available open space. These tenements
were then packed to unbelievable densities with
immigrant workers—first Irish, then German,
Jewish, Italian, and Polish—who could afford
no other housing on the pitiful wages they
made working 12 hours a day, six days a week.
Slums provided the immigrant laborers with
housing close to the factories, but at a horren-
dous price in terms of health and quality of life.

Twentieth-Century Dispersion

While 19th-century technology fostered concentration, technologies of the last hundred
years have fostered metropolitan-area dispersion. Three technological inventions heavily
contributed to this change: the telephone,
electricity, and transportation advances, especially the electric streetcar, the automobile,
and the truck. The telephone meant that city
business could be conducted other than by
face-to-face contact or messenger. It enabled

Box 3.1   A Note on Urban Pollution

It is revealing, if depressing, to recognize that the problems of pollution and environmental destruction are not new to North American cities. Until late in the 19th century most American cities, such as Baltimore and New Orleans, still relied on open trenches for sewage. The only municipal garbage collection provided by most cities until after the Civil War was that provided by scavenging hogs and dogs and other carrion eaters. Colonial Charleston even passed an ordinance protecting vultures because they performed a public service by cleaning the carcasses of dead animals.* In 1666 a Boston municipal ordinance ordered the inhabitants to bury all filth, while "all garbage, beasts, entrails, etc.," were to be thrown from the drawbridge into Mill Creek.† Colonial Boston's system of burying what one could and throwing the rest into the nearest river was used by many cities well into the modern era. The beautiful Canadian city of Victoria is still fighting environmental orders to stop dumping all its raw sewage untreated into the Pacific Ocean.

A description of Pittsburgh dating from the late 19th century details its air pollution in terms that suggest air pollution was good for health:

> Pittsburgh is a smoky, dismal city, at her best. At her worst, nothing darker, dingier or more dispiriting can be imagined. The city is in the heart of the soft coal region; and the smoke from her dwellings, stores, factories, foundries, and steamboats, uniting settles in a cloud over the narrow valley in which she is built, until the very sun looks coppery through the sooty haze. According to a circular of the Pittsburgh Board of Trade, about twenty per cent, or one-fifth of all the coal used in the factories and dwellings of the city escapes into the air in the form of smoke. . . . But her inhabitants do not seem to mind it; and the doctors hold that this smoke from the carbon, sulphur, and iodine contained in it, is highly favorable to the lung and cutaneous diseases, and is the sure death of malaria and its attendant fevers.‡

Public waterworks were luxuries found in few communities until well after the Civil War. Medium-size cities such as Providence, Rochester, and Milwaukee relied entirely on private wells and water carriers. Sanitation fared little better.§ Until the twentieth century, bathrooms were all but nonexistent in the congested slums.

* Carl Bridenbaugh, *Cities in the Wilderness*, Capricorn Books, New York, 1964, p. 18.

† "Victoria Told to Clean up it's Act," *Calgary Herald*, July 22, 2006, pA13.

‡Willard Glazier, *Peculiarities of American Cities*, Hubbard, Philadelphia, 1884, pp. 322–33.

§Blake McKelvey, *The Urbanization of America, 1860–1915*, Rutgers University Press, New Brunswick, N.J., 1963, p. 13.

---

businesses to locate their factories separate from their offices.

Electricity meant factories no longer had to be next to a steam plant. Power could be brought in from a distant electric plant. Before the electric streetcar, separation of places of living from places of work was a luxury restricted to the affluent or well-to-do. Nineteenth-century suburbs developed along commuter railroad lines and were the private preserves of those who had both the time and the money to commute. The North Shore suburbs of Chicago are an example. Common people, on the other hand, walked or rode the horse streetcars to work. At the beginning of the 20th century, the average New Yorker lived a quarter mile, or roughly two blocks, from his or her place of work. Chicago at that time contained 1,690,000 inhabitants, half of them living within 3.2 miles of the city center.[30]

The electric streetcar changed all this. Perfected in 1888 in Richmond, Virginia, the streetcar moved twice as fast as the horse-drawn car and had over three times the carrying capacity. The new system of urban transportation was almost immediately adopted everywhere. By the turn of the century horse car lines, which had accounted for two-thirds of all street railways a decade earlier, had all but vanished. Electric trolleys accounted for 97 percent of all mileage in 1902, with 2 percent still operated by cable car lines and only 1 percent by horse cars.[31]

The result was the rapid development of outer areas of the city and the proliferation of

Note the traffic congestion in downtown Philadelphia of 1897. Pedestrians, streetcars, carriages, and wagons all compete for space. National Archives

new middle-class streetcar suburbs.[32] With one's home along the streetcar line, it was possible to live as far as 12 miles from the central business district and commute relatively rapidly and inexpensively. This led to an outward expansion of the city and the establishment of residential suburbs in strips along the right-of-way of the streetcar line. Those with high positions in the electric traction industry, and corrupt politicians with influence, made fortunes when streetcar lines were built to outlying areas where they just happened to own all the vacant lots.

We should keep in mind that technology is not an economically or politically neutral force.

The benefits of streetcar—and later automobile—technology especially assisted the middle classes in establishing ethnically and racially exclusive suburban neighborhoods. (For elaboration see Chapter 6, The Suburban Era.)

Land lying between the "spokes" formed by the streetcar lines remained undeveloped. The cities thus came to have a rather pronounced star-shaped configuration, with the points of the star being the linear rail lines.[33] This is a shape cities would hold until the era of the automobile.

Where street rail lines intersected, natural breaks in transit took place and secondary business and commercial districts began to develop. These regional shopping areas were the equivalent of the peripheral shopping centers of today. With the coming of the automobile, the city areas between the streetcar lines filled in, and by the 1920s most of the major eastern cities had completed the bulk of their building. The depression of the 1930s effectively stopped downtown building; thus, many central business districts remained basically unchanged until building resumed again in the early 1960s.[34] Outlying suburban areas similarly saw little change until the post–World War II suburbanization boom (Chapter 6).

POLITICAL LIFE

Corruption and Urban Services

Urban corruption has a long American history. In 1853, New York was described in *Putnam's Monthly* as possessing "Filthy streets, the farce of a half-fledged and inefficient police, and the miserably bad government, generally, of an unprincipled common council, in the composition of which ignorance, selfishness, impudence and greediness seem to have an equal share." Over the following score of years the venality and urban politics became synonymous. As Arthur Schlesinger charitably put it, "This lusty urban growth created problems that taxed human resourcefulness to the utmost."[35] A particularly high price was paid in the area of municipal governance. Political institutions that were adequate under simplified rural conditions but inadequate to the task of governing a complicated system of ever-expanding public services and utilities presented an acute problem. The contemporary observer Andrew White was more direct: "With very few exceptions the city governments of the United States are the worst in Christendom . . . the most expensive, the most inefficient, and the most corrupt."[36] Or, as the noted British scholar James A. Bryce put it, "There is no denying that the

government of cities is the one conspicuous failure of the United States."[37]

Boss Tweed of New York, who plundered the city of up to $200 million, was even more explicit: "The population is too helplessly split into races and factions to govern it under universal suffrage, except by bribery or patronage or corruption."[38] The political machines were renowned for graft and voting fraud. Immigrants were encouraged to "vote early and often" for the machine candidates.

Political Bosses

Although the political bosses emptied the public treasury, they also provided poorer citizens with urban services, jobs, and help in solving problems. The bosses were buffers between slum dwellers and the often hostile official bureaucracy. In return for votes, the boss provided not abstract ideals but practical services and benefits. The boss was the one to see when you needed a job, when your child was picked up for delinquency, or when you drank a bit too much and were arrested for drunkenness. The boss would arrange something with the police at the station house or even "go your bail" if the offense was serious. The boss was certain to attend every wedding and wake in the neighborhood, and often provided cash to get the newlyweds going or cover funeral expenses for a widow. The boss produced.

As Boston ward heeler Martin Lomasney straightforwardly expressed it, "There's got to be in every ward somebody that any bloke can come to—no matter what he's done—to get help. Help, you understand; none of your law and justice, but help."[39]

In managing the city the bosses distinguished between dishonest graft and honest graft, or "boodie." The former would include shakedowns, payoffs, and protection money for illegal gambling, liquor, and prostitution. "Boodie," on the other hand, involved using your control over contracts for municipal services and tax assessments to maximize your advantage. In a famous passage, the boss George Washington Plunkitt explained how it worked:

> Just let me explain by examples. My party's in power in the city, and its going to undertake a lot of public improvements. Well, I'm tipped off, say, that they're going to lay out a new park at a certain place. I see my opportunity and I take it. I go to that place and I buy up all the land I can in the neighborhood. Then the board of this or that makes its plan public, and there is a rush to get my land, which nobody cared particular for before. Ain't it perfectly honest to charge a good price and make a profit on my investment and foresight? Of course it is. Well, that's honest graft.[40]

In an urban environment committed to the principle of free enterprise, politicians saw no reason for all the profits to go to business-people rather than politicians.

While the "better classes" viewed all machine bosses as rogues and thieves, the bosses were apparently far more personable and friendly than the elite captains of industry in the business community. A study of 20 city bosses described them as warm and often sentimental men who had come from poor immigrant families. All were naive urbanites, and most were noted for loyalty to their families.[41] The political machine provided a route for social mobility for bright and alert young immigrants. Police departments were also an avenue of upward mobility for first- and second-generation European immigrants.

Without the aid of the ward bosses, the new immigrants would have had an even rougher time than they did. For the immigrants, boss rule was clearly functional. As expressed by the sociologist Robert Merton, "The functional deficiencies of the official structure generate an alternative (unofficial) structure to fulfill existing needs somewhat more effectively."[42]

Immigrants' Problems

The role of immigrants is treated in detail in Chapters 9 and 10. Suffice it to say here that the dimensions of the European immigrant flood are hard to overemphasize—probably more than 40 million persons between 1800 and 1925. From the 1840s onward, waves of immigrants landed in the major northeastern ports. The first of the mass ethnic immigrations was that of the Irish, who were driven from home in the late 1840s by the ravages of the potato blight. Later, Germans and Scandinavians poured into the Midwest, particularly after the development of steamships and the opening of the railroads to Chicago.

Immigration accelerated after the Civil War, spurred on by the need for industrialization. This was a period of industrial and continental expansion. Between 1860 and 1870, 25 of the 38 states took official action to stimulate immigration, offering not only voting rights but also sometimes land and bonuses.[43]

By 1890 New York had half as many Italians as Naples, as many Germans as Hamburg, twice as many Irish as Dublin, and two and a half times the number of Jews as Warsaw.[44] The traditions, customs, religion, and sheer numbers of these immigrants made fast assimilation impossible. Between 1901 and 1910 alone, immigration officials counted over 9 million immigrants. These newcomers came largely from peasant backgrounds. They were packed into teeming slums and delegated to the lowest-paying and most menial jobs. Native-born Protestant Americans suddenly became aware of the fact that 40 percent of the 1910 population was of foreign stock—that is, immigrants or the offspring of immigrants.[45] The percentage was considerably higher in the large northern industrial cities, where over half the population was invariably of foreign stock.

To WASP (White Anglo-Saxon Protestant) writers around the turn of the century, the sins of the city were frequently translated into the sins of the new immigrant groups pouring into the ghettos of the central core. Slum housing, poor health conditions, and high crime rates were all blamed on the newcomers. Those on the city's periphery and in the emerging upper-class and upper–middle-class suburbs associated political corruption with the central city. Native-born Americans tended to view city problems as being the fault of the immigrants, frequently Catholic or Jewish, who inhabited the central-city ghettos. Even sympathetic reformers such as Jacob Riis portrayed central-city slums as anthills teeming with illiterate immigrants. The masses in the ghettos were said to be a threat to democracy.[46] (The Great Migration of African Americans from the rural South to the urban North will be discussed in detail in Chapter 9.)

Reform Movements

The writing of "muckrakers" like Lincoln Steffens, who in his articles on "The Shame of the Cities" exposed municipal corruption, gave considerable publicity to the grosser excesses of municipal corruption, such as deals with utility franchises. To destroy the power of the bosses and their immigrant supporters, reforms were pushed in city after city. Reformers of the period had a distinctly middle-class orientation. Social reformers such as Jane Addams, who founded Hull House to teach immigrants "Americanism" and job skills, and Margaret Sanger, who in 1916 opened the first birth control clinic for immigrants in Brooklyn (today Planned Parenthood), were upper-class or upper–middle-class city dwellers who saw themselves as having a mission to "save" the lower classes. To the general public the problems of the city were viewed then, as today, as problems of and by the poor in the central core.

While the bosses represented personalized politics, reform represented abstract WASP goals such as good citizenship, efficient administration, and proper accounting. The Progressive Movement at the turn of the 20th century, at least in its urban manifestation, was in many respects an attempt by the upper middle class to reform the inner city. This, of course, meant white, Protestant, middle-class groups regaining political power. Political reformers joined with businesspeople in organized groups such as the National Municipal League to "reform" city government by getting rid of the ethnic political bosses.

The National Municipal League provided model charters and moral impetus. By 1912 some 210 communities had dropped the mayor and city-council system and adopted the commission form of government. In 1913 Dayton adopted the first city-manager system, and during the following year 44 other cities followed suit. Under the city-manager system, a nonpolitical manager was appointed to run the city in a businesslike manner. However, in the larger cities the political machines, while they lost a few battles, managed to weather the storm. The coming of World War I directed crusading energies into new channels, and the Roaring Twenties was not a decade noted for municipal reform. While there were exceptions, such as William Hoan, the reform socialist mayor of Milwaukee, many cities during the 1920s had a colorful and corrupt mayor like James ("Gentleman Jimmy") Walker in New York or Big Bill ("The Builder") Thompson in Chicago.

However, in spite of all the city's problems the 1920s marks the first "modern" decade. As of 1920 half the U.S. population was urban, but, more importantly, the decade marked the beginning of the modern age. The car, the telephone, and the radio all became part of middle-class life during the 1920s. While the clothes styles and cars may look strange to us today, the people thought and acted in modern ways. By comparison, earlier decades seem out of another era.

URBAN IMAGERY

Ambivalence

America has never been neutral regarding its great cities; they have been either exalted as the centers of vitality, enterprise, and excitement or denounced as sinks of crime, pollution, and depravity. Our present ambivalence toward our cities is nothing new; even the founding fathers had great reservations about the moral worth of cities. The city was frequently equated by writers such as Thomas Jefferson with all the evils and corruption of the Old World, while an idealized picture of the yeoman farmer represented the virtue of the New World. Thomas Jefferson expressed the sentiments of many of his fellow citizens when he stated in 1787 in a letter to James Madison,

> I think our governments will remain virtuous as long as they are chiefly agricultural; and this will be as long as there shall be vacant land in any part of America. When they get piled upon one another in large cities, as in Europe, they will become corrupt as in Europe.[47]

In a famous letter written in 1800 to Benjamin Rush, Jefferson even saw some virtue in the yellow fever epidemics that periodically ravaged seaboard cities. Philadelphia, for example, lost over 4,000 persons, almost 10 percent of its population, in the epidemic of 1793. Jefferson wrote to Rush:

> When great evils happen I am in the habit of looking out for what good may arise from them as consolations to us, and Providence has in fact, so established the order of things, as that most evils are the means of producing some good. The yellow fever will discourage the growth of great cities in our nation, and I view great cities as pestilential to the morals, the health, and the liberties of man.[48]

This, however, is not the entire picture, for in spite of these sentiments Jefferson proposed a model town plan for Washington, D.C., and after the War of 1812 he came to support urban manufacturing. Also, although in his writings Jefferson advised against sending Americans to Europe for education lest they be contaminated by urban customs, he himself enjoyed visiting Paris and was a social success there. Other Americans were similarly inconsistent.

Benjamin Franklin, never one to be far from the stimulation, pleasures, and excitement of the city, went so far as to say that agriculture was "the only honest way to acquire wealth . . . as a reward for innocent life and virtuous industry." Ben Franklin was many things during his long, productive life, but never a

farmer; and his own way of life indicates that he never considered an innocent life or conventional virtue to be much of a reward. Writers as diverse as de Tocqueville, Emerson, Melville, Hawthorne, and Poe all had strong reservations about the city.[49] In the 20th century the famous architect Frank Lloyd Wright carried on the anti-urban ideology by referring to cities as "a persistent form of social disease." According to de Tocqueville:

> I look upon the size of certain American cities, and especially on the nature of their population, as a real danger which threatens the future security of the democratic republics of the New World; and I venture to predict they will perish from this circumstance, unless the Government succeeds in creating an armed force which while it remains under the control of the majority of the nation, will be independent of town population, and able to repress its excess.[50]

Cowley's line "God the first garden made, and the first city Cain" expressed an attitude toward cities shared by many Americans. Thoreau, sitting in rural solitude watching a sunset, is an acceptable image. Thoreau, sitting on a front stoop in Boston watching the evening rush hour, creates an entirely different image.

Americans, even while pouring into urban areas, have traditionally idealized the country. A Gallup poll indicated that, given the choice, almost half of American adults say they would move to towns with fewer than 10,000 inhabitants or to rural areas.[51] The clearing of the wilderness by the pioneers, and the taming (eradication) of savages—human and animal—were considered highly laudable. By contrast, the building of cities by the sweat and muscle of immigrants was ignored. It is as if we consider the history of the immigrants somewhat discreditable and thus best forgotten.

During the late 19th century vigorous attacks on the city came from writers such as Josiah Strong, who condemned it as the source of the evils of "Rum, Romanism and Rebellion." Strong's book *Our Country* sold a phenomenal—

Box 3.2   *Carl Sandburg's Chicago*

Probably the most quoted image of the raw vitality, strength, and brutality of the early 20th-century American city is Carl Sandburg's poem "Chicago."* An excerpt follows:

> Hog Butcher for the World,
> Tool Maker, Stacker of Wheat,
> Player with Railroads and the Nation's
> Freight Handler;
> Stormy, husky, brawling,
> City of the Big Shoulders:
> They tell me you are wicked and I believe them, for I have seen your painted women under the gas lamps luring the farm boys.
> And they tell me you are crooked and I answer: Yes, it is true I have seen the gunman kill and go free to kill again,
> And they tell me you are brutal and my reply is: On the faces of women and children I have seen the marks of wanton hunger.
> And having answered so I turn once more to those who sneer at this my city, and I give them back the sneer and say to them:
> Come and show me another city with lifted head singing so proud to be alive and coarse and strong and cunning.

> Flinging magnetic curses amid the toil of piling job on job, here is a tall bold slugger set vivid against the little soft cities;
> Fierce as a dog with tongue lapping for action, cunning as a savage pitted against the wilderness,
> Bareheaded,
> Shoveling,
> Wrecking,
> Planning,
> Building, breaking, rebuilding,
> Under the smoke, dust all over his mouth, laughing with white teeth,
> Under the terrible burden of destiny laughing as a young man laughs,
> Laughing even as an ignorant fighter laughs who has never lost a battle.
> Bragging and laughing that under his wrist is the pulse, and under his ribs the heart of the people,
> Laughing!
> Laughing the stormy, husky, brawling laughter of Youth, half-naked, sweating, proud to be Hog Butcher, Tool Maker, Stacker of Wheat, Player with Railroads and Freight Handler to the Nation.

*Carl Sandburg, *Chicago Poems,* Holt, New York, 1916.

---

for that date—175,000 copies. He effectively mirrored the fears of small-town Protestant America that urban technology and the growth of foreign immigrant groups were undermining the existing social order and introducing undesirable changes such as political machines, slums, and low church attendance. Several excerpts give the general tone of his "Rum, Romanism and Rebellion" argument:

> The city has become a serious menace to our civilization. . . . It has a particular fascination for the immigrant. Our principal cities in 1880 contained 39.3 percent of our entire German population, and 45.8 percent of the Irish. Our ten larger cities at that time contained only nine percent of the entire population, but 23 percent of the foreign. . . .
> Because our cities are so largely foreign, Romanism finds in them its chief strength. For the same reason the saloon together with the intemperance and liquor power which it repre-

sents, is multiplied. . . . Socialism centers in the city, and the materials of its growth are multiplied with the growth of the city. Here is heaped the social dynamite; here roughs, gamblers, thieves, robbers, lawless and desperate men of all sorts congregate; men who are ready on any pretext to raise riots for the purpose of disruption and plunder; here gather the foreigners and wageworkers who are especially susceptible to socialist arguments; here skepticism and irreligion abound; here inequality is the greatest and most obvious, and the contrast between opulence and penury the most striking; there the suffering is the sorest.[52]

An extremely influential lecture by Frederick Jackson Turner just before the turn of the 20th century, "The Winning of the West," also struck a responsive chord: it glorified the pioneer and the virtues of the West. Needless to say, such homage was not paid to tenement dwellers working under oppressive conditions, who were simply trying to raise decent families. Today, television and other media perpetuate the same myth when giving us drama after drama set in the 19th-century American West, but nothing about the 19th-century American city dweller. The cowboy or pioneer sodbuster, not the factory hand, is the American hero. Criticism of the city contained some contradictory premises, although these were generally not noticed: while it was being castigated for not exhibiting rural or agrarian values, it was also being taken to task for failing to be truly urban and reach the highest ideals of an urban society. In short, the city was at the same time supposed to be both more rural and more urban.

Distrust and dislike of the city crystallized in the later part of the 19th century around the issue of the free coinage of silver, with silver representing the agrarian West and gold the commercial and industrial cities of the East. William Jennings Bryan's campaign for the presidency in 1896 was a major attempt by the rural anti-urbanites to gain national political power. As Bryan put it in his famous "cross of gold" speech, "Burn down your cities and leave our farms, and your cities will spring up again as if by magic; but destroy our farms, and the grass will grow in the streets of every city in the country."[53] By the 20th century Bryan's day had passed, and although rural fundamentalism still had some strength, it was no longer a commanding ideology. The city, not the farm, represented the future.

Myth of Rural Virtue

The myth of agrarian virtue continues to live in politics. One of President Calvin Coolidge's campaign photographs in 1924 showed him posing as a simple farmer haying in Vermont. However, the photograph said more than was intended, for the president's overalls are obviously fresh, his shoes are highly polished, and if one looks carefully, one can see his expensive Pierce Arrow, with Secret Service men waiting

to rush him back into Washington, D.C., once the picture-taking at a Virginia—not Vermont—farm was completed.[54] Within more recent times President Ronald Reagan similarly posed for publicity photos of himself cutting wood on his "ranch," while Bill Clinton ran as a small-town boy from Hope, Arkansas. Similarly, George W. Bush wore a cowboy hat when campaigning and portrayed himself as growing up in a small town and exemplifying small-town family values. Actually he was raised in a cosmopolitan Eastern urban environment.

Demographically, since 1920 America has been a nation of urban dwellers, and with every census the percentage urban climbs higher. Only 1.6 percent of the nation's population still resides on farms.[55] Even the fifth of the population that does not live in metropolitan places is clearly tied to an urban way of life. As noted in Chapter 1, the profits of wheat farmers, cattle ranchers, dairy farmers, and other agribusiness professionals are tied more to government price-support and subsidy systems than to weather or other natural factors. In 2000 the $28 billion paid in farm subsidies accounted for fully half of all the money made by farmers.[56] In states such as Montana the reality is that federal subsidies provide the great bulk of rural income.

Today our picture of how rural life is lived and the nature of basic rural virtues is the creation of mass media based in cities. Television shows written in New York and produced in Hollywood try to create an image of small towns filled with friendly folk with "down home" wisdom, rather like a Norman Rockwell painting. Urban advertising also hits hard at the same bogus theme—commercials often depend heavily on nostalgia, with old cars, fields of wheat, the old farmhouse, and the front porch swing.

What all this reflects is a deep ambivalence regarding cities and city life. A Gallup poll indicates that only 19 percent consider city life to be the ideal. Suburbs (24 percent), small towns (34 percent), and farms (22 percent) are all rated higher.[57] As a people, we glorify rural life but we live in metropolitan areas. North America is the most urbanized of the continents (excluding Australia), but our attitude toward cities is frequently unrealistic. We live urban, but we sometimes treat our major cities as though we don't trust them and wish they would stop causing problems.

SUMMARY

European colonists arriving in North America found a land without cities. While Native Americans sought to live within the environment, the colonists sought to dominate nature. Early settlement was primarily in towns. New England towns such as Boston and Newport were cultural and religious as well as commercial centers. Middle Colonies cities such as New York and Philadelphia had environmental advantages, which they turned to commercial advantage. In the South reliance on slave labor inhibited the development of an urban middle class. Canadian towns were garrisons and trading posts more than manufacturing places.

North American colonial cities represented only a small fraction of the population, but politically and socially the towns were dominant. The American Revolution was largely town based. Early 19th-century American cities were largely commercially based and located along waterways. During the second half of the 19th century, the technology of the railroad overcame environmental limitations. The railway, and railway-based towns, opened up the West. Cities were at the forefront of settlement.

The Civil War (1861–1865) saw northern cities develop as industrial centers, as opposed to mercantile or trade centers. Steam power encouraged urban concentration. For efficiency, industrial factories were located surrounding the city center. The factories were on rail lines that not only moved in raw material and shipped finish products but also brought

in the coal that fed the steam boilers that produced the factories' power. Factory laborers working 12-hour days were packed into surrounding tenements. Most of the late 19th- and early 20th-century workers were recent immigrants from eastern and southern Europe, and were commonly blamed for the crowded slum conditions under which they were forced to live.

Political bosses and their political machines provided necessary services to the new immigrants—and did it with a human face. Reform politics at the turn of the 20th century often represented WASP attempts to reclaim control of the cities. City-manager systems, for example, were designed to remove power from immigrant-dominated city councils and to put power into the hands of an appointed city manager.

Americans have long been ambivalent about their great cities. Founding fathers such as Thomas Jefferson feared large cities, and 19th-century WASP writers and politicians denounced the city as a center of "Rum, Romanism and Rebellion." America still has a myth of urban vice and rural virtue. Contemporary politicians attempt to portray themselves as having small-town roots and values.

REVIEW QUESTIONS

1. What were the major English settlements in North America and how did they differ?

2. How did early Canadian settlements differ from those in what would become the United States?

3. What was the role of cities in the United States prior to the Civil War?

4. What was the role of technology in shaping the spatial pattern of American cities between the Civil War (1865) and 1920?

5. What was the role played by transportation technology in developing cities west of the Mississippi River?

6. How did the electric streetcar change the spatial and social patterns of American cities?

7. What was the role played by political bosses in 19th- and early 20th-century American cities?

8. What was the impact of immigration on the 19th-century American city?

9. What were the goals of early 20th-century urban reform movements and what impact did they have?

10. How has the myth of rural virtue affected American politics and urban policies?

NOTES

1. Some estimates range as high as 10 million Native Americans prior to the arrival of Europeans, but whatever the initial indigenous population, smallpox, cholera, and other European-introduced diseases rapidly destroyed most of the population.

2. Not everyone agrees with this view. Shepard Krech, in *The Ecological Indian: Myth and History,* Norton, New York, 1999, says the image of the ecological Indian as a preserver of the environment is unsubstantiated myth and far from scientific reality.

3. Lewis Mumford would not agree with this statement. Mumford saw New England villages and towns as the last flickering of the medieval order. See, for example, Lewis Mumford, *Sticks and Stones: A Study of American Architecture and Civilization,* Liveright, New York, 1924.

4. John Smith, *The General Historie of Virginia, New England, and the Summer Isles,* University Microfilms, Ann Arbor, Mich., 1966 (first published in London, 1624), p. 72.

5. *Bradford's History of Plymouth Plantation* (William T. Davis, ed.), Scribner, New York, 1908, p. 96.

6. Howard P. Chudacoff, *The Evolution of American Society,* 5th ed., Prentice-Hall, Saddle River, N.J., 2000, chap. 1.

7. Carl Bridenbaugh, *Cities in the Wilderness,* Capricorn Books, New York, 1964.

8. Quoted in Kenneth T. Jackson and Stanley K. Schutty (eds.), *Cities in American History: The First Century of Urban Life in America,* 1625–1742, Knopf, New York, 1972.

9. Carl Bridenbaugh, quoted in Charles N. Glaab and A. Theodore Brown, *A History of Urban America,* Macmillan, New York, 1967, pp. 25–26.

10. Howard P. Chudacoff and Judith E. Smith, *The Evolution of American Urban Society,* 5th ed., Prentice-Hall, Saddle River, NJ, 2000.

11. Ibid., p. 27.

12. Richard Frame, "A Short Description of Pennsylvania in 1692," in Albert Cook Myers (ed.), *Narratives of Early Pennsylvania, West New Jersey, and Delaware,* Scribner, New York, 1912; reprinted in Ruth E. Sutter, *The Next Place You Come To: A Historical Introduction to Communities in North America,* Prentice-Hall, Englewood Cliffs, N.J., 1973, p. 90.

13. Constance McLaughlin Green, *The Rise of Urban America,* Harper & Row, New York, 1965, p. 21. For further information on Charleston, see David A. Smith, "Dependent Urbanization in Colonial America: The Case of Charleston, South Carolina," *Social Forces* 66:1–28, September 1987.

14. Peter McGahan, *Urban Sociology in Canada,* 3rd ed., Harcourt Brace, Toronto, 1995, p. 46.

15. Glaab and Brown, op. cit., p. 21.

16. Green, op. cit., p. 51.

17. Sam Bass Warner Jr., *The Urban Wilderness: A History of the American City,* Harper & Row, New York, 1972, p. 16.

18. Quoted in James H. Cassedy, *Demography in Early America: Beginnings of the Statistical Mind,* Harvard University Press, Cambridge, Mass., 1969, pp. 154–55.

19. P. L. Ford, *The Works of Thomas Jefferson,* Putnam, New York, 1904, pp. 503–504.

20. Charles N. Glaab (eds) *The American City: A Documentary History,* Dorsey, Homewood, IL, 1963, p. 65.

21. Chudacoff and Smith, op. cit., p. 20.

22. Nelson M. Blake, *A History of American Life and Thought,* McGraw- Hill, New York, 1963, p. 156.

23. Christopher Tunnard and Henry Hope Reed, *American Skyline: The Growth and Form of Our Cities and Towns,* New American Library, New York, 1956, p. 59.

24. Sam Bass Warner Jr., *The Private City: Philadelphia in Three Periods of Its Growth,* University of Pennsylvania Press, Philadelphia, 1968, p. 13.

25. Bryant Robey, "Two Hundred Years and Counting: The 1990 Census," *Population Bulletin* 44:1, April 1989, p. 7.

26. For an impact of all these changes see Witold Rybczynski, *City Life,* Simon & Schuster, New York, 1995.

27. Arthur M. Schlesinger, "The City in American History," *Mississippi Valley Historical Review,* 27:43–66, June 1940.

28. Josiah Strong, *Our Country: Its Possible Future and Present Crisis,* Baker and Taylor, New York, 1985, p. 206.

29. Janice Perlman, "Mega Cities and New Technologies," paper presented at XI World Congress of Sociology, New Delhi, India, July 1986.

30. Paul F. Cressey, "Population Succession in Chicago: 1898–1930," *American Journal of Sociology* 44:59, 1938.

31. Glaab and Brown, op. cit., 2nd ed., p. 144.

32. For an excellent account of this phenomenon, see Sam Bass Warner Jr., *Streetcar Suburbs: The Process of Growth in Boston, 1870–1900,* Atheneum, New York, 1970. Also see Kenneth T. Jackson, *Crabgrass Frontier,* Oxford University Press, New York, 1985; and J. John Palen, *The Suburbs,* McGraw-Hill, New York, 1995.

33. Richard Hurd, *Principles of City Land Values,* The Record and Guide, New York, 1924.

34. For more on central business districts, see Chapter 11: Cities and Change.

35. Schlesinger, op. cit.

36. James Bryce, *Forum,* vol. X, 1890, p. 25.

37. James Bryce, *The American Commonwealth,* vol. 1, Macmillan, London, 1891, p. 608. Reprinted by Putnam, New York, 1959.

38. Arthur M. Schlesinger, *Paths to the Present,* Macmillan, New York, 1949, p. 60.

39. Quoted in Lincoln Steffens, *The Autobiography of Lincoln Steffens,* Literary Guild, New York, 1931, p. 618.

40. Chudacoff, op. cit., p. 163.

41. Harold Zink, *City Bosses in the United States: A Study of Twenty Municipal Bosses,* Duke University Press, Durham, N.C., 1930, p. 350.

42. Robert K. Merton, *Social Theory and Social Structure,* Free Press, Glencoe, Ill., 1957, p. 73

43. Zink, op. cit., p. 350. For an excellent study of the role of a 20th-century boss, see Andrew Theodore Brown and Lyle W. Dorset, *K.C.: A History of Kansas City, Missouri,* Pruett Publishing, Boulder, Colo., 1978.

44. Glaab and Brown, op. cit., p. 125.

45. Donald Bogue, *The Population of the United States,* Free Press, Glencoe, Ill., 1969, p. 178.

46. Jacob Riis, *How the Other Half Lives: Studies among the Tenements of New York,* Scribner, New York, 1890; republished by Corner House, Williamstown, Mass., 1972.

47. Quoted in Glaab, op. cit., p. 38.

48. Andrew A. Lipscomb and Albert E. Bergh (eds.), *The Writings of Thomas Jefferson,* vol. X, The Thomas Jefferson Memorial Association, Washington, D.C., 1904, p. 173.

49. Morton White and Lucia White, *The Intellectual Versus the City,* Harvard and M.I.T. Presses, Cambridge, Mass., 1962. Quoted in Glaab, op. cit., p. 38.

50. Alexis de Tocqueville, *Democracy in America,* Henry Reeve (trans.), New York, 1839, p. 289.

51. Gallup poll, *New York Times,* October 8, 1989.

52. Strong, op. cit., chap. 11.

53. Glaab and Brown, op. cit., p. 59.

54. Richard Hofstadter, *The Age of Reform: From Bryan to FDR,* Knopf, New York, 1955, p. 31.

55. Bureau of the Census, "Condominium Status and Farm Residence," *Current Population Reports,* 1995, p. 2.

56. Timothy Egan, "Failing Farmers Learn to Profit from Wealth of U.S. Subsidies," *New York Times,* December 24, 2000, p. 1.

57. Gallup poll, op. cit. p. 89.

CHAPTER 4

Ecology and Political Economy Perspectives

Prediction is difficult. Especially about the future.
Casey Stengel

OUTLINE

Introduction
Development of Urban Ecology
    Invasion and Succession
    Criticisms of Ecology
    Role of Culture
Burgess's Growth Hypothesis
    Concentric Zones
    Limitations
Sector and Multiple-Nuclei Models
Urban Growth Outside North America
The Postmodern City: The Los Angeles School
Political Economy Models
Political Economy Assumptions
Examples of the Political Economy Approach
    The Baltimore Study
    Urban Growth Machines
    World Systems Theory and Globalization
Challenges
Summary

INTRODUCTION

Much has been written of the American city: its spatial physical structure, its forms of social organization, its peoples and lifestyles, and its problems. The sociologist Louis Wirth suggested that these various topics could be viewed empirically from three interrelated perspectives: (1) as a physical structure comprising a population base, a technology, and an ecological order; (2) as a system of social organization involving a characteristic social structure, a series of social institutions, and a typical pattern of social relationships; and (3) as a set of attitudes and ideas, and a constellation of personalities engaging in typical forms of collective behavior, and subject to characteristic mechanisms of social control.[1] In this chapter we shall be concerned with the first two of these perspectives: the spatial and social structure of the city and how it affects and is affected by the city as a system of social organization. We will also examine how those espousing political economy or world systems theories of urban development see sociospatial patterns, not as the outcome of ecological forces, but as a result of the contradictions and conflicts in capitalist society. Wirth's third area of focus, urbanism as a system of lifestyles and values, will be discussed in Chapter 7: Urban Lifestyles.

DEVELOPMENT OF URBAN ECOLOGY

The classical urbanization model, urban ecology (sometimes called "human ecology"), developed out of a concern with the form and development of the modern American city, and particularly with the relationship between the community's social and physical structure. Early urban ecology is associated with the so-called Chicago School of scholars working at the University of Chicago in the first half of the 20th century. Members of the Chicago School were concerned with systematically documenting both the patterns of urban change and the consequences of these changes for social institutions such as the family. Led by researchers such as Robert Park, Ernest Burgess, and Roderick McKenzie, the Chicago School produced a prodigious number of studies.

The interest of the Chicago sociologists was not simply in mapping where groups and institutions were located, but also in discovering how the sociological, psychological, and moral experiences of city life were reflected in spatial relationships. As expressed by McKenzie, human ecology "deals with the spatial aspects of symbiotic relationships of human beings and human institutions."[2]

Park was interested in how changes in the physical and spatial structure shaped social behavior. He felt that "most if not all cultural changes in society will be correlated with changes in its territorial organization, and every change in the territorial and occupational distribution of the population will effect changes in the existing culture."[3]

Ecology in its broadest sense is the study of the relationships among organisms within an environment. It is the study not of the creatures and objects themselves but rather of the relationships among them. The community together with its physical habitat form an "ecosystem." Park and Burgess gave particular importance to the role played by competition, especially economic competition, in shaping the city's physical and social organization. The Chicago School's emphasis on competition came not from Marx's analysis of capitalism so much as from the ecological models being used to study the then-new subjects of plant and animal ecology. Ecological reasoning thus traces its theoretical underpinnings to Charles Darwin's research on evolution.

Urban ecology is concerned with examining the independence and interdependence of specialized roles and functions (recurrent patterns of behavior) within the society. In examining the relationship between people and their environment and people within their environment, the level of analysis focuses on the aggregate level. The issue is the properties of populations rather than the properties of the individuals who constitute them. Thus, it is based on the study of groups rather than individuals—and this focus on the group or aggregate is basic to sociology, as opposed to disciplines such as psychology in which the focus is on the individual. Urban ecology does not—and cannot—explain the beliefs, values, and attitudes of individuals while they are performing certain activities.[4]

Classical ecological theories of the human community were consciously based on evolutionary theories explaining plant and animal development. Just as a person driving from the desert into the mountains finds that different soil, water, and temperature affect the bands of growth of the plants; by analogy, in a drive from a city's business district to its outlying suburbs, there are differing zones of development. In all these theories, *competition* played a core role.

In the city, as a consequence of economic competition for prime space, there emerged distinct spatial and social zones. The internal structure of the city thus evolved not as a consequence of direct planning but through competition, which changed areas through the ecological processes of invasion, succession, and segregation of new groups (e.g., immigrants) and land uses (e.g., commercial use displacing residential use). Economic competition was thus seen as the engine driving the spatial and social organization of the city.

Ecologically oriented sociologists of the Chicago School stressed the social as well as the economic aspects of competition for urban space. They also stated that within the city individuals and groups also compete for *power* and for control of particular neighborhoods or space. In their study of ethnic and racial neighborhoods, they examined the relationship between residential proximity and social equality. They found that in the large city, where one's social position is not widely known to everyone, spatial distance is often substituted for social distance—thus the importance of a fashionable address in the "right" neighborhood.

Note that ecological models place emphasis on competition and changing technology. By comparison, neo-Marxist and political economy models emphasize the deliberate planned actions of government officials and economic elites in shaping urban patterns. Both ecological and political economy models have in common the belief that change occurs through conflict. They differ in whether the source of that conflict comes more from economic competition or from deliberate planned political and economic decisions.

Invasion and Succession

The history of the American city is the story of the *invasion* of one land use or population by another. Chicago School ecologists were concerned with how change in community areas comes about. The end result when one group or function finally takes the place of another is called *succession*.[5] None of the patterns of land use within a city are permanently fixed, although sometimes zoning laws attempt to fix them. Areas once characterized by single-family houses have been converted to apartment, commercial, or industrial use—and sometimes today back to residential use; this is succession. Viable communities always are in the process

of changing. Ecological patterns are dynamic. Cities that do not change become historical tourist attractions or stagnant backwaters.

Today one of the most spectacular instances of invasion and eventual succession is found in urban ethnic changes. Today, the new ethnic group "invading" an area is often Latino or Asian. Another example of population invasion is the flow of limited numbers of affluent young whites to inner sections of the central city. This in-migration is not headed to areas of new housing, but rather to older neighborhoods in a state of some decline. This rehabilitation, or "gentrification," of the central-city neighborhoods is discussed in Chapter 11: Cities and Change.

Early sociologists of the Chicago School were particularly interested in segregated urban areas. They called these areas *natural areas,* since they were supposedly the results of ecological processes rather than of planning or conscious creation by any government unit. When zoning laws were established, the regulations generally recognized such natural areas of apartment houses, single-family neighborhoods, commercial areas, warehouse districts, and the like so as to maintain existing land-use patterns. A number of minor sociological classics, such as Wirth's book *The Ghetto* and Zorbaugh's book *The Gold Coast and the Slum,* deal with so-called natural areas.[6] (The so-called defended neighborhoods discussed in Chapter 7: Urban Lifestyles might be considered a contemporary version of a natural area.)

Criticisms of Ecology

As noted earlier, the heavy emphasis on competition in traditional human ecology, plus the nonsocial nature of some of the variables, disturbs contemporary political economy critics. Those taking a political economy approach see the city shaped more by deliberate political decisions than do ecologists who put more emphasis on economic competition. Political economy scholars argue that spatial patterns are the result of deliberate actions taken by capitalists, or that they are the outcome of the contradictions in capitalist development.[7]

A less valid criticism made of ecology is that it borrows concepts from other disciplines. As one critic put it, "As the ecologists have admitted, practically all their basic hypotheses have been derived from natural science sources—and the influence of certain geographers and economists is apparent."[8] To such critics the multidisciplinary base of human ecology is a weakness rather than a source of strength. However, as expressed by Leo Schnore, "the central role given to organization—both as dependent or independent variable—places ecology clearly within the sphere of activities in which sociologists claim distinctive competence, i.e., analysis of social organization."[9]

Role of Culture

Not everyone has agreed with ecology's macro-level focus. The "sociocultural" school of ecology places renewed emphasis on cultural and motivational factors in explaining urban land-use patterns. Urban cultural scholars believe that both human ecology and political economy approaches overemphasized economic factors while ignoring cultural and social-psychological variables. Cities, they stress, are places that have meaning and symbolic values to those who use them. Symbolic places help define a city's culture and identity, and symbolically structure people's lives.[10] Walter Firey for example, demonstrated in a study of land use in central Boston that many acres of valuable land in the central business district had been allowed to remain in uneconomic use, such as parks and cemeteries.[11] He suggested that "sentiment" and "symbolism" play an important part in maintaining areas such as Boston Common.

BURGESS'S GROWTH HYPOTHESIS

The most famous product of the spatial-organizational concerns of the Chicago School is Burgess's concentric-zone hypothesis, first presented in 1924.[12] We still discuss the Burgess hypothesis today because it provides a good model of American urban growth up until roughly 1970, and the patterns set in that earlier time still strongly influence how most cities look today. Later models of urban growth all use the Burgess model as a point of departure. Burgess said that city growth was not random or haphazard but the consequence of ecological factors.

The Burgess hypothesis suggested that industrial cities grew radially through a series of concentric zones: from the most valuable land of the central business district (CBD) through the zone of transition, the zone of working men's homes, and the zone of better residences to the commuter zone (see figure 4.1). Competition for prime space, plus demographic considerations such as population growth and social factors such as social power and prestige (used to explain elites' moves to the suburbs), were the factors that drove the model.

When introductory sociology students are exposed to the concentric-zone hypothesis it is all too frequently as a static picture of city structure. This is unfortunate, for what Burgess was positing was a *growth* model, not a model of how things are as much as a model of how things change—changes such as from the simpler preindustrial model in which there is no clear segregation of city land for specific functional purposes, to the complex industrial and postindustrial city pattern of segregated land usages (e.g., central business district, and different residential and commercial zones). Burgess's hypothesis is a model, and only a model or "ideal type," of how industrial cities evolve spatially as a result of competition for prime space.

Burgess suggested that the most valuable property goes to those functions that can use space intensively and are willing to pay the costs. Thus the ecologist would expect the land located at the center of the transportation network to be occupied by intensive space users

Figure 4.1   Developed in the 1920s, Burgess's zonal hypothesis provided a model of how cities grew from center to periphery during much of the 20th century, and contemporary cities still reflect the pattern.

Central business district: downtown Denver. iStockphoto

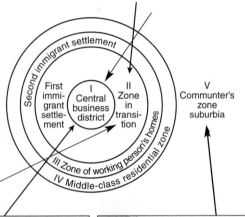

Zone in transition: Cincinnati Over-the-Rhine. Al Behrman/AP Images

Upscale suburban homes. © Al Campanie/The Image Works

From *The Growth of the City: An Introduction to a Research Project,* 1924.

such as department stores, major business headquarters, and financial institutions. An economic model of land use developed by William Alonso points out that those who can pay the most occupy CBD land.[13] Costs include not only land purchase price but also taxes and nuisances (congestion, noise, pollution, etc.) from other nearby land users. In the industrial city of the first half of the 20th century, centrally located land was taken by economic units, such as department stores, that could effectively use space and that profited from heavy pedestrian traffic. Production-oriented activities at that time were in the next ring out; and residences were the least centralized.

Most residential users cannot pay the high cost of central location and do not want the pollution, noise, and congestion of such a location. In inner areas higher land costs are compensated for by density of use. Through crowding, a slumlord can compensate for higher costs by densely using the land. Since land in outer suburban areas is less valuable, less intensive use, such as single-family houses on large lots, becomes economically feasible. Thus, as you move out from the center of the city toward the periphery, land values and rental per acre tend to grade downward, while the rental per housing unit grades upward. Consequently, there is often an inverse relationship between the value of land and the economic status of those who occupy it. Where people live spatially reflects their position socially.

Concentric Zones

So that they can serve as a baseline from which to examine more recent patterns of change, zones are presented here essentially as they existed during the first two-thirds of the 20th century.

Zone 1 was the central business district: the economic and transportation center of the city. The heart of the zone was the retail shopping district, with its major department stores, theaters, hotels, banks, and central offices of economic, political, legal, and civic leaders. Today, most American cities, such as Baltimore, Detroit, and Omaha, lack even a single downtown department store.[14] Meanwhile, the urban function of providing downtown office space and convention centers is increasing.[15] Fifty years ago the outer fringes of the CBD with its lower rents contained the wholesale business district: markets, warehouses, and storage buildings. Today these old warehouse districts are often the site of trendy restaurants and apartments.

Until the inner city deindustrialization of the 1970s, Zone 2—the zone in transition—contained both older factory complexes, many from the 19th century, and an outer ring of deteriorating tenement neighborhoods. The zone in transition was the point of entry for immigrants. Immigrants settled in the cheap housing near the factories because they could not compete economically for more desirable residential locations. The zone in transition was known as an area of high crime rates and social disorganization.

As the twentieth century immigrants moved up in socioeconomic status, they moved out spatially and were in turn replaced by newer immigrants. Thus, a nonrandom spatial structure or pattern emerged, with groups of lower socioeconomic status being most centrally located. Today most of the inner city warehouses have been either destroyed by urban renewal or turned into gentrified neighborhoods prized for their central location.

Zone 3 was the zone of "working people's homes." This was the area settled by second-generation families, the children of the immigrants; it was the place where one moved to from the inner core. Typically, blue-collar families shown on TV sitcoms resided in Zone 3.

Zone 4, named the "zone of the better residences," was the outer city zone of the great middle class—small-business owners, professional people, sales workers, and those holding white-collar jobs. However, even in the 1920s this zone was changing from a community of single-family houses to one of apartment build-

---

Box 4.1   Ecology of the City: The Barbary Coast of San Francisco

The Chicago School spoke of "natural areas" by which they meant social areas that developed without the aid of planning or design. During the 19th and early 20th centuries the most notorious of the natural areas were the vice areas, commonly located just outside the central business district. Among the most famous of these districts were Storyville in New Orleans, the Levee in Chicago, Five Points in New York, and the "Barbary Coast" in San Francisco. Such districts were eventually put out of business more by technological change than by the famous "Societies for the Suppression of Vice." The automobile and the telephone, for example, put fixed-location brothels out of business by making possible the "call girl." More recently, the availability of X-rated videos at suburban video stores, X-rated cable channels, and over 100,000 porno websites has put central area porno theaters out of business.

What follows is a 19th-century writer's view of vice in San Francisco.* Like many "reformers" of that era he seems to enjoy lingering over the sins of the city.

> In the early days of San Francisco, Barbary Coast was the place of refuge and security for the hundreds of criminals that infected the city. When they had passed within its boundary, they were strongly fortified against any assault that the officers of the law might lead against them. . . . Then villains of every nationality held high carnival there. The jabber of the Orient, the soft-flowing tone of the South Sea Islander, the guttural gabbing of the Dutch, the Gallic accent, the round full tone of the son of Africa, the melodious voice of the Mexicano, and the harsh, sharp utterances of the Yankee, all mingled in the boisterous revels.
>
> It was the grand theatre of crime. The glittering stiletto, the long blade bowie knife, the bottle containing the deadly drug, and the audacious navy revolver were much-used implements in the plays that were there enacted. . . .
>
> Were the restraining power of the law and public sentiment removed, Barbary Coast to-day could soon develop the same kind of outlawry that made it notorious in the primitive days. . . . Barbary Coast is the haunt of the low and the vile of every kind, The petty thief, the house burglar, the tramp, the whoremonger, lewd women, cut-throats and murderers, all are found there. Dance-houses and concert saloons, where bleary-eyed men and faded women drink vile liquor, smoke offensive tobacco, engage in vulgar conduct, sing obscene songs, and say and do everything to heap upon themselves more degradation, unrest and misery are numerous. Low gambling houses thronged with riot-loving rowdies in all stages of intoxication are there. Opium dens, where heathen Chinese and Godforsaken women and men are sprawled in miscellaneous confusion, disgustingly drowsy, or completely overcome by inhaling the vapors of the nauseous narcotic are there. Licentiousness, debauchery, pollution, loathsome disease, insanity from dissipation, misery, poverty, wealth, profanity, blasphemy, and death are there. And Hell, yawning to receive the putrid mass, is there also.

*B. E. Lloyd, *Lights and Shades in San Francisco,* San Francisco, 1876, pp. 78–79.

---

ings (that is, there was an invasion of new land-use patterns).

Burgess's final zone was the "commuter zone" or suburbs. Before World War II the commuter zone was comprised of upper-middle-class and upper-class dormitory suburbs. Here were found the traditional suburban life patterns: the husband leaving in the morning for the city and returning in the evening; the wife raising the children, maintaining the house, and participating in civic affairs. Chapter 6: The Suburban Era discusses the many changes in suburban lifestyles.

Burgess's model has had considerable practical consequences. For example, while few real estate agents realize it, the Burgess-based filter-down housing model, which suggests that housing and neighborhoods inevitably filter from higher status to lower-status populations, was used by realtors to determine housing values. As Chapter 11: Cities and Change details, this resulted in policies of disinvestment in central cities.

Urban gentrification, by contrast, turns Burgess's pattern inside out. Today not only older residences, but also central city commercial property and warehouses are being converted into housing.

Limitations

Over the years Burgess's hypothesis has come under criticism on both theoretical and empirical grounds. It has been charged that Burgess's zonal boundaries, "do not serve as demarcations in respect to the ecological or social phenomena they circumscribe, but are arbitrary divisions."[16] This is an overstatement, but it is clear that Burgess's zones are not homogeneous units. However, when evaluating Burgess's hypothesis, we have to keep in mind that he was proposing a "model" or "ideal type" of what American cities would look like if other factors did not intervene— but of course other factors do intervene. Burgess's own statements make it clear that he recognized the effects of distorting factors. He said:

> If radial extension were the only factor affecting the growth of American cities, every city in this country would exhibit a perfect exemplification of these five urban zones. But since other factors affect urban development (including) situation, site, natural and artificial barriers, survival of an earlier use of a district, prevailing city plan and its system of transportation, many distortions and modifications of this pattern are actually found.[17]

The question, then, is not whether the zonal pattern is an exact description, for it obviously is not. The question is whether the growth patterns of American cities were described by Burgess's model. Empirical tests have mostly supported his hypothesis.[18] A rough version of Burgess's model does appear to have held up, at least for larger and older American cities, up until the suburban era of the 1970s.[19] On the other hand, a more mixed pattern was found in Canada's 11 largest cities.[20] As we will see in later chapters, in recent decades North American growth

(both population and economic) has been taking place in the suburbs, not in the central city.

SECTOR AND MULTIPLE-NUCLEI MODELS

There are also variations of the zonal model. Based on his study of 142 cities, Homer Hoyt proposed a "sector theory."[21] Hoyt said that rather than urban growth progressing through rings, growth takes place in fairly homogeneous pie-shaped wedges or sectors that extend from the center toward the periphery of the city. A pattern of land use was said to develop in which each use—industrial, commercial, high-income residential, or low-income residential—tended to push out from the city core in specific sectors that reflected the early land use in that sector. The sectors cut across concentric zones.

Thus, high-income housing could radiate from the core in one wedge, a racial ghetto in a second, industrial firms next to it in a third, and working-class residences in a fourth. The sector theory focuses attention on the role of transportation arteries. Although originally developed to explain city patterns, the sector theory perhaps better explains outer development out along interstate and other major highways. It is a useful modification of the Burgess hypothesis when discussing the post-war development of suburbs.

The multiple-nuclei theory of spatial growth, on the other hand, rejects the idea of a single-centered city altogether. Instead it holds that as a city grows it develops distinct centers of activity, and that in contemporary cities these different land uses have different centers. Chauncy Harris and Edward Ullman argued that land-use patterns developed around what were originally independent nuclei.[22] Four factors were said to account for the rise of the different nuclei:

1. Certain activities require specialized facilities. Retailing, for example, requires a high degree of accessibility.
2. Like activities group together for mutual advantages, as in the case of the central business district.
3. Some unlike activities are mutually detrimental or incompatible with one another. For example, it is unlikely that high-income or high-status residential areas will locate close to heavy industry.
4. Some users, such as storage and warehousing facilities, which have a relatively lower competitive capacity to purchase good locations, are able to afford only low-rental areas.[23]

Today, the multiple-nuclei hypothesis provides a better description of the entire metropolitan area than it does of the central city. Contemporary suburbia, with nuclei of outlying shopping malls, office and industrial parks, edge cities, and residential neighborhoods, does indeed exhibit a multinucleated pattern when seen from the air.

Amos Hawley stressed the importance of transportation networks in his multinucleated theory of growth.[24] He noted that within metropolitan areas there is not one retail business district, but rather a hierarchical, multinucleated system of districts. Second- and third-rank business districts particularly develop at transportation intersections where traffic converges from four directions. We will explore this further in the next chapter, Chapter 5: Metro and Edge City Growth.

URBAN GROWTH OUTSIDE NORTH AMERICA

The Burgess concentric-zone pattern of urban growth, which suggests an increasing status gradient as one goes from city core to periphery, has never been a very satisfactory model for explaining urban growth outside North America.[25] Rather, in cities with a nonindustrial heritage, there appears to be an inverse zonal hypothesis. That is, in such cities, it is common to find a pattern in which upper-class and upper-middle-class groups occupy the city proper and poor in-migrants settle on the "suburban" periphery.[26] Housing projects in Paris, for instance, are not located in the central city, but in the suburbs. In developing countries the poor often live in squatter shantytowns. These *favelas, barriadas, gecekondulas,* or *bustees* can be found on the periphery of almost every major city in Latin America, Africa, and Asia.

Burgess's theory does not appear to be applicable to older European cities.[27] In the established cities of Europe the elites preempted the prestigious central locations, and the poor were forced to live in more peripheral locations. Manufacturing and commerce, when located within the city, were restricted to specific areas. Thus, in London the central districts of Westminster, Marylebone, and Kensington have continued to retain their upper-class airs for two centuries. Moscow, before the Russian Revolution, clearly had the urban structure of a preindustrial city with its inverse zonal pattern.[28]

As European cities industrialized during the 19th century, central land was already filled, so heavy industry was confined to "suburban" areas where there was sufficient land. Thus, Paris has a concentration of automobile and aircraft factories to the south and east of the city. The poorest areas of Paris are not in the city, but in the government-built public housing suburbs where many Islamic newcomers live. The suburbs, not the central city, were the location of the 2005 Paris riots. Throughout Europe suburbs are more likely to house immigrant newcomers. It is the inner-city middle-class districts which support conservative policies and candidates—exactly the opposite of the American stereotype.

Gideon Sjoberg sees the European pattern of identification of high-status groups with central city location as a persistence of a "feudal tradition" that is not present in American

Box 4.2 A Note on Urbanization and Environment

Our discussion of the ecology of the city would be incomplete without mention of the effect of cities on the physical environment. The actual physical shape of cities has been sharply modified by human design. Much of contemporary Boston, for instance, was underwater at the time of the American Revolution. One of the former underwater zones is known today as Back Bay. Chicago in similar fashion created an Outer Drive and lakefront park system out of filled land. In other cases cities have sunk. Pumping out subsurface groundwater and other fluids has led, as in parts of cities such as Houston, Long Beach, and Phoenix, to subsidence. In the Long Beach case, from 1937 through 1962 some 913 million barrels of oil, 482 million barrels of water, and 832 billion cubic feet of gas were extracted, causing parts of this heavily urbanized area to sink as much as 27 feet.[*]

Cities also create atmospheric changes. Buildings and paved streets retain heat, and urban areas become heat islands, as anyone who has spent a hot summer day in the central city knows. What is less well known is that the condensation nuclei produced by activity in cities increase cloudiness and precipitation over cities.[†]

Also, by covering the ground with buildings, paved roads, and parking lots, urban development in effect waterproofs the land surface. Rainfall cannot be normally absorbed into the soil; instead, storm runoff must be handled by massive systems of storm sewers. The paving over of city and suburban areas, by preventing water absorption, increases the risk of severe flooding.

Those living in coastal areas subject to hurricanes, or in localities that flood, or on earthquake-prone fault lines, are particularly sensitive to the extent to which we are subject to the laws of nature. During the last 15 years both San Francisco and Los Angeles suffered major earthquake damage. By far the most tragic event was the 2005 destruction of most of New Orleans by Hurricane Katrina. New Orleans suffered thousands of deaths and social disintegration into chaos. New Orleans lost over 80 percent of its homes, and today some of the city remains an abandoned wasteland.

Cities, of course, are notorious for their contribution to air pollution. One of the worst examples occurred in London in 1952 when a disastrous temperature inversion kept a deadly smog over the city for a week. Some 4,000 Londoners died of smog-related causes before the smog lifted. Today London has strict air pollution controls; the air is getting cleaner, and the city's sooty fogs are a thing of the past.

In the United States, a nationwide study tracking the health histories of 552,138 adults in 151 metropolitan areas was released in 1995.[§] The good news is that, due to the Clean Air Act, air quality had improved dramatically since 1982. The bad news is that after factoring in each subject's age, sex, occupational exposure to pollution, obesity, and alcohol use, living in a city having high sulfate and fine-particle levels raised the risk of premature death by 15 and 17 percent respectively. Living in high-pollution cities such as Los Angeles, Denver, or Salt Lake City can substantially shorten life. Houston, thanks to Texas's weak environmental controls, has the nation's most polluted air. California, by contrast, in 2006 passed very strict laws mandating pollution reductions.

Today, the most serious air and other pollution problems occur in the cities of the developing world. Rapidly industrializing China has virtually no pollution controls. (To avoid being embarrassed by Beijing's filthy air during the 2008 Olympics the Chinese government ordered the city's industries to shut down two weeks prior to the games.) Every fall Indonesia is covered by a pall of smoke from forests being illegally burned to clear the land, and the dirty cloud also covers Singapore and Malaysia. Just breathing the air in Mexico City during the winter is equivalent to smoking two packages of cigarettes a day.

---

[*]Donald Eachman and Melvin Marcus, "The Geologic and Topographic Setting of Cities," in Thomas Detwyler and Melvin Marcus (eds.), *Urbanization and Environment: The Physical Geography of the City,* Duxbury Press, Belmont, Calif., 1972, p. 46.

[†]Rid Bryson and John Ross, in Detwyler and Marcus, op. cit., p. 63.

[‡]Robert Kates, Ian Burton, and Gilbert F. White, *The Environment as Hazard,* Oxford University Press, New York, 1978; and Stanley A. Changon, et al., *Summary of Metromex,* vol. 1; *Weather Anomalies and Impacts,* Illinois State Water Survey, Urbana, 1977.

[§]Curt Suplee, "Dirty Air Can Shorten Your Life, Study Says: Death Rate Much Higher in Worst Cities," *Washington Post,* March 10, 1995, pp. A1 and A15.

cities. In his view, "In many European cities, including those in Russia, the persistence of the feudal tradition has inhibited suburbanization because high status has attached to residence in the central city."[29]

However, New York doesn't have a feudal tradition, but it still has a pattern of the well-to-do locating in certain areas of Manhattan. Cosmopolites, whether in London, Paris, San Francisco, Vancouver, or New York, simply prefer to live where they can easily get to work, where they can find a full cultural life, and where they can easily get a cappuccino or find a deli open at 1:00 A.M. It can be argued that, in Europe or elsewhere, upper-status urban populations live in the city because they feel it is an exciting and attractive place to live.

THE POSTMODERN CITY: THE LOS ANGELES SCHOOL

Probably the most discussed new way of looking at cities is provided by the so-called Los Angeles School of urban scholars. Scholars of the Los Angeles School such as Michael Dear, Michael Davis, and Edward Soja set themselves up in direct opposition to the Chicago School.[30] What they suggest is that Los Angeles, with its fragmented spatial and social pattern is the model for the future. The culturally and socially diverse Los Angeles metro area is not an exception to the pattern, they argue; it, rather than Chicago with its dominant central core, is the new pattern. That is, L.A. and southern California are "a polyglot, polycentric, polycultural pastiche that is deeply involved in rewriting American urbanism."[31]

Thus, the L.A. School turns the older Chicago School on its head by arguing that the multicultural way of life is the new postmodern norm in which the periphery is now the core. As Charles Jencks writes, "Los Angeles, like all cities, is unique, but in one way it may typify the world city of the future: there are only minorities. No single ethnic group, nor way of life,

nor industrial sector dominates the scene. Pluralism has gone further here than in any city in the world and for this reason it may well characterize the global metropolis of the future."[32] Los Angeles is not an exception to the rule; it is the rule.

The assertion that Los Angeles represents the new paradigm for the city has not been without critics. Robert Beauregard suggests, for instance, that the overuse of superlatives and the suggestions that Los Angeles is the "first" on one or another measure slips from science into an academic boosterism that is at odds with empirical research and critical theory.[33] This problem emerges when writers lose the critical mindset in which a city illuminates some important urban trend in the making, replacing it with superlatives to suggest the city in question is the prototype of a new pattern.[34] Debate over the empirical accuracy and theoretical contributions of the Los Angeles School is certain to continue.

We now go on to examine political economy models, for just as the Chicago zonal hypothesis was part of a larger ecological model, the Los Angeles School is usually seen as being subsumed under the larger heading of political economy models.

POLITICAL ECONOMY MODELS

With its premise that economic competition for space produces the spatial order of cities, urban ecology remained the dominant model of urban change until the 1970s, when it was challenged by the emergence of political economy paradigms. Political economy advocates argue that you have to look beyond the city to national (and possibly world) patterns to understand massive changes such as city declines, suburbanization, or deindustrialization. Some argue that such neo-Marxist conflict-based models now have become the dominant paradigm.[35]

A note on terminology: In the 1970s, models critical of capitalist patterns were commonly identified by their advocates as being neo-Marxist, in the 1980s they were referred to as the "new urban sociology," and since the 1990s they have commonly been referred to as "urban political economy." These name changes often (but not always) reflect real theoretical changes. Today there is some difficulty making statements that cover all political economy adherents.

While some of those using the political economy identification remain Marxist or neo-Marxist, some others clearly are not. For example, Manuel Castells, whose seminal Marxist analysis, *The Urban Question,* provided a basic critique of existing urban sociology and the theoretical underpinning for Marxist urbanism, in later works revised his thinking away from his earlier class conflict–based Marxist approach.[36]

What is common to the political economy perspective is that it focuses on the role played by human agency, and especially the actions of the corporate economic elites and political institutions that do their bidding. Political economy emphasizes, not impersonal economic forces producing uniform ecological patterns, but how urban systems are structured to give

advantage to some groups and disadvantage to others.

As put by supporters, "Like urban ecology, political economy is concerned with systems of dominance and subordination operating across spatial boundaries. Unlike urban ecology, these systems are seen as driven by the actions (or inactions) of particular groups pursuing their particular interests, sometimes with a vengeance. The focus is on how various political economic systems usually operate, which groups tend to hold more power, and who tends to benefit and who is likely to lose from 'the way things are' in cities."[37]

Urban political economy thus looks at social power and how urban decisions favor the powerful at the expense of others. Also, while the focus of the Chicago School urban researchers initially was on cities of North America and the developed world, urban political economy has given considerable attention to cities in the developing world, especially cities in Latin America.

Figure 4.2, prepared by David Smith and Michael Timberlake, presents a schematic

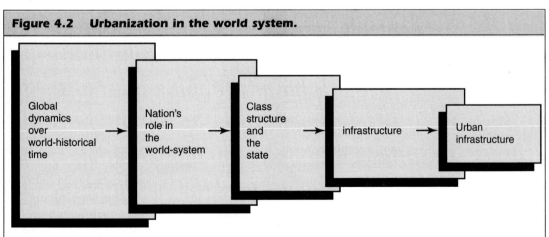

Figure 4.2   Urbanization in the world system.

Global dynamics over world-historical time → Nation's role in the world-system → Class structure and the state → infrastructure → Urban infrastructure

Model of how macrostructures set the parameters for urban development. The image of smaller "windows" of possible variability, instead of deterministic causal arrows, is chosen because this figure is intended to provide a general theoretical orientation for research (i.e., to point to the key elements), rather than pretend to provide a verifiable model for testing.

Source: David A. Smith and Michael F. Timberlake. Chapter 5, *The Urban World,* 5th ed. 1997.

description of key elements in the political economy perspective. The figure shows how macrostructures establish ever-narrower parameters for urban outcomes and infrastructures going from the global world system down to the specific infrastructure of a city. The city's (or nation's) role is seen as being shaped and constrained by the particular historical period or particular economic specialization required during times of economic expansion or contraction. Thus, while ecological approaches are likely to rely on the statistical analysis of large data sets, political economy is more likely to look to case studies of particular cities emphasizing how political struggles and decisions shape the urban social and built environment.

POLITICAL ECONOMY ASSUMPTIONS

All theoretical models are built on assumptions. The following five underlying assumptions are taken from the work of Joe Feagan and have been modified and simplified somewhat by David Smith and Michael Timberlake.[38]

1. *Cities are situated in a hierarchical global system, and global linkages among cities help define the structure of the world system.* Cities and urban life in both developed and developing countries are largely shaped by their specific location and involvement in the world system. Groups in some areas, both historically and in the present day, "exploit" groups and resources in other regions. As a result, major social differences (e.g., patterns of urbanization) across the globe have much to do with how the region fits into this international division of labor and with how local systems of class, race/ethnicity, and gender relations have developed in connection with the operation of the world system.

2. *The world system is one of competitive capitalism.* This world system is driven, to a significant degree, by the logic of capitalism and is, therefore, competitive. Locally based actors (e.g., local politicians and business people) attempt to outbid one another for access to capital, cheap labor, and resources. Competitive capitalism when transmitted to geographical space involves the creation and destruction of the land and built environment we term "cities." It also leads to the concentration and shifts of populations *within* urban space into neighborhoods, slums, and suburbs.

3. *Capital is easily moved; locations of cities are fixed.* Gains and losses are usually calculated within corporations. Owners and managers of companies act to maximize the profitability and ensure the survival of their firms. Actions to do this often include moving capital (in the form of factories and production facilities, corporate offices, etc.) from one location to another to attempt to improve the "bottom line." Investments and disinvestments often have profound effects on the locals and localities, many of which are cities. This can lead to "capital drain" and "deindustrialization" in these places.

4. *Politics and government matter.* The state in modern capitalist states is linked to the economic processes that form cities. Both local and national politics play a major role in setting the rules and "greasing the skids" for business profitability. Contrary to the assumption that capitalist economies are driven by a free market, states fundamentally help determine the flow of capital over the globe, including from one city or region to another. The policies of political jurisdictions—on corporate taxes, road building, the regulation of workers, and so on—help define the local business climate, which in turn strongly influences patterns of urban growth or decline.

5. *People and circumstances differ according to time and place, and these differences matter.* Specific economic and state forms do not develop automatically or inevitably. They develop as the results of conscious actions taken by social classes, acting together or singly, in particular historical or structural circumstances. In other words, cities are shaped by real flesh-and-blood people making decisions in particular situa-

tions. Decisions are made by people, not "variables" or "social forces." People may support or oppose the existing system, or they may support alternatives.

EXAMPLES OF THE POLITICAL ECONOMY APPROACH

Now that the major characteristics of the political economy approach have been defined, we will look at some examples of how it is applied.

The Baltimore Study

David Harvey, a Marxist geographer, in a well-known study analyzed the real estate market in Baltimore as an example of how capitalists, motivated by profit, use government programs to change the spatial use of the city.[39] Harvey suggested that the capitalist economy builds the city it needs, and it uses government policies and programs to protect its profits and investments. Real estate investors see little financial sense in putting capital into decaying and poorer neighborhoods. Profits are greater in high-rent neighborhoods and outer suburbs. Thus, they deliberately disinvest in the central city. In effect, they create blight.

Government urban renewal programs using public funds are used to physically restore blighted areas and put in infrastructure improvements so that real estate investors can again make a profit. According to Harvey, financial capital (investment capital) rather than industrial capital (business or manufacturing capital) determines the future of the city. Urban growth or urban blight are not some sort of automatic processes. Rather, they are the consequences of directed actions by financial capitalists seeking to maximize profit without regard to the needs of the urban population.

Harvey also argued that capitalism consistently produces more surplus investment than can be used (chronic over accumulation) and that changes in the built environment such as suburbanization, gentrification, and urban renewal are ways of using surplus capital.[40] Private mass market housing is also used as a means of preventing population unrest and providing social stabilization.

Urban Growth Machines

John Logan and Harvey Molotch present a conflict-based, but non-Marxist, analysis of urban growth. They say that an "urban growth machine" ideology influences American urban growth.[41] Pushed by bankers, developers, corporate officials, and real estate investors, the growth machine ideology influences local governments to view cities, not as places where people live, work, and have social relationships, but solely as a place where it is necessary to create a "good business climate."

A good business climate means that a growth machine is created in which increasing the value of commercial property comes ahead of community values, neighborhood needs, or a livable city. In their terms, "Cities become organized enterprises devoted to (raising) the aggregate rent levels through the intensification of land usage."[42] Municipal officials constantly broadcast the advantages of growth, such as a larger tax base and more jobs, while ignoring problems of growth, such as greater traffic congestion, environmental damage, higher home costs, and loss of community.

Local residents, in contrast to business and local government officials, see their neighborhoods as places for living and often wish to maintain their character through controlling traffic flows, restricting building heights, and keeping open spaces. Their communities are social space to them, not just economic sites. Conflict comes when local populations seek to limit negative impacts of growth on their community while the growth machine defines all growth that raises property values as good growth.

Local governments are largely in the pockets of major economic interests. Thus, revitalizing the city means downtown improvements for business, not assistance to local communities. Inner-city poverty is ignored unless it affects business. The global economy means that local groups have less political influence. Business interests are less tied to local areas and concerned with local needs. Industrial capital goes where the profits are greatest. The sole question in urban land use thus becomes "Will it make money?" rather than "Is it good for the city?" The assumption of the political economy model is that profit shapes the city. A 2010 example of how an urban growth ideology can produce a boom-bust cycle is Las Vegas.

World Systems Theory and Globalization

When taken to the level of the global economy, urban political economy is often associated with world systems theory. World systems theory suggests that what happens to individual cities is not a result so much of what happens in their own region as to where these cities fit into the world hierarchy of cities. Capitalism organizes cities around the globe into overarching geopolitical and economic systems.[43] It is important to note that, "the key nodes in the international system are (global) cities, not nations."[44] Globalization is all about which cities will dominate economically.

Cities of the economically developed "core" of North America, Europe, and Japan—especially New York, London, Paris, and Tokyo—are home to multinational corporations that dominate the world economy. The core region is seen as exploiting the rest of the globe. The professionals working for the corporations make good livings, and the urban areas in which they live have a wide range of housing and social choices.

Countries in the "peripheral" underdeveloped Third World provide raw materials and raw labor. Their cities have small elites living in luxury and large numbers living in slums in poverty. Executives working for international businesses see themselves as trying to transform the cities into high-tech business centers, while the "others," who Saskia Sassen defines as immigrants, minorities, and women, see their claims for a decent life ignored.[45] As of 2010 the average worker in the developing world makes less than $2 a day. Third World cities offer few social amenities to their poorer residents. Cities in "semi-peripheral" countries such as Brazil, Argentina, and most of Eastern Europe fall in between. They are tied to the core, but lack the control and resource base of core cities.

World systems theory, then, emphasizes that there is a hierarchy of cities in the world, and this hierarchy is based upon the economic power the city commands. The ability of a city to attract global investments ultimately determines its rank order among world cities.[46] Major core global cities manage the global economy and offer the most advanced financial, service, and production operations. This global hierarchy produces inequalities among world cities.

World systems theory implicitly assumes that so long as world capitalism continues to dominate the globe the existing core–periphery system of inequality will persist. On the other hand, critics point out that recent history suggests countries can change their economic position. South Korea and Taiwan, for example, have moved from underdeveloped to economically developed in a generation. Brazil is also moving toward "core" status. The strength of political economy and world systems models is that they focus attention on the historical context and political issues. Contemporary political economy faces the challenge of continuing to develop as the urban world changes.

Challenges

The challenge of the political economy model is to adapt what began as a neo-Marxist model to a world that has largely abandoned Marxism.[47] Since 1989 most "socialist" regimes have collapsed, and even China, while retaining the socialist title, has largely adopted a capitalist economic model. However, the political economy model need not be wedded to a neo-Marxist perspective. Works such as John Logan's on urban growth machines point out how local political action becomes less effective in an era of transnational capital and an international division of labor.[48] Local people have little power and leverage when confronting international corporations quite willing to move jobs abroad to save money, even if it destroys local communities. Such scholarship expands the political economy model.

Similarly, ecologists need to develop models that focus more on the social patterns and economic structure of the early 21st century than on those of the early 20th century. The challenge for urban theorists is to move beyond old issues and revise both the current ecological and political economy models so that they speak to a 21st-century world.

SUMMARY

Cities can be viewed as (1) a physical structure, (2) a system of social organization, or (3) a set of attitudes and ideas. This chapter is concerned with the first two: the relationship between the spatial and social organizational aspects of urban places. The two major models describing how this occurs are the ecological model and the political economy model.

Urban ecology traces its underpinnings to Darwin's research on evolution and stresses the role played by competition within the urban environment. The history of the American city tells of the invasion and succession of one group or land use by another. The most famous product of the Chicago ecological school is Burgess's "concentric zonal" urban growth model.

Ernest Burgess suggested cities grow through a series of concentric zones. Occupancy of prime land goes through competition to the users willing to pay the highest costs, either economic or in terms of congestion and pollution. Zone 1 was the central business district (CBD), Zone 2 a factory and tenement zone of transition, Zone 3 an area of working people's homes, Zone 4 an area of middle-class

residences, and Zone 5 the suburbs. Homer Hoyt suggested an alternative "sector theory" model in which growth proceeds out from the center not through rings but in fairly homogeneous pie-shaped wedges. The Burgess hypothesis reasonably describes American urban growth prior to the 1970s. It does not prove a particularly useful model for non-American cities.

The Los Angeles school suggests that L.A., with its multicultural population and its dispersed non core spatial organization, is the model of the postmodern city of the future. Political economy models challenge the economic competition emphasis of ecological models. Since the 1970s conflict-oriented political economic models—originally Marxist based—have stressed the importance of power. Conflict models emphasize the crucial role played worldwide by capitalist economic systems. Political economy models look to issues of power and how corporate economic elites and political institutions make decisions that favor global corporate interests at the cost of individuals.

Logan and Molotch provide a conflict-based, but non-Marxist, analysis of urban growth. They suggest that an "urban growth machine" ideology influences local governments to view cities not as places where people live and work but solely as a place where it is necessary to create "a good business climate." This means that increasing the value of land comes ahead of community values, neighborhood needs, or the livability of the city.

When applied to the global economy, political economy is commonly associated with "world systems theory" which suggests that cities' economic viability depends on where they fit into the world hierarchy of cities. Cities at the economically developed "core" of North America, Europe, and Japan contain the multinational corporations that control the world economy. Peripheral third world countries are permanently relegated to marginal status and exploited for their raw materials and cheap labor. Traditional world systems theory suggests that as long as capitalism persists, the core–periphery inequality will continue and countries can't change from one status to the other. However, recent history indicates that some countries such as South Korea and Taiwan have moved from periphery to core status. World systems theory is changing as economic realities change.

REVIEW QUESTIONS

1. What is meant by an urban ecology approach to the city?

2. How have patterns of invasion and succession shaped American cities, and how do they affect cities today?

3. What is the Burgess zonal hypothesis, and what does it say about the growth pattern of American cities?

4. Does the evidence support or contradict the Burgess Hypothesis?

5. What are the sector and multinuclei models of urban growth and how do they differ from the Burgess model?

6. Are growth patterns outside North America different, and if so how?

7. How does the Los Angeles School suggest the postmodern city differs from the Chicago School model?

8. What are the assumptions of political economy models of cities?

9. What is the urban growth machine ideology, and how does an urban growth machine model differ from the political economy approach?

10. What is world systems theory, and what are its assumptions?

NOTES

1. Louis Wirth, "Urbanism as a Way of life," *American Journal of Sociology* 44:18–19, July 1938.

2. Roderick D. McKenzie, *The Metropolitan Community,* McGraw-Hill, New York, 1933.

3. Robert Park, *Human Communities: The City and Human Ecology,* Free Press, New York, 1952, p. 14.

4. Some members of the "sociocultural" school of human ecology would dispute this statement.

5. The term *function* as used by sociologists means patterns of activities that depend on other activities. *Structure* is the orderly arrangements of the parts that make up the whole, the loci within which the functions or activities are performed.

6. Louis Wirth, *The Ghetto,* University of Chicago Press, Chicago, 1928; and Harvey W. Zorbaugh, *The Gold Coast and the Slum,* University of Chicago Press, Chicago, 1929.

7. Mark Gottdiener, *The Social Production of Urban Space,* University of Texas, Austin, 1985.

8. Warner E. Gettys, "Human Ecology and Social Theory," in George A. Theodorson (ed.), *Studies in Human Ecology,* Harper & Row, New York, 1961, p. 99.

9. Leo Schnore, "The Myth of Human Ecology," *Sociological Inquiry* 31:139, 1961

10. Lyn Lofland, *The Public Realm: Exploring the City's Quintessential Social Territory,* Aldine de Gruyter, 1998; and Daniel Monti, *The American City: A Social and Cultural History,* Blackwell, Malden, Mass., 1999.

11. Walter Firey, "Sentiment and Symbolism as Ecological Variables," *American Sociological Review* 10:140–148, 1945.

12. Ernest W. Burgess, "The Growth of the City: An Introduction to a Research Project," *Publications of the American Sociological Society* 18:85–97, 1924.

13. William Alonso, "A Theory of Urban Land Market," in Larry Bourne (ed.), *Internal Structure of the City: Readings on Space and the Environment,* Oxford University Press, New York, 1971, pp. 154–159.

14. J. John Palen, *The Suburbs,* McGraw-Hill, New York, 1995, p. 182.

15. For a detailed analysis of CBD changes in Baltimore and in Hamburg, Germany, see Jurgen Friedrichs and Allen C. Goodman, *The Changing Downtown: A Comparative Study of Baltimore and Hamburg,* Walter de Gruyter, New York, 1987.

16. Milla R. Alihan, *Social Ecology,* Columbia University Press, New York, 1938, p. 225.

17. Ernest W. Burgess, "Residential Segregation in American Cities," *Annals of the American Academy of Political and Social Science* 140:108, November 1928.

18. Leo F. Schnore and Joy K. O. Jones, "The Evolution of City–Suburban Types in the Course of

a Decade," *Urban Affairs Quarterly* 4:421–422, June 1969; Joel Smith, "Another Look at Socioeconomic Status Distributions in Urbanized Areas," *Urban Affairs Quarterly* 5:423–453, June 1970; and Lee J. Haggerty, "Another Look at the Burgess Hypothesis: Time as an Important Variable," *American Journal of Sociology* 76:1084–1093, May 1971.

19. J. John Palen and Leo F. Schnore, "Color Composition and City–Suburban Status Differences," *Land Economics* 41:87–91, February 1965.

20. Kent P. Schwirian and Marc D. Matre, "The Ecological Structure of Canadian Cities," in Kent P. Schwirian (ed.), *Comparative Urban Structure*, Heath, Lexington, Mass., 1974.

21. Homer Hoyt, "The Structure and Growth of Residential Neighborhoods in American Cities," U.S. Federal Housing Administration, Washington, D.C., 1939.

22. Chauncy Harris and Edward Ullman, "The Nature of Cities," *The Annals of the American Academy of Political and Social Science* 252:7–17, 1945.

23. Ibid.

24. Amos H. Hawley, *Urban Society: An Ecological Approach*, Wiley, New York, 1981.

25. Bruce London and William G. Flanagan, "Comparative Urban Ecology: A Summary of the Field," in John Walton and Louis H. Masotti (eds.), *The City in Comparative Perspective: Cross-National Research and New Directions in Theory*, Sage, Beverly Hills, Calif., 1979, pp. 41–66.

26. Gideon Sjoberg, *The Preindustrial City*, Free Press, New York, 1960, pp. 97–98.

27. London and Flanagan, op. cit., p. 56.

28. Walter F. Abbott, "Moscow in 1897 as a Preindustrial City: A Test of the Inverse Burgess Zonal Hypothesis," *American Sociological Review* 39:542–550, August 1974.

29. Gideon Sjoberg, "Cities in Developing and in Industrial Societies: A Cross-Cultural Analysis," in Philip Hauser and Leo F. Schnore, *The Study of Urbanization*, Wiley, New York, 1965, p. 230.

30. See, for example, Michael Davis, *City of Quartz: Excavating the Future in Los Angeles*, Verso, New York, 1990; Michael Dear, *The Postmodern Urban Condition*, Blackwell, Oxford, 2000; Michael Dear (ed.), *From Chicago to L.A.: Making Sense of Urban Theory*, Sage, Thousand Oaks, Calif., 2001; and Edward W. Soja, *Postmodern Geographics: The Reassertion of Space in Critical Social Theory*, Verso, New York, 1989.

31. Michael Dear, "Los Angeles and the Chicago School: Invitation to a Debate," *City and Community* 1(1):6, 2002.

32. Charles Jenks, *Hetropolis: Los Angeles, the Riots and the Strange Beauty of Hetro-Architecture*, St. Martins, New York, 1993, p. 7.

33. Robert A. Beauregard, "City of Superlatives," *City and Community* 2(3):183–199, 2003.

34. Anthony M. Orum, "Editorial Introduction," *City and Community* 2(3):179, 2003.

35. Mark Godinnier and Joe Feagin, "The Paradigm Shift in Urban Sociology," *Urban Affairs Quarterly* 24(2):163–187, 1988; David A. Smith, "The New Urban Sociology Meets the Old: Rereading Some Classical Human Ecology," *Urban Affairs Review* 30(3):432–457, 1995.

36. Manuel Castells, *The Urban Question*, MIT Press, Cambridge, Mass., 1977, and *The City and the Grassroots*, University of California Press, Berkeley, 1983.

37. David A. Smith and Michael F. Timberlake, "Urban Political Economy," in J. John Palen, *The Urban World*, 5th ed., McGraw-Hill, New York, 1997, p. 110.

38. Joe Feagin, *The Free Enterprise City*, Rutgers, New Brunswick, N.J., 1988, chap. 2; David A. Smith and Michael F. Timberlake, op. cit., 1997, p. 116.

39. David Harvey, *Social Justice and the City*, Johns Hopkins Press, Baltimore, 1973.

40. David Harvey, *Consciousness and the Urban Experience: Studies in the Theory and History of Capitalist Urbanization*, Johns Hopkins University Press, Baltimore, 1985.

41. John Logan and Harvey Molotch, *Urban Fortunes: The Urban Economy of Place*, University of California Press, Berkeley, 1987.

42. Ibid., p. 13.

43. Immanuel Wallerstein, *The Capitalist World-Economy*, Cambridge University Press, New York, 1979.

44. Mark Abrahamson, *Global Cities*, Oxford University Press, New York, p. 2.

45. Saskia Sassen, *Cities in a World Economy*, Pine Forge, Thousand Oaks, Calif., 2000.

46. I am Indebted to Mila Zlatic for stressing this point.

47. David A. Smith and Michael F. Timberlake, op. cit. p.127.

48. John Logan and Harvey Molotch, op. cit.

CHAPTER 5

Metro and Edge City Growth

Woe to them that join house to house.
Woe to them that lay field to field till there be no place.
Isaiah 5:8

OUTLINE

Introduction
Metropolitan Growth
    In-Movement: 1900 to 1950
    Out-Movement: 1950 into the
        21st Century
Commuting and Communication
Canadian Urban Regions
Postindustrial Central Cities
Edge Cities
    Edgeless and Private Edge Cities
    Boomburgs
    Suburban Business Growth
    Malling of the Land
    Malls and "Street Safety"
Nonmetropolitan Growth
    Diffuse Growth
    National Society
The Rise of the Sunbelt
    Population and Economic
        Shifts
    Regional Consequences
    Sunbelt Problems
Movement to the Coasts
Summary

INTRODUCTION

The United States is undergoing profound urban changes. In this chapter, three major transformations are emphasized. The first is the metropolitan area (and beyond) replacing the city as the major urban unit. Eighty-three percent of the population now lives in metropolitan areas. The 2010 census showed nine-tenths of all U.S. growth occurring in metropolitan areas. However, the year 2000 may have been the zenith. The Census Bureau reports that from 2000 to 2004 a full 18 of the 25 largest metropolitan areas had more people move out than move in.[1] The New York, Los Angeles, and Chicago metro areas—the three largest metro areas—lost the most residents.

The second change is the increasing dominance of edge cities as a major locus of metropolitan growth. While some inner cities struggle economically, edge cities, even during the Great Recession, did better. The metro areas whose economies did the worst were those that previously had had huge house price booms, or those dependent on the auto industry.[2] Ninety percent of the nation's office space is

Figure 5.1   Rate of Net Migration by Metropolitan and Micropolitan Statistical Areas, 2000 to 2010

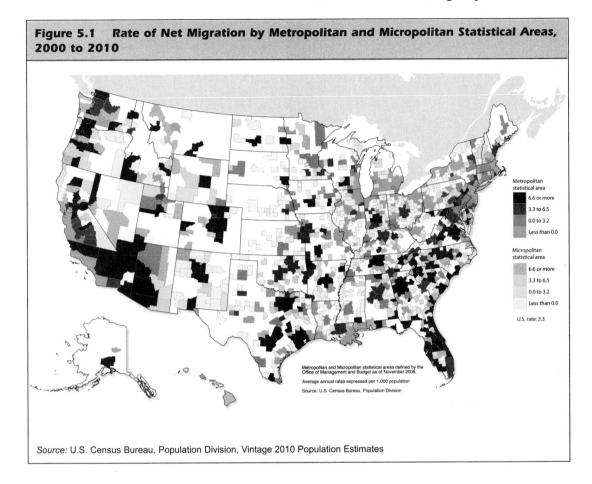

Metropolitan
statistical area

6.6 or more

3.3 to 6.5

0.0 to 3.2

Less than 0.0

Micropolitan
statistical area

6.6 or more

3.3 to 6.5

0.0 to 3.2

Less than 0.0

U.S. rate: 3.3

Metropolitan and Micropolitan statistical areas defined by the
Office of Management and Budget as of November 2008.

Average annual rates expressed per 1,000 population

Source: U.S. Census Bureau, Population Division

Source: U.S. Census Bureau, Population Division, Vintage 2010 Population Estimates

now in suburbia or beyond, much of it in outlying office parks along the interstates. While it twists the language, edge cities are now the center of most urban area economic activity. Note that figure 5.1 shows growth, often major growth, in metro areas outside central cities. By contrast, central cities are growing slower or even declining.

The third change is the three-decades-long population and industry shift toward the sunbelt and the nation's east and west coastlines

(see figure 5.2). Generally the move has been toward warmer climes. Urban sprawl, which is the product of these changes, will receive major treatment in Chapter 12: Housing Patterns, Sprawl, and Smart Growth.

METROPOLITAN GROWTH

Let us begin by looking at the metropolitan areas where over four out of five Americans

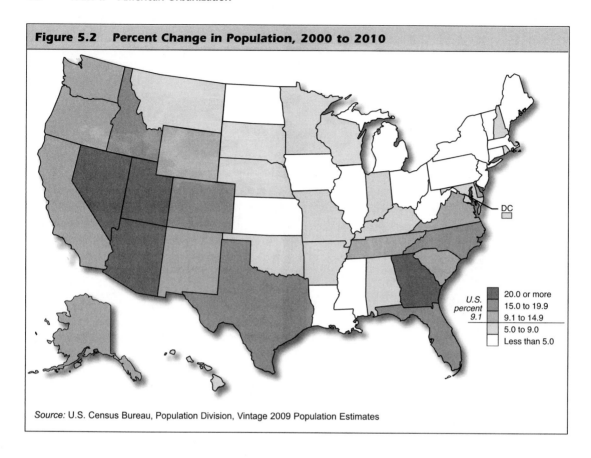

Figure 5.2   Percent Change in Population, 2000 to 2010

U.S. percent 9.1

20.0 or more
15.0 to 19.9
9.1 to 14.9
5.0 to 9.0
Less than 5.0

Source: U.S. Census Bureau, Population Division, Vintage 2009 Population Estimates

lived as of 2010. Metropolitan areas now house 250 million of the nation's 308 million population. Over half of all Americans live in the 37 largest "Metropolitan Statistical Areas" having a population of 1 million or more. The nine largest metropolitan areas, each with a population of more than 5 million, now hold almost a third of U.S. residents. New Jersey is entirely covered by metropolitan areas, while in seven other states—California, Maryland, Connecticut, Rhode Island, Florida, Massachusetts, and New York—over 90 percent of the population lives in metropolitan areas. In Idaho, at the other extreme, only 20 percent of the population lives in metropolitan areas.

The 20th century was a period of dramatic metropolitan growth and ascendancy. A hundred years ago the era of the frontier was closed, and it was clear that future national growth would have a metropolitan nexus. People were moving off the farms and out of the small towns into the cities. Rural counties were being depopulated, while population in the central cities was rapidly increasing.

The pattern was one of population growth concentrating in ever-larger metropolitan areas. The census of 1910 recognized this centripetal (inward) population movement by establishing 44 ad hoc "metropolitan districts" whose boundaries extended beyond those of the central city. A century ago, roughly one-third of the nation's population already resided in these newly defined metropolitan areas.

If changes in the definition of metropolitan areas are taken into account, virtually all the population growth during the 20th and 21st centuries occurred in metropolitan areas. Exceptions were a brief revival of non-metropolitan growth during the 1970s and some rural rebound during the 1990s. However, while this non-metro population is technically defined as living outside of metropolitan areas, it does not represent a return to farming or older rural ways of life. Rather, many of the new non-metropolitan residents live rural but are employed urban. Others are retired and live in retirement-oriented communities within commuting distance of the city. All these are part of an exurbia sprawl that extends metropolitan influence to virtually the entire population.

Metropolitan dominance had been foreseen by scholars as far back as the 1920s in the pioneering works of perceptive writers such as Gras and McKenzie.[3] They foresaw that the city per se was yielding its influence to a larger unit: the metropolitan area. The consequence of the rural out-migration is reflected in Bureau of Census figures (see table 5.1 and figure 5.1). On the eve of World War II, (1940) a fifth of the American population still lived on farms; by 2000 this figure had shrunk to under 2 percent.[4] In the fifty years from 1920 to 1970, the net out-migration from farms to cities was 29 million people.[5] Today, fewer than one person in sixty lives on a farm. For the overwhelming majority of Americans, the family farm, which was so much a part of our national heritage, is history.

In-Movement: 1900 to 1950

The first half of the 20th century saw a massive population implosion or in-gathering of population into metro areas. During this era the central city population often expanded beyond its legal bounds into suburbs. However, the central city clearly remained dominant over its metro area. While the central city increasingly found its *physical* expansion contained by surrounding suburbs, the social and economic *influence* of the central city expanded. Once independent, outlying towns, villages, and crossroad markets found themselves engulfed in an urban network. The local bank became a branch of a large city bank; local papers were replaced by metropolitan dailies; and local businesses went under, unable to compete with metropolitan-based firms. Some previously independent communities became satellite towns, while others specialized as bedroom suburbs for those who worked in the city. The consequence was the emergence during the first half of the century of the era of the city-dominated metropolitan unit.

Table 5.1	**The Top Ten Metropolitan Statistical Areas of 2008**		
Metropolitan Statistical Area	**2008 Population Estimate**	**2008 Ranking**	**2000 Ranking**
New York–Northern New Jersey–Long Island, NY–NJ–PA	19,006,798	1	1
Los Angeles–Long Beach–Santa Ana, CA	12,872,808	2	2
Chicago–Naperville–Joliet, IL–IN–WI	9,569,624	3	3
Dallas–Fort Worth–Arlington, TX	6,300,006	4	5
Philadelphia–Camden–Wilmington, PA–NJ–DE–MD	5,838,471	5	4
Houston–Sugar Land–Baytown, TX	5,728,143	6	8
Miami–Fort Lauderdale–Pompano Beach, FL	5,414,772	7	6
Atlanta–Sandy Springs–Marietta, GA	5,376,285	8	11
Washington–Arlington–Alexandria, DC–VA–MD–WV	5,358,130	9	7
Boston–Cambridge–Quincy, MA–NH	4,522,858	10	10

Source: U.S. Census Bureau, Population Division, 2009

Box 5.1   Defining Metropolitan Areas

The Census Bureau has a number of ways of defining different-size metropolitan areas. Traditionally, the federal government has defined metropolitan areas in two ways: as urbanized areas and as Metropolitan Statistical Areas. The building unit of urbanized areas was population density, while the building blocks of metropolitan areas are counties. The 2010 census essentially used this system, and census-based data released since the census uses this format. In 2003 the system for defining Metropolitan Statistical Areas (MetroSAs) was redefined to reflect the decentralization of employment and population within metro areas.* A new concept of Micropolitan Statistical Areas (MicroSAs) was also introduced. The result has been some confusion among researchers and policymakers. There is no need to foster this confusion on students. Thus, to minimize confusion, and to allow for historical comparisons, we will use the pre-2003 definitions in this text unless otherwise noted.

Urban. The U.S. Census Bureau defines as "urban" all census block groups or blocks that have a population density of at least 1,000 persons per square mile.

Urbanized Areas. According to the Census Bureau definition, an urbanized area consists of a central city, or cities, of 50,000 or more and the surrounding closely settled territory, whether incorporated or unincorporated. The term, thus, refers to the actual urban population of an area regardless of political boundaries such as county or state lines. The 2000 census also created a new category of areas over 10,000 but under 50,000, which it calls **Urban Clusters.** The 2000 census recognized 1,371 "urbanized areas" and "urban clusters." All residing in the urbanized area are considered urban, but the population is also divided into those in the "central city" and those in the remainder of the area, or "urban fringe." The proportion of a state's population living in urbanized areas at the last census varied from 85 percent in New Jersey to 15 percent in Vermont.

Metropolitan Statistical Areas. Metropolitan Statistical Areas (MetroSAs, or MSAs) are what are most commonly referred to when speaking of metro areas. They are officially designated by the U.S. Office of Management and Budget. A "Metropolitan Statistical Area" is a county or group of counties having at least one urbanized area of 50,000 or more population, plus adjacent territory that has a high degree of social and economic integration with the core as measured by commuting ties. In New England, where there are no counties, MSAs consist of townships and cities instead. Since 2003, MSAs with a single core city having at least 2.5 million are designated "Metropolitan Divisions."

As of 2005 the 361 MSA areas in the U.S. held 83 percent of the national population. New Jersey was the most metropolitan state with 100 percent of its population living in metro areas. Arizona was second with 88 percent, and Nevada third with 86 percent. (Non-urban space in both these states is very much open.)

Newly defined smaller **Micropolitan Statistical Areas** have at least one urban cluster of at least 10,000 but less than 50,000 population, plus adjacent territory that has a high degree of social and economic Integration with the core as measured by community ties. The 577 micropolitan statistical areas in 2005 contained 10 percent of the total population.

Combined Statistical Areas. In 2003 a new set of census areas called "Combined Statistical Areas" (CSAs) were created. Basically, CSAs are combinations of two or more Metropolitan Statistical Areas. They also can include a MetroSA and one or more Micropolitan Statistical Areas. As of 2005 there were 124 CSAs.

All these variously defined metropolitan areas can cross state lines. The New York CSA, for example, includes portions of New Jersey and Connecticut. The Philadelphia CSA includes, in addition to the section in Pennsylvania, portions of Maryland, Delaware, and northeast New Jersey. In 1990, the term *Metropolitan Area* (MA) became the overall umbrella term covering MetroSAs and CSAs.

Canada. Canada's definitions are a bit different. In Canada an "urban area" is any area that has more than 400 persons per square kilometer and has 1,000 people. As of 2005 Canada had 33 large metropolitan areas called Census Metropolitan Areas (CMAs). Each CMA in Canada has a total population of at least 100,000, including an urban core with a population of at least 50,000.** CMAs usually consist of many smaller municipalities.

---

*. For a discussion of the new U.S. definitions, see: William H. Frey, Jill H. Wilson, Alan Berube, and Audrey Singer, "Tracking American Trends into the Twenty-First Century: A Field Guide to the New Metropolitan and Micropolitan Definitions," in Alan Berube, Bruce Katz, and Robert E. Lang, eds., *Redefining Urban & Suburban America, Vol.III*, Brookings Institution, Washington, D.C., 2006, pp. 191–234.

**. "Portrait of the Canadian Population in 2006: Subprovincial Population Dynamics," *Statistics Canada*, www2.statcan.ca/english/census 06/analysis

In the American city prior to the 1960s, industry was concentrated in an inner belt located between the central business district (CBD) and the better residential areas. However, central city factory expansion was both difficult and expensive. Assembly lines or other factory operations had to be fitted into existing buildings, and moving goods from floor to floor was a serious problem. Moreover, land surrounding the factory was already occupied, which meant that whatever was already on the land had to be bought and torn down before the factory could expand. Transportation also was an increasing problem. Trucks had to move down busy city streets before lining up to wait to get into too few loading docks. Parking space for workers' cars developed into another major headache.

Factories until the mid-20th century had stayed in the city because they had no choice. They needed access to rail lines to ship their goods, and most workers did not have private cars, but rather came to work on public transportation. Similarly, until the 1970s, downtown was where the major department stores and retail outlets were located. For major shopping one went downtown, usually by public transit.

Out-Movement: 1950 into the 21st Century

Today, the geography of work and shopping have been turned upside down. Most shopping, service establishments, and manufacturing firms now have suburban addresses. Decentralization of people, shopping, offices, and manufacturing has been the pattern since the last half of the 20th century. Not since the 1970s have downtowns accounted for over half the nation's sales. Today downtowns average less than 10 percent of metro area employment.[6]

Suburban shopping malls—only a handful existed 50 years ago—now number about 50,000 and dominate retail sales. With over three-quarters of employed suburbanites working in suburbs, old commutation patterns (residents of suburbs commuting to the central city) have also broken down. Since 1980 the average commute has not been from suburb to city but from suburb to suburb. Downtown is no longer the major metropolitan employment site. Today, 90 percent of metro areas office space is not in the downtown, but suburban. Many of the offices are in suburban office parks.

The last half of the 20th century saw a massive flow of urban business, manufacturing, housing, and retail trade from the center toward the periphery, a pattern that continues today. This change did not happen overnight. Actually, for a century, with annexation taken into account, the population of outer "suburban" areas has grown faster than that of central cities.[7] Almost all metropolitan growth during the last century took place in the suburban ring beyond the central city. Today, roughly two-thirds of the metropolitan area population lives in the suburbs. (This suburban decentralization is further treated in Chapter 6, The Suburban Era.) Even growth in non-metropolitan areas has been highest in counties having metropolitan characteristics and/or experiencing overspill from metropolitan counties. The exurbia areas of overspill, or sprawl, particularly those along interstates, simply confirm the patterns of metropolitan dominance.

COMMUTING AND COMMUNICATION

Without technological breakthroughs in electrification, transportation, and communication the 20th century outward flow of urban population wouldn't have been possible. The 19th-century city was based on steam power, which could only be transported short distances. The cities of the 20th and 21st centuries are based on electricity and petroleum. Massive use of electric power, automobiles, trucks, telephones, Internet, cell phones, and iPads dramatically increased the movement of persons, goods, and ideas.

Research shows that the factor most closely related to a city's growth during the first half of the 20th century was the extent of its transportation network with other cities.[8] The auto was critical to urban growth. The automobile provided mobility to the average urban dweller and encouraged rapid settlement of previously inaccessible areas on the periphery of the central city. Henry Ford's Model T changed, not just the way we move, but the way we live. The automobile went from being a toy of the rich to a middle-class necessity. Automobile registration in the United States increased from 2.5 million in 1915 to 9 million in 1920 and 26 million in 1930. Following World War II, car ownership became common in working-class as well as middle-class families. As of 2006 the 300 million Americans (including children) had 237 million registered vehicles. The auto now dominates American life. Roughly one-third of all city land is devoted to the movement or the storage of vehicles. Roads, garages, car dealerships, parking lots, and truck facilities define urban areas.

As of 1920 a Chicago study indicated that the average distance from home to workplace was only 1.5 miles.[9] With the coming of the automobile, the maximum distance that workers could live from their place of employment and commute within an hour increased from a dozen miles to perhaps 25 miles or so. (Theoretically, the automobile more than doubled the commuting radius, but the practical realities of poor roads and traffic congestion set lower limits.) However, far more important today than the actual distance from work is the commuting time. Today the average one-way commute is about 24 minutes; the longest average commute time of 39 minutes is endured by New Yorkers. According to the Census Bureau, New Yorkers spend 6.7 days a year commuting to work.[10] (See figure 12.1.)

What the automobile did for people, the truck did for goods. Prior to the 1920s there really was no alternative to the railroad for moving intercity goods. There was no road system beyond city limits. Following World War I the Army sent a convoy of trucks coast to coast to demonstrate the need for national roads. It took the Army convoy 62 difficult days to cross the country. Leading the 1919 Washington to San Francisco convoy was Lt. Colonel Dwight Eisenhower. (Later, when he became President, Eisenhower signed the bill creating the national Interstate System, which now bears his name.)

Trains went from city to city, but roads go everywhere. Trucks were free of fixed routes and fixed schedules, needed no elaborate fixed terminal facilities, and could make door-to-door pickups and deliveries. No longer was it necessary for the factory to be on the rail line. The major advantage of motor transport is its lower cost per mile for short hauls within a day or two of the city. In train transport, on the other hand, the lowest cost per mile was, and is, for the longest trips. The motor truck advantage was increased considerably by the building of new public roads. Railroads, by contrast, pay for their own construction and maintenance. The interstate expressway system, begun during the late 1950s, dramatically extended the trucks' advantage. Today, virtually all short-haul goods are shipped by truck. Goods that are needed overnight are increasingly shipped by air.

What the motor vehicle did for transportation, the telephone did for communication. Today when digital cell phones and PDAs are commonplace, it is useful to remember that not until 1920 did over half of all homes have telephones. And until the last 20 years or so long-distance phoning was quite expensive.

Today technology goes anywhere and geographical isolation no longer means isolation from mainstream technology. There is more than a touch of truth in the joke that the West Virginia state flower is the satellite dish. Businesses and offices no longer have to be in central-city locations in order to have adequate communication availability. During recent decades, widespread use of air-delivery services such as FedEx, and the universal use of computers for data transfer, have further weakened the need for a central-city business location. E-mail, cell phones, the Internet, and fax mean a central location is no longer a business requirement. Business sprawl, as well as residential sprawl, is the new pattern. Once physically inaccessible locations now have addresses on the information superhighway.

CANADIAN URBAN REGIONS

Canada is now 80 percent urban, and four major Census Metropolitan Areas (CMAs) now hold half of Canada's population. The 2006 Census showed that just over half of Canadians live in southern Ontario's so-called Golden Horseshoe around Toronto, Montreal and environs, the Vancouver area on the West Coast, and the Calgary-to-Edmonton corridor in Alberta.[11] These four areas, holding over 17 million people in 2007, are growing far faster than the country as a whole. (A five year jump of 7.6 percent as compared to 0.5 for the rest of the country.)

These four urban regions are magnets for people, jobs, and services. They are also more ethnically diverse than the rest of Canada. Demographically, the four major metro areas look more like each other than like the rest of the country. Immigrants, who make up the main source of Canada's growth, flow mainly into these four major metropolitan areas. This is especially true of Toronto, which boasts that 45 percent of its population has immigrated from another country. This makes Toronto more diverse than New York City. In North America only Miami, with its large number of Cuban and other Latin newcomers, has a higher proportion of immigrants than Toronto.

POSTINDUSTRIAL CENTRAL CITIES

The changes noted above have radically altered the relationship between central cities and their suburbs. Cities no longer dominate in population, services, or employment. In the U.S., the overall population of central cities remains about the same, but the overall data masks real changes. Losses in northern and eastern cities have been offset by growth and annexations in newer southern and western sunbelt cities. Suburbs, on the other hand, continue to grow. There are now over three suburbanites for every two central-city residents. Once dominant cities have lost most of their blue-collar manufacturing jobs. Pittsburgh, the Steel City, for example, hasn't had steel mills in decades. Cities have lost both well-paying union jobs and the entry-level jobs through which poorer city dwellers traditionally entered the labor market. This is not a recent change. Thirty years ago there already were almost twice as many persons employed in manufacturing in the suburbs as in cities.

Decentralization to fringe locations has been somewhat selective. Operations that require large plants and large amounts of ground space per worker are drawn toward the periphery. Obsolete central-city plants cannot compete economically with new, custom-designed single-story facilities. Intel, for instance, builds its factories around the product. Automobile plants, chemical firms, steel mills, and petroleum refineries also require large areas of fringe land for their newer operations. The American auto plants of the last decades have been built not in Detroit but in rural Tennessee, South Carolina, Alabama, and Mississippi. In 2003 Nissan opened its largest U.S. plant in Clinton, Mississippi.

Generally, production and distribution have decentralized as markets have decentralized. Wholesaling has decentralized as well, since wholesaling and warehousing require large spaces. The use of trucks and air rather than railroads for transportation also means more flexible outer locations become possible. By locating businesses outside the congested city core, near the interstate expressways and airports, businesses reduce transportation costs. Rapid transportation provides a form of storage en route.

On the other hand, the city still has some advantages. Finance, advertising, legal services, management, educational institutions, and government generally have shown less inclination to decentralize. While manufacturing, retail trade, and wholesaling typically have large space-per-employee requirements, most managerial, clerical, professional, and business functions are highly space-intensive. City offices can pack white-collar workers in cubicles, and then efficiently stack them floor upon floor, in high-rise office buildings.

Central cities are far from dead. While downtowns have clearly lost much of their retailing function CBDs have been experiencing new business construction. The last decade has witnessed a downtown office building boom in cities such as New York, Chicago, Phoenix, Atlanta, Houston, and Seattle. Boston, for example, has undergone a renaissance, moving from being a casualty of the manufacturing shutdown of the 1970s to becoming a model today of high-tech and service industries.[12] Meanwhile, 21st-century Chicago before the recession had its biggest building boom since the 1920s.

Management, finance, government, and law still remain at the center of the city because they do not require great amounts of space per worker and they need access to one another; a downtown location makes far more sense when services are oriented not to individuals but to other organizations. In the CBD, communications are easy and informal—business may be conducted over lunch, for example—and there are many services and economies available outside the firm itself. Outside specialists are readily accessible to cover areas such as advertising, legal services, accounting, tax information, and mailing.

Firms located on the periphery must provide all sorts of services often not required of those in the center, such as parking lots, cafeterias, and medical services. Top management may also remain in the city so that it does not become isolated from the informal information networks regarding competitors, government policy, and buying patterns that are always found when a number of firms in the same sort of business are located in the same area. Even in an era of Twitter and computer-based information systems, face-to-face contact remains important.

Downtowns also have become major entertainment, tourist, and convention sites. New downtown hotels and convention centers are common to midsized and large traditional tourist cities. Since the 1990s downtowns have again become fun places to be. As cities have dropped their crime rates their tourist business has soared. From 1970 to 1990 alone, the 38 largest urban areas added more than 300 downtown hotels, and more than a hundred cities have built convention centers.[13] In New York's Lower Manhattan, for example, a 92-acre business, hotel, and entertainment complex named Battery Park City has been constructed at the cost of $1.5 billion.[14] Even Harlem, which for years suffered disinvestment, is now showing major commercial investment in large retail businesses. Ex-President Clinton has his offices in Harlem. (See Chapter 11, Cities and Change, for more on gentrification in Harlem).

Overall, however, the growth of urban-office white-collar employment has not been able to compensate fully for major blue-collar and retail trade losses. And the recession beginning in 2007 devastated blue-collar jobs. Today some cities are in financial distress, while other American cities are in reasonable financial condition (see Box 7.2 Brain-Gain Cities).[15]

Newer post-automobile cities are far more "suburban" and spread out than older pre-automobile cities.[16] Research indicates that older metropolitan areas have seen sharp decreases in density in their central cores, whereas newer post–World War II cities never had high-density apartment neighborhoods in their central cities.[17] The result is a national pattern of moderate- to low-level density throughout metropolitan areas—in effect, the suburbanization of the central cities. This pattern of sprawling "suburban-like" cities is most evident in the newer cities of the South, Southwest, and West.

EDGE CITIES

The 21st-century pattern is one of what have been called edge cities. The term *edge cities* was coined by Joel Garreau in 1991 to describe the pattern of evolving new multiple urban cores increasingly found in the outer rings of metropolitan areas.[18] Edge cities can be viewed as an extension of the multiple-nuclei model of urban growth. Currently North America has approaching 300 edge cities, usually anchored by a mall or malls. While the boundaries of edge cities are often imprecisely defined, edge cities do have certain common characteristics.[19] Edge cities generally are located well beyond the old downtowns, and usually they are found at the intersection of two major highways, one often being an interstate. In size they are much larger than any single mall, and while they may include limited housing (sometimes in gated communities), edge cities are predominantly retail and business centers. Edge cities commonly have more retail stores than found in old downtowns and, unlike downtown, are usually totally automobile dependent. According to Garreau's criteria, edge cities have to have at least 5 million square feet of leasable office space and at least 600,000 square feet of retail space (about the size of a large mall with three anchor stores and 80 to 100 smaller shops).

Edge cities are the culmination of three major suburban changes that have taken place in metro areas over the last 50 years. These changes represent three overlapping waves of out-movement from the central city. The first out-movement, starting in the 1950s, was the flow of young ex-GIs and their wives to new suburban homes. (The post-war suburban housing boom is fully discussed in Chapter 6: The Suburban Era, so we will only touch on it here.) It is enough to say here that this movement to the suburbs continues today and has transformed North America from an urban to a suburban continent.

The second wave, beginning in the 1960s, was the out-movement of retail trade, especially the out-movement of the large department stores that have anchored the new suburban shopping malls since the 1970s. The malling of the land continues to the present day and will be discussed later in this chapter.

The third wave became a major force in the 1970s and still continues today. This is the out-movement of businesses and manufacturing from inner-city factories and firms to suburban business or industrial parks. Most economic activity is now suburban based. The bulk of the nation's blue-collar as well as white-collar jobs are now located in the suburbs.

Edgeless and Private Edge Cities

Edge cities are difficult to define since they don't look like we think cities should look, nor are they politically organized like cities. From earliest history cities have had clearly defined boundaries, often demarcated by an enclosing wall. However, while edge cities have jobs, shopping, and entertainment, they usually lack any clearly definable borders. Unlike legally defined cities and suburbs, there are no signposts to tell you when you are entering or leaving. *Edge cities do not have clearly defined legal edges.*[20] They lack municipal boundaries because they are not actually legal entities. Legally they often are non-place places, having names but not legal status. Tysons Corner in Virginia outside of Washington, D.C., is one of the nation's largest edge cities, having more office space than Tucson and more major retailing than Washington itself, but Tysons Corner, even with its over 100,000 jobs, doesn't appear as a municipality on Virginia state maps. Legally, Tysons Corner is just another part of Fairfax County.

Not being legal municipalities, edge cities have another strange characteristic for a place called a city: they have no civic order or elected government. Being private places they are not governed by municipal legislation, codes, or ordinances. They are private property, governed, not by elected representatives, but by corporate policy. Tysons Corner—like Dallas's Las Colinas, Los Angeles's Marina Del Rey, and Boston's Burlington Mall—are, in effect, *private cities* unto themselves.

What makes these places a sharp break with the past is not that they are planned, newer, shinier, or enclosed with air conditioning, but that they are *private domains* rather than incorporated, legally defined areas. The old downtowns, whether planned or unplanned, are public spaces open to all. The rules that govern public dress and behavior are found in ordinances passed by elected officials. Edge cities, for all their open courtyards and fountains, and all their calling themselves "town centers," are fundamentally different.

Basic questions, such as who can be in an outer-city office park or shopping mall and what they can or cannot do while there, are determined not by civic ordinance but by private corporate policy. The new outer cities are administered by company decree. They may be safe, but they are not democratic. They are privately managed city-states controlled and managed by a financial, rather than a municipal, corporation.

Remarkably, this major shift of our outer cities from public to private control has taken place almost completely without public notice, discussion, or debate. The once-public city has been privatized without discussion. Residential areas within edge cities are sometimes even walled off and "gated" with private security guards restricting entrance.

Boomburgs

While edge cities are not incorporated places, "boomburgs" is a name given to extremely fast-growing suburban *incorporated places* that have populations over 100,000 but are *not* the largest city in the metro area. Boomburg suburbs typically have been growing in double-digits, but while they have housing, retail centers, and entertainment venues they lack the dense business cores found in traditional cities. As of 2003 the U.S. had fifty-three boomburg suburbs.[21] Most are found in the Southwest. The Los Angeles, Dallas, and Phoenix metro areas contain 60 percent of the nation's boomburg suburbs. Many of these are large master-planned community developments. The five fastest growing during the last decade are: Gilbert in the Phoenix metro area, North Las Vegas and Henderson in Las Vegas, Chandler in Phoenix, and Irvine in Los Angeles. Future dramatic growth of boomburg suburbs in the Southwest is likely to be constrained by limited water supplies. The mortgage crisis starting in 2008 hit boomburgs especially hard.

Suburban Business Growth

The building of the interstate expressway system over the last 45 years gave industry a genuine alternative to a central-city location. Goods could now be cheaply and rapidly moved by truck rather than rail. Outer suburban land was cheap, and the taxes were low. Importantly, manufacturing plants could be designed from the inside out. A common pattern is to lay out an assembly line all on one level and then simply build walls around the workspace. The size and shape of the building is determined by the needs of the factory rather than by the size and shape of a lot or of an existing plant.

Thus, in the decades following World War II industry increasingly leapfrogged over intermediate city residential areas and moved directly from the inner city to suburban industrial parks. When a firm was serving only local markets, a central-city location, with its ease of access to all parts of a city, made sense. Such a location also was necessary if the major transport between cities was done by rail. Today, however, firms with national markets usually seek a location on or near an interstate expressway.

The industrial park has supplanted the city factory, with twice as many manufacturing jobs now located in suburbs as in central cities. Not only manufacturing but also white-collar jobs have been suburbanized. The earlier suburbanization of population provided a suburban workforce, a workforce that now commutes to work by auto. In turn, the location of most jobs in suburbs encouraged even more workers to move to new suburban tract type housing developments.

Today, employment of all sorts is most likely to have a suburban zip code. Over 90 percent of new office space is built in suburbs. Outer Dallas, for example, has three times the office space of the central business district, while suburban Atlanta has twice the office space of the center city. Even in the New York metropolitan area, northern New Jersey now has more office space than Manhattan. Nor are suburban offices simply back-office operations seeking low rentals; the executive suite has come to the suburbs. For example, Plano, Texas, north of Dallas, was a small residential suburb two decades ago. Today it is a business center and the national headquarters for five major corporations: Frito-Lay, Electronic Data Systems, Murata Business Systems, Southland Life Insurance, and J. C. Penney. J. C. Penney moved its headquarters to Plano from New

Willis Tower (formerly Sears Tower), Chicago. Symbolizing the suburban shift, in 1992 Sears moved its headquarters out of Sears Tower (the tallest building in the United States) in downtown Chicago to the suburban office park in Prairie Stone, some 35 miles northwest of the city. iStockphoto

Sears Prairie Stone. Courtesy of Sears

York City. The suburban economy is substantially service oriented, often with its marketplace patterns being nationally or internationally, rather than locally, focused.

Sears is an example of the suburban shift. In the 1970s Sears consolidated its operations in the then world's tallest building, the new 110-story Sears Tower in downtown Chicago. However, as Sears was placing its head in the clouds, its network of urban-based stores increasingly lost touch with suburban customers. Now Sears has gone suburban. In 1992 Sears moved all of its 5,000 merchandise- group employees of Sears Tower to suburban Hoffman Estates, 35 miles northwest of Chicago. The new Sears headquarters, named Prairie Stone, occupies a former soybean field and boasts 200 acres of reconstructed prairie and wetlands. The highest building is six stories high.

Growth of outer metropolitan-area private economies is increasingly driven by job growth in high-end service industries such as information technology, biomedical research, and business services. Suburban Fairfax County, Virginia, outside Washington, D.C., now has some 2,000 high-tech firms.[22] It also in 1997 became the richest county in America. The major per capita locations of Internet addresses are not the cities of New York, Los Angeles, or Chicago. The places with the largest per capita number of .com, .net, and .org addresses are suburban Herndon and Fairfax Counties in Virginia, both housing edge cities of Washington, D.C.

As suburbs have gone from being primarily residential areas to being the primary location of shopping, manufacturing, and office space, the old Burgess hypothesis of economic growth moving out from the CBD through a series of zones has become history. Business, retail trade, and homeowners all have leapfrogged to the outer ring of the metro area. Suburbs have become the new commercial and economic cores of metropolitan areas, and as a result our spatial models of the metropolitan area have gone from core–periphery models to multinucleated or multicentered models.

Malling of the Land

If the dominant urban symbol for the middle of the 20th century was the skyscraper, the dominant symbol for the beginning of the 21st century is the shopping mall. As expressed by Kowinski, "More than locations for consumption, malls have become the signature structure of the age."[23] Some, such as the economist Tyler Cowen, even praise the commercial culture of the mall as the best of all possible worlds.[24] You may love the malls, or believe

Submarine rides are a feature of the huge West Edmonton Mall, Alberta, Canada. The mall has a hotel with a "red neck" room, where the bed is on the back of a pickup truck. © James Marshall/Corbis

their consumerism values represent all that is wrong with North America, but it is impossible to discuss contemporary metropolitan life without discussing the role of the shopping mall. The larger malls have become social as well as retail centers. They have become America's town centers and main streets. Shopping centers from convenience centers to massive malls now account for almost three-quarters of the nation's non-automotive retail sales.

Shopping centers are actually a rather new development. The first shopping center, as we understand the term, was Country Club Plaza, developed in 1923 in Kansas City. At the end of World War II, there were only eight shopping centers in all of North America. The first of the modern malls surrounded by parking places was Northgate, which opened on the edge of Seattle in 1950. The first enclosed mall, Southdale Center was built in 1956 just outside Minneapolis in Edina, Minnesota. Southdale Center, designed by the architect Victor Gruen, was refurbished and enlarged to 1.3 million square feet for its 50th anniversary in 2006. The now-ubiquitous food courts were first introduced by the Rouse Company in the early 1970s.

Today North America's 50,000 shopping malls are an integral part of the suburban landscape and range in size from small strip malls to monsters such as Canada's West Edmonton megamall, which is the size of 115 football fields and has 800 shops, 19 movie theatres, 110 places to eat, a 355-room hotel, the world's largest indoor amusement park, a five-acre lake with the world's largest wave machine, and parking for over 200,000 cars. Malls sometimes almost become cities unto themselves. San Jose, California, has an enclosed air-conditioned center that includes 130 stores, 27 restaurants, and 9,000 parking spaces. Houston's Galleria, which initially set the pattern for the multiuse malls to follow, is modeled after a 19th-century gallery in Milan, Italy; it has three levels, and in addition to the usual department stores, restaurants, and shops, it also includes an athletic club with 10

air-conditioned tennis courts and a jogging track. (Some small college athletic departments would gladly exchange their facilities for those of the shopping mall.) It is connected to two high-rise office buildings and a 404-room hotel.

Malls, with their fountains, film festivals, and wine tastings, have come a long way from the mercantile stores of the last century. The shopping mall is replacing Main Street as the core of the community. Increasingly, the malls serve social as well as commercial functions. (Reflecting this, a shopping mall in the author's metro area changed its name from "Chesterfield Mall" to "Chesterfield Town Centre.")

Malls, with their "mall rats" and "mall bunnies," provide a place for young adolescents to gather and socialize. At the other end of the age spectrum, the mall also provides a safe and weather-free place for seniors to walk and socialize.[25] As downtowns have faded as centers of retail trade, dining, and entertainment, the shopping mall has become the contemporary public space version of the ancient Greek agoras.

Malls and "Street Safety"

Malls are designed to exude an image of being a comfortable, safe, and secure place. In good part this is done by excluding from the mall any persons or activities that might seem disruptive or disturbing. The strength of traditional downtowns is their ability to produce surprise and excitement, of not knowing what is around the next corner. Malls, by contrast, emphasize total predictability. No street musicians, no religious speakers, no one soliciting for charity, and no activities that might in any way disturb or offend any customers. For all their open courtyards and talk of being "town centers," malls are rigorously private, and thus can ban from the property teenagers who are disruptive, panhandlers, and bag ladies. No one has a right to walk into a mall just because they feel like going there. (The Mall of America bans unaccompanied teenagers on weekend nights.) The mall police enforce

---

Box 5.2   The Ultimate Malls

A Goliath of a shopping mall is the West Edmonton Mall in Edmonton, Alberta.* Edmonton is a city of a million persons, but during after-Christmas sales the mall alone draws as many as a quarter of a million people a day to its site on the cold Canadian prairie. This mall attracts 20 million people a year in a country of 33 million people. Visitors come to see a shopper's fantasyland. There are some 800 stores, 110 restaurants, 19 movie theaters, and even a Caesar's Palace Bingo Parlor, as well as the world's largest indoor amusement park, with 24 rides including two 13-story-plus roller coasters. There are, additionally, an 18-hole miniature par-46 golf course, an NHL-size ice rink, and a dolphin lagoon. And set in a balmy 86-degree atmosphere, the world's largest indoor wave pool boasts a sand beach, palm trees, and 22 water slides. On a lower level, the mall also houses an aquarium. All this in often-frigid northern Alberta.

The most spectacular feature, however, is the mall's 200-foot artificial lake. At one end of the lake, a replica of Christopher Columbus's ship, the *Santa Maria,* rests on a coral reef, illuminated by a giant skylight. At the other end of the lake, children and parents line up to cruise the 20-foot-deep lake in one of four 25-person submarines. The mall actually has more submarines than the Canadian Navy.

But there is an even larger mall. In 1992 the Ghermezian brothers, who built the West Edmonton Mall, opened a United States version in Bloomington, Minnesota (south of Minneapolis), called the "Mall of America." The Mall of America as of 2006 covered 4.2 million square feet. It had 520 stores, 14 movie screens, and 46 places to eat. Its Knott's Berry Farm Camp Snoopy has a 7-acre indoor amusement park, including a half-mile-long rubber-wheeled roller coaster, a log flume ride, and a Hormel cookout area named Spamland. Inside the mall Dinosaur Walk Museum has more than 60 life-sized dinosaurs and interactive displays. Underwater Adventures Aquarium houses a 1.2 million gallon aquarium and the world's largest shark collection. The Mall of America has 400 live trees, 300,000 plants, and a 4-story waterfall. It also has its own zip code, police, doctors, dentists, and a public school for the children of the mall's 10,000 employees.

In spite of all this the Mall of America had slipped to third place in retail footage by 2007. To reclaim its number-one status the Mall of America plans to *double* its size. In addition to adding more retail shops, Phase II will add a 6,000-seat music theatre, an ice rink, and 3 hotels.**

Where all this will end is a matter of professional dispute. Some see entertainment malls as a new model, while others believe that the megamall, like the brontosaurus, is the final gasp of a concept that has been pushed to excess. So far the "Build it and they will come" approach seems to be working.

* Partially based on material in J. John Palen, *The Suburbs,* McGraw-Hill, New York, 1995, pp. 199–201

** "Mall of America Plans to More than Double Size," Associated Press, March 27, 2007.

---

the image of the mall as a secure place into which outside problems don't intrude. They may even patrol parking lots in highly visible vehicles with revolving flashing lights.

However, while the mall security staff may wear the uniforms, badges, and even weapons of police, they usually are "rent-a-cop" private security officers dressed to look like police officers. Their role is basically public relations. In most states security guards lack police powers to arrest. They can only hold someone until the real police arrive. Similarly, the stop signs on mall roads, while looking official, are only advisory since the mall rights-of-way are private, not municipal or state roads.

To maintain their image of safety, malls use their advertising clout to see that crimes committed on mall property are not reported on local TV or in the local newspaper. Malls and their stores are major media advertisers. In reality malls have problems with car theft, robbery, and occasionally even rape, but to acknowledge that malls have crimes other than shoplifting would damage the illusion that both mall operators and their patrons seek to maintain.

NONMETROPOLITAN GROWTH

Historically, metropolitan areas in the United States have grown faster than nonmetropolitan areas. The classic ecological model implicitly assumed continued movement of population from rural hinterlands to metropolitan areas. This clearly was the case for the first 70 years of the 20th century, when the metropolitan sector—core or fringe—was growing while rural areas consistently lost population. However, during the 1970s, for the first time, rural counties not only stopped declining but increased in population. Metropolitan dominance was said to be challenged by an emerging pattern of increased dispersion and deconcentration.[26] However, during the 1980s talk of a "rural renaissance" largely faded, since the 1980s saw metropolitan areas again growing considerably faster than nonmetropolitan areas.

The 1990s saw some rural rebound, and by decade's end some 71 percent of rural counties were growing again.[27] This pattern has continued into the 21st century. The Census Bureau reported in 2006 that since 2000 18 of the 25 largest metro areas saw more people move out than move in.[28] The few exceptions were in the South and Southwest.

Diffuse Growth

Is the growth of nonmetropolitan population a sign of a return to older and simpler rural ways? Are we about to experience a rural renaissance? No. We are experiencing a transformation in settlement patterns, but this does not represent a rebirth of rural ways of life. Rather, what we are witnessing is the outmovement of population into a new form of community that is more diffuse.[29] Most of the rural rebound has been due to in-migration by previous metro area residents rather than natural increase. What this means is that the fastest growth is in the sprawling exurbs.

There is a rural-residence preference among the in-movers, some of whom are retired. Businesses are also locating in rural areas. (L.L. Bean operates from a small town in rural Maine, and Lands' End from a town in rural Wisconsin).

The most rapidly growing nonmetropolitan areas are those economically tied into the metropolitan nexus, but legally outside the metro area. Often these outer sprawl exurb areas can't be clearly defined as suburb, small town, or rural countryside. What is not taking place is a "rural renaissance" or "rural rebound." Both the proportion and the absolute number of persons actually engaged in agriculture continue to decrease. Farm population dropped about one-quarter during the last decade, and today fewer than 2 percent of the U.S. population remains on farms. Clearly, any rural rebound does not mean a return of the family farm or to agricultural pursuits.

Additionally, some rural growth is now related to providing recreational and retirement opportunities for metropolitan residents. Thus, nonmetropolitan growth can be best seen not as something totally separate from urban areas but rather as an extension of the metropolitan area's influence beyond the daily commuting range. More than 50 years ago, Louis Wirth noted that urbanism—that is, urban behavior patterns—had become the American way of life. Today it is far more so. Even isolated towns in Montana boast drive-in gourmet coffee stands.

As we continue to expand into a national metropolitan society, distinctions between metropolitan and nonmetropolitan areas become even more blurred. Growing nonmetropolitan areas don't look all that different from metro area exurbs.

National Society

We are rapidly moving toward a national metropolitan system in which old differences cease to make a difference. The pattern of discrete metropolitan concentrations is being challenged by an emerging pattern of increased dispersion and metropolitan de-concentration. Metropolitan areas are no longer even semi-independent. Local banks run by local bankers who knew their customers have largely been replaced by a handful of national banks. National digital cell-phone networks, e-mail, the Internet, Twitter, and FedEx and its competitors have further reduced the friction of space.

While at the turn of the century the commuter railroad and streetcar made it possible for a vanguard of businesspeople to move their residences from the city, commuter air travel now puts a premium on accessibility to an airport. Today the significant factor is no longer distance. Distance now is measured not in miles or kilometers, but by time. The question "How far is it?" commonly anticipates a temporal rather than spatial response: How long does it take to get there? Increased mobility of goods, persons, and ideas suggests that a new urban phase—a national urban system—is being created.

Air shuttles tie cities together: a commuter between New York and Chicago or Los Angeles and San Francisco is able to catch a flight in either direction almost every half hour from dawn to dusk. Ironically, shuttle flights linking San Diego, Los Angeles, and San Francisco make it easier (and faster) to move between these cities than around Los Angeles itself. It is one of the peculiarities of modern life that the air shuttles from city to city can offer more frequent, and even faster public transportation than that often available within cities themselves. Increasingly, we don't even physically commute; rather we telecommute. Physical distance is losing importance.

The emerging pattern of a national metropolitan society forces us to rethink traditional assumptions. Half a century ago, Otis Dudley Duncan suggested that the concept of a "rural–urban continuum" was losing empirical validity.[30] Today, emerging nonmetropolitan growth patterns suggest that the concept of a metropolitan–nonmetropolitan continuum is also losing utility. New patterns contradict the old assumption that the social and economic factors of urbanization are a consequence of the distance from the point of population concentration. This change has yet to be fully reflected in federal policy or research.[31]

Contemporary distinctions between metropolitan and nonmetropolitan are becoming more blurred with each passing decade. In the contemporary information society, it is becoming more difficult to distinguish metropolitan and nonmetropolitan residents on the basis of occupations, consumer habits, and degree of sophistication.[32] In many respects the metropolitan–nonmetropolitan differences have ceased to make a difference. Whether we live in a metropolitan area or not, we are all part of a metropolitan society.

THE RISE OF THE SUNBELT

Population and Economic Shifts

One of the most dramatic urban changes of the last 40 years has been the historic shift of population and power from the old industrial heartland of the Northeast and North-central regions to the metropolises of the West and the South (see table 5.2). The Census Bureau reports that as of 2008, of the 100 fastest growing counties, 70 percent were in the South. The growing southern rim, commonly known as the sunbelt, extends roughly from Virginia on the east through the states of the South and Southwest, up through California on the west. The rise of Houston from a steamy Texas town of little economic interest to its role as the oil capital of the world typifies the pattern of sunbelt growth.[33] Houston, with just over 2 million people, is now the nation's fourth largest city. It is exceeded in size only by New York, Los Angeles, and Chicago. Without the technology of air conditioning this transformation would have been impossible.

A striking example of the growing sway of the sunbelt is that Peoria, Illinois—long touted by comedians, politicians, and marketers as the quintessential heartland city—has been passed in size by the lesser-known Peoria, Arizona. As of 2006 the sunbelt Phoenix suburb of Peoria had grown to 138,143 residents while the Illinois rustbelt Peoria had declined to 112,936. The old question, "How will it play in Peoria?" takes on an entirely new meaning. Today, which Peoria provides the truer mirror of America?

Since the 1970s the population below the Mason–Dixon Line and west of the Rockies has outpaced that of the nation. However, the housing recession hit the western and southern sunbelt states especially hard. Previously boom cities such as Phoenix found themselves with a glut of unsold homes. Still, as of 2010 the 50 fastest-growing metro areas were concentrated in the West and South.[34] Meanwhile, older economic areas of the Midwest and the Northeast remain economically comparatively stagnant. These

older northern areas are sometimes collectively referred to as the frostbelt, snowbelt, or rustbelt. The term *rustbelt* refers to the decline of the heavy manufacturing cities that during much of the 19th and 20th centuries defined America's industrial might. However, by the 1970s the dominant northern cities were experiencing deindustrialization. California, Texas, and Florida are projected to account for 45 percent of the United States' net population change between now and 2025.[35] Table 5.2 indicates that all save two of the 10 fastest-growing metropolitan areas are in the West or South. In fact, nearly all of the 40 fastest-growing metro areas are in the West or South.[36]

This is a huge transformation since until 40 years ago the South was an economic backwater. Now, population and businesses are moving to the South and Southwest. Businesses are said to be attracted to such areas by a "good business climate," by which is meant lower wages, lower taxes, lower land costs, and a lower rate of unionization. The sunbelt as an energy-producing area also enjoys a cost advantage, particularly when oil costs are high. The milder climate requires less energy for

Table 5.2	**Population Estimates for the 10 Metropolitan Statistical Areas with the Largest Numeric Increase: 2007 to 2008**			
Rank in numeric change	Metropolitan statistical area	Population estimates		Change Number
		2008	2007	
1	Dallas–Fort Worth–Arlington, TX	6,300,006	6,153,474	146,532
2	Houston–Sugar Land–Baytown, TX	5,728,143	5,597,958	130,185
3	Phoenix–Mesa–Scottsdale, AZ	4,281,899	4,165,921	115,978
4	Atlanta–Sandy Springs–Marietta, GA	5,376,285	5,261,296	114,989
5	Los Angeles–Long Beach–Santa Ana, CA	12,872,808	12,784,612	88,196
6	New York–Northern New Jersey–Long Island, NY–NJ–PA	19,006,798	18,922,571	84,227
7	Chicago–Naperville–Joliet, IL–IN–WI	9,569,624	9,496,853	72,771
8	Austin–Round Rock, TX	1,652,602	1,592,590	60,012
9	San Francisco–Oakland–Fremont, CA	4,274,531	4,216,125	58,406
10	Washington–Arlington–Alexandria, DC–VA–MD–WV	5,358,130	5,302,295	55,835

Source: U.S. Census Bureau, Population Division, 2009

heat (this is only partially offset by higher air-conditioning costs).

Quality-of-life factors such as warmer winters and the chance to engage in outdoor activities—such as playing golf most of the year—also play a role. Also, the racial climate has improved markedly. Some sunbelt cities also have been able to annex outlying areas before they develop. This means the cities are less financially stressed because they can include within their city boundaries most new "suburban" development. By contrast, almost all northern cities have had to deal with fixed city boundaries since roughly the 1920s, or even earlier in the case of cities in the Northeast.

Over the last quarter of a century sunbelt cities such as Charlotte, Atlanta, Orlando, Dallas–Fort Worth, San Antonio, Albuquerque, Phoenix, and San Diego have all become world-class locations. Greater Los Angeles, in terms of economic activity and cultural influence, is now challenging New York. Some argue that Los Angeles will be the leading western-hemisphere city of the 21st century.

Regional Consequences

The consequences of interregional population shifts have been dramatic. The South, which historically always had migratory outflows of population, now is the fastest-growing region in the nation. During this same period, once-economically powerful industrial cities of the North have experienced declines in both population and economic influence. In 2006 North Carolina displaced New Jersey from the ranks of the 10 most populous states.[37] Northern cities often are suffering real declines. For example, the central city of St. Louis now has only as many people as it did in 1890, Cleveland now has as many as during World War I, and Detroit now has no more than in 1920.

This does not mean all northern cities and metro areas are in economic decline;

most clearly are not. What it does mean is that population is flowing south and west, attracted by new jobs, a mild climate, a lower cost of living, and a lifestyle stressing outdoor living. While the North and Midwest still have more corporate headquarters, there is clear movement toward the South and the West.[38]

The fastest-growing sunbelt industries are service industries such as real estate and tourism, plus the newer, highly skilled industries such as electronics, energy, and aircraft. These often have a preference for a location in the Southwest, particularly suburbs of major cities. Federal-level political decisions, such as locating the space agency in Houston and the national center for silicon research in Austin, have strongly reinforced growth trends. Even after base cutbacks, military budgets disproportionately directed monies and employment to areas with substantial military basing, i.e., the South. Also, retirees often head south, especially to the states of Florida and Arizona. The Great Recession beginning in 2007 slowed this trend, but it is likely to resume with better economic times.

Sunbelt populations are more likely to vote conservative and are less likely to support liberal political candidates or policies—excepting firm support of Social Security by the retired elderly. The political implications of the sunbelt clearly gaining political influence and power can be seen in figure 5.3. The 2010 census-based reapportionment will see Texas gain four seats in the House of Representatives, Florida gain two, and Arizona, Georgia, Nevada, Utah, Washington, and South Carolina each gain one seat. These are states that usually vote Republican. New York and Ohio will loose two seats, while New Jersey, Michigan, Iowa, Louisiana, Massachusetts, Missouri, Illinois, and Pennsylvania, meanwhile, will each lose a seat.

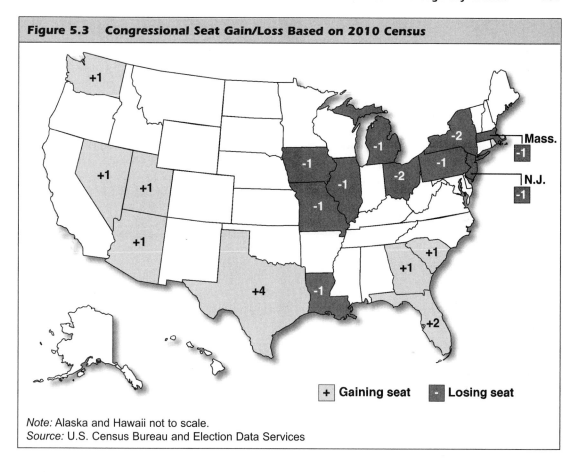

Figure 5.3   Congressional Seat Gain/Loss Based on 2010 Census

+ Gaining seat   − Losing seat

Note: Alaska and Hawaii not to scale.
Source: U.S. Census Bureau and Election Data Services

Political power clearly is shifting south and west. Many political writers see this benefitting Republicans.[39]

Sunbelt growth is not a consequence of runaway northern industries that abandoned the industrial heartland to build low-wage nonunion plants in the South.[40] Rather than attracting older smokestack industries, the sunbelt states developed new economic activities. As summed up by Kirkpatrick Sale, the writer who first used the term *sunbelt*:

> In broad terms there has been a shift from the traditional heavy manufacturing long associated with the industrial belt of the Northeast to the new technological industries that have grown up in the Southern Rim—aerospace, defense, electronics.[41]

Newer cities of the sunbelt, partially because of the office-at-home phenomenon, also require far less office space. Greater New York has some 27 feet of office space per person. In Greater Los Angeles, by comparison, the figure is a mere 15 square feet per person. Telecommuting is becoming more common, and the consultant subculture often works at home.

Sunbelt Problems

The sunbelt, however, is not all sunshine. Breakneck growth has brought not only jobs but also massive urban sprawl, huge traffic congestion, overtaxed water and sewer systems, rising air pollution, and widespread environmental degradation. Houston, for example, has some of the worst air pollution in the nation. Additionally, auto congestion, water supplies, and sewage disposal problems are growing ever more severe.[42]

Cities such as Houston, Dallas, San Antonio, Albuquerque, Phoenix, and San Diego have all had to cope with phenomenal growth, and the responses have not all been similar.[43] During the last decade, sunbelt metro areas were most likely to be overbuilt, and thus they were hit hardest by recession. Sunbelt cities are pressured to expand schools, social services, water plants, roadways, and waste treatment facilities. All these require financing. At the same time, citizen groups are lobbying for limits on taxes. Traditionally, cities of the sunbelt have had low taxes but also have provided lower-level services, especially for poorer residents. Today, city officials are caught by newcomers having contradictory expectations of northern-level services and southern-level taxes. How a state chooses to spend its resources helps determine the future of its cities. In the mid-1990s, for example, Texas voters approved issuing bonds to build new prisons, but turned down issuing bonds for building new schools. Texas now has, proportionately, the world's largest prison population. However, it is doubtful whether having new prisons rather than new schools is going to be more helpful for the long-run future of the state.

It should also be remembered that sunbelt cities are not automatically immune to the population declines that affected frostbelt cities. While 86 percent of the U.S. cities in the Northeast and 66 percent of those in the industrial North-central region lost population during the last decade, this was also true of 26 percent of the South's cities and 12 percent of the West's. A sunbelt location does not prevent people from moving out. Some long-term problems are emerging. Low wages once gave the sunbelt a competitive advantage. However, not only have sunbelt wages gone up, but in a global economy firms that once moved to Alabama or the Carolinas now move to Mexico, Southeast Asia, or

China. Nothing is guaranteed. For example, boom areas such as Las Vegas and San Diego, which had red-hot property values until mid 2006, saw real estate prices tumble in 2007. As of 2010, Las Vegas led the nation in housing foreclosures.

Finally, in building a high-technology economy, some parts of the South and Southwest still have academic systems that need upgrading, particularly at the primary and secondary school levels. In general, the South and Southwest have been less willing to invest the necessary tax money in developing their human capital. Teachers are comparatively poorly paid and public school systems often lag behind the rest of the nation. High-tech firms require well-educated workers. A condition Mercedes-Benz placed on opening its auto plant in Alabama was that the local school system be upgraded. Unless the South invests more in education it may again see itself outshone by northern and central regions with better-supported public educational systems at the primary, secondary, and university levels.

Geography is not destiny. There is nothing necessarily permanent about the sunbelt boom. In a global economy economic success increasingly depends not on geography, but on having an educated and flexible labor force. Businesses seeking just a cheap labor force move to China.

MOVEMENT TO THE COASTS

The early 21st century continues to show movement toward the Atlantic, Gulf, and at a slower rate, Pacific shorelines. More than 41 million Americans, one in seven persons, now lives in a county abutting the eastern or southern seaboard.[44] And this figure does not include those with vacation homes on the shore. The shoreline strip is growing significantly faster than the rest of the country (a partial exception are western states such as Arizona and Nevada). All the way from Maine to Texas, seaside property is burgeoning. Wealth generated by a strong economy, and more flexible work arrangements such as telecommuting, are resulting in more and more people living permanently near the shore.

Seasonal resort towns are turning into sprawling fulltime communities. Cape Cod, Massachusetts, for example now has a year-round population of 225,000. The Outer Banks of North Carolina a decade ago were largely deserted after Labor Day; now even a Wal-Mart has been built on the sand banks. Less mass movement to the beach has taken place on the West Coast. Especially in California the beaches and bluffs along the Pacific generally have state protections against private development. Also on the West Coast, the south-flowing California current keeps all but the most southern California beaches chilly, even in summer. Along the East Coast, on the other hand, the water is kept warm by the north-flowing Gulf Stream. However, Mother Nature is not always benign on the warmer Atlantic and Gulf Coasts. Since 1995 there has been a sharp rise in hurricanes. The risk of another major killer hurricane such as Katrina, which devastated New Orleans in 2005, is at an all-time high. Also, human caused disasters such as the 2010 BP oil spill can destroy ocean base of economies.

The costs of coastal living are not just paid by those living on the water's edge. New populations at the beach mean that existing taxpayers have to subsidize new water, sewer, and road systems. Major state roads have to be built so that when a dangerous storm hits, evacuation gridlock does not result. One of the reasons people are willing, literally, to build their castles on the sand in high-risk coastal areas is because they don't have to pay many of the costs of building in these high-risk areas. Federal disaster and insurance programs help them out if a hurricane, storm, or even coastal erosion damages or wipes out their property.

This is known as the "moral hazard" problem. It occurs when existing federal programs, by protecting against loss, inadvertently create the very problem they were designed to prevent. Since government foots much of the bill for coastal disasters, people can afford to move to unstable coastal areas.

Given these circumstances it is not surprising that we are rushing like lemmings toward the sea. The National Flood Insurance Act provides up to $350,000 insurance for properties private insurance firms will not cover. Currently it covers over 5 million properties valued at over $700 billion. The federal government even pays for bringing in sand to rebuild beaches. Although the program has come under attack as being environmentally unsound, the U.S. Army Corps of Engineers spends $80 million a year just to rebuild beaches. The Federal Emergency Management Agency (FEMA) estimates that even without storms some 30,000 coastal homes sit on land that will be under water by 2030.[45]

SUMMARY

Metropolitan areas are replacing cities as the major urban unit, and within metro areas suburban edge cities are the locus of growth. The first half of the 20th century saw a major inflow of population into metro areas, with the central city clearly dominating the metro area economically, socially, and demographically.

Since the mid-20th century, movement has been toward the periphery (and beyond). Suburban areas have experienced dramatic growth. Today over 60 percent of metro-area populations live in suburbs, and in some metro areas the figure is far higher. As of 2005 there were 361 Census Bureau–defined Metropolitan Statistical Areas (MSAs). Canada has 27 Metropolitan Areas with a urban core population of at least 100,000.

The growth of metro areas during the 20th century is closely related to technological breakthroughs in transportation and communication. Automobile registration has gone from 2.5 million in 1915 to one car for every two people today. Not until 1920 did half of all Americans have telephones. Today digital cell phones, PDAs, and smart phones are commonplace, and businesses no longer require a central-city location. Decentralization to fringe locations has been somewhat selective. Downtowns, with their high-rise buildings, are still cost-effective for finance, advertising, legal services, and management operations that have limited space requirements.

As the 21st century opens, cities from New York to Chicago to Atlanta to Phoenix are experiencing downtown office building booms. However, the greatest growth is taking place in America's approximately 250 suburban edge cities. Edge cities are hard to define because they lack clearly defined legal edges. They are usually not legal entities but placeless places. Edge cities also differ from central cities insofar as edge cities are legally private places without any civic order or elected government. This privatization of the edge cities has taken place largely without public debate or even discussion.

The majority of blue-collar as well as white-collar employment is now suburban. Northern New Jersey has more office space than Manhattan, and most industry has a suburban zip code. Suburban shopping malls have become the dominant metropolitan symbol for the beginning of the 21st century. Today there are 50,000 shopping malls that have replaced Main Street as the center of the community. Malls are designed to project a safe and secure image, and activities or persons that management views as potentially disruptive are banned from the corporate-owned and -managed malls.

Nonmetropolitan growth is again taking place, but it does not represent a rural renaissance or return to farm life. Some nonmetropolitan growth is the result of sprawl from metropolitan areas and some is occurring in outlying areas providing recreational and retirement opportunities for metro-area residents. Economically and socially we are becoming a national society.

For the last 40 years, growth in the sunbelt has outdistanced that of the nation. The sunbelt stretching from Virginia through the South and Southwest to California generally benefits from lower energy costs and quality-of-life advantages such as warmer winters. Sunbelt economic growth has not been the result of capturing runaway northern industries but of developing new economic activities in aerospace, electronics, and technology. A recent population movement is toward coastal locations. One in seven Americans now lives in a county that abuts the shore. Coastal living is accelerated by the federal government largely funding insurance against storm losses and other costs of building in high-risk coastal areas.

REVIEW QUESTIONS

1. How is the metropolitan area replacing the city as the major urban unit?

2. What was the major population flow within metropolitan areas during the last half century and how did it differ from the pattern of the first half of the 20th century?

3. How does the Census Bureau define urbanized areas, metropolitan statistical areas, and consolidated metropolitan statistical areas?

4. What economic activities have decentralized from central cities and which have not?

5. How are edge cities defined and where are they located?

6. What are the primary characteristics that distinguish edge cities from traditional city cores?

7. How do malls differ from traditional downtown shopping?

8. How has the sunbelt changed in the 30 years since it was first named and discussed?

9. What currently are the major regional population shifts and what are the consequences?

10. What problems face the sunbelt?

NOTES

1. U.S. Census Bureau, Population Estimates Program, Population Division, Washington, D.C., April 2005.

2. Brookings Institution, "December 2010–MetroMonitor: Tracking Economic Recession and Recovery in America's 100 Largest Metropolitan Areas," www.brookings.edu/reports/2010/0615.

3. Norman Scott Brien Gras, *Introduction to Economic History,* Harper, New York, 1922; and Roderick McKenzie, *The Metropolitan Community,* McGraw-Hill, New York, 1933.

4. U.S. Bureau of the Census, "Residences of Farms and Rural Areas: 1990," *Current Population Reports,* series P-20, no. 457, 1992, p. 2.

5. U.S. Bureau of the Census, U.S. Department of Commerce, "Population Profile of the United States: 1981," *Current Population Reports,* series P-20, no. 394, Washington, D.C., September 1982, p. 7.

6. Larry S. Bourne, "Commuting," in William van Vliet, ed., *The Encyclopedia of Housing,* Sage, Thousand Oaks, CA, 1998, p. 72.

7. J. John Palen, *The Suburbs,* McGraw-Hill, New York, 1995.

8. Mark LaGory and James Nelson, "An Ecological Analysis of Growth between 1900 and 1940," *Sociological Quarterly* 19:590–603, 1978.

9. Beverly Duncan, "Factors in Work–Residence Separation: Wages and Salary Workers, 1951," *American Sociological Review* 21:48–56, 1956.

10. U.S Census Bureau News, *American Community Survey,* www. census.gov, February 24, 2004. National Resources Committee, *Technological Trends and National Policy,* U.S. Government Printing Office, Washington, D.C., 1937.

11. "Highlights from the 2001 Census of Population," *Statistics Canada,* statcan.ca May 20, 2003.

12. Barry Bluestone and Mary Huff Stevenson, *The Boston Renaissance: Race, Space, and Change in an American Metropolis,* Russell Sage Foundation, New York, 2000.

13. Bernard Frieden and Lynne B. Sagalyn, *Downtown Inc.: How America Rebuilds Cities,* M.I.T. Press, Cambridge, 1989.

14. David Dunlap, "Filling in the Blanks at Battery Park," *New York Times,* Feb. 7, 1999, p. RE2.

15. Richard Florida, *The Rise of the Creative Class,* Basic Books, New York, 2002.

16. Rob Kling, Spencer Olin, and Mark Poster (eds.), *Posturban California: The Transformation of Orange County Since World War II,* University of California Press, Berkeley, 1991.

17. Thomas A. Guterbock, "Suburbanization of American Cities of the Twentieth Century: A New Index and Another Look," paper presented at meeting of the American Sociological Association, Toronto, 1982.

18. Joel Garreau, *Edge City: Life on the New Frontier,* Doubleday, New York, 1991.

19. Ibid., p. 425.

20. J. John Palen, op. cit., p. 187.

21. Robert E. Lang, "Are the Boomburgs Still Booming?" in Alan Berube, Bruce Katz, and Robert Lang (eds.), *Redefining Urban & Suburban America, Vol III,* Brookings Institute, Washington, D.C., 2006, p. 84.

22. Samantha Friedman, "Behind the Monuments: Taking a Sociological Look at Life in the Nation's Capital," *Footnotes,* American Sociological Association, 28:1, July/August 2000.

23. William S. Kowinski, *The Malling of America,* Murrow, New York, 1985, p. 22.

24. Tyler Cowen, *In Praise of Commercial Culture,* Harvard University Press, Cambridge, Mass., 1998.

25. Dawn Graham, "Going to the Mall: A Leisure Activity for Urban Elderly People," *Canadian Journal of Aging* 10:345–358, 1991.

26. William H. Frey, "Migration and Metropolitan Decline in Developed Countries," *Population and Development Review* 14:595–628, December 1988.

27. Kenneth M. Johnson, "The Rural Rebound," *Reports on America,* Population Reference Bureau, September 1999.

28. Rick Lyman, "Surge of Population in the Exurbs Continues," *New York Times,* April 20, 2006.

29. John Herbers, *The New Heartland,* Times Books, New York, 1986.

30. Otis Dudley Duncan, "Community Size and the Rural–Urban Continuum," in Paul K. Hatt and

Albert J. Reiss (eds.), *Cities and Society*, Free Press, New York, 1957, pp. 35–45.

31. The Department of Agriculture, for example, divides nonmetropolitan counties into six types; they "describe a dimension of urban influence in which each succeeding group is affected to a lesser degree by the social and economic conditions of urban areas. This includes the influence of urban areas at a distance as well as within counties themselves.

32. William Parker, Frisbie, and John D. Kasarda, "Spatial Processes," in Neil Smelser (ed.), *Handbook of Modern Sociology*, Sage, Beverly Hills, CA, 1988, p. 636.

33. Joe R. Feagin, *Free Enterprise City: Houston in Political–Economic Perspective*, Rutgers University Press, New Brunswick, N.J., 1989.

34. PRN Newswire, "50 Fastest-Growing Metro Areas Concentrated in West and South," prnewswire.com, June 21, 2010.

35. Paul Campbell, Census Bureau, "Population Projections: States, 1995–2025," *Current Population Reports*, P25-1131, May 1997, p. 2.

36. U.S. Census Bureau, "Metropolitan Areas Ranked by Percent Population Change: 1990–2000," Internet Release date: April 2, 2001.

37. Haya El Nasser, "Southern Growth Leads USA," op. cit.

38. Sally K. Ward, "Trends in the Location of Corporate Headquarters, 1969–1989," *Urban Affairs Quarterly* 29:468–478, 1994.

39. Josh Kurte, "New Census Helps GOP to a Degree," *New York Times*, Greenwire.com, December 22, 2010.

40. Larry Sawers and William K. Tabb (eds.), *Sunbelt/Snowbelt: Urban Development and Regional Restructuring*, Oxford University Press, New York, 1984.

41. Kirkpatrick Sale, *Power Shift: The Rise of the Southern Rim and Its Challenge to the Eastern Establishment*, Random House, New York, 1975, p. 5.

42. Joe R. Feagin, "Tallying the Social Costs of Urban Growth under Capitalism: The Case of Houston," in Scott Cummings (ed.), *Business Elites and Urban Development*, SUNY Press, Albany, 1989, pp. 205–234.

43. Richard M. Bernard and Bradley R. Rice (eds.), *Sunbelt Cities: Politics and Growth since World War II*, University of Texas Press, Austin, 1983.

44. "Growth Reshapes Coast," *USA Today*, July 21, 2000, p. 1A.

45. Owen Ullman, "Facing Mother Nature's Fury," *USA Today*, July 24, 2000, p. 6A.

CHAPTER 6

The Suburban Era

The country life is to be preferred, for there we see the works of God, but in the cities little else but the works of men.
William Penn, Reflections and Maxims

OUTLINE

Introduction
Suburban Dominance
Emergence of Suburbs
    The 19th Century
    Electric Streetcar Era: 1890–1920
    Annexation
    Automobile Suburbs: 1920–1950
    Mass Suburbanization: 1950–1990
    Metro Sprawl: 1990–2010
Causes of Suburban Growth
    Postwar Exodus
    Non-Reasons
Contemporary Suburbia
Categories of Suburbs
    Persistence of Characteristics?
    Ethnic and Religious Variation
    High-Income Suburbs
    Gated Communities
    Common-Interest Developments
    Working-Class Suburbs
    Commercial Definitions
Exurbs
Rurban Areas
Characteristics of Suburbanites
Suburban Poverty
The Myth of Suburbia
Minority Suburbanization
    Suburban Diversity
    Black Flight
    Integration or Resegregation?
Latino Suburbanization
Asian Suburbanites
Summary

INTRODUCTION

The 21st century is a suburban century. For more than 30 years America has had more suburbanites than city dwellers. Moreover, since 1997 an absolute majority of the population has lived in suburbs, and today 55 percent of the population is suburban. Suburbs have changed from being fringe locations from which commuters go to the city to being the modal areas where people work, live, shop, and recreate. Indeed, a role reversal has occurred between cities and suburbs—young singles, widows, and other non-family households now outnumber married-with-children homes in the suburbs. While cities overall still have higher rates of poverty, the number of suburban poor as of

115

2010 exceeded the city poor by 1.6 million.[1] Suburbs now house one-third of the nation's poor. Suburbs have radically changed, while many of our images of suburbia have remained set in the past.

The suburban revolution has changed suburbs from being residential places on the periphery to being the residential, economic, and commercial centers of a new metropolitan form. Moreover, if the polls are to be believed, substantial numbers of those still living in large cities would prefer not to be. One poll indicated that 60 percent of those living in New York, half (48 percent) of those in Los Angeles, and 43 percent of those in Boston would move out of the city if they could.[2]

SUBURBAN DOMINANCE

Economically, the suburbs now rule. We shop at some 50,000 suburban malls. Downtown department stores, by contrast, remain open in only a handful of cities. Suburbs also are where most of us work. Two-thirds of metropolitan office space and two-thirds of the nation's manufacturing jobs are in the suburbs.

Politically, suburban voters are in the majority, and their interests now set national and state agendas. Big-city bosses like Mayor Richard J. Daley of Chicago played a major role in choosing and electing presidents such as John Kennedy and Lyndon Johnson. Today presidential candidates primarily address themselves to the interests and concerns of suburbanites. President Barack Obama tailored his 2008 election campaign to the needs and interests of white middle-class suburbanites.

That the suburban shopping mall has replaced downtown as a shopping site is commonly recognized. What is less known is that factory employment now also has a suburban zip code—twice as many manufacturing jobs are located in suburbs as in the central city. The city factory has been supplanted by the suburban industrial park. White-collar office

jobs have also suburbanized. Outer Dallas has three times the office space of the central business district. Downtown Atlanta has a skyline of new office buildings, but suburban Atlanta has twice the office space. Even in the New York metropolitan area, northern New Jersey has more office space than does Manhattan. As noted earlier in the text, in 1992 Sears moved its 5,000 merchandise-group employees out of Sears Tower to suburban Hoffman Estates, 35 miles to the northwest beyond O'Hare Airport. The new location, named "Prairie Stone," boasts more than 200 acres of reconstructed prairie and wetlands, and no building is more than six stories high.

Such out-movement of offices, manufacturing, and shopping has turned Burgess's zonal hypothesis inside out and created a multinucleated pattern of outer suburban centers or edge cities. Suburbs have been transformed from being primarily outlying residential areas to being the nation's new economic and commercial cores. The suburbs are no longer "sub." While it twists the language a bit, suburbs are now the nation's demographic and economic centers.

EMERGENCE OF SUBURBS

How did this major change occur? Writing at the end of the 19th century, Adna Weber concluded that the most hopeful sign in American urbanization was the "tendency . . . toward the development of suburban towns," for "such a new distribution of population combines at once the open air and spaciousness of the country with the sanitary improvements, comforts, and associated life of the city."[3] This image of the suburb as a green or pleasant oasis with its single-family homes, neighbors, children, dogs, and bikes—all within commuting range of the city—is one that still has force. Suburbs have been called "bourgeois utopias."[4] Intellectuals may scorn such a suburban vision, but scorned or not suburbs have transformed the landscape demographically, organizationally, and in lifestyle.

Suburbs have been growing faster than central cities for a century. (Remember, though, that *suburban* as defined by the Bureau of the Census simply means territory inside the metropolitan area that lies outside the central city. Some of the more outlying areas might not ordinarily be considered suburban.) Officially the U.S. became a nation of suburbanites in 1970 when the census showed that for the first time suburban areas of metro areas exceeded central cities in population size and growth rate. Virtually the entire metropolitan area increase since that time has occurred in suburbs. (The total central-city population increase between 1970 and 2000 was less than 100,000 for all the nation's central cities put together.)

The switch to being a suburban nation came after World War II. In 1920 only 15 percent of all Americans were suburbanites, and the percentage was only 20 percent by 1940. It increased to 24 in 1950, and then shot up to 33 percent in 1960, 40 percent in 1980, 52 percent in 2000, and 54 percent in 2005.

The following sections first discuss the emergence of suburbs, then their organizational and demographic aspects, then the question of suburbia as a way of life, and, finally, the increasing role of minorities in suburbs.

The 19th Century

As noted in Chapter 3: The Rise of Urban America, the American city of the 19th century was compact, had high density, and could be walked rather quickly. Major suburbanization was not possible prior to the transportation advances of the 19th century that permitted population dispersal. The first to move out were the wealthy, who built "suburban" communities out along the railroad lines radiating from the city.[5] Initially, some of the homes were summer villas, but it was not long before families remained year-round and businessmen were commuting daily by train.[6] These expensive

railroad commuter suburbs were to provide an idealized rural refuge from the clamor of the city.[7] As advertised by a promotional piece of over a century ago:

> The controversy which is sometimes brought, as to which offers the greater advantage, the country or the city, finds a happy answer in the suburban idea which says, both—the combination of the two—the city brought to the country. The city has its advantages and conveniences, the country has its charm and health; the union of the two (a modern result of the railway), gives to man all he could ask in this respect. The great cities that are building now, all have their suburban windows at which nature may be seen in her main expressions—and these spots attract to them cultured people, with their elaborate and costly adornments.[8]

As this quotation suggests, the first American suburbs were generally upper-class villages of substantial country homes. The quotation also notes the importance of the railroad. In the absence of a reliable transportation technology, one could venture no farther from the railway station than one could conveniently walk, or be driven by carriage. Suburbs were thus strung out along the rail lines like beads on a string. Chestnut Hill on Philadelphia's Main Line was an early example of this pattern. Chicago's North Shore was another. Only those who could afford both the time and money to commute could combine an urban occupation with a rural residence. This began social class polarization between city and suburb.

Electric Streetcar Era: 1890–1920

The rapid adoption of the electric streetcar around the close of the 19th century allowed the middle class to move out to the new suburban developments springing up along the streetcar corridors. Boston, for example, as of 1850 was a walking city extending at most 2.5 miles from city hall. The coming of the electric streetcar in 1888 changed the spatial configuration of Boston and other American urban areas from that of a compact city to that of a star-shaped urban area.

By 1900 the streetcar meant one could live as far as 12 miles from the central business district. Moreover, one could ride the entire line for a five-cents fare. Using the streetcars, the middle-class population could separate where they worked from where they lived, just like the wealthy had been able to do earlier by using the railroads. Development, both residential and commercial, occurred along the fingers of the electric streetcar tracks, while the interstices remained empty and undeveloped.[9]

The electric streetcar, not the automobile, made middle-class suburbanization possible.

Annexation

Annexation was the major means of adding to the city during the last part of the 19th century. New suburban housing developments on the edges of the cities, such as Hyde Park (President Obama's neighborhood) on Chicago's south side were commonly annexed to the central city once they were built up. In 1889 Chicago annexed a massive area of 133 square miles on its south side. Such annexations were usually sought by suburban residents. Before the 20th century, suburbs sought to be annexed by the city in order to benefit from its superior fire protection, schools, and roads; to gain access to city water supplies (both for drinking and fires); and to use city sewer systems.

However, by the early 20th century, the pattern had generally reversed: suburbs increasingly actively sought "home rule" and opposed annexation. In many cases, the desire for suburban autonomy was directly linked to suburbanites' desires to remain free of the graft, corruption, political bosses, and the ethnic political influence of the central city. Keeping control over land use and taxes was also very important, as was maintaining influence over the local schools. Home rule meant that WASP

(white Anglo-Saxon Protestant) suburbanites could exclude from their suburban schools the immigrant Irish, Italian, Polish, and Jewish children found in the central cities. While the city was ethnically and religiously diverse, suburbs could remain Anglo-Saxon Protestant havens.

The fragmentation of governmental units within the metropolitan area thus became part of the American system. The 25 metropolitan districts defined by the census of 1910 showed the new future pattern. A full quarter of the metropolitan population already lived outside the core city. By the time of World War I the pattern was one of ethnic working-class populations residing in the central city, while more affluent white-collar workers commuted. To move out was to move up.

The division between city and suburbs is a legal distinction that over time has become a sociological division. While local municipal boundaries are significant in many ways—including financing, taxing, and schools—other social, organizational, ecological, and demographic criteria can be used to distinguish different regions within the metropolitan area. Some of these criteria are population density, the proportion of single-family dwellings, and distance from the center of the city. However, none of these alternative schemes has gained anywhere near the acceptance of the traditional city–suburb division. Today the city line is commonly viewed as a social and economic boundary as much as a legal boundary.

Automobile Suburbs: 1920–1950

Widespread adoption of the automobile greatly accelerated suburbanization. Car registrations, which had been 2.5 million in 1915, jumped to 9 million in 1920 and then skyrocketed to 26.5 million in 1930. (Today there are 235 million cars and two thirds of families have two or more autos). Henry Ford changed the car from a plaything of the rich to an everyday means of transportation. Ford's assembly lines did more than produce cars; they brought a revolution that changed the face of the nation. Ford had produced 16 million Model Ts by the time production switched to the Model A in 1927. At that time one of every two vehicles on the road was a Ford Model T.

Automobile usage meant that previously inaccessible land was open for suburban development. No longer was it necessary to be located along a railroad or streetcar line; commuters willing to pay the costs in money and time could drive their own cars to work and live where they pleased. The result was a middle-class suburban housing boom.

Ironically, the automobile was initially praised as solving the serious pollution problem caused by horses. Each horse produced 15 to 26 pounds of manure and several gallons of urine a day. In New York at the beginning of the 20th century, this meant 2.5 million pounds of horse manure and 60,000 gallons of urine each day. Manure littered the streets and provided a breeding ground for disease-carrying flies. Some 41 horses a day also died in the street. Thus, the automobile was viewed as a far less polluting form of transportation.

Popular upper-middle-class and affluent auto suburbs of this era—the Grosse Pointes, Shaker Heights, and Winnetkas—established an image of suburbs as places of substantial single-family houses surrounded by lawns free of crabgrass, and inhabited by white Anglo-Saxon Protestants of upper-middle-class income and educational levels. Voting Republican was frequently included in this image. These affluent suburbs established an image of suburbia as being "the good life," an image that developers still use to sell even the most humble suburban houses.

Suburbs built before World War II were sharply distinguished according to income, occupation, religion, and ethnicity. Developing suburbs often used zoning laws, which had come to be widely adopted following the pioneering New York City Zoning Resolution of 1916, to prevent the building of inexpensive homes on small lots. Restrictive racial, religious, and ethnic covenants included in deeds were also widely used to exclude "undesirable" groups such as blacks, Asians, Jews, and, occasionally, Catholics.

Pre–World War II suburbs had the advantage of appealing to the long-standing anti-urbanism of Americans—suburbs were supposedly closer to nature and thus better places to live, while at the same time close enough to the city to have all the advantages of the urban life that the suburbanite didn't really want to abandon. Suburban houses built during this period reflect the romanticism of their owners. Styles were widely eclectic; houses half-timbered in the grand English Tudor style were built next to pillared Georgian colonial houses and Spanish-Moorish villas. To their owners, these homes were far more than mere housing; they represented the romantic idealization of an earlier non-urban era. "A man's home was his castle," where he could live, if not as a lord, at least as a latter-day country gentleman—and all without being isolated from the advantages of modern city life such as electricity and connection to city water, sewer, and gas lines. Newer suburban homes had access to city services such as electricity and gas well before older, poor inner-city neighborhoods.

Actually, most of the suburban homes built during the 1920s were not grand estates but rather more utilitarian and moderately priced bungalows. Such one- or two-story homes were small, but efficiently laid out, and could be managed without servants. Bungalow homes suggested not wealth but solid middle-class comfort. To real estate developers, the adoption of automobiles was a boon, for it meant that open land lying between the rail and streetcar axes was now available for residential development. The ideal was that every family (or at least every middle-class family) should have a single-family home (and mortgage).

The middle-class and upper-middle-class character of this development meant that American cities were assuming a spatial configuration

Robert Rehm and his family living in the suburb of Levittown, N.Y., in 1951 was described by the Census Bureau as the "Average American." "He is a semi-skilled worker; has a wife and two children; has an average income of around $3,000; owns a refrigerator, radio, and telephone; and is paying on his home." Bettmann/Corbis

in which movement out was increasingly being associated with movement up. By the 1920s the social distinction between cities and suburbs was set.[10]

Mass Suburbanization: 1950–1990

The pent-up housing demand that had been frustrated first by the depression of the 1930s, and then by World War II, burst in a suburban flow by 1950—a momentum that has carried to the present day. Following the war the exodus of whites from the city included not only the rich and well-to-do but also large numbers of middle-class families and even working-class families.

Across the country once largely rural areas such as Los Angeles County saw massive conversion of rural tracts and orchards to suburban subdivisions. New families flowed to the suburbs seeking detached single-family houses in homogeneous look-alike residential areas. This movement was made possible by liberalized lending policies of the Federal Housing Administration

(FHA) and the new Veterans Administration (VA) loans. Often no down payment was required for purchasing a new home in a suburban subdivision. The consequence, as discussed later in this chapter, was a de facto national housing policy of government-subsidized movement to suburbia. (Canada has no similar national mortgage subsidy plan, nor does Canada allow a tax deduction for mortgage interest.)

As noted in Chapter 5: Metro and Edge City Growth, postwar suburbanizing families were rapidly followed by retailers who discovered that retail shopping malls were far more lucrative than their older stores in the declining central business districts. Business and industry similarly leapfrogged to the suburbs in order to benefit from newer plants, increased space, lower taxes, and access to the new freeways.

The rapidity with which farmers' fields were converted to single-family housing developments is well known. Builders of tract developments transformed huge areas of rural land into instant suburbia. Homes in Levittown, the prototypical postwar development, built 30 miles east of New York City on 4,000 acres of potato fields on Long Island, cost $6,900 in 1948, which even then was a real bargain. For this amount you purchased an identical 720-square-foot home having a 12-by-16-foot living room, a kitchen, two bedrooms, a bath, and a stairway leading to an unfinished attic that could be finished. All interiors were exactly alike, and there were four facades with different colors for external variety. To the ex-GIs and their wives, often living doubled-up with parents in a city apartment, such homes were a dream come true. The Levitt brothers revolutionized homebuilding, being the first to use a version of assembly-line techniques to mass produce some 17,500 houses for 80,000 people. On the West Coast, Lakewood Village, south of Los Angeles, was even larger, housing more than 100,000 persons in 16 square miles. Most suburban developments were, of course, far smaller.

The aesthetically vapid nature of many of these tracts of "little boxes" has been justly con-

demned. On the other hand, it should be kept in mind that the city neighborhoods from which many middle-class and lower-middle-class people migrated were far from being architectural gems. Look-alike uniformity was not a suburban invention. Most city streets have similar-type housing. For most families, a move to a suburban subdivision meant a move to a better house.

The titles of many suburban subdevelopments built after World War II—Rolling Meadows, Apple Orchard Valley, Oak Forest Estates—are really epitaphs for what was destroyed by the housing developments. I lived for two years in a suburban Washington, D.C., apartment complex of several hundred units named Seven Oaks Farm. The farm had been plowed under by the housing project, and there were only three oaks—mere saplings hardly three feet tall. Country names are used to suggest an openness and rural nature—a nature that vanishes as soon as the subdivision is built. But, of course, suburban developments named Congested Acres Estates or Flood Plains Hollow, while perhaps more accurately named, would not have the same sales appeal.

Metro Sprawl: 1990–2010

Across the nation, year by year, acre after acre of once rural land is relentlessly being consumed by urban sprawl. *Sprawl* is the term commonly used to refer to the automobile-dependent, low-density housing and commercial development taking place in the outer reaches of metropolitan areas (see Chapter 12: Housing Patterns, Sprawl and Smart Growth). Developers love new outer areas for their quick profits and ease of building, and the new homeowners like having more space for less money. Sprawl, however, is inherently economically inefficient, wasteful of time and resources, and destructive of the environment. Sprawl means the outlying parts of metropolitan areas, whether surrounding Atlanta, Phoenix, Salt Lake City, Denver, San Antonio, or Los Angeles, increasingly look the

The Rancher in Levittown
$59 A MONTH
No Down Payment for Veterans!

▶ The famous Rancher of Levittown is now being built in two more sections of Levittown. When these are sold there will be no more Ranchers; we haven't any more room for them.

▶ It's a beauty of a house that's priced unbelievably low at $8990. Carrying charges are only $59 monthly, and veterans need absolutely no down payment. Non-veterans need only a total of $450 down. Can you think of anything much easier than that?

▶ The house at $8990 comes with two bedrooms, but you can have a third bedroom for only $250 more. If you're a veteran you still don't need any money down, and a non-veteran needs only $100 more. We think that's a bargain, don't you?

▶ Of course, you're not buying just a house. You own the ground—60 x 100—beautifully landscaped. You have access to the community-owned swimming pools, recreational areas, etc.

▶ Your house itself is charming, cheerful, and convenient. Such things as a four-foot medicine chest completely mirrored, picture windows from floor to ceiling, an outside garden storage room, a Bendix washer, an oil-fired radiant heating system, complete rock-wool insulation—all add to your comfort and enjoyment.

▶ Get your application in as soon as possible. Occupancy may be any time from January thru May. You pick the month. You'll need a good-faith deposit of $100, but you'll get it back at settlement if you're a veteran; credited against your down payment if you're a non-veteran.

▶ O, yes, we almost forgot! Total settlement charges are just $10! See you soon, folks!

Furnished Exhibit Homes open every day until 9 P. M.

Levitt and Sons
INCORPORATED
U. S. ROUTE 13 • LEVITTOWN, PA. • Telephone WINDSOR 6-1100

Philadelphia Inquirer—November 14, 1954   Camden Courier-Post—November 13, 1954
Philadelphia Bulletin—November 12, 1954   Trenton Times—November 12, 1954

Note the no down payment for veterans, low monthly payments, and $10 total closing costs touted in this 1954 advertisement for the new Levitown being built outside Philadelphia.
(Courtesy of Levitt Homes)

Levittown house ad. Courtesy of Levitt Homes

same, with open scars where farms and forests once stood, new large houses (often in gated communities), and look-alike shopping centers surrounded by huge asphalt parking lots.

With dispersed growth often comes larger new homes, but also congestion and gridlock. Paradise is being paved. The average commuting time in Atlanta is 80 minutes, and commuting time is expected to increase to an hour and a half.[11] For those on the exurban edge times are even longer.

In 1950 Scottsdale, Arizona, was a tiny suburb of Phoenix with barely 2,000 people living in its one square mile. Today Scottsdale is three times the size of San Francisco, and the commute into Phoenix is far from the fast scenic desert drive it once was. It can take an hour to drive from Scottsdale to Phoenix. Phoenix is becoming what it most feared: another Los Angeles. Actually, at 469 square miles Phoenix sprawls over more space than does Los Angeles. Phoenix, where people once moved seeking clean desert air, now has some of the dirtiest air in the nation outside of Houston and southern California. Those with health problems are increasingly warned to stay inside because of air pollution.

During the housing boom that lasted until 2007 outer ring suburbs grew rapidly. However, during the subsequent severe housing recession outer ring homes were the slowest to sell. Inner ring suburbs and cities fared somewhat better.

Sprawl has moved to among voters' top concerns nationally, along with the economy, crime, taxes, and education. Nonetheless, in spite of spreading talk of "smart growth" and the "new urbanism," sprawl—so far—is the pattern for the 21st century. This issue will be discussed at length in Chapter 12: Housing Patterns, Sprawl, and Smart Growth, and in Chapter 13: Planning, New Towns, and New Urbanism. For now we will return to our discussion of how we became a suburban nation, and what this means for the future.[12]

CAUSES OF SUBURBAN GROWTH

Postwar Exodus

How did the US become a suburban nation? Why the postwar suburban exodus? Six factors largely account for the postwar suburban boom.

First, and most important, government policies—whether by intent or not—acted to directly subsidize suburban growth. New Veterans Administration (VA) loan guarantees made mortgage loans available to veterans at rates below those for conventional mortgages. A similar Federal Housing Administration (FHA) program that made loans to non-veterans had made some 22 million new home loans by 1994. (Canada had a small program for veterans-only.) VA loans could be obtained with no money down and a 25-year repayment schedule. Prior to this time mortgages commonly required 50 percent down and could only be obtained for five years with a balloon payment at the end. However, with the government guaranteeing housing, loan banks suddenly were competing to make loans to middle- and lower-middle-class families that they otherwise would have ignored.) Both VA and FHA programs required that communities be "homogeneous areas," thus reinforcing racial segregation.

Developers streamlined the application process so all the paperwork could be completed during a Sunday drive to see the model house at the proposed development. The VA and FHA initially made loans only on new houses, and once a developer's model home was approved, all similarly built homes automatically qualified. Not surprisingly, young families flocked to subsidized suburban houses.

Second, beginning in the late 1950s the federal government further subsidized out-movement by financing the construction of a system of metropolitan expressways. The resulting national interstate freeway system has been described by a secretary of commerce as "the

The affluent increasingly isolate themselves in suburban gated communities. © 1000words/ Dreamstime.com

greatest public works program in the history of the world."[13] Since the federal government paid 90 percent of the construction costs, city mayors pushed for having new freeways cut through their cities in order to bring shoppers downtown. They forgot that the new roads would go both ways. Without the federally funded freeways many of the new suburban developments would have been impossible to reach.

Third, in the eastern and northern sections of the country, almost all the land within the legal boundaries of the city had already been developed by the 1950s. This is both the most obvious and the most overlooked factor in explaining suburban growth. Most established cities couldn't annex, and without annexation all additional growth of the urban area would, by definition, *have* to be suburban growth. The depression years of the 1930s saw little building, and private home building was prohibited during World War II. Thus by the 1950s there was a tremendous pent-up demand for new metropolitan-area housing, and most available open land was, by definition, suburban.

Fourth, overall suburban housing costs were initially lower than costs in central cities. With a city housing shortage, buying older homes in the city required larger down payments. To new families just becoming economically established, this was a major consideration. Young marrieds went to the suburbs not for togetherness or to escape the city, but because new houses in suburban subdevelopments were frequently cheaper than housing in the city.

Today, when closing costs commonly run thousands of dollars, it is useful to remember just what a bargain the new suburban homes were. The *total* closing costs for a 1954 Levitt-built home was $10. Taxes in the new suburbs were generally lower than in the central city. Many suburban developers did not include in their purchase price tax-supported "extras" such as city water, sewers, sidewalks, street lighting, parks, and museums. Thus, the initial front-end costs of housing were frequently lower and easier to finance in the newer "package" suburbs than in the central city.

Fifth, suburbanization was "caused" by demographic changes. Prosperity and the return of veterans created a "marriage boom" that was quickly followed by a "baby boom." In the decade after the war, some 10 million new households were created. The existing housing in cities could not absorb large numbers of additional families. New city housing had not been built in decades, existing housing was badly overcrowded, and landlords were not inclined to be tolerant of young children. Thus, young couples with children were forced toward the suburbs, since they were not welcome as renters in city apartments and could not afford to purchase city houses. The suburban "baby-boom" children (born between 1947 and 1964, the "baby-boom" years) created a need for new housing—a need that suburban developers were delighted to fill.

Sixth, survey data show decisively that most Americans prefer the newer single-family houses on their own lots that are most commonly found in the suburbs. Even those who see suburban sprawl as a result of deliberate decisions made by powerful capitalists acknowledge that people want suburban single-family homes.[14] Planners and architects may feel that such housing defiles the landscape, but the public overwhelmingly prefers suburban sprawl to high-rise luxury apartments or even townhouses. This is true even of those without children. Given a choice, North Americans would rather live in single-family housing outside the city. Most families residing in apartment buildings view their tenancy as a temporary step before moving to a single-family house. If a suburban single-family home is too expensive, a suburban townhouse or even a garden apartment complex may substitute.

Among other things, this means that North Americans are getting pretty much what they want in housing design. Suburban subdevelopments succeed because even when alternatives are open, most people prefer suburban locations. The fact that many professional urban planners and architects deplore the cookie cutter "little boxes all in a row" has had little impact on most of the population. Residents perceive individuality and differences even in the largest look-alike sub-developments.

Non-Reasons

There is a tendency to project contemporary factors back into the past. Thus, the "cause" of suburban growth is frequently equated in the popular media with the decline of cities. Contributing to this decline are said to be the deterioration of central-city services, poorer-quality city schools, higher urban crime rates, and the high proportion of minorities in city neighborhoods. The problem is that *none* of these factors had much impact during the first two decades of massive postwar suburbanization.

This is not to say that urban decay, poor schools, race, and crime don't affect contemporary suburbanizing. However, "commonsense" explanations such as "white flight" had only minimal impact on the massive post-war suburbanization before the late 1960s. The reason white flight was not a major factor is because, prior to the Fair Housing Act of 1968, all city housing in the U.S. was racially segregated. Residential segregation was the law in the South, and enforced even more rigorously by custom and practice in the North. Since whites lived in completely segregated all-white neighborhoods, the idea of massive white flight from minorities made no sense prior to the 1968 open housing legislation. Black and whites were in separate housing pools, and publicly sanctioned racial segregation kept blacks within specific racially segregated neighborhoods. The massive postwar suburban growth during the 1950s and 1960s represents more a movement *toward* values associated with suburbanization—privacy, space, cleanliness, and other amenities—than a fleeing from perceived central urban ills.[15]

Nor were people fleeing city economic or social problems during the first two decades of suburban boom after World War II. Cities during this period were doing reasonably well in terms of taxes, schooling, and crime. Today we may associate cities with higher crime rates, but that was not the case in most cities during the 1930s, 1940s, 1950s, and early 1960s. For example, New York City in 1942 had only 44 murders in the entire city including gangland hits and family fights. It is important not to automatically project contemporary patterns into the past. From the 1920s through the 1950s uptown Harlem nightclubs were filled nightly with affluent white New Yorkers who went "Up to Harlem" after the downtown clubs closed. The streets of Harlem were safe for both whites and blacks at 2:00 A.M.

A cliché of movies of the 1930s, 1940s, and 1950s (especially musicals) was a young couple strolling through Central Park at midnight (and breaking into song and dance as the Irish cop strolling his beat looked on). At that time Central Park was quite safe at night for couples.

CONTEMPORARY SUBURBIA

Suburbia today is remarkably diverse. There are affluent commuter suburbs, working-class suburbs, suburbs of condominiums, industrial-park suburbs, and commercial edge cities. Historically, suburbs were considered "sub" because they were not economically self-supporting but rather were appendages of the central city, serving as dormitories. Suburban residents had to commute to the central city in order to earn their livelihood. Today the Phoenix suburb of Mesa has a larger population than Minneapolis.

That no longer holds: today suburbs are the major centers of employment. Even three decades ago in New York City, the legendary citadel of the commuter, only one-fifth of the suburban workers actually commuted into New York City. Our image of the suburbs, obviously, has not caught up with reality. Today's suburban commuter is much more likely to commute to another suburb than to the central city. Three-quarters of suburbanites who work now work in the suburbs. One is over twice as likely to commute between suburbs than to commute from suburb to city.

There are now more large corporate headquarters in areas surrounding New York City than in the city itself. In terms of number of Fortune 500 corporations, Fairfield County, Connecticut, alone is second nationally to New York City. For two decades corporate headquarters have been moving south and suburban.[16] As a result, reverse commuting is becoming more common. One now lives in Dallas, Los Angeles, New York, or Chicago while working not downtown, but beyond the city limits. Moreover, suburbs are increasing their lead as places of employment.

Washington, D.C., as the nation's capital, enjoys an employment advantage over most older cities. While other cities were losing jobs, Washington added them. Yet the District, which held half of all metropolitan jobs in 1970, by 2000 was down to only a quarter of metropolitan-area workers. Three-quarters of Washington-area workers actually work in the Virginia or Maryland suburbs. In fact, of the 230,000 Washington area jobs added between 1990 and 2005 a remarkable 45 percent were located in Fairfax County, Virginia.

Figures such as these definitely indicate the increasingly diversified notion of suburbia. The old image of the suburb as an exclusive area of single-family homes is obsolete. Even putting aside the questions of commercial and industrial construction and examining only residential building, it is clear that suburbs are building up as well as out. High-rises and apartment units—whether rentals or condominiums—for young singles and the elderly have become increasingly commonplace. Suburban apartment complexes are now accepted as a part of suburbia. In spite of rising suburban housing costs and central-city "gentrification," there has been no real decline in the movement to the suburban periphery.[17] The outmovement of shopping malls, industrial parks, and suburban office complexes, in fact, means that moving "closer to the action" often means moving out rather than in.

CATEGORIES OF SUBURBS

Suburban growth is not as chaotic as it might seem. While suburbs may vary in many respects, there is a predictable pattern to the variation. There are persistent systematic differences that contribute to predicting the development of suburban areas. Suburbs can be differentiated in many ways: old versus new, rich versus poor, incorporated versus unincorporated, ethnic versus WASP, growing versus stagnant, residential versus commercial. Suburban settlements are so diverse that no single typology can adequately encompass them all.

Suburbs also differ systematically with regard to housing characteristics. Residential suburbs have the highest proportion of new housing, the highest percentage of owner-occupied units, and the highest percentage of single-family units; the employment suburbs are lowest on these measures. Older typologies that distinguished between those suburbs that function essentially as dormitories—"residential" suburbs— and those that are basically manufacturing or industrial areas—"employment" suburbs—no longer fit the polycentered nature of contemporary suburbia.

Suburbs also can be distinguished on the basis of lifestyle, separately from their legal definition as a suburb. Old industrial suburbs and poor minority suburbs, for example, don't fit the conventional image of suburban lifestyle, yet they are legally suburbs. On the other hand, a place such as River Oaks, inside Houston, is very suburban in lifestyle but is legally within the city. Similarly, Buckhead in Atlanta fits our image of a suburb far closer than that of a city district.

Persistence of Characteristics?

Since World War II most neighborhoods within central cities have undergone profound changes in terms of the characteristics of the residents and often even the physical structures. We take it for granted that city neighborhoods will change in socioeconomic status over time. One-time prosperous neighborhoods are expected to decline and possibly be rebuilt or gentrified. This model of local community status change is basically a lifecycle model. The previously discussed Burgess concentric zonal theory posited neighborhood change due to competition for land and the outgoing movement of affluent populations.[18]

However, when our focus shifts to suburbs, the assumption of status change is replaced by the assumption of status consistency. It is as if suburbs are not subject to the same laws of aging and change. The status persistence model suggests that early in a suburb's history its socioeconomic status tends to fix its position in the metropolitan area's ecological structure. Research done by Reynolds Farley and by Avery Guest indicates that there is considerable persistence in characteristics over time in the suburbs, especially older established suburbs.[19] The socioeconomic status of individual suburbs was generally the same as it had been 20 or 40 years earlier. In fact, a sound prediction of the educational level of a suburb can be made if one knows the school attendance rate of the high school-age population of 40 years earlier. Guest's later research indicated that suburban persistence was most pronounced in the mid-twentieth century period.

Individual suburbs are thus said to change far less than central cities. For example, Darien, Connecticut; Wilmette, on Chicago's North Shore; Chevy Chase, just outside Washington; Grosse Pointe Shores near Detroit; and Beverly Hills, surrounded by Los Angeles, occupy positions of social status remarkably similar to the positions they occupied in 1920. Farley suggests that suburban persistency may result because a suburb originally establishes a distinct social composition, so that the people who tend to move to it have socioeconomic characteristics similar to those already there.

John Logan and Mark Schneider, on the other hand, found that there were wide regional variations in suburban persistence, and suburban employment improved the relative income level of poorer suburbs.[20] John Stahura found that as suburban growth rates slowed in the 1970s there was a tendency toward crystallization of the status differences between suburbs.[21] Thus, unless circumstances change, it does not appear that there will be major changes in the status ranking of suburbs.

Wealthy suburbs do appear to be relatively immune to downward changes in status. An elite suburb such as Lake Forest, north of Chicago, has maintained its position for well over a century. Suburbs can also maintain their position by using their considerable resources to control who can move into the suburb.[22] This can be done through high tax rates or by passing zoning regulations that mandate certain size homes and/or large-size lots. Such practices have the effect of excluding the non-wealthy. Wealthy suburbs are also able to employ their social prestige of being exclusive areas to attract prestigious residents. Upper-income suburbs thus use their political knowledge and power to protect and enhance the value of their investments.

A political power model is usually associated with scholars taking a conflict perspective, while the status persistence model is usually associated with those holding an ecological model. However, in this instance both approaches seem to reinforce rather than contradict each other. Older and more affluent suburbs have had the greatest success in maintaining their favored position. There also is regional variation. Specifically, in the North and Midwest involuntary annexation of suburbs had ceased by the beginning of the 20th century, while in much of the Southwest annexation is still possible. Thus one would expect to find the greatest number of affluent suburbs practicing exclusionary zoning in the North and Midwest.

Demographically, even more important than keeping "undesirables" out is attracting new high-status residents. Here a self-fulfilling prophesy seems to occur for affluent suburbs. A suburb having an established reputation as a high-status area employs its social prestige to attract new high-status residents. Realtors also play a major role by steering higher income newcomers toward what are perceived as the more prestigious areas. Reputation creates a reality that in turn reinforces reputation. In this fashion older suburbs such as Beverly Hills maintain their upper-status positions.

Ethnic and Religious Variation

Within the metropolitan area different ethnic, religious, and racial groups historically often followed specific patterns of suburbanization. In Atlanta, for instance, blacks went south and whites went north. "Spillover" black suburbs were often extensions of the black ghettos across the city boundary. In Chicago, Polish heritage populations moved from the near north side, to the northwest side, and into northwest suburbs such as Niles. The Chicago Jewish housing pattern was from poor central neighborhoods to the north side, and then middle-class Jews moved into northwest suburbs such as Skokie, and wealthy Jews moved along the North Shore to Glencoe and Highland Park. Italian heritage populations, on the other hand, moved progressively west, and in time into western suburbs such as Melrose Park. WASPs, by contrast, moved up the North Shore to Evanston, Wilmette, and Winnetka. Thus, the pattern of ethnic inner-city neighborhoods was in modified form carried to the suburbs.

High-Income Suburbs

The 19th century saw the first examples of exclusive suburbs designed as refuges for the wealthy. Then, as now, upper-status suburbs usually featured large imposing homes built on extensive properties that were screened off from casual external observation by shrubbery and trees. Today new upper-class suburbs are often gated. Generally high-status suburbs have been located at the outer suburban edges, but there are some clear exceptions, such as centrally located Grosse Pointe, bordered by Detroit, and Beverly Hills, surrounded by Los Angeles.

However, what gives most upper-status suburbs their character is not so much their housing style as their style of life and demographic patterns. Demographically high-income suburbs tend to have a somewhat older median-age population and a lower proportion of women employed in the labor force. Particularly in the East and Midwest, the older elite suburbs were, and in many cases still are, socially WASP communities. Older elite suburbs have never been home to believers in multiculturalism. Traditionally, racial minorities and those whites having southern or eastern European ethnic heritage were automatically disqualified for residency, as were Jews and Catholics. When the Kennedy family bought a large home in Hyannis Port, Massachusetts, several neighbors moved out on the grounds that with the coming of the Irish Catholic Kennedy family the community was surely going downhill. Opposition remained even after John Kennedy became president of the United States. Similarly, one of the richest suburbs in the country, Kenilworth on Chicago's North Shore, both has a median family income over $200,000 and a reputation for discouraging Catholics and Jews as residents. Catholics and Jews who were excluded from WASP suburbs often responded by founding their own exclusive suburbs and country clubs. For example, on Chicago's North Shore wealthy Jewish families developed Glencoe and Highland Park as heavily Jewish suburbs.

In today's newer upper-income growth suburbs, ethnicity and religion tend to have lesser relevance, so long as one has sufficient cash. The Census Bureau announced in 2006 that the most affluent county in the U.S. was not an old established area, but fast-growing Loudoun County (median household income $98,483) in northern Virginia.[23] Loudoun County is essentially a bedroom community for Washington, D.C., professionals and their young children. Similarly, in the affluent sub-

urbs of Texas and southern California one's heritage and religion is of little importance compared to one's bank balance. Elsewhere in the world Jews and Arabs may be in deadly conflict, but in Beverly Hills wealthy Arabs and wealthy Jews live as neighbors. (The majority population, as well as the mayor, in 2010 Beverly Hills are Iranian Jews.)

Another change is that wealthy suburbs are no longer solely communities of single-family homes. Luxury high-rise condominiums increasingly are found in newer suburbs for the well-to-do.

As a cautionary note, there is a tendency to equate the high costs of housing with affluent residents. This is generally the case, but it can be misleading insofar as it might suggest that counties with the highest housing costs, such as those in California, necessarily also have the highest percentages of affluent householders. For example, even the comfortably-off have trouble affording a house in Santa Barbara, California, where the median house sales price was 1.2 million dollars in 2007. Unbelievably, subsidized housing was built in Santa Barbara for families earning as much as $177,000.[24] In Palo Alto (surrounding Stanford University) the average house sale price is over $1 million. While Silicon Valley has many wealthy, it also has many in other economic strata.

The census indicates that the counties having the most affluent householders are still concentrated on the East Coast. Of the 20 counties having the greatest proportion of population with households earning $100,000 or more, fully half are found in the suburban ring of the New York Consolidated Metro Area. Leading the list is Westchester County, New York. Just behind are Morris County, New Jersey; Fairfield County, Connecticut; and Nassau County, New York. Another four counties—Loudoun, Virginia; Montgomery, Maryland; Fairfax, Virginia; and Howard, Maryland—are in the Washington, D.C.–Baltimore suburban ring. Only a quarter of the top 20 are west of the Mississippi. Marin and San Mateo Counties in the San Francisco metropolitan area ranked 5th and 16th respectively, Santa Clara County (San Jose) was 19th, and Orange County in southern California just made the list at 20th.

Gated Communities

A newer form of exclusive suburb is the gated community. While exclusive communities are nothing new, and cities such as St. Louis and Toronto have long-standing gated communities, the number of such communities and the number of people living in them definitely are new.[25] As of 2001, over 20,000 gated communities housing over 8 million people had been built, especially in the Southwest, California, and Florida. Some 15 percent of the new housing in the South now is in gated communities. The well-to-do in other areas are quickly following the pattern.

Gated communities are no longer largely for retirement areas. They now are being built in the suburbs of the largest metropolitan areas. Moreover, within cities, four out of five new housing developments are now gated. These are self-segregated areas that are physically walled-off from their neighbors with access only through roads controlled by electronically controlled gates or security guards in guardhouses. In such communities it is definitely not "a free country." Those not possessing a valid pass are refused entry.

For some, living behind the walls is part of a fortress mentality that seeks to exclude anyone who might possibly be disruptive or threaten their quality of life. The gates are supposed to exclude crime and protect property values. They also promote social and economic segregation.[26] Inside the walls you can live in an exclusive cocoon where property values are protected without your having to look at poor people who are not gardeners or servants. Others see gated communities as a way of affirming their own affluence and status. The gates don't serve so much as a physical barrier as a symbol of who belongs and who does not. They are the chosen insiders; all others are outsiders. Finally, some gated communities, especially in southern and southwestern states, are retirement communities where children, and other tax-consuming residents under age 55, are barred by community bylaws. No children means no noise or other disruptions of life, but more importantly, no children means no schools. And no schools means no school taxes.

Common-Interest Developments

Most gated communities are legally what are known as CIDs or common-interest developments. Although not all CIDs are gated, CIDs are private, self-governing, homeowner-membership associations to which everyone in a development must belong as a condition of purchase. CIDs are essentially private governments that set the rules for the community. For a monthly mandatory association fee, the CID provides its members facilities within the community that can include parks, swimming pools, community buildings, and even golf courses. Within the community the CID also performs what are usually thought of as government functions, such as policing, street maintenance, and even trash collection.

CIDs are not a fringe development. They represent a major social change and are rapidly proliferating. In 2000 they already included more than 200,000 developments housing over 42 million people. Local governments like CIDs because they save money by privately providing services that otherwise would have to be paid for by taxpayers. The local government is relieved from its usual service obligations. The downside for CID residents is that common-interest developments have a reputation for being highly autocratic and undemocratic. Theoretically, CID directors are periodically elected by the homeowners. However, in reality the directors usually are a small, self-perpetuating group.

Courts have held that since homeowners voluntarily agree to CID restrictions when joining the association, the CID can enforce detailed regulations that local governments cannot. And if a homeowner doesn't follow all CID regulations (such as prohibitions against flying more than one flag on Flag Day—a local case in the author's metro area) the CID can fine the offender or use the general membership funds to take the dissident to court. CID regulations are usually quite specific, detailing everything from what color you can paint your front door, to what plants you can put in your garden, to whether you can be fined for leaving your garage door open. Moreover, the CID homeowners' association agreement, which each homeowner signs when moving into the CID, provides that if an individual sues the CID and loses, the CID can seize his or her home to ensure payment of any court penalties or fees.

Moving into a CID community means that you can remove yourself from the rest of the metro area and live in a privatized, totally predictable, socially segregated, homogeneous community. For this, however, you have to be willing to surrender some personal freedom, taste, and individuality. Many affluent homebuyers apparently like the trade-off.

Working-Class Suburbs

Before the mass suburbanization following the Second World War, working-class suburbs were older industrial factory suburbs. An example would be Cudahy, south of Milwaukee, Wisconsin, which was established when the Milwaukee city government refused to allow Patrick Cudahy to build a stockyard and slaughterhouse works within the city. Another example would be the working-class suburb of Cicero, west of Chicago. Cicero achieved national notoriety during the 1920s as the headquarters of Al Capone's operations when a short-lived reform administration in Chicago temporarily forced The Outfit to move its headquarters to the suburbs. Most prewar working-class suburbs, however, were simply factory towns. Plain, but generally well-kept, houses with small yards were the norm.

Following World War II, GI loans allowed blue-collar workers, as well as the traditional middle class, to successfully apply for long-term mortgages. It is sometimes forgotten that the new postwar working-class suburbanites that followed the factories to the suburbs were not fleeing decaying city neighborhoods. More often than not, they were somewhat reluctantly leaving tight ethnic neighborhoods with high levels of social interaction.

Bennett Berger studied the lifestyle of some 100 blue-collar Ford assembly workers and their families who were forced to move from Richmond, California, to the suburb of Milpitas, California, north of San Jose in order to work at a new Ford automobile plant.[27] He found that suburbanization had little or no effect on the workers' style of life. They did not see the move in terms of social mobility; they had no great hopes of getting ahead in their jobs. They had no illusions of wealth; their wage level was dependent on the union contract. As a consequence of becoming suburbanites, they didn't change their political affiliation (81 percent Democrat), go to church more, or join community organizations. They participated only minimally in formal groups. What they did do is continue their traditional working-class pattern of tight, informal socialization with long-term friends and neighbors. In brief, they lived life patterns quite similar to those workers living in blue-collar central city neighborhoods. Their new suburban homes were not seen as way stations on the road to social mobility, but rather as permanent places of residence.

Now many of these postwar blue-collar suburbs are experiencing the same job losses, tax losses, and physical decline suffered by central cities. But they have fewer resources and are less able to cope. Losses of suburban industrial and manufacturing jobs mean that those living in older inner-ring suburbs have to make long commutes to service jobs in outlying edge suburbs. The automobile factory in Milpitas that triggered the move Berger described itself was closed in 1983 for being technologically out-of-date. Some 2,400 auto workers lost their jobs and the community declined. However, Milpitas was in the path of a growing Silicon Valley and by the 1990s sprouted scores of new manufacturing plants (largely electronic). The actor Tom Selleck and his father bought the Ford site for $100 million, and in 1994 a giant shopping mall opened on the site of the abandoned Ford assembly plant. Today, once-blue-collar Milpitas is distinctly up-scale.

Most blue-collar suburbs aren't so lucky. As factories and then businesses close, the commercial tax base sharply erodes. As a result, class divisions between types of suburbs are becoming sharper, rather than blurring. Older working-class suburbs with their low-cost housing were those most likely to attract minority families escaping the city. Deteriorating job prospects for blue-collar workers in a postindustrial economy means that such workers can now find themselves trapped in aging suburbs with high service needs and a declining tax base. Some inner suburbs are struggling to cope with unemployment, strained public schools, rising crime, and deteriorating housing.[28] Poverty rates are now increasing faster in suburbs than in central cities. Poorer suburbs lack both the tax base of other suburbs and the basic amenities and public services found in the central city.

Commercial Definitions

Since defining a model-type suburbanite, or a model suburban lifestyle, is becoming less and less possible, one way out of the difficulty is not to even try. Rather than seeking overall similarities, business-oriented researchers now more often focus on the differences that will aid politicians and marketers to fine-tune their advertising campaigns to meet specific needs and markets. A marketing research firm named Claritas has developed a system that places every zip code in the country into one of 40 different types of communities on the basis of the dominant economic, family lifecycle, and ethnic racial characteristics of households and the physical characteristics of the areas in which they live.[29]

In effect Claritas has tried to create homogeneous ethnographic areas, what Chicago School sociologists of the 1920s referred to as "natural areas." They have done this using statistical cluster analysis techniques to explain the relationship between physical space and social behavior. These areas have become a virtual Bible for market researchers, but thus far they have had limited use by academics more concerned with universality of standards.

The strength of the system is that it provides fairly detailed information on areas as small as zip codes, but the limitation is that some of this detail may be spurious. This is because postal zip codes are sometimes anything but homogeneous, and the cluster analysis technique gives the average characteristics for the area. Therefore, if population or housing characteristics are diverse within the area, there is a serious risk of committing the "ecological fallacy" of attempting to predict the behavior of individuals from the characteristics of an area. The more homogeneous the zip code, the greater the validity of the coding. Of the 40 lifestyle communities Claritas identifies, a dozen have a suburban location. From upper income to lower these areas and their characteristics are, roughly:

> Blue-Blood Estates—The wealthiest neighborhoods of largely suburban homes.
>
> Furs and Station Wagons—Newer-money metropolitan bedroom suburbs.
>
> Pools and Patios—Older upper-middle-class suburban communities.
>
> Gray Power—Upper-middle-class retirement suburbs.
>
> New Beginnings—Outer city or suburban areas of single complexes, garden apartments, and well-kept bungalows (single or childless).
>
> Two More Rungs—Comfortable multiethnic suburbs.
>
> Blue-Chip Blues—More affluent blue-collar suburbs.

Young Suburbia—Outlying child-rearing suburbs.

Young Homesteaders—Exurban boom towns of younger midscale families.

Levittown, U.S.A.—Aging postwar working-class tract suburbs.

Rank and File—Older blue-collar industrial suburbs.

Norma Rae–Ville—Older industrial suburbs and mill towns, primarily in the South.

EXURBS

The term *exurb* refers to the upper-middle-class settlement that is taking place in outlying semi-rural areas beyond the second ring of densely settled subdivisions. Fringe exurban areas have more widely separated homes, often with woods between, and the homes tend to be large and expensive. Sometimes exurbanites settle around old villages or small towns. In fact, the "in" place for longer-range commuters fleeing suburbia is older small towns.[29] The inflow of newcomers is not always greeted enthusiastically by existing residents who welcome the influx of new money, but not necessarily new ideas as to how to improve school systems and roads.

Exurbanites as a rule are affluent, well-educated professionals. Sometimes these individuals work in fields such as communications, advertising, and publishing that allow them to work at home and avoid daily commuting by using their PCs, fax machines, and cell phones to stay in touch with their offices. These are not country folk. Basically exurbanites are urbane seekers of the American Dream who want to reside in rustic settings. They are urbanites living in the country. They want to move out of the city but not away from its advantages and services. If their base is New York, they may live in Fairfield County, Connecticut, or northern New Jersey; if the office is in Philadelphia, then Bucks County, Pennsylvania; and if in San Francisco, then Marin County, California.

Unfortunately, the study of exurbia that first gave the area its name, *The Exurbanites*, presents a caricature of suburban lifestyles.[30] Exurbanites were portrayed as hyperactive, upwardly mobile strivers who are desperately trying to find meaning in their lives by moving out of the city. Working in highly competitive industries where the standards for judging performance are subjective and fickle, they seek solace by escaping the city. According to the stereotype, living in exurbia also puts considerable pressures on wives, who find themselves locked into a schedule of maintaining the house and providing shuttle service for children and commuting husbands while attempting to maintain their own careers and interests.

If the above sounds familiar it is because this general outline has served as the plot for dozens of novels, television soaps, and movies. The TV show *Desperate Housewives* is a contemporary version. The problem is that broad stereotyping is often taken as a scientific reflection of reality rather than inventive fiction. Contemporary novels such as Chang-rae Lee's *Aloft*, probing the dark underside of life on Long Island, simply perpetuate the myth. [31]

Demographic characteristics offer no support for the belief that exurbanites are significantly different from other same-status suburbanites. A 1999 study by Nelson and Sanchez using American Housing Survey data debunks the idea that exurbanites differ significantly from other suburbanites.[32] In reality exurbs have a way of turning into reluctant suburbs as more and more people move into the same area, all seeking to escape urban life.

RURBAN AREAS

Harder to pin down are those places beyond the exurbs that are *not* oriented toward a major city. While by official definition these areas may still be within a metropolitan area, the orientation of residents is more rural than urban. Housing in these in-between areas that are not truly rural, but are probably never destined to become suburban, is sometimes of marginal quality. This is the home of the double-wide. Some of those living in such "rurban" areas are barely getting by economically in spite of low housing costs and low taxes. It is not uncommon for rurban residents to commute long distances to work at low-income jobs. They are anything but affluent suburban commuters. They are people on the economic margins living in marginal areas.

Adding to the confusion over what is suburban are places such as outlying college towns that the census has defined as metropolitan but that are not really urban in character. One of these is Centre County, Pennsylvania, the home of Pennsylvania State University. Because of its population, Centre County is a metropolitan area named State College, but it is clearly neither urban nor suburban. The county includes a widely dispersed and mixed population having a wide range of interests and occupations. There are 165 acres for every person in the metropolitan area.[33] The consequence is a metropolitan area that is known for its hiking trails, numerous lakes, trout streams, and mountains.

In practice, residential suburbia, to say nothing of the commercial and business edge cities discussed in Chapter 5, has become remarkably diverse, so diverse in fact that calling an area "suburban" doesn't really tell us much anymore. As suburbia has come to house and employ the largest segment of the American population, the characteristics that define a "typical suburb" and "typical suburbanites" have become even more difficult to define.

CHARACTERISTICS OF SUBURBANITES

Who, then, are the suburbanites, and does the popular image of suburbanites as being white, middle-class homeowners with children fit the facts? Not really. Suburbs are now a microcosm of America. Suburbanites do tend to be homeowners. Approximately three-quarters of sub-

urban housing units are owner occupied, as compared with half of those in the cities. Homeownership usually provides greater economic security, not to mention tax benefits. However, young singles, elderly widows, and other such "non-family households" now outnumber married-with-children homes in the nation's suburbs.

SUBURBAN POVERTY

In terms of poverty, central-cities' and suburbs' numbers have changed places. By 2005 the suburban poor outnumbered their city counterparts by at least 1 million.[34] As of 2010, there were 1.6 million more suburban poor than city poor. Cities, and even rural areas, have traditionally had programs to elevate poverty. Suburbs, by contrast, are served by fewer social service organizations. Suburban poor are both less served and less seen. The collapse of housing values has hit newer suburban areas particularly hard. Declining property values have reduced local government revenues, just when needs were increasing. Suburbia today is no longer the promise land. Suburbs today are not overrun with children. With the maturation of the baby boomers, suburbs ceased to be baby factories. Suburbs are growing, but the number of children under 18 is declining. Inner-city areas, especially black and Latino neighborhoods, actually have more children per household. The big difference, however, is not in the numbers of suburban and city children, but in the fact that suburban children are far more likely to live in two-parent families. Twice as many city children as suburban children live in families headed by a single female parent. This is in part the reflection of the racial composition of cities since over two-thirds of black infants are born to single mothers. Child poverty is found in a third of city households, but less than a quarter of suburban households.,

The most pronounced difference between cities and suburbs remains their racial composition. In spite of heavy black suburbanization the percentage of blacks in suburbs is only half of what would be expected given random distribution. (Black suburbanization trends are discussed later in this chapter.)

THE MYTH OF SUBURBIA

Over the years the suburbs have become more than mere places of residence. Suburbia has become endowed with a long list of physical and even psychological attributes: ranch-style houses; neat lawns; SUVs; good schools; clean, safe neighborhoods; a small town atmosphere; and overscheduled parents and children. This caricature has been called the "myth of suburbia," the myth being the belief that there is, in fact, a uniquely suburban way of life.[35] According to the myth of suburbia, people living in suburbs are, or become, somehow different from those who remain in the city. Upon moving, non-communicative people become friendly neighbors and Democrats become Republicans.

These myths refuse to die. For example, both the public and popular writers continue

to assume that suburbanites are more likely to vote Republican.[36] The reality is that suburban voters tend to be independents who vote on the basis of issues rather than party. Bill Clinton won the suburban vote in both 1992 and 1996, Al Gore won slightly more suburban votes than did George W. Bush in 2000, and Barack Obama won the suburban vote in 2008.

Postwar stereotypes of suburbia were frequently less than complimentary. The suburban way of life was supposedly one of wide lawns and narrow minds in which family life was child-oriented rather than adult-oriented. Critics described the suburban family as surrendering all individuality and creativity. Funnier is Malvina Reynolds' 1963 folksong *Little Boxes* (made famous by Pete Seeger, and was used for the opening of the TV show "Weeds"). (See box 6.1.)

In terms of lifestyle, suburbanites—particularly those in the newer suburbs—were said to be gregarious. Numerous parties were interspersed with extensive informal visiting or neighboring. Togetherness was a way of life. Organizationally, suburbanites were said to be hyperactive joiners, with hobby groups, bridge

---

Box 6.1   The Suburbs in Song

Little Boxes

Little boxes on the hillside,
Little boxes made of ticky tacky,
Little boxes on the hillside,
Little boxes all the same.
There's a green one and a pink one
And a blue one and a yellow one,
And they're all made out of ticky tacky,
And they all look just the same.
And the people in the houses
All went to the university,
Where they were put in boxes
And they came out all the same,
And there's doctors and lawyers,
And business executives,
And they're all made out of ticky tacky,
And they all look just the same.
And they all play on the golf course
And drink their martinis dry,

And they all have pretty children
And the children go to school,
And the children go to summer camp,
And then to the university
Where they are put in boxes
And they come out all the same.
And the boys go into business
And marry and raise a family
In boxes made of ticky tacky
And they all look just the same.
There's a green one and a pink one
And a blue one and a yellow one,
And they're all made out of ticky tacky
And they all look just the same.

From the song, "Little Boxes"
Words and music by Malvina Reynolds
Copyright 1962 Schroder Music Co. (ASCAP)
Renewed 1990.
Used by permission. All rights reserved.

Box 6.2   Case Study: Levittown

Probably the most thoroughly studied suburb is discussed in *The Levittowners*, Herbert Gans's case study of the social organization of the third Levittown, built in New Jersey, east of Philadelphia.* The various Levittowns were prototypes of the postwar "package suburbs" that can be found near all of the country's larger cities. Levitt and Sons, Inc., originally built for a lower-middle-class market, but over the years the size of their houses and their prices have increased considerably. The Levittown Gans studied later changed its name to Willingboro to escape the Levittown stereotype.

Gans's findings were based on interviews and on his own observations, made while living in Levittown for two years. Gans suggests that the sociability found within the community was a direct result of the compatibility or homogeneity of the backgrounds of the residents (discussed in the text as compositional theory). Homogeneity was most evident in terms of age and income. But diversity in regional backgrounds, membership in ethnic groups, and religious beliefs provided variety for the community. Even the similarity in income did not indicate as much homogeneity as the statistics indicated, for one family might be headed by a skilled worker at the peak of earning power, another by a white-collar worker with some hope of advancement, and a third by a young executive or professional just at the start of a career. Active sociability emerged only when neighboring residents shared common tastes and values, were similar with regard to race and class, and shared similar beliefs regarding child-raising practices. Residents saw family togetherness as a positive attribute of the community. Parents and children all felt that they spent more time together as a family. Residents of the mass suburb were generally content with their housing, lifestyle, and general environment. Although the popular literature is rather heavy with criticism of suburban anomie (normlessness) and malaise, boredom was not a serious problem in Levittown.

However, the community was particularly hard for teenagers, owing to the lack of recreational facilities and places to go. It was designed for families with young children, not adolescents. Thus, bedrooms were small and lacked the privacy or soundproofing necessary to allow teenagers to have their friends visit.

Gans found that suburbanites differed little from similar city dwellers. Overall, Gans's description of Levittown shows a community that was not overly exciting but that generally met the needs of its residents. The worst thing that could be said about the community was that for anyone with cosmopolitan tastes, it was rather dull. But, then, Levittowns weren't built for cosmopolites.

David Popenoe's later examination of another Levittown community across the Delaware River from Philadelphia, came to similar conclusions.** Residents spent their leisure time in locally based informal activities with friends and in watching television, rarely going into downtown Philadelphia. Life was comfortable, family-based, and not overly exciting. As in Gans's study, Popenoe suggests that young teenagers found the residential environment most wanting. While Levittown does have recreational facilities such as pools and parks, it, like many similar suburbs in the United States, has few places just to hang out and see and be seen.

The historian Barbara Kelly's 1990s restudy of Levittown found essentially what Gans had found more than three decades earlier. Kelly says, "I went to Levittown expecting to find people who lived in cookie cutter houses living cookie cutter lives. I went to find women who were stunted and men who were emasculated, and instead I found people who were extremely grateful to be where they were, who took their homes and expanded them as they moved into the middle class, and along the way their lives expanded with them."+

Today the original Levittown on Long Island has urban-style problems of crime and an aging physical plant, but overall is doing well. Given the original similarity of all the housing, the homes look remarkably diverse. Virtually all the homes have been enlarged and changed over the years. In fact, when in the mid-1990s it was decided to designate Levittown as a National Historic Landmark, it was very difficult to find an original home that had not been modified or expanded. Willingboro today is a diverse community. It is two-thirds black, and one in eight residents is 65 or older.

*. Herbert J. Gans, *The Levittowners*, Vintage Books, New York, 1967.

**. David Popenoe, *The Suburban Environment: Sweden and the United States*, University of Chicago, Chicago, 1977.

+. Barbara Kelly, *Expanding the American Dream: Building and Rebuilding Levittown*, State University of New York Press, Albany, 1993.

clubs, neighborhood associations, and church-related social activities taking up several nights a week. On top of this, there was a proliferation of women's groups, scout troops, and *kaffeeklatsches*. Husbands were said to spend their weekends cutting grass, watching football games, picking up kids, going to parties, going to church, and watching more football games.

This myth of suburbia now has been replaced with a new myth that sees the compulsive group conformity of the postwar years replaced by competitive self-advancement and manic self-fulfillment. Status and money supposedly are the new suburban icons. The home is less a place to relax than a site for showcasing goods. Middle-class suburbia is said to have gone "from glorifying group bonding to glorifying individual happiness and achievement."[37]

For all the talk, the number of scholars studying suburbs remains limited. The urban racial and fiscal crises of the late 1960s and 1970s resulted in "urban research" becoming defined as research on the inner city. The vacuum left by the absence of hard research on suburban lifestyles was filled with popular books and articles dealing with suburban conformity, adultery, alcoholism, divorce, and plain boredom. Even the best of the American literature on suburban life (e.g., John Updike's short stories and novels) paints a highly selective picture.

The best known of the postwar studies was William H. Whyte's influential book *The Organization Man*.[38] Unfortunately, many of Whyte's imitators were not as careful. Early suburban studies suffered from three liabilities. *First*, the postwar suburban studies were highly selective, focusing attention on the large new subdivisions built for young families, and paying little attention to industrial suburbs, working-class suburbs, or even older established suburbs. The end result was that the image of suburbia was loaded by emphasizing brand new tract-housing suburbs. *Second*, it appears that some of the communities chosen for study were selected precisely because they were in some respects

atypical and thus presumably more interesting. *Third*, many of the observations were based on a single look at a suburb immediately after the first wave of settlement. Another look 10 or 20 years later, after the community had "matured," would almost certainly show a different picture.

The reality is that although suburbs have greatly changed, our ways of looking at them haven't. Suburbia, housing over half the nation's population, has become diverse. Over half of the nation's poor live in suburbs. Over half of all Asians, approaching half of all Hispanics, and over one-third of African Americans are now suburbanites. Nonetheless, TV, movies, and novels miss the ethnic and racial mix that has become the reality of contemporary suburbia.[39] Suburbs have outgrown their clichés.

MINORITY SUBURBANIZATION

Post–World War II suburbs lost their social-class exclusiveness, but not their racial exclusiveness. Blacks were noticeable by their absence. Suburban zoning laws mandating large lot and dwelling sizes were used to keep out both the poor and minorities. The general conclusion of researchers was that black suburbanization was increasing, but only marginally.[40] Latino and Asian suburbanization was largely ignored.

Suburban Diversity

However, the last two decades have seen considerable change. While one still hears reference to "lily-white suburbs," and the media often give the impression that minorities reside overwhelmingly in central-city neighborhoods, the reality is that roughly half (47 percent) of the minorities in the nation's 102 largest metropolitan areas live in the suburbs.[41] (See tables 6.1 through 6.3.)

The 21st century shows ethnic diversity spreading to the suburbs. Suburbs are increasingly multiethnic and multiracial. Breaking the

Table 6.1   Suburban Regions Ranked by % Black in 2000 (50 largest suburban regions by total population

Rank	1990	2000	Rank	1990	2000
1 Atlanta, GA MSA	18.8	25.6	26 Las Vegas, NV–AZ MSA	6.8	7.5
2 Washington, DC–MD–VA–WV PMSA	18.8	22.9	27 Detroit, MI PMSA	4.3	6.6
3 Richmond–Petersburg, VA MSA	17.9	21.3	28 Monmouth–Ocean, NJ PMSA	6.2	6.3
4 New Orleans, LA MSA	17.7	21.0	29 Hartford, CT MSA	3.8	6.1
5 Fort Lauderdale, FL PMSA	13.3	20.6	30 Tampa–St. Petersburg–Clearwater,		
6 Miami, FL PMSA	18.8	20.4	FL MSA	4.0	5.8
7 Newark, NJ PMSA	15.7	17.8	31 Cincinnati, OH–KY–IN PMSA	4.5	5.7
8 Baltimore, MD PMSA	10.4	14.9	32 Sacramento, CA PMSA	4.2	5.7
9 Greenville–Spartanburg–Anderson			33 Pittsburgh, PA MSA	4.1	5.3
SC MSA	13.6	14.6	34 San Diego, CA MSA	3.8	4.6
10 West Palm Beach–Boca Raton,			35 Fort Worth–Arlington, TX PMSA	3.5	4.5
FL MSA	10.9	13.7	36 Seattle–Bellevue–Everett,		
11 New York, NY PSMSA	11.1	12.6	WA PMSA	1.9	3.9
12 St. Louis, MO–IL MSA	9.5	12.5	37 Denver, CO PMSA	2.9	3.9
13 Orlando, FL MSA	9.4	12.4	38 San Francisco, CA PMSA	4.7	3.7
14 Charlotte–Gastonia–Rock Hill,			39 Kansas City, MO–KS MSA	2.2	3.7
NC–SC MSA	10.6	10.9	40 Rochester, NY MSA	2.5	3.5
15 Houston, TX PMSA	8.9	10.7	41 Grand Rapids–Muskegon–Holland,		
16 Cleveland–Lorain–Elyria, OH PMSA	8.0	9.7	MI MSA	2.6	3.4
17 Philadelphia, PA–NJ PMSA	7.8	9.7	42 Phoenix–Mesa, AZ MSA	2.2	3.1
18 Dallas, TX PMSA	7.3	9.7	43 Minneapolis–St. Paul, MN–WI MSA	1.1	2.9
19 Chicago, IL PMSA	6.4	8.8	44 Boston, MA–NH PMSA	1.7	2.8
20 Nassau–Suffolk, NY PMSA	7.1	8.7	45 Buffalo–Niagara Falls, NY MSA	1.4	2.4
21 Oakland, CA PMSA	7.4	8.4	46 Indianapolis, IN MSA	1.3	2.2
22 Los Angeles–Long Beach, CA PMSA	8.4	8.2	47 Orange County, CA PMSA	1.4	1.7
23 Bergen–Passaic, NJ PMSA	7.5	8.1	48 Milwaukee–Waukesha, WI PMSA	0.7	1.6
24 Middlesex–Somerset–Hunterdon,			49 Portland–Vancouver, OR–WA PMSA	0.6	1.3
NJ PMSA	6.4	8.0	50 Salt Lake City–Ogden, UT MSA	0.5	1.0
25 Riverside–San Bernardino, CA PMSA	6.1	7.9			

total minority figures down into the Census Bureau racial/ethnic group categories of white, black, Asian, and Hispanic (the last being defined by the Census as an ethnic rather than a racial category), the data indicate considerable ethnic change in the suburbs. In the nation's 102 largest metro areas somewhat under three-quarters of whites (73 percent) reside in the suburbs, but suburbs house 4 of 10 blacks (39 percent), the majority of Asians (55 percent), and half (49 percent) of the nation's Latinos.[42]

However, while whites are still more likely to be suburban residents, minority suburban growth rates considerably outdistance those for whites. Between 2000 and 2006 the white pop-

ulation of large city suburbs grew 7 percent. During the same period the black suburban population grew 24 percent, the Asian American population 16 percent, and the Latino suburban population 60 percent.[43]

With 4 of 10 metro-area blacks having a suburban rather than a central city address, African American suburbanization is a social fact. As a group black suburbanites have income levels slightly below white suburbanites, but twice those of black city dwellers. Old patterns of token suburban integration have been replaced by major population transfers. A major example is the Atlanta metro area, where during the last decade the number of

Table 6.2   Suburban Regions Ranked by % Hispanic in 2000 (50 largest suburban regions by total population)

Rank	1990	2000	Rank	1990	2000
1 Miami, FL PMSA	46.0	55.8	26 Washington, DC–MD–VA–WV PMSA	4.9	8.5
2 Los Angeles–Long Beach, CA PMSA	37.8	44.7	27 Portland–Vancouver, OR–WA PMSA	3.4	7.8
3 Riverside–San Bernardino, CA PMSA	26.2	38.3	28 Atlanta, GA MSA	1.8	6.8
4 San Diego, CA MSA	19.8	27.0	29 Hartford, CT MSA	3.1	6.1
5 Houston, TX PMSA	14.7	22.8	30 Monmouth–Ocean, NJ PMSA	3.7	5.8
6 Orange County, CA PMSA	16.0	22.3	31 New Orleans, LA MSA	4.7	5.2
7 Phoenix–Mesa, AZ MSA	18.5	21.0	32 Seattle–Bellevue–Everett, WA PMSA	2.4	5.1
8 Las Vegas, NV–AZ MSA	9.3	19.3	33 Grand Rapids–Muskegon–Holland,		
9 San Francisco, CA MSA	14.8	19.1	MI MSA	1.9	4.0
10 Oakland, CA PMSA	13.2	18.6	34 Boston, MA–NH PMSA	2.2	3.5
11 Fort Lauderdale, FL PMSA	8.6	17.5	35 Charlotte–Gastonia–Rock Hill,		
12 Bergen–Passaic, NJ PMSA	11.3	17.3	NC–SC MSA	0.6	3.4
13 Orlando, FL MSA	8.0	16.4	36 Kansas City, MO–KS MSA	1.7	2.9
14 Dallas, TX PMSA	8.9	15.3	37 Philadelphia, PA–NJ PMSA	1.7	2.8
15 Denver, CO PMSA	8.8	14.2	38 Greenville–Spartanburg–Anderson,		
16 New York, NY PMSA	8.3	13.3	SC MSA	0.6	2.8
17 West Palm Beach–Boca Raton,			39 Richmond–Petersburg, VA MSA	1.1	2.3
FL MSA	7.1	12.3	40 Rochester, NY MSA	1.3	2.2
18 Sacramento, CA PMSA	8.4	12.0	41 Detroit, MI PMSA	1.4	2.1
19 Chicago, IL PMSA	5.5	11.3	42 Milwaukee–Waukesha, WI PMSA	1.0	2.1
20 Middlesex–Somerset–Hunterdon,			43 Minneapolis–St. Paul, MN–WI MSA	0.9	2.1
NJ PMSA	6.9	11.2	44 Baltimore, MD PMSA	1.3	2.0
21 Newark, NJ PMSA	7.0	10.8	45 Cleveland–Lorain–Elyria, OH PMSA	0.9	1.5
22 Fort Worth–Arlington, TX PMSA	6.1	10.7	46 Indianapolis, IN MSA	0.9	1.5
23 Nassau–Suffolk, NY PMSA	6.0	10.3	47 St. Louis, MO–IL MSA	1.0	1.4
24 Tampa–St. Petersburg–Clearwater,			48 Buffalo–Niagara Falls, NY MSA	0.9	1.3
FL MSA	6.0	9.8	49 Cincinnati, OH–KY–IN PMSA	0.5	1.0
25 Salt Lake City–Ogden, UT MSA	4.4	8.5	50 Pittsburgh, PA MSA	0.4	0.6

African American suburbanites more than doubled from slightly under half a million to 1.2 million. More dramatic than the numerical increases was that by 2000, one of four Atlanta suburbanites was black, and four-fifths (79 percent) of all African Americans living in the Atlanta metro area lived in the suburbs. For Washington, D.C., three-quarters of the metro area black population is suburban.

The critical question today is not whether African Americans will suburbanize, but whether future black suburbanization will reflect increasing housing integration or the growth of more affluent, self-segregating black suburbs. The average Atlanta African American suburbanite has a 56 percent chance of living in a majority black suburban neighborhood.[44]

The major suburban African American growth nationwide is not in the older inner-ring suburbs but rather in the newer suburbs on the suburban edge. Prince George's County, Maryland, south and east of Washington, D.C., is two-thirds black and has more black residents than Washington itself. And most of these residents are middle-class or above.

Blacks (and to a lesser extent Hispanics, but not Asians) live in suburbs that have lower proportions of whites, and lower average-income levels than would be predicted using socioeconomic characteristics alone.[45] Decades of racial

Table 6.3   Suburban Regions Ranked by % Asian in 2000 (50 largest suburban regions by total population)

Rank	1990	2000	Rank	1990	2000
1 Oakland, CA PMSA	12.1	18.9	28 Detroit, MI PMSA	1.5	3.1
2 San Francisco, CA PMSA	13.5	18.6	29 Monmouth–Ocean, NJ PMSA	1.9	3.1
3 Orange County, CA PMSA	10.1	14.9	30 Fort Worth–Arlington, TX PMSA	1.7	2.9
4 Los Angeles–Long Beach, CA PMSA	11.5	14.6	31 Fort Lauderdale, FL PMSA	1.4	2.8
5 Middlesex–Somerset–Hunterdon,			32 Richmond–Petersburg, VA MSA	1.6	2.6
NJ PMSA	5.6	11.8	33 Hartford, CT MSA	1.4	2.6
6 Seattle–Bellevue–Everett, WA PMSA	4.8	9.5	34 Phoenix–Mesa, AZ MSA	1.3	2.5
7 Bergen–Passaic, NJ PMSA	5.1	8.7	35 New Orleans, LA MSA	1.6	2.4
8 Washington, DC–MD–VA–WV PMSA	5.3	8.0	36 Tampa–St. Petersburg–Clearwater,		
9 Sacramento, CA PMSA	4.9	7.9	FL MSA	0.9	2.1
10 San Diego, CA MSA	5.0	6.8	37 Rochester, NY MSA	1.2	2.0
11 Las Vegas, NV–AZ MSA	2.9	6.0	38 Kansas City, MO–KS MSA	0.9	1.8
12 Houston, TX PMSA	3.7	5.8	39 Miami, FL PMSA	1.4	1.8
13 Chicago, IL PMSA	3.3	5.3	40 West Palm Beach–Boca Raton,		
14 Riverside–San Bernardino, CA PMSA	3.8	5.0	FL MSA	1.0	1.8
15 Portland–Vancouver, OR–WA PMSA	2.6	5.0	41 Grand Rapids–Muskegon–Holland,		
16 New York, NY PMSA	3.6	4.9	MI MSA	0.8	1.8
17 Dallas, TX PMSA	2.5	4.9	42 Milwaukee–Waukesha, WI PMSA	0.8	1.7
18 Newark, NJ PMSA	3.0	4.8	43 Cleveland–Lorain–Elyria, OH PMSA	1.1	1.7
19 Boston, MA–NH PMSA	2.2	4.4	44 St. Louis, MO–IL MSA	1.0	1.7
20 Nassau–Suffolk, NY PMSA	2.3	3.9	45 Buffalo–Niagara Falls, NY MSA	1.0	1.5
21 Atlanta, GA MSA	1.8	3.8	46 Greenville–Spartanburg–Anderson,		
22 Denver, CO PMSA	2.2	3.7	SC MSA	0.6	1.3
23 Baltimore, MD PMSA	2.1	3.5	47 Indianapolis, IN MSA	0.8	1.3
24 Salt Lake City–Ogden, UT MSA	1.9	3.4	48 Cincinnati, OH–KY–IN PMSA	0.6	1.3
25 Philadelphia, PA–NJ PMSA	1.8	3.2	49 Charlotte–Gastonia–Rock Hill,		
26 Minneapolis–St. Paul, MN–WI MSA	1.6	3.2	NC–SC MSA	0.5	1.2
27 Orlando, FL MSA	1.7	3.2	50 Pittsburgh, PA MSA	0.5	1.0

segregation have ensured that suburbs remain predominately white. Also, suburbs are mostly white because whites constitute the overwhelming majority of the population. Thus, so long as whites continue to live in suburbs, the suburbs will retain their mostly white complexions.

Black Flight

White flight to suburbs is largely history. For the last two decades the exodus of middle-class families leaving the city for the suburbs has been disproportionately black. In Washington, D.C., for example, over half the households departing Washington for the suburbs are black.[46] The smaller numbers of households moving into the District are overwhelmingly white. As a result of black suburbanization both a decreasing number and decreasing proportion of the African American population is living in central cities. As a result major cities such as New York, Los Angeles, Philadelphia, and Washington, D.C., have had declines in their numbers of black residents. The last decade witnessed heavy black flight from Detroit.[47] Large central cities continue to have a high proportion of blacks only because of somewhat higher black birthrates. Interestingly, the white population is increasingly dispersing to exurbia, small towns, and even rural areas, while a growing proportion of the black population is living in suburbs. Upper- and middle-class whites who want to move to suburbs have already done so. Remaining central-city whites, whether they are there by choice or economics, will remain city folk. New York, Chicago, and Los Angeles added whites between 2000 and 2010.

Integration or Resegregation?

Does increasing black suburbanization represent housing integration or merely the growth of suburban African American enclaves? Research prior to the 1980s substantially showed a pattern of black spillover from central cities into older inner-ring suburbs.[48] Suburban blacks were more likely to live in suburban communities that had lower average family income, less adequate housing, and strained local finances.

However, the last three decades show less of the racial displacement of the invasion–succession model, and more of the parallel growth of both racial groups. Overall, suburbs are becoming more diverse racially. Racial spillover is not today's pattern in major metropolitan areas. The reality is that rather than invasion–succession, with one group supplanting another, stable multiracial suburbs are now more common.[49] The old model of the racial tipping point has less and less empirical validity.[50]

However, the invasion–succession model of racial change retains adherents in spite of its decreasing validity. Rather than spillover, the pattern now is more likely to be a leapfrog effect with blacks moving over older suburbs into newer subdivisions on the periphery.[51]

It also should be noted that not all suburban blacks want to live in racially integrated neighborhoods. To significant numbers of African Americans, "fair housing" means nondiscrimination in housing purchases, not integration.[52] While research shows that blacks are generally more open to integrated housing than whites, some African Americans are making affirmative decisions to live in predominantly black suburbs. Among these are affluent black suburbs such as Rolling Oaks in the Miami area, Brook Glen and Wyndham Park near Atlanta, and many of the newer outer subdivisions in Prince George's County outside Washington, D.C. Black suburbanites in such areas often say they find it more comfortable to live with black neighbors.[53]

The changes noted above suggest that while racial equality has not yet arrived, suburban middle-class blacks are becoming more similar to suburban middle-class whites. In metropolitan areas of a million or more, black suburban families have incomes 55 percent higher than the average for blacks living in the city.

The overall pattern offers both hope and discouragement. Old patterns of suburban racial segregation are increasingly becoming history, but four decades after the Fair Housing Act of 1968, racial steering by real estate agents and discrimination by banks, lending institutions, and insurance companies still persists. Suburban racial changeover is no longer automatically triggered by the presence of minority residents, but whites continue to exhibit reluctance to move into predominantly minority areas. Racial steering by real estate agents and discrimination against minorities by mortgage institutions still continues. Higher-income blacks still have significantly higher rates of home loan rejections than do same income whites. However, in spite of all the obstacles, African American suburbanization is the contemporary reality.

LATINO SUBURBANIZATION

The Hispanic-origin population of the United States, according to Census Bureau estimates, numbered 43 million or 14 percent of the total U.S. population in 2006.[54] (See Chapter 10: Diversity: Hispanics, Asians, and Native Americans.) Latinos are the nation's largest minority population, and half the Hispanics in the United States today are suburbanites.[55] For the last two decades Hispanics have accounted for over a quarter of all suburban growth. Latino suburban growth is greatest in the areas of the country showing the greatest economic growth. Half of all Latinos live in either California or Texas. The eight metropolitan areas having the greatest number of Latino suburbanites are all in the sunbelt: five in California, two in Texas, and one in Florida. The Los Angeles metropolitan area counts over 2 million suburban Latinos.

For Hispanics suburban residence is closely associated with higher income levels.[56] Suburban residence is also associated with less spatial segregation, and more association with non-Hispanic whites.[57] Among the fastest-growing Hispanic suburbs are the predominantly Cuban growth areas in Florida, especially the areas surrounding Orlando and Fort Lauderdale. Hispanics constitute 57 percent of the suburban population of metropolitan Miami, and 45 percent of the suburban population of Los Angeles. Half of New Jersey's population growth since 1990 is Latino.

Cities of the Southeast such as Charlotte and Atlanta are now points of destination for Latinos. Atlanta's Latino population exploded from 55,000 in 1990 to 269,000 in 2000. Of that number only 19,000 live in the city of Atlanta while 250,000 are suburbanites. Thus, while nationally half of all Latinos are suburbanites, in Atlanta the figure is an overwhelming 93 percent. The Latino future is increasingly a suburban future.

ASIAN SUBURBANITES

Asian Americans as of 2010 constitute 5 percent of the U.S. population. Asians, who numbered 14 million in 2010 (dramatically up from 7.3 million in 1990), are the most suburban minority group, with 6 of 10 Asians in America living in suburbs. Unlike earlier immigrant groups who first settled in the city, over half of all current Asian immigrants bypass the city and go directly to the suburbs. A 2001 Brookings Institute study showed half the Asian immigrants in the Washington, D.C. area settled in outer suburbs.[58]

Asian immigrants having educational skills tend to move directly into those suburban neighborhoods where employment and schooling opportunities for children are greatest. The suburbs are where the best employment opportunities are found and a majority of the suburban-bound immigrants speak fluent English and hold advanced degrees. Asian Americans living in the suburbs have average household incomes 25 percent higher than Asian American populations in the central city.[59] Central city populations are both less educated and more likely to be illegal immigrants.

Generally Asians live in suburbs that have a strong Asian presence but are not predominantly Asian. An exception is the east Los Angeles suburb of Monterey Park, which is the first Chinese suburb in America. Monterey Park, a suburb of 60,000, which was 80 percent Chinese in 2000, has experienced a series of growth and land-use controversies as it has been transformed from a low-density suburb to a more urban, high-density "Little Taipei."[60]

Part of the controversy reflects cultural differences in the use of land. Americans value open spaces around suburban houses, while Taiwanese and Hong Kong newcomers are accustomed to a more urban environment, and thus build more urban-looking buildings right up to the property line and pave over front yards for auto parking. (For further discussion of Asian Americans, see Chapter 10: Diversity: Hispanics, Asians, and Native Americans.) Asian Americans do not constitute a majority of all suburban residents in any wider geographic area. However, they do constitute more than 10 percent of the northern California residents of San Francisco and Oakland, the southern California metro areas of Los Angeles and Orange Counties, and the Middlesex-Somerset-Huntington suburban area of New Jersey.

SUMMARY

The 21st century is a suburban century. At mid-20th century, less than one-quarter of the U.S. population was suburban. Today 55 percent of Americans live in suburbs. The first 19th-century suburbs were generally well-to-do communities along railroad lines. The rapid spread of the electric streetcar a century ago allowed the middle class to move out to the new streetcar suburbs.

The automobile suburbs of 1920 to World War II were often affluent places of well-built single-family homes. Our image of suburbia is still shaped by this era. Although American suburbs have existed for over 150 years, mass suburbia is a post–World War II phenomenon. Federal government lending policies contributed heavily to subsidizing suburban growth. Suburbs have changed dramatically over the past quarter of a century from overwhelmingly residential areas to the nation's primary shopping, office, and manufacturing locations. The last two decades in particular have been characterized by metropolitan sprawl.

The major cause of the postwar suburban housing boom was subsidized no- or low-money-down Veterans Administration (VA) and Federal Housing Administration (FHA) loans. Also contributing were federal-government-subsidized expressways, lower suburban housing costs, and the fact that most city land was already developed. Couples sought single-family homes with yards as the postwar marriage boom was followed by a baby boom. White flight from the cities was not a cause of suburbanization for the first 25 years after the war since city neighborhoods were racially segregated by law or custom until the 1968 Open Housing legislation.

Today suburbia is remarkably diverse. Older established suburbs have often changed less than city neighborhoods and retained their status positions due to restrictive zoning and attraction of new high status residents. Gated suburban communities now house more than 8 million people. Most are self-governing common-interest developments (CIDs) that are essentially private governments setting binding rules for the community. Many postwar factory-based working-class suburbs are now experiencing declines as manufacturing plants close. Exurbs are upper-middle-class settlements that are taking place in outlying rural or small town areas beyond the second ring of suburbs. Rurban areas, by contrast, are economically marginal rural areas that are not socially oriented toward the central city.

The "myth of suburbia" is that there is a unique suburban way of life and that suburban dwellers are essentially different from city dwellers. Suburbs now house four of ten African Americans, 55 percent of Asian Americans, and half the nation's Latinos. For 30 years African Americans have been suburbanizing from a smaller base but at a faster rate than whites. Today 4 of 10 metro area blacks are suburbanites. Suburbia has long since ceased to be "lily white." African American suburbanization is a fact of metropolitan life. The 2000 Census documented 1.2 million African American suburbanites in the Atlanta metro area. The crucial question is whether future black suburbanization will increase housing integration, or whether it will promote the increase of more affluent, self-segregating black suburbs. Today flight from the nation's largest cities is disproportionately middle-class black flight.

Latinos, with a population of 43 million, are now the nation's largest minority. Latinos account for one-quarter of all suburban growth, and Hispanic suburban growth is greatest in sunbelt states (especially California, Texas, and Florida). The Latino future is a suburban future.

Asian Americans are most likely to be suburbanites. Affluent Asian immigrants bypass the central city and move directly to suburban areas experiencing economic growth. Asians generally live in suburbs that have an Asian presence but are not majority Asian.

Over the decades suburbs have taken justified criticism as being all-white communities, but suburbs increasingly are multiracial and multiethnic. Ironically, the suburbs now have the opportunity to achieve what the cities have largely failed to accomplish: establish stable, economically viable, and racially and ethnically integrated communities.

REVIEW QUESTIONS

1. How did 19th-century suburbs differ numerically, economically, and socially from post–World War II suburbs?

2. What role did the electric streetcar play in the development of suburbia?

3. What were the major reasons for post–World War II suburban growth?

4. How did the Veterans Administration (VA) and Federal Housing Administration (FHA) change residential housing patterns?

5. What frequently mentioned common-sense "causes" of suburbia played minor roles in the 25 years following World War II (from 1945)?

6. What are some of the categories of suburbs discussed in the text?

7. What is the "Myth of Suburbia"?

8. According to extensive research, how did residents of Levittown differ from city dwellers?

9. Are suburbs still lily-white or have they become multiracial and multicultural?

10. How do minority suburbanization patterns differ among African Americans, Latinos, and Asian Americans?

NOTES

1. Scott W. Allard and Benjamin Roth, *Strained Suburbs: The Social Service Challenges of Rising Suburban Poverty*, Metropolitan Opportunity Series, No. 8, Brookings Institute, Washington, D.C., October 11, 2010.

2. William Schneider, "The Suburban Century Begins," *Atlantic Monthly*, July 1992. p. 33.

3. Adna Ferrin Weber, *The Growth of Cities in the Nineteenth Century*, Macmillan, New York, 1899, pp. 458–59.

4. Robert Fishman, *Bourgeois Utopias: The Rise and Fall of Suburbia*, Basic Books, New York, 1987.

5. For a history of American suburbanization, see Kenneth T. Jackson, *Crabgrass Frontier: The Suburbanization of the United States*, Oxford, New York, 1985. The book is strongest in its descriptions of suburbanization prior to 1950.

6. E. Digby Baltzell, *Philadelphia Gentlemen: The Making of a National Upper Class*, University of Pennsylvania Press, Philadelphia, 1979, p. 197.

7. In preindustrial cities such as the American cities prior to the Civil War, respectable people lived downtown. The peripheries of urban centers were disreputable shantytowns for the lower classes and those on the margins of society. Until the 19th century, in the terms of the *Oxford English Dictionary*, a suburb was "a place of inferior, debased, and especially licentious habits of life." In Tudor London, houses of prostitution moved to the outskirts, and so a whore was named a "suburb sinner," and it was an insult to call a person a "suburbanite." See Fishman, op. cit., pp. 6–7.

8. "North Chicago: Its Advantages, Resources, and Probable Future," reprinted in Charles N. Glaab, *The American City*, Dorsey, Homewood, Ill., 1963, pp. 233–234.

9. Sam B. Warner Jr., *Streetcar Suburbs*, Harvard and M.I.T. Presses, Cambridge, Mass., 1962.

10. The existence of another type of prewar suburb—the working-class industrial suburb—was conveniently overlooked.

11. David Firestone, "Suburban Comforts Thwart Atlanta's Plans to Limit Sprawl," *New York Times*, November 21, 1999, p. 30.

12. For an overview of suburbia, see, J. John Palen, "Suburbia," in Karen Christensen and David Levinson (eds.), *Encyclopedia of Community*, Sage, Thousand Oaks, CA, 2003, vol. 3, pp. 1354-1360.

13. Mark Reutter, "The Lost Promise of the American Railroad," *Wilson Quarterly*, Winter, 1994, p. 28.

14. Joe R. Feagin and Robert Parker, *Building American Cities*, Prentice-Hall, Englewood Cliffs, NJ, 1990, p. 15.

15. For a brief overview of suburbanization see: J. John Palen, "Suburbanization," in Willem van Vliet (ed.), *The Encyclopedia of Housing*, Sage Publications, Thousand Oaks, Calif., 1998, pp. 567–569.

16. Sally Ward, "Trends in the Location of Corporate Headquarters, 1969–1989," *Urban Affairs Quarterly* 23:469–478, 1994.

17. Barry Edmonston and Thomas Guterbock, "Is Suburbanization Slowing Down? Recent Trends in Population Deconcentration in U.S. Metropolitan Areas," *Social Forces* 66:905–925, 1984.

18. Ernest Burgess, "The Growth of the City," in Robert Park, Ernest Burgess, and Roderick McKenzie (eds.), *The City,* University of Chicago Press, Chicago, 1925, pp. 47–62.

19. Reynolds Farley, "Suburban Persistence," *American Sociological Review* 29:38–47, 1964; and Avery M. Guest, "Suburban Social Status: Persistence or Evolution," *American Sociological Review* 43:251–264, 1978.

20. John R. Logan and Mark Schneider, "Stratification of Metropolitan Suburbs, 1960–1970," *American Sociological Review* 46:175–186, 1981.

21. John M. Stahura, "Suburban Socioeconomic Status Change: A Comparison of Models, 1950–1980," *American Sociological Review* 52:268–277, 1987.

22. John R. Logan, "Growth, Politics, and the Stratification of Places," *American Journal of Sociology* 84:404–415, 1978.

23. Justin Fox, "The Federal Job Machine: How Did America's Richest Region Get That Way? Uncle Sam," *Time,* February, 19, 2007, p. 48.

24. Edward Lewine, "Subsidized Houses for Rich People," *Key, New York Timers Real Estate Magazine,* Spring 2007, p. 54.

25. J. Edward Blakely and Mary Gail Snyder, *Fortress America: Gated Communities in the United States,* Brookings Institution, Washington, D.C., 1997.

26. Setha Low, *Behind the Gates: Life, Security, and the Pursuit of Happiness in Fortress America,,* Routledge, New York, 2003.

27. Bennett M. Berger, *Working Class Suburbs,* University of California Press, Berkeley, 1960.

28. Daniel Pinlott, "As Cities Revive, America's Poor Are Forced to the Periphery," *Financial Times,* April 4, 2008, p. 7.

29. Michael Weiss, *The Clustering of America,* Tilden Press, New York, 1988.

30. A. C. Spectorsky, *The Exurbanites,* Berkeley, New York, 1957.

31. Chang-rae Lee, *Aloft,* Riverhead, New York, 2004

32. Arthur C. Nelson and Thomas W. Sanchez, "Debunking the Exurban Myth: A Comparison of Suburban Households," *Housing Policy Debates* 10:689–709, 1999.

33. John Herbers, *The New Heartland: America's Flight beyond the Suburbs and How It Is Changing Our Future,* Times Books, New York, 1986.

34. Alan Berube and Elizabeth Kneebone, "Two Steps back: City and Suburban Poverty Trends 1999–2005," Brookings Institute, www.brook.edu/ Dec. 7, 2006.

35. Bennet M. Berger, "The Myth of Suburbia," *Journal of Social Issues* 17:38–49, 1971; Herbert J. Gans, "Urbanism and Suburbanism as Ways of Life: A Re-evaluation of Definitions," in Arnold Rose (ed.), *Human Behavior,* Houghton-Mifflin, Boston, 1962.

36. William Schneider, "The Suburban Century Begins," *Atlantic,* July 1992, p. 35.

37. Nicholas Lemann, "Stressed Out in Suburbia," *Atlantic,* November 1989, p. 46.

38. William H. Whyte, *The Organization Man,* Doubleday (Anchor), Garden City, N.Y., 1956.

39. Samuel G. Freedman, "Suburbia Outgrows Its Image in the Arts," *New York Times,* February 28, 1999, p. AR1.

40. George Sternlieb and Robert W. Lake, "Aging Suburbs and Black Home-Ownership," *Annals of the American Academy of Political and Social Science* 422:105–117, 1975; Karl E. Taeuber, "Racial Segregation: The Persisting Dilemma," *Annals of the American Academy of Political and Social Science* 422:87–96, 1975; and Leo F. Schnore, Carolyn D. Andre, and Harry Sharp, "Black Suburbanization 1930–1970," in Barry Schwartz (ed.), *The Changing Face of the Suburbs,* University of Chicago Press, Chicago, 1976, pp. 69–94.

41. William H. Frey "Melting Pot Suburbs," in Bruce Katz and Robert E. Lang (eds.), *Redefining Urban and Suburban America,* Brookings Institution Press, Washington, D.C., 2003, pp. 155–179.

42. Ibid.

43. William Frey quoted in *The Economist,* May 31, 2008, p. 27.

44. Edward L. Glaeser and Jacob L. Vigdor, "Racial Segregation: Promising News," in Bruce Katz and Robert E. Lang (eds.), *Redefining Urban and Suburban America,* Brookings Institution Press, Washington, D.C., 2003, pp. 211–234.

45. Richard Alba and John Logan, "Minority Proximity to Whites in Suburbs: An Individual Level Analysis of Segregation," *American Journal of Sociology* 98:1388–1427, 1993.

46. A study by George Grier of the Washington Consumer Survey reported in D'Vera Cohn, "D.C. Losing Longtime Residences to Suburbs, Study Finds," *Washington Post,* February 26, 1998, p. C1.

47. Alex Kellogg, "Black Flight Hits Detroit," *Wall Street Journal,* June 5–5, 2010, pp. 1, 12.

48. John M. Stahura, "Changing Patterns of Suburban Racial Composition," *Urban Affairs Quarterly* 23:448–460, 1988.

49. Barrett A. Lee and Peter B. Wood, "Is Neighborhood Racial Succession Place Specific?" *Demography* 28:37, 1991.

50. Nancy A. Denton and Douglas S. Massey, "Patterns of Neighborhood Transition and a Multiethnic World: U.S. Metropolitan Areas 1970–1980," *Demography* 28:41–63, 1991.

51. Morton D. Windsberg, "Flight from the Ghetto: The Migration of Middle Class and Highly Educated Blacks to White Neighborhoods," *American Journal of Economics and Sociology* 44:411–421, 1985.

52. Andrew Wiese, "Neighborhood Diversity: Social Change, Ambiguity, and Fair Housing Since 1968," *Journal of Urban Affairs* 17:107–129, 1995.

53. David J. Dent, "The New Black Suburbs," *New York Times Magazine,* June 14, 1992, p. 23.

54. J. June Kronholz, "Hispanics Gain in Census," *Wall Street Journal,* May 10, 2006, p. A6.

55. Robert Suro and Audrey Singer, "Changing Patterns of Latino Growth in Metropolitan America," in Bruce Katz and Robert E. Lang, *Redefining Urban and Suburban America,* Brookings Institution Press, Washington, D.C., 2003, pp. 181–210.

56. William Frey and Alden Speare, *Regional and Metropolitan Growth and Decline in the United States,* Russell Sage Foundation, New York, 1988, pp. 311–316.

57. Douglas Massey and Nancy Denton, "Trends in Residential Segregation of Blacks, Hispanics, and Asians," *American Sociological Review* 52:802–825, 1987.

58. Mary Beth Sheridan and D'Vera Cohn, "Immigrating In, Settling Out," *Washington Post,* April 25, 2001, p. A1.

59. William P. O'Hare, William H. Frey, and Dan Fost, "Asians in the Suburbs," *American Demographics,* May 1994, p. 34.

60. Timothy P. Fong, *The First Suburban Chinatown,* Temple University Press, Philadelphia, 1994.

Part III

METROPOLITAN LIFE

CHAPTER 7

Urban Culture and Lifestyles

What is the city but the people?

Shakespeare, Coriolanus

OUTLINE

Introduction
Social Psychology of Urban Life
    Early Formulations
    The Chicago School
    "Urbanism as a Way of Life"
Reevaluations of Urbanism and
    Social Disorganization
    Determinist Theory
    Compositional Theory
    Subcultural Theory
Characteristics of Urban Populations
    Age
    Gender
    Race, Ethnicity, and Religion
    Socioeconomic Status
Urban Lifestyles
    Cosmopolites
    Unmarried or Childless
    Gay Households
    Ethnic Villagers
    Neighborhood Characteristics
    Deprived or Trapped
A Final Note of Caution
Summary

INTRODUCTION

Now we turn from the spatial and macro-level construction of the city to a consideration of the city as a unique social organizational form and social milieu. In short, the culture of the city, urbanism rather than urbanization. Here we ask questions such as these: What are the characteristics of urban dwellers? Do urbanites differ from ruralites or small-town residents? Do cities produce a unique way of life or psychological outlook?

We all carry stereotypes of the "typical" city dweller and the "typical" suburbanite. Think for a moment about the pictures that come to your mind when you think of central-city residents. Is it an image of an affluent and sophisticated couple, a young minority male, or, perhaps, the young people on *Friends* or *How I Met Your Mother.* The reality is that there isn't any one city lifestyle. The hallmark of the city is its diversity. Certainly, cities differ from towns and rural areas not only in their size and patterns of economic activities but also in their tone, texture, and pace. Heterogeneity, variety, and change are givens, as is a potpourri of different occupations, social classes, cultural backgrounds, and interests. As expressed eight decades ago in the first major social science reference work:

> The city has more wealth than the country, more skill, more erudition within its bounds, more initiative, more philanthropy, more science, more divorces, more aliens, more births and deaths, more accidents, more rich, more poor, more wise men and more fools.[1]

As noted in Chapter 3: The Rise of Urban America, Americans have long been ambivalent about cities and city life. On one hand the city is praised as the height of civilization—the new Athens—and the center of progress, energy, and enterprise. But more frequently the city is characterized as the source of crime, corruption, and social disorganization—the repository of all the problems of the society:

> The city is not only Zion, the city of God; it is Babylon, the scarlet woman. On the one hand, we have the opposition of urbane splendor and culture with rural cloddishness and savagery; on the other hand, we have the opposition of urban vice, corruption and cruelty, as against rural virtue and purity. The Bible, to take but one instance furnishes us with innumerable examples of this deep ambivalence towards the city. It is at once the house of God and the house of iniquity. Amos, the herdsman, denounces it; Jeremiah weeps over it; Christ is crucified for it. One of the great threads through the Bible is the destruction and rebuilding of the city—a pattern which is wholly characteristic of the age of civilization.[2]

The contrast between urban and rural ways of life was a basic part of urban studies for much of the 20th century. The terms used to define the dichotomy sometimes differed, but the underlying content remained remarkably similar; the country represented simplicity, the city complexity. Rural areas were typified by stable rules, roles, and relationships, while the city was characterized by innovation, change, and disorganization. The city was the center of variety, heterogeneity, and social novelty, while the countryside or small town represented tradition, social continuity, and cultural conformity. The stereotype also included a view of city people as possessing greater sophistication but less real warmth and feeling.

Implicit, and sometimes explicit, in this viewpoint was that modern mass society was destroying close attachments to kin and community. In their place were being substituted uprooted, isolated, and alienated individuals who were free of traditional bonds but alone in the big city. An excellent portrayal of this view is Charlie Chaplin's classic film *Modern Times,* in which the helpless worker is literally swallowed up and spit out by the faceless factory machine. Cities fared badly in popular descriptions during the last half of the 20th century. Urban decay and violence were said to be the inevitable fate of once-mighty American cities.[3]

Here we won't debate the inherent biases that occur when emotionally loaded terms such as *warmth, friendliness,* and *community* are associated with smaller rural and suburban places, while terms such as *anonymity, alienation,* and *isolation* appear to be reserved for large cities. What is important for our purposes is to understand the influence such beliefs, even if inaccurate, have had on traditional and contemporary views of urban life.

SOCIAL PSYCHOLOGY OF URBAN LIFE

Early Formulations

The specter of the city as the source of isolation and alienation for the individual, and of social problems and collapse for the society, is far from new. As noted in Chapter 1, The Urban World, classical social theorists such as Ferdinand Tönnies, Karl Marx, Émile Durkheim, Max Weber, and Georg Simmel all discussed the decline of local attachments and the rise in their place of mass urban society.[4] The changes were frequently presented in terms of logical constructs or models, which sociologists refer to as "ideal types."

Among the most noteworthy of these dichotomies, in terms of its impact upon later urban research, was Tönnies's elaborate description of the shift from *gemeinschaft*—a community where ties were based upon kinship (that is, personal ties and relationships)—to *gesellschaft*, a society based on common economic, political, and other interests. *Gemeinschaft* communities, according to Tönnies, were smaller places where people knew one another and reacted to one another as members of the group, rather than as someone playing a specific role such as merchant or banker. *Gesellschaft* societies, on the other hand, are far more goal-oriented and impersonal, with money and contractual relationships dominating. Thus, in contractually based societies we expect to have a leaking roof repaired by the roofer offering the best price, not by cousins who automatically do it for free because they are relations.

The German social theorist Max Weber made similar distinctions between "traditional society" and "rational society"—that is, the substitution in modern society of formal rules and procedures for earlier, more spontaneous, patterns. The prime ideal type of rational behavior was institutionalized bureaucracy since bureaucracies have formal job descriptions and rules for appointment and promotion. Bureaucracy, in its best sense, thus promotes predictability and uniformity.

The French theorist Émile Durkheim distinguished between societies based on "mechanical solidarity" and those based on "organic solidarity." For Durkheim, the old mechanical social order was one in which all had similar interests and carried out similar tasks. This was the case in traditional rural areas where all the peasants led similar lives. They got up at the same time, planted the same way, and followed the same seasonal patterns.

Organic solidarity of urban places was by contrast based not on everyone doing the same things but on a division of labor. An analogy was made to the body, where different organs perform different functions, and thus by specializing create a more efficient organic system.

Karl Marx also discussed the dichotomy between the urban and the rural. For Marx, the emergence of urban-based capitalism meant destruction of the older agrarian-based social order. Market-based relations replaced feudal relationships, and industrial capitalism encouraged the exploitation and alienation of urban workers. Eventually this would result in the workers developing a class consciousness and uniting to overthrow their capitalist oppressors. The workers' new unity was based, though, on common interest rather than having a common interest based on residing in similar areas.

There are significant differences among the frameworks, but note that all the comparisons have an implicit time frame in which rural areas represented the past—sometimes in a glorified form (the "good old days") and the city represented the present, with its impersonal technology and division of labor.

The Chicago School

American urban scholars were influenced by the European theorists, but even more by the changes they saw occurring in the cities where they lived. This was especially true of members of the so-called Chicago School of sociology, assembled during the 1920s at the University of Chicago. These scholars were concerned with examining scientifically the changes produced by urbanization. Seeing the apparent confusion of urban life among urban immigrants, they focused on the way urban life disrupted traditional ties to kin and community. Some of their writings on such diverse phenomena as juvenile delinquency, organized vice, ethnic community ghettos, and the nature of the city's ecological growth have become sociological classics. Writings such as *The Ghetto* (Wirth), *The Gold Coast and the Slum* (Zorbaugh), and *The Polish Peasant in Europe and America* (Thomas and Znaniecki) are descriptive gems giving insights into this unique period in the urbanization of the United States.[5]

Writers of the Chicago School were especially influenced by Georg Simmel's earlier vision of the social–psychological consequences of city life—a lifestyle where, as a result of city size, calculated sophistication would replace close and meaningful relationships.[6] Simmel suggested that the pace of city life and the overwhelming number of stimuli in the city result in a state of mental overstimulation and excitement.

Simmel said that shifting internal and external situations produce constant nervous stimulation and that as a result city dwellers have difficulty in maintaining an integrated personality in social situations where the reference points are constantly changing. As a result they seek to protect themselves by anonymity and sophistication. Calculating expediency takes the place of affective feelings and personal relationships. One is forced to become blasé in the urban environment in order to protect one's psyche from overstimulation.

> If so many inner reactions were responses to the continuous external contacts with innumerable people as are those in the small town, where one knows almost everybody one meets and where one has a positive relation to almost everyone, one would be completely atomized internally and come to an unimaginable psychic state.[7]

Simmel's belief that the city produces "nervous stimulation" among its inhabitants, and of the socially disorganizing and disruptive effects of urbanism as a way of life, keeps being reinvented. For example, it is the basis for Alvin Toffler's popular book *Future Shock* and can be found in Stanley Milgram's use of the concept of "psychic overload."[8] The term *overload* comes from systems analysis, where overload occurs when the system cannot process inputs because they are coming too fast or because there are

too many of them. Under such circumstances, system adaptations or shutdown are said to occur. This is essentially Simmel's argument of a century ago being restated using a more contemporary analogy.

An interesting contemporary testing of the consequences of urban life has been done by Robert Levine, who compared the pace of life in 36 American cities.[9] What he discovered was that cities do differ. Northeasterners in larger cities generally walk faster, talk faster, and check their watches more than those on the slower-paced West Coast. A follow-up study in 36 American cities of people's willingness to help someone in a chance encounter on a city street found that people were most helpful in small and medium-sized cities in the Southeast, and least helpful in the large cities of the Northeast and the West Coast.[10] New York came in last. Thus, there does seem to be some, at least superficial, support for Simmel's views. The faster urban pace literally does affect our lives.

"Urbanism as a Way of Life"

The classic formulation of how urbanization fosters innovation, specialization, diversity, and anonymity is found in Louis Wirth's essay "Urbanism as a Way of Life."[11] This is still the most influential urban sociology essay ever written. Using Simmel's ideas as a foundation, Wirth argued that the city created a distinct way of life—called "urbanism"—that is reflected in how people dress and speak, what they believe about the social world, what they consider worth achieving, what they do for a living, where they live, with whom they associate, and why they interact with other people.

Wirth further suggested that urbanization and its components—size, density, and heterogeneity—are the independent variables that determine urbanism, that is, shape urban behavior and lifestyles. Moreover, the relationship is linear: the larger, denser, and more heterogeneous the city, the more prevalent is urbanism as a way of life. As a way of life, urbanism was viewed by Wirth (and others) as economically successful but socially destructive:

> The distinctive features of the urban mode of life have often been described sociologically as consisting of the substitution of secondary for primary contacts, the weakening of bonds of kinship, the declining social significance of the family, the disappearance of the neighborhood, and the undermining of the traditional basis of social solidarity. All of these phenomena can be substantially verified through objective indices.[12]

Some characteristics of the urban way of life as described by Wirth are:

1. An extensive and complex division of labor replacing the artisan who participated in every phase of manufacture.
2. Emphasis on success, achievement, and social mobility as morally praiseworthy. Behavior becomes more rational, utilitarian, and goal-oriented.
3. Decline of the family (increased divorce) and weakening bonds of kinship, with previous family functions transferred to specialized outside agencies (schools, health and welfare agencies, commercial recreation).
4. Breakdown of primary groups and ties (neighborhood) and substitution of large, formal, secondary group-control mechanisms (police, courts). Traditional bases of social solidarity and organization are undermined, leading to social disorganization.
5. Relation to others as players of segmented roles (bus driver, shop clerk) rather than as whole persons—i.e., there is a high degree of role specialization. Utilitarian rather than affective relationships with others. Superficial sophistication as a substitute for meaningful relationships leading to alienation.
6. Decline of cultural homogeneity, and an increasing diversity of values, views, and

opinions. The emergence of subcultures (ethnic, criminal, sexual) that are at variance with the larger society. Greater freedom and tolerance, but also decline in sense of common community.
7. Spatial segregation into disparate sections on the basis of income, status, race, ethnicity, religion, and so on.

REEVALUATIONS OF URBANISM AND SOCIAL DISORGANIZATION

Determinist Theory

Not surprisingly, many of Wirth's characteristics read like a catalog of contemporary social changes. Wirthian social disorganization theory is sometimes referred to as "deterministic theory." It is deterministic insofar as urbanization is said to more or less automatically produce the characteristics of urbanism as a way of life. Sometimes this is called the *community lost* perspective.

Wirth's essay "Urbanism as a Way of Life" still influences both professional and popular thought about cities. We now know that the early sociologists of Wirth's day (the 1920s and 1930s), in their fascination with the socially disorganizing aspects of urban life, underplayed the role of the city as a social integrator and underestimated the strength of traditional ways of life. William F. Whyte's excellent study of street life in an Italian slum of Boston was one of the few to stress that urban neighborhoods had sociocultural continuity and maintained traditional cultures.[13] Today, some writers are still predicting the imminent disappearance of these same traditional lifestyles. Ethnic affiliations that were supposed to have vanished long ago, and are continually being pronounced dead, seem somehow to be constantly reviving.

We can now see how Wirth's views suffered from not fully recognizing the degree to which his generalizations were limited both by historical time and by the differing composition and variety of urban areas. Herbert Gans, for instance, questions Wirth's diagnosis of the city as producing anomic, goal-oriented, segmented role relationships. Gans says, "Since the theory argues that all of society is now urban, *his analysis does not distinguish ways of life in the city from those in other settlements within modern society.*"[14]

Gans suggests that Wirth's "urbanite" is a member of a mass society, a representative of urban-industrial society rather than of the city itself. In other words, Wirth tended to confuse urbanization with general modernization of the society. Additionally, Gans believed there was not enough evidence either to prove or to deny the posited relationship among size, density, heterogeneity, and social disorganization.

Some data, however, do support the contention that urbanism per se affects social behavior. Urbanism, for example, does appear to increase tolerance for unpopular ideas and interests.[15] Also, research by Levine in 36 American cities found that the best predictor of the willingness of passing pedestrians to perform simple acts of assistance such as returning a dropped pen or mailing a stamped and addressed envelope left on a sidewalk was population density.[16] People proved the most helpful in small and medium-sized cities in the Southeast and least helpful in large cities. New Yorkers were least willing to help. The claim that urbanism negatively affects mental health is also unfounded. Mental health appears to be better in urban rather than rural areas.[17]

Extensive research by White and Guest shows that while in urban areas ties are more voluntary, the level of urbanization has little effect on the amount of contact one has with significant others.[18] Urban dwellers have as much contact with their friends as do rural residents. Moreover, urban residents have relationships with others that are as full and meaningful as the relationships of those in small towns.[19] The conventional wisdom is simply wrong in painting city people as being more alienated and

isolated. Knowing fewer persons in a community does not necessarily lead to atomization or isolation.[20] Today most of one's social contacts may be on Facebook.

Compositional Theory

One alternative to Wirthian determinist theory is compositional theory. Gans suggests that the city is composed of not just one urban way of life but rather a wide variety of lifestyles. Wirth's characterization of the disorganizing aspects of urban life applies only to some inner-city residents: the composition of the group is important. Research on inner-city neighborhoods by Elijah Anderson, for example, shows that high-crime areas have their own moral codes and rules of behavior (especially for young men).[21] These codes sometimes differ radically from those of the larger city. Residents of the outer city, on the other hand, have a lifestyle that resembles the lifestyle of suburbanites.

These outer-city neighborhoods, and even most inner-city populations, consist "mainly of relatively homogeneous groups, with social and cultural moorings that shield [them] fairly effectively from the suggested consequences of number, density, and heterogeneity."[22] In other words, there is not just one urban way of life but many urban lifestyles.

Gans thus argues that more important to the individual than the size, density, or heterogeneity of the larger population is the nature of his or her local community and primary groups. Rather than living in the city per se, people actually live in what the early Chicago School called a "mosaic of social worlds." Some of these local social worlds, far from producing alienation, act to protect their members from negative outside influences. Thus, differences in behavior are said to be consequences not of place of residence, but rather of the social and economic characteristics of the group. In this view urbanization itself has no effects; middle-class city dwellers, for example, are seen as virtually identical to middle-class suburbanites.

Subcultural Theory

A third perspective, known as "subcultural theory," is especially identified with Claude Fischer. Unlike Gans, Fischer argues that space does matter, and there is something different about cities. Fischer thus agrees with Wirth that the urban area does shape social life. However, Fischer turns Wirth's ideas on their head by suggesting that urbanization, rather than destroying social groups as Wirth suggested, strengthens and intensifies subcultural groups.[23]

Only large cities contain enough people to provide the critical mass of people necessary to allow subcultures to emerge. Urban life, in fact, creates new social worlds or subcultures. Only in the city can one find a subculture of model-train enthusiasts or tuba players. The effect of the city is greatest for the smallest groups who would not find enough members other than in large cities. The city doesn't produce alienation and normlessness. Rather, it promotes new subcultures. Gay subcultures, for example, thrive in larger urban centers.[24] The city acts to intensify experiences. Contrary to what Gans says, Fischer maintains that being middle class in a small town is not the same as being middle class in a city of several millions. Place does matter.

CHARACTERISTICS OF URBAN POPULATIONS

Age

The demographics of urban populations differ from those of rural and smaller places. Urban populations are younger than their rural counterparts. This is particularly true of cities in developing countries, but it is also true of North America. (This subject is dis-

Lesbian couple in their kitchen. © Bill Bachmann/Photo Edit

cussed further in Chapter 14: Developing Countries.) City populations are younger not because they have high birthrates and thus more children; that is not the case. Rather, cities attract immigrants, and immigrants tend to be young adults. This in turn means that cities have a smaller proportion overall of children and elderly. (A partial exception is poor, inner-city, minority neighborhoods that have a high proportion of children but fewer elderly.) Because cities have more young adults they have more of the activities in which young adults engage. This means more bars (for singles and otherwise), more places of entertainment (movies are an activity primarily of the young), more crime (those ages 16 to 25 commit most crime), and more social change (younger populations are less bound by tradition).

Gender

The pattern of urban–rural sex ratios differs for developed and developing countries. Less-developed countries have a higher proportion of urban males because young men come to the city, leaving women behind to care for the farms. In African cities, for instance, there are often three males for every two females. Unmarried men tend to be less socially integrated than are husbands, and to have weaker social commitments to the community. Young males also engage in higher rates of socially disruptive behavior such as drunkenness, gambling, prostitution, and crime. (This was the history of the American West before the arrival of settlers with families. Frontier towns were rowdier before churches and the school marm arrived.) Alaska is the state with the highest proportion of males.

In developed countries, on the other hand, there is a higher likelihood that single women will leave rural areas for city jobs. In farm-based areas and in small towns, high school graduation is a time of leaving. Young women in particular have little option but to go elsewhere for jobs, training, or further schooling. Often the only option at home is to get married. The result is that greater numbers of women leave for urban places. The TV show *Sex in the City* was based on the premise that attractive, educated young women had difficulty finding enough marriageable males in large cities such as New York.

Race, Ethnicity, and Religion

Cities are more racially, ethnically, and religiously heterogeneous than small towns or the countryside. Small towns may be largely one race, religion, and ethnic group, but cities are far more mixed. In cities, even groups that are proportionately only a small part of the urban population can band with enough similar persons to constitute a minority group. This ethnic, racial, and religious mosaic led Louis Wirth to describe heterogeneity (along with size and density) as one of the basic characteristics of the city.[25]

In the city, ethnic and racial differences also raise the potential of intergroup cleavage, competition, and conflict. Greater religious and ethnic heterogeneity can lead to greater tolerance, but it does not have to do so. Tolerance is greater when race, ethnicity, and religion lose force as the primary way of identifying persons. Even when people look similar to outside observers, sharp ethnic or religious differences may cause conflict. In areas of centuries-old ethnic strife such as the Balkans, for example, religion still is the major way of defining one's group membership.

Sharp cleavages are most likely to occur when racial, ethnic, and religious boundaries also represent socioeconomic status boundaries. An example would be when most of the poor are also of the same ethnic or racial background. Claude Fischer argues that urban places actually foster heterogeneity beyond race, ethnicity, and religion since only with urban concentrations can smaller groups achieve a "critical" mass and thus become active subcultures in their own right.[26] Thus only in the city can you find subcultures devoted to classic viola music, backgammon, or S&M. Urban places thus not only tolerate diversity, they create it.

Socioeconomic Status

As the discussion at the opening of this chapter indicates, the city is a place of extremes, a site of both extreme wealth and poverty. Occupation and education show a similar spread. North American cities have been losing middle-class residents since World War II, and increasingly house those at the extremes. Once-

Box 7.1   Montreal and the "Quiet Revolution"

Canada has been defined as "two solitudes" or "two nations warring within one state."* Until 1970, French-speaking Montreal, Quebec, was Canada's financial and commercial center, the role now played by English-speaking Toronto, Ontario. Why the change? For 200 years after the British took Canada in 1765, anglophone (English-speaking) economic and political dominance of Montreal went unchallenged so long as the province of Quebec remained agrarian. In Montreal an informal arrangement between the government and the Catholic church resulted in businessmen of English background dominating the economy, while the culture remained traditional and francophone. Social control of the French-speaking areas and population was de facto conceded to the conservative Catholic clergy and lower officials.

Then in the 1960s dramatic social and political changes known as the *Quiet Revolution* began. With greater urbanism, pressures began to develop for economic and social change. The growing new middle class of French-speaking white-collar workers in the public sector saw their upward mobility blocked by anglophone dominance. At the same time blue-collar industrial workers began to develop a clear sense that they were being exploited by anglophone capitalists. As the French-speaking population became more urban in outlook, centuries-old rural-based social patterns began to crumble. In 1964 the Ministry of Education replaced the Catholic Church's control of public education. Changes in birth rates reflect the dramatic social changes of the *Quiet Revolution.* As of the late 1950s Quebec had the highest birthrate of any developed nation. Today Quebec has one of the lowest in the world, far below replacement level. Today only half the Quebec population marries, while close to half of those that do marry divorce.

The major symbols of francophone political ascendancy were the 1976 election of the separatist Parti Quebecois, and the passage the next year of Bill 101, which mandated that all communication in both public and private sectors had to be in French. In spite of the Canadian government's official policy of bilingualism, French was proclaimed the official language of Quebec. Just as the old structure of Montreal society had excluded francophones from control, Bill 101 excluded anglophones. English was barred from public schools and a "language police" established to ensure that English was not used in business places. One consequence was the virtually total replacement of English-speaking officials, businesspeople, and professionals with French speakers. Another consequence was a massive hemorrhaging of finance and business offices and money from Montreal to Toronto from the 1970s to the 1990s. Toronto prospered from the inflow and now clearly is the economic center of Canada.

Growing Quebecois identity also raised the question of Quebec's political independence. In 1970, 44 percent of the Quebec population defined themselves as French-Canadian and 34 percent as Canadian. By 1990, 59 percent identified themselves as Quebecois, while only 28 percent saw themselves as French-Canadian, and a low 9 percent called themselves Canadian.** In 1995 a referendum on sovereignty in Quebec brought out 94 percent of all voters, of whom 50.6 percent voted to remain in Canada. (The vote was not simply a gesture; France secretly had agreed to recognize Quebec if a majority voted for sovereignty.) Since 1995, pressures for independence have receded, and Canadian Supreme Court rulings have made sovereignty more difficult. Montreal, the most cosmopolitan city in North America, has also been showing increasing signs of economic prosperity. As time goes on even the language issue is becoming less divisive. In 1993 Quebec passed Bill 86, which allowed English to again be used for commercial signs, provided that French predominates. Symbols often reflect changing attitudes. In 1998, without announcement or fanfare, the Canadian flag once again began flying in front of Montreal's City Hall. Young Montrealers today are more concerned with economic issues.

*Part of the following is based on Harry A. Hiller, *Canadian Society: A Macro Analysis,* 3rd ed., Prentice Hall Canada, Toronto, 1996, pp. 212–230.

**Andre Blais and Richard Nadeau, "To Be or Not to Be Sovereignist: Quebecker's Perennial Dilemma," *Canadian Public Policy* 18:89–103, 1992.

solid middle-class neighborhoods have declined, reflecting the fact that the middle-class is barely treading water. Working-class families are even worse off with a 25 percent decline in the income of blue-collar males from the 1970s to 2010. As a result of the recession middle-class neighborhoods are suffering while poorer neighborhoods are doing even worse.

Overall city income averages tend to hide sharp individual and neighborhood variations in socioeconomic status. Cities increasingly house the richest and the poorest. A 2006 study done for the Brookings Institution showed that middle-income neighborhoods declined from 58 percent of all metropolitan neighborhoods in 1970 to 41 percent in 2000.[27] Moreover, in the 12 largest metropolitan areas only 23 percent of central city neighborhoods were middle-income, down sharply from 45 percent in 1970.[28] Middle-class neighborhoods, particularly in central cities, have declined even faster than the middle-class population in cities.

In urban areas, socioeconomic-status criteria such as income, education, and occupation tend to supplant family, ethnicity, religion, and the other ways of ordering people used in more traditional small towns.

URBAN LIFESTYLES

While cities generally have the highest rates of social problems, this clearly is not the same as saying that all central-city populations, or even wide areas of the city, have high rates of personal alienation and social disorganization. Some groups thrive in central-city locations. Inner-city working-class ethnic groups, for instance, live lives that, far from being disorganized, are probably more organized and integrated than those of other city dwellers. Characterizations of depersonalization, isolation, and social disorganization simply do not fit. Gans describes four general urban lifestyles, which he calls cosmopolite, unmarried or childless, ethnic villager, and deprived or trapped. [29]

Cosmopolites

Cosmopolites are urban sophisticates, most often having incomes to match their lifestyles. These are people who love city life. They live in urbane neighborhoods without really knowing their neighbors. New York's Upper East and West Sides, Chicago's Lake Shore and Lincoln Park, and San Francisco's Pacific Heights and Nob Hill are examples. Cosmopolites are almost always well-educated, and they value both the cultural life and the social privacy of the city. They are very much of the city, but do not display any of the isolation and alienation that Wirth associated with city life.

Unmarried or Childless

This group of central-city dwellers overlaps with the cosmopolites. Usually they are younger and apartment dwellers rather than owners. *Yuppies* (young urban professionals) and *dinks* (dual income, no kids) fall in this category, as does the cast of *Friends*. Many urban gays also fit the category. Both gay and straight fit into what David Brooks refers to as the new social class of *"BOBOs,"* by which he means the emerging upper-class that combines sturdy bourgeois standards of work and order with a nonjudgmental bohemian love of ease and emancipation.[30] For this economically successful group, brains have replaced money and accomplishment trumps religion and wealth. Having a killer resume is the ideal, and the group defines itself more by its "socially responsible" patterns of consumption than by production. In consumption, having the "right" stainless steel kitchen stove is better than buying jewelry. Pleasures are also utilitarian and practical, such as running an hour a day, in order to be fitter for work. BOBOs can be found in trendy suburbs and university towns such as Ann Arbor, Michigan (places Brooks calls "Latte Towns"), but central areas of large cities are also natural locations. Like cosmopolitans, the unmarried and childless do not exhibit the negative consequences of "urbanism as a way of life." They thrive on urban life.

Gay Households

A significant city population that Gans overlooked is made up of gay households. There

Box 7.2   Brain-Gain Cities

All the talk about city problems and economic downturn obscures the fact that some cities are growing both in people and economic vitality. Richard Florida argues that the failing and prospering cities don't divide along rustbelt–sunbelt considerations as much as by whether they attract and hold educated and talented young workers.* Cities that attract smart young people such as Ann Arbor, Austin, Atlanta, Boston, Chicago, Denver, Minneapolis, San Diego, San Francisco, Seattle, Raleigh and Durham in North Carolina, and Washington, D.C., are prospering. Whether in the North or South, these are technology-rich cities where the work tends to be smart, the culture cool, and the environment clean. Even in economic downturns "brain-gain" cities hold young educated entrepreneurs betting on the next step in the knowledge-based economy.

Brain-gain cities look to the future rather than the past. They tend to have a higher percentage of residents who are culturally creative—artists, writers, and musicians—as well as visible gay communities. A dominant research-based university is also a common feature. There is also a high percentage of college-educated, foreign-born residents. Brain-gain cities also share pedestrian-oriented neighborhoods, good restaurants, live music, and theatre.

Florida has developed a "creativity index" to measure how a city is likely to succeed in today's creative economy.** The index measures high-tech output and patent growth; degree of racial integration; concentration of foreign-born and gay couples; the percentage of the workforce in occupations such as education, computers, business, medicine, and law; and the percentage of artists, writers, musicians, designers, and "creatives."

Florida argues that the struggle between brain-gain and brain-loss cities is accelerating. Cities such as Boston, Minneapolis, Portland, and Austin routinely poach talent—and the future—from cities such as Baltimore, Cleveland, Milwaukee, Saint Louis, and San Antonio. In this "winner take all" competition, city population growth is not as important as the nature of the growth. The winning cities are those gaining college graduates. Las Vegas, the nation's fastest-growing city, attracts more high school dropouts than college graduates. The winner cities are places where young people want to be, which translates into luring more bright, young, educated people. Brain-drain cities lose their best at graduation or soon after.

Finally, it should be noted that the technologically rich and culturally cool places Florida discusses offer opportunities to young, well-educated newcomers. They offer far less to working class, blue collar, or lower level white collar, workers.

*Richard Florida, *The Rise of the Creative Class: And How It's Transforming Work, Leisure, Community, and Everyday Life,* Basic Books, New York, 2002.

**Ibid.

---

are estimated to be some 8.8 million gay, lesbian, or bisexual persons in the United States.[31] The 2000 census reported that 1.2 million people defined themselves as part of a gay or lesbian couple. This is more than a 300 percent increase from 1990, but census experts believe it reflects not so much an increase in the number of same-sex couples as an increase in people's comfort and honesty about their sexual orientation. The 2010 census data, when published, is expeced to show major increases over 2000 numbers. The cities of San Francisco, New York, Los Angeles, and Washington, D.C., rank highest in the number of heavily gay urban neighborhoods. In Canada, Vancouver, the scenic "San Francisco North," possibly has a higher proportion of gays than San Francisco. According to the U.S. census, gay male households are more likely to live in downtown gay neighborhoods, while lesbians more commonly reside in suburban areas.

Ethnic Villagers

Working-class neighborhoods, far from being characterized by depersonalization, isolation, and social disorganization, often exhibit a high degree of social interaction among residents. This is particularly the case when the neighborhood is dominated by a single ethnic group. Those living in such organized inner-city neighborhoods have been referred to as

Latino neighborhood activity—couple dancing at Three Kings festival in Calle Ocho or "Little Havana," in Miami. © Jeff Greenberg/The Image Works

"urban villagers" or "urban provincials." These inner-city neighborhoods, whatever their predominant group, embody more of the family and peer orientation of a homogeneous small town than the attitudes of an impersonal large city. Ethnic villagers, although they live in the city, try to isolate themselves from what they consider to be the harmful effects of urban life. Whether they are Irish in South Boston, Italian in South Philadelphia, or Mexican in East Los Angeles, they resist the encroachment of other ethnic or racial groups. Such working-class neighborhoods place heavy emphasis on kinship and primary-group relationships and often resent the secondary formal control mechanisms of the larger city. Some of these Italian, Puerto Rican, Mexican, Asian, or Eastern European enclaves are no larger than a census tract, but some are quite extensive. Chicago claims the largest Polish population outside Warsaw; Cleveland's Hungarian population is said to be second only to that of Budapest. Similarly, Miami is a major Cuban city

and Los Angeles's Mexican population is third behind that of Mexico City. Los Angeles's Asian population numbers over a million.

Several decades ago it was thought that tight ethnic urban neighborhoods were only anachronistic survivals from earlier times. Urban villagers were thought to represent only "bypassed pre-industrial locals," left behind by modern society.[32] The irony is that in the 21st century new ethnic areas are bringing vitality to American cities. One-third of New York's population is foreign born and half are foreign born or the children of foreign born. In Toronto a full 44 percent are foreign born.

Outsiders sometimes mislabel urban villages as "slums" because the buildings are old and may not appear from the exterior to be in good condition. Often they are better than they appear, but even when an area is physically deteriorated, its social fabric may still be strong.[33] (Later in the chapter we will discuss disorganized urban neighborhoods.) Urban villagers remain in older neighborhoods in spite of the obvious physical limitations and external conditions of the housing because moving to the suburbs would mean leaving the tight-knit social neighborhood. Studs Terkel quotes the mother of six children living in the near West Side of Chicago expressing the affection urban villagers have for their neighborhoods:

> I got everybody on this block that would do something for me. If one of my children were sick, I wouldn't feel any compunction of waking up the man across the street to take me to the hospital. He expects this. . . . I know friends of ours, who've moved away from here, who bitterly lament their predicament now. They've got beautiful homes—I guess the city planners would say they've done better for themselves. . . . to me, we're more concerned about people.[34]

(The next few pages focus on settled working-class neighborhoods and their norms. Use this material to compare the type of neighborhood described with neighborhoods with which you are personally familiar.)

Neighborhood Characteristics

Territoriality. Inner-city neighborhoods generally have a strong sense of territory. The residents, although living near the center of a large metropolis, still manage to remain socially and psychologically isolated from the rest of the urban area. Those living in inner-city areas often have very restricted mental maps of their own neighborhoods. The city outside the neighborhood is viewed as a foreign land—and a potentially hostile one—into which one ventures only when necessary. Even in cosmopolitan New York there are people living in Staten Island who have rarely been to Manhattan—and have no real desire ever to go there.

Ordered Segmentation. Ecologically settled ethnic areas are usually characterized by ordered segmentation. That is, each ethnic group carefully and specifically defines its territory. Boundaries between different ethnic groups,

while invisible to the outsider, are well-known and respected by the local residents. Gerald Suttles, in his study of the Taylor Street area of Chicago, points out that the Italian, Mexican, Puerto Rican, and black groups living in the area had their own provincial enclaves and conducted their daily lives within these known borders.[35] Within these territorial units, one is safe and comfortable. Business establishments—particularly bars, but even grocery stores—are viewed by local inhabitants as being the exclusive property of a single minority group. Outsiders are made to feel unwelcome unless they are there as guests. Community facilities such as parks are often seen as "belonging" to one group. The movement of one group into the social area of another is likely to lead to violence or the threat of violence.

Peer-Group Orientation. The primary integrative mechanism of stable inner-city ethnic neighborhoods is the peer group—that is, a group made up of members of the same age and sex who are at the same stage of the life-cycle. The peer group, be it a gang of adolescents or a clique of married friends and relatives of the same sex, provides a vital buffer between the individual and the larger society.

Gans has described the relationship of the peer-group society to the larger world as follows:

> The life of the West Ender takes place within three interrelated sectors: the primary group refers to that combination of family and peer relationships which I shall call the *peer group society.* The secondary group refers to the small array of Italian institutions, voluntary organizations, and other social bodies which function to support the workings of the peer group society. This I shall call the *community.* . . . The out-group, which I shall describe as the *outside world,* covers a variety of non-Italian institutions in the West End, in Boston, and in America that impinge on his life—often unhappily to the West Ender's way of thinking.[36]

The peer group sets standards for behavior, acts as a filter through which one can obtain information, reduces anonymity, and tells the individual that he or she belongs. Frequently, ingroup membership is signified by a distinctive way of dressing and/or locally distinctive speech patterns. The priority of personal relationships over goal-oriented relationships is stressed. The absence of material wealth is rationalized: luxurious consumer goods are associated with the outside world and a cold, impersonal, friendless way of life.

Family Norms. Family life in middle-class families is child-oriented, but in settled, ethnic, working-class areas family life is generally adult-oriented. The child is not the center of the family as in many middle-class and upper-middle-class families, where everything is adjusted to the child's needs, schedule, and general "development." Rather the role of children is to stay out of the way and behave. Girls are expected to start helping their mothers around the home, frequently by caring for younger siblings. Boys are given more freedom to roam the streets. Children soon pick up the notion that the home is the preserve of the mother. Leisure activities for males often focus on the local tavern, which is the major social institution for many blue-collar workers.[37]

Unlike middle-class professionals, sociability for adults does not revolve around occupation or involve a search for new or different friends. The basis for gathering with others is not occupation but kinship or long-standing friendship and association (the traditional upper class also stresses the importance of family relationships). Parties in the upper-middle-class sense—gatherings for which invitations are given and at which you expect to meet people you do not know—are not part of the local lifestyle. As one West Ender put it, "I don't want to meet any new people. I get out quite a bit all over Boston to see my brothers and sisters, and when they come over, we have others in, like neighbors."[38] Husband and wife are not expected to communicate as extensively as in the middle-class family model. Husbands and

wives are expected to have separate interests, activities, and friends.

Housing. Housing often does not have the same meaning in established ethnic working-class neighborhoods that it has in suburban middle-class areas. For the middle class, how one decorates one's home is viewed as an extension of one's personality. The home is a reflection of one's tastes and style of life. The working-class home, on the other hand, is not primarily viewed as a status symbol. Homes may be old but are quite comfortable. Rents are usually well below the average for the city. Social closeness among neighbors is encouraged by the tendency of local landlords to rent apartments to their married children, relatives, and friends. The goal is a "respectable" neighborhood in which neighbors are of the same general ethnic, religious, and economic background.

Imagery and Vulnerability. Blue-collar ethnic neighborhoods, although physically a central part of the city, manage to maintain a psychological distance between themselves and other areas. They are "in" but not "of" the city. The neighborhood is considered friendly, while the city is considered cold and hostile. Residents' negative images of major urban institutions are remarkably similar to those of small-town dwellers, who also feel powerless in the face of the large urban-oriented bureaucracies that control much of their lives.

The peer-group orientation of working-class urban neighborhoods leaves them vulnerable to change induced from the outside. The emphasis within the community on personal relations makes residents ill-equipped to participate in large-scale formal organizations or communitywide activities. One learns from the peer group how to get along with others, but not how to organize or deal effectively with an outside bureaucracy. A traditional distrust of politicians and a lack of knowledge about how to lobby on the level of city government further handicap the working-class neighborhood. Suburban upper-middle-class groups are by training and inclination well equipped to organize ad hoc committees for any purpose under the sun. Working-class people are used to working within an environment of limited size, oriented toward persons more than organizations. Except in cases where a powerful communitywide ethnic church exists, there is no large-scale organization that has the power both to organize and to speak for the neighborhood in its dealings with the larger city. Urban ethnics do not turn to outside bureaucratic structures in time of trouble. They distrust the city hall bureaucracy and that of the courts. They feel that, whatever happens, they are going to lose. They are right, and their lack of knowledge of how to fight the system makes it all the easier for city hall and other outside interests to have their way.

This means that the community as a whole may not be able to respond effectively as a unit to threats to its existence. In the past, the threat might be urban renewal or an urban expressway that cuts it apart. Today, it is more likely to be plans for displacing the residents so the area can be gentrified by the upper middle class. A peer-group society based on ethnicity, age grading, dominance of a single sex, and limited territoriality is at a considerable disadvantage when it necessarily comes into contact and confrontation with large-scale, complex, bureaucratic society.

Deprived or Trapped

Unlike urban villagers, the deprived live in slums of despair. For the 15 to 20 percent of the population who are the bottom (unskilled manual workers, people with unstable and erratic work histories, the homeless, and those on long-term welfare, particularly if they are members of minority groups), the slum has the character more of an urban jungle than an urban village. Such areas have high rates of residential instability, with the population sharing little but the physical area. They are there because they have no alternative. Poverty, crime, and welfare dependence result in an area suffering from "hyperghettoization."[39]

Unstable slums thus differ not just because they house the very poor. Residents are not simply poorer, although that is also the case—they are in many ways excluded from the social system that includes both the rich and the blue-collar workers of stable slums. Most of the residents of unstable slums are for all practical purposes excluded from the economic and social life of the larger society. Life in such an environment is not an attempt to maximize advantages but rather an attempt, frequently unsuccessful, to minimize the harsh negative realities of everyday life. Drug dealing is often a major route of economic mobility. Residents are surrounded by others who are out to exploit them whenever possible. They are considered fair game by everyone from landlords to hustlers to drug dealers.

An excellent description and analysis of such ghetto life is provided by Elijah Anderson in his 14-year study of two Philadelphia neighborhoods.[40] Anderson discusses the effect of drugs, and how communities develop their own norms and behaviors regarding sexual activity and family life. Young males, in particular, have a code of street etiquette or street behavior aimed at getting and keeping respect. In order to successfully move on the streets males have to learn the "street wisdom" of how to signal their intentions to others through words, body language, and facial expressions.

Such knowledge is essential in an atmosphere where every encounter is viewed as a test of respect, respect for which one is willing to fight to the death. Violence under such a system becomes normative. "Because public interactions generally matter for only a few critical seconds, people are conditioned to rapid scrutiny of the looks, speech, public behavior, gender, and color of those sharing the environment."[41] A lack of jobs, which might provide an alternative lifestyle, virtually ensures that the cycle of illegitimacy, drugs, crime, and violence will continue.

The sex codes by which many inner-city young men operate make sexual conquests a game youths play to gain respect from their male peers. Having a number of girlfriends and offspring gives males street status. Babies in this system become the "consolation prizes" for the unwed mothers who have been promised marriage and settling down.

However, in the late 1990s the booming economy for the first time began to bring substantial numbers of young black men with less than high school education—many burdened with prison records—into the paid labor force. A major study of 322 metropolitan areas showed both young black employment and entry-level wages up dramatically.[42] Employment rates for young black males reached a 27-year high. The challenge is to maintain job growth in an era when reasonable-paying new manufacturing jobs are disappearing. Minimum wage service jobs don't provide a living, and the Great Recession starting in 2007 even destroyed many of these low-paying jobs.

Without access to entry-level jobs that pay a living wage, the deprived and trapped will remain an isolated semi-permanent underclass. Also virtually invisible in most discussions of inner-city ghettos are the responsible, working, adult males who continue to espouse and practice traditional values of responsibility and hard work.[43] Stable working-class males continue to provide a moral authority and serve within the community as role models of decency and respectability. Most inner-city poor are committed to earning a living and struggling to support themselves and their families on minimum wage jobs.[44]

Housing Problems. The middle class may view housing as an extension of one's personality, and the working class may see the house as a place of comfort, but for the urban underclass the house is basically a place of refuge. Urban poor, particularly those stored in public housing projects, have to be constantly on guard against violence against themselves and their possessions. Assaults, robberies, and muggings are a constant danger in stairwells, corridors, laundry rooms, and even apartments. In addition to physical violence, symbolic violence on the part of building supervisors, social workers, and others who perform caretaker services for the lower classes is also endemic in slums and public housing.

To the extent that the world is seen as consisting of dangerous others, the very act of making friends involves risks for the lower-class person. Lower-class persons are constantly being exploited, and thus it is not surprising that many view the world as threatening. In the words of a researcher, "To lower-class people the major causes stem from the nature of their own peers. Thus a great deal of blaming goes on and reinforces the process of isolation, suspiciousness, blaming and shaming."[45]

As those having economic strength or potential flee unstable slums, the isolation of those who are left behind and locked into poverty increases.[46] It can result in the "hyper-ghettoization" noted earlier. Thus decreases in discrimination can actually heighten the isolation between the very poor and other strata of blacks. Poverty and economic instability lock the urban underclass at the bottom as effectively as discrimination once did. Certainly the feeling of being ignored and bypassed while all around others rise can lead to explosions of frustration—or worse, despair and violence—not only against oneself but also against one's children. The bondage of unstable slums is made doubly oppressive by the relative prosperity of those outside their boundaries.

A FINAL NOTE OF CAUTION

Urbanism as a way of life is remarkably diverse. It includes the wealthy, gentrifying communities of straights and gays, tightly organized ethnic neighborhoods, and disorganized slums.

There is no single urban lifestyle per se. It is important to distinguish between the different urban lifestyles, and not just speak of "the city" as if it were all of one pattern.

SUMMARY

This chapter focuses on the city as a unique social organizational form and social milieu. Prior to World War II the contrast between urban and rural ways was an implicit part of urban studies; cities represented complexity and change while rural areas represented simplicity and stability. Classical European social theorists such as Ferdinand Tönnies, Karl Marx, Émile Durkheim, Max Weber, and Georg Simmel all developed dichotomous "ideal types" contrasting simpler rural social organization with the goal-oriented and impersonal urban division of labor. Simmel, with his belief that the city produced a "mental stimulation" leading to "atomization" and alienation of city dwellers had a particularly strong impact on the Chicago School.

A number of empirical community studies by the Chicago School were summed up in Louis Wirth's seminal essay "Urbanism as a Way of Life." Wirth argued that urbanization, as typified by size, density, and heterogeneity, creates unique urban behaviors and a lifestyle he termed *urbanism*. Urbanism, according to Wirth, often produced social disorganization and was characterized by the substitution of secondary for primary contacts, the weakening of the bonds of kinship, the weakening of the family, and the undermining of the traditional basis of social solidarity and community.

Wirth's views have influenced sociological and popular thought for over half a century, but his generalizations were limited both by the historical time in which he wrote and by the fact that not all urban areas are equally impacted by urbanism. An alternative to Wirthian deterministic theory is Herbert Gans's compositional theory. Gans suggests that the disorganizational aspects of urbanism are limited to some inner-city residents and that a group's socioeconomic composition is a better predictor of behavior than its spatial location in the metropolis. Place doesn't matter.

A third perspective, known as subcultural theory, has become dominant in recent years. Associated with Claude Fischer, subcultural theory suggests that urbanization, rather than destroying groups, as Wirth suggested, actually provides a critical mass of persons to allow subcultures to emerge. Urbanization strengthens and intensifies subcultural groups. Place matters, but it is the opposite of what Wirth suggested.

Urban populations tend to be demographically younger, more female, and more racially, ethnically, and religiously heterogeneous. Sharp cleavages occur when racial, ethnic, or religious boundaries also represent socioeconomic status boundaries. In cities socioeconomic differences tend to supplant other, more traditional ways of ordering people. Prospering "brain-gain" cities are technologically rich and culturally attractive. They attract and hold young college graduates, the culturally active, and gay populations.

There is not one urban lifestyle but many. Four categories suggested by Gans include cosmopolite, unmarried or childless, urban villager, and the deprived or trapped. We add a fifth category of gay households. Cosmopolites are upper-income urban sophisticates who choose the social life and the social privacy of the city. They show none of the social isolation or alienation Wirth associated with urban life. The unmarried or childless are a younger group (such as the cast of *Friends*) overlapping with cosmopolites. Gay-oriented central-city neighborhoods are an increasing feature of middle- and larger-size cities. Established working-class ethnic neighborhoods of ethnic villagers often exhibit a high degree of social organization and little of the social disorganization Wirth associated with city life. They live in stable neighborhoods and peer groups play a major role in tying ethnic villagers to their local community.

By contrast, the deprived and trapped live in slums of despair. The 15 to 20 percent of the city population on the bottom (those with erratic work histories, those on long-term welfare, the homeless) do exhibit the alienation and isolation Wirth described. They are essentially excluded from the urban social system that includes both the well-to-do and blue-collar workers living in stable urban neighborhoods. Simple generalizations about the city as a whole are thus best avoided. The city has many lifestyles.

REVIEW QUESTIONS

1. What did the 19th- and early 20th-century social theorists suggest regarding the impact of the city on personal and social life?

2. What were some of the major characteristics of "urbanism as a way of life"?

3. Is the Wirthian "urbanism as a way of life" model supported by the data or not?

4. How does compositional theory differ from Wirthian deterministic theory?

5. How does subcultural theory differ from Wirthian deterministic theory?

6. What factors distinguish "brain-gain" cities from "brain-loss" cities?

7. What are the different urban lifestyles discussed in the text and how do they affect urban attitudes?

8. What is meant by the statement that stable inner-city ethnic groups have a peer-group orientation?

9. How do urban working-class family norms differ from those of upper-middle class professionals?

10. How does the social attitude toward housing of deprived inner-city residents differ from that of middleclass populations?

NOTES

1. William B. Munro, "City," in *Encyclopedia of the Social Sciences,* Macmillan, New York, 1930, p. 474. For a far more sophisticated contemporary view see: Daniel Monti, *The American City: A Social and Cultural History,* Blackwell, Malden, MA, 1999.

2. Kenneth E. Boulding, "The Death of the City: A Frightened Look at Postcivilization," in Gino Germani (ed.), *Modernization, Urbanization, and the Urban Crisis,* Little, Brown, Boston, 1973, p. 265.

3. Robert A. Beauregard, *Voices of Decline: The Postwar Fate of U.S. Cities,* Blackwell, Cambridge, Mass., 1993.

4. For a detailed discussion of social theories, see George Ritzer, *Sociological Theory,* 5th ed, McGraw-Hill, New York, 2000.

5. Louis Wirth, *The Ghetto,* University of Chicago Press, Chicago, 1928; Harvey W. Zorbaugh, *The Gold Coast and the Slum: A Sociological Study of Chicago's Near North Side,* University of Chicago Press, Chicago, 1929; William I. Thomas and Florian Znaniecki, *The Polish Peasant in Europe and America,* 5 vols., University of Chicago Press, Chicago, 1918–1920.

6. Georg Simmel, "The Metropolis and Mental Life," in *The Sociology of Georg Simmel,*" Kurt H. Wolff (trans.), Free Press, Glencoe, Ill., 1950.

7. Ibid., p. 415.

8. Alvin Toffler, *Future Shock,* Random House, New York, 1970; Stanley Milgram, "The Experience of Living in Cities," *Science* 167:1461–1468, March 13, 1970.

9. Robert Levine, "The Pace of Life," *Psychology Today,* October 1989, pp. 42–46.

10. Robert V. Levine, "The Kindness of Strangers," *American Scientist* 91(3), May–June 2003, American Scientist Online.

11. Louis Wirth, "Urbanism as a Way of Life," *American Journal of Sociology* 44(10):8, July 1938.

12. Ibid., p. 21.

13. William F. Whyte, *Street Corner Society,* University of Chicago Press, Chicago, 1943.

14. Herbert J. Gans, "Urbanism and Suburbanism as Ways of Life: A Reevaluation of Definitions." in J. John Palen and Karl Flaming (eds.), *Urban America,* Holt, Rinehart and Winston, New York, 1972, p. 185.

15. Thomas C. Wilson, "Urbanism and Tolerance: A Test of Some Hypotheses Drawn from Wirth

and Stouffer," *American Sociological Review* 50(1): 117–123, 1985.

16. Robert V. Levine, "The Kindness of Strangers," *American Scientist,* 91(3):223-226, Summer 2003.

17. Leo Srole's comments in Tim Hacker, "The Big City Has No Corner on Mental Illness," *New York Times Magazine,* December 16, 1979, p. 136.

18. Katherine J. Curtis White and Avery M. Guest, "Community Lost or Transformed? Urbanization and Social Ties," *City and Community,* 2(3): 239–259, September 2003.

19. Claude Fischer, *To Dwell among Friends: Personal Networks in Town and City,* University of Chicago Press, Chicago, 1982, pp. 59–60.

20. William R. Freudenburg, "The Density of Acquaintanceship: An Overlooked Variable in Community Research?" *American Journal of Sociology,* 92:27–63, July 1986.

21. Elijah Anderson, *Streetwise: Race, Class, and Change in an Urban Community,* University of Chicago Press, Chicago, 1990.

22. Gans, op. cit., p. 186.

23. Claude Fischer, "Toward a Subcultural Theory of Urbanism," *American Journal of Sociology* 80:1319–1341, 1975.

24. John D'Emilio, *Sexual Politics, Sexual Communities: The Making of a Homosexual Minority in the United States, 1940–1970,* University of Chicago Press, Chicago, 1983.

25. Louis Wirth, "Urbanism as a Way of Life," *American Journal of Sociology* 44(10):8, July 1938.

26. Claude Fischer, *The Urban Experience,* Harcourt Brace Jovanovich, San Diego, 1984, pp. 36–37.

27. Jason C. Booza, Jackie Cutsinger, and George Galster, *Where Did They Go? The Decline of Middle-Income Neighborhoods in Metropolitan America,* Living Cities Census Series, Brookings Institution, Washington, D.C., June 2006, p. 1

28. Ibid.

29. Gans, op. cit.

30. David Brooks, *BOBOs in Paradise: The New Upper Class and How They Got There,* Simon & Schuster, New York, 2000.

31. For review of the literature see: Japonica Brown-Saracino, "LGBTI in CUSS," *CUSS* Newsletter, Community & Urban Section, American Sociogiocal Association, Fall/Winter, 2008/09, p. 1, 4–9. Also see Jan Christensen, "Welcome to the Grayborhood," *Advocate,* June 20, 2006, pp. 65–70.

32. Melvin M. Webber, "The Post-City Age," in J. John Palen (ed.), *City Scenes,* Little, Brown, Boston, 1977, p. 314.

33. Gerald D. Suttles, *The Social Order of the Slum: Ethnicity and Territory in the Inner City,* University of Chicago Press, Chicago, 1968.

34. Quoted in Studs Terkel, *Division Street: America,* Pantheon Books (Avon ed.), New York, 1967, p. 198.

35. Suttles, op. cit.

36. Gans, op. cit., pp. 36–37.

37. E. E. LeMasters, *Blue Collar Aristocrats,* University of Wisconsin Press, Madison, 1975; and William Kornblum, *Blue Collar Community,* University of Chicago Press, Chicago, 1974, p. 80.

38. Gans, *The Urban Villagers,* p. 75.

39. Loic J. D. Wacquant and William J. Wilson, "The Cost of Racial and Class Exclusion in the Inner City," *Annals of the American Academy of Political and Social Science,* 501:8–25, 1989.

40. Elijah Anderson, *Streetwise: Race, Class, and Change in an Urban Community,* University of Chicago Press, Chicago, 1990

41. Ibid.

42. Sylvia Nassar (reporting on research by Richard Freedman and William Rogers), "Booming Job Market Draws Young Black Men into Fold," *New York Times,* May 23, 1999, p. 1.

43. Mitchell Duneier, *Slim's Table: Race, Respectability, and Masculinity,* University of Chicago Press, Chicago, 1992.

44. Katherine S. Newman, *No Shame in My Game: The Working Poor in the Inner City,* Random House, New York, 2000.

45. Lee Rainwater, "Fear and the House-as-Haven in the Lower Class," in J. John Palen and Karl H. Flaming (eds.), *Urban America,* Holt, Rinehart, and Winston, New York, 1972, p. 319.

46. William Julius Wilson, *When Work Disappears,* Knopf, New York, 1996.

CHAPTER 8

The Social Environment of Metro Areas: Strangers, Crowding, Homelessness, and Crime

Hark, hark, the dogs do bark
Beggars are coming to town
Some in rags and some in tags
And some in velvet gowns.
Traditional nursery rhyme

OUTLINE

Introduction
Dealing with Strangers
Codes of Urban Behavior
    Neighboring
    Neighbors and Just Neighbors
Defining Community
Categories of Local Communities
Density and Crowding
    Crowding Research
    Practical Implications
Homelessness
    Characteristics of the Homeless
    Social Problems
    Disappearing SRO Housing
Urban Crime
    Crime and Perceptions of Crime
    Broken Window Theory
    Crime and City Size
    Crime and Male Youth
    Crime and Race
    Crime Variations within Cities
    Crime in the Suburbs
Summary

INTRODUCTION

In the last chapter we saw how Simmel, Wirth, and the classic Chicago School emphasized the disruptive and socially disorganizing aspects of the size, density, and heterogeneity of cities. A century ago Simmel stressed the degree to which one can become alienated in a city of strangers. Although we saw that this was an overstatement, a question still remains: How do people outside their own defended neighborhood or "turf" cope with large numbers of other people whom they do not know? How do we learn to operate in an urban world of strangers in which we are largely anonymous?

In London, social custom dictates queuing while waiting for the bus. © Oli Scarff/Getty Images

Here we look at that question as well as issues of urban crowding, homelessness, and crime.

DEALING WITH STRANGERS

Lyn Lofland suggests that we cope by identifying strangers on the basis of two factors: their *appearance* and their *spatial location* in the city.[1] We examine strangers and they "look us over" in order to place us in space. Our clothing, jewelry, hairstyles, and even how we walk are all external symbols of who we are and our social position. In earlier eras, legal codes and customs often decreed what one could or could not wear. "Clothes make the man" was a statement of social position. Velvet gowns, for example, were reserved for those of rank, while commoners were restricted to plain cloth, as attested to by the nursery rhyme at the chapter opening. In ancient Rome the white toga was a sign of Roman citizenship. Colors also have been used historically to signify position. Royalty in Europe wore royal purple; in China only

the emperor wore yellow. Professions also had their unique garb, such as the academic robes of the professor.

Today professorial robes are worn only on ceremonial occasions such as convocations, but that does not mean we no longer wear distinctive clothing. Not only priests, nurses, bus drivers, and soldiers wear uniforms or have dress codes. We still wear a "uniform," but the signs may be more subtle, such as a designer's symbol on one's shirt. Clothing also indicates social rank. Business executives wear dark-blue Brooks Brothers suits; professors wear a tweed jacket with no tie; and students wear jeans. There are preppy uniforms and subculture uniforms. Even entrepreneurs in start-up software companies wear "uniforms"—anything more formal than a T-shirt automatically marks one as an outsider. On supposedly homogeneous college campuses, business students dress differently from art students, jocks differently from fraternity brothers, and blacks sometimes differently from whites. These dress codes help us identify strangers as being similar to or dissimilar from ourselves.

In large contemporary metro areas where other people are not known to us location also plays a major role. Where we see people in the city helps us identify strangers. Young people on a college campus are assumed to be students, and conservatively dressed middle-aged persons in an office district are assumed to be businesspeople. Passengers in airports are assumed to be of higher status than passengers in the city bus station; suburbanites are assumed to be of higher status than those in slum neighborhoods.

Of course, errors are made because location and dress are not certain signs of a stranger's position. Initial conversation with a stranger is often an attempt to identify socioeconomic status. One often hears the social-class question "What do you do for a living?" or "What's your line of work?" The college-age student's version of this is "Where do you go to school?" What conversation follows, if any, depends on the answer received. Another way of making ourselves more comfortable in public spaces is to turn them into semiprivate spaces. The urban villagers discussed in the last chapter turn street corners, parks, and bars into private places. Throughout the city and suburbs certain groups in effect "own" certain turf and make public space private.

Ray Oldenburg argues that cities are losing their informal gathering places that provide a "home away from home."[2] Bars and beauty parlors and local stores provide a "third place," an informal gathering spot that is not home or work. He says there must be neutral-ground urban places where you can come and go as you please and feel comfortable as more than a faceless consumer. Urban coffee shops such as Starbucks often fill the role of providing "third place" informal public habitats.

CODES OF URBAN BEHAVIOR

The late Erving Goffman pointed out that even supposedly random activity is not without a system. Even such urban activity as walking down a street has a whole set of social rules.[3] People do not just walk down the street at random; rather, there is an intricate code of pedestrian behavior. For example, pedestrian traffic sorts itself into two clear streams. In North America, pedestrians as well as drivers keep to the right, and they "watch their step" by avoiding obstacles such as light posts and other people on the sidewalk. Pedestrians also adjust their speed to avoid collisions; faster traffic moves to the outside lane. Pedestrians expect others to follow the "rules of the road" and negatively sanction those who break the rules by bumping into someone (a nasty look or a "Why don't you watch where you're going?"), and they apologize for their own infractions ("Oh, sorry").

Rules differ by culture. Where auto traffic stays to the left (e.g., England, Japan), local pedestrian traffic does likewise. (Tourists from the United States and Europe often try to move to the right in England, causing general confusion.) In Great Britain one queues up for a bus; in the United States one waits in an informal line. However, in North America people keep mental track of who has waited longest. Those pushing ahead get a dirty look or comment. In Western cultures a man is traditionally expected not to shove ahead of a woman (New York males jumping ahead into a vacant cab is an exception). In Israel, Korea, and China, on the other hand, there is no queuing of any sort. Pushing to the head of the line is accepted. In Great Britain those on escalators leave the left lane open for those who are in a hurry and wish to pass. Signs above the escalators coming up from the underground subways remind people to stay right. Not to do so is considered rude. In North America, on the other hand, couples stand side by side on escalators and to push past is considered rude. Thus, even pedestrian behavior follows generally internalized rules. Coping in the city is made easier by a whole series of informal rules which we follow, but of which we are not normally conscious.

Neighboring

We have seen that city life does not automatically destroy close personal relationships. People are part of social networks. However, neighboring studies do suggest that, on the whole, large-city dwellers know fewer of their neighbors than do residents of smaller places.[4] Most of us, after all, do not live in tight-knit ethnic urban enclaves. Studies of vital urban neighborhoods raise two questions: First, what characteristics distinguish the city dweller who is likely to neighbor? Second, what social conditions tend to turn people who live near each other into real neighbors?

Claude Fischer offers several hypotheses on both these questions.[5] First, he suggests that persons who neighbor are likely to be raising a family. Children engage parents in neighboring activities (e.g., PTA, Girl Scouts), children meeting other neighborhood children facilitate their parents meeting, and having children increases the likelihood that a parent will be home during the day to neighbor. Second, and related to this, neighborly people are likely to be home during the day, perhaps retired or caring for children. Third, neighborly folk tend to be older and more settled. Fourth, neighboring people tend to be homogeneous, to share common race, ethnicity, occupations, interests, and lifestyles. Working-class persons tend to rely more on neighbors than do members of the middle class.

Further research, however, has questioned if having children and having someone home during the day are truly good predictors of neighboring, particularly in central cities.[6] In cities, as opposed to suburbs, neighboring may be seen as helping out in a crisis rather than regular interaction.

Finally, research indicates that the longer one has been a neighborhood resident, the greater the likelihood of neighborhood involvement.[7] Since urbanites are more mobile than those living in other places, and more likely to be working during the day and living in heterogeneous neighborhoods, it is understandable that city dwellers on the whole are less likely to be involved with their neighbors.

Neighbors and Just Neighbors

Fischer, drawing on the existing research, suggests that the social, as opposed to personal, conditions that turn "just neighbors" into "real neighbors" tend to be found less commonly in cities. Three conditions encourage "real" neighboring. The first is functional interdependence. In rural America this involved mutual help with barn raising, harvesting, or meeting joint local needs. A suburban activity that generates social cooperation today is neighborhood crime-watch patrols. A second condition encouraging involvement is the preexistence of other relationships and bonds. Relatives and people who have same-age children, do similar-type work, who share the same ethnicity, and who worship together have already existing bonds that being neighbors simply strengthens. Third, Fischer suggests some people neighbor because they have fewer alternatives. The elderly and mothers with small children may have reduced mobility and thus form relationships with those nearby. Since large-city dwellers are less likely to have such functional interdependence and do have more alternatives, old-fashioned neighboring is less common for them.

On a similar theme Robert Putnam in his much-discussed book, *Bowling Alone,* has suggested that recent decades have witnessed declining membership in civic and social organizations, and an erosion of social capital.[8]

This view, however, may be unduly pessimistic. The U.S. Census Bureau's American Housing Survey indicates that neighborhood pride remains alive and well.[9] Moreover, satisfaction with neighborhood life cuts across owners and renters in all regions. Homeowners expressed particularly high neighborhood satisfaction levels.

DEFINING COMMUNITY

The term *community* has been used for many years but not really defined. Unfortunately, there is no single or even most common usage. Anthropologists dealing with localized semi-isolated populations generally have found the concept of community more useful than do sociologists researching contemporary urban areas, where the boundaries between distinct groups or patterns of activities are often blurred. Today the term *community* has lost much of its descriptive preciseness and efficiency. It is applied arbitrarily to everything from one block in a neighborhood to those who use Facebook to the international community. Community has become an elastic social and theoretical concept holding diverse meanings.[10]

Contemporary urbanites can have "community without propinquity" (nearness). On the other hand, *community,* as used by ecologists, is usually defined as a territorially localized population that is interdependent with regard to daily needs. This usage implies a territorial unit, as opposed to other uses of the term such as "community of scholars" or "religious community," or "Internet community." *Community* as used by most sociologists refers to a spatial or territorial unit.[11] Communities provide a link between the family and primary group and the larger society. Communities edit and interpret reality on the local level so it seems manageable to community members.

In the writings of the Chicago School, the term *community* was often a synonym for urban neighborhood. However, two of the most important pre–World War II community studies focused on small cities as the unit of analysis. Robert and Helen Lynd's famous *Middletown* and *Middletown in Transition* studies focused on the transformation of life in Middletown (Muncie, Indiana) as a result of absorption into an industrially oriented community.[12] The Lynds documented the decline of control by the community over its own destiny. However, in spite of the economic shocks of the depression, Middletown residents did not become radicalized, but retained complacency and belief in traditional values. A restudy done 50 years later in the 1970s found that, to a remarkable degree, Middletown's values were unaffected by the decades.[13] While the city was no longer economically in control of its own destiny and was heavily beholden to the federal government, the traditional values and normative structure still persisted. A more recent update of life in Middletown (and America in general) with comparisons to earlier periods in Middletown can be found in Caplow's *The First Measured Century.*[14]

Another classic community study, W. Lloyd Warner's *Yankee City* (Newburyport, Massachusetts), dealt with the degree to which the movement from craft work by individuals to mass industrial production led to a breakdown of a sense of community.[15] Local power and control, Warner suggested, had gone from ownership and control by local family-owned firms to large outside corporations. Accompanying this, he also suggested that the social structure became more rigid and there was decreased social mobility among workers. The historical accuracy of the latter points, however, has been strongly challenged.

There is currently no consensus on the significance of community in modern social life. Some, such as Suzanne Keller and Claude Fischer, suggest that urbanites engage in activities on the basis of interest rather than propinquity, and that today neighborhood serves only minimal functions.[16] One might borrow eggs or a cup of sugar from neighbors or call on them in an emergency, but for everyday life, local attachments are seen as being quite limited. Those taking this view would agree with Roland Warren that the strengthening ties to extra community systems orient them in important and clearly definable ways toward larger systems outside the community. The result is that the model of a spatially delineated, relatively independent, and self-sufficient community is less and less relevant to the modern scene.[17] Larger networks for some have made the spatial unit of the neighborhood no longer important.[18] Others see urban neighborhoods continuing to play a sometimes significant, if changing, role.[19]

CATEGORIES OF LOCAL COMMUNITIES

A number of types of local communities have been defined in the professional literature, among them these:

1. The defended neighborhood.
2. The community of limited liability.
3. The expanded community of limited liability.
4. The contrived or conscious community.[20]

The *defended neighborhood* is an area that residents feel is their turf.[21] "Functionally, the defended neighborhood can be conceived of as the smallest spatial unit within which co-residents assume a relative degree of security on the streets as compared to adjacent areas."[22] The defended neighborhood thus is the place where people feel safe and secure. As such, it may or may not have a name or be recognized by government. Those within the defended neighborhood assume a common residential identification and identity.

The *community of limited liability* was first described by Morris Janowitz and later elaborated on by Scott Greer.[23] The concept of the community of limited liability emphasizes the voluntary and limited involvement of residents in the local community. The amount of emotional investment in the area, or investment of time or resources, is dependent on the degree to which the community meets the needs of individuals. If the needs are not met, the individual might withdraw psychologically and socially, if not physically. Voluntary organizations play important roles in defining and defending issues common to communities of limited liability. Communities of limited liability usually have names and boundaries that are recognized by local planning agencies and government. Local organizations, and particularly the local community press, have a vested interest in maintaining the identity and boundaries of the area. The community of limited liability thus is defined by commercial interests and government agencies more than by internal community awareness, as is the defended neighborhood.

The *expanded community of limited liability* is more fragmented and diffuse than the community of limited liability. It is a larger area composed of multiple communities. The boundaries of such an area usually are defined by external or government institutions. The expanded community may take in whole sections of the city, such as the east side or the north side. As such, it has little real cohesion as an actual unit.

The *contrived or conscious community* is an area—new or developing—in which builders, financiers, public agencies, and sometimes residents set out consciously to create a community image. Boundaries are clearly laid out, and the housing in the area may even be identical—e.g., all apartments or all townhouses or all public housing. The name of the area is usually given by the builder rather than emerging from the community. Conscious communities tend to be more homogeneous than other communities. Residents in such developments may all be young singles, families with children, or retired elderly. Ethnic and racial conformity, and similarity of social class, are also more common in both urban and suburban conscious communities. Some conscious communities are even gated.

DENSITY AND CROWDING

The Chicago School saw high urban rates of density as a social problem. In fact, urban crowding and high density have long been seen as the cause of social pathology. Historically, high density (the number of people per acre, block, or other geographical unit) and crowding (the number of people per room, usually in housing) have been cited as a cause of epidemics, contagion, crime, and moral degradation.[24] The engravings of Hogarth, the novels of Dickens, and primitive health statistics all tell the same unfortunate tale—high density means disorganization and disease. As graphically expressed by Charles Dickens in *Oliver Twist,*

> They walked on, for some time, through the most crowded and densely inhabited part of the town; and then, striking down a narrow street more dirty and miserable than any they had yet passed through, paused to look for the house which was the object of their search. The houses on either side were high and large, but very old, and tenanted by people of the poorest class: as their neglected appearance would have sufficiently denoted, without the concurrent testimony afforded by the squalid looks of the men and women who, with folded arms and bodies

half doubled, occasionally skulked along. A great many of the tenements had shopfronts; but these were fast closed, and mouldering away; only the upper rooms being inhabited. Some houses which had become insecure from age and decay, were prevented from falling into the street, by huge beams of wood reared against the walls, and firmly planted in the road; but even these crazy dens seemed to have been selected as the nightly haunts of some houseless wretches, for many of the rough boards which supplied the place of door and window, were wrenched from their positions, to afford an aperture wide enough for the passage of a human body. The kennel was stagnant and filthy. The very rats, which here and there lay putrefying in its rottenness, were hideous with famine.[25]

Almost every social evil—air pollution, the loss of community, the lack of response of neighbors to cries for help—has been attributed to urban density and overcrowding.[26]

Crowding Research

Experimental animal studies tend to support the view that high density and crowding produce a long list of physical and behavioral pathologies. In fact we probably know more about the behavior of rats under conditions of crowding than we do about that of city dwellers. John Calhoun's now famous article "Population Density and Social Pathology" indicates that in experiments with Norway rats, pathological states develop under conditions of crowding even when there is an abundance of food and freedom from disease and predators.[27] In Calhoun's experiment, even when all the above needs of the rats were met, a behavioral sink or downward spiral developed in which infant mortality increased, females didn't build proper nests or carry infants to term, and homosexuality and even cannibalism occurred. When the experiment was terminated, the rat population was well on the way to extinction.

Unfortunately, there is a tendency to try to transfer findings from animal studies to human populations. Sometimes there is even an assumption that what holds for Norway rats automatically applies to humans. For example, one writer suggests:

> The implications of animal and human studies are clearcut. Just as the offspring of frustrated mother rats, part of whose pregnancy was spent trapped in problem boxes with no exits, carried an emotional disturbance throughout their own lives, so too many children of frustrated human mothers, trapped by urban slums, show behavioral manifestations of emotional disturbance.[28]

This analogy repeats the "commonsense" view of the effects of density and crowding.

The problem is that the commonsense view is both simplistic and inaccurate. A considerable body of sociological and psychological research on density indicates that it does *not* have any clear and definite association with human pathology.[29] Density research is a classic case: What everyone "knows to be true" is simply not supported by the data. The effects of interior household crowding on social relationships and mental health also are very limited.[30]

What is clear is that one's social background and experience play a major role in how "high density" is defined. Upper-middle-class populations, for example, have been socialized to view crowding as a problem, and personal space as natural and necessary. Community studies of working-class populations indicate, on the other hand, that residents of city neighborhoods often view high density as a positive sign of community involvement and vitality rather than an indication of social disorganization.[31] Contact with others is viewed positively, as a sign of belonging, rather than negatively, as a sign of crowding. Inner-city youngsters from such areas are more comfortable being with others than being alone. Gans reports how social workers in the West End of Boston were forced to abandon a summer program that gave inner-city boys a chance to spend a vacation exploring nature at an unpopulated section of Cape Cod.[32] The boys could not understand why anyone would want to

On the fifth anniversary of Hurricane Katrina, New Orleans city neighborhoods were still in disarray. Here, a slab of a destroyed home is shown next to a newly constructed home in the "Make It Right" housing complex in the Lower 9th Ward across from the levee that broke after Hurricane Katrina hit. "Make It Right" is a humanitarian project of actor Brad Pitt that provides sustainable, affordable housing designed by world-class architects. Even though these homes offer a bright spot, the surrounding area is still full of blight. Adding insult to injury, the April 2010 BP oil spill in the Gulf of Mexico affected some of the same areas and depleted local resources for recovery even further. © Julie Dermansky/Corbis

spend time in such a lonely spot. They were accustomed to, and thrived on, crowded and noisy street life. The boys wanted to be where the action was. They were emotionally uncomfortable with wide vistas and open unused space.

Similarly, while much of the population of crowded and noisy Shanghai, Hong Kong, and Singapore may want larger apartments, they do not want to be isolated or set apart from the crowd. (While living in Singapore, I found myself craving empty, quiet spaces. By contrast, a student of mine from Singapore found it very difficult to adjust to the non-urban University of Virginia. She found the open space disorienting and longed for high buildings, concrete sidewalks, and urban noise.) In North America, some people choose a camping vacation of backpacking into the wilderness, miles from anyone, while others prefer to settle for weeks in commercial RV campgrounds where the density is higher than in city slums.

In North America, middle-class and working-class populations may also vary in how they orient themselves to a common spatial feature, such as streets. For working-class urban groups, much daily activity takes place in the streets; streets are seen as living space, a place to talk and gather with others in the neighborhood. Streets serve a vital social function. Upper-middle-class groups, on the other hand, are far less likely to see streets as performing a social function. In their view streets are corridors to be used to travel from place to place, and they think people should be kept off the streets, lest they interfere with rapid movement. Today, the New Urbanism housing movement, to be discussed in Chapter 13, seeks to restore streets to their earlier social role.

Thus, contrary to the common assumption, density or crowding does not necessarily have either a negative or positive impact on urban life. It all depends on how the level of crowding is socially defined. Urban densities, for example, have been decreasing for 100 years, but there has been no corresponding decrease in urban social problems. Freedman suggests that the effect of density and crowding is to "intensify the individual's typical reactions to the situation."[33] Thus, being crowded with friends may produce positive reactions, although the same degree of crowding with those one dislikes may produce negative reactions. People do not respond to density or crowding in an automatic or uniform way.

Practical Implications

For 25 years William H. Whyte examined with telephoto camera and recorder what makes some urban spaces "work," while others clearly do not. Why are some areas socially popular while other planned places go unused?[34] What he discovered is that what most attracts people is other people. Rather than trying to escape crowds, people move toward areas of highest per-person density. Observing from hidden perches, researchers mapped location and duration of conversations. Whyte discovered that most take place "right smack in the middle of the pedestrian traffic stream."[35] Moreover, people who begin conversations on the fringe drift into the traffic flow, not out of it.

A practical consequence of this is that street musicians and sidewalk vendors—those whom store merchants, police, and city hall work so hard to remove—actually contribute to the social and economic vitality of a streetscape. On the other hand, so-called incentive zoning, which allowed developers to add extra stories to skyscrapers if they provided ground-level setbacks with parks or plazas, often resulted simply in the creation of dull unused zones. Sunken plazas turned out to be particularly little used.

Whyte's research led to New York City's making three important changes in its commercial zoning that have helped restore lively (and safe) street life. First, every new building must, on the street level, have retail shops (no blank walls or huge, dull lobbies). Second, there must be access to the street-level shops from the street (no turning your back on the street). Third, street-level windows must be transparent (to avoid the blank-wall-facing-the-street effect). These relatively minor changes have made the newer buildings more livable than those built in the 1960s and 1970s, and the streetscapes friendlier than they were.

Whyte argued against city planners' or architects' "ideal" streetscapes. As he pronounced, "It's all in such goddam good taste! You need a touch of glitz. You need something like Trump Tower."[36] We have learned that urban sociologists can discover what makes cities livable, but sometimes the answers are counter to the sterile versions officials might see as an ideal or model cityscape.

HOMELESSNESS

The number of homeless goes up and down with the economy. It is estimated that one in 200 were homeless at some time during 2010.[37] There was also an increase in families in shelters due to the loss of jobs and housing during the Great Recession.

Each year as colder weather approaches, the media feature stories on the most disadvantaged of all urban populations, the homeless. Data about the homeless are subject to dispute, basically for two reasons. First, the homeless are a transient demographic population about whom data are both difficult to obtain and often unreliable. Second, homelessness is a highly politicized issue. For example, the Washington-based Community for Creative Non-Violence, an advocacy group for the homeless, has estimated that there are at least 2 million homeless people nationwide. This figure is widely quoted in the media but is based on estimates by advocates, not on research. What is generally agreed upon is that today's shelters have far too few beds to accommodate all of

Street people in Paris are provided tents for sleeping on the street. Francois Mori/AP Images

those in need, and that life on the street can be truly life threatening.

Studies traditionally have put the number of homeless in the 400,000 to 500,000 range. Jencks estimated the number of homeless at approximately 400,000 while Rossi, in a solid study estimated the number of homeless on a given night at roughly half a million persons.[38] A 2000 report by the Department of Housing and Urban Development (HUD), based on surveys and interviews with homeless assistance providers, came up with similar figures.[39]

However, HUD in 2007 released the most detailed and thorough major study ever done of homelessness. HUD estimated the number of persons in shelters each night at 335,000, and the total number in shelters, transitional housing, or on the street any night as 754,000 persons.[40] Given the quality of this study the larger numbers have to be considered definitive.

Characteristics of the Homeless

Who is homeless has changed over the decades. Forty years ago, the homeless population was heavily made up of older, possibly alcoholic, skid-row men with acute personal problems.[41] Then, the stereotype of the skid-row wino was supplanted by that of the bag lady who had been deinstitutionalized from a psychiatric hospital and left to pick through refuse bins.[42] A more recent stereotype of who is on the streets is the image of a delusional, drug-taking panhandler.

The HUD reports give a clearer picture of the characteristics of the contemporary homeless. Some 66 percent of the homeless are single (compared to 15 percent in the total population), 68 percent are male, 80 percent are aged 25 to 54, 28 percent have less than a high school education, and 23 percent are veterans.[43] Racially, blacks are overrepresented, with

41 percent of those on the street being white, 40 percent black, 11 percent Hispanic, and 9 percent other. Males on the street are more likely to be white, while homeless families are more likely to be headed by women.

During the recession the proportion of families who are homeless increased. One-third of the homeless are children. In New York City more than 13,000 children spend their nights in shelters.[44] Homeless families, particularly two-parent families and employed people are part of the less visible hidden homeless problem. Homeless families' problems are largely economic, but there is special concern over homeless females on the street who are IV drug users. The combination of IV drug use and unsafe sex makes AIDS infection a major health concern. Three-quarters of female AIDS infection comes from IV drug usage. Child abuse or child abandonment also is a serious problem.

Social Problems

A frequently heard statement among advocates for the homeless is that the homeless are "just like you and me," except for having the bad luck of being homeless. This statement has the good intention of invoking sympathy and support for the homeless, but it is *not* accurate. Most homeless have high levels of social disabilities. Four of 10 street people admit to having spent time in jail. The federal HUD figures are probably the most reliable. They report that 62 percent of the homeless have problems with alcohol, 58 percent of the homeless have drug abuse problems, and 57 percent have mental-health problems.[45] In terms of official records, more than four of five have been in a mental hospital or detoxification unit, have been convicted by the courts, or receive clinically high scores on the psychotic thinking scale.[46]

What the above picture indicates is that those who end up on the streets often have very high levels of social disabilities. Many have multiple personality problems. Most grew up in problem families or foster care. Social isola-

tion is endemic, with 6 in 10 never having married and most of the remainder being separated or divorced. Strained or very minimal relations with family and relatives is the usual pattern. Some who work with the homeless claim that academics often downplay the seriousness of street people's problems in an attempt to not "blame the victim."[47]

What is beyond dispute is that the homeless are marginalized in a North American urban society that has little interest in providing them the broad-based (and expensive) treatments they require. It is far easier and cheaper simply to ignore them. The deindustrialization of the economy, the deinstitutionalization of the mentally ill, and the dismemberment of urban welfare systems have left the homeless without even the marginal supports of decades past.

Public attitudes toward, and tolerance of, the homeless, and especially homeless panhandlers, has hardened during the last decade. Increasingly, the homeless are viewed by many citizens not as victims, but as a threat to public order. Homeless shelters have had to develop strict policies to deal with the major behavior problems of drug usage and fighting in the shelters. Crack or crystal meth use is a particular problem for shelters since it makes users aggressive and violent. Those who violate shelter policies are expelled from the shelters. Tough anti-vagrancy measures also have been taken in some of the previously most tolerant cities. New York has gotten tough with aggressive subway panhandlers and squeegee men who aggressively offer to clean car windshields for money. Once-liberal Seattle has made it illegal to sit on downtown public sidewalks during business hours and can ban from public parks those found sleeping in them. In Atlanta a person asking more than twice for money can be arrested, and tolerant San Francisco now arrests those urinating in public and tickets people for "camping in public" (sleeping in a public park or in a doorway). In Orlando, in 2006, after a law banning panhandling was struck down, a ordinance was passed to stop feeding programs for the homeless by making it illegal to feed more than 25 people in public parks.[48] Las Vegas in 2006 went even further by criminalizing giving food to even a single transient in any city park. Not surprisingly, both these ordinances are being challenged in the courts. However, what they represent is a decreasing tolerance for street people, especially those seen as a public nuisance.

Disappearing SRO Housing

For some of the homeless, being on the street is simply the result of the decrease in marginal, but affordable housing. In the past many of the economically marginal, who did not live in family units, lived in single-room-occupancy (SRO) residential hotels. However, the number of SRO units has sharply decreased by over 80 percent during the last two decades. Central city buildings frequently were either torn down, or converted into more expensive condo units. Making the problem worse was the fact that at the same time private SRO units were disappearing, federal funding for low-cost housing was being severely decreased. During the Reagan and senior Bush years (1980 to 1992), federally subsidized programs were cut a massive 70 percent. The result is that today the economically marginal have fewer places to live than they did twenty-five years ago.

However, there are some bright spots. Some homeless have not only survived on the street, but have created their own alternative social communities.[49] Also, cities are beginning to build at least a limited number of new or renovated SRO residential hotels. These so-called supportive SROs are generally run by community development corporations and other nonprofit organizations. They provide a clean room but tolerate no drug or alcohol use. In addition to decent housing, the supportive SROs offer a structured support system that often includes biweekly medical clinics, alcohol and drug treatment, and job counseling. And they seem to be working. Moreover, they are relatively inexpen-

sive to operate. Even with all renovation and social service costs included, they cost one-fifth the cost of incarceration and just over half of what it costs to warehouse someone in a shelter.[50]

There is a new realism as to the possibility of quick-fix answers to homelessness. To the extent that most homelessness is the result of a whole web of problems, there may not be "a solution" to homelessness any more than there is "a cause." A primary need is for more affordable low-cost SRO housing, but in addition there is a need for substance-abuse treatment, education, job training, medical care, and counseling to deal with an interrelated complex of problems.

In today's political and social climate there is little chance of such comprehensive programs being implemented on a sufficient scale to make a real impact. Thus, homelessness will remain a North American disgrace.

URBAN CRIME

It is impossible to discuss the contemporary urban environment without talking about crime. In any discussion of what is happening in American cities the topic of crime is sure to be near the top of the list. Surveys show that most Americans worry about crime. Fears about personal safety remain for urban residents in general and inner-city residents in particular. People are afraid of both urban violence and the unpredictability of such violence. Some of these fears are fed by media attention to high-profile events such as school shootings and the so-called "reality-based" crime shows on TV. Whatever the cause, it is generally assumed that living in the city means living with crime, that you can't have one without the other.

Crime and Perceptions of Crime

Crime, however, is a topic upon which people's perceptions of what is happening and the reality of what is actually happening differ considerably. The reality is that Department of Justice statistics show urban crime between 1993 and 2010 experienced not increases but *sharp declines*.[51] The declines were especially great for serious crimes. The Uniform Crime Report (UCR)—which is data collected by the FBI about crimes known to the police—indicates continued declines in all crime categories.[52] The National Crime Victimization Survey (NCVS), which is a yearly survey of 134,000 people in 77,200 households about their victimization from crime, showed similar sharp drops in both violent and property crimes. Crime in 2008 was at a thirty year low. Canada showed similar declines in violent and property crimes.

In 2005 and 2006, murder and robberies increased. The murder rate in large cities increased 10 percent between 2004 and 2006.[53] Philadelphia, Houston, Cleveland, Detroit, and Las Vegas saw particularly high jumps. Most criminal-justice experts suggest that crime-rate increases largely reflect two factors. First, there developed some complacency in fighting crime following years of decreasing rates. Second, the Bush administration's slashing of federal funds for local policing meant there were fewer police on the street. As the number of police decreases, crime tends to increase. Since 2006 crime rates have again been decreasing.

Overall what the variations in urban crime rates tell us is that crime and cities do *not* necessarily go together. Over the past 25 years urban crime rates have been both quite high, and quite low. City size and crime are not directly related.

Broken Windows Theory

The two-decade long decline in crime rates in large cities usually is attributed to the combination of effective computer-based community policing, the decline of crack cocaine markets, shrinking of the teenage population (young adults commit most crimes), and stiffer sentencing for crimes of violence. Many also give credit for the crime decline to the application of community policing based on the "broken windows theory" developed by the social scientists James Q. Wilson and George Kelling.[54]

The broken windows theory suggests the best way to control crime is to prevent it, and the best way to prevent crime is not by concentrating police efforts on solving major crimes, but focusing on preventing minor quality-of-life offenses such as drinking in public and public vandalism. This counter-intuitive approach suggests that it is the feeling of public order that acts to dent criminal behavior. The broken windows theory says that when one window is broken in an abandoned building soon after all the windows become broken—that is, public disorder leads to a breakdown of public order. The essence of broken windows theory is that neighborhood disorder and decay, if left unchecked, combined with public drinking and vagrancy, signal to criminals that no one is watching, and crime can take place. The theory argues that people fear a sense of disorder, and by creating a sense of order in a neighborhood crime can be prevented.

The broken windows theory was first applied on a large scale in New York where cops were put back walking beats on the street, and miscreants arrested for minor offences such as public drinking. It turned out that many of those stopped for minor offenses were carrying illegal weapons or flouting existing arrest warrants. The application of zero-tolerance policies, together with using computers to check suspects and to target areas of emerging crime, generally is credited with much of New York's drop in crime.[55] However, some argue that other factors, such as the end of murderous turf wars among crack dealers, were of more importance.[56]

Also the good news about lower crime rates very much does not mean that America is now a crime-free Eden. Far from it. The United States still has the highest crime rate of any developed nation, excluding Russia. Some 16,000 Americans die each year as victims of homicide, and more than 15,000 of these deaths are caused by handguns. There are now over 200 million handguns in America. By comparison,

L. A. gang members with guns flashing signs. In Los Angeles since adopting community policing in 2003, gang-related murders have dropped sharply. © A. Ramey/PhotoEdit

in Canada, where handguns are banned except for sport, there are fewer than 200 yearly handgun deaths.

It also should be noted that crime-statistics data have many problems. The Uniform Crime Reports are far from uniform in coverage since only crimes known to the police are reported. This means that while virtually all homicides are reported, many burglaries and larcenies are not. Rape is particularly underreported. In order to get better data on the actual number of offenses, the Justice Department carries out a National Crime Victimization Survey (NCVS), which, as noted previously, gets its data from interviews with roughly 134,000 people living in 70,000 randomly selected households nationwide. The National Crime Victimization Survey reports that only about one-third of all crimes are actually reported to the police. Roughly half of all violent crimes are reported, but only slightly more than one-quarter of all thefts, and only one-fifth of all rapes. About half the violent crimes are committed by someone the victim knew. The National Crime Victimization Survey shows the rate of reported crimes is increasing. The NCVS shows the same pattern of declining crime levels over the last decades as does the Uniform Crime Report.

Crime and City Size

The belief that the larger the city, the higher the crime rate is an urban myth. While we often think of crime and large cities going together, high rates of urban crime and violence have not always been associated. Large-city life *per se* doesn't cause crime. During the 1940s and 1950s, for example, New York City had a murder rate that fluctuated around 50 homicides a year. New York, with 7.5 million people in 1942, had only 44 homicides, and that included all mob hits, street murders, and domestic homicides. By contrast 40 years later, in 1994, New York had more murders of cabbies than the total of all murders in the city in 1944. New York's murder rate peaked at 2,420 in 1993. In 2007, it was 801, and in 2008, 836.[57] This is very low for the U.S., although still high by international standards.

The United States' homicide rate is higher than that of other developed countries. It is 17 times that of equally urban Japan, and 10 times that of France, or heavily urban Germany. Most cities in developing countries are fairly safe, with murder rates more like those of New York in the 1950s. The exceptions are some Latin American and sub-Saharan African cities. Most cities elsewhere in the world are safer than those in the United States.

Size does not mean high crime. A decade and a half ago New York was a media example of out-of-control urban crime. Today New York is one of the safest cities in the nation with crime rates lower than those of more than 140 other American cities. Today, New York has much less street crime than London. The general belief is that the largest cities have the highest crime rates, but the reality is that cities of over a million average lower crime rates than do cities of between 100,000 and 1 million persons. The highest crime rates by a good margin are found in cities of 250,000 to 500,000 population.

Crime and Male Youth

Crime is an activity of the young. Forty-five percent of all crimes, except murder, are committed by people under 18, and three-quarters are committed by those under 25. The most likely age for being arrested is 16; 15, 17, and 18 are the next most likely ages. (White-collar crimes that require training or skill, such as embezzlement, investment fraud, and counterfeiting, are most likely to be committed by older persons.) Crime is also still largely a male activity, with about 80 percent of all arrests and 90 percent of arrests for violent crimes being males. Disputes that once resulted in fistfights now may lead to gunfire. The number of juvenile homicide offenders almost tripled between 1985 and 1994, and gun-related murders of juveniles increased fourfold. In 1995 the Office of Juvenile Justice

and Delinquency predicted that the number of juvenile offenders would double by 2010.[58] Fortunately, that didn't happen, and since 1995 juvenile crime rates, excepting gang-related, have been decreasing rather than increasing. However, even if the crime "rates" stay at the current level, some increases in the "number" of crimes could occur since the number of juveniles in the population will increase 31 percent this decade.

Crime and Race

Historically, poor newcomer groups to the city, especially those who have suffered discrimination, have used crime as an alternate route to social mobility. The changing ethnic and racial composition of those committing crimes roughly reflects changes in the social and economic position of various American minorities. Thus, by the early 20th century Yankee gangs were being replaced by Irish and Jewish gangs. They in turn were replaced by Italians, who in turn were replaced by African Americans, and most recently Colombians, Mexicans, Asians, and Russians.

Crime and race are linked in many people's minds—the standard image is of black males preying on middle-class whites. The reality is that whites mostly commit crimes against whites and blacks against blacks. The most common crime in large cities is black-on-black crime. Some 84 percent of violent crimes committed by blacks have black victims. According to the Gallup poll, blacks feel less secure than whites, both when walking the streets and when in their homes. Blacks are more fearful of crime than are whites. And they have reason for their fears. Blacks, even in suburbs, are more exposed to property, and especially violent, crime.[59] Robbery is the only largely interracial crime, with 45 percent involving a black offender (almost always a young male) and a white victim (usually a middle-aged white male).

Blacks are more than five times as likely to be homicide victims as are whites. Since 1989

Box 8.1   Street Etiquette

In *Streetwise,* Elijah Anderson discusses the norms or rules of street conduct or street etiquette local people use to avoid conflict.* This excerpt discusses how adults living in the Philadelphia neighborhood he calls Village-Norton respond to young males.

> The residents of the area, including black men themselves, are likely to defer to unknown black males, who move convincingly through the area as though they "run it," exuding a sense of ownership. They are easily symbolically perceived as inserting themselves into any available social space, pressing against those who might challenge them. The young black males, the "big winners" of these little competitions, seem to feel very comfortable as they swagger confidently along. Their looks, their easy smiles, and their spontaneous laughter, singing, cursing, and talk about the intimate details of their lives, which can be followed from across the street, all convey the impression of little concern for other pedestrians. The other pedestrians, however, are very concerned about them. . . .
>
> Because public interactions generally matter for only a few crucial seconds, people are conditioned to rapid scrutiny of the looks, speech, public behavior, gender, and color of those sharing the environment. . . . The central strategy in maintaining safety of the streets is to avoid strange black males. The public awareness is color-coded: white skin denotes civility, law abidingness, and trustworthiness, while black skin is strongly associated with poverty, crime, incivility, and distrust. Thus an unknown young black man must be readily deferred to. . . . Middle-income blacks in the Village, who also are among the "haves," often share a victim mentality with middle-income whites and appear just as distrustful of black strangers. Believing they are immune to the charge of racism, Village blacks make some of the same remarks as whites do, sometimes voicing even more incisive observations concerning "street blacks" and black criminality. . . .

*Elijah Anderson, *Streetwise: Race, Class, and Change in an Urban Community,* University of Chicago Press, Chicago, 1990.

---

each year there have been more black homicide victims than white victims. African Americans are 12 percent of the population, but they make up just over half the homicide victims and 56 percent of the offenders. Data from the National Center for Health Statistics show black-on-black homicide to be the leading cause of death among black men aged 16 to 34. With the declining overall crime rate, male African American victimization rates have dropped 50 percent in recent years, but they are still unreasonably high. Today one of every 68 black males can expect to be murdered during the course of a lifetime.[60]

In addition to having the highest victim rate, African American males also have the highest probability of being an offender. In 1996, for example, black males aged 14 to 24 were just over 1 percent of the population, but they were 17 percent of the homicide victims and 30 percent of those convicted of murder.[61] Overall, black males account for half of those arrested for violent crimes, just over half of those arrested for murder and non-negligent manslaughter, and more than half of those arrested for forcible rape.[62] Some 25 percent more young black men now are in prison than are in college.[63] There is a clear crisis when Justice Department figures show one-third of young black males aged 20 to 29 in prison, on probation, or on parole.

This often leads to racial profiling where young, non-criminal black men are routinely stopped and automatically viewed with suspicion. Young black males feel they are frequently stopped for DWB ("driving while black"). As box 8.1 indicates, uncertainty and caution about the intentions of young urban males have become urban characteristics.[64] African Americans have low arrest rates for white-collar crimes such as tax evasion, fraud, and embezzlement. This largely reflects occupational discrimination, which historically kept blacks out of positions where large funds are controlled. A reasonable hypothesis would be that as black income and occupational levels increase, street crime by blacks will decline and white-collar crime will increase.

Crime Variations within Cities

Crime rates within urban areas generally reflect Burgess's hypothesis insofar as crime rates tend to be highest in central-city neighborhoods and to decrease as one moves toward the periphery. Research done by the Chicago School during the first half of the 20th century also demonstrated a high concentration of criminal activity in the central city—a phenomenon they attributed to the "social disorganization" of such areas, as typified by high poverty and welfare rates, low levels of education, broken homes, and other social ills.[65] Since that time, the concept of social disorganization has been superseded by other less value-laden explanations, but the pattern of decreasing street crime rates as one moves toward the urban periphery has been confirmed. White-collar crime, such as investment fraud, is more concentrated in upper-class suburban populations.

The pattern of higher crime rates being found in inner-city areas has held while the occupants, and even the physical look, of the area have changed completely. This consistency does not mean that these neighborhoods or their locations somehow create crime. Rather, it suggests that the inhabitants of these areas—whether European immigrants at the turn of the century, blacks after World War II, or Mexicans and other Latinos today—have been subject to the same pressures. An excellent study of Latino gangs by Sanchez Jankowski shows that gangs still occupy territorial boundaries and provide an organizational framework for their members.[66]

As Chapter 7: Urban Lifestyles pointed out, not all central-city neighborhoods have gone through the cycle of invasion and reinvasion by new groups—a cycle which hinders the development of social control by family, peers, and neighbors. Inner-city areas that have not been invaded by disadvantaged newcomers are often among the most stable, low-crime areas in the city.

Crime in the Suburbs

One of the more commonly heard explanations for fleeing cities is higher urban crime. The assumption is that suburbs are relatively crime-free. This assumption is no longer true. As newspaper stories document, crime rates in the suburbs are increasing. Nor are suburbs immune from violent crime. The Columbine High School murders occurred in an upper-middle-class suburb. Still, suburban crime rates are one-third those of the nation's cities.[67] Suburban crime tends to be less violent than city crime. Someone living in the city is more likely to be murdered and more likely to be robbed than a suburban resident. The most frequently reported single crime in suburbs is bicycle theft—a problem if it is your expensive trail bike that is stolen, but not equivalent to being mugged or shot.

Moreover, within the suburbs, crime is not randomly distributed, but rather it is concentrated in lower-income suburbs whose characteristics most closely approximate the central city. Older, inner-ring suburbs abutting the central city generally have higher rates than outlying areas. Around Chicago, 10 suburbs accounting for 15 percent of the suburban population account for 40 percent of the murder and a majority of the armed robberies, assaults, and rapes. These suburbs have burglary rates three times as high as the 10 richest suburbs of Chicago, indicating that "Them that hasn't, gets taken." High-crime suburbs tend to have low-income or minority residents. Higher crime rates are also found in suburbs having places that attract crime, such as large shopping centers and business parks. Automobile theft is the most common crime at malls, but robbery and even rape also occur. It is hard to imagine a better location than a large parking lot for an auto thief to steal an auto for parts or to ship abroad for sale.

Affluent suburbs keep crime rates down by restricting certain economic activities and populations (fewer minority, poor, and unemployed). Thus, in effect, they deflect crime to lower-status areas. Upper-income residential areas are particularly able to control street crime by restricting the influx of outsiders.[68] Increasingly, upper-income communities are even physically gated.

SUMMARY

Cities are filled with strangers, but we cope by identifying people by their dress and location. There are also clear codes of behavior or informal rules that govern urban behavior. People are part of social networks, and those who neighbor are likely to share common traits, such as ethnicity or religion, and have other bonds, such as young children.

There is no consensus on either the definition of *community* or its significance for modern life. For the Chicago School sociologists, *community* was often a synonym for "urban neighborhood." The Middletown study of Muncie, Indiana, has had numerous follow-ups for three-quarters of a century. Communities can be categorized as either defended communities, communities of limited liability, expanded communities of limited liability, or contrived and/or conscious communities.

Density and crowding have long been commonly thought to be a major cause of negative social behavior, but research indicates little relationship between crowding and social behavior. Problems that occur in controlled animal studies do not occur in real-life studies of humans. People socially define what they consider crowding.

New research released by HUD in 2007 suggests homelessness in the United States affects 754,000 persons a night. Males are more likely to be homeless than females, and roughly a third of the homeless are children. More than half of the adult homeless have serious mental problems, have spent time in prison, and/or have drug abuse and/or alcohol problems. Minorities are overrepresented among the homeless. The homeless are likely to be single, have high rates of social disabilities, and be isolated from family members. Recent years have seen a decrease in single-room-occupancy (SRO) housing availability, and some homelessness is simply due to lack of such housing. City governments are becoming less tolerant of panhandling and stricter in the enforcement of vagrancy and panhandling laws. Public-use spaces, such as parks and plazas, are being reclaimed.

Urban areas have not always had high crime rates, and urban crime rates sharply decreased between 1992 and 2008. New York today is a relatively safe city with a crime rate lower than most other American cities. Violent crime is largely committed by young males. African American males have both the highest probability of being a crime offender and of being a crime victim. Suburban crime rates are increasing, but suburban crime is overwhelmingly property crime. Suburbs still have less violent crime than do cities.

REVIEW QUESTIONS

1. What two factors does Lyn Lofland suggest we use when identifying strangers in metro areas?

2. What is the distinction between "neighbors" and "just neighbors?"

3. What is meant by "community of limited liability?"

4. What are the social effects of density and crowding?

5. How do the popular and social science views of the effects of crowding differ?

6. How have the numbers of the homeless changed over the last few decades?

7. Who is homeless and what are the demographic characteristics of the homeless?

8. What have been the patterns over the last decade regarding urban crime rates?

9. What is the relationship between city size and city crime rates?

10. What is the broken windows theory, and how does it suggest we combat crime?

NOTES

1. Lyn Lofland, *A World of Strangers*, Basic Books, New York, 1973.

2. Ray Oldenburg, *The Great Good Place: Cafes, Coffee Shops, Community Centers, Beauty Parlors, General Stores, Bars, Hangouts and How They Get You Through the Day*, Paragon House, New York, 1989.

3. Erving Goffman, *Relations in Public*, Basic Books, New York, 1971.

4. Claude S. Fischer, *The Urban Experience*, 2nd ed., Harcourt Brace Jovanovich, New York, 1984.

5. Ibid., pp. 130–31.

6. Carol J. Silverman, "Neighboring and Urbanism: Commonality versus Friendship," *Urban Affairs Quarterly* 22:312–328, December 1986.

7. John D. Kasarda and Morris Janowitz, "Community Attachment in Mass Society," *American Sociological Review* 39:328–339, June 1974.

8. Robert D. Putnam, *Bowling Alone: The Collapse and Revival of American Community*, Simon & Schuster, New York, 2000.

9. U.S. Bureau of the Census, "Neighborhood Pride: Most People Like Where They Live," *Census Brief* CENBR/98–3, May 1998.

10. "2009 Annual Meeting Theme: The New Politics of Community," *Footnotes*, Sept./Oct. 2007, p. 5.

11. For a discussion of use of community, see Suzanne Keller, "The American Dream of Community: An Unfinished Agenda," *Sociological Forum* 3:167–183, Spring 1988.

12. Robert S. Lynd and Helen Merrell Lynd, *Middletown*, Harcourt, Brace, New York, 1929; and *Middletown in Transition*, Harcourt Brace, New York, 1937.

13. Theodore Caplow, Howard Bahr, Bruce Chadwick, Reuben Hill, and Margaret Holmes Williamson, *Middletown Families: Fifty Years of Change and Continuity*, University of Minnesota Press, Minneapolis, 1982.

14. Theodore Caplow, Louis Hicks, Ben J. Wattenberg, *The First Measured Century*, AEI Press, Washington, D.C., 2001.

15. W. Lloyd Warner, *Yankee City*, Yale University Press, New Haven, Conn., 1963; for a critique, see Stephen Thernstrom, "Yankee City Revisited: The Perils of Historical Naiveté," *American Sociological Review* 30:234–242, April 1965.

16. Suzanne Keller, *The Urban Neighborhood*, Random House, New York, 1968; and Claude S. Fischer, *The Urban Experience*, Harcourt, Brace, Jovanovich, New York, 1976.

17. Roland L. Warren, *New Perspectives on the American Community*, Rand McNally, Chicago, 1977.

18. Barry Wellman, "The Community Question: The Intimate Networks of East Yorkers," *American Sociological Review* 84:1201–1231, 1979.

19. Albert J. Hunter, *Symbiotic Communities: Persistence and Change in Chicago's Local Communities*, University of Chicago Press, Chicago, 1974.

20. For information and discussion of types of communities, see Dennis E. Poplin, *Communities*, 2nd. ed., Macmillan, New York, 1979.

21. See for example Elijah Anderson, *Streetwise, Race, Class, and Change in an Urban Community*, University of Chicago, Chicago, 1990.

22. Gerald Suttles, *The Social Construction of Communities*, University of Chicago Press, Chicago, 1972, p. 57.

23. Morris Janowitz, *The Community Press in an Urban Setting*, University of Chicago, Chicago, 1952; and Scott A. Greer, *The Emerging City: Myth and Reality*, Free Press, New York, 1962.

24. See A. D. Biderman, M. Louisa, and J. Bacchus, *Historical Incidents of Extreme Overcrowding*, Bureau of Social Science Research, Washington, D.C., 1963.

25. Excerpt from Charles Dickens, *The Adventures of Oliver Twist*, Chapman & Hall, Ltd., London, pp. 42–43, 1868.

26. See James Q. Wilson, "The Urban Unease," *The Public Interest* 12:25–39, 1968; James A. Swan, "Public Responses to Air Pollution," in Joachim F. Wohlwill and Daniel H. Carson, *Environment and the Social Sciences*, American Psychological Association, Washington, D.C., 1972, pp. 66–74; Robert Buckout, "Pollution and the Psychologist: A Call to Action," in

Joachim F. Wohlwill and Daniel H. Carson, *Environment and the Social Sciences*, pp. 75–81; and B. Latane and J. M. Darley, *The Unresponsive Bystander: Why Doesn't He Help?* Appleton-Century-Crofts, New York, 1970.

27. John B. Calhoun, "Population Density and Social Pathology," *Scientific American* 206:139–148, February 1960.

28. Shirley Foster Hartley, *Population Quantity vs. Quality*, Prentice-Hall, Englewood Cliffs, N.J., 1972, p. 76.

29. For an overview of available research, see Claude Fischer, Mark Baldassare, and Richard Ofshe, "Crowding Studies and Urban Life: A Critical Review," *Journal of the American Institute of Planners* 41:406–418, November 1975; and Jonathan Freedman, *Crowding and Behavior*, Viking, New York, 1975. Also see Harvey M. Choldin and Dennis Roncek, "Density, Population Potential, and Pathology: A Block Level Analysis," *Public Data Use* 4:19–30, July 1976.

30. O. R. Galle and Walter R. Grove, "Crowding and Behavior in Chicago, 1940–1970," in J. R. Aiello and A. Blaum (eds.), *Residential Crowding and Design*, Plenum, New York, 1979, pp. 23–40.

31. Herbert J. Gans, *The Urban Villagers*, Free Press, Glencoe, Ill., 1962; Gerald Suttles, *The Social Order of the Slum*, University of Chicago Press, Chicago, 1968; and Michael Young and Peter Willmott, *Family and Kinship in East London*, Penguin Books, Baltimore, 1962.

32. Gans, op. cit.

33. Freedman, op. cit., p. 90.

34. William H. Whyte, *City: Rediscovering Its Center*, Doubleday, New York, 1989.

35. Stephen S. Hall, "Standing on Those Corners, Watching All the Folks Go By," *Smithsonian*, February 1989, p. 123.

36. Ibid.

37. NPR, "All Things Considered," December 30, 2010.

38. Christopher Jencks, *The Homeless*, Harvard University Press, Cambridge, MA., 1994, p. 16; and. Peter H. Rossi, *Down and Out in America: The Origins of Homelessness*, University of Chicago, 1989. Also see James D. Wright, *Address Unknown: The Homeless in America*, Aldine de Gruyter, Hawthorne, N.Y., 1989.

39. U.S. Department of Housing and Urban Development, *Homelessness: Programs and the People They Serve*, Government Printing Office, Washington,

D.C., 2000, and *Practical Lessons: The 1998 Symposium on Housing Research*, Government Printing Office, Washington, D.C., 1999.

40. U.S. Department of Housing and Urban Development, *Annual Housing Assessment Report*, Community Planning and Development, www.hud.gov/offices/cpd/homeless/ahar.cfm, Feb. 27, 2007.

41. Donald J. Bogue, *Skid Row in American Cities*, University of Chicago, Community and Family Study Center, Chicago, 1963; Carl I. Cohen and Jay Sokolovsky, *Old Men of the Bowery: Strategies for Survival among the Homeless*, Guilford Press, New York, 1989.

42. For an examination of deinstitutionalization and its consequences, see Michael J. Dear and Jennifer R. Wolch, *Landscapes of Despair: From Homelessness: Programs and the People They Serve*, op. cit. *Deinstitutionalization to Homelessness*, Polity Press, Oxford, 1987.

43. *Homelessness: Programs and the People They Serve*, op. cit.

44. Jennifer Egan, *To Be Young and Homeless*, *New York Times Magazine*, March 24, 2002, p.23.

45. Homelessness: Programs and the People They Serve, op. cit.

46. Peter H. Rossi and James D. Wright, "The Urban Homeless: A Portrait of Urban Dislocation," *The Annals* 501:137, January 1989.

47. Alice S. Baum and Donald W. Burnes, *A Nation in Denial: The Truth about the Homeless*, Westview, Boulder, CO., 1993.

48. Todd Lewan, "Do Not Feed the Homeless," *Richmond Times-Dispatch*, February 4, 2007, p. A4.

49. David Wagner, *Checkerboard Square: Culture and Resistance in a Homeless Community*, Westview Press, Boulder, 1993.

50. Lynette Holloway, "With a New Purpose and Look, S.R.O.s Make a Comeback," *New York Times*, November 10, 1996, pp. 1, 44.

51. U.S. Department of Justice, Bureau of Justice Statistics, *Serious Violent Crime Levels Declined Since 1993*, http://www.ojp.usdoj.gov/bjs/glance/cv2.htm, January 24, 2007.

52. U.S. Department of Justice, *Crime in the United States, 2008*, Government Printing Office, Washington, D.C., 2009.

53. Associated Press, "Murder Rate Up in Big Cities," *New York Times*, March 9, 2007, p. A9.

54. James Q. Wilson and George L. Kelling, "Broken Windows," *Atlantic Monthly*, March 1982, pp. 29–36; and James Q. Wilson, *Thinking about Crime*, Basic Books, New York, 1983.

55. Eli B. Silverman, *NYPD Battles Crime: Innovative Strategies in Policing,* Northeastern University Press, Boston, 1999.

56. Andrew Karmen, *New York Murder Mystery: The True Story behind the Crime Crash of the 1990s,* New York University Press, 2001.

57. U.S. Department of Justice, *FBI Uniform Crime Reports, 2008,* Government Printing Office, Washington, D.C., 2009.

58. U.S. Department of Justice, *Juvenile Offenders and Victims: A National Report,* Office of Juvenile Justice and Delinquency Prevention, Washington, D.C., 1995.

59. Richard Alba, John Logan, and Paul Bellair, "Living with Crime: The Implications of Racial/Ethnic Differences in Suburban Location," *Social Forces* 73:395–434, 1994.

60. U.S. Department of Justice *1999 Uniform Crime Report,* Government Printing Office, Washington, D.C., p. 282.

61. James A. Fox, "The Calm before the Storm?" *Population Today* 24:4, September 1996.

62. William Julius Wilson, *The Truly Disadvantaged: The Inner City, the Underclass, and Public Policy,* University of Chicago Press, Chicago, 1987.

63. Bill Maxwell "Grim Statistics for African-American Men," *International Herald-Tribune,* January 11, 2004, p. 3F.

64. Elijah Anderson, *Streetwise: Race, Class, and Change in an Urban Community,* University of Chicago Press, Chicago, 1990.

65. Clifford R. Shaw and Henry D. McKay, *Juvenile Delinquency in Urban Areas,* University of Chicago Press, Chicago, 1942.

66. Martin Sanchez Jankowski, *Islands in the Street: Gangs and American Urban Society,* University of California Press, Berkeley, 1991.

67. "US Central City and Suburban Crime Rates Ranked," *Demographia,* www. demographia.com/db-crime99.htm, January 21, 2007.

68. John M. Stahura and John J. Sloane III, "Urban Stratification of Places, Routine Activities and Suburban Crime Rates," *Social Forces,* 66(4): 1102–1118, 1988.

CHAPTER 9

Diversity: Women, Ethnics, and African Americans

Those who do not wish to partake in the American experiment ought not settle in America. America must be kept American.
President Calvin Coolidge, 1924

OUTLINE

Introduction
Women in Metropolitan Life
    Female Domesticity
    Gendered Organization of Residential
        Space
    Feminist Housing Preferences
    Cohousing and Downsizing
    Current Housing Choices
    Gendered Public Spaces
    Workplace Changes
White Ethnic Groups
    Immigration
First-Wave Immigrants
    Second-Wave Immigrants
    Third-Wave Immigrants
    "Racial Inferiority" and Immigration
African Americans
    Historical Patterns
    Population Changes
    Slavery in Cities
    "Free Persons of Color"
    Jim Crow Laws
    "The Great Migration"

Moving South
Urban Segregation Patterns
    Extent of Segregation
    Housing Discrimination
21st-Century Diversity
    The Economically Successful
    The Disadvantaged
Summary

INTRODUCTION

This chapter and Chapter 10 examine the issues of gender, race, and ethnicity in the metropolitan area. Specifically, we will be examining the changing status of women, African Americans, Latinos, Asians, ethnics, and Native Americans. For organizational convenience this chapter will focus on women, ethnic immigrant groups, and African Americans. The next chapter will concentrate on the minority groups showing the most dramatic contemporary growth, Latinos, Asians, and Native Americans. Given the considerable overlap between the two chapters they should be read not as distinct chapters, but as two mutually reinforcing sections of a single topic. Our concern is not so much with idiosyncratic bits of information as with the overall general patterns.

In this chapter our focus is on women in metro areas, ethnics, and African Americans whose futures are bound to the urban scene. The changing place of women in metropolitan life opens the chapter. Also discussed in this chapter are white ethnics and African Americans. These groups differ from one another in numerous respects; what they have in common is that historically they have been relatively powerless compared to WASP males. Women, ethnics, and African Americans have all, until very recently, been dismissed as unimportant or marginal to the mainstream of urban America. Although women are a demographic majority, their historically marginal status is a measure of social position and life chances, not numbers.

WOMEN IN METROPOLITAN LIFE

Women are often discussed as a minority not because of their numbers (women both live longer and outnumber men in North America), but because of their historically subordinate role. Space in urban places has historically been gendered space, and women have utilized and conceptualized urban space differently than men.[1] The fact that men's and women's places in, and experience of, the city have not been the same has been largely ignored. Urban research over the years has focused almost exclusively on the place and space of men in urban order. For example, when the Chicago School sociologists examined the impact of the city on newcomers, it was the urban experiences of males that was the focus of discussion. The less publicly visible roles of women in North American cities tended to make them invisible in urban research. The identification of men's space with

public places (work) and women's with *private* places (home) contributed to this division.

Female Domesticity

In early rural-based America there was no sharp division between home and work. On the farm everyone—including children—worked. However, with the spread of industrialization and the factory system in the 19th century, it became economically possible for the first time for growing numbers of urban middle-class women to be removed from the nonhousehold labor force. (Keep in mind that poorer women have always been in the labor force, working long hours for low pay.)

As middle-class women left the labor force a new definition of women's role emerged. The dirty and overcrowded 19th-century industrial city was Gomorrah—a world of heavy work, men, factories, and vice. By contrast, women's world (at least for the upper and middle classes) was portrayed as being centered on the family-based suburban cottage with garden and picket fence as portrayed in Currier and Ives prints. The middle-class home came to be defined not just as lodgings, but as sacred space where, under the wife's tutelage, men would be civilized and children would be raised in health and virtue. The world of work was increasingly defined as a man's world, while the domestic world of home was defined as a woman's world.

The 19th-century ideology of *female domesticity* suggested that nature itself determined that the home was the "woman's sphere," and that women were particularly physically, morally, and spiritually equipped to nurture. The home was to be the social linchpin around which all else revolved. As Catherine Beecher said in her very influential *Treatise on Domestic Economy*, "Surely it is a pernicious and mistaken idea, that the duties which tax a woman's mind are petty, trivial, or unworthy of the highest grade of intellect and moral worth. . . . Every woman should imbibe from early youth, the impression, that she is training for the care of the most important, most difficult, and the most sacred and interesting duties that can possibly employ the highest intellect."[2] Proper management of the home influenced national character and thus was an activity of the highest social order.

Physical spaces inside upper-class and middle-class homes came to be identified by gender. Nineteenth-century homes did not have living rooms to be used by everyone in the family. Rather, on the first floor father had his study (and if wealthy, library, billiard, and smoking rooms) while mother had her drawing room (where women withdrew after dinner) where she formally entertained her female guests. Kitchens were used by wives or servants, but were out-of-bounds for the husband.

For the middle and upper classes it was only the parlor and dining room that were not gender designated for primary use by one sex. Upstairs the separation of rooms by gender was even more complete. Couples often had separate bedrooms. Off the wife's bedroom was a sunlit corner known as the "morning room," where the female householder had her breakfast and where she informally visited with women friends during the morning. Children's bedrooms were gender designated as being for boys or girls, while the nursery was for young children, their nanny, and occasional visits by the mother.

Gendered Organization of Residential Space

Nineteenth-century Victorian social and spatial patterns were substantially modified by the new "progressive" 20th-century models of family behavior. The early 20th-century progressive-era household ideology was not one of separateness, but of shared domesticity. For the rising middle class it was the family, not just the mother and children, that was seen as the basic family unit. In practice this meant that husbands, wives, and children shared common

time and space. Open floor plans, centralized heating, and the removal of sliding doors between small downstairs rooms opened the house up spatially and socially. The new larger living room, in which all family members could gather, came to replace the smaller parlor and sexually separate reception rooms. Floor plans were designed to produce a more cohesive family. Especially after dinner family members were expected to informally congregate in the living room. Father, mother, and children were not necessarily engaged in the same activities; it was enough that they were all gathered around the family hearth. Popular magazines such as *Good Housekeeping* and *The Ladies' Home Journal* constantly stressed the advantage to children of such family living patterns, as did the *Dick and Jane* school readers widely used throughout the nation from the 1920s to the 1970s.

The early 20th-century new and smaller bungalow-style homes with central heating and electric fixtures particularly appealed to younger couples. The compact bungalows were built with all the modern conveniences of the time, indoor bathrooms, electric sockets, central heating, and often gas connections for hot water and a gas kitchen stove. (Keep in mind that at the time of World War I (1914–1918) three-quarters of American homes still lacked electricity.) Electricity was more common in the newer outer-city and suburban bungalow homes. By the 1920s they had the new laborsaving electric appliances such as electric washing machines, electric vacuum cleaners, electric irons, and even electric toasters. Laborsaving appliances meant heavy labor around the home was sharply reduced. No longer was it necessary to have a washerwoman—or yourself—do the backbreaking labor of heating water on a wood or coal stove, washing the clothes in huge vats, and then ironing everything with irons heated on the stove.

The bungalow-style homes with their laborsaving appliances reduced both heavy labor and chore time around the home and provided the possibility of free time for middle-class women. By reducing time-consuming home drudgery the new technologies contributed to an ongoing social revolution. The magazines of the day noted that women now had "free time" to devote to charity work, social activities, education, or even a career. Middle-class women still were expected to be housewives and mothers, but by the 1920s there was at least the possibility of having both a career and a home. None of this is to suggest that new inventions and new technologies alone brought about new social and work patterns, but technological advances did for the first time make it possible for women to get out of the home. Married women could have careers without automatically being thought negligent wives and mothers. Until the 1970s most married women would remain at home, but it no longer was a practical necessity.

More recently, technology again has brought another revolution regarding home and work. People are moving back from office to home-based working. Telecommuting, at least for a couple of days a week, is becoming more common. Not surprisingly, it is especially popular among mothers holding professional jobs who have small children. The emerging 21st-century pattern is for the home and workplace once again to become the same. Whether this is seen as an advance or not often depends on individual circumstances.

Feminist Housing Preferences

From the 1920s to the present, popular magazines have equated the suburban home with attaining the American Dream, but this clearly has *not* been the view of feminists. Early 20th-century feminists saw suburban homes as producing patriarch-designed drudgery and isolation.[3] To break this pattern feminists advocated forming collective organizations and making responsibilities for domestic housework, laundry, and cooking communal responsibilities. Many of these ideas were quite progressive and form the basis for communal housing found in Scandinavia and elsewhere today. For instance,

the early 20th-century feminist-based community of Llano del Rio in southern California was designed without kitchens or laundries in the homes. Rather, there was a communal cooking and eating area and a common laundry building. The goal was to remove household drudgery and give the wife free time for other, more rewarding activities. The unseen irony was that this was accomplished for the middle-class women by having all the cooking, cleaning, and heavy washing done by poorer women. Apparently it never occurred to the early advocates of communal living that gender liberation was being accomplished at the cost of class and race discrimination.

Cohousing and Downsizing

Contemporary communities that share common facilities and where residents seek to know one another and cooperate communally are known as *cohousing*.[4] Cohousing communities are not communes, they are intentional communities. Advocates of cohousing with shared community kitchens, dining areas, and laundries stress the importance of tasks being shared by the partners.

Cohousing communities have smallish private houses (usually 20 to 30 in number) but share common community buildings and backyard space. These communities are commonly designed and managed by their residents and owned as condominiums. They usually are designed and built to be earth friendly.

Today, cohousing projects are most commonly found in Scandinavia and the Netherlands. There are increasing numbers of cohousing projects in North America, such as Eco Village, in affluent Loudoun County, Virginia. As of 2007, there were 1,300 cohousing communities in North America.[5] Others aren't joining communities but simply downsizing their housing to minimalist levels. The Small House Society is for those who live in 1,000 square feet and less.[6] Reducing one's carbon footprint by downsizing is a growing movement.

Current Housing Choices

Not until the late 1960s was sociological research done on gendered housing preferences. A number of well-done studies indicated that males were more pleased with suburban living than were wives. For instance, Gans, in his Levittown study, found that while only 3 of 10 husbands favored living in the city "if not for the children," this was true for twice as many wives. Claude Fischer found that husbands, who left their suburban communities to work, had wider networks of friends and colleagues than did wives with more restricted local socializing.[7] William Michelson in his research on Toronto found that women expressed greater satisfaction living in urban residential neighborhoods than in suburban areas.[8] Where urban crime and the quality of schools were not major problems, the urban access to public services and transportation were major pluses. Feminists writing on the effect of housing environments also emphasized that the burden of suburban isolation fell heavily and unfairly on women.

However, times and conditions change. The days when suburbs were solely residential are past. Today, suburbs house most of a metropolitan area's retail trade, business activity, and employment. Moreover, three-quarters of women with school age children no longer stay home full-time, but are now employed outside the home. The era in which women remained isolated in suburban homes, without access to cars, culture, or community, is a cliché of decades past. Contemporary suburban women don't have the problem of suburban isolation and being trapped at home with too much free time and nothing to do. Today, women commuting to work in their autos worry about being overworked and overscheduled, without any free time for themselves. For contemporary women having time alone at home is not a problem; rather it is viewed as a relief when it occurs.

As a consequence, women's post–World War II preference for urban over suburban res-

Women have now ascended to some of the highest public offices available. Secretary of State Hillary Rodham Clinton was a frontrunner in the 2008 U.S. presidential election until her campaign was overtaken by that of Barack Obama. U.S. Department of State photo

idential locations no longer applies. Daphne Spain's examination of 32,000 responses to the federal government's Annual Housing Survey overwhelmingly indicates that for over two decades women have preferred single-family suburban homes.[9] For most women, concerns over urban crime and poor quality public education have more than offset earlier urban advantages. Another factor is that most American young adults, male and female, have grown up in suburbs, and they are most comfortable with the environment they know.[10] Gender differences in housing preferences represent an earlier era.

Gendered Public Spaces

There was little research on women in public space before the 1970s. Early urban research largely ignored women; their traditional home-based roles meant they were less publicly visible.[11] Urban public space was for "town women" (prostitutes) or poor working women, and both populations were restricted to marginal urban space. Middle-class women, on the other hand, as defenders of the home, had moral superiority, but social subordination.[12] For respectable women to commonly occupy public space implied abandonment of hearth and home.

In contemporary urban areas men and women are still sometimes spatially segregated in ways that reduce women's access to information, knowledge, and power. We still assign gender to some places in the workforce, and male space frequently is where the information and knowledge that influence decisions and determine who holds power can be found.[13] Most managerial knowledge does not come from reading books, but from observation and relationships with older mentors in shared business space. Traditionally this meant that younger men learned from older male role models. Only now is gender segregation being overcome and are women gaining access to the workplace spaces and experiences that determine who exercises power.

Workplace Changes

A major study of women and the workplace by Suzanne Bianchi and Daphne Spain provides statistical details about the major changes that are taking place in the work lives of American women.[14] They paint a picture of slow but clear progress to work equality with men. The possibilities for managerial or professional women are particularly strong. However, even within the 500 occupational categories used by the census, men and women in the same categories often cluster into different specialties. Men's oc-cupational goals tend to be more sex-typed than those of women. Men are more likely to be loners; place higher preference on status, power, and money; and have a willingness to take risks. Women more often value creativity, working together with people, and helping others. Bianchi and Spain found that women make different choices about schooling, jobs, and family, which means they amass less human capital in the workforce. Women also continue to face greater constraints in the workforce.

A major constraint is that married women in the workforce also still carry the major responsibility for home and child care. This amounts to a second job or a second shift.[15] Women's role within the family as the manager of the home and primary child-care provider limits occupational flexibility and mobility, and thus career advancement. Questions of child care and even commuting time and distance between home and workplace differ for men and women.[16] Mothers feel a greater need to be closer to home in order to get home in emergencies and provide supervision for children after school or day care. Suburban office and industrial parks benefit from this reserve labor force of suburban female workers who wish to work close to home. Online home-based workers are heavily female. For increasing numbers of professional women with young children the home and the workplace are becoming one.

Women are increasingly visible in the public realm. In government women are occupying more and more elective and appointed public offices. In the United States it generally appears that larger urban places are more likely to elect women. In cities of 25,000 or more, women hold just under one-quarter of the seats as council members or alderpersons.[17] Larger city councils of more than nine persons also favor higher female representation. It should also be noted that as this is being written Hillary Clinton is Secretary of State. Increasingly, women's place is in the public space.

WHITE ETHNIC GROUPS

Immigration

As the chapter's opening quotation by President Coolidge indicates, America has not always welcomed newcomers with open arms. There is a story (probably apocryphal) that President Franklin Roosevelt enraged a Daughters of the American Revolution (DAR) convention during the 1930s by addressing them as "Fellow Immigrants." If so, he was only stating what is frequently forgotten: That is, all groups—including American Indians—were once newcomers. The only difference is in time of arrival. Indians or First Peoples came across the Bering Strait land bridge perhaps 15,000 to 20,000 years ago, while Europeans first came in significant numbers less than 400 years ago, as did the first Africans. Many of the most recent arrivals have been Hispanic or Asian. Most of these latter groups are first- or second-generation newcomers.

It may be a cliché to state that America is a nation of immigrants, but it is sometimes forgotten that the American immigration was the largest mass migration in the history of the world. Precise data are lacking, but probably some 45 million immigrants arrived in the United States prior to the restrictive immigration laws of the 1920s. (Currently we are adding yearly a million legal residents and perhaps 600,000 unauthorized.) We will never know the exact number of early immigrants, or their precise ethnic distribution, since record-keeping was minimal. Table 9.1, giving the ancestry of U.S. groups, should be taken as an approximation. In some cases overworked immigration officials automatically listed all newcomers on a ship as being of the same nationality as the ship. Thus, those on a ship from Hamburg were automatically German. Reflecting class bias, foreign first-class passengers did not count as immigrants, but rather as visitors until early in the 20th century. (This meant they did not have to

Table 9.1	Largest 10 Ancestries of U.S. Population Groups, 1820–2000	
Reported Ancestry	**Number**	**Percent of Population**
All Countries	64,599,082	100.0%
Germany	7,156,257	11.1
Mexico	5,819,966	9.0
Italy	5,431,454	8.4
United Kingdom	5,247,821	8.1
Ireland	4,779,998	7.4
Canada	4,453,149	6.9
Russia	3,830,033	5.9
Austria	1,842,722	2.8
Hungary	1,675,324	2.6
Philippines	1,460,421	2.3

Source: 1998 Statistical Yearbook of the Immigration and Naturalization Service, Washington, D.C., 2000.

go through Ellis Island or other immigration centers.) While a greater portion of the U.S. population was foreign born a century ago, the actual number of immigrants is now at record levels. The proportion of immigrants in the population today is twice as high as it was in 1970. Today almost 1 in 10 United States residents is foreign born, a proportion similar to that in 1850 when the Census Bureau first asked people their place of birth. During the last decade the foreign-born population grew by 27 percent, nearly four times as fast as the 7 percent increase in the native-born population. In 2005 there were 37 million foreign born in the U.S.[18]

FIRST-WAVE IMMIGRANTS

There is a loose pattern of association between higher social status and the early arrival of ancestors on these shores. (The exception is African Americans who, in spite of their early arrival, remained a separate caste excluded from white society.) Most early European immigrants were of British Isles background. At the time of the Revolutionary War some nine-tenths of the new nation's white population traced their ancestry to the British Isles: English, Scotch, or Northern Irish (called Scotch-Irish to distinguish them from Catholic Irish). Even cosmopolitan New York was dominated by English customs, laws, values, and mores. Protestantism in various forms was, in effect, the national religion.

The founding fathers strongly supported free and open migration. However, immigrants were not welcomed without reservations. George Washington's view was that:

> The bosom of America is open to receive not only the Opulent and Respectable Stranger, but the oppressed and persecuted of all Nations and Religions, whom we shall welcome to participation of all our rights and privileges, if by decency and propriety of conduct they appear to merit the enjoyment.[19]

Washington was more liberal in his admission criteria than many of his contemporaries (his successor, John Adams, dramatically lengthened the waiting period for citizenship), but even Washington's statement has a final clause that says, in effect, "if we think they behave themselves."

Second-Wave Immigrants

The second wave of ethnic immigration ran from roughly 1820 to 1880. The Irish were the first large-scale group of migrants. Serious Irish immigration began in 1820 and sharply accelerated in the mid-1840s when millions of Irish fled the potato famine in Ireland. The famine caused more than a million deaths by starvation in Ireland, and another million or so impoverished Irish peasants immigrated to America. The Irish were closely followed by the Germans and somewhat later the Scandinavians. These groups are collectively called the "old immigrants" to distinguish them from the earlier settlers—overwhelmingly of British origin.

The Germans, in spite of the fact that they played cards and insisted on drinking beer on Sunday—shocking some bluenoses—after a rough start fared rather well. They earned a reputation for industriousness, thrift, and orderly living—although they rioted in Chicago in 1855 when the mayor banned the sale of beer on Sunday. Easing assimilation was the fact that the majority of Germans were Protestant.

The Irish had greater problems, for not only were they viewed as recalcitrant, papist rowdies, but also they voted Democratic and were the poorest of the poor. Poor Irish, rather than more valuable slaves, were used in hazardous work in the South. As a New Orleans riverboat captain explained to a famous northern visitor in the 1850s, "The niggers are worth too much to be risked here; if the Paddies are knocked overboard or get their backs broke, nobody loses anything."[20] Irish laborers built many of the nation's railroads, and a saying of the time was, "An Irishman is buried under every tie." Confronted by discrimination—"No Irish Need Apply" was found in Boston help-wanted ads—the Irish organized themselves. For the immigrant Irish, the route to social mobility was said to be through becoming one of the three P's: "priest, politician, or policeman"; and by the latter part of the 19th century, the Irish controlled the city halls in the cities where they lived in significant numbers. Stereotypes also softened as more and more of the Irish became skilled workers. By the 1880s it was a common saying that "A good worker does as much as an Irishman."[21]

Third-Wave Immigrants

A third wave of ethnic immigration took place between 1880 and the 1920s. While the ethnic groups of the second wave came from northern and western Europe, those of the third wave came largely from southern and eastern Europe. After 1880, increasing numbers of immigrants had Slavic, Polish, Jewish, Italian, or

Greek heritage. During the 1860s less than 2 percent of all immigrants came from southern or eastern Europe; by the 1890s southern and eastern Europe were the source of a majority (52 percent) of all immigrants. By the first decade of this century 7 of 10 immigrants came from southern or eastern Europe. Today all European migration is much reduced and only one-twentieth of all immigrants comes from Europe. With the open farmlands largely taken, virtually all the southern and eastern European immigrants stayed in the cities—as had the Irish before them.

For the last half of the 19th century and first half of the 20th century, the majority of the urban population was foreign born or first-generation American. As of 1900, only half (51 percent) of the country's population was native white and of native parentage. In eastern seaboard cities such as New York and Boston, more than three-quarters of the population was of foreign stock (the census term for foreign-born or second generation).

The strong negative reaction of WASP rural and small-town America to the nation's cities was closely linked to the perceived "foreignness" of the cities. Cities were considered places of "rum, Romanism, and rebellion." Nineteenth-century writers and preachers such as Josiah Strong raised the clarion call against the menace of cities teeming with foreigners:

> The City has become a serious menace to our civilization. . . . . It has a peculiar attraction for the immigrant. . . . While a little less than one-third of the population of the United States was foreign by birth or parentage, sixty-two percent

Immigrants arriving third class (steerage) at Ellis Island had to undergo a complete physical examination. First-class passengers were not considered immigrants so did not have to undergo examination. Library of Congress

of the population of Cincinnati was foreign, eight-three percent of Cleveland, sixty-three percent of Boston, eighty percent of New York and ninety-one percent of Chicago. . . . Because our cities are so largely foreign, Romanism finds in them its chief strength. For the same reason the saloon, together with the intemperance and the liquor power which it represents, is multiplied in the city.[22]

To ethnocentric WASP Americans, the new immigrants were alien races about to overwhelm American institutions and cities. First, they were coming from what were considered the most backward areas of Europe—regions that did not have self-government and thus by implication were incapable of self-government. Second, their customs and even food habits differed greatly from the Anglo-Saxon-Teutonic norm of earlier settlers. Third, their religions were different. They were more likely to be Catholic, Eastern Orthodox, or Jewish than Protestant. Finally, they came in large numbers, were concentrated in the cities, and thus were highly visible. (The technology of larger and faster steamships spurred immigration. The *Titanic* was built to make money not as a first-class liner but primarily to transport steerage immigrants to America.)

By the time the third-wave immigrants arrived, the frontier had closed and the best farmlands were taken. Of necessity the new immigrants became industrial factory workers. Easy assimilation of the immigrants was retarded not only by their overwhelming numbers but also by their concentration in ethnic ghettos—in the inner-city zone of transition. Residence near the factories in central-city tenements reflected economic necessity, but it also reflected the desires of the immigrants to have their own communities where they could follow traditional customs removed from Anglo-Saxon hostility. The consequence was the development of ethnic neighborhoods that were socially isolated from the larger city. The social organization of one such Italian neighborhood, with its strong peer-group relationships,

is described in William F. Whyte's sociological classic, *Street Corner Society*.[23]

As noted in Chapter 3: The Rise of Urban America, middle-class WASP attempts to remove the political bosses and reform the city generally meant removing power from the central-city immigrants. In the early 20th century the city-manager system, in which an appointed WASP city-manager replaced the elected ethnic mayor, was seen as an urban reform.

"Racial Inferiority" and Immigration

Before the turn of the 20th century, arguments to restrict immigration were largely based upon (1) the ethnocentric assumption of the superiority of American ways and (2) the assumption that American industrial society represented a higher evolutionary form than the backward regions of Europe. Nonetheless, "the wretched refuse of your teeming shore" were felt to be convertible into the American mainstream. As the *Philadelphia Press* commented in 1888, "The strong stomach of American civilization may, and doubtless will, digest and assimilate ultimately this unsavory and repellent throng. . . . In time they catch the spirit of the country and form an element of decided worth."[24]

However, around the turn of the century a new argument, that of racial inferiority, was added to the argument for exclusion. At that time the term *race* meant ethnicity or nationality rather than color, so that such terms as the "Polish race" and the "Italian race" were used to describe "races." "Experts" of the time agreed that the new immigrants were genetically inferior to the Anglo-Saxons who, combined with Germans, Scandinavians, and other first-wave immigrants had formed the "American race." Discovering genetics, they jumped to the conclusion that not only were hair color, size, and bone structure genetically transferable, but also disposition, creativity, criminality, poverty, illiteracy, and all social behavior. "Blood would tell"—

and what they believed it told was that Anglo-Saxon America was genetically committing "race suicide" by allowing in unrestricted numbers of inferior races such as Poles, Italians, Slavs, and other eastern and southern Europeans. The racist conclusion seemed clear: "To admit the unchangeable differentiation of race in its modern scientific meaning is to admit inevitably the existence of superiority in one race and of inferiority in another."[25]

According to E. A. Ross, a leading sociologist of the time, even the appearance of the American population was likely to deteriorate: "It is unthinkable that so many persons with crooked faces, coarse mouths, bad noses, heavy jaws, and low foreheads can mingle their heredity with ours without making personal beauty yet more rare among us than it actually is."[26] While this sounds absurd today, the importance of the genetic argument cannot be overstressed. These genetic beliefs were held not just by a lunatic fringe but by major scholars with national influence.

The genetic argument contributed to the restrictive "racial"-based immigration laws of 1921 and 1924, the National Origins Act of 1929, and the McCarran–Walter Act of 1952. (President Truman vetoed the latter as discriminatory, but Congress passed it over his veto.) The intent of the immigration acts was to discriminate. Southern and eastern Europeans were reduced from 45 percent of all immigrants under the already restrictive law of 1921 to 12 percent under the law of 1924. Northern and western Europeans were welcome—particularly if they were Protestant. About 85 percent of the quota went to northwest Europe, and roughly half the total quota went to three countries: England, Germany, and Ireland. Eastern and southern Europeans were given minimal quotas. While Great Britain's quota was 65,721 per year, that for Italy was only 5,802. Not until 1968 were the "racial" quotas eliminated. Canada followed a similar pattern with its "white Canada" immigration policy until 1967.

Today, all those with European background are commonly placed in the same Euro-American category. Research indicates that the differences between northern European immigrant groups and southern and eastern European groups has largely disappeared.[27] Fourth-wave immigrants began arriving after 1968 when the old ethnic preference system was dropped. The majority of these newest immigrants are Hispanic or Asian. They will be discussed in the next chapter.

AFRICAN AMERICANS

African Americans numbered 36 million as of the 2000 U.S. census—more than the total population of Canada.[28] Today the figure is 38 million. Blacks are classified by the census as a racial group. However, scientists today hold that racial categories are more myth than science and that race is far more a social than a biological construct.[29] Nonetheless, while biologically meaningless, race continues to have social meaning because it is a difference that is usually immediately visible as an identifier. In 21st-century America, race still counts.

Historical Patterns

The first blacks in the American colonies were not slaves but indentured servants. That meant that they—like the more numerous white indentured persons—had to serve for a given time, usually five to seven years, in bondage or indentureship before they became legally entitled to own property. However, for blacks this system—particularly in the South, where plantations required large labor forces—rapidly evolved into one of perpetual servitude. In 1661 Virginia passed a law allowing perpetual slavery, and two years later the Maryland colony declared that "all Negroes or other slaves within the province, to be hereafter imported, shall serve during life."

The fundamental conflict between America's social and political philosophy of freedom and equality on the one hand and the practice of social inequality on the other was aptly characterized by Gunnar Myrdal as the "American dilemma."[30] Two centuries earlier, Thomas Jefferson (who owned slaves while also apparently fathering children with Sally Hemmings, a female slave) had referred to slavery as justice in conflict with avarice and oppression.

Population Changes

As Table 9.2 indicates, at the time of the first census in 1790 blacks made up one-fifth of the total population. In spite of a high rate of natural increase, the proportion of blacks in the population declined during the 19th century because of heavy European immigration. As noted earlier, large-scale European immigration was restricted during the 1920s, and since that time African Americans have been increasing as a proportion of the population. African Americans currently constitute one-eighth (12.9 percent) of the population.

The black population was—until the 20th century—overwhelmingly rural and southern.

Table 9.2	African American Population in the United States by Number and Percent, 1790 to 2010	
Year	Number	Percent of Total Population
1790	757,000	19.3
1800	1,002,000	18.9
1850	3,639,000	15.7
1900	8,834,000	11.6
1930	11,891,000	9.7
1940	12,866,000	9.8
1950	15,042,000	10.0
1960	18,860,000	10.6
1970	22,672,570	11.2
1980	25,969,000	11.8
1990	31,517,000	12.3
2000	35,231,000	12.8
2010	39,906,000	12.9

*Figures differ slightly from text due to assignment of persons checking two or more races.

Source: U.S. Census Bureau.

The Civil War and the extensive political and social upheavals of Reconstruction made but slight change in this pattern. As recently as 1910, 9 of 10 blacks still lived in the South, and 73 percent of blacks were rural. Then 50 years of heavy black migration from the South to the North made African Americans the nation's most urban population by the 1960s. Today black migration is again taking place, but now it is to the metropolitan South from the urban North. African American migrants especially are moving into the suburbs of large southern metro areas.[31] Today more than 4 out of 5 of the blacks living in the Atlanta metro area are suburbanites.[32]

Slavery in Cities

Slavery was basically a rural institution, founded upon the plantation economy. Plantation owners vigorously opposed the use of slaves in urban manufacturing, fearing that it would undermine the South's "peculiar institution." As a consequence, slavery declined in the large southern cities prior to the Civil War (1861–1865). (Richmond's iron works were an exception.) The reason for the decline was not economic but social:

> While plantation slaves were typically field hands or house servants, urban slaves engaged in a wide variety of occupations, skilled as well as unskilled, in addition to those who worked as domestic servants for their owners. A very large number of slaves were hired out to work for others, the arrangement being made either by the slave owners or the slaves themselves.[33]

The system of slaves being "hired out" or hiring themselves to others and sharing the income with their owners meant that the urban slave was, in the words of the great black leader, Frederick Douglass, "almost a free citizen."[34] Also, escaping from slavery was far easier in the cities; so, to prevent runaways urban slaveholders had to rule with a light hand. In the cities slaves and owners often had an informal contract in which the slave, through the sharing of his or her earnings, "purchased" some degree of freedom.

"Free Persons of Color"

It is an error to think that before the Civil War all southern blacks were slaves. On the eve of the Civil War, roughly one of eight blacks was a "free Negro," and most of these lived in cities, usually in border states. In Richmond, Virginia, the capital of the Confederacy, in 1860 one-fifth of the city's black population were "free persons of color," and one-fourth of the city's blacks (including some slaves) owned their own small homes. This growing population of "free persons of color" created serious problems for the slave states, for although most "free persons" did poorly in economic terms, they were still free men and women and thus a threat to the system.

A handful of the southern antebellum free blacks were slave owners themselves. An extreme was William Ellison of South Carolina, who owned more slaves than all but the richest white southerners and lived in the former home of a governor of South Carolina.[35] However, such persons were anomalies. In Virginia the 1830 census data indicate that perhaps some 1,000 free blacks were themselves slaveowners.[36] Many only "owned" their spouse whom they had bought out of slavery.

The descendants of free persons of color dominated leadership roles in the black urban community until the Civil Rights Movement of the 1960s. While Booker T. Washington was indeed "up from slavery," few other early black leaders were. W.E.B. DuBois, for example, was a Harvard graduate, and, like the other founders of the National Association for the Advancement of Colored Persons (NAACP), had no experience with slavery.

Jim Crow Laws

Segregation of public facilities was not characteristic of the pre- or post-Civil War urban South. Jim Crow laws, which established separate railway cars, streetcar seating, dining areas,

rest rooms, and even doorways for blacks, were largely a product of the years between 1890 and 1910.[37] During these years literacy tests and poll taxes disenfranchised blacks. Illiterate whites were protected by grandfather clauses (you could vote if your grandfather did, thus excluding blacks). Laws also were passed to separate the races in schools and public facilities. In the 1896 case of *Plessy* v. *Ferguson,* the Supreme Court ruled that segregation was legal. Segregation meant that in urban places where one's social position wasn't known to all in the community, physical distance could be used to signify social distance. The pernicious doctrine of "separate but equal" was not finally eliminated until the famous 1954 case of *Brown* v. *Board of Education of Topeka,* in which the Supreme Court ruled that "separate educational facilities are inherently unequal."

"The Great Migration"

Major black immigration from the rural South to the urban North occurred from World War I to the 1960s. World War I (1914–1918) cut off the North's tide of European immigrant labor at the same time northern industries were being flooded with war orders. A new source of unskilled factory labor had to be found. Northern industries sent recruiters south to encourage blacks to migrate north to "the promised land." In some cases, one-way railroad tickets were even provided. Recruiters were accused of "stirring up the negroes" and were unwelcome in southern communities. For example, a licensing regulation in Macon, Georgia, required each labor agent to pay a $25,000 fee and obtain recommendations from 10 local ministers, 10 manufacturers, and 25 merchants. Elsewhere, methods were more direct. Labor recruiters were shot or tarred and feathered.

The pull of northern industrial jobs, combined with the boll weevil's destruction of cotton crops and the mechanization of agriculture, encouraged what became known as "The Great Migration." Cotton production was shifting out of the old South to the West and Southwest, and field-hand labor was no longer as necessary. Between 1910 and 1920 the five states of the deep South—South Carolina, Georgia, Alabama, Mississippi, and Louisiana—lost 400,000 blacks through out-migration. (Poor whites were also out-migrating at this time.)[38]

This was an extremely substantial migration, but it should be kept in perspective. Between 1910 and 1960 somewhat under 5 million blacks left the South, largely for the big cities of the North. This is a great number of people but fewer than the waves of European immigrants that inundated American shores during the first years of the 20th century. For example, between 1900 and 1910 some 9 million immigrants entered the United States.

The "great migration" had three major migratory streams. The first was from the Carolinas, Georgia, and Florida up the East Coast to key locations such as Washington, Philadelphia, New York, and Boston. The second was from Mississippi, Arkansas, and part of Alabama into the Midwestern cities of St. Louis, Detroit, Chicago, and Milwaukee. The third stream was from Texas and part of Louisiana to Los Angeles and the West Coast.

The depression of the 1930s both cut off employment opportunities in the North and stemmed the flow of immigrants to the cities. But the resurgence of industry during World War II again accelerated the pace of migration, and migration north continued into the 1950s and 1960s. By the 1960s Chicago housed more blacks than all of Mississippi, and the New York metropolitan area had more blacks than any state of the old South.

Moving South

This period of mass migration from the South to the North is history. Today, African Americans' migration is in the opposite direction, out of northern central cities and toward the South. According to Census Bureau figures, by the 1980s there were already over a million more blacks moving south than moving north.[39] The last two decades have seen record black migra-

tion to the suburbs of the South's booming metropolitan areas, especially Atlanta, Houston, Dallas–Fort Worth, and Miami. Some two-thirds of African American population growth is now taking place in the South.[40] Since 1990 roughly a million blacks have moved south.

Those moving to the sunbelt are using many of the same migratory routes used by their grandparents decades earlier to move north. The same economic conditions of better jobs and living conditions that attract whites to the sunbelt also attract blacks. Additionally, in another reversal, the racial atmosphere in the South is now perceived to be often better than that in northern cities. The Pew Research Center found in 2003 that southern blacks were more likely than non-southern ones to say that discrimination today is rare.[41] The earlier "great migration" north was overwhelmingly one of unskilled workers. However, since the 1980s it is young, college-educated blacks who are those most likely to move south. Black urban professionals find more employment opportunities, more affordable housing, and a more congenial social and cultural atmosphere. Between 1990 and 2010 Atlanta's African American population more than doubled. The 2010 census showed that Atlanta's suburbs added half a million new black suburbanites between 2000 and 2010.

The 2010 census showed an acceleration in the pattern of middle-class African Americans moving to southern metro areas. Atlanta, Dallas, Houston, Charlotte, Raleigh, Miami, and Tampa all showed large gains. At the same time cities in the North and West such as New York, Los Angeles, Chicago, Cleveland, and Detroit all experienced African American population declines. Chicago, for example, between 2000 and 2010, lost 17 percent of its black population.

URBAN SEGREGATION PATTERNS

Extent of Segregation

Segregation of all racial and ethnic groups into ghettos was a common experience of early 20th-century newcomers to the cities. Anti-black, anti-immigrant, and anti-Catholic political movements, from the Know-Nothing Party of the 19th century to the Ku Klux Klan of the 1920s, attempted to keep newcomers "in their place" socially and physically. Their "place" commonly was the old and overcrowded housing in the central area near the factories. As members of white ethnic groups prospered, they then moved out of the ghetto into outlying neighborhoods with better-quality housing, and so social and residential segregation decreased.[42]

By contrast, blacks, who entered the poorest central-city ghetto neighborhoods during the early 20th century, remained restricted to such "black belts."[43] For blacks the pattern was one of race overriding economics. For a couple of decades it has been noted that upper-income Hispanics have suburbanized more than comparable-income blacks. Recent research following how immigrants in New York fare over time indicates that the old "color line" that separated blacks from whites is shifting to one that also separates blacks from Hispanics and all other non-blacks.[44]

We are still a segregated society, but a two-year extensive Census Bureau study, as well as research during the last decade by Douglas Massey and Nancy Denton, confirms still high, but declining, urban segregation levels.[45] These studies measure changes in segregation levels over time using the "dissimilarity index," which measures the percentage of a group's population that would have to change residences for each neighborhood to have the same percentage of that group as the city as a whole. Using this measure, in which a score of 100 would be total segregation, a score of around 60 would indicate low segregation while one of 90-plus would indicate virtual total segregation. Segregation indexes for American cities go back to 1940, and a substantial number of studies based on the dissimilarity index document slow but gradually declining incidences of segregation.[46]

Over time regional segregation patterns have changed dramatically. Research done by Reynolds Farley and William Frey, examining the trends in the 232 metropolitan areas having significant black population, suggests that today the highest contemporary segregation levels are not found in the South but in the North.[47] The lowest segregation levels now are found in growing southern and western metro areas experiencing significant housing construction. On the other hand, the central cities and the older suburbs surrounding older northern industrial cities have shown little change and remain highly segregated. The newer southern and southwestern suburbs, are now more integrated. That the early 21st century would see southern cities less segregated than cities in the North definitely was not something predicted by most social scientists.

Housing Discrimination

Until the 1968 Fair Housing Act the federal government directly encouraged racially restrictive neighborhoods. The Federal Housing Authority (FHA) developed a model *protective or restrictive covenant,* which was a document that was attached to a deed to prevent sale of the property to the listed restricted racial and/or ethnic groups. FHA manuals advocated preventing integrated neighborhoods in order to supposedly prevent "declining property values." Restrictive covenants were widely used. During the 1940s roughly 80 percent of the residential property in Chicago had racially restrictive covenants. In 1948 the Supreme Court, in *Shelly v. Kraemer,* ruled that racially restrictive covenants could not be enforced through the courts. However, they continued to have social force, and did not become illegal until the 1968 Fair Housing Act.

Another common means of maintaining separate black and white housing markets was for banks and other lending institutions to *redline* neighborhoods undergoing, or thought to be about to undergo, racial change. Redlined neighborhoods were defined as high-risk areas, and thus few if any mortgage or home improvement loans were available. This, of course, created a self-fulfilling prophesy.

Title VIII of the 1968 act prohibited realtors and financial institutions from employing such discriminatory mechanisms to maintain dual markets for separate white and minority home buyers. Nonetheless, discriminatory practices sometimes still can be found.[48] The first decade of the 21st century saw banks practicing *reverse redlining*. Financial institutions targeted poor—usually minority—financially unsophisticated populations with home loans that were all but certain to fail. Questionable loans with high front-end costs were bundled and then sold to Fannie Mae and other investors as class A loans. Financial institutions pocketed huge profits, while poor homeowners were left with unpayable high-interest loans for more than their property was worth. The result has been high foreclosure rates.

The Obama family in the Green Room of the White House. The Obamas epitomize the growing success and socioeconomic mobility of the new black middle class elite. White House photo

21ST–CENTURY DIVERSITY

The Economically Successful

It does not make sense to speak of the African American population as if all 38 million share similar characteristics. As the African American scholar, Henry Louis Gates Jr., puts it, "There are now two nations in America, and those two nations—one hopeless and one full of hope—are both black."[49] The numbers of middle-class and affluent blacks are increasing, while at the same time those at the bottom are slipping ever further behind. While intact black families are increasingly middle class or above, impoverished inner-city families (frequently female-householder families) are becoming more isolated. One consequence of this division is that median (half above, half below) income, education, and occupation data for the entire black population (while statistically accurate) fail to reflect both the growing prosperity of the black middle class and the deepening poverty and desperation of the truly poor underclass. Exam-

ining each group separately helps us to better understand what is occurring.

There always has been a small upper-class black elite, belonging to Links (a national upper-class social club) and whose children belong to Jack and Jill (an invited, members-only organization for upper-class black children). Historically this small elite has kept to itself and remains largely unknown, both to whites and poorer blacks.[50]

However, far more significant sociologically is the growing African American middle class. The good news is that black income is up and unemployment levels are down. The Census Bureau reported a decade ago that blacks statistically were no more likely than whites to drop out of high school, and college-educated blacks were as likely as whites to hold executive, administrative, or managerial jobs.[51] Half of black heads of households own their own homes and some 88 percent of blacks aged 25-29 have completed high school. Married college-educated African-Americans under 40 have all but closed the income gap with similarly educated whites. According to the Census Bureau, black women with college degrees earn more than similarly educated white women.[52] Overall though, the pattern is one of moving forward but still being behind. Census Bureau data show that black family incomes have been increasing at a stronger rate than whites, but black median family income levels still remain below white median white family income levels.[53]

While the income gap between middle-class blacks and whites is closing, the wealth gap persists. When wealth and accumulated assets are the measure, the difference between blacks and whites is very large. African Americans still control only one-quarter of the assets whites do.[54] The black and white middle classes often live in different physical and social worlds. Based on a three-year examination of an all-black middle-class neighborhood in Chicago, Mary Pattillo-McCoy shows that middle-class African American families still face greater obstacles and pressures than economically equivalent white families.[55] Similarly, in a new work Wilson and Taub suggest that income doesn't bridge other differences, with urban neighborhoods being likely to remain divided racially and culturally. [56]

One development is that a major gender gap is developing between the educational levels of African American women and men. Currently black women are twice as likely to have a bachelor's degree or a master's degree as black males. According to the American Council on Education, a quarter of college-age black men attend college. By contrast, 35 percent of black women and 36 percent of all 18–24-year-olds attend college.[57] Black male graduation rates are the lowest of any minority group. In our increasingly technologically oriented society this gender gap has potentially profound economic and social consequences. It suggests that the declining marriage rates for educated black females are not likely to soon reverse given the smaller number of equal-education black males.

The Disadvantaged

Poor blacks are not doing well. Unlike middle- and working-class blacks they have not benefited from the educational and employment opportunities of affirmative action. The poor, especially the welfare poor, know they are being bypassed while others are moving ahead. The population referred to as the underclass or the truly disadvantaged are essentially outside the system of social mobility. Their numbers include unskilled dropouts, drug addicts, and teenage mothers on welfare and their children. These groups are increasingly excluded from the economic patterns that have benefited both the black and white middle class.

Black poverty is increasingly feminized. While intact black families continue to move out of poverty, two-thirds (66 percent) of black families headed by divorced or never-married women are now below the poverty level ($20,650 for a family of four in 2007). To look at it another way, of all poor black families, 7 of 10 are headed by women. William Julius Wilson and others argue that the crisis of the inner city is increasingly one of an economic underclass rather than one of race.[58] Racism explains why working-class blacks are especially vulnerable, but the changes in the economy are the critical key to the problems of the underclass or truly disadvantaged. Most scholars now agree with Wilson's contention that the crisis occurred not because a "welfare ethos" took over, but because the economic structure of the inner city collapsed, and the resulting economic exclusion led to social collapse. Thus, welfare reforms cannot work without providing living-wage jobs for those leaving welfare. Deindustrialization since the 1970s has led to rustbelt cities of the North losing two-thirds of their manufacturing workers. The movement abroad of decent-paying blue-collar manufacturing jobs eliminated a major source of employment for urban working-class males. Blacks were hit especially hard since poor minorities were disproportionately concentrated in the inner cities where the manufacturing plants closed. The absence of traditional entry-level lower-skilled jobs means that it is increasingly difficult for those without technical skills to climb the socioeconomic ladder.

Once an area collapses economically, joblessness follows. In Chicago's poverty ghetto it resulted by the early 1990s in adult unemployment rates over 60 percent.[59] The absence of jobs is made even worse by the absence of adult working males who can provide knowledge of available jobs, and assistance in entry into the workforce. People tend to learn about employment opportunities through employed relatives and friends, and the truly disadvantaged don't have this opportunity. Further, massive joblessness weakens the perception that there is a relationship between going to school and getting a job. This in turn decreases academic aspirations for young males who see no purpose in attending classes. The link between school and work is broken.

Once a neighborhood collapses economically, social collapse also follows. To those without jobs that pay a living wage, and who are stigmatized by race and alienated from the rest of society, the very streets become a place of constant challenge. A young male's safety in the streets is often based on how much "respect" he garners. An elaborate, informal, but well-known code of the street develops that specifies how young males should dress, behave, and talk.[60] To young males who have nothing else, reputation is worth fighting or even dying for. As joblessness increased among urban blue-collar blacks, the number of marriageable men also decreased, and divorce and illegitimacy increased. The pool of marriageable—that is, reasonably economically secure—men dropped sharply. Poverty undermined family strength and increased the number of female-headed families. As a consequence marriage and illegitimacy rates have changed radically over the last third of the 20th century. In 1960 two-thirds (65 percent) of black women aged 30 to 34 were married, but by 1990 this had reversed to where 61 percent were not married. This in turn impacted a change in marital status. Out-of-wedlock births jumped from one-quarter of all black births in 1960 to 68 percent in 1994. In the late 1990s out-of-wedlock births began slowly to decline, and that slow decline has continued into the early 21st century.

If economic expansion takes place during the coming decade there is some hope for the urban disadvantaged. If it does not, the United States will continue to separate into two societies: one multiracial and increasingly prosperous, and the other disadvantaged, often dark skinned, and surviving in semi-permanent poverty.

SUMMARY

This chapter focused on the changing status of women, white ethnic groups, and African Americans. Women are a minority not because of their numbers (there are more women than men in North America) but because of their historical subordination. In early rural-based America there was no sharp division between home and work. On farms everyone worked. In 19th-century American cities middle-class women were removed from non-household labor and domestic space became women's space. The ideology of *female domesticity* suggested that by nature women were physically, morally, and spiritually equipped to nurture. Space inside homes was defined by gender, with libraries and studies being "men's space" and kitchens, drawing rooms, and morning rooms being solely "women's space."

The 20th-century home, with its living room housing all family members, represented the "progressive" family model of shared domesticity. Influential popular magazines such as *Good Housekeeping* and *Ladies' Home Journal*, as well as the *Dick and Jane* school readers, emphasized the importance of the suburban family home as representing the "American Dream."

Space reflects social patterns. Contemporary communities that emphasize equality by sharing community kitchens, dining areas, and laundries are known as cohousing. Cohousing projects exist in North America, but they are most common in Scandinavia.

Women's postwar housing preferences research indicated that husbands were more pleased with suburban living than wives. Today gender difference in housing preferences no longer exists. For women, concerns over urban crime and poor-quality urban schools more than offset advantages of urban access. Also, most North American young adults have grown up in suburbs, and jobs and retail shopping are now most likely to have a suburban location. Postwar women's concerns about suburban isolation and too much free time have been supplanted by contemporary concerns over long job commutes and not enough free time. Only now is gender segregation in public spaces being overcome, and women are gaining access to workplace spaces that determine who exercises power.

Everyone in North America is an immigrant or descendent of immigrants. The only difference is in time of arrival. Immigration numbers are now at record levels. The foreign-born population is growing four times as fast as the native-born population. The first wave of immigrants, Colonial-era Americans, came largely from the British Isles. Second-wave immigrants (1820 to 1880) were largely from northern and western Europe, especially Ireland and Germany. They were not welcomed with open arms. Third-wave immigrants came between 1880 and 1920, mostly from southern and eastern Europe. They largely worked in central-city factories and lived in nearby tenements. Immigration laws passed in the 1920s and in effect until 1968 were based on the assumption that eastern and southern Europeans were biologically inferior to earlier immigrant populations. Fourth-wave immigration since 1968 comes mainly from Asia and Latin America.

African Americans (numbering 40 million) first came to America as indentured servants, but that soon changed to permanent slavery. Slavery was basically a rural institution; in cities slaves often contractually "hired out." On the eve of the Civil War one in eight blacks was a "free person of color." Racial segregation of public facilities was not from the pre–Civil War period but came as a consequence of Jim Crow laws passed at the turn of the 20th century.

Major out-migration from the rural South to the urban North began during the First World War (1914–1918) as a consequence of labor demands of northern factories. Five million blacks left the South due to "the great migration" from World War I to the 1960s. Today, African American migration is from the North to southern metro areas, especially suburbs. Housing segregation, north and south, was supported by federal government lending policies until the 1968 Fair Housing Act. Today, the highest levels of housing segregation are found in the old industrial cities of the North, while newer cities of the South and West have the lowest segregation levels. This was not predicted by social scientists.

The African American population is educationally and economically divided between an increasingly affluent middle and upper-middle class and a disadvantaged population (often living in city female-headed families). The economic and social gap between the two populations is increasing. The poor need jobs that pay a living wage.

REVIEW QUESTIONS

1. Why are women discussed as a minority?

2. What are the contradictory images of women from frontier times to the contemporary era?

3. What is the ideology of "female domesticity" and how did it affect housing patterns and designs?

4. What is meant by the gendered organization of space?

5. Compare the experiences of second-wave immigrants (1820–1880) with that of third-wave immigrants (1880–1920s)?

6. How was U.S. immigration legislation from the 1920s to the 1960s influenced by the assumed "racial inferiority" of third-wave immigrants?

7. How did slavery in cities differ from plantation slavery?

8. What was the "Great Migration" and how did it impact American cities?

9. How have urban racial segregation patterns in American metro areas changed over the last 25 years?

10. What did Henry Louis Gates mean when he said, "There are now two nations in America, and those two nations—one hopeless and one full of hope—are both black"?

NOTES

1. Kristine B. Miranne and Alma H. Young (eds.). *Gendering the City: Women, Boundaries, and Visions of Urban Life,* Rowman & Littlefield, Lanham, Md., 2000.

2. Catherine Beecher, *Treatise on Domestic Economy,* Marsh, Capen, Lyon, and Webb, Boston, 1841, p. 144.

3. Dolores Hayden, *The Grand Domestic Revolution: A History of Feminist Designs for American Homes, Neighborhoods, and Cities,* MIT Press, Cambridge, Mass., 1981.

4. Charles Durrett, "Cohousing," in Karen Christensen and David Levinson (eds.) *Encyclopedia of Community,* Sage, Thousand Oaks, Calif. 2003, pp. 194-198, and Dorit Fromm, "Cohousing," in Willem van Vliet (ed.), *The Encyclopedia of Housing,* Sage, Thousand Oaks, Calif., 1998, pp. 54–58.

5. Bret Schulte, "Just Don't Call Them Communes," *U.S. News & World Report,* August 13, 2007, p. 32.

6. Zosia Bielski, "Keeping Down with the Jones," *Globe and Mail,* August 28, 2010, p. 14.

7. Herbert Gans, *The Levittowners,* Vintage Books, New York, 1967, p. 272, and Claude Fischer, *The Urban Experience,* Harcourt Brace Jovanovich, New York, 1976.

8. William Michelson, *Environmental Choice, Human Behavior and Residential Satisfaction,* Oxford University Press, New York, 1977.

9. Daphne Spain, "The Effect of Changing Household Composition on Neighborhood Satisfaction," *Urban Affairs Quarterly* 23:581–600, 1988.

10. Sylvia F. Fava, "Residential Preferences in the New Suburban Era: A New Look," *Sociological Focus* 21:109–117, 1985.

11. Lyn Lofland, "The Gendered War against Public Space: Consequences for Community," paper presented at the 1995 Annual Meeting of the American Sociological Society, p. 5.

12. Christine Wright-Isak and Sylvia Fava, "Women in Metropolitan Life," Chap. 11 in J. John Palen, *The Urban World,* 5th ed., McGraw- Hill, New York, 1997, p. 274.

13. Daphne Spain, *Gendered Spaces,* University of North Carolina Press, Chapel Hill, 1992.

14. Suzanne M. Bianchi and Daphne Spain, "Women, Work, and the Family in America," *Population Bulletin,* 51:14–27, December 1996.

15. Arlie Hochschild, *Second Shift,* Avon, New York, 1997.

16. Susan Hanson and Geraldine Pratt, *Gender, Work, and Space,* Routledge, New York, 1995.

17. Susan McManus and Charles Bullock, "Electing Women to Public Office," in Judith Garber and Robyne Turner (eds.), *Gender in Urban Research,* Thousand Oaks, Calif., 1995, p. 162.

18. Phillip Martain and Eiizabeth Midgley, "Immigration: Shaping and Reshaping America, 2nd ed." *Population Bulletin,* 6:4, December 2006, p. 7.

19. Quoted in the President's Commission on Immigration and Naturalization, *Who Shall We Welcome?* U.S. Government Printing Office, Washington, D.C., 1953.

20. Frederick Law Olmsted, *The Cotton Kingdom,* Modern Library, New York, 1969, p. 215.

21. John Higham, *Strangers in the Land,* Atheneum, New York, 1977, p. 26.

22. Josiah Strong, *Our Country,* rev. ed., Baker and Taylor, New York, 1891, chap. 11.

23. William F. Whyte, *Street Corner Society,* University of Chicago Press, Chicago, 1943. See Chapter 7: Urban Lifestyles, for a review of material on inner-city communities. For a more contemporary historical view of Italian Americans, see Stefano Luconi, *From Paesani to White Ethnics,* State University of New York, Albany, 2001.

24. Quoted in Higham, op. cit., p. 63.

25. Madison Grant, *The Passing of the Great Race,* New York, 1921, p. XXVIII.

26. E.A. Ross, *The Old World in the New,* Century, New York, 1914, p. 287.

27. Stanley Lieberson and Mary C. Waters, *From Many Strands: Ethnic and Racial Groups in Contemporary America,* Russell Sage Foundation, New York, 1988.

28. The 36.4 million includes 1.76 million people who also checked at least one other race. The census reports 34.7 million just checked black.

29. Ivan Hannaford, "The Idiocy of Race." *Wilson Quarterly,* Spring 1994, pp. 8–35; and David L. Wheeler, "A Growing Number of Scientists Reject the Concept of Race," *Chronicle of Higher Education,* February 17, 1995, pp. A8, A9, A15.

30. Gunnar Myrdal, *An American Dilemma,* Harper & Row, New York, 1944.

31. William H. Frey, "Migration to the South Brings U.S. Blacks Full Circle," *Population Today* 29: 1–4, May/June, 2001.

32. U.S. Census Bureau, "Race and Hispanic Origin, Census 2000 Brief," Government Printing Office, Washington, D.C., March 2001.

33. Thomas Sowell, *Race and Economics,* David McKay Company, New York, 1975, p. 12.

34. Richard C. Wade, *Slavery in the Cities: The South 1820–1860,* Oxford University Press, New York, 1964.

35. Michael P. Johnson and James L. Roark, *Black Masters: A Free Family of Color in the Old South,* Norton, New York, 1984.

36. Philip J. Schwarz, "Emancipators, Protectors, and Anomalies: Free Black Slaveholders in Virginia," *Virginia Magazine of History and Biography* 95:317–338, 1987.

37. C. Van Woodward, *The Strange Career of Jim Crow,* Oxford University Press, New York, 1966.

38. For more on the Great Migration see: Isabel Wilkerson, *The Warmth of Other Suns,* Random House, New York, 2010; and Peter M. Rutkoff and William B. Scott, *Fly Away,* Johns Hopkins, Baltimore, 2010.

39. U.S. Bureau of the Census, "The Black Population of the United States: March 1988." *Current Population Reports,* series P–20, no. 442, November 1989.

40. William H. Frey, "Migration to the South brings U.S. Blacks Full Circle," *Population Today* 29(4):1, 2001.

41. A Special Report on the American South, "The Central Question: Race Relations are No Longer Black and White, *The Economists,* March 3, 2007. p. 6.

42. Richard D. Alba, *Ethnic Identity: The Transformation of White America,* Yale University Press, New Haven, Conn., 1990.

43. For an excellent early study of life in Chicago's black ghetto, see St. Clair Drake and Horace Cayton, *Black Metropolis,* Harcourt, Brace, New York, 1945.

44. Emile Rosenbaum and Samantha Friedman, *The Housing Divide: How Generations of Immigrants Fare in New York's Housing Market,* New York University Press, New York, 2006.

45. Daniel H. Weinberg and John Iceland, *Racial and Ethnic Residential Segregation in the United States: 1980-2000,* U.S. Census Bureau, Washington, D.C.; and Douglas Massey and Nancy Denton, *American Apartheid: Segregation and the Making of the Underclass,* Harvard University Press, Cambridge, MA, 1993.

46. Karl E. Taeuber and Alma F. Taeuber, *Negroes in Cities: Residential Segregation and Neighborhood Change,* Aldine, Chicago, 1965; Annemette Sorenson, Karl E. Taeuber, and Leslie J. Hollingsworth Jr., "Indexes of Racial Residential Segregation for 109 Cities in the United States, 1940 to 1970," *Sociological Focus* April 1975, pp. 125–42; Thomas Van Valey, Wade Clark Roof, and Jerome E. Witcox, "Trends in Residential Segregation: 1960–1970," *American Journal of Sociology* 82:826–844, 1977; Karl E. Taeuber, "Racial Residential Segregation in 28 Cities, 1970–1980," Center for Demography and Ecology, University of Wisconsin Working Paper 83–12, 1983; Michael J. White, *American Neighborhoods and Residential Differentiation,* Russell Sage Foundation for the National Committee for Research on the 1980 Census, New York, 1988; and Edward L. Glaeser and Jacob L. Vigdor, "Racial Segregation: Promising News," in Bruce Katz and Robert E. Lang (eds.), *Redefining Urban and Suburban America,* Brookings Institution Press, Washington, 2003, pp. 211–234.

47. Reynolds Farley and William H. Frey, "Changes in the Segregation of Whites from Blacks During the 1980s: Small Steps toward a More Integrated Society," *American Sociological Review* 59: 23–45, 1994.

48. Douglas Massey and Nancy Denton, op. cit.

49. Quoted in Michael Martin, "Harvard Black Scholar Laments Those Left Behind," *Richmond Times–Dispatch,* February 16, 1997, p. C1.

50. Lawrence Otis Graham, *Our Kind of People: Inside America's Black Upper Class,* Harper-Collins, New York, 1999.

51. U.S. Bureau of the Census, *The Black Population of the United States: March 1994,* pp. 2–20, no 480, 1995.

52. Associated Press, "Data Shows Gaps In Women's Income," *Wall Street Journal,* March 28, 2005, p. A9.

53. Michael Stoll, *African Americans and the Color Line,* Russell Sage, New York, 2004.

54. Melvin L. Oliver and Thomas M. Shapiro, *Black Wealth/White Wealth: A Perspective on Racial Inequality,* Routledge, New York, 1995.

55. Mary Patillo-McCoy, *Black Picket Fences: Privilege and Peril among the Black Middle Class,* University of Chicago Press, Chicago, 1999.

56. William Julius Wilson and Richard P. Taub, *There Goes the Neighborhood: Racial, Ethnic, and Class Tensions in Four Chicago Neighborhoods,* Knopf, New York, 2006.

57. Bill Maxwell, "Grim Statistics for African-American Men," *Herald Tribune,* January 11, 2004, p. 3F.

58. Loic J. D. Wacquant and William Julius Wilson, "The Cost of Racial and Class Exclusion in the Inner City," *The Annals* 501:17, 1989.

59. William Julius Wilson, *When Work Disappears,* Knopf, New York, 1996, p. 1.

60. Elijah Anderson, *Code of the Street: Decency, Violence, and the Moral Code of the Inner City,* W. W. Norton, New York, 1999.

CHAPTER 10

Diversity: Hispanics, Asians, and Native Americans

Goddamn New York, it is filled with Jews and Catholics and blacks and Puerto Ricans. There is a law of the jungle where some things don't survive. So maybe New York shouldn't survive. Maybe it should go through a cycle of destruction.

President Richard M. Nixon, from the 1972 Nixon Watergate Tapes, released December 2003

OUTLINE

Introduction
    Fourth-Wave Immigrants
    Recent Immigration Impact on Cities
    Melting Pot or Cultural Pluralism
Latino Population
    Legal Status
    Growth
    Diversity
Mexican Americans
    Mexican Diversity
    Education
    Urbanization
    Housing and Other Patterns
    Political Involvement
Puerto Ricans
Asian Americans
    A "Model Minority"?
    Asian Residential Segregation
    The Case of Japanese Americans
    The Internment Camps
    Japanese Americans Today
Native Americans
    Nonurban Orientation
    Movement to Cities
Summary

INTRODUCTION

The following pages review the changing status of metro-area Hispanics, Asians, and Native Americans. These are the populations replenishing American cities.

America is becoming far more multicultural and multiracial. All minorities combined comprise more than a third of the nation's population, up from a quarter in 1990. One in five U.S. residents is either foreign born or first generation. The U.S. minority population numbers more than 100 million.[1]

The state of California provides a quick look at where we may be going as a nation in terms of ethnic change. California has a history of leading the nation in demographic and social trends. Thus, a look at contemporary California gives an indication of what much of the rest of the nation can expect. As of 2010, the Census Bureau reported that 58 percent of the state's population was minority. In California non-Hispanic whites became a "minority" population in 2000. California's population now is 36 percent Hispanic, 14 percent Asian, and 9 percent African American. Hawaii, New Mexico, Texas, and Washington, D.C., are the nation's other majority-minority localities. By 2015 non-Hispanic whites will also be a numerical minority in Florida. Based on Census Bureau projections half the nation will be "minority" by 2050.

The rate of ethnic change is increasing. California now is a majority-minority state. It is also home to more than one-third of all legal immigrants to the United States and half those who enter illegally. Some 35 years ago California's famous Silicon Valley (Santa Clara County) was 82 percent non-Hispanic white. Today whites comprise less than half of the population of Silicon Valley; Hispanics represent 24 percent of the population; Asians 23 percent; and African Americans 4 percent. Immigrants provide much of America's cutting-edge computer-related technology. The workforce at Silicon Valley's dot-coms is heavily Asian, especially Chinese and Indian. Data from Dun & Bradstreet indicate that 29 percent of the post-1995 Silicon Valley start-ups are headed by Asians. It is worth noting that Cisco Systems' San Jose headquarters' workforce is 45 percent Asian, while Sun Microsystems and Hotmail were started by Indian entrepreneurs.

Fourth-Wave Immigrants

The majority of the nation's newest or "fourth-wave" immigrants are Hispanic or Asian. During the last census decade the number of foreign-born Hispanic residents grew 34 percent while the number of foreign-born Asians shot up 40 percent. Currently, Hispanics make up 51 percent of the legal immigrant population, and Asians constitute 30 percent.[2] (Actual Hispanic figures are somewhat higher due to approximately 12 million non-documented Hispanics.) This means four of five legal immigrants now come from Asia and Latin America (primarily Mexico). Canada, on the other

hand, has proportionately higher immigration rates, but the great majority of immigrants to Canada come from Asia, with only a small proportion being Hispanic. Since the birthrate of native-born Canadians is below replacement level, all of Canada's current population growth can be attributed to immigration and to the fertility of immigrants.

The era of mass European migration to North America ended roughly 90 years ago. Today less than 5 percent of America's yearly million-plus immigrants come from Europe. Ellis Island is now a museum. Los Angeles International Airport (LAX) is the Ellis Island of the 21st century. Immigrants are concentrated in California, New York, Florida, Texas, Illinois, and New Jersey. However, most recently non-"gateway" states as diverse as Georgia, North Carolina, Minnesota, and Iowa have seen dramatic increases in their immigrant populations.

In the cities of the East and the Midwest the majority of the European white ethnic populations now have been dispersed outward from ethnic neighborhoods. This has led some to view the ethnic neighborhoods, as described in Chapter 7: Urban Lifestyles, as simply historical remnants of bypassed ways of life. However, ethnic neighborhoods are far from gone. The difference is that today's immigrant neighborhoods are most likely to be Hispanic or Asian.

Recent Immigration Impact on Cities

The role of immigrants in shaping the American city of the 19th and early 20th centuries is well known. Less well known is the impact of the subsequent declines in immigration and the resurgence of urban immigration, especially during the last decade. From the 1920s to 1970s, sharply curtailed immigration meant central-city declines because those who moved out could not be replaced with newcomers. Today vibrant immigrant neighborhoods are again the pattern in cities such as New York, Toronto, Miami, Chicago, Houston, Los

Angeles, San Francisco, and Vancouver. During the last decade New York City would have lost 5 percent of its population were it not for new immigrants. Immigrant populations are replacing central cities' population losses and adding to the tax base. In some cases they are also revitalizing inner-city neighborhoods. Immigrants are particularly attracted to large cities such as New York, Toronto, Los Angeles, Vancouver, Chicago, and Miami.

Research done by the Fannie Mae Foundation shows that immigrants will account for almost one-quarter of all new households in the U.S., and this figure is far higher in port-of-entry or gateway cities.[3] Figure 10.1 shows the racial and ethnic composition of the United States in 2010, with projections for 2025 and 2050. In addition to the 880,000 legal U.S. immigrants each year, approximately 300,000 permanent nondocumented, or illegal immigrants, enter the country, for a net increase of 1.25 million persons a year.[4]

Immigrants, and the children of immigrants, now account for over half the United States population growth. In larger cities they may account for most of the growth. In the case of Miami the largely immigrant Latino community has evolved into the dominant population group. Half of greater Miami's population is Hispanic, and 60 percent of that is Cuban. Miami has become a bilingual city that is economically and socially being shaped by Latin immigrants.[5] Only 30 percent of Miami's population is non-Hispanic white. (Among North American cities Toronto has the second highest proportion of immigrants at 44 percent.) In similar fashion Asian immigrants are changing West Coast cities such as Los Angeles and Vancouver.

Melting Pot or Cultural Pluralism

Assimilation or integration into American society through a "melting pot" was the model that guided the early studies of the Chicago School

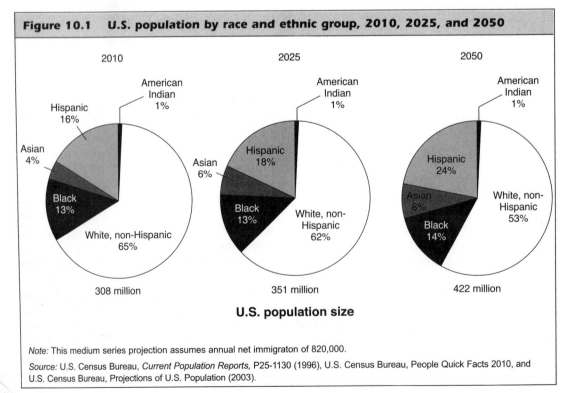

Figure 10.1   U.S. population by race and ethnic group, 2010, 2025, and 2050

2010 — 308 million
Hispanic 16%
American Indian 1%
Asian 4%
Black 13%
White, non-Hispanic 65%

2025 — 351 million
American Indian 1%
Hispanic 18%
Asian 6%
Black 13%
White, non-Hispanic 62%

2050 — 422 million
American Indian 1%
Hispanic 24%
Asian 8%
Black 14%
White, non-Hispanic 53%

U.S. population size

Note: This medium series projection assumes annual net immigraton of 820,000.

Source: U.S. Census Bureau, *Current Population Reports*, P25-1130 (1996), U.S. Census Bureau, People Quick Facts 2010, and U.S. Census Bureau, Projections of U.S. Population (2003).

sociologists. The melting pot model was implicit in Burgess's zonal hypothesis discussed in Chapter 4. The melting pot assumed that as second- and later-generation populations moved toward the urban periphery, they would lose much of their ethnic identification. In fact, as European-origin groups have moved into the middle class, ethnic differences have faded and a generalized "European" background has emerged.[6]

During the 1970s the melting-pot metaphor was largely replaced by that of *cultural pluralism.* Cultural pluralism suggests the metaphor of a salad bowl rather than a melting pot. While an extreme view of the melting pot assumed all ethnic cultures would die out, the extreme cultural pluralist view is that all racial and ethnic cultures should remain distinct. Trying to "Americanize" newcomers or to push English as a national language is seen as "cultural genocide." Attempts to assimilate new immigrants are denounced as racist.[7] However, since 9/11 there has been increased public debate as to whether separatist pluralism fosters cultural and political extremism.

Does ethnicity really make a difference in the attitudes, values, or lifestyle of second- and later-generation whites and Asians now living in the suburbs? Research by Reynolds Farley on today's second-generation European and Asian immigrants suggests not. It shows that they are making rapid social and economic progress.[8] Most social scientists suggest that for predicting a person's behavior and future, knowing their social class is far more useful than knowing their ethnicity. A number of years ago Scott Greer suggested that ethnicity had lost real meaning when increasing proportions of the population have mixed ancestry. He stated that, "The romantic idealization of the ethnic bond persists, despite the difficulty many Americans have in deciding which ethnic background is the right one."[9] Tiger Wood's background, for example, is Thai, Chinese, Jamaican, European, and others. Research by Jaret and Reitzes indicates that for both whites

and those of multiracial background the importance of racial-ethnic identity is decreasing.[10] In the U.S. African Americans are only now becoming part of the melting pot. However, for poorer persons of color residing in inner-city ghettos, the most appropriate model may not be the melting pot, or cultural pluralism, but internal colonialism.

LATINO POPULATION

Immigration is an issue that is splitting the country. Hispanics are now America's largest minority population.[11] In 1980 the Latino population was only slightly more than half the size of the African American population, but dramatic growth resulted in the Census Bureau designating Latinos as the nation's largest minority group in 2003.[12] The 2000 census counted 35.3 million Hispanics, about 3 million more than the Census Bureau had predicted. The Census Bureau estimated this had increased to 48 million Latino Americans in 2009.[13] Those of Hispanic origin account for 16 percent of the national population, and this figure includes the Census Bureau's estimate of 12 million undocumented or unauthorized immigrants, the majority of whom are Hispanic. Hispanics now account for half of those being added yearly to the U.S. population. The Census Bureau defines Hispanic as being an ethnic rather than a racial category and Hispanics can be of any race.[14] The Latino population currently is growing five times faster than the population as a whole (see figure 10.2). It is projected that before 2050 one of every four Americans will be Latino.

Superficial changes can already be seen such as the popularity of Latino music and foods—the United States now consumes more tortilla chips than French fries and uses more salsa than ketchup. A more substantive visible change is the growing use of Spanish, including signage in business establishments and stores such as Sears and McDonald's.

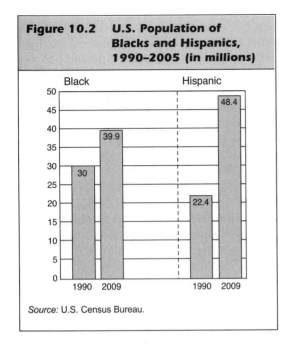

Figure 10.2 U.S. Population of Blacks and Hispanics, 1990–2005 (in millions)

Source: U.S. Census Bureau.

Legal Status

A noticeable response to the growing Latino population can be seen in Arizona's 2010 anti-immigration law, which mandates that police stopping anyone who could be in the country illegally (i.e., Latinos) must check their immigration status. The constitutionality of the law is currently being tested in the courts.

Currently, undocumented immigrants make up slightly more than 4 percent of the population, but their babies represent twice that number, or 8 percent of all births.[15] Latinos account for about 85 percent of the births to undocumented immigrants. There now are some 4 million children who have U.S. citizenship as a result of being born in the United States to undocumented immigrants. Whether or not the children who are born in the United States are guaranteed automatic citizenship under the 14th Amendment is an issue certain to come before the Supreme Court.

Growth

The Latino population is growing by an extraordinary 1.4 million a year, five times the national average. In a big change, as of 2005 more Latino growth came from births rather than immigration. This is partially because of the Hispanic population's young age structure (a 2005 median age of 27.2 years, 10 years below the non-Hispanic white average of 36.2). Two-thirds of the Latino population is under age 35. This means far more of the Hispanic population is of childbearing age. Additionally, Latino birthrates are about 50 percent higher than the U.S. average. Thus, Latino growth will continue to occur even if immigration, legal and undocumented, ceases.

The result of both Hispanic and Asian immigration is a new multicultural society taking form along the Pacific Coast. Latinos now constitute one-third of California's population, and Hispanic-origin births now constitute half of all births. A sign of changing patterns came in 1998 when "José" replaced "Michael" as the most popular name for newborn boys in both California and Texas. By 2020 Hispanics are projected to outnumber non-Hispanic whites in both states. Before the end of the 21st century, the United States will probably be the largest Spanish-speaking country in the world.

Latinos are concentrated geographically (see table 10.1). Over half the Hispanic population of the United States is clustered in two states: California and Texas; most of these immigrants are from Mexico or Central America. One in three Latinos calls California home. The 2000 census showed New York with the third-largest Hispanic concentration; there were roughly 3.6 million Hispanics counted in the New York metropolitan area. Puerto Ricans, who used to represent the great bulk of New York–area Hispanics, now number about 2 million, or somewhat over half of all Hispanics. New York is now home to increasing numbers of Dominicans, Colombians, and Cubans. The Washington, D.C., metro area had 432,000 Latinos counted by the 2000 census. Florida similarly has a growing Cuban population with over a million Latinos in the Miami metropolitan area and a growing Puerto Rican population in Orlando. Some 27 percent of Chicago's popula-

Table 10.1 **States Ranked by Hispanic Population, 2000**					
Rank	State	Hispanic Population, 2000	Hispanic Population, 1990	Numeric Change	Percent Change	Percent Hispanic
1	California	10,459,616	7,704,348	2,755,268	35.8	31
2	Texas	6,045,430	4,339,874	1,705,556	39.3	30
3	New York	2,660,685	2,213,943	446,742	20.2	14
4	Florida	2,334,403	1,574,148	760,225	48.3	15
5	Illinois	1,276,193	904,449	371,744	41.1	10
6	Arizona	1,084,250	688,355	395,895	57.5	22
7	New Jersey	1,027,277	747,737	279,540	37.4	12
8	New Mexico	708,407	579,227	129,180	22.3	40
9	Colorado	603,582	424,309	179,273	42.3	15
10	Massachusetts	390,947	287,561	103,386	36.0	6

Source: Population Estimates Program, Population Division, U.S. Census Bureau.

tion is Hispanic, the largest group being 700,000 Mexican Americans.

Latinos, however, are beginning to spread out to smaller metro areas. Hispanic migrants are transforming smaller communities where a decade or so earlier they were all but invisible. Raleigh-Durham, for example, now has more than 100,000 Hispanics. Georgia had about 100,000 Hispanics in 1990; today the figure is over a million. In Dalton, Georgia, the percentage of Hispanic students has gone from 1 percent to 42 percent. Latino communities are now growing in places where they weren't previously found, such as Kentucky, Kansas, and Iowa.[16]

The Latino population is more concentrated in metropolitan areas than either the white or black populations. Some 84 percent of Latinos live in metro areas. There are more than 4.7 million Latinos in Los Angeles County alone.[17] Hispanics in Houston now outnumber both blacks and whites. Miami, as a consequence of Cuban in-migration since the 1960s, has gone from being a declining winter resort for the elderly to the "Capital of the Caribbean." Latinos make up three-fifths of Miami's population; Cubans alone number more than 1 million.

While the Hispanic population is metropolitan, it isn't solely urban. Latinos are rapidly suburbanizing. Within metropolitan areas the Hispanic population is more evenly distributed than the black population. As of the 2010 census, more than half of the Latino population resided in suburbs. Hispanics account for a quarter of all suburban population growth.

Diversity

The difficulty in discussing Hispanics in the United States is that in many ways Latinos aren't an ethnic group at all. Rather *Latino* is an umbrella term that covers everyone speaking a common language although they come (or their forebears came) from two dozen different countries and cultures. Latinos include everyone from middle-class Mexican Americans in California to Tejanos (Texas Mexicans) to poor Chicago Puerto Ricans to successful Cubans in Miami. Thus, Latinos are very heterogeneous with regard to place of origin, economic status, and social variables. The label *Hispanic* or *Latino*, by suggesting commonality, obscures the diversity of people sharing the label. Nationally, a common Latino subcommunity doesn't really exist.

Most Hispanics define themselves by their original nationality, while others prefer the more generic *Latino*. Some 65 percent of the U.S. Hispanic population has Mexican heritage, 13 percent come from Central or Latin

America, 10 percent is from Puerto Rico, 5 percent is Cuban, and 7 percent other. As a group Latino males make approximately two-thirds the income of non-Hispanic whites, while Latina women make four-fifths that of non-Hispanic white women. The Spanish-speaking population as a whole is better off economically than blacks, but below non-Hispanic whites. One-quarter of blacks are below the poverty level; this is true of 22 percent of Hispanics and 8 percent of non-Hispanic whites.[18]

This general comparison, however, masks wide variations among those of different Spanish-speaking backgrounds. Puerto Ricans, with a high proportion of female-headed households, earn the least; Mexican Americans earn slightly more; and Cuban Americans—many of whose families left Cuba with marketable business and professional skills—earn considerably more. Cuban American income levels now slightly exceed those of the general population.

Contributing to the comparatively low economic position of many Latinos are their low levels of education. According to Department of Education figures some 4 of 10 Hispanic adults have less than a high school education.[19] More worrisome, one-third of current students fail to finish high school. (As of 2005 only 12 percent of Latinos had completed college, compared to 31 percent of non-Hispanic whites, 18 percent of African Americans, and 49 percent of Asians.) In the United States, lack of a high school diploma means virtual exclusion from most contemporary employment, so many Hispanics are employed in the so-called secondary labor market of marginal jobs and illegal enterprises. While older immigrants, especially Cubans, sometimes arrived in the United States with skills, recent immigrants (especially Dominicans and Salvadorians) are largely unskilled and have especially low educational levels. Thus it is feared that they will have more employment problems, will have lower-than-average incomes, and will spend more time on welfare than other immigrant groups. However, keep in mind that the Latino population is very diverse. Cuban Americans, for example, now

have college graduation rates equal to those of non-Hispanic whites.

MEXICAN AMERICANS

Today approximately two-thirds of all Hispanics are Mexican Americans. Mexican immigrants have earned a reputation as hard workers. Stereotypes of Mexican Americans as largely agricultural workers are quite erroneous. While many Hispanic immigrants have rural roots, 90 percent of California's residents of Mexican descent are urban dwellers. Los Angeles County today has over 4.7 million Latinos (most of whom are of Mexican background). This is without fully counting all the "undocumented aliens" in the heavily Spanish-speaking East Los Angeles area. There are more Latinos than blacks in Los Angeles. The city is 40 percent Latino, 37 percent Anglo, 13 percent African American, 9 percent Asian, and 1 percent Native American.

Mexican Diversity

Anglos may see the Mexican American community as uniform, but that is not the view from the inside. There isn't even a mutually acceptable term used to define the group. California-born, second- and third-generation, poor, barrio-living Latinos call themselves *Chicanos,* while middle-class Mexican Americans shun the term. Within the two largest Mexican American populations, California Mexican Americans (*Californios*) differ radically from Texas Mexican Americans (*Tejanos*). Both disagree over whose culture is more authentically Mexican American.

Tex-Mex has a heritage of both its own unique foods and its own music, a combination of country and *ranchera.* More importantly, *Tejanos* have often been in the United States for generations, while *Californios* are often more recent arrivals. In south Texas many Anglos speak Spanish, and intermarriage has a long tradition. Tex-Mex populations also tend to be far more conservative socially than *Californios* on questions of family, abortion, and even immigration.

Traditionally, Mexicans (and Anglos) made a broad distinction between the upper-class "Spanish" and the lower-class "Mexicans." "Spanish" ancestry has traditionally been considered more prestigious than "Mexican" ancestry, and "Indian" ancestry is at the bottom. This attitude has roots deep in the early colonial history of Mexico under the Spanish Crown. (The Spanish colonial social system is discussed further in Chapter 16: African and Latin American Urbanization.) The gracious Spanish grandee of a California rancho (e.g., Zorro) typifies the first stereotype. Mexicans, by contrast, were stereotyped as lazy peasants. Particularly disparaged are recent Mexican immigrants. Residing in the country as undocumented workers and working in menial jobs, undocumented Mexicans constitute one of the poorest-educated segments of the population. The social distinction between "Spanish" and "Mexican" serves the sociological function of allowing the former to be accepted into the businesses, homes, and even families of Anglo society, while discrimination and exploitation of lower-class "Mexicans" continues.

Education

Low educational levels are a major barrier to economic advancement. Mexican Americans have lower median levels of education than African Americans. Poor knowledge of English tends to shunt Mexican American newcomers toward low-paying jobs with limited chances for advancement. However, poorer academic performance is not simply the result of being handicapped by not knowing English since the Latino population most likely to speak Spanish at home is Cubans, the group who have the highest educational levels.

For families without steady employment, frequent moving disrupts children's education. Hispanic immigrants often have completed little formal education in their home countries. Only 44 percent of foreign-born Hispanic adults are high school graduates, compared to 70 percent of U.S.-born Hispanic adults.[20] Current immigrants from Mexico have lower educational levels than Mexican immigrants of earlier generations.

The question is whether the current low-education Mexican and Central American immigrants will remain stuck in low-paying jobs once they become familiar with the U.S. labor market. There are some positive signs. Today Latino (and especially Mexican) workers are helped by a growing reputation as being good, responsible workers. Newcomers sometimes hold two jobs in order to leverage themselves into the middle class.

Urbanization

The rapid urbanization of the Mexican American population has made the problems of social and economic adjustment more acute. Today Los Angeles has more people of Mexican ancestry than any other city in the Americas except Mexico City and Guadalajara. Clearly, the Mexican American's future is an urban future. More recently, the geographical movement out of the Southwest is not only migration out of a region; it is a symbol of the inevitable change from rural to urban residence, and rural to urban ways of life.

Until the recent national debate over immigration Mexican Americans had generally attracted less attention than had other minority groups. The relatively low profile maintained by Mexican American city dwellers can be partially attributed to the fact that a significant proportion of the newcomers are undocumented immigrants who therefore are not seeking attention. Despite the low-level income, housing, and services they experience in U.S. cities the standard of living is still superior to the destitute *barrios* of the Mexican *municipios*. Living is also better than in the *barrios* in Mexico along the American border region where many United States manufacturing plants have relocated in order to profit from wages that average one-quarter of those in the United States.

Congresswoman Loretta Sanchez (D-CA) is one of a growing number of Latinos serving in the U.S. Congress. Her representation of Orange County, California, reflects the increasing diversity of the U.S. population overall, and especially the influx of Latinos into major urban areas. Office of Loretta Sanchez photo

Housing and Other Patterns

The crowded *barrios* of California and Texas are where new arrivals are most likely to settle. Poverty is common in the urban *barrios*, or "hoods," and Chicano "homeboy" gangs remain a serious problem. Gang-related drug use and crime are common in the hoods.[21] Los Angeles County is estimated to have as many as 40,000 gang members. For Mexican Americans there are wide variations in patterns of physical segregation. Segregation levels are high in large cities having large Latino populations.[22] Outside of the border states, economics plays an increasing part in determining residential patterns.

Political Involvement

Mexican Americans are still underrepresented in the halls of political power, but signs point to increased political activity. The National League of Cities says Hispanics nationally hold only 4 percent of mayoral and council seats (blacks hold 14 percent and whites 81 percent).[23] Mexican Americans got a big boost in 2005 when Antonio Villaraigosa, a one-time high school barrio dropout, became mayor of Los Angeles.

Mexican Americans are divided as to viewing themselves as a distinct minority group, or as individual Americans who share the speaking of Spanish. Chicanos often look to black groups as an example of how they should organize, while assimilated middle-class Mexican Americans resist the minority-group label. Overall, political awareness and voting is increasing. Latinos now constitute 12 percent of the voters in Texas, and 15 percent of those in California, and their numbers are increasing. In 1996, Orange County, California, long considered a conservative WASP bastion, voted out their entrenched nine-term right-wing Republican Congressman. He was defeated by Loretta Sanchez, a Latina Democrat who still holds the seat a decade and a half later. Orange

County is now one-third Latino, and 45 percent of the county's residents speak a language other than English at home.[24]

Nonetheless, it is the number of Latino voters, rather than population numbers, that is most important. Some 12 million Latinos have non-legal status, and only 35 percent of all legal Mexican-born immigrants are citizens and thus able to vote. Also most Latinos live in solidly Republican states such as Texas or solidly Democratic states including California, where Latino voting numbers aren't enough to shift party control. Latinos, for instance, number 30 percent of generally reliably Republican Arizona, but so far they account for only a relatively small number of voters.

Also, Latino groups don't all vote the same. While California and Texas Mexicans generally vote Democratic, Cubans in Florida vote overwhelmingly Republican. Other Florida Latinos vote largely Democratic. One could make the argument that the split in the Florida Latino vote in the 2000 election contributed to George W. Bush's being sworn in as president. While Gore won the national popular vote, Bush's eventual victory was based on a contested 500-vote margin in Florida, where his brother was governor. Controversy remains about whether or not Florida counted all votes from black and non-Cuban Latino areas.

PUERTO RICANS

Puerto Ricans, with about 10 percent of Hispanics, are the second-largest Hispanic minority in the United States. Puerto Ricans differ from other Spanish-speaking Americans in one significant respect: Puerto Ricans have been American citizens since 1917. Thus, there is no question regarding their legal citizenship. Mainland Puerto Ricans are almost totally urban. Some 96 percent of mainland Puerto Ricans reside in metropolitan areas, especially in New York City and Orlando, Florida. According to the Census Bureau, as of 2008, Florida had more Puerto Ricans than New York, reversing the heavy concentration of Puerto Ricans in New York City. Puerto Rican family income is the lowest among all Hispanic groups, with one-third of Puerto Rican families living in poverty. Puerto Ricans are even more hard-pressed than blacks.

Like blacks, but unlike other Hispanics, Puerto Ricans have a high proportion of female-headed families. Over four of ten (44 percent) of all Puerto Rican families are headed by a woman without a husband present. Puerto Rican women also are less likely to be in the labor force than other Hispanic women. Following World War II, over a million Puerto Ricans moved to New York City. Most of them worked in the city's manufacturing plants. As of the 1960s Puerto Ricans in New York owned some 4,000 businesses, many of them in Spanish Harlem. During the 1970s and 1980s the industrial base of the city withered away, leaving many Puerto Ricans unemployed. Today economic advancement strongly favors those having white-collar skills and higher levels of education. Upgrading overall educational levels is essential. Puerto Rican political involvement tends to be low compared with that of other immigrant groups—perhaps because Puerto Ricans can migrate back to Puerto Rico when facing tough times.

ASIAN AMERICANS

Asian Americans are fast increasing in numbers. Between 1990 and 2010 the Asian American population more than doubled. Census figures indicate the Asian American population increased to 15 million in 2010. Because of heavy recent immigration, the foreign-born Asian population is now half again as large as that of native-born Asian Americans. Immigrants from Asia represent almost half of all legal immigrants coming to the United States and the majority of Canada's immigrants. Asian Americans now account for 5 percent of the nation's population.[25]

The Asian American population is overwhelmingly metropolitan with 94 percent living in metropolitan areas compared to 80 percent

Asian Americans have risen to the top of every enterprise from government to business to the arts, often in urban contexts. Here, former Washington, D.C., schools chancellor Michelle Rhee testifies on Capitol Hill. © Susan Walsh/AP Images

of the overall population.[26] Asians are highly concentrated on the West Coast with 54 percent of all Asian Americans living in the western United States. Four of 10 of all those of Asian background are living in California. The metropolitan Los Angeles Asian population numbers over a million. Vancouver and Toronto are the major destinations for Asians immigrating to Canada.

As figure 10.3 shows, Asian Americans have diverse origins. The earliest Asian immigrants were largely Chinese and Japanese men who worked as railway workers, laborers, and farmers. The largest contemporary ethnic group is Chinese, followed by Filipino, Asian Indian, Vietnamese, Japanese, and Korean. Metropolitan North American Asian groups are diverse culturally and economically. No "one size fits all" statements apply. Nonetheless, there are some commonalities. One of the most noticeable is a strong belief in education. High school completion rates not only outstrip other minorities but also are higher than those for whites. Nearly 9 of 10 of those over 25 have

completed high school, and almost half of young adults 25 to 29 have at least a college degree.[27] Some four out of ten students at the University of California, Berkeley, are Asian. Asian Americans have twice the proportion graduating from college as do whites.[28]

A "Model Minority"?

Economically Asian Americans are prospering. As a group, Asian Americans have for decades had the highest average family income levels of any census group. For example, as of 1996 the median family income for Asian Americans was $3,000 more than for non-Hispanic whites, $18,000 above Hispanics, and nearly $20,000 above the median family income for African Americans.[29] Within the Asian population there is a great economic range, with Japanese Americans having the highest income levels, and the more recently arrived Vietnamese the lowest.

Asians have prospered in a number of occupations. Among the better known are Kore-

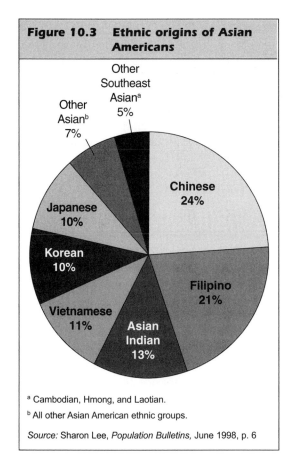

Figure 10.3   Ethnic origins of Asian Americans

Other Southeast Asian[a]
5%

Other Asian[b]
7%

Chinese
24%

Japanese
10%

Korean
10%

Filipino
21%

Vietnamese
11%

Asian Indian
13%

[a] Cambodian, Hmong, and Laotian.

[b] All other Asian American ethnic groups.

Source: Sharon Lee, *Population Bulletins,* June 1998, p. 6

dren are more likely to be raised in intact families having close family ties. They are also more likely to grow up in families with multiple workers. The role played by having extended households with multiple workers is very positive in raising household income.[31] Being a "model minority," however, can sometimes bring its own problems. The open hostility that earlier generations of Asian immigrants encountered sometimes is now replaced by more subtle types of prejudice. The relative success of Asian Americans means that they are now sometimes encountering a "glass ceiling." Ironically, much of this comes because Asian Americans are perceived not as a "problem" minority, but as a "super minority."

Although as "honorary whites" they may be the model minority when compared to experiences of other minorities such as blacks and Latinos, they may still be considered foreigners when compared to whites.[32] In the same way that Euro-Americans have adopted a common white identity, people of Asian ancestry may be coming to adopt a common Pan-Asian ancestry.

Asian Residential Segregation

American urbanization reveals a strong association between ethnicity and race on one hand and patterns of urban residential segregation on the other. In the classic North American pattern of urban settlement described in Chapter 3: The Rise of Urban America, the point of entry for poor immigrants was the tenement district surrounding the core of the city. As the newcomers' economic conditions improved, the more established immigrants moved outward, leaving their tenements to be occupied by a wave of more recent immigrants. The first Asian immigrants were Chinese laborers brought to America to build the transcontinental railroad, but with the completion of the railroad the 1882 Chinese Exclusion Act forbade further immigration. Those of Chinese background were restricted to living in Chinatowns, which initially were viewed as being a combination of mystery, vice, and inscrutable Oriental

ans as grocery and liquor store owners, Vietnamese owning restaurants, Asian Indians in medical fields and running quick-stop stores, and Filipinas as nurses. The economic success of metro-area Asian immigrant groups has been linked partially to an ethnic enclave economy that gives newcomers a start.[30] Although an enclave economy that sells largely to the ethnic group limits contacts with the larger economy, it provides an environment where non-English speakers can obtain employment.

Asian newcomers also have high levels of human capital due to household composition. Asian Americans are more likely than other ethnic and racial groups to live in supportive family households. Some 78 percent of Asian households are family households as compared to 70 percent for combined white and African American households. Asian American chil-

ways of life. By the 1930s Chinatowns began to have a still exotic, but more cosmopolitan, image, an ethnic "city within a city," but a city still plagued by low-prestige, low-paying jobs.[33]

Following World War II, Chinatowns declined as populations aged and upwardly mobile younger populations moved out. Revival of immigration during recent decades has brought new life to ethnic enclave economies, but most new poorer immigrants, although living in crowded housing, do not form traditional Chinatowns.[34] During recent decades Asian immigrant groups have been instrumental in bringing indirect urban renewal and reversing blight in city neighborhoods. For example, small commercial strips have been revitalized by Korean grocery stores and Chinese restaurants. Pooling capital, often through small revolving credit associations, has aided Asians in establishing small businesses.

Today, well-educated Asian immigrants bypass the city entirely and move to the economically developing suburban edge cities. Immigrants from China and India with advanced degrees typically have suburban residential addresses. Of the more than 50,000 Koreans who live in the metro area of Washington, D.C., less than 1,000 actually live in the District. Asians commonly live with those of similar ethnic background in suburbs that have a strong Asian presence but are predominantly white. An exception is the Los Angeles suburb of Monterey Park in which four-fifths of the residents are ethnic Chinese. Monterey Park is the first Chinese suburb in America.[35]

The Case of Japanese Americans

Whenever one starts making generalizations about minorities, one is brought up short by the example of the Japanese Americans. Japanese Americans, who during World War II were a hated minority, are now among the nation's most successful, and prosperous, citizens. Japanese Americans have been notably successful in adapting to the values, behaviors, and expecta-

tions of the American system. Harry Kitano's oft-quoted statement, "Scratch a Japanese American and find a white Anglo-Saxon Protestant," is generally accurate.[36] What makes this all the more remarkable is that Japanese Americans have had to overcome severe discrimination—discrimination that included being forcibly driven from their homes and businesses during World War II and being incarcerated behind barbed wire in "relocation camps."

The Internment Camps

The entry of the United States into World War II on December 7, 1941, resulted in anti-Japanese hysteria. It was popularly believed that a Japanese fifth column existed, conducting sabotage on orders from Tokyo. Interestingly, considering their later political development, such well-known liberals as Earl Warren and Walter Lippmann were among the most vocal for relocating the Japanese, while one of the few public officials to denounce the rumors of sabotage as "racist hysteria" was J. Edgar Hoover, the director of the FBI.

The public clamor for action was met in February 1942 when President Roosevelt signed Executive Order 9066. The order designated military areas from which military commanders could exclude persons because of national security. The order also authorized the construction of inland "relocation centers." It was quickly implemented. On March 2, 1942, General De Witt, commander of the Western Defense Area, ordered all persons of Japanese ancestry to be evacuated from the three western coastal states and part of Arizona. He summed up his feelings when he said, "Once a Jap, always a Jap." The evacuation order included children with as little as one-eighth Japanese ancestry. Two-thirds of those ordered to leave their homes were citizens of the United States. They were each allowed to take one suitcase with them as they were herded by army troops into assembly centers and then shipped to 1 of 10 inland relocation camps. More than 110,000 of the 126,000 Japanese in this country were put in these camps—regardless of their citizenship.

No such action was taken against those of German and Italian ancestry on the East Coast, nor was any action taken against the Japanese on the strategic islands of Hawaii, where the Japanese made up a full 37 percent of the population. Long after the war, it was officially admitted that no Japanese American had committed a single subversive act anywhere within the United States. But for as long as three years many Japanese Americans lived in dismal tarpaper shacks in deserted, inhospitable areas of California, Arizona, Idaho, Wyoming, Utah, and Arkansas, surrounded by barbed wire and machine guns. The inmates were let out only on "seasonal leaves"—which was a euphemistic way of saying that they were used as cheap labor on local farms. Jobs in the camps paid from $16 to $19 a month. In 1942 the Federal Reserve Bank of San Francisco estimated the Japanese Americans' financial loss—abandoned or cheaply sold stores, farms, and businesses—at $400 million. The United States government eventually paid settlement claims at the rate of 5 to 10 cents on the dollar. In 1988, the U.S. government issued an apology to those interred in the camps and two years later made symbolic payments of $20,000 to each person so treated.

Life in the camps radically changed the structure of Japanese American society. The second generation, or Nisei, who spoke English and were citizens, quickly filled most of the local leadership positions, displacing the older Issei, or first generation. Ironically, the Nisei could fill a host of leadership positions that anti-Japanese discrimination on the West Coast would have made unavailable to them on the outside. After the war many Nisei chose to move east, where their skills and abilities had a better chance of recognition, rather than back to the more ghettoized West Coast.

One of the many paradoxes of this period was that the 442nd Regimental Combat Team—the most-decorated American unit in World War II—was composed of Japanese Americans. More than 1,000 of the men in the 442nd had enlisted directly from the internment camps to fight for the country that had forcibly removed them from their homes and livelihood. (A further irony was that the Japanese American volunteers were sent to Camp Shelby in the racially segregated state of Mississippi. Since all public facilities were either "white" or "colored," the governor had to decide which the Japanese were. He decided that during their stay in Mississippi they were "white.") The 442nd war cry, "Go for Broke," is a part of American history. Less well known is the fact that the average IQ of the unit was the highest (119) for a combat group and that the 442nd had more college graduates than any other comparable unit in the armed forces. The Nisei earned, in blood, the grudging respect of other GIs. In action in Italy and France, the unit suffered 9,486 casualties—or more than 300 percent of its original infantry strength. The 442nd was known as the "Christmas tree" outfit because of all the medals it earned for bravery.

Japanese Americans Today

Since the war Japanese Americans have had a record of upward mobility. The group is almost entirely metropolitan in residence. While in 1940 more than one-quarter of all Japanese Americans were laborers, today this figure is only an insignificant number. Among all American groups the Japanese rank first in income and education. The generations born since World War II have become all but totally acculturated. With an out-marriage rate of more than 50 percent, Japanese Americans are a clear case of assimilation.[37] Soon after arrival, Japanese Americans stopped teaching their children the Japanese language, and over the years Japanese customs have been abandoned in favor of American models. The breakdown of distinctive ways of life is a mixed blessing. On the positive side, Japanese Americans now participate fully in all aspects of national life. However, it is more than a little ironic that in an urban world that is seeking a sense of community, Japanese Americans, who prospered because of their strong community and family systems, would see their distinctive culture disappear.

NATIVE AMERICANS

Native Americans, or in Canadian terminology, "First Peoples," have until very recently not fared well. By omission, we have in essence denied that the Indian has a heritage other than that portrayed in old John Wayne movies on cable television. Not until recent decades have there been popular books telling history from the Indians' side, such as *Bury My Heart at Wounded Knee.*[38] Such works have helped to restore our perspective, but valuable as they are, they do not confront one basic problem: our tendency always to refer to Indians in the past tense, as if they had disappeared with the buffalo and the frontier. They didn't disappear: they were simply ignored and forgotten.

Native Americans or First Peoples—from Algonquin to Cherokee to Lakota to Navajo— are heterogeneous in patterns of social organization and in their world view. The major justification for subsuming such diversity under the generic term *Indian* is that the white society has consistently done this for several centuries and the majority population has responded similarly to all groups it has labeled *Indian*. Recently intertribal and pan-Indian groups have begun to stress common Indian roots and refer to themselves as "Indians."

Nonurban Orientation

North American Indians have traditionally been rural based and oriented. As noted in Chapter 3: The Rise of Urban America, the first colonists saw Indians as part of the physical environment, to be mastered and tamed like the forests and wild animals. The Indians' anti-urban orientation—they lived in nomadic bands or small villages—left them particularly vulnerable to exploitation. Indians were systematically exterminated by Indian wars, destruction of the buffalo, and most importantly, by epidemics of European diseases against which they had no immunity. By 1890, when the first federal census of Indians was taken, their population had been reduced to 250,000, most barely surviving on government reservations. In 1915 the Census Bureau predicted that "full blooded" American Indians would disappear.[39]

Today, the "vanishing red man" is vanishing no more. The 2000 census figures put the Native American population between 2.5 and 4.1 million.[40] The larger number includes those who also included themselves in another racial category. More persons are identifying themselves as Indian on census forms. What this doesn't tell is how many of these have a majority (or any) Indian ancestry. Native Americans remain one of the nation's poorest populations, falling just ahead of Hispanics and African Americans.[41] As with other poor groups, the poorest families are maintained by a single-parent householder. This represents 27 percent of all Indian households. Twenty years ago Native Americans were the poorest group in the United States.[42] While only a few reservations are rich in natural resources, some tribal groups have become relatively well-off during the last decades due to the establishment of reservation gambling casinos. The very small Pequot tribe (375 members) opened Foxwoods Resort Casino in 1992 in Ledyard, Connecticut, and it now grosses over $1 billion a year.[43] Nationally, gambling is now the major reservation employer. Indian "sovereignty" under treaties means many state (and some federal) laws do not apply on Indian reservations. Nor do reservations have state sales taxes, so cigarettes and auto gas can be sold at discount prices. Within the last decade some previously poor tribes have become affluent on gambling and selling nontaxed items. Indian craft items have also become quite popular. Native American education levels are rising; two-thirds of adults are now high school graduates.[44] At present almost all Indian children are attending school, but the quality of the education, particularly in reservation schools, remains suspect. There are wide variations in educational levels among reservations. Overall, Blackfeet and Hopi have the highest rates, while Navajo have the lowest.

Movement to Cities

Native Americans today remain the nation's most rural ethnic group with only half living in cities and one-third still residing on reservations. However, it is likely that the number of American Indians living in cities is under-counted by the census.[45] Native Americans leave the reservations for the cities because most reservations offer no economic future, only illiteracy, poverty, and alcoholism, all too frequently terminated by an early death. Recently on some reservations, gambling casinos have provided an income base. Between 1930 and 2010, the native-born minority group that experienced the greatest degree of urbanization was not, as is commonly thought, blacks but rather Native Americans. As of 1930, only 10 percent of the Indian population lived in metropolitan areas, and as recently as 1960, 7 of 10 Indians were estimated to be rural. Indians have been moving to cities in general rather than to any one city. Some 15 cities in the country have Native American populations of more than 10,000, but in no large city do Indians account for more than 5 percent of the population. The largest urban Indian populations are found in Los Angeles, San Francisco, New York, Phoenix, and Seattle.

The not-uncommon pattern of shuttling between city and reservation hinders effective urban organization. Tribal differences and lack of stable urban Indian populations have worked against the creation of tight ethnic social communities such as those of European immigrants. Shuttling back and forth also interferes with holding stable city jobs. The Bureau of Indian Affairs encourages urban migra-tion because although life in the city may not be grand, it is usually superior to the cycle of acute poverty that is the lot of most of those on the reservation. While the earnings of urban Native Americans are less than those of urban whites, they are substantially more than what rural Native Americans earn.

Urban Native Americans often live in poorer central-city neighborhoods, much as newer immigrant groups do. Persons whose ancestry is Indian but who have been assimilated into middle-class America may not identify themselves as Native Americans except under particular circumstances, such as the distribution of funds from selling tribal lands, or profits from gambling enterprises. Such individuals have Indian ancestry, but in their behavior, attitudes, and daily life, they are indistinguishable from their neighbors. These culturally assimilated Indians are sometimes referred to by other Indians as "apples"—"red on the outside and white on the inside." More than one-third of Indians now marry non-Indians, and in many tribes outside the Southwest it is difficult to find pure-blood Native Americans.

Urban ways can produce a cultural bind for some Native Americans. Most (but not all) Indian cultures stress cooperation over competition. This places some Indian heritages at variance with the larger American culture, with its emphasis on the moral virtue of competition and economic success. American Indians who want to remain Indian are caught in a dilemma: they desire educational and employment opportunities, but they want to live according to Indian ways that can make it difficult to take advantage of such opportunities. The problem of being pulled between two cultures is, of course, not unique to Native Americans. The rural and anti-urban orientation of most Native American cultures, however, gives special sharpness to the issue of cultural separateness versus assimilation. North American policymakers in both Washington and Ottawa have also vacillated: they seem unable to decide whether Indians should be encouraged to remain tribal nations, with separate cultures, or whether First Peoples are better served by urban relocation.

SUMMARY

The United States will be half minority by 2050. Hispanics, at 48 million, are now America's largest minority population. About half the Latino growth is due to immigration. Half the Latino population is concentrated in California and Texas. Some 84 percent of the Hispanic population resides in metro areas.

The various Hispanic populations differ considerably in socioeconomic characteristics. Generally, Mexican Americans, who compose almost two-thirds of all Latinos, have low educational and income levels, as do Puerto Ricans. Some 4 of 10 adult Hispanics have less than a high school education. Education levels are the lowest among immigrant Mexican Americans. By contrast, Cuban Americans have income and educational levels slightly above those of non-Hispanic whites. Immigrants, particularly in Texas and California, are most likely to settle in crowded *barrios* where "homeboy" gangs are a problem. Middle-class Hispanics are likely to be suburbanites. Housing segregation is highest in the largest metro areas.

Politically, Hispanics are being increasingly courted as the nation's most numerous potential "swing vote." Mexican American and Puerto Rican Latinos tend to vote Democratic, while Cubans overwhelmingly vote Republican. Unlike other Hispanic groups, all Puerto Ricans have American citizenship. Mainland Puerto Ricans have relatively low educational levels, and the highest proportion of female-headed families (44 percent) among all Latino populations. There is no single common Latino experience. Diversity is the norm.

North American immigration since 1968 comes mainly from Asia and Latin America. Without current immigration, large cities such as New York would have lost rather than gained population in the last decade. For Americans of European or Asian origin, ethnicity is less significant than social class as a predictor of social behavior.

Asian Americans are not the largest minority, but they are fast growing. Asian Americans are sometimes characterized as a "model minority," with twice the proportion graduating from college as whites, as well as the highest income levels of any census group. Sometimes Asians are subject to a "glass ceiling." The status of a minority group can change radically as did that of Japanese Americans. During World War II Japanese Americans suffered severe discrimination, including all West Coast residents of Japanese ancestry being removed from their homes and sent to inland "relocation camps." Out of the camps, the most decorated army outfit of World War II was recruited, the famous 442nd Regimental Combat Team. Today Japanese Americans have been almost totally acculturated and have lost their language and customs. They are the nation's most prosperous ethnic population.

Native Americans, with their traditional non-urban orientation, have not fared well during the 19th and most of the 20th centuries. Twenty years ago Native Americans were the nation's most rural and its poorest population. More recently some tribal groups have prospered economically due to the establishment of reservation-based gambling casinos. Partially because of this, the population identifying themselves as Native American has grown considerably faster than natural increase would permit. In spite of widespread movement to cities, Indians remain North America's most rural ethnic group, with only half living in cities and one-third still living on reservations. Native Americans are sometimes conflicted between the demands of their native heritages and those of competitive metropolitan America.

REVIEW QUESTIONS

1. What is the current size of the Latino population? Describe its growth and geographical distribution?

2. Describe the diversity within the Hispanic population and the differences among Mexican, Puerto Rican, and Cuban populations.

3. Describe the size, regional location, and socioeconomic characteristics of the Mexican American population.

4. How do segregation levels of Latinos compare with those of African Americans?

5. What is the current growth pattern for Asian American populations, and where is growth taking place?

6. What are the differences within the Asian population in terms of socioeconomic status? Which group is at the top and which at the bottom?

7. What were the consequences for Japanese Americans of their internment in camps during World War II?

8. What is meant by the term *model minority* and what are some of its disadvantages?

9. What is the current demographic and economic status of Native Americans?

10. How has movement to cities impacted Native Americans?

NOTES

1. U.S. Census Bureau, CB10-FF.12, May 5, 2010.

2. U.S. Census Bureau, "1-in-5 U.S. Residents Either Foreign-Born or First Generation, Census Bureau Reports," www.census.gov/ Press Release, 3/12/02

3. Dowell Myers, "Immigration: Fundamental Force in the American City," *Housing Facts & Findings,* Fannie Mae Foundation, Winter 1999, p. 5.

4. U.S. Bureau of the Census, "Population Projections of the United States by Age, Sex, Race, and Hispanic Origin, 1993 to 2050," *Current Population Reports,* P–25, no. 1104, Washington, D.C., 1993.

5. Alejandro Portes and Alex Stepick, *City on the Edge: The Transformation of Miami,* University of California Press, Berkeley, 1993.

6. Richard D. Alba, *Ethnic Identity: The Transformation of White America,* Yale University Press, New Haven, 1990.

7. For recent critiques of assimilation as racist, see Bill Ong, *To Be an American: Cultural Pluralism and the Rhetoric of Assimilation,* New York University Press, New York, 1997; for a defense, see Peter D. Salins, *Assimilation, American Style,* New Republic Books, New York, 1997.

8. Reynolds Farley, "A New Look at Second Generation Immigrants," a paper read at the annual meetings of the Population Association of America, New York, March 25, 1999.

9. Scott Greer, "The Faces of Ethnicity," in J. John Palen, *City Scenes,* Little Brown, Boston, 1977, pp. 147, 157.

10. Charles Jaret and Donald C. Reitzes, "The Importance of Racial- Ethnic Identity and Social Setting for Blacks, Whites and Multiracials," *Sociological Perspectives* 42:711–737, 1999.

11. U.S. Census Bureau "Hispanics and Asian Americans Increasing Faster than Overall Population," U.S. Census Bureau, Washington, D.C., June 14, 2004, p. 1.

12. Rogelio Sanz, *Latinos and the Changing Face of America,* Russell Sage, New York, 2004.

13. "Statistical Portrait of Hispanics in the United States," Pew Hispanic Center, Washington, D.C., 2009, Table 1.

14. There is no consensus on how the Hispanic-origin population should be addressed. Government documents use *Hispanic* while academics often use *Latino.* To resolve this question the Census Bureau ran a special race/ethnic group survey in the *Current Population Survey* of May 1995. It found that 58 percent of the Hispanic-origin respondents preferred *Hispanic,* 12 percent favored *Latino,* and 12 percent *Spanish origin.*

15. Jeffrey S. Passel and Paul Taylor, "Unauthorized Immigrants and Their U.S.-Born Children," Pew Hispanic Center, Washington, D.C., August 2010, p. 1.

16. Victor Zuniga and Rubin Hernandez-Leon, *New Destinations: Mexican Immigration in the United States,* Russell Sage, New York, 2005.

17. U.S. Census Bureau, Public Information Office, B09-76, July 2, 2010.

18. U.S. Census Bureau, "Income Stable, Poverty Up Census Bureau Reports" Bureau of the Census, Washington, D.C., Aug. 26, 2003.

19. U.S. Census Bureau, "College Degrees Nearly Doubles Annual Earning, Census Bureau Reports," Census Bureau, Washington, D.C., March 28, 2005.

20. Kelvin M. Pollard and William P. O'Hare, "America's Racial and Ethnic Minorities," *Population Bulletin*, Population Reference Bureau, Washington, D.C., September 1999, p. 30.

21. For a study of homeboy gangs, see Martin Sanchez-Jankowski, *Islands in the Street: Gangs and American Society*, University of California Press, Berkeley, 1991; for an earlier view see Joan W. Moore, *Homeboys: Gangs, Drugs and Prison in the Barrios of Los Angeles*, Temple University Press, Philadelphia, 1978.

22. Lewis Mumford Center, *Ethnic Diversity Grows, Neighborhood Integration Is at a Standstill*, www.albany.edu/mumford/census, April 3, 2001.

23. Media General News, "Hispanics Gain Ground as Leaders and Voters," *Richmond Times-Dispatch*, May 22, 2005, p. A9.

24. Adam Nagourney, "Orange County Is No Longer Nixon Country," newyorktimes.com., August 30, 2010.

25. U.S. Census Bureau, Public Information Office, "Minotiry Population Tops 100 Million," www.census.gov., May 18, 2007.

26. Sharon M. Lee, "Asian Americans: Diverse and Growing," *Population Bulletin*, 53:14, June 1998.

27. U.S. Census Bureau, *Educational Attainment in the United States: March 1997, Current Population Reports*, P20–505, 1999, p. 3.

28. Robert Gardner, Bryant Robey, and Peter Smith, "Asian Americans: Growth, Change, and Diversity," *Population Bulletin* 40:4, October 1995.

29. Lee, op. cit., p. 28.

30. Min Zhou and John R. Logan, "Return on Human Capital in Ethnic Enclaves: New York City's Chinatown," *American Sociological Review* 54:809–820, 1989.

31. Sharon M. Lee and Barry Edmonston, "The Socioeconomic Status and Integration of Asian Immigrants in the 1980s," in James P. Smith and Barry Edmonston (eds.), *The New Immigrants: Economic, Fiscal, and Demographic Effects of Immigration*, National Academy Press, Washington, D.C., 1997.

32. Mia Tuan, *Forever Foreigners or Honorary Whites? The Asian Ethnic Experience of Today*, Rutgers University Press, New Brunswick, N.J., 1998.

33. Chalsa M. Loo, *Chinatown: Most Time, Hard Time*, Praeger, New York, 1991.

34. Hsiang-Shui Chen, *Chinatown No More: Taiwan Immigrants in Contemporary New York*, Cornell University Press, Ithaca, 1992.

35. Timothy P. Fong, *The First Suburban Chinatown*, Temple University Press, Philadelphia, 1994.

36. Harry H. L. Kitano, *Japanese Americans: The Evolution of a Subculture*, Prentice-Hall, Englewood Cliffs, N.J., 1976, p. 3.

37. Herbert Barringer, Robert W. Gardner, and Michael J. Levin, *Asian and Pacific Islanders in the United States*, Russell Sage Foundation, New York, 1993.

38. Wounded Knee was the final episode of the Indian wars. In 1890, 300 Lakota Sioux were massacred by the U.S. army. See Dee Alexander Brown, *Bury My Heart at Wounded Knee: An Indian History of the American West*, Holt, Rinehart and Winston, New York, 1971. Wounded Knee was also the site of an unsuccessful militant political occupation by Indians in 1973. Today the major economic activity on the reservation is a gambling casino.

39. C. Matthew Snipp, "Demographic Comeback for American Indians?" *Population Today*, November 1996, p. 63.

40. U.S. Census Bureau, "Overview of Race and Hispanic Origin," *Census 2000 Brief*, Washington, D.C., March 12, 2001.

41. Kelvin M. Pollard and William P. O'Hare, "America's Racial and Ethnic Minorities," *Population Bulletin*, September 1999, p. 31.

42. C. Matthew Snipp, *American Indians: The First of This Land*, Russell Sage, New York, 1989.

43. Kim Isaac Eisler, *Revenge of the Pequots: How a Small Native American Tribe Created the World's Most Profitable Casino*, Simon & Schuster, New York, 2001.

44. U.S. Bureau of the Census, *Population Profile of the United States 1995*, Government Printing Office, Washington, D.C., 1996, p. 51.

45. Susan Lobo, *Urban Voices: The Bay Area America—Indian Community*, University of Arizona Press, Tucson, 2002.

Part IV

METRO ISSUES, HOUSING, SPRAWL, AND PLANNING

CHAPTER 11

Cities and Change

Where you find both good and evil, there you find a city.
Hindu Proverb

OUTLINE

Introduction
The Urban Crisis: Thesis
Urban Revival: Antithesis
A Political Economy Look at the Urban Crisis
21st-Century City Developments
    New Patterns
    Central Business Districts
    Mismatch Hypothesis
    Downtown Housing
    Fiscal Health
    Crumbling Infrastructure
    Neighborhood Revival
Gentrification
    Government and Revitalization
    Who Is Gentrifying?
    Why Is Gentrification Taking Place?
    Displacement of the Poor
Decline of Middle-Income Neighborhoods
Successful Working Class Revival
Summary

INTRODUCTION

There is confusion and dispute about the future of the city. It is a cliché that we live in an age of urban crisis. Crime, racial division, pollution, congestion, and alienation are all attributed in one degree or another to urban life. A planner during the mid-20th century described Los Angeles as "a federation of communities coordinated into a metropolis of sunlight and air."[1] No one makes such claims today. More common are books on Los Angeles, such as *City of Quartz,* that paint a dark picture of the L.A. metropolis as a location of Dickensian extremes.[2] The same is said to be true of other cities. Certainly there is no lack of prophets to passionately catalog urban ills.

THE URBAN CRISIS: THESIS

Are cities, particularly large cities, doomed? The last decades of the 20th century heard voices raised everywhere proclaiming the inevitable decline, if not death, of the city.[3] In 1990 the mayor of Los Angeles warned, "If we do not save our cities we shall not save the nation."[4] Some urban scholars were no less pessimistic, contending that the worst still lies ahead. Thirty years ago George Sternlieb stated, "The Newarks of America are forecasts of things to come, and if we want to understand the probable future that faces many of our older cities, then we will first have to get clear on what is happening—has happened—in places like Newark."[5] Contemporary 21st-century predictions of urban collapse can be found in Fred Harris's and Lynn Curtis's *Locked in the Poorhouse,* while Joel Kotkin has been writing for a decade that talk of urban revival is mostly hype.[6]

Are these pessimistic predictions accurate? For much of the end of the 20th century it looked like they might be. Well-paying manufacturing jobs left the older cities, and it seemed that the cities no longer provided entry-level opportunities or upward mobility for unskilled newcomers such as African Americans and Hispanics. The crisis was seen as a permanent long-standing one of opportunity, rather than a short-term one of fiscal management.[7] As both black and white middle-class taxpayers and their dollars departed, municipal payrolls and public assistance expenditures increased. Growing numbers of poor residents needed expensive services while depressing revenues. Cities were becoming polarized between the affluent and the poor. (The income of one in five New Yorkers is below the poverty line.) Aging city properties also require more fire and police protection, and older street, lighting, and sewer systems require more maintenance. Pessimists saw cities as having their vital signs maintained by external life support systems. The 1992 eruption of looting and burning in South-Central Los Angeles set off by a police beating seemed to confirm the worst fears. The resulting 58 deaths, 5,600 businesses suffering losses, and approximately 15,000 arrested seemed to suggest the country was about to re-experience the widespread urban destruction of the late 1960s.

URBAN REVIVAL: ANTITHESIS

Then an interesting thing happened. Starting in the early 1990s urban crime began to drop sharply across the country, urban economies did better, urban housing upgraded, and the quality of urban life noticeably improved. The last two decades have witnessed a rebirth of hope. Urban crime declined nationwide by over half between 1992 and 2010. At the same time cities from Columbus to Memphis to Miami to Los Angeles rediscovered their downtowns, and the renovation of selected older neighborhoods picked up. The media discovered that the city was not only alive, but healthy. An urban renaissance was taking place. Suddenly the urban crisis was said to have left town and the slumming of the suburbs became the problem. Downtowns were again said to be full of people and showing economic vigor.[8] Young dual-income couples rediscovered the city as a place of residence. In New York City the seedy Times Square and drug-infested 42nd Street of two decades ago have been revitalized as a sparkling new entertainment district. Across the country new professional sports parks were built in the city—be it Camden Yards in Baltimore, U.S. Cellular Field (Comiskey Park) in Chicago, or Pac Bell Field in San Francisco.

Even Washington, D.C.—which in 1995 was effectively bankrupt, and facing collapsing services in spite of having 1 of every 12 city residents on the city payroll—now is on an economically sound footing and showing clear signs of both physical and social improvement. Moreover, the recession and housing bust kept people from moving to the suburbs. The U.S. Census Bureau reported cities such as New York, Chicago, Dallas, Denver, and Seattle in 2010 posted their highest growth rates in a decade.[9] Even economically hard hit Las Vegas and Phoenix saw population gains.[10]

A POLITICAL ECONOMY LOOK AT THE URBAN CRISIS

Why did first the urban crisis, and then possibly urban revival, occur? Political economy theory suggests the changes are deliberate.

The South Bronx has been rebuilt from the devastation of the 1980s (above) to a pleasant neighborhood of row houses and apartments. Below are the Villa Maria homes on Fox Street in the South Bronx. Photo credits: above, © Michael Lipack/NY Daily News Archive via Getty Images; below, © M. Graff/The Image Works.

Political economy academics hold that city problems do not occur in a vacuum, and city problems cannot be examined separately from the political, historical, and, particularly, economic system of which they are a part. Manuel Castells has argued, for example, that not only is the crisis of the cities real, but the decay of the central cities, their fiscal insolvency, and the flight to the suburbs all are inevitable and necessary consequences of a capitalistic economic system.[11]

The quest for ever-greater profits by large monopolistic corporations is seen as leading to government policies such as government-insured mortgages and subsidies for expressways. Corporations—and their wealthy managers—thus could move to the suburbs, where land costs and taxes were lower, while they still maintained the economic benefits of being near the central city.

The fiscal crisis of cities thus was not seen as the consequence of costly public services, too many public service jobs, and too much welfare, as conservative economists argued. Rather, the near "bankruptcy" of cities is the result of the corporations' rejection of increased taxes to pay for social services. The result is the abandonment and destruction of largely poor areas of the city, while corporations concentrate on issues important to themselves such as downtown redevelopment.[12] Social movements by the poor are either repressed or bought off. The consequence is said to be a future where the urban crisis is sharpened and mass repression and control become inevitable adjuncts of an exploitative metropolitan model.

Political economists similarly analyze gentrification not as a result of the decisions of individual homebuyers, but as a conscious product of land-based interest groups able to control the real estate market.[13] Thus, investment capital was systematically moved out of inner cities and into suburbs because suburban profit rates were higher. The subsequent deterioration of inner-city neighborhoods led to the development of a rent gap, which in turn made it possible for capital to return to the central city seeking profits. The ownership class benefits from these decisions, while the costs of gentrification fall upon the urban poor in the form of displacement. Advocates of a non-Marxian political economy approach similarly see gentrification as a conscious action by business groups that act to ensure profits by maintaining an urban "growth machine" that boosts downtown economic development at the cost of neighborhoods.[14]

21ST-CENTURY CITY DEVELOPMENTS

New Patterns

Overall, the economic and social health of cities shows a mixed pattern. The Census Bureau reports that even after the recession, the fastest growing metro areas are concentrated in the West and South.[15] Older industrial strongholds had the largest losses. While some city populations may have been falling, the per-capita income of residents went up compared to those in the suburbs. The cities are gaining economic ground and housing prices are holding ground. What this means is that smaller, wealthier households are increasing in number while larger, poorer families are not.

Overall the state of the cities is fiscally and—perhaps equally importantly—psychologically healthier than a decade or two ago. Bright new downtown developments and rebuilt and revitalized neighborhoods are signs

of hope. There are also clear signs of well-off and upper-middle-class movement into older city neighborhoods. For example, Brooklyn, perennial second fiddle to Manhattan, has become the hot new-housing center of New York City. Brooklyn's neighborhoods, pocked full of old buildings and weed-choked lots just two decades ago is building and rehabbing at a furious rate.

On the debit side, poor and moderate-income families with children are doing less well. The real estate decline beginning in 2008 has decreased the amount of affordable housing. Overall, the homeownership rate for families with children is lower than it was 40 years ago.[16] Also, fiscally there is still an outflow of tax dollars, older cities continue to lose manufacturing jobs, and the cost of services is rising. Crime and drug-related violence, while down from the highs of the early 1990s, still fray the social fabric. Some neighborhoods are physically experiencing regeneration, but deterioration of the physical infrastructure (e.g., water mains and sewers) remains an expensive, if often unseen, problem. Meanwhile, the national political climate does not favor new urban programs.

During the 21st century, it seems clear, not all cities are going to experience similar situations. Some will prosper, while others will not. For example, declines in population may reflect urban deterioration, or may, as in Boston or Pittsburgh, spur the development of new urban roles as cultural and service centers. Cities such as Camden and Gary may remain stagnant regardless of valiant efforts to reverse the process. On the other hand, cities such as New York, Chicago, Dallas, and Los Angeles are economically vibrant, while Charlotte, Boston, Denver, and Seattle are prospering. Older cities such as Baltimore, Cleveland, Milwaukee, and Philadelphia have experienced problems, but also retain considerable vigor and attractiveness.

The urban renaissance is uneven, but clearly more prevalent than a decade ago. As

---

Box 11.1   New Orleans: An America Tragedy

On August 2005 New Orleans suffered the worst natural city catastrophe in American history. Hurricane Katrina, a Class 3 hurricane, breached New Orleans levies and flooded the city. What was a natural disaster soon turned into a man-made debacle due to the incompetence of both local officials and the Federal Emergency Management Agency (FEMA). The tragedy was further compounded by the apparent indifference of President Bush who, without anyone fully in charge of relief efforts, stayed on vacation for several days after the tragedy.

Katrina left over 2,000 dead and the city's physical structure in shambles. Overall Katrina left 181,000 Gulf region homes and apartments destroyed, and hundreds of thousands of people uprooted. In New Orleans the poor suffered most with neighborhoods such as the low-lying Ninth Ward experiencing total destruction. Compounding New Orleans' physical devastation was a total social breakdown. As Katrina's flood waters lashed the city, all semblance of law and order disappeared. The city descended into weeks of chaos, violence, and looting. Several thousand people who took refuge in the Superdome had to endure days without food, medical assistance, or any police protection from predators. Local government and policing essentially disappeared, and federal efforts were both tragically late and inadequate. City facilities and services were essentially wiped out. Of the city's eight pre-Katrina hospitals only two partially survived.

A half decade after Katrina the French Quarter is again crowded with tourists for Mardi Gras, but the situation remains grim in many of the city's 72 neighborhoods. Outside the affluent Garden District, some neighborhoods still remain vacant, without electricity, water, or sewage service. Federal disaster assistance allocated for the city was tied up in bureaucratic red tape. The federal government allocated $4.6 billion to help people rebuild their homes and 107,000 applied, but by 2007 only 630 had received money.* Not until 2007 were the first two new houses built in the Ninth Ward, and they were built by ACORN, a nonprofit housing organization. Local elected officials constantly speak of the city coming back, but they have proved to be largely incapable of producing actual results. Returnees face the obstacles of few schools, limited health care facilities, and very high violent crime and murder rates. Nor do experts agree as to how the city should be rebuilt.** The roles of planning and of public housing are especially strongly debated.

In the weeks following the storm at least 300,000 New Orleans residents left the city. Many were evacuated to Houston and other cities. Only a limited number have returned. As of 2010 estimates of New Orleans' population hover around 250,000. This is about half of its pre-Katrina size of 445,000. Most demographers and economists expect future population gains to be small and the city never to regain its previous population.*** The once-proud Crescent City may be destined to be a smaller place, known largely for good restaurants and the Mardi Gras celebration.

* Associated Press, "New Orleans a 'Disaster' Report Says," *Richmond Times-Dispatch*, Feb.26, 2007, p.A4.

** Susan Greenbaum, "Comments on Katrina"; Sudhir Alladi Venkatesh, "Sociology and Katrina"; and Xavier de Sousa Briggs, "After Katrina: Rebuilding Places and Lives," in *Community and Society*, 5(2):107–128, 2006.

*** Adam Nossiter, "New Orleans of Future May Stay Half Its Old Size," *New York Times*, January 21, 2007, p. A1.

Chapter 7 indicated, "brain-gain" cities that attract and hold young educated workers are faring the best.

Central Business Districts

In evaluating what is happening in cities, it helps to distinguish between what is occurring in the economic heart of the city—the central business district (CBD)—and what is happening in residential neighborhoods. As suburban shopping malls have proliferated, downtown sales have declined. Aging downtown stores closed because they could not effectively compete with suburban shopping malls. Even wealthy San Jose, located in the Silicon Valley and with the highest house prices of any city in the country, after spending $1.2 billion on downtown redevelopment had a 2007 CBD office vacancy rate of 21 percent.[17]

On the other hand, CBDs generally have been reasonably successful in retaining business and government offices. Prior to 2008, downtowns were experiencing a boom in high-rise construction. Chicago's downtown, for example, is experiencing its greatest growth in 80 years. Following 9/11 Lower Manhattan sprouted new buildings; downtown Los Angeles underwent new construction.

Downtown buildings use space effectively. Offices concerned with processing knowledge and information find it easy to move vertically from floor to floor. Downtown remains a location of choice for insurance firms, financial and legal services, government, and administrative headquarters of all sorts. Manufactured goods, on the other hand, move goods much easier horizontally. Thus, new manufacturing facilities seek outlying locations with plenty of horizontal space. Downtowns no longer process goods; rather, they process information.

Across the country cities are actively promoting downtown convention centers as an economic growth strategy. The last decade has witnessed city after city building convention centers and encouraging downtown hotel construction in order to attract conventions and trade meetings. Middle-sized cities now attract meetings that once were held in a handful of the largest cities. Downtown shopping malls such as Harbor Place in Baltimore and Quincy Market in Boston also draw tourists. Downtown markets can be found in Denver, San Antonio, Portland (Oregon), Seattle, and a host of other cities. Cultural activities, art, music, and theatre centers are also part of the urban development strategy.

Overall, the picture is mixed. Downtown stores will never again have the unchallenged control of retail trade they exhibited during the centralizing era of the streetcar and subway; but so long as the downtown is a major white-collar employment center, the CBD will be a profitable location for selected retail sales.

Mismatch Hypothesis

There is a catch, however, to all this downtown CBD economic development. Central-city offices provide new jobs—but only for those possessing specific white-collar skills. City factories and manufacturing plants continue to move to the suburbs—or, more frequently, abroad. The so-called "mismatch hypothesis" is that cities have blue-collar job seekers and white-collar job opportunities.[18] A mismatch exists between central-city residents' job skills and the type of information-age jobs being created in the city. Stagnant or declining inner-city manufacturing sectors offer scant employment opportunities for new workers with limited educational backgrounds and/or job experience. The availability of entry-level jobs that once attracted disadvantaged migrants to the cities has dropped precipitously.

Compounding the difficulty is that the cities experiencing the greatest loss of entry-level jobs over the past two decades have often been those with the largest minority populations. The result is school dropout rates, welfare dependency, and unemployment rates higher than national averages, as blue-collar employment opportunities contract and college-degree, white-collar opportunities expand.

Thus, depending on the worker's education and skill level, one can make both the case that urban job opportunities are expanding, and the case that urban job prospects are worsening.

Downtown Housing

The last decade has seen many cities make a major effort to transform downtowns into residential as well as business locations. Luxury condominiums located in converted factories and new high-rise towers are becoming commonplace. City administrations seek downtown residents in order to promote downtown shopping, restaurant, and cultural activities after 5 PM.

In the last decade downtown population in major U.S. cities increased about 10 percent. Manhattan experienced 8 million square feet of older commercial space going condo between 2001 and 2006.[19]

The most successful North American city in bringing residents back downtown is Vancouver. While most cities in the U.S. would be delighted to have 2 to 4 percent of their residents living downtown, Vancouver has nearly 20 percent—and gaining.[20] Virtually all this has happened in the last 20 years as a result of rewriting zoning laws to encourage downtown residences. Moreover, the residential boom includes not just singles, couples, and empty-nesters, but a substantial number of families with children. In short Vancouver has the vibrant, safe, and glamorous downtown that every city seeks.

Ironically, the very success is causing problems. Since high-rise condos are cheaper to build than office building projects, virtually no new office buildings are being built. The concern is that without some balance Vancouver will suffer as a center of commerce, business, and jobs. In a decade or two, it could be a place where many people live, but few work. Vancouver also has the dubious distinction of being the most expensive city in which to buy a home in the English-speaking world.

Almost all North American cities would love to have some of Vancouver's "problems," with people moving into the downtown. Nonetheless, the issue of downtown residents competing with business for space is real in Vancouver. There is also the tax issue. Since commercial properties pay proportionally higher taxes than residences, having too many people living downtown means the tax base could suffer in the long run. However, at this point this is far from an issue for North American cities. What most cities need are far more downtown residents.

Fiscal Health

While "saving the cities" was a major emphasis of federal programs 35 years ago, today municipalities are largely left to sink or swim on their own. During the Reagan years (1980 to 1988)

federal aid to cities was cut sharply. Also, while President Clinton (1988–1996) spoke in favor of urban-based programs, his budgets did not restore funding. President George W. Bush showed no interest in funding urban programs, especially programs that mostly benefited Democratic-voting central-city residents. President Obama has the interest, but in an era of major federal deficits, lacks the funding.

Without federal help cities have substantially abandoned their earlier programs to fight poverty and solve social problems. Rather, municipalities increasingly focus on the day-to-day delivery of core services. Some see this as a positive move insofar as it means the city is concentrating efforts on those things it can do well and cutting back on those things it does less well, such as solving social and personal problems.[21] Others see it as abandonment of poor urban populations and areas. City mayors, both Republican and Democratic, have been privatizing city services. Under some circumstances this has improved services and saved money. For example, Chicago's Mayor Daley (the son of *the* Mayor Daley) privatized the towing of autos abandoned on city streets. Previously it cost the city to tow each auto; now the city is paid for each abandoned car private towing companies tow away.

Cutting services and costs, however, is not the only reason for municipal financial solvency. Local governments also have been raising more revenues through higher property tax assessments. Cities still remain squeezed between growing expenditures due to an aging infrastructure and a concentration of higher-need populations on one hand, and a slower-growing tax base on the other. The larger the city, the greater the financial burden. Per capita debt is more than twice as high in cities of more than 1 million as in smaller cities. City administrators are concerned that cities are being stuck with higher tax burdens and unfunded state and federal mandates while their tax bases shrink. Of every dollar of taxes, 65 cents go to the federal government, 20 cents go to the states, and only the remaining 14 cents go to local governments.[22] Today, successful local governments are those that receive community support (i.e., taxes) for necessary services.

Crumbling Infrastructure

Generally overlooked is the question of cities' physical infrastructure. The most severe problem is often antiquated water and sewage systems. In New York, bursting water mains and collapsing streets have become commonplace, yet relatively little is being done to remedy this. At the present level of construction, it would take more than 200 years to replace New York City's streets and water mains and 300 years to replace its sewers. Nor is New York alone; Philadelphia's sewers are falling apart, while Boston and Houston are plagued with hemorrhaging water mains. The Department of Environmental Protection estimates that more than a million Americans become ill each year due to sanitary sewer overflows. Municipal sewage plants release 51 million pounds of toxic chemicals into public waters yearly. Atlanta, for example, has problems with sewage backup. Milwaukee, in 2000, discharged more than a billion gallons of raw sewage into Lake Michigan.[23] In 2004 the Milwaukee sewage district released 4 billion gallons of sewage, the worst release in modern times. Unbelievably, the Canadian city of Victoria as of 2010 was still dumping untreated sewage into the Pacific.

How and why do such problems occur? The major reason is that it is relatively easy for politicians to ignore infrastructure needs until the problems become massive. Local and state politicians trying to cut taxes invariably raid infrastructure funds. This creates huge and expensive problems for the next generation, but it is relatively safe politically, for it is only when infrastructure fails that it attracts attention.

The problem, though, doesn't just go away. A U.S. Conference of Mayors study released in 2000 reported that 80,000 acres of land, more than Pittsburgh and Minneapolis combined, are polluted with toxic chemicals and deserted.[24] These urban sites, known as "brownfields," are both unsightly and dangerous. Such land can be cleaned, but banks and real estate developers are sometimes reluctant to clean and redevelop the land because they fear possible lawsuits from inadequate cleanup.

Neighborhood Revival

The purpose of the post-war urban renewal programs was to rebuild cities' inner cores to encourage middle-class residency. The effort was largely unsuccessful. Talk of a "back to the city" movement was not followed up by actual movement. As Chapter 6: The Suburban Era documents, the major population movement has long been outbound rather than directed toward the central city. The assumption has been that those having the choice (i.e., middle-class homebuyers) shun the central city for the suburbs. As noted in Chapter 7: Urban Lifestyles, Gallup polls supported the view of suburban preference.[25]

However, the outward spread of suburbs has generated a countervailing pressure to recycle and rebuild older central-city neighborhoods. There now is a clear movement, especially by young professionals, toward residence in the central city.

The gentrification movement is taking place in older neighborhoods that are recycling from a period of decay. Middle-income and upper-middle-income couples are buying and restoring old homes. Additionally, coalitions of local government and community local nonprofit housing corporations have been restoring homes in poorer neighborhoods and bringing buildings and neighborhoods back to life. Easier credit terms, community reinvestment activities, and the ability to shift risk to

Box 11.2   Harlem Uneasily Confronts Gentrification

Some city neighborhoods are now gentrifying at a much more rapid pace. For decades Harlem has been a microcosm of urban problems: increasing crime, drugs, welfare, social and physical deterioration. Once the epicenter of black culture and noted for the artistic Harlem Renaissance of the 1920s, by 1990 the once-proud and vibrant neighborhood had sunk into social dissolution and physical decay. Outdoor drug markets and crack houses openly did business with drug buyers lining up on the street. Physically, more and more buildings were being abandoned. By 1990 the only fresh paint being applied in Harlem was gang graffiti. The surviving poor residents had lost all hope. Old and young had become accustomed to public gun battles and losing friends to vendettas.

Then in 1994 change began coming to Harlem. At first it was slow, but by 2007 a flood of newcomers had come and Harlem was gentrifying. Harlem has always enjoyed a number of advantages. It occupies a prime Manhattan location with easy commutes downtown. Moreover, its brownstones and apartment buildings were originally constructed to high standards. Only their initial quality had allowed them to survive decades of neglect. Middle- and working-class blacks only reluctantly abandoned Harlem as its crime rates skyrocketed and it became an unsafe place to live.

The change in Harlem's future can be linked to the police department's beginning in 1994 an extensive precinct-based assault on both violent crime and quality-of-life crime. Major drug dealers were shut down and even minor infractions such as publicly smoking marijuana or urination on the street landed perpetrators in jail. Identification was demanded of young men hanging out, even in front of their own buildings. Portable computers allowed police to immediately check anyone they stopped for outstanding warrants. As a result of regular pat-downs, the carrying of guns radically decreased as did open drug dealing, public drinking, and even hanging out in public.

The tough police tactics produced strong resentment among young males, but it also dropped the 32nd Precinct homicide rate to a third of what it

had been, from 52 homicides in 1994 to 17 in 2000.* Young men reluctantly credit the police for making the carrying of weapons "outdated." As crime declined, newcomers flocked to buy and restore Harlem's low-cost housing.

However, some residents view the dramatic upgrading of their community with unease as well as hope. The anxiety is because revitalization is also bringing some measure of racial integration.** Whites are moving into a community that African Americans have long considered theirs. Increasing racial and ethnic diversity has produced wariness and unease, even among some African American scholars who previously lamented white abandonment of the city. The mixed feelings are expressed by the sociologist Mary Pattillo, who once lived in Harlem: "If Harlem becomes integrated, is it still Harlem in the way everybody says Harlem and has a vision of it? I would like Harlem to stay a black neighborhood and a strong black cultural space. But my political and policy opinion is that I know that segregation allows neighborhoods to be strangled."†

Further complicating and confusing what is happening in Harlem is that racial changes are also often class changes. Middle- or upper-middle-income whites are moving into what was a lower-income minority community. While appreciating the increased safety, civility, and physical improvement of the neighborhood, longer-term residents wonder whether rising property values will eventually force them out. And even if that doesn't occur will a racially integrated Harlem be the same place? Will the control, customs, and way of living shift from that of a black community to a multiracial community? Will Harlem revive but lose its black soul? One sign of the dramatic rapidity of Harlem's change is that in 2001, ex-President Bill Clinton moved his office and staff into new business space in Harlem.

*Amy Waldman, "In Harlem's Ravaged Heart, Revival," *New York Times,* February 18, 2001, p. 15.

**Janny Scott, "White Flight, This Time toward Harlem," *New York Times,* February 25, 2001.

†Ibid., p. 20.

the secondary real estate market have all contributed to increased gentrification activity.[26] (See Chapter 12: Housing Patterns, Sprawl, and Smart Growth for a discussion of HOPE VI

housing programs.) The last decade has seen the rapid expansion of gentrification with cities such as Boston, New York, Chicago, and San Francisco having experienced "turbo gentrifi-

In Chicago new and old homes sit side-by-side. Sally Ryan/*New York Times*/Redux

cation." This is when professionals and business investors compete for homes in a "hot" urban neighborhood.

GENTRIFICATION

Today, the "right" neighborhood is sometimes not previously used residences but old city warehouse or factories that have been converted into upscale apartments and condos. Gentrification is especially likely to take place in areas with good transportation and having accessibility to the central core. Older residences undergoing restoration often have historic or architectural merit. While the homes may be in disrepair when purchased, they were originally constructed to standards generally unavailable in new suburban houses. Neighborhoods such as Brooklyn in New York, Lincoln Park West in Chicago, and Haight-Ashbury in San Francisco are examples of once-marginal neighborhoods that now are "in" places to live.

Middle-class in-movement to older central-city neighborhoods challenges the classical Burgess model of growth (discussed in Chapter 4: Ecology and Political-Economy Perspectives). The filtering down economic model proposes that this in-movement should not be occurring. Rather, under the Burgess model older central-city residences should filter down to the economically marginal. Also, according to the original Burgess model, central-city residential property is vacated for commercial or industrial usage. Today, the pattern is the reverse; formerly commercial buildings and warehouses are being rehabilitated as residences. The SoHo section of New York, for instance, contains older commercial structures that have been transformed into stylish homes. Throughout North American cities commercial-to-residential transformations have become the norm. However, most of the regeneration is occurring in older residential neighborhoods. Neighborhoods such as Ansley Park in Atlanta, the Fan in Richmond, New Town in Chicago, Five Points in Denver, Montrose in Houston, the Mission District in San Francisco, Capitol Hill in Washington, D.C., and Tribeca in New York are physically more robust than they were two decades ago.

Often overlooked in discussing neighborhood revitalization is the regeneration of working-class neighborhoods. Even the term *gentrification* suggests that newcomers are young professionals of higher income and status than existing residents. This is not always the case. Upgrading of working-class neighborhoods is often less dramatic because newcomers, while often younger, are not that different from existing residents in terms of ethnic or social-class characteristics.[27] Physical improvements may be slow to show in city data since working-class residents may make home improvements without getting building permits. The important point is that local residents have accomplished neighborhood improvement without middle-class influx and without the displacement of existing residents.

Government and Revitalization

In the postwar years the federal government sponsored urban clearance and renewal and supported "redevelopment authorities" concerned with rebuilding the economic and physical structure of the central city. By contrast, until recently urban gentrification has been funded almost entirely by the private sector. Initially municipal governments played a negative role in urban gentrification. During the 1970s and early 1980s, when gentrification or revitalization was just getting established, negative municipal policies often served as a catalyst to bring neighbors together. Whether it was failure to enforce building codes; inadequate police protection; poor garbage collection and sanitation; or just general neglect of the area, the lack of appropriate government action

often brought residents together in opposition to city hall.

Today, municipal governments overwhelmingly support gentrification, largely because it brings more affluent taxpayers. However, there is considerable dispute as to the role government housing policies are playing in contemporary low-income urban gentrification. Wyly and Hammel argue for the crucial role played by low-income housing assistance, while John Kasarda, Brian Berry, and Peter Marcuse remain far more doubtful whether changes in mortgage lending have changed the gentrification process.[28]

Who Is Gentrifying?

Descriptive accounts suggesting that urban renovators are disillusioned suburbanites returning to the city from the suburbs are in error. Although one commonly hears the phrase "return to the city," most in-movers actually come from other areas of the city. The best predictor of an affluent in-mover is someone who already lives in a central-city location.[29] Thus, gentrifiers are perhaps better described as "urban stayers," than as "urban in-movers."

Renovators are generally young or middle-aged adults, childless, white, urban-bred, well-educated, employed in professional or managerial positions, and earning middle-class to upper-middle-class incomes.[30] Many are "DINKS" (dual income-no kids). However, research suggests that it is the older community residents who are best integrated into neighborhood social networks and have high levels of community participation.[31]

Why Is Gentrification Taking Place?

Three factors help to explain urban revitalization.

Demographic Changes. Today young adults more often live independently, and there are relatively high rates of separation and divorce. Where in the past there would be one household of several people, today there is often fragmentation into several households, each containing fewer people, which increases housing demands. The census has documented the decline in marriage, later age at marriage, increases in unmarried couples, and declines in the number of young children per family.[32]

Other demographic changes include more nontraditional living arrangements, later birth of the first child, increasing entry of both single and married women into the labor force, and a rising number of dual-wage-earner families. Taken together these factors represent a decline of the sort of "familism" that played such an important part in the postwar flight to the suburbs. The post–World War II American ideal of a suburban home, your own backyard, and good schools neatly met the needs of new families with children. However, this option has far less appeal for contemporary two-career couples without children. Inner-city living is particularly attractive for gays and nontraditional households. To the extent that aggregate demographic changes are producing more nontraditional family units than ever before, we have partial explanation of urban revitalization of central-city neighborhoods.

Economic Changes. Economic considerations, particularly for single persons or two-income households, often encourage a central-city location. Commuting costs, in terms of time as well as money, can be especially high when both partners commute to work. If one or both works downtown, commuting time can be cut substantially, and public transit often can be used, saving second car and parking fees. Suburban home heating and cooling expenses in an era of rising energy costs also are expensive. Couples are rediscovering what their grandparents knew: heating and/or cooling a two-story townhouse with buildings on either side is more efficient than heating and/or cooling a single-story, freestanding ranch-style home.

Revitalizing existing city housing also can be less expensive than new construction on the suburban periphery. This is especially the case if the new urban homeowners are willing to put in sweat equity by doing some rehabilitation and upgrade work themselves. Most important, mortgage funds for city properties are more likely to be available.

Lifestyle Choices. Urban living is "in." City households often are not "typical" two-children families. Young couples are postponing, and sometimes sidestepping, matrimony. Childbearing, likewise, is being postponed. Gentrifiers espouse an urban lifestyle that emphasizes urbanity, historical preservation, architectural design, and urban amenities such as good local restaurants. The potential quality of the housing units, the greater convenience to central-city work, and the availability of adult amenities associated with the central city dovetail well with the needs of the increasingly numerous, smaller-sized, adult-oriented households. Inner-city living has a special appeal to the gay community.

A serious liability of many central-city neighborhoods—the low quality of city schools—does not weigh as heavily on urbanites without children. The availability of cultural and social activities and shorter commuter time are more important. Establishments and activities that low-density suburban areas tend to ban, such as late night bars, restaurants, and grocery stores, are just the things that give high-density urban areas their vitality. A growing number of middle-class urbanites are, in effect, voting for sticking with their image of good city life.

After postwar decades in which newer homes were more or less automatically judged better, older restorable houses are now considered more desirable. To central-city aficionados, the ones to be pitied are those suburbanites who remain trapped in outlying suburban housing subdevelopments.

Displacement of the Poor

Local boosters and politicians support gentrification because it raises tax revenues. On the other hand displacement can potentially create havoc for poorer incumbent residents. Is gentrification making the poor urban nomads, priced or pushed out of their neighborhoods?

There is no question that gentrification displaces lower-income residents. Anecdotal evidence suggests displacement can be especially difficult for poor elderly householders. Frequently, it is stated that lower-income black residents are being replaced by middle- and upper-income black residents.[33] Displacement, however, needs to be placed in perspective. The impression is sometimes given that prior to the onset of revitalization in a community both the neighborhood and its population were stable and secure. This assumption is usually inaccurate. While displacement of long-term neighborhood residents certainly does occur, those displaced are most often low-income renters, and low-income renters as a group have high residential mobility. For example, according to census data, nearly 40 percent of all renters move at least once a year. For the lower-income, especially those who rent from month to month rather than under long-term leases, moves are very frequent. Low-income areas undergoing revitalization thus commonly have high levels of residential mobility. Even before gentrification such areas also have high levels of household displacement due to eviction.

While displacement can have high emotional costs, some of those displaced by gentrification find moving has long-term benefits. Research findings (as opposed to newspaper statements) usually indicate that the majority of those displaced move to nearby housing of better quality, but they pay more after moving.[34]

Research also indicates that long-term residents generally view neighborhood changes positively. Elderly property owners do face higher property assessments, but higher assessments mean that their property is sharply appreciating in value, and now can be sold at a good profit. This provides some older homeowners an opportunity to sell and more comfortably retire elsewhere. When examined closely some of the hand-wringing over too-rapid economic upgrading of urban neighborhoods has a bit of an "Alice in Wonderland" quality to it. Ironically, some of those who are the first to condemn middle-class flight from the city are the same ones complaining about the middle-class moving into gentrifying central-city areas. Their complaint is that too many middle-class buyers are moving in and too much housing is being upgraded.

Regardless, gentrification is likely to be an increasing urban occurrence during the first decades of the 21st century. However, the importance of gentrification lies not so much in its amount, but in that it represents a reversal of a long-term trend against middle- and upper-middle-class city residence.

DECLINE OF MIDDLE-INCOME NEIGHBORHOODS

All the good news about cities is challenged by a sobering but little noticed fact: urban middle-income neighborhoods, the icon of the American dream, are not doing well. The number of middle-income neighborhoods is shrinking. While for the 100 largest metro areas in the U.S. middle-income neighborhoods made up six out of ten (58 percent) of all metropolitan neighborhoods in 1970, they made up only four out of ten (41 percent) in 2000.[35] Rising income inequality has led to rising income segregation. Neighborhoods are becoming more and more economically homogeneous, with the affluent living with affluent and lower-income living with lower-income. In 1970 over half (55 percent) of lower-income families lived in middle-income neighborhoods. By

2000 this was down to just over a third (37 percent) of poorer families living in middle-income areas.[36]

While much attention and research has focused on both the well-to-do and the poor communities in cities, very little notice has been given to the "hollowing out" of middle-class neighborhoods. Moderate-income communities, once the backbone of the city, are becoming less numerous. This is a serious problem. Suburban middle-income populations, and suburban middle-class communities have been more likely to retain their middle-income profile.

SUCCESSFUL WORKING-CLASS REVIVAL

Is it possible for cities to provide decent housing for low-income working-class residents? Across the country local governments, together with local nonprofits, have stepped in to build homes for lower-income working-class populations. Working with community groups and local nonprofit housing corporations, the city of New York, for example, has worked a quiet revolution, building just during the early 1990s some 50,000 new residences in what had been the most devastated areas of the city.[37] This was a massive undertaking because by the 1980s large areas of the South Bronx, Harlem, and Brooklyn had become littered with the burned-out hulks of more than 5,000 abandoned buildings.

Rather than just trying one program, the city tried a number of approaches to revitalize abandoned buildings and vacant land that it had come to own through foreclosures. Some of the vacant shells of buildings were given over to private developers for rehabilitation, some were given to churches and nonprofit community groups, and some rehabilitation was done by large city-hired construction companies. It turned out that the top-of-the-line city-hired companies had major cost overruns and that smaller firms with rehabilitation experience were more effective. Private rehabilitation with government subsidies was effective, but by far the best results have been obtained by locally run community action groups and nonprofits. By 2000 more than 3,000 abandoned apartment houses, with some 44,000 apartment units had been rebuilt. Additionally, over 100,000 units had been moderately rehabilitated in occupied buildings. Also, some 16,000 one-, two-, and three-family new houses were constructed on vacant city-owned land and sold to working families.[38]

However, success wasn't automatic. Initially, much against the wishes of community organizers, the city filled buildings with homeless families. Local organizers argued that it was foolhardy to put so many poor and troubled families together. As the level of experience with revitalization of inner-city areas has grown, the city has learned from its mistakes. Now more working families are being intermixed with poor families. There is also more effort now on scattered-site infilling of littered vacant lots.

The overall result of New York's efforts has been a true inner-city success story. Twenty years ago anyone taking Interstate 95 through New York on the Cross-Bronx Expressway saw acres of abandoned apartment buildings. The impotent city administration tried unsuccessfully to hide this by painting shutters and flowerpots on the plywood-covered windows facing the expressway. Today these now-restored buildings have been brought back to full occupancy. What was vacant wasteland now houses rows of attached single-family townhouses. New York City has in effect reinvented abandoned neighborhoods by building more than 100,000 new housing units 2010.

SUMMARY

It is part of the "common knowledge" about cities that we live in an age of urban crisis. However, the last decade actually shows the quality of urban life improving. Crime rates are down, and central cities are showing economic vigor. Political economy models see the decline of the central city and the flight to the suburbs not as a result of individual choices, but as the inevitable consequence of a capitalistic economic system. Urban decline and decay are seen as the deliberate abandonment of the central city for corporate profit. Gentrification is similarly seen not as individual actions, but as the conscious economic policy of business and government elites.

The first years of the 21st century show some older industrial cities—such as Portland, Oregon, and Pittsburgh—reinventing themselves. Others, such as Camden and Gary, have not. The urban renaissance is real, but uneven. Some city populations may be decreasing, but their share of affluent professionals is increasing. Housing quality is increasing, but the working-class have problems with housing affordability. Central business districts (CBDs) have lost their retail trade dominance, but have been more successful in retaining business and government offices. Downtowns no longer process goods, they process information.

The 21st century shows downtowns still vital. Across the country downtown office buildings and downtown cultural and convention centers have been constructed. The goal of downtown housing also is becoming a reality in many North American cities. Vancouver may, in fact, have a problem with too many people moving into downtown residences.

Within cities there is a mismatch between the information-age jobs being created and the entry-level skills of poorer central-city residents. The entry-level manufacturing jobs that once attracted disadvantaged ethnic and minority groups to the city no longer exist. Also the federal programs that helped support cities 25 years ago are largely gone and unlikely to return. In order to remain solvent, municipalities today concentrate on providing basic city services at the lowest possible cost. This may include privatizing some city services, such as garbage collection. A growing problem is that city infrastructure problems have largely been ignored and much-needed major upgrades put off.

Gentrification of older city neighborhoods is now a widespread urban phenomenon. However, it doesn't involve all city neighborhoods and does not represent a "back to the city" movement. Those gentrifying or revitalizing older decaying neighborhoods are, demographically, young or middle-aged adults without children. Single or gay households are also attracted to the urban adult advantages of shorter commuting time and easily available restaurants and bars. Gays are particularly attracted to gentrifying neighborhoods. The generally poor quality of urban schools and the lack of urban play space weigh less heavily on households that do not have school-age children.

The moderate pace of gentrification in most cities means that the displacement of the poor has, to date, not been a grave problem. Those displaced are usually poor short-term renters rather than long-time neighborhood occupants. Research shows those displaced by gentrification move to better, but higher cost, rental housing.

A largely unnoticed urban housing problem is the substantial decline in the number of middle-income urban neighborhoods. Middle-class neighborhoods are being "hollowed out" with more homogeneous affluent and more poor communities. This is an increasingly serious problem. A bit of good news is that we have discovered that it is possible for cities to provide good-quality housing for low-income residents. Over the last 20 years New York has built more than 100,000 new housing units in the once-devastated South Bronx, Harlem, and Brooklyn. Using a combination of government, nonprofit building corporations, and private funds, more than 25,000 one-, two-, and three-family townhouses have been constructed and more than 50,000 apartment units rehabilitated. The most successful buildings are those self-managed by the residents and local nonprofit housing corporations.

REVIEW QUESTIONS

1. What is the urban crisis thesis and the urban revival antithesis and what is the current situation?

2. How does the political economy approach explain the urban crisis?

3. What is the "mismatch hypothesis" and how does it impact urban vitality?

4. What is the current status of gentrification and who is gentrifying?

5. What positive and negative changes are occurring as a result of gentrification in Harlem?

6. Why and where is gentrification taking place?

7. Is displacement of the poor a major consequence of gentrification, and how serious is the problem?

8. Is there currently a sizable "back to the city" movement, and why or why not?

9. What has been New York's experience with urban rehabilitation of the South Bronx?

10. How would you relate the text statement that the urban crisis "is a long-standing one of opportunity (lack of employment), rather than a short-term one of fiscal management" to problems in urban America?

NOTES

1. R.M. Fogelson, *The Fragmented Metropolis: Los Angeles 1850-1930,* Harvard University Press, Cambridge, Mass., 1967, p. 163.

2. Mike Davis, *City of Quartz,* Vintage, New York, 1992.

3. Robert A. Beauregard, *Voices of Decline: The Postwar Fate of U.S. Cities,* Blackwell, Cambridge, Mass., 1993.

4. William Schneider, "The Suburban Century Begins," *Atlantic Monthly,* July 1992, p. 34.

5. George Sternlieb, "The City as Sandbox," *The Public Interest* 4(25):14, Fall 1971.

6. Fred R. Harris and Lynn A. Curtis (eds.), *Locked in the Poorhouse: Cities, Race, and Poverty in the United States,* Rowman & Littlefield, Blue Ridge Summit, Pa., 2000, and Joel Kokin, "Urban Revival Remains Wistful Hope," *Washington Post,* April 28, 2002; and "The Myth of Superstar Cities," *Wall Street Journal,* Feb. 13, 2007, p. A25.

7. Gregory R. Weihner, "Rumors of the Demise of the Urban Crisis Are Greatly Exaggerated," *Journal of Urban Affairs,* 11(3):225–242, 1989.

8. Sandra Jones, "Loop Lights Up with A Retail Wick," *Chicago Tribune,* Aug. 20, 2006, Section 5, p. 1.

9. Conor Dougherty, "Cities Grow as Housing Bust Slows Movement to Suburbs," *Wall Street Journal,* June 23, 2010, p. A5.

10. Ibid.

11. Manuel Castells, "The Wild City," *Kapital State* 4–5:2–30, Summer 1976.

12. Scott Cummings (ed.), *Business Elites and Urban Development,* State University of New York, Albany, 1988.

13. Neil Smith and Michele LeFaivre, "A Class Analysis of Gentrification," in J. John Palen and Bruce London (eds.), *Gentrification, Displacement and Neighborhood Revitalization,* State University of New York Press, Albany, N.Y., 1984; and Neil Smith and Peter Williams (eds.), *Gentrification of the City,* Allen and Unwin, London, 1986.

14. John Logan and Harvey Molotch, *Urban Fortunes: The Political Economy of Place,* University of California Press, Berkeley, 1987.

15. PR Newswire, "50 Fastest-Growing Metro Areas Concentrated in West and South," prnewswire.com, June 21, 2010.

16. Associated Press, "New Mixed on Home Ownership," *Richmond Times-Dispatch,"* May 19, 2004, p. C1.

17. "Downtowns: Where the Lights Aren't Bright," *The Economist,* March 3, 2007, p. 40.

18. John Kasarda, "Urban Change and Minority Opportunities," in *The New Urban Reality,* Paul Peterson (ed.), Brookings Institution, Washington, D.C., 1985, pp. 33–67.

19. Alan Herenhalt, "Extreme Makeover," *Governing.com,* www. governing.com, Dec. 27, 2006.

20. Ibid.

21. Nathan Glazer, "Fate of a World City," *City Journal,* Autumn 1993.

22. William Tucker, *Insight,* September 6, 1993, pp. 18–22.

23. David Whitman, "The Sickening Sewer Crisis," *U.S. News & World Report,* June 12, 2000, p. 17.

24. Traci Watson, "Brownfields Mar U.S. Cities," *USA Today,* February 24, 2000, p. 1.

25. Gallup Organization, "Your Kind of Town," *New York Times,* October 8, 1989, p. 8.

26. Elvin K. Wyly and Daniel J. Hammel, "Cities and the Reinvestment Wave: Understanding Markets and the Gentrification Housing Policy," *Housing Facts & Findings* 2:11, Spring 2000.

27. J. John Palen and Chava Nachmias, "Revitalization in a Working-Class Neighborhood," in J. John Palen and Bruce London (eds.), *Gentrification, Displacement and Neighborhood Revitalization,* State University of New York Press, Albany, N.Y., 1984.

28. Elvin K. Wyly and Daniel J. Hammel, "Islands of Decay in Seas of Renewal: Housing Policy and the Resurgence of Gentrification," *Housing Policy Debate,* 10:711–771, 1999; John D. Kasarda, "Comments on Elvin K. Wyly and Daniel J. Hammel's Islands of Decay in Seas of Renewal: Housing Policy and the Resurgence of Gentrification," *Housing Policy Debate* 10:773–781, 1999; Brian J. L. Berry, "Comment on Elvin K. Wyly and Daniel J. Hammel's Islands of Decay in Seas of Renewal: Housing Policy and the Resurgence of Gentrification—Gentrification Resurgent" *Housing Policy Debate* 10:783–788, 1999; and Peter Marcuse, "Comment on Elvin K. Wyly and Daniel J. Hammel's Islands of Decay in Seas of Renewal: Housing Policy and the Resurgence of Gentrification," *Housing Policy Debate* 10:789–797, 1999.

29. Daphne Spain, "Why Higher Income Households Move to Central Cities," *Journal of Urban Affairs* 11:283–299, 1989.

30. Daphne Spain and Shirley Laska, "Renovators Two Years Later: New Orleans," in J. John Palen and Bruce London (eds.), *Gentrification, Displacement and Neighborhood Revitalization,* State University of New York Press, Albany, N.Y., 1984, p. 108.

31. Chava Frankfort-Nachmias and J. John Palen, "Neighborhood Revitalization and the Community Question," *Journal of the Community Development Society* 24:1–14, 1993.

32. U.S. Census Bureau, Census 2000, Table DP-1 Profile of General Demographic Characteristics for the United States: 2000, census.gov.2001.

33. Lesley Williams Reid and Robert M. Adelman, "The Double-Edged Sword of Gentrification in Atlanta," *Footnotes,* 31:1 and 8, April 2003.

34. Chava Nachmias and J. John Palen, Neighborhood Satisfaction, Expectations, and Urban Revitalization," *Journal of Urban Affairs* 8:51–62, 1986.

35. Jason C. Booza, Jackie Cutsinger, and George Galster, "Where Did They Go? The Decline of Middle-Income Neighborhoods in Metropolitan America," *Brookings Institution,* June 2006, p. 1.

36. Ibid.

37. Alan Finder, "New York Pledge to House Poor Works a Rare, Quiet Revolution," *New York Times,* April 30, 1995, pp. 1, 40.

38. Larry Keating and David Sjoquist, "Bottom Fishing: Emergent Policy Regarding Tax Delinquent Properties," *Housing Facts & Findings,* Fannie Mae Foundation 3:1, 2001, pp. 1, 5–8.

CHAPTER 12

Housing Policies, Sprawl, and Smart Growth

We shape our buildings, and afterwards our buildings shape us.

Winston Churchill

OUTLINE

Introduction
Housing in the 21st Century
    Mobility
    Housing Costs
    Changing Households
Changing Federal Role
    Federal Housing Administration (FHA)
        Programs
    Subsidizing Segregation
    Upper- and Middle-Class Housing
        Subsidies
Urban Redevelopment Policies
    Critique of Urban Renewal
    Phasing Out Public Housing
Urban Homesteading
Rent Vouchers: Section 8
HOPE VI Projects
Tax Credits
Designing for Safety
Growth Control
Suburban Sprawl
    Auto-Driven Sprawl
    Amount of Sprawl
    Costs and Consequences
Smart Growth
    Advantages
    Legislation
Summary

INTRODUCTION

We are now coming out of the greatest housing downturn since the Great Depression. However, owning one's own home is still a central goal of most North Americans. A house today is seen basically as a home rather than an investment. Until the post–World War II era, most householders were renters. Not until about 1950 were half of all families homeowners. As of 2010 the census reported that two-thirds (67 percent) of all householders were homeowners and some four-fifths of married couples were homeowners. (Householders share the same dwelling but aren't necessarily married.) Renters now constitute only one-third of all households, and—significantly—about 40 percent of all rental units have a female head of household. Seventy-five percent of all white households live in their own homes, but less than half (46 percent) of blacks and half of (49 percent) Hispanics do so.[1] These figures were higher prior to the housing recession. Home ownership rates are now down to the level they were in the 1990s.[2]

HOUSING IN THE 21ST CENTURY

Anyone driving through any North American metro area during recent decades can't help but see the number of new housing units. Between 1975 and 2010 the housing stock increased at a rate more than twice as fast as the population. Just the last 10-year growth in U.S. housing units represents more than the entire housing stocks of Canada, the United Kingdom, or France. As a result much of America's housing is relatively new. One-quarter of all the dwelling units in the United States have been built in the last 15 years.

Some two-thirds of the housing increase of the last two decades occurred in the sunbelt, with the three states of California, Florida, and Texas alone accounting for more than 6 million additional units. New homes are mostly in the suburbs—8 of 10 new homes are located in the suburbs or nonmetropolitan territory.

The median age (half older, half younger) of houses in the United States is 30 years, and the median overall quality is high. As recently as 1950 only half of American homes had central heating and one-quarter didn't have flush toilets. Less than 1 percent had air conditioning. Today central heating and flush toilets are all but universal, and many people have air conditioning. Living space has also increased—97 percent of living units have less than one person per room. This is a great improvement over the crowded post–World War II era. Living space has increased 25 percent since 1960. Over one-fifth of all homes have seven or more rooms.

Mobility

Contrary to what many people think, we are not moving more. We are becoming more res-

identially stable. Mobility decreased, not increased, during the last 50 years.[3] The 2010 Census reported that the sluggish economy and housing recession led to long-distance moves hitting a new low.[4] Younger people, especially college grads, found themselves locked down, unable to move to jobs or buy homes. The economic recession, with its job losses and uncertainty has further dropped mobility. Longer term residential stability is due to home ownership, an aging population, and women's participation in the labor force. When both partners are employed it is more difficult to pull up stakes and relocate. This is particularly the case when homes have lost value to the point that owners owe more than the house could be sold for (negative equity). Lower mobility might result in deeper community ties and greater participation in local politics and schools. But it also makes it harder to relocate to better job markets.

Housing Costs

The cost of becoming a homeowner has gone up from what it was in your parents' or grandparents' day. A way to show the changes in costs while controlling for inflation is to examine the portion of a worker's pay required to buy the average home. In the mid-1950s, the average 30-year-old male worker could carry a mortgage on a median-priced home for 14 percent of his gross earnings.[5] Thirty years later it took a full 44 percent of his gross earnings to make the monthly payment on a median-priced home. Today new workers often are saddled with larger educational debts, and it's more difficult to qualify for a mortgage. Today both partners must work to purchase the average house, one that in the 1960s could be purchased with one income (although, as noted earlier, today's houses are larger). The question of whether or not a spouse with children works outside the home often is determined not so much by choice as by economic necessity. Today, renting is not only a necessity for more young people, it also makes more sense economically.

Housing prices vary considerably from area to area. One region of the country where housing prices have skyrocketed is California. The median 2007 price for a house in Santa Barbara was $1.2 million. Families that would be middle-class in many other places—making more than $75,000 a year—are essentially excluded from the housing market. In Silicon Valley federal figures for 2000 defined a family of four making under $53,100 as "poor" (add $10,000 more for today).[6] Two of five valley residents can't even afford to rent the average two-bedroom apartment. Teachers, police officers, firefighters, and even working people in tech industries cannot afford to live where they work. Even following the housing market meltdown, the 2009 median house price in Los Altos, California, was $1,475,000, and the median price in Palo Alto, California, was $1,222,500.[7]

Baby boomers start hitting age 65 in 2011 and by 2030 more than 70 million people will be over 65. The housing market can expect major changes as many older couples downsize into retirement housing, some of it in age-restricted communities.

Changing Households

There are somewhat more than 95 million households in the United States. The Census Bureau recognizes two types of households: family (a householder and one or more other persons related by blood, marriage, or adoption) and non-family (a householder living alone [84 percent of non-family householders] or with persons not related). Household arrangements are changing from what many think of as the traditional family. Today married families with children constitute less than half of all families. (This is primarily due to the number of "empty nester" couples.) Family size, at 2.6 persons per household, has been level since 1980, but that figure is down substantially from the 3.2 persons of the 1960s.

Married-couple families have dropped from 87 percent of all family households in 1970 to three-quarters today. During this same time the number of families maintained by a woman without a husband present has doubled. Beginning in the late 1980s, for the first time there were more families without children at home than with children. One-quarter of all white children under 18 and two-thirds of all black children under 18 live with one parent.[8] About 1 in 8 adults lives alone, and 6 in 10 of these are women. More elderly women than elderly men live alone, reflecting the higher mortality rates for men. The census reports that 10 percent of all opposite-sex couples are unmarried.[9] In 1970 the figure was only 1 unmarried couple for every 100 married. Of particular interest to many college students is the high number of "return nesters." Approximately 61 percent of young males and 48 percent of females ages 18 to 24 live at home with their parents (women marry at younger ages and, thus, are less likely to still be living at home). A 2010 Pew Center report documented a 33 percent increase in multi-generational adult households.[10]

CHANGING FEDERAL ROLE

Federal housing programs are in flux—even the Secretary of the Department of Housing and Urban Development (HUD) recommended in 1995 that HUD get out of the business of managing public housing. The United States government's official housing policy was formulated in 1949. It states that it is the aim of the government to realize the goal of a decent home and a suitable living environment for every American family.

However, in the more than half century that this has been official policy, no administration has taken this statement as a guideline for clear and decisive action; rather, they have been viewed as long-range goals. Today—as when the policy was written into law—safe and decent housing at affordable prices remains but a dream for all too many Americans.

Housing in America has traditionally been considered a private rather than a public concern, and the whole concept of involvement by the federal government in the housing of its citizens is fairly recent in the United States. Nor is the concept of government support for housing universally accepted, a situation much different than that in European countries.

It took the massive economic collapse of the Great Depression of the 1930s to involve the federal government with housing issues. During the Depression, residential construction dropped by 90 percent and downtown skyscrapers stood vacant. Even the prestigious Empire State Building in New York City was unable to fill most of its offices. Franklin D. Roosevelt's administration came into office committed to reviving the economy through federal intervention, a new and radical approach at that date. In order to get a sick housing industry on its feet and encourage "builders to build and lenders to lend" the government engaged in extensive "pump priming" in the housing area.

The Housing Act of 1937, for example, established a slum-clearance program and created the United States Housing Authority, which built some 114,000 low-rent public housing units before the program was ended during World War II. However, it was never clear whether the goal of the programs of the 1930s was to put people to work or to provide new housing for those lacking "standard" dwellings. Whatever the purpose, the result was that some of the worst deteriorated slums were cleared, and every substandard unit of housing that was cleared was replaced with a standard unit.

The 1930s housing programs differed from later efforts in at least two respects: first, only public housing was built on land that was cleared, not shopping centers or office buildings; second, the housing projects were generally quite successful—many of them are still well maintained today. Their success can be attributed first to their design (few were over four stories high, giving the buildings the atmosphere of family apartment buildings where neighbors knew each other), and second to the fact that residents initially were either working or seeking work while temporarily employed by the government's Works Progress Administration (WPA). Until the 1960s projects did not house poor families on welfare.

Federal Housing Administration (FHA) Programs

During the Depression, the government, through the Housing Act of 1934, created the Federal Housing Administration to insure home loans. After World War II, the Veterans Administration also made loans (VA loans) to veterans, which were guaranteed by the government. Under such schemes, banks and lending institutions still decided who would get loans—the FHA or VA acted to insure the bank against loss if the buyer defaulted. This system encouraged lending institutions to make loans to buyers they would otherwise reject.

After World War II, the FHA and the VA for the first time insured mortgages given to working-class and lower-middle-class families who wanted to buy homes. The consequence was a federally insured urban exodus to the new suburban subdivisions as discussed in Chapter 6: The Suburban Era. The FHA program both encouraged and subsidized white suburbanization. As recently as the 1980s about half the outstanding mortgage debt on single-family homes was insured by either the FHA or the VA. By 1995 the FHA had insured some 22 million home purchases. The post-2007 collapse of the subprime housing market saw FHA loans increase. By 2010 the FHA was backing nearly half of all home-purchase loans, which was a record high.

The government-sponsored urban renewal program was designed to hold middle-class white families in the central city. The government was thus simultaneously trying to hold the middle class in cities, while subsidizing them to leave. Currently, Fannie Mae, a semi-government corporation, provides support for low-interest loans to low-income home buyers. Fannie Mae bought many bad subprime loans, contributing to the post-2007 housing meltdown.

Subsidizing Segregation

For years government housing policies directly encouraged racial segregation. After World War II, suburbs (with FHA encouragement) used restrictive covenants to exclude blacks and other "undesirables" who it was feared might lower property values and threaten the FHA's investment. From 1935 to 1950 FHA regulations expressly forbade issuing loans that would either permit or encourage racial integration.

> The Federal Housing Administration's official manuals cautioned against "infiltration of inharmonious racial and national groups," "a lower class of inhabitants," or "the presence of incompatible racial elements" in the new neighborhood. . . . Zoning was advocated as a device for exclusion, and the use was urged of racial covenants (attachments to deeds prepared by the FHA) with a space left blank to be filled in by the builder for the prohibited races and religions.[11]

Government policy thus directly encouraged "white-only" suburbs and held blacks in the inner city. Restrictive racial covenants were declared illegal by the 1968 Fair Housing Act. Redlining, a practice by which lending institutions refuse to make loans in minority or mixed-race areas, has also been declared illegal. However, insurance redlining, a practice in which insurance companies make it more difficult and/or expensive to obtain insurance coverage in minority areas, still persists.

Upper- and Middle-Class Housing Subsidies

In the United States today we have anything but a laissez-faire housing policy. Almost all financing for new houses or apartments involves fed-eral government support in one way or another. The largest federal tax subsidy is the middle- and upper-class tax break of mortgage interest deduction on federal taxes. As of 2009 the mortgage interest deduction benefit amounted to a huge entitlement costing the government $80 billion.[12] No such government housing entitlement is available in Canada. Additionally, in the U.S. property taxes paid by homeowners (but not by renters) can be deducted from federal taxes. The direct and indirect consequence of these subsidies plus depreciation write-offs costs the U.S. Treasury more than $131 billion a year. These federal subsidies were designed to help families to purchase homes, and they certainly prop up the housing industry. Various proposals over the years for replacing the U.S. tax structure with a single "flat tax" have floundered once people realize that a flat tax means the end of homeowner's tax breaks.

For several decades, there has been talk about a "back to the city" movement. But that is all it has been—talk. Now, however, partially because of the collapse of the suburban "McMansion" trend of the first half of the last decade, there does appear to be signs of younger dual-income families seeking somewhat more manageable, affordable, and convenient, central-city housing. The 21st century may be notable for the revival of the city.

URBAN REDEVELOPMENT POLICIES

After World War II it was widely recognized that cities were headed for trouble if the federal government didn't intervene. Housing was in poor shape, and downtowns were showing age and wear. Problems were particularly acute on the deteriorating downtown fringe areas. It was generally felt that the expense of buying, tearing down, and rebuilding in the inner city was not economically feasible for private developers.

Liberals and conservatives in Congress had radically different ideas of what government should do. The eventual result was a classic American compromise. The Housing Act of 1949 contained both a public housing section, which liberals had lobbied for, and an urban development section, which conservatives and business people had sought. Urban renewal was seen as being both good for business and good for the city. Commercial and financial interests in the central cities supported urban renewal because they saw the renewal areas as providing the downtown with a buffer, or *cordon sanitaire*, against encroachment by slums. Moreover, since the occupants of the urban renewal housing were expected to be families with substantial purchasing power it was expected they would help stimulate retail trade. Thus, the purpose of urban renewal was not to rebuild the area for the old residents, but rather to change land-use patterns.

The urban redevelopment section of the 1949 Urban Renewal Act was a radical break with past housing policies in that it provided for the use of public funds to buy, clear, and improve the renewal site, after which the ownership of the land would again revert to the private sector. When the renewal area was approved, the authorities were given the power to buy properties and, in cases where the owner refused to sell at a market price, to have the property condemned through the government's right of eminent domain, with compensation paid.

Once the city acquired all the land in the renewal area, the existing buildings were cleared (or rehabilitated under later modifications of the act). New streets, lights, and public facilities were then installed, and finally the land was sold to a private developer who agreed to build in accordance with an approved development plan. The developer paid only about 30 percent of what it had cost the local government to purchase, clear, and improve the land. This so-called "write-down" was the difference between what the land had cost the public and what it was sold for to the private developer. Two-thirds of the city's loss was made up in a direct subsidy from the federal government.

Thus, the control of the program was basically local, while most of the funds were federal.

Since the purpose of urban redevelopment was to change patterns of land use for the benefit of the city as a whole, there was no requirement that destroyed housing had to be replaced with housing for people with a similar income level. In fact, once the dwelling units within the renewal area were demolished and cleared, the land could be used for a shopping center, a park, or an office building. By the time urban renewal largely ended in the 1970s, over one-third of the federal funds were being used for nonresidential projects.

In 2005 the Supreme Court in *Kelo v. the City of New London* ruled that private land could be taken from one private party by eminent domain and sold to another private party in order to foster economic development. This ruling set off a furor in Congress and in state legislatures where the outcry was that private land was being taken for other private-, rather than clearly "public use."[13] In virtually every state legislation has been introduced (and mostly passed) to shore up restrictions on the use of eminent domain.

Critique of Urban Renewal

Much of the confusion and downright contradiction in urban renewal programs were a result of the mixture of three different goals. These were increasing low-cost housing while eliminating slums, revitalizing the central city, and creating planned cities through community renewal programs. Today the impact of urban renewal projects is seen as decidedly mixed. It never was able to meet its own expectations, and its long-term impact has been less than proponents or critics expected.[14] Finally, it is only fair to say that the urban renewal program had some notable successes, such as the comprehensive renewal effort in New Haven, the Southwest Project in Washington, D.C., the Western Addition in San Francisco, Society Hill in Philadelphia, and Hyde Park–Kenwood in Chicago. The vast majority of the renewal sites were blighted, dilapidated, filthy slums that no one wants to bring back. Even critics of urban renewal concede that the grossest mistakes were made by the earliest projects and that, as the program matured, it profited from earlier errors. It is agreed that the most glaring weakness of urban renewal programs was the displacement of large numbers of low-income families without adequate provision for their relocation.

Phasing Out Public Housing

High-rise public housing projects are now being phased out. There are about 3.4 million persons currently living in 1.2 million public housing units (this is roughly 1.5 percent of the nation's housing stock). Public housing was originally designed to provide standard-quality housing for those who could not afford decent, safe housing on the private market. One of the basic unwritten assumptions of the program was that by changing a family's place of residence you could also change the way people behaved. Advocates of social planning supported public housing as a means of social up-

lift. Tearing down slum housing was seen as a way of destroying the crime, delinquency, drunkenness, and lax morals that were considered to be associated with the slum housing. Once again, technology was going to solve social problems—a naive belief of long standing in America. This can be characterized as "architectural determinism" or what I've called "salvation by bricks and mortar." Public housing erected during the 1930s was built as much to give workers jobs as to eliminate slums. Projects were filled mainly with working-class families who were there because, owing to the Depression, family heads could not get regular work and thus could not find adequate housing elsewhere. After World War II, as these families moved up and moved out, the projects lost their sound working-class image.

By the mid-1960s families living in projects were mostly female headed, on welfare, and without any reasonable expectation of moving into the middle class. The low levels of education and training among these project residents, coupled with regulations that placed low limits on how much a family could earn and still qualify for public housing, meant that those

Implosion of Edward W. Scudder housing project in Newark, N.J. The razing is part of a plan to demolish and replace deteriorated high-rise apartments. Michael Sypniewski/ AP Images

who were at all upwardly mobile moved on, while those who were not mobile stayed. The policy of evicting successful families also meant that in the largest projects successful adult role models were virtually nonexistent. This had disastrous results for children, whose images of successful adults were those involved in drugs, gambling, or prostitution. As inner-city projects became the residence of last resort for the permanently poor, the public at large became disillusioned with public housing. It obviously wasn't remaking the poor into middle-class citizens. As caustically expressed by one writer, "They're the same bunch of bastards they always were."[15]

Public housing construction and finance costs were paid by the federal government, but local housing authorities were to provide operating and maintenance out of tenant rents. Congress, however, put a cap of 25 percent of tenant income on what tenants could pay (raised to 30 percent in the Reagan years) and so had to provide operating subsidies to the nation's 3,000 local housing authorities.[16] The subsidies, though, never covered the needs, and projects badly deteriorated to the point where many units became unlivable. A three-year study ordered by Congress reported in 1987 that $21.5 billion would be needed to repair and restore the nation's public housing units.[17]

In the late 1990s the Clinton administration began tearing down high-rise housing projects and replacing them with mixed-income low-rise units. Nationwide, some 150,000 public housing units were demolished between 1994 and 2006. Many of the most notorious high-rise projects, such as Chicago's massive Cabrini-Green housing project, are now history. Cabrini-Green now is a neighborhood of mixed working-class and low-income families living in low-rise units.

URBAN HOMESTEADING

Urban homesteading programs turn over abandoned and foreclosed homes to those who

agree to stay for a period of years (at least three) and bring the homes up to code standards within two years. Urban homesteading programs conjure up the image of the hardy pioneers, who, under the Homestead Act signed by President Lincoln, were given 160 acres of western land if they could stick it out for five years. Urban homesteaders, on the other hand, are not supposed to build on the land but to rebuild inner-city neighborhoods.[18] The first urban homesteading program (and still one of the most active) began in Wilmington, Delaware, in 1973. Others followed in Philadelphia, Baltimore, Detroit, and Saint Louis. Offering homes at nominal fees such as $100, urban homesteading programs implicitly recognize that by definition there is no market for abandoned property. Thus it is given away to those who agree to improve and use it. The Housing and Community Development Act of 1974 got the federal government into the business of transferring residential properties to local governments for homesteading. Federally funded programs were discontinued in 1992.

The record of urban homesteading has been mixed. While the concept sounds ideal, there are some major limitations:

First, homesteading involves a limited number of homes. Programs to date are only a drop in the bucket, with only approximately 75,000 homes having been rehabilitated by the homesteading mechanism. (By comparison, 150,000 inner-city homes and apartments are abandoned annually.)

Second, by the time government action is taken, most abandoned properties are beyond the point of economic rehabilitation. Professional and amateur looters strip homes to the shell, and vandals deface what isn't taken. Fires are also common, and no one wants to rehabilitate a burned-out hulk. Unlike gentrification, urban homesteading often occurs in less desirable areas without historic or other distinction.

Third, there is the cost factor. Title to the property may come cheap, but rehabilitation costs big money. Even when owners use "sweat equity" (i.e., their own labor), rehabilitation loans commonly run from $50,000 to over $200,000. Thus urban homesteading is definitely not the answer for the urban poor.

Fourth, as a home rehabilitation program, urban homesteading does not affect multifamily apartments, where the bulk of the poor are housed.

Fifth, for loans, of course, lenders are necessary, and financial institutions have been reluctant to invest in rehabilitating abandoned slum properties. Thus low-interest municipal loans or loans guaranteed by the municipality appear to be essential.

Finally, there is no point in rehabilitation of one home if the remainder of the neighborhood consists of vandalized burned-out buildings. There has to be an overall change in the neighborhood, simultaneously renovating a substantial number of homes while providing reasonable public services and police protection. Habitat for Humanity discovered in Chicago that if it just rehabilitated a few homes in an area, those homes would soon also be beset by major problems.

Nonetheless, urban homesteading has had some psychological as well as physical impact on cities. While it is not the answer to most urban housing problems, homesteading has provided a psychological lift. An additional "nonlegal" form of homesteading is "walk-in homesteading," or urban squatting. Until a decade ago this was a politically important movement in European countries such as Holland, Germany, and Sweden. Today, nonprofit CDCs (Community Development Corporations) are the major force rebuilding urban neighborhoods that have experienced tax delinquency and abandonment.[19]

RENT VOUCHERS: SECTION 8

Public housing programs were replaced in large part by the Section 8 Program of rent certificates or vouchers, which allows tenants to shop for private-market housing units. The landlord enters into a subsidy contract with the government, and the tenant pays no more than 30 percent of his or her income as rent, with the rent subsidy making up the balance. As of 2000 more than 1.4 million families nationwide received Section 8 vouchers, but many families, especially in large cities, couldn't find units with rental prices low enough to qualify. To correct this, the Department of Housing and Urban Development (HUD) has increased voucher amounts to substantially boost the number of apartments open to Section 8 users.[20]

The consensus seems to be that vouchers are better as social policy than as housing policy. Vouchers do little to encourage the construction of new low-income housing. Nonetheless, with public housing generally viewed as a failed policy, rent vouchers are becoming more common. The Section 8 Program has been very popular with landlords and particularly developers. However, the program has had some tough times. Dishonest officials and influence peddlers stole billions meant to house needy families .Massive mismanagement and fraud in the Department of Housing and Urban Development led to losses of $8 billion. Former Interior Secretary James Watt pleaded guilty in 1995 to receiving $420,000 in kickbacks for pushing approval for questionable new projects. Since then the program has worked reasonably well.

HOPE VI PROJECTS

Recognizing the failure of public housing, Congress in 1992 created the Urban Revitalization Demonstration Program, commonly known as HOPE VI, in order to transform distressed public housing developments. The idea was to give public housing authorities (PHAs) the tools necessary to reform public housing. To do this PHAs sought to eliminate the preferences for the very poorest, and to establish mixed-income communities with different types of working tenants. They also eliminated the one-for-one replacement of demolished units that had effectively stopped any new building, and used public–private partnerships to build mixed-income housing.[21] Powers to do this were made permanent in what is known as the 1998 Act.

HOPE VI projects involve social as well as physical changes. The goal is to provide stable sustainable communities for those cycling from welfare to work—not an easy task. Areas undergoing HOPE VI projects invariably are poor areas occupied by racially segregated populations. Changing community makeup inevitably means displacing some current poor residents and there are legitimate concerns over land grabs by developers.[22] Designs for HOPE VI projects assume that social behavior is linked to architectural design. (See the following section on The Meaning of Space for elaboration.) Existing failed high-rise projects

are torn down, and the area is rebuilt with a mixture of low-rise building and townhouses.

HOPE VI is partially based on the sociologist William Julius Wilson's linking of social behavior to the concentration of poverty. Wilson's research indicates that when neighborhood poverty rates exceed a certain level, social and behavioral collapse follow.[23] Thus, it is assumed that in order to integrate poor inner-city residents into the social and economic fabric of the city, concentrations of the poor either have to be physically dispersed, or new mixed-income neighborhoods developed. HOPE VI projects focus on accomplishing the latter. The assumption is that more than buildings have to be rebuilt.

Given the newness of the program it is impossible to make a final judgment as to the effectiveness of HOPE VI projects, but after a decade there are positive signs. Still, it is a chal-

HOPE VI projects, such as this one on the west side of Chicago, seek to reduce the concentration of very poor residents by replacing high-rise public housing projects with sustainable public-private low-rise communities. © Camilo Vergara

lenge to create viable mixed-income projects in areas where only low-income public housing projects existed.

HOPE VI requires resident participation in planning redevelopment. Public housing residents invariably oppose neighborhood change because some residents will necessarily be displaced. Acrimony was bitter over destroying the notorious Cabrini-Green high-rises in Chicago and rebuilding the area as a low-rise mixed-income community. However, in spite of setbacks, Cabrini-Green, and other new mixed-income projects across the nation, appear to be successful.

TAX CREDITS

In order to encourage the private rehabilitation of older central-city areas, in 1981 Congress passed a rehabilitation tax-credit program. Under the program investors who renovate old structures can qualify for tax credits. The amount of the credit depends on the age and the historical or architectural significance of the structure. This program has been a boon to older cities. Under the program central-city office buildings have been restored, old hotels revitalized to their 19th-century glory, and factories converted into rental apartments or commercial space. The 1986 revision of the tax code allowed renovation of a historic structure to qualify for a 20 percent tax credit. The increasing visibility of downtown housing in rehabilitated buildings is economically viable due largely to the use of tax credits.

DESIGNING FOR SAFETY

Physical planning has social consequences. And, as noted in earlier chapters, physical space often has different meanings to different groups. Understanding the symbolic uses of space can certainly be of practical use to architects and planners. Public housing in par-

ticular can be designed to minimize rather than maximize feelings of deprivation and isolation from the community at large. Traditional high-rise projects too often were not only dull and monotonous, but also dangerous to the inhabitants.

Large open areas outside the projects frequently became "no man's lands" after dark, while within the buildings the corridors, washing rooms, and even elevators were unsafe. Architectural design can increase the security and livability of projects. One of the simplest changes is to build low-rise buildings (six stories at most) where no more than a dozen families share the same stairwell and thus know who should or should not be present. Oscar Newman suggests that some other elements that can help provide security are:

1. Defining territorial space in developments to reflect the areas of influence of the inhabitants. This works by subdividing the residential environment into zones toward which adjacent residents easily adopt proprietary attitudes.
2. Positioning apartment windows to allow residents to naturally survey the exterior and interior public areas of their living environments.
3. Using building forms that avoid the stigma of peculiarity that allows others to perceive the vulnerability and isolation of the inhabitants.
4. Enhancing safety by locating residential developments in functionally sympathetic urban areas immediately adjacent to activities that do not provide continued threat.[24]

The effect of planning can be seen by comparing the Brownsville and Van Dyke housing projects in New York, which are separated only by a street. The low-rise Brownsville buildings, although older, have significantly fewer problems of crime and maintenance than the high-rise Van Dyke buildings. This is in spite of the fact that the average density per acre of the two projects is virtually identical. The difference appears to be that the Brownsville projects, with their 6-story buildings and 3-story wings, are humanly manageable and controllable to a far greater degree than the 13- and 14-story Van Dyke projects across the street. Architectural design alone, however, does not prevent crime. An absence of social relationships among residents, fear, and a sense of futility may result in residents not becoming involved.[25] Social involvement produces safety. One way to augment building safety is to have areas visible to residents and design barriers that discourage entry by those who don't belong.[26] The next chapter offers a fuller discussion of how design can help promote safe neighborhoods.

Finally, it is helpful to keep in mind that even the best-designed cities and housing cannot solve social and economic problems. Unemployment, high dropout rates from school, drug usage, and crime cannot be expected to vanish simply because of redesigned buildings. Making cities more attractive and livable is a noble goal in and of itself.

GROWTH CONTROL

For years it was part of the American creed that bigger is better. City boosters, as a matter of course, bragged that their town or city was growing faster than neighboring places. Now that is changing, and rapidly growing communities are seeking ways of limiting growth. Residents of growing suburban areas in particular have concerns about future growth. (The recent housing recession, beginning in 2007, has made growth control far less of an issue.)

Studying responses of citizens in Orange County, California, Mark Baldassare found that over half his sample cities had environmental concerns such as traffic congestion and environmental deterioration, while one-third had

economic worries such as maintaining property values and keeping down government costs and taxes.[27]

Those groups favoring land-use control, such as the Sierra Club, argue that uncontrolled sprawl has destroyed the physical and cultural environments and that indiscriminate gobbling up of land by developers has to be controlled. Opponents deplore a "pull up the gangplank" approach on the part of established communities that resist change in their way of life. Those against growth controls range from the National Association of Home Builders (NAHB) to the National Association for the Advancement of Colored People (NAACP). While the home-building industry is concerned about the effect of building restrictions on the profits of developers, the NAACP is concerned that imposing environmental protections (e.g., requirements for municipal sewers and water hookups rather than septic systems and wells) will drive up prices and exclude blacks. Opponents of growth controls say that the real question is whether those already in the area can infringe on what they see as a constitutional right to settle where one chooses.

To date, only a limited number of environmentally active communities (usually in the South and West) have actually tried to put lids on growth. Decisions by the courts seem to indicate that while a town can't simply ban all growth, it can try to control its future. This is what most citizens also favor. Research shows strong suburban support for slow growth, but little support for no growth.[28] Charging builders' fees or "proffers" to help pay for new homes using local road, sewer, water, and school services is becoming a more common practice. Research indicates that municipal zoning and other techniques to control growth have only a modest effect. Stating goals and accomplishing them are not the same thing.[29] (Smart growth and the New Urbanism are discussed in Chapter 13: Planning, New Towns, and New Urbanism.)

SUBURBAN SPRAWL

Growth and sprawl are not identical. *Sprawl* means unbridled and poorly planned, spread-out, low-density, auto-dependent, residential development. This development "leapfrogs" over open spaces. Its trademark is strip or leapfrog commercial and residential development, each zoned into separate areas. Sprawl means huge consumption of environmentally sensitive land, total reliance on automobiles, and often fragmented government. Outer regions of metro areas are, as a consequence of sprawl, experiencing severe environmental costs; commuting headaches; and social, race, and class isolation.[30]

Sprawl occurs when land usage expands dramatically faster than population growth. Census 2000 figures showed that the average size of the nation's 100 largest cities had grown to roughly 168 square miles, or triple the average city size in 1950.[31] The greatest expansion has been in southern and western cities, but they are not alone. The Greater Toronto Area (GTA) is projected to double in physical size in the next twenty years.[32] That means urbanizing 200,000 more acres of prime agricultural land. However, the housing meltdown has slowed sprawl.

Auto-Driven Sprawl

Implicit in outlying areas undergoing sprawl is that all travel for any purpose must be by auto. In Atlanta, for example, the majority of business and residential sprawl is taking place to the north of the city, but the only public transit goes south. Common ills of sprawl are the unholy trio of traffic congestion, air pollution, and massive destruction of the natural environment. Long traffic commutes not only contribute to frustration and air pollution; they also take time away from family and work. The average American driver spends 443 hours per year, or the equivalent of 55 eight-hour work-

days, behind the wheel.[33] Fuel lost to traffic jams provides six days of driving for every car in the country. Census data indicate New York City residents average 38 minutes each day getting to work.[34] This means they spend one full week each year commuting. (See figure 12.1.) They are not alone. Washington, D.C., commuters have seen their time stuck in traffic increase to 46 hours a year, while metro Seattle today has twice the daily auto trips per household it did in 1990. Traffic is making millions sick and tired, but gridlock is going to increase unless we act to control sprawl.

Amount of Sprawl

A few figures give some sense of the magnitude of sprawl. In the last 50 years Pennsylvania has lost more farm and open land to sprawl than the entire states of Connecticut and Rhode Island. The city of Phoenix, at 469 square miles (and growing), is already almost half as large as Rhode Island.[35] Michigan's 10 expanding urban areas are consuming land at six times the population growth rate. In the Atlanta metro area the momentum and consequences of sprawl are becoming catastrophic. The Atlanta Regional Commission estimates that 1 percent in population growth results in 10 to 20 percent growth in land consumption.[36] Every day in metro Atlanta another 50 acres are plowed under for development. In Atlanta the daily commute already is 36.5 miles, the longest in the nation. Partially as a result Atlanta is severely out of compliance with federal clean-air standards. And Atlanta is far from alone.

One of the unfortunate characteristics of sprawl is that it occurs not only in metro areas that are growing but also in metropolitan areas that are losing overall population. Ohio provides an example. Between 1990 and 1996 metropolitan Akron lost 37 percent of its population. Nonetheless, the amount of developed metro land area expanded 65 percent.[37] Similarly, since 1970 Cleveland and Cincinnati both

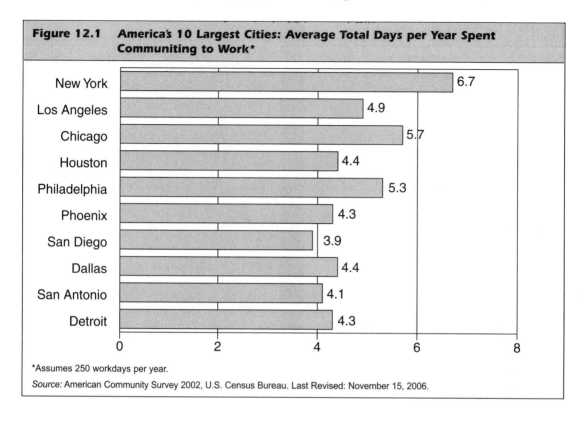

Figure 12.1   America's 10 Largest Cities: Average Total Days per Year Spent Communiting to Work*

*Assumes 250 workdays per year.

Source: American Community Survey 2002, U.S. Census Bureau. Last Revised: November 15, 2006.

have seen their metro populations decline while their outlying land consumption continues to accelerate.

Costs and Consequences

Sprawl has been with us for years, but what has changed is that it is now increasingly a process that is spiraling out of control.[38] Remember that sprawl is far more than just low-density development or growth. Sprawl occurs when land use increases much faster than does the growth of population. It is the seemingly unstoppable spread of ever more developments, producing more and more congestion, escalating tax rates, and consuming more and more of the landscape. To give an example, for two decades the Los Angeles metro area has been increasing its land area more than 10 times faster than its population. The result is that the Los Angeles area, bounded by ocean, mountains, desert,

and federal land, has run out of room. Ironically, this has led to infill developments, and as of 2000 the Los Angeles area had the eighth lowest level of new sprawl in the United States, built up New York had the nation's lowest metro sprawl level, and Atlanta had the highest.

By 2000 we had built over 4 million miles of roads in America, most of them in rural areas.[39] Much of the highway-induced sprawl has been directly financed by the federal government. During the last half of the 20th century the federal government spent eight times as much money to build sprawl-inducing highways as to support space-conserving mass transit.[40] The destruction of woodlands, wetlands, and wildlife habitats has been massive. Florida has lost half its original wetlands, and the U.S. Fish and Wildlife Service estimates that more than 90 percent of California's coastal system has been developed.[41] The American Farmlands Trust estimates that we continue to lose nearly 1 million acres of farmland and open space each year. Building more expressways just compounds the problem. Building more roads is like giving a fat man a bigger belt.

Sprawl also has heavy social and economic costs for already existing communities. It encourages disinvestment in older communities and increases economic and racial segregation by concentrating poverty in inner-city neighborhoods and older, first-ring suburbs. First-ring suburbs on the city edge are often most impacted since they lack both the central city's infrastructure and its commercial and industrial tax base. This makes such suburbs very vulnerable to disinvestment. Sprawling population dispersion also puts small, locally owned shops and restaurants out of business; shopping and dining are instead concentrated in national chains located in or near regional malls. Sprawl enriches developers but heavily costs taxpayers by requiring increased taxes to pay, not only for new roads, but also for sewers, police and fire department services, and new schools. Meanwhile, existing facilities and schools in more densely settled non-sprawl areas are either underused or closed. So far, only the housing recession has been able to halt sprawl.[42]

SMART GROWTH

Sprawl is not inevitable. The term *smart growth* covers a variety of efforts to shape growth so sprawl is limited. Smart growth assumes that while growth is inevitable, low-density suburban sprawl and "leapfrog" development are not. Smart growth "encompasses a range of measures intended to encourage development that offers transportation options, preserves open space and revitalizes older communities."[43] The basic idea of smart growth is to use all land resources, whether recycled urban "brownfield" or infill land or raw suburban "greenfield" land, as effectively as possible. To do this, development is concentrated in agreed-upon growth zones while open land is protected in conservation zones. The goal is to limit wasteful and expensive leapfrog suburban sprawl.

Housing strategies to accomplish this include the use of infill housing in urban areas and higher-density housing in suburban subdivisions. The latter encounters especial opposition since it goes against the common suburban pattern of larger and larger lots. Suburbanites (and suburban governmental units) have a long history of opposing higher density housing for fear it will damage property values and bring in lower-quality residents. They associate higher-density housing with undesirable community characteristics. In reality though, examples of high-income, high-density suburbs already exist. Los Angeles, for instance, contains the highest-density suburbs in the nation.[44] Los Angeles also has the highest gross population density of the nation's twenty largest metropolitan areas.[45]

Advantages

Higher-density designs can result in positive advantages, such as greater sense of community, walk-to schools, lower crime, and moderate taxes. Home buyers are quite willing to accept a bit smaller private lot for a better neighborhood environment, a sense of place, and community amenities. In locations with high housing costs and long commutes, such as California's Silicon Valley, planned higher-density communities offer a better quality of life than that associated with a long commute to an expensive exurb.[46] Among smart growth projects, developers see higher-density urban infill projects as far less risky than smart growth development of outlying suburban greenfields.[47] They view multiple-use projects as inherently risky, and therefore necessitating a relatively high required rate of return. Urban infill projects are seen as most likely to generate a fast cash flow.

From the standpoint of the purchaser, as long as the urban infill unit is large enough and comes with sufficient parking, security, and pri-

---

Box 12.1   Sprawl versus a Suburban Mother

The reaction of suburban residents toward sprawl is beginning to change as they suffer the impact of un-bridled growth. As expressed by Julie Harley, a 39-year-old mother of two who moved to the Atlanta subdivision of Alpharetta in 1994 when the area was mostly horse farms and trees, "People who visited us five years ago say, 'I couldn't find your house.' The roads have all gotten wider, they've knocked down all the trees. The kids cry when they see the bull-dozers. They say, 'When I grow up I'm gonna be president and I'm not going to let them cut down any more trees.'"* Commuting has become a nightmare. In order to beat the traffic to Atlanta's Hartsfield-Jackson airport her husband has to leave the house at 5:30 A.M. for a 9:00 A.M. flight. Harley, a nonprac-ticing lawyer, has found that the Fulton County zon-ing board responds more to well-connected develop-ers than to citizens. For example, a hard-won

moratorium on new development in the county was lifted the next day for developers who already had "land disturbance permits." And the zoning board turned out hundreds of such permits to build in spite of the moratorium. Developers are major contribu-tors to politicians' PACs (political action committees) and reelection campaigns. As Harley says, "We are in the middle of a moratorium, and there is twice as much building as before."** Moreover, taxes, which are low for first arrivals, skyrocket as roads and schools have to be built. Subdivisions a few years old are left to choke on their growth without adequate infrastructure, while the developers move on to the next interstate exit.

*. Ellen Florian, "Oh No, It's Spreading," *Newsweek*, July 19, 1999, p. 26.

**. Ibid.

---

vacy, such urban infill housing has real advan-tages. It is often closer to employment and cul-tural and social amenities. Such housing partic-ularly appeals to working women, non-married couples, childless couples, gays, and some empty-nesters. It is convenient, involves only short commutes, and has low maintenance re-quirements. Convenient housing at higher den-sities also has an appeal to those who work from their homes. The next chapter will discuss New Urbanism as a form of smart growth.

Legislation

A number of states from Maryland to Ten-nessee to Colorado have enacted some version of smart growth legislation. Portland, Oregon, has had an effective smart growth plan setting metropolitan growth limits for more than a decade and a half. However, the evidence thus far is that statewide smart growth laws have been a bust. This is largely because the laws, such as Maryland's celebrated program, have

no teeth to force local governments to comply, and because builders have little economic in-centive to redevelop older urban neighbor-hoods.[48] Florida's plan was substantially gutted by the Republican legislature in 2000 after heavy construction and highway industry lob-bying. Similarly, Oregon's legislature has passed legislation to weaken Portland's smart growth policies.

Smart growth approaches are not a panacea. Legislation favoring constructing planned suburban communities at higher den-sities and designing to promote a sense of com-munity are not going to eliminate all suburban sprawl. However, eliminating regulatory zon-ing barriers to higher-density developments would be a good first step. Political pressure to prevent sprawl is clearly spreading. Voters in states as diverse as New Jersey and California have recently approved smart growth policies to limit sprawl, but until more states do so, sprawl—with all its environmental, economic, and commuting liabilities—will remain the dominant suburban building system of the 21st century.

SUMMARY

Four-fifths of American couples are now homeowners. Whites are more likely to be homeowners than African Americans or Hispanics, and 40 percent of renters are female householders. Housing costs (and quality) are up from your parents' era, but overall housing costs have been stable for the last decade because generally lower interest rates have compensated for higher home costs. Household size at 2.6 persons is at an all-time low, and there are now more families without children than with children at home.

The federal government goal of "a decent home and a suitable living environment for every American family" has never been fully put into action. During the Depression the federal government cleared slums and built a limited number of housing projects, many of which remain successful more than 60 years later. Postwar Federal Housing Administration (FHA) loans insured some 22 million home purchases. One of the nation's largest tax subsidies is the $58 billion mortgage interest and property tax deductions available to those purchasing homes. Canada has no such subsidy.

The Housing Act of 1949 was designed to promote urban renewal through government land clearance and then resale of the land at a "write-down" of approximately two-thirds of the cost of development. Urban renewal destroyed many older urban neighborhoods and displaced their residents, but it did also rebuild some of the nation's worst slums.

Public housing is being phased out. High-rise public housing projects are both dangerous and socially isolating. Since 1995 more than 150,000 high-rise units have been leveled. Urban homesteading has had relatively little application. Abandoned properties are often beyond saving, and while a property is essentially free, rehabilitation can run $200,000. It is not a program for low-income renters. Tax credits for renovating old structures have contributed greatly to increasing the amount of downtown housing in many cities.

Replacing public housing have been Section 8 rent vouchers, which allow users to shop for private-market units. The amount paid by vouchers often has been below the amount required to obtain decent housing. Vouchers also do little to encourage the building of new low-cost housing. A promising federal program, permanently funded by the 1998 Act, is HOPE VI. The goal of HOPE VI is to replace high-rise projects with new low-rise mixed-income communities. The program is based on the twin assumptions that architecture can affect behavior and that poverty concentrations create social disorganization. Thus far HOPE VI programs appear successful.

Concerns over controlling suburban growth are growing. Most communities don't want to stop growth, just make it manageable. Suburban sprawl of low-density, automobile-dependent, outer subdivisions is causing destruction of the environment, economic and racial segregation, and increased commuting times. Sprawl is causing outer metro areas to expand land usage at a rate 10 times or more that of population growth. New York City residents spend a full week a year commuting to work. Today the average commute in Atlanta is 36.5 miles, and the American spends an average of 55 eight-hour workdays driving. Sprawl has only been slowed by the housing recession.

Smart growth is the term applied to efforts to stop leapfrog low-density suburban sprawl while stressing higher-density multiple-use infill housing projects. Such projects meet the needs of many nontraditional as well as traditional families. However, developers view them as economically more risky investments than standard subdivisions. Political support for smart growth developments is growing.

REVIEW QUESTIONS

1. Are Americans becoming more or less residentially mobile?

2. What changes in FHA lending policies have occurred since World War II regarding racially integrated neighborhoods?

3. How have federal government policies regarding housing projects changed over the last 20 years?

4. What factors limit the success of urban homesteading programs?

5. What is the goal of HOPE VI housing projects, and how do they differ from traditional public housing?

6. How is sprawl different from metropolitan growth?

7. What are the characteristics of sprawl?

8. What is meant by the term *smart growth*?

9. How do smart growth communities differ from traditional suburbs?

10. What lobbying groups oppose smart growth, and why do they do so?

NOTES

1. U.S. Census Bureau, "Residential and Home Ownership First Quarter 2010," *U.S. Census Bureau*, Washington, D.C., Table 7, April 26, 2010.

2. "A House Has Become Just a Home, Not an Investment," *Globe and Mail*, August 28, 2010, p. B3.

3. Claude S. Fischer, "Ever More Rooted Americans," *City & Community* 1:2, June 2002, pp. 175–193.

4. William H. Frey, "Population Migration Declines Further: Stalling Brain Gains and Ambitions," *State of Metropolitan America*, Brookings Institution, January 12, 2011.

5. Frank Levy, *Dollars and Dreams: The Changing American Income Distribution*, Russell Sage, New York, 1987.

6. Evelyn Nieves, "Many in Silicon Valley Cannot Afford Housing, Even at $50,000 a Year," *New York Times*, February 20, 2000, p. 20.

7. *Silicon Valley Daily*, "Median California Home Price $304,520 in November." California Association of Realtors, December 26, 2009, p. 2.

8. U.S. Census Bureau, "Households, Families, Marital Status, and Living Arrangements: March 1998," *Current Population Reports*, series P–20, no. 514, 1999.

9. Sharon Jayson, "Census Reports More Unmarried Couples Living Together," *USA Today*, July 28, 2008, p. 1.

10. Pew Research Center, "The Return of the Multi-Generational Family Household." http://pew-socialtrends.org, March 18, 2010.

11. Charles Abrams, *The City Is the Frontier*, Harper & Row, New York, 1965, p. 61.

12. Barbara Kiviat, "The Case Against Home Ownership," *Time*, September 6, 2010, p. 43.

13. Cindy Elmore, "The Pain and Prosperity of Eminent Domain," *Marketwise*, Issue III, 2005, pp. 2–7.

14. Jon C. Teaford, "Urban Renewal and Its Aftermath," *Housing Policy Debate* 11:443–465, 2000.

15. Michael Stegman, "The New Mythology of Housing," *Trans-Action* 7:55, January 1970.

16. Allen Hays, "Housing Subsidy Strategies in the United States: A Typology" in Elizabeth Huttman and Willem van Vliet. (eds.), *Handbook of Housing and the Built Environment in the United States*, Greenwood Press, New York, 1988, p. 184.

17. "H.U.D. Disputes Cost of Fixing Public Housing," *Washington Post*, August 4, 1988, p. 1.

18. Mittie Olion Chandler, "Urban Homesteading," in Willem van Vliet, (ed.), *The Encyclopedia of Housing*, Sage, Thousand Oaks, CA, 1998, pp. 610–612.

19. Larry Keating and David Sjoquist, "Bottom Fishing: Emergent Policy Regarding Tax Delinquent Properties," *Housing Facts & Findings*, Fannie Mae, 3:1, 2000, pp. 1, 5–8.

20. Donna Rogers, "HUD Expands Voucher Limits," *Richmond Times–Dispatch*, September 17, 2000, p. K1.

21. Jerry J. Salama, "The Redevelopment of Distressed Public Housing: Early Results from HOPE VI Projects in Atlanta, Chicago, and San Antonio," *Housing Policy Debate* 10(1): 96–97, 1999.

22. Elvin K. Wyly and Daniel J. Hammel, "Islands of Decay in Seas of Renewal: Housing Policy and the Resurgence of Gentrification," *Housing Policy Debate* 10(4):739–740, 1999.

23. William Julius Wilson, *When Work Disappears: The New World of the Urban Poor,* Knopf, New York, 1996.

24. Oscar Newman, *Defensible Space,* Macmillan, New York, 1972, p. 9.

25. Sally Merry, "Defensible Space Undefended: Social Factors in Crime Control through Urban Design," *Urban Affairs Quarterly* 16:397–422, 1981.

26. Timothy D. Crowe and Diane L. Zahm, "Crime Prevention through Environmental Design," *Land Development,* Fall 1994, pp. 22–23.

27. Mark Baldassare, *Trouble in Paradise,* Columbia University Press, New York, 1986

28. Mark Baldassare, "Suburban Support for No-Growth Policies," *Journal of Urban Affairs* 12:197–206, 1990.

29. John Logan and Min Zhou, "Do Suburban Growth Controls Control Growth?" *American Sociological Review* 54:461–471, June 1989.

30. For a general discussion see Gregory D. Squires (ed.), *Urban Sprawl: Causes, Consequences & Policy Responses,* Urban Institute Press, Washington, D.C., 2002.

31. Associated Press, "Largest U.S. Cities Grow by Leaps and Land Grabs," Sept. 28, 2002.

32. Catherine Vakil and Riina Bray, "From the Suburbs a Parade of Horrors," *National Post, Canada,* April 27, 2005, p. A17.

33. Sierra Club, "Sprawl Increases Traffic on Our Neighborhood Streets and Highways," www.sierraclub.org/sprawl/factshet.asp, accessed November 24, 2000.

34. U.S. Census Bureau, "New York Had Longest Commute to Work in Nation," www.census.gov/Press-Release, Feb. 25, 2004.

35. Sierra Club, "Smart Choices or Sprawling Growth," op. cit.

36. Atlanta Regional Commission reported by Ellen Florian, "Oh No, It's Spreading," *Newsweek,* July 19, 1999, pp. 24–25.

37. Sierra Club, "What Is Sprawl?" 1999 Report, www.sierraclub.org.

38. Donald D. T. Chen, "The Science of Smart Growth," *Scientific American,* December 2000, p. 85.

39. Sierra Club, "Smart Choices or Sprawling Growth: A 50-State Survey of Development," Fall 2000, www.sierraclub.org., accessed Nov. 20, 2000.

40. David Rusk, "Saving Farms and Saving Cities: Sprawl, Race, and Concentrated Poverty," *Community News,* MSU Center for Urban Affairs, Spring 1999, p. 5.

41. Chen, op. cit., p. 86.

42. Richard Florida, "How the Crash Will Reshape America," *The Atlantic,* March 2009, pp. 44–56.

43. Donald D. T. Chen, op. cit., p. 87.

44. Karen A. Danielsen, Robert E. Lang, and William Fulton, "Retracting Suburbia: Smart Growth and the Future of Housing," *Housing Policy Debate* 10:513–540, 1999.

45. Dowell Myers and Alicia Kitsuse, *The Debate over Future Density of Development: An Interpretive Review,* Lincoln Institute of Land Policy, Cambridge, MA, 1999.

46. Karen A. Danielsen, Robert E. Lang, and William Fulton, op. cit.

47. Joseph E. Gyouroko and Witold Rybcynski, "Financing New Urbanism Projects: Obstacles and Solutions," *Housing Policy Debate,* 11:733–750, 2000.

48. Rebecca Lewis, Garrit-Jan Knaap, and Jungyul Sohn, "Managing Growth with Priority Funding Areas: A Good Idea Whose Time Has Yet to Come," *Journal of the American Planning Association,* 7:457–478, 2009.

CHAPTER 13

Planning, New Towns, and New Urbanism

Let there be one man who has a city obedient to his will, and he might bring into existence the ideal polity about which the world is so incredulous.
Plato, The Republic

OUTLINE

Introduction
    Ancient Greece and Rome
    Renaissance and Later Developments
American Planning
    Washington, D.C.
    19th-Century Towns
    Early Planned Communities
    Parks
    The City Beautiful Movement
    Tenement Reform
20th-Century Patterns
    The City Efficient
    Zoning and Beyond
    Master Plans to Equity Planning
    Crime Prevention through Environmental
        Design
European Planning
    Planning and Control of Land
    Housing Priorities
    Transportation
    Urban Growth Policies
    The Dutch Approach
New Towns
    British New Towns
    New Towns in Europe
American New Towns
    Public-Built New Towns
    Federal Support for New Towns
    Private New Towns: Reston, Columbia,
        and Irvine
    Research Parks
New Urbanism or Traditional Neighborhood
   Developments
    Celebration
    Creating Community
    Limitations
Summary

INTRODUCTION

This chapter discusses urban planning in different eras and various forms. New Towns and the New Urbanism are given particular attention. Remember to read this chapter not as a distinct unit, but as part of a larger explanation of urban process. Note how our discussion of Roman and Renaissance planning ties in with Chapter 2: The Emergence of Cities, while coverage of the American planning experience continues the discussion in Part II: American Urbanization.

Urban planning is not a new development. The Bible, in Genesis 11:4, tells of one of the earliest attempts at urban planning:

> And they said, "Come let us build us a city, and the tower the top of which may reach unto heaven; and let us make ourselves a name, lest we be scattered upon the face of the whole earth."

As we all know, the Tower of Babel was not successful as a form of urban planning in spite of the fact that it did have full citizen participation. The hope is that some of our more modest contemporary attempts will be more successful.

Ancient Greece and Rome

Ancient cities, as indicated in Chapter 2: The Emergence of Cities, were rarely based on a plan or even a general concept of what the city should be. The Greeks, who appreciated organization and structure in other aspects of their lives, gave little attention to the physical arrangement of their communities. In classical Greek cities, the main thoroughfares were generally planned as processional avenues, but residential development was undisciplined and chaotic. Rhodes, with its avenues radiating from a center, was something of an exception. What planning did take place was limited to the central municipal area which contained the principal monuments, temples, and stately edifices.

Aristotle tells us that Hippodamus of Miletus, who lived in the fifth century B.C., was the first city planner. According to Aristotle, in planning Athens' port city of Piraeus:

> He planned a city with a population of 10,000 divided into three parts, one of the skilled workers, one of farmers, and one to defend the state. The land was divided into three parts: sacred, public, and private supporting in turn the worship of the gods, the defense of the state, and the farm owners.[1]

Note that provision was made for farming within the city walls, a very necessary consider-ation during periods when the city was under siege.

The Romans were somewhat more successful than the Greeks at planning their towns. But as discussed in Chapter 2, beyond the city center Rome showed very limited evidence of planning, but provincial Roman towns, with their central square and gridiron layout established a model that still can be seen in most American cities today. That Roman provincial cities (and our football fields) were modeled after the gridiron pattern of encampment used by the Roman legions is not surprising since much of provincial Roman town planning was done by military engineers. It has been said that these outpost towns were so similar that if a Roman centurion were dropped in the middle of any one of them, he could not tell which town he was in.

The largest of the planned Roman cities was Constantinople, the "Rome of the East," which the emperor Constantine built to glorify his reign and escape the fate of previous emperors at the hands of Roman mobs.

Renaissance and Later Developments

The fall of the Roman Empire in the West meant the death of western urban planning for virtually a millennium. The Renaissance (14th to 16th centuries) revived planning in cities. Star-shaped models were especially popular; in 1593 Vicenzo Scamozzi actually built a small city, Palma Nova, in the shape of a nine-pointed star.

Planners in the 16th and 17th centuries often designed stylized and static artificial communities. Geometric form rather than natural-ness was the goal. The epitome of symmetrical perfection was Versailles, the magnificent home of the French kings, whose gardens, palaces, and town were planned as a unit.

The English also made attempts, largely unsuccessful, at town planning. In 1580 Queen Elizabeth proclaimed restrictions on London's

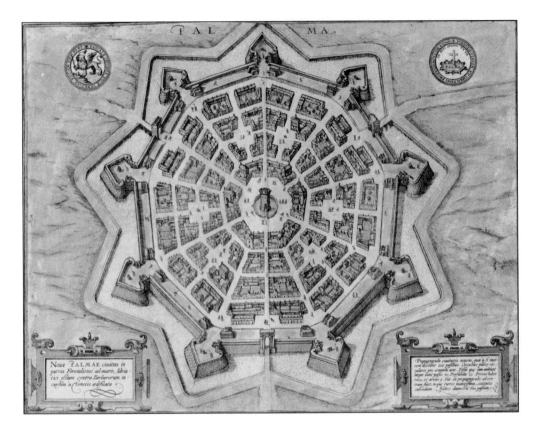

The Italian Renaissance city of Palma Nova was designed as a nine-pointed star. The points were military defense positions. British Library

growth that were designed to give the city a greenbelt of open land and thus prevent crowding and poverty.[2] This policy—which foreshadowed the 20th-century greenbelt towns discussed later in this chapter—failed, although it was backed by royal statute. Probably the most noteworthy master plan was that designed by Christopher Wren for rebuilding London after the disastrous fire of 1666. However, his plan was ignored in the rush to rebuild the city.

The 19th-century redesign of Paris must be listed among the more successful attempts at city planning. The beauty of Paris today is not accidental but the result of 17 years of rebuilding directed by Baron Haussmann under the sponsorship of Napoleon III (1852–1870).

Boulevards such as the Champs-Elysées were cut through festering slums, squares were laid out, and the city was planned for separate industrial and residential areas. However, the rationale for the changes was not solely aesthetic; the broad boulevards were also designed to provide clear fields of fire for cannon so that city districts could be isolated in times of civil insurrection.

AMERICAN PLANNING

Within the next 30 years the United States population is projected to grow by 30 million. That is the equivalent of constructing 60 new cities of 500,000. Would we prefer these places be planned or will sprawl simply continue? Urban planning in the United States is usually regarded as a 20th-century development, but as early as 1672 Lord Ashley Cooper instructed that Charles Town be laid out "into regular streets for be the buildings never so mean and thin at first, yet as the town increases in riches and people, the void places will be filled up and the buildings will grow more beautiful." Philadelphia was laid out according to a gridiron pattern. Today, the area surrounding Independence Hall once again shows the original pattern intended by William Penn. North American colonial cities as disparate as Quebec in the north and James Oglethorpe's Savannah in the south began their existence as planned enterprises.

Washington, D.C.

Pierre L'Enfant's plan for Washington, D.C., is the best-known example of North American town planning during the 18th and 19th centuries. L'Enfant's original design, produced in 1791, called for broad, sweeping diagonal boulevards overlying a basic gridiron pattern of major avenues. L'Enfant himself was removed in 1792, after numerous disputes, and his contention that his plan was "most unmercifully spoiled and altered" is largely accurate. For example, he planned a broad boulevard along the Potomac to be lined with gardens; these have never been seen except on his own detailed maps. He even had a plan to divert the river, making it flow toward the Capitol, whence it would be routed over a 40-foot waterfall and then back to its original course.[3] It is probably fortunate that this particular feature was never constructed.

For much of the 19th century, muddy Washington remained, in Charles Dickens's words, "a city of magnificent intentions." Washington's oppressively hot, unhealthful summers did not encourage year-round residence. On the eve of the Civil War, when Lincoln assumed the presidency, Washington was still a half-finished quagmire, packed with members of Congress, lobbyists, job seekers, prostitutes, gamblers, and hangers-on while Congress was in session, and deserted when it was not. There was no classical Washington Mall during the 19th century.

Near the end of the 19th century a revival of interest in L'Enfant's original plan gave us the Mall with the beaux arts neoclassical style of government buildings found in the capital today. Until the railway lines were put underground at the end of the 19th century, railway lines actually ran across the Mall in front of the Capitol. Among L'Enfant's legacies are Washington's numerous traffic circles. Any tourist who has ever had the folly of driving into the city is not likely to forget the traffic circles, which disorient even the most experienced drivers.

19th-Century Towns

During the 19th century little creative energy went into designing the rapidly multiplying new towns. New western settlements were built as if God had intended that streets always be laid out in a grid, at right angles to each other. The gridiron pattern, in which plots could easily be divided, was well suited to the feverish speculation that accompanied the nation's early growth; most town promoters were speculators whose major interest in the new communities was quick profit. "The open lot and speculation have always gone hand in hand."[4] The Federal Land Ordinance of 1785 encouraged the gridiron pattern, since it divided all lands west of the Appalachians into units of one square mile to facilitate their sale to settlers.[5] In the American and Canadian West, towns were commonly divided into four quarters with numbered avenues going east to west while numbered streets ran north to south. If hills got in the way, as for example in San Francisco, streets were simply cut up one side and down the other rather than following the natural contour of the land.

By the early 20th century the rectangular grid had come to be identified with the American city.

It is in America that the persistence of uniform right-angled streets has been most marked. Here the universality of the plan's adoption, and the rigidity of adherence to it, has been such that Europeans, forgetting the long history of rectangular street planning refer to it now as the American method.[6]

Roads strongly influence the pattern of development of a city. A circular pattern, with roads leading from the center like the spokes of a wheel, focuses attention on the center of the city. It is a system "beloved by chieftains, emperors, priests, and popes."[7] Washington, D.C., and Detroit were both designed on modified wheel patterns. The gridiron system, with its square lots, has always facilitated subdivision and thus is the model used in industrial and business-oriented cities in North America and elsewhere (Johannesburg, South Africa, is an example).

In the new frontier towns, housing was as predictable as the pattern of streets. The same American businesspeople who prided themselves on their originality and inventiveness in business created towns that were dull and repetitive. Every town had its Main Street, Oak Street, and Elm Street. Chicago, largely reduced to ashes by the 1871 Chicago Fire, was one of the few cities insisting that new residences be built of brick or stone.

Early Planned Communities

Historically, totally planned communities have not fared well in North America. In the early 19th century, Lowell, Massachusetts, for all its early promise as an idealistic community, quickly deteriorated into just another New England mill town. Pullman, Illinois, was designed in the 1880s as an experiment in both well-managed labor relations and town planning. In the words of its founder and sole owner, George Pullman, "With such surroundings and such human regard for the needs of the body as well as the soul the disturbing conditions of strikes and other troubles that periodically convulse the world of labor would not be found here."[8] George Pullman proved to be a poor prophet. Pullman is today best known because of the bitter strike there in 1894, a strike that was finally broken by the National Guard.

Of the new communities organized around religious or political–philosophical doctrines— New Harmony, Indiana, and Oneida, New York, for example—only Salt Lake City has grown and prospered, largely because it had, under Brigham Young, a very tight and well-run social organization. It also had an excellent environmental location along the trail to the California gold fields. An early 20th-century attempt to create a feminist planned community was Alice Austin's "Socialist City" of Llano del Rio in southern California.[9] The homes were built without kitchens and backed up on a communal eating area. This latter feature was intended to relieve housewives of the drudgery of cooking. The planned community, like most utopian communities, was underfinanced and went bankrupt in 1917. As a sidelight, it might be noted that such early feminist communities often had a distinctly middle-class orientation. Middle-class women would be relieved of cooking and heavy cleaning, with that work to be done by lower-class women servants.

Parks

One of the brightest aspects in the rather discouraging story of 19th-century urban planning is the work of Frederick Law Olmsted. In 1857, after much controversy, he began building Central Park on 843 acres of wasteland on the outskirts of New York City. The site was hardly promising, for, as Olmsted described it, much of it was a swamp "seeped in the overflow and mush of pigsties, slaughterhouses, and boneboiling works, and the stench was sickening." Olmstead turned the landscape itself into architecture with rolling hills and winding paths. Not only did Central Park serve the function of providing "lungs" for the city, but it inspired other cities to copy New York's successful plan. Parks were built across the country, and some of them, such as the park systems of Kansas City, Milwaukee, Chicago, Philadelphia, and San Francisco, have become invaluable city assets. Olmsted also designed Montreal's central Mont Royal Park.

There was a pronounced profit as well as an aesthetic motive in creating parks since adjacent property greatly increased in value. Thus, major real estate developers favored the construction of parks and parkways. Private interests favored public spaces that increased property values.

The City Beautiful Movement

Perhaps the most pronounced effect on the design of American cities came from the "City Beautiful" movement that emerged from the World's Columbian Exposition (or World's Fair) held in Chicago in 1893. The Columbian Exposition was Chicago's attempt to show the world that it was no longer a ramshackle town surrounding stockyards, but a booming modern metropolis. City leaders were determined to make a good impression, so Daniel Burnham was placed in charge of assembling the nation's leading architects and landscape designers. Their goal was to create a modern wonder: the famous White City, lit at night by the then-new electric light bulbs. The Columbian Exposition marked the first major use of alternating current, and the Fair had its own million-dollar generating plant which used three times as much electricity as the entire city of Chicago. All the Fair buildings—with the exception of the Transportation Building, designed by the great architect Louis Sullivan—were designed in a semi-classical beaux arts style.

The classical buildings of White City, combined with harmoniously planned lagoons and grounds, created an overwhelming impact even for the architecturally sophisticated. As the author Hamlin Garland wrote to his parents back home on the farm, "Sell the cookstove if necessary and come. You *must* see the Fair."[10] Some 27 million people (in a nation of 67 million) came to view the 200 buildings of exhibits on 533 lakeside acres.

The Fair's famous Ferris wheel dwarfed later versions. Ferris's original wheel carried some 2,100 passengers in 36 cars as large as small streetcars that held 60 people each. Everyone who saw the Columbian Exposition went home deeply impressed. Today the White City lives on in literature since the White City was transformed by the writer L. Frank Baum into the Emerald City in Oz, forever there at the end of the Yellow Brick Road just beyond the rainbow.

The majestic size of the Columbian Exposition buildings neatly meshed with the optimistic and expansionist mood of the country at the turn of the century. Strong, powerful buildings were a way of expressing the fever of imperialism and material success then sweeping the land. The United States was (Americans believed) blessed by God with a "manifest destiny" to rule.

White City, with its magnificence and grandeur, started a trend; for decades it became customary to design all government buildings in neoclassical beaux arts style. As a result of the City Beautiful movement, there is not a major city in the United States without at least one government building—a city hall, court, train station, or library—designed to roughly resemble a Roman temple. Cleveland, St. Louis, Detroit, Los Angeles, San Francisco, and especially Washington, D.C., were strongly affected by the City Beautiful movement. Many of the government buildings were poor imitations, but among the better products of the neoclassical revival are, in addition to the Washington Mall, the famous civic center in San Francisco, the Museum of Science and Industry in Chicago, and the Benjamin Franklin Parkway in Philadelphia. The latter terminates at a majestic neoclassical art museum (where in the Rocky movies he runs up the museum stairs). It must be pointed out that the City Beautiful movement paid attention almost exclusively to public spaces such

The World Columbian Exhibition with its monumental public architecture influenced the "City Beautiful" movement and public architecture for the first half of the 20th century. Frances Benjamin Johnston/Library of Congress

as city centers; there was little concern for housing or neighborhoods.

Parks, which have already been discussed briefly, were related to—though not an integral part of—the City Beautiful movement. A number of elaborate parks systems, tied together by attractive boulevards, were developed to further beautify the city. The excellent city parks of Chicago, Kansas City, and Washington, D.C., are largely a result of the early-20th-century trend for planned public development.

The model City Beautiful plan was Daniel Burnham's Chicago Plan, created at the request of Chicago's business leaders in 1909. Burnham's master plan for the city (It Is still the plan) proposed a massive civic building program of museums; a central feature of this plan was an extensive network of city parks tied together by a system of grand, tree-shaded boulevards. Chicago's landmark Lake Shore Drive, built on filled land remains today as one

example. It is worth noting that pressure for developing the plan came from business and civic leaders rather than city government. Burnham captured the mood of the age when he ordered his staff to "make no little plans, they have no magic to stir men's souls."

The nation's capital also profited from the City Beautiful emphasis on planning public buildings and public spaces. L'Enfant's long-neglected design for Washington, D.C., was revived, and Burnham and other architects prepared plans for the beautification of Washington from which we now have the present-day "federal triangle" of government buildings plus the Mall between the Capitol and the Lincoln Memorial.

At about the same time Ottawa was being designed as Canada's national capital. However, in Canada the building style was not classical. Rather, as a British colony Canada looked to Victorian England and tried to suggest the

Gothic style of the English Houses of Parliament. The overall result is one that suggests order rather than power.

The City Beautiful movement can be criticized on aesthetic grounds, but it did have a concept of the city as an integrated whole and a vision of what it could be. It was a solid, conscious, and sincere attempt to improve the urban environment. The greatest weakness of the City Beautiful movement was that it almost totally ignored the problem of housing, particularly that of the slums.

Tenement Reform

The early 20th century saw a movement by social reformers such as Jane Addams to improve the quality of life in inner-city slums. (Also influenced were the later Chicago School of urban scholars.) Among other things, social reformers were concerned with protecting immigrant populations by passing model tenement laws to correct some of the worst abuses in the design and construction of older tenements. To reformers such as Jacob Riis, the slum was the enemy of the home and of basic American virtues. To quote Riis:

> You cannot let men live like pigs when you need their votes as freemen; it is not safe. You cannot rob a child of its childhood, of its home, its play, its freedom from toil and care, and expect to appeal to the grown-up voter's manhood. The children are our to-morrow, and as we mould them today so will they deal with us then. . . . The slum is the enemy of the home. Because of this the chief city of our land [New York] came long ago to be called "The Homeless City." When this people comes to be truly called a nation without homes there will no longer be any nation.[11]

The answer at that time appeared clear: destroy the slum and you will destroy the breeding ground of social problems. Symptoms of social disorganization such as alcoholism, delinquency, divorce, desertion, and mental illness were to be cured, or at least

greatly reduced, through the provision of better housing and more open spaces for the young. This belief in salvation by bricks and mortar fit in neatly with the American belief in the unlimited potential of technology. Note the following 1905 assertion:

> Bad housing is tremendously expensive to a community. It explains much that is mysterious in relation to drunkenness, immorality, poverty, crime and all forms of physical and social decline. Improved dwellings are the best guarantee of civilization. They help conserve the family institution, which is the underlying basis to society. In great cities especially there is no more important phase of civic welfare.[12]

Many desperately needed housing improvements were made as a result of the campaigns of the reformers, but crime, violence, and alcoholism were not banished as a result. The relationship between housing and social behavior is complex and unfortunately not amenable to simple bricks-and-mortar solutions. Nonetheless, we keep being disappointed when housing programs such as public housing don't also produce changes in social behavior.

20TH-CENTURY PATTERNS

The City Efficient

The golden age of urban planning and reform of politics died with the entry of the United States into World War I. Holistic visions of the city's future such as the City Beautiful movement provided did not fare well in the postwar laissez-faire atmosphere of the 1920s. As a result, the emphasis shifted from the city beautiful to the city efficient. Bold urban planning was replaced by city engineering. During the 1920s, the city was viewed as an engineering problem, and planners became technicians concerned with traffic patterns, traffic lights, and sewer systems. The city was viewed as a machine, and the goal was to keep the machine running smoothly. To this end planning and land-use regulation through zoning became accepted functions of local government.

Zoning and Beyond

The concept of the city as an evolving organic unit was also overshadowed by the development of zoning, a new planning tool. Zoning, which became a force in the United States with the New York City Zoning Resolution of 1916, was originally seen as a device to "prevent the intrusion of improper uses into homogeneous areas." "Improper" use of land meant not only industrial and commercial establishments, but also lower-class housing. It was an attempt to segregate land use and freeze "non-compatible" uses out of upper-middle-class neighborhoods. What made zoning significant was that now "bad" usages could be controlled by law. The effect of the first zoning laws was mainly negative—that is, to keep unwanted types of buildings or usages from an area. Zoning boundaries in many cases recognized the existence of "natural areas" as described by the early human ecologists, and then went a step further and tried to prevent additional change in these areas. The 1921 Standard State Zoning Enabling Act, which was issued by the federal government, advised state legislatures to grant the following power to the cities:

> For the purpose of promoting health, safety, morals, and the general welfare of the community, the legislative body of cities and incorporated villages is hereby empowered to regulate and restrict the height, number of stories, and size of the buildings, and other structures, the percentage of the lot that may be occupied, the size of the yards, courts, and other open spaces, the density of the population, and the location and use of buildings, structures, and land for trade, industry, residence, or other purpose.[13]

In practice, zoning was commonly used for social purposes of producing racial, social, and economic exclusivity. Zoning was used before the Fair Housing Act of 1968 as a means of enforcing racial segregation.[14] Even when used for land-use zoning the results often were unfortunate (see box 13.1). For example, cities often overzoned for commercial usage, which unintentionally pushed new residential developments to the suburbs.

After World War II, subdivision regulations often became the main control device in controlling land use in new suburban areas. Today, CIDs (common-interest developments) are commonly used to control all aspects of a project's development.

Interestingly, New York City, which pioneered zoning, has now moved to a hands-off policy, except when prodded by a complaint or where there is an issue of public safety.[15] New York's virtual ignoring of zoning laws began because of budget cuts, but it became policy when it was realized that zoning was hurting the city more than it was helping. When artists and others in the 1970s started to move into abandoned industrial properties in SoHo, the question, "Who is hurt?" came up. Residential use seemed better than empty buildings, even if the use was "out of code." Now lower Manhattan's old commercial and industrial zones have been reborn. They house not only residents but trendy restaurant and shopping areas, as well as most of the city's 1,500-plus media-related computer companies. While New York's zoning laws technically remain, the reality is that zoning in New York has been abandoned.

Houston, Texas, as of 2010, is the only major city in North America without any zoning laws. However, Houston does not look noticeably different from other cities because the market mechanism allocates the downtown land to business and commercial usage while outlying land is used for residential purposes. It is not economically feasible to deviate from the normative pattern of land use. Also, deed restrictions on land use are a de facto equivalent of zoning. More than 10,000 deed restrictions cover more than two-thirds of the city; they are most often enforced in wealthy neighborhoods along Memorial Drive and in River Oaks.

Master Plans to Equity Planning

The idea of the city efficient can be seen in the master plans for city development that became the hallmark of city-planning agencies from the 1920s to the 1970s. The purpose of the master plan was to coordinate and regulate all phases of city development; but in practice the preparation of the plan frequently became an end in itself, since the planners rarely had any real authority over the direction of urban development. The plan, even if formally adopted by the city council, was not legally binding unless backed up by specific zoning and other laws.

In defining neighborhoods, physical criteria were used almost exclusively. In the words of Herbert Gans:

> The ends underlying the planners' physical approach reflected their Protestant middle-class view of city life. As a result, the master plan tried to eliminate as "blighting influences" many of the land uses and institutions of lower class and ethnic groups. Most of the plans either made no provision of tenements, rooming houses, second hand stores, and marginal loft industry, or located them in catchall zones of "nuisance uses," in which all land uses were permitted. Popular facilities that they considered morally or culturally undesirable were also excluded.[16]

The death blow for many a master plan was the upsurge of urban renewal and other development plans after World War II. These development schemes were frequently put forward by business groups or the federal government with no concern for the city's general plan as such. Conflicts between the static master plan and specific development proposals, especially those with federal funding, were almost always resolved in favor of the specific proposals.

The urban riots and social upheavals of the 1960s and 1970s shook up the planning profession and led to advocacy planning for less-favored urban populations.[17] Planning became more socially responsive. Today most planners question the utility of creating citywide plans unless the plans can have direct influence on the future development of the city. Neighborhood-level plans are often more useful. Not infrequently neighborhood-level groups use neighborhood-level plans to block unwanted changes such as institutional expansion, or to redirect city resources to the neighborhood level. So called "equity planners" consciously try to change the bureaucracy to move power and decision-making away from elites and to mobilize low-income and working-class residents. The work of equity planners focuses on the short term rather than on long-range comprehensive planning. Advocates of equity planning tend to see it as another form of politics.[18] In the last decade planners' interest in social issues has declined, but physical planning still has social consequences.

Crime Prevention through Environmental Design

As noted in box 13.1, the work of Jane Jacobs encouraged planners to think about how a mix of land usages, shorter blocks, and 24-hour activity might contribute to lower crime levels. Earlier in the text we examined how physical space often has different symbolic meanings to different groups. The physical environment is not neutral but can be used to increase or decrease various behaviors. Contemporary concern with the question of crime control dates to the publication of Oscar Newman's book *Defensible Space*.[19] He used his sociological knowledge to emphasize design factors that would contribute to a sense of having control over one's environment.

In recent years interest in crime prevention through environmental design (CPTED) has revived. City or suburban neighborhoods use design to augment safety by providing natural access control with house fences and shrubs,

Box 13.1   Jane Jacobs: A Prophet in Her Time

Twenty-five years after its first publication, Jane Jacobs's *The Death and Life of Great American Cities* remains the classic critique of zoning and one of the great books of urban planning.* Jacobs was one of those rare people whose writings actually changed how things are done. Using Greenwich Village in New York City as an example (she later lived in Toronto), Jacobs argued that the mixed housing and commercial usages and the resulting congestion—factors that orthodox planners deplored—are the very reason why the area has retained its buoyancy and unique character over time. Cities, she suggested, are natural economic generators of diversity and incubators of new enterprises, and attempts by planners to zone various activities into distinct areas only work toward dullness and eventual stagnation both economically and socially.** Jacobs's ideas have had a major impact on planning. The city of Toronto has largely adopted her approach.†

Jacobs said that four conditions are indispensable if diversity and liveliness are to be generated in a city: 1. The district, and indeed as many of its internal parts as possible, must serve more than one primary function, preferably more than two. These must ensure the presence of people who go outdoors on different schedules and are in the place for different reasons. 2. Most blocks should be short—that is, streets and opportunities to turn corners must be frequent. 3. The district must mingle buildings that vary in age and condition, including a good proportion of old ones so that they vary in the economic yield they must produce. This mingling must be fairly close-grained. 4. There must be a sufficiently dense concentration of people, for whatever purposes they may be there. This includes dense concentration in the case of people who are there because of residence.††

Jacobs saw the physical environment of the city directly affecting city life and argued for a mix of social activities and populations to increase neighborhood vitality. By advocating mixed populations and land usages she directly challenged one of the basic tenets of traditional city planning. Jacobs argued that providing a mixture of functions— residence, work, entertainment—ensures that eyes are constantly on its streets, maintaining safety. Research appears to support the view that such diversity does contribute to lower crime rates.††† This diversity of use further means that uniquely urban specialty shops can oper-

ate profitably because considerable traffic passes their doors. Short city blocks provide for alternative routes and use of different streets, with the result that a cross-section of the public passes the doors of the smaller specialty operations.

Old buildings are needed, since, as Jacobs puts it, "Old ideas can sometimes use new buildings. New ideas must use old buildings." New buildings are limited to enterprises that can support the high costs of construction and rent. Old buildings not only provide space for new enterprises; they also break the visual monotony, and they can house cozy stores that provide gossip and a place to leave your keys as well as merely selling goods. Finally, the dense concentration of people in an area contributes to its vitality and liveliness. Jacobs suggests that it is not accidental that the district in San Francisco with the highest dwelling density is the popular North Beach–Telegraph Hill section. High building density does not, of course, necessarily mean crowding. Medium density areas fail to provide liveliness and safety, and they have none of the advantages of low-density, suburban areas.

In Jacobs's view, the population and environmental characteristics of a neighborhood shape its social character: Great cities are not like towns, only larger. They are not like suburbs, only denser. They differ from towns and suburbs in basic ways, and one of those is that cities are, by definition full of strangers. . . . Even residents who live near each other are strangers, and must be, because of the sheer number of people in small geographical compass. The bedrock attribute of a successful city district is that a person must feel safe and secure among all these strangers. He must not feel automatically menaced by them. A city district that fails in this respect also does badly in other ways and lays up for itself, and for its city at large, mountains on mountains of trouble.+

A criticism of Jacobs is that her preoccupation with street safety makes her oblivious to other urban problems. Also many critics say that she ignores the growing power and presence of large corporations in shaping urban real estate.++ Jacobs can also be criticized for not really dealing with the question of racial change in the city. Nonetheless, the importance of her work should not be underemphasized.

(continues)

Box 13.1   Jane Jacobs: A Prophet in Her Time *(concluded)*

Because of her influence, the planners of today are far more conscious of the social impact of design and planning decisions. Her message that cities are for people has for decades directly affected the practice of urban planning. Jane Jacobs died in 2006, but her ideas regarding planning continue to have influence.

* Jane Jacobs, The *Death and Life of Great American Cities,* Random House, New York, 1961.

** For an analysis of Jacobs's views, see Andrew Sancton, "Jane Jacobs on the Organization of Municipal Government," *Journal of Urban Affairs* 22:463–471, 2000; and

Harvey M. Choldin, "Retrospective Review Essay: Neighborhood Life and Urban Environment," *American Journal of Sociology* 48:457–463, 1978.

† Amrita Daniere, "Canadian Urbanism and Jane Jacobs," *Journal of Urban Affairs* 22:459–461, 2000.

†† Jane Jacobs, op. cit.

††† E. P. Fowler, "Street Management and City Design," *Social Forces* 66:365–389, December 1987.

+ Jacobs, op. cit., p. 300.

++ R. Montgomery, "Is There Still Life in the Death and Life," *Journal of the American Planning Association* 64:269–274, 1998.

---

as well as physical design elements, to discourage entry except by those who belong there.[20] Natural surveillance can be increased by placing windows so open areas can be observed. Lighting and landscaping can also be used to promote unobstructed views. Finally, territorial behavior can be encouraged by using sidewalks, porches, and landscaping to define the boundaries between what is public space and what are private areas. The goal is to increase surveillance and human activity in order to decrease the opportunity for crime.

Street design also can play a role since criminals prefer locations with high traffic that permit anonymity and easy escape. Streets that are well maintained and landscaped, and especially those that slow down traffic and discourage pass-through traffic, discourage criminal activity. Sometimes something as simple as blocking off a street at one end can produce noticeable improvements. Importantly, none of the above requires walling off a community or adding police; they are attempts to produce safe and livable communities without resorting to gates or guards.

EUROPEAN PLANNING

Now let's take a few pages to see how planning is done in Europe. This will provide a point of comparison with U.S. planned towns discussed later in this chapter. Lacking the land resources of the United States, Europeans have been more concerned with conserving their resources and preventing unlimited growth. The desires of the individual builder are more subject to the criteria of the public welfare. The major ways in which European planning differs from American planning are these:

1. Government planning is expected and accepted as necessary.
2. There is greater governmental control of land.
3. Housing subsidies are commonplace.
4. Public transportation is widely used.

The United States, by contrast, has yet to formulate a national, state, or even regional land-use policy. Ironically, some of those who most oppose government land-use policies as "socialistic" are often the strongest supporters of stringent, detailed controls in their own local communities. They live in subdivisions (gated or not) that regulate all physical details such as lot sizes, home sizes, building materials, type and placement of fences, where cars can be parked, colors the house can be painted, and even whether residents can leave their garage door open. The question, then, is not planning or no planning, it is at what level and for whose benefit the planning is done.

Planning and Control of Land

Some European cities enjoy the advantage of control over their own municipal lands. Stockholm began buying land in 1904 outside the city limits. This land has long since been annexed to the city, so that Stockholm is now in the position of owning about 75 percent of the land within its administrative boundaries. The city rarely sells its land; instead, it leases the land on 60-year renewable leases to both public and private developers. The money earned from the leases pays off the cost of the loan used to buy the land, and the municipality has the additional advantage of profiting directly from increases in land values. The public, rather than private land speculators, thus profits from the increased value of the land. If the city wants the land after the 60-year lease is up, it must go to court and prove that the land is needed for the public interest. Then it must pay the leaseholder the value of any buildings on the property. Such a system would not be politically acceptable in the United States or Canada, where landowners' private profit is valued.

Europe also has a tradition of urban planning. For example, for half a century Stockholm has been developing a system of subcenters or "minicities," built one after another along rapid-transit lines extending in five directions from the old city center. Each subcenter contains between 10,000 and 20,000 inhabitants and is served by its own community services, schools, and shops. These subcenters are seen not as independent towns, but as satellites with easy access to the center city. Blocks of flats, frequently high-rises, are built within 550 yards of a transit station; detached and terrace-style housing is built beyond the apartments up to about 1,000 yards from the station. Cars are routed through green areas surrounding the living areas. In addition to subcenters, "main centers" are built at appropriate inter-

vals. Each main center, with a larger shopping mall, theaters, and a major transit station, has a supporting population of between 50,000 and 100,000 persons within 10 minutes by automobile or public transit.

Students should keep in mind that land-use systems are not socially neutral. Private laissez-faire land ownership tends to further the gap between rich and poor. Western European nations, by contrast, place greater emphasis on providing a minimum economic floor for all and minimizing social inequality.

Housing Priorities

The postwar western European housing shortage came to an end by the 1980s. Attention then shifted from building programs to an emphasis on the quality of the urban environment. During the postwar period there was heavy emphasis on clearing slums and war-damaged central areas and on building new towns on the urban periphery. Outside of England, these new towns were often high-rise in nature. A welfare-state approach also led to the construction of largely rent-controlled and rent-subsidized units. By 1980, for example, council housing—that is, public housing—accounted for one-third of the entire housing stock in Great Britain. The conservative government under Margaret Thatcher (1979 to 1990) began selling council houses to their occupants. Today approximately a fifth of Great Britain's housing is council housing.

Throughout western Europe, increased affluence plus an interest in central-city living is leading to the rehabilitation and revitalization of older inner-city housing stock. High-rise housing projects are in disfavor, and the focus is on gentrification of older neighborhoods. Governments increasingly place heavier emphasis on "private market housing," although most new "private market" residential buildings in Europe are subsidized in one way or another in order to hold down costs and maintain quality. Germany and the Netherlands have elaborate programs for loans to nonprofit housing organizations; Great Britain has rent rebates; and Sweden has an annual housing allowance for all families with two or more children, plus other housing subsidies. In Sweden only 35 percent of all housing built since World War II has been constructed solely by the private sector. Some 44 percent of the housing in Holland is publicly supported in some fashion. Housing costs in most western European countries take less than 25 percent of family income because of subsidies. This is excellent by American standards. The trade-off is higher taxes, which European populations have chosen over a lower level of services.

Transportation

Cars are relied on extensively in low-density American metro areas with their commitment to dispersed single-family houses. On the other hand, in more densely populated European cities, where most people reside in apartment buildings (typically of three or four stories), public transit is the norm. Even in affluent Sweden, which has a per capita income approximating that of Canada, and where 90 percent of the households own an auto, about half of the trips to or from work in Stockholm are made by public transit.[21] There is excellent public-subsidized subway and ground transportation. Stockholm's public transportation actually offers a free taxi ride if public transportation is delayed 20 minutes or more.[22]

In order to decrease auto usage many European cities such as Stockholm, Oslo, and London use congestion pricing. That is, they charge motorists to drive into the center of the city. So far congestion charges have speeded up traffic. In 2006 London further expanded the inner zone into which you have to pay to drive. New York City mayor Michael Bloomberg has proposed adopting congestion pricing of $8 per car per day. It has minimal chance of adoption.

For many European cities with narrow streets and limited garages, the convenience of driving is often outweighed by the problem of where to park. An average European city may have only half the autos of its American counterpart, but these cars can cause immense congestion and parking problems. Fortunately, mass transit in London, Paris, and anywhere in Holland, Germany, or Scandinavia is remarkably fast and efficient.

Urban Growth Policies

While the United States does not have a national land-use or growth policy, European countries do. Great Britain, France, Italy, the Netherlands, and Sweden are all seeking to stem migration to the largest centers. Although the measures haven't been entirely successful, they have slowed the movement from smaller to larger places. In Britain the goal has been to stem the so-called drift to the south—out of Scotland and Wales and into the area centering on London. In France, the goal has been to lessen the domination of Paris; in Italy, to develop the economy of the depressed south, or Mezzogiorno; in the Netherlands, to save the remaining green areas; and in Sweden, to halt the flow out of more northern areas into Stockholm and the south.

Manufacturers are given economic incentives to invest in depressed areas needing growth. In addition, controls are increasingly imposed upon adding factories or offices to places where growth isn't wanted. For example, the Netherlands puts higher taxes on buildings in the cities of Amsterdam, Rotterdam, and The Hague. Another policy is to relocate government offices to areas where growth is desired. Sweden is relocating one-quarter of its government offices outside of Stockholm—a policy that definitely does not appeal to the government bureaucrats who have to move.

It is difficult to see any urban growth and redistribution policy ever being implemented in the United States. There is no clamor for action by Washington, and programs by individual states are unlikely to be effective. If one state imposed tough controls, a company could—and probably would—simply up and move to another state that did not. Thus, while European programs for dispersion of growth have been somewhat successful, they are unlikely to be copied in North America. Our decentralized system also has a flexibility lacking elsewhere. The economic and housing growth in sunbelt states reflects a de facto decentralization of people and power from older established northern and eastern cities.

The Dutch Approach

Americans who fear that metro areas of the United States are turning into unrelenting sprawl should find it instructive to see how the Dutch are coping with similar problems. The Netherlands is the most densely populated country in Europe, with 1,030 persons per square mile. If the United States had this population density, it would have a population of over 3.7 billion. The problem in the Netherlands is aggravated by the fact that the majority of the Dutch population is found in a megalopolis about 100 miles in diameter, including Amsterdam, Rotterdam, and The Hague. This conurbation is known as the *randstad*, or "rim city."

It is possible, nonetheless, to reach the open countryside in half an hour's time from the center of any of the cities in the *randstad*. In spite of their limited land the Dutch lead remarkably uncluttered lives. Urban sprawl such as that found in the United States is virtually unknown. That is because when a city such as Amsterdam stops, it stops abruptly. It is quite common at the city's edge to see massive blocks of high-rise apartments overlooking cows peacefully grazing in open fields. The Dutch have kept their towns compact, and valuable woods and fields are kept as a reserve for the use of all.

A system of local, regional, and—finally—national controls prevents urban sprawl. If a local development is in conflict with the regional plan and if the differences cannot be resolved at that level, the question then goes to

the national level for a decision. There is no national plan as such; rather, there are national guidelines that influence the regional plans and the city development plans. An attempt is made to avoid rigidity, and plans are constantly being modified—within the national guidelines—to meet new situations and needs. Without controls, the remaining green space between The Hague, Rotterdam, and Amsterdam would soon be filled.

NEW TOWNS

Throughout the centuries, humans have had visions of creating new towns free from the problems of older cities. The term "utopia" originated as the title of a book (1516) by Thomas More, which gave his version of how a new continent of new towns should be organized. Here the emphasis is on new towns that have actually been built, beginning with the English new towns program and then discussing European alternatives, and, finally, American examples. (For examples of Asian new towns see the sections on Singapore and Pudong in Chapter 15: Asian Urban Patterns.)

British New Towns

The new town movement owes its origins to Ebenezer Howard (1850–1928), an English court stenographer who proposed building whole new communities in a book called *Garden Cities of Tomorrow* (1902).[23] Howard's new towns were not to be simply another version of suburbs. Rather, they were to be self-contained communities of 30,000 inhabitants that would have within their boundaries ample opportunities not only for residence but also for employment, education, and recreation (see figure 13.1). The towns were to be completely planned, with all land held in public ownership to prevent speculation. Frederick Osborn, a major proponent of new towns, described them as follows:

Figure 13.1   Garden city and rural belt model

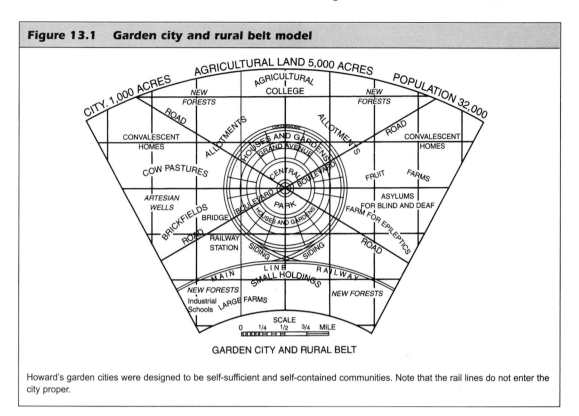

GARDEN CITY AND RURAL BELT

Howard's garden cities were designed to be self-sufficient and self-contained communities. Note that the rail lines do not enter the city proper.

Howard's Garden City is to be industrial and commercial with a balanced mixture of all social groups and levels of income. Areas are worked out for the zones: public buildings and places of entertainment are placed centrally, shops intermediately, factories on the edge with the railway and sidings. Houses are of different sizes, but all have gardens and all are within easy range of factories, shops, schools, cultural centers, and the open country. Of special interest is the central park and the inner Green Belt or Ring Park, 420 feet wide, containing the main schools with large playgrounds and such buildings as churches.[24]

Howard's garden cities were a reaction against the urban abuses of the industrial revolution in England. His new towns were not to be extensions of the morally and socially polluted city but self-sufficient towns with all necessary amenities, where one could enjoy the benefits of a healthful country life. The garden city was fundamentally anti-urban in its basic conception. It was to solve the problem of the great cities largely by abandoning them and starting over with a fresh environment. In Howard's words:

> There are in reality not only, as is so constantly assumed, two alternatives—town life and country life—but a third alternative in which all the advantages of the most energetic and active town life, with all the beauty and delight of the country, may be secured in perfect combination.[25]

The most distinctive feature of the garden cities was that beyond the city there was an encircling greenbelt of natural fields and woodlands that the town owned and could never sell. This greenbelt could not be encroached upon for housing, business, industry, or even farming, although it could be used for pasturage. Because of this feature, garden cities are also known as "greenbelt cities." The greenbelt not only provided the residents exposure to nature, it also was intended to prevent the city from growing beyond its planned limit of 30,000 inhabitants.

Nor was the internal design of the garden city left to chance. Strict zoning was central to Howard's basic scheme. The residential city was divided into five neighborhoods or wards, each with approximately 5,000 residents. Each was to have its own centrally located school and community subcenter, and every attempt was to be made to keep all houses within walking distance of factories, schools, churches, shops, and, of course, the open country.[26]

The whole site, including agricultural land, was to be under quasi-public or trust ownership to ensure planning control through leasehold covenants. When the population outgrew the prescribed size and area, another new town was to be created with its own sacrosanct greenbelt. As with the ancient Greeks, problems of growth were to be handled by colonization rather than by extending city boundaries.

First Towns. The concept of garden cities would have gone the way of other utopian plans had Howard not been an activist as well as a visionary. In 1902, with the aid of the newly formed Garden City Association, he established the first garden city at Letchworth, some 30 miles north of London.[27] This initial venture was plagued by many difficulties, the principal one being that the site was poor. Another problem was the difficulty of finding investors for a project that limited dividends to a maximum of 5 percent per year. In fact, it was 20 years before the shareholders received any dividends at all.[28] The understandable reluctance of industry to move out to the new town meant that residents largely became commuters to London—a situation directly opposed to Howard's conception.

Land for a second new town—Welwyn Garden City—was secured in 1920. Welwyn Garden City suffered financial crises for many years, but it eventually surmounted them. Today it is a pleasant and prosperous community of 50,000 residents about 25 minutes by rail from London.

Government Involvement. Were it not for World War II, Howard's garden cities would probably have remained a quaint experiment. However, World War II, with its extensive destruction in the heart of London, led to the Greater London Plan of 1944, with new towns as one part of a four-part policy. The policy included (1) a greenbelt around London to halt continuous metropolitan growth, (2) new towns to house the expanding urban population, (3) redevelopment of inner-city areas, conforming to higher standards than had existed previously, and (4) an attempt to control the location of employment and to prevent everyone from building in London.[29]

The British government became directly involved in building new towns through the New Towns Act of 1946. In the back of everyone's mind was the fact that London had suffered grievously from bombing during the war and that new towns would disperse both population and industry at numerous smaller nodes rather than create one massive target in London. Government involvement in new towns meant that building on a large scale was now possible, and compulsory purchase of land from private owners for building the town was also available.

The involvement of the British government, however, meant that the new towns would differ in significant ways from Howard's original scheme. First, the development corporation was appointed by and answerable to the central government, not to the town. Second, the size range was pushed upward—first to 60,000, and then up to 250,000 in cluster cities. This is far from Howard's limit of 30,000. Third, no provision was made for nearby land to be used only for agriculture. "As far as access to the countryside is concerned the new towns do not differ from most other settlements in Britain."[30] Finally, the concept of a city providing all its own employment was also abandoned, in practice if not in theory, although the new towns are certainly not designed to be commuter suburbs. They are basically manufacturing centers, with approximately half the population in manufacturing and the other half in trade, the services, and the professions.

The first of the English government-sponsored new towns, Stevenage, was begun in 1947. Among other innovations, it had the first pedestrian shopping mall in Britain and neighborhoods designed to separate pedestrian walkways from contact with automobile and truck traffic. While the new towns have been successful economically, they have not significantly altered social behavior. New-town residents have no fewer class prejudices and social problems than their counterparts not living in new towns.[31] The early expectation that planned communities could determine people's behavior has not been met. What the new towns do provide is a decent community. Some 34 new towns, housing some 4 million persons, have been completed in Great Britain. This means that only 5 percent of Britain's housing construction after World War II has taken place in new towns. Still, the British are pleased with their new towns program.

New Towns in Europe

European countries, including Sweden, Finland, the Netherlands, and Russia, built new towns after World War II. The Russian development of new towns was part of broad schemes for national development and the decentralization of industry. Many of their earlier new towns were connected with hydroelectric power projects and then expanded into manufacturing centers. The Russian new communities were company towns where the goal was not to build more humane environments but to provide housing for factory workers.

In Sweden and the Netherlands, the new communities were designed to be closely tied to the central city, and to serve as residential—not employment—areas. Scandinavian new towns such as Vallingby, Farsta, and Taby are basically residential and shopping areas. Unlike the British new towns, they are constructed along rapid-transit lines so that they will be an integral part of the city's life; they are not designed to be independent and self-contained employment units. European new towns are really extensions of the older city into the countryside, rather than attempts to create new rural or suburban utopian communities.

All European new towns have in common the fact that they were initiated, planned, and financed by the government. While there has occasionally been some financing from cooperatives, unions, or even private sources, the land and the facilities built on it have been owned either directly by the local government or indirectly by the government through quasi-public corporations chartered by the national government to build and administer the town.

Throughout Europe high-rise apartment buildings are generally used in new towns, not only to make economical use of the land because land costs are high but also to avoid suburban sprawl and to provide open spaces for recreation and enjoyment of the natural environment. In Sweden, Finland, and the Netherlands more than 80 percent of the units are in blocks of flats. English new towns, on the other hand, built more than 80 percent single-family homes.

Although postwar Swedish new towns such as Vallingby and Farsta were constructed to deliberately high densities, the communities have an openness and closeness to nature that residents find appealing. While there are no private yards there are many walkways, trees, and common open spaces. Swedish new towns built during the 1970s and 1980s have a far more negative image. The brick-sided walk-up apartments were replaced with six- to eight-story concrete-slab buildings—many more than a block long. Such slab cities have been criticized as "inhuman environments" and social disasters. Built in parallel rows, they present a very sterile and uninviting appearance. Only the color of the buildings distinguishes one group from another. (After dark all the colors look alike, a fact I once discovered when I got lost trying to locate the building where I was staying as a guest.)

Social problems associated with new towns—and the high cost of building them—have resulted in European nations ending new town building. For example, today the high-rise new towns on the outskirts of Paris house a high concentration of North African and other Muslim immigrants. In the eyes of many French these high-rise areas are havens of crime, drugs, and Islamic political subversion.[32] In 2005, rioting broke out in the suburban high-rises of Paris. To some Europeans the outer city is viewed as negatively as some Americans view the inner city.

AMERICAN NEW TOWNS

Public-Built New Towns

Radburn, New Jersey, opened in 1929, is the archetype of the American planned new town. Radburn was built by a nonprofit to encourage community and control auto usage by putting everything close at hand. Homes were clustered close together and car traffic travels around the town perimeter. Park land is only a few steps from everyone's door, and cars are parked on narrow streets going to the back doors. The last houses in Radburn were built in 1936, but the community today remains such an attractive location that houses rarely remain for sale more than 48 hours.[33]

It is sometimes forgotten that during the 1930s the United States government designed, financed, built, and for a decade managed three planned greenbelt towns surrounded by areas of open land. Like Howard's garden cities, the greenbelt towns were an attempt to create an idealized less-urban past. The government had three main objectives in building new towns:

1. To demonstrate a new kind of suburban community planning that would combine the advantages of city and country life.
2. To provide good housing at reasonable rents for moderate-income families.
3. To give jobs to thousands of unemployed workers that would result in lasting economic and social benefits to the community in which the work was undertaken.

The three American greenbelt towns were Greenbelt, Maryland, outside of Washington, D.C.; Green Hills, Ohio, near Cincinnati; and Greendale, Wisconsin, just south of Milwaukee. They were basically demonstration projects. (An interesting note is that bureaucrats in Washington somehow mixed up the blueprints, so the homes with basements designed for wintry Wisconsin were authorized for Cincinnati, while the cement-slab homes designed for Cincinnati were built outside Milwaukee.)

Plans called for the towns to be composed of neighborhood units and to have their own industry, as in the British model, but first a shortage of funds and then World War II kept them basically commuter suburbs. After World War II, the private housing lobby convinced Congress that having the government involved in building and renting low-rent homes was socialistic and a danger to the free-enterprise system. Public Law 65 of 1949 mandated that all the homes built by the government be sold. The greenbelts surrounding the towns—which had become valuable land with the expansion of the metro areas—were sold. Much of Greendale's greenbelt, for example, is now occupied by privately developed housing tracts and a shopping center. In Greenbelt, Maryland, college students are buying in due to its closeness to the University of Maryland.

Federal Support for New Towns

The late 1960s brought riots and burning to major American cities. This encouraged Congress to support new communities free from urban blight and suburban sprawl. New towns require heavy front-end outlays for land purchase and infrastructure long before the first house is built or sold. Congress in 1968 and 1970 voted federal funds and technical aid to developers and—most importantly—guaranteed each developer's bonds. By 1974, 12 projects had issued bonds for a total of $252 million in federally guaranteed debentures. At this critical point the nation was hit both with an energy crisis and a depressed housing market. Developers found themselves caught with expensive front-end costs and no customers. At that point the Ford administration announced that government support would end. The new towns were cut loose to sink or swim. Only one made it.

The federal government acquired all but one of the new towns by foreclosure and sold the assets at a total loss of $570 million. This loss was the government's own doing, since it deliberately underfunded the towns and then pulled back at a critical juncture. By contrast, the British do not anticipate that government-built new towns will be self-supporting for the first decade and a half. There is no sign that the United States government is willing to make such a commitment. It is not likely there will be any U.S.-government new-town programs in the foreseeable future.

Private New Towns: Reston, Columbia, and Irvine

Among the best-known and most successful American new towns are Reston, Virginia, just west of Washington, D.C.; Columbia, Maryland, near Baltimore on the way to Washington, D.C.; and Irvine in southern California. All were financed privately, rather than by the government. Irvine, however, differs from the other two: while it was built on new-town principles, it never had a commitment to economic or racial diversity.[34] It was designed from the first to be an upper-class community.

Reston, which was founded in 1964, is an unincorporated planned community of 56,000. Paths and woodlands run through Reston, and it has a large number of corporate offices and other "clean" industries. Reston, like other privately financed new towns has from the first had a distinctly upper-middle-class character. The average buyer in Reston is between 30 and 40 years old, is the head of a family with two children, and has an annual median income over $90,000. Two-thirds of the adults in Reston are at least college educated. One of six Reston residents is a minority and Reston has several hundred units of federally subsidized housing. Architecturally, Reston uses contemporary designs. Although Reston's founder had attempted to integrate the community economically by placing middle-income and more expensive houses side by side, this approach was abandoned as not being economically sound. Reston also has a downtown designed to resemble traditional downtowns. Although Reston was developed before "New Urbanism" as such existed, it anticipated New Urbanism guidelines.

Columbia, Maryland, the second new town, 20 miles from Washington, D.C., was developed by the Rouse Company. Architecturally, Columbia looks more like a traditional development since there is no unifying architectural style. Columbia covers 15,600 acres and will eventually house 110,000 people.[35] As of 2000 it had some 80,000 residents living in nine "villages." Columbia represents an investment of over $3 billion. Wooded areas and pathways run throughout the town. Like most new towns, it is organized into neighborhoods. Each neighborhood has some 900 houses, and each has its own elementary school and recreational facilities, including a swimming pool, a neighborhood center, and a convenience store. Four neighborhoods are combined to form a "village" of about 3,500 units, which has an intermediate or middle school, a meeting hall, larger and more varied shops, and a supermarket. These are all designed to cluster around a small plaza with benches and a fountain. There is also a larger shopping center for the whole community in the downtown city center, which contains office buildings and larger department stores.

Socially, Columbia has made a conscious effort to be a racially integrated community: one-third of the residents are black. Income integration has generally not been as successful. Subsidized units are not clustered as in Reston, but are spread over five different sites to avoid the creation of a low-income ghetto. Within the community, use of automobiles is discouraged by providing walkways and bicycle paths that are both more direct and not in physical contact with roads. Nonetheless, cars are as numerous as in other suburbs, and the parking lots of the shopping centers are filled.

Research Parks

Another form of planned community is the business-oriented research park. Perhaps the most famous of these, the Research Triangle, was founded over three decades ago on a 6,700-acre tract in the Raleigh–Durham–Chapel Hill area of North Carolina. The Research Triangle is run by a state-created foundation that owns and operates the research park.

Research Triangle has come to be an exclusive address. Today, the campus-like park is home to more than 50 high-technology companies with more than 30,000 employees, at least one-quarter of whom must be directly engaged in research. To get into the Research Triangle a company must buy at least eight acres of parkland, its building cannot be high-rise, it has to meet architectural standards, and it can cover no more than 15 percent of the property. Nearby communities try to replicate the atmosphere of the Research Triangle Park by establishing construction restrictions on everything from the size of buildings to that of McDonald's arches (the latter are usually banned).

Communities seek office and research parks because they bring nonpolluting, high-tech, and high-paying employment to the area. There are, however, real limits to the number of such enterprises possible in a region.

NEW URBANISM OR TRADITIONAL NEIGHBORHOOD DEVELOPMENTS

The most discussed contemporary housing development is building new communities according to Traditional Neighborhood Development or "New Urbanism" criteria. New Urbanism developers and planners follow smart growth practices. They turn away from the subdivision development practices of recent decades and model their plans on those of closely built old-fashioned small towns. The basic New Urbanism tenet is that communities should be complete and integrated, containing not only housing but also shops, businesses, parks, schools, and civic facilities. (This is the opposite of traditional zoning.) All these activities should be within walking distance of one another and of public transportation. New Urbanism communities are designed to minimize auto usage. Garages, for instance, which often dominate the front of conventional suburban houses, are moved to the rear facing a service drive. This move makes the house and sidewalk more inviting. All this costs 10 percent to 20 percent more than traditional developments.[36]

The pioneers of neo-traditional New Urbanism development are the Miami architects Andrés Duany and Elizabeth Plater-Zyberk. They believe that design affects whether or not a place develops a sense of community.[37] In order to combat the negative social as well as design effects of sprawl they advocate building deliberately "old-fashioned"–style homes placed on narrow grid streets that encourage walking, and keeping shopping on the intimate scale of a small town. The image of the New Urbanism is one of homes on tree-lined streets, where one can walk to nearby corner shops to buy a quart of milk or eat out. The goal is to move away from a subdivision to the more personal scale of a walking small town.[38] New Traditional Neighborhood Developments are designed to be comfortable communities with varied architecture and a 19th-century scale. They are expressly designed to encourage neighborliness. Examples include Seaside on the Florida Panhandle (the setting for the perfect town of the 1998 Jim Carrey movie *The Truman Show*); Harbor Town, on an island in the Mississippi River across from downtown Memphis; and Laguna West, south of Sacramento.

A suburban New Urbanism community designed to combat sprawl and produce a sense of community through the purposeful design of compact neighborhoods is the 352-acre Kentlands in Gaithersburg, Maryland, northwest of Washington, D.C. More urban and contemporary in design would be RiverPlace, located along the Willamette River in downtown Portland, Oregon. Other Traditional Neighborhood Development communities include Baldwin Park, built on an old Navy base in Orlando, and McKenzie Towne, opened in 1995 outside Calgary in Canada.

Celebration

A New Urbanism project not designed by Duany and Plater-Zyberk that has received considerable attention is Celebration, built by the Walt Disney Company outside Orlando. Celebration is basically a reproduction of an old-fashioned Midwest town.[39] When homes in Celebration first opened for sale in 1995, people lined up for a 1 in 10 chance to buy a home at a price more than one-third above the market price to live in a Disney community where many aspects of their lives would be controlled. The Disney Company, for instance, not only specified the color of the curtains residents can hang in their windows (white), but those who accepted a free phone and computer live with a "Zeus Box" that monitors every phone call they make and every website they visit. Celebration is no longer owned by Disney. It definitely is not a community for those with average incomes. Home prices generally range just below a mil-

lion dollars. In one area Disney's plans failed. The company went to great affirmative-action lengths to encourage minorities in order to prevent Celebration from becoming racially homogeneous. However, Celebration is only one percent black and 6 percent Hispanic.[40]

Nor is everything quite what it seems in Celebration. For example, the town plays recorded bird songs through outside speakers since the local birds are not melodious enough. And at Christmas the town center is layered with artificial snow.

Creating Community

It is not the housing styles but the handling of autos that set New Urbanism developments apart from standard suburban designs. They reject most post–World War II suburbanization as nonfunctional for people. Thus, New Urbanism strongly opposes the subdivision idea of curvilinear streets that discourage walking and feed all of a subdivision's traffic into a single access road. Rather than deadend cul-de-sacs, New Urbanism communities are connected by traditional right-angle grids so there are multiple ways of getting somewhere.[41] This limits traffic on any one street. Streets in New Urbanism communities are deliberately kept narrow to discourage auto usage, and sidewalks are mandated to encourage walking. Typical suburban front-access garages are moved from the fronts of houses—where they look ugly, discourage walking, and prevent neighborhood interaction—to rear garages opening on rear alleys or service drives.

New Urbanism communities are deliberately built to higher densities and with a mix of income levels, policies anathema to typical suburban developers. Houses may be large, but they occupy smaller lots than in typical suburbs. This is done to produce a community environment, encourage walking, and save space for numerous small parks and playgrounds. Homes are designed not to stand alone but to be part of a community. For example, to encourage sociability, homes in Seaside are required to have shallow front lots and usable front porches.

Rather than the typical subdivision zoning, which segregates housing from commercial activities, Traditional Neighborhood Development communities are designed to encourage a mixture of people and activities in order to create lively streets. A mixture of housing types is encouraged, and small stores may even be found at corners. Strip-mall shopping centers are banned, as is the suburban practice of every shopping area having a large asphalt parking area in front for cars. Rather, shared parking lots are put behind the stores. New Urbanism towns are designed to project a strong pedestrian, user friendly attitude. The design goal is to provide an inviting, livable, and walking public environment as well as secure and comfortable private home environments. As such, the New Urbanism derives some of its inspiration from the ideas of Jane Jacobs (see box 13.1).

There are signs that some "smart growth" and New Urbanism ideas are taking hold. Suburban developers love cul-de-sacs because many of them sell quickly at a premium price, however, New Urbanism critics say they funnel cars into clogged arterial routes and restrict access of emergency vehicles. Virginia, as of 2009 required that all new subdivisions have "connectivity" to through streets, or the state won't provide maintenance or snowplow services.[43]

Limitations

Critics of the New Urbanism question whether suburbanites are willing to give up their subdivisions with wide lots for higher-density small towns. Architectural critics also say New Urbanism is nostalgic and unimaginative. After Hurricane Katrina the New Orleans neighborhood of Gentilly asked Andrés Duany to prepare a plan for rebuilding. He did so for free, but local planners objected saying the plan was backward looking.[42]

There is also the question of whether businesses in the downtown sections of Traditional Neighborhood Developments can compete economically with the strip malls and Wal-Marts just down the road. Will people be willing to reduce their reliance on autos? Nineteenth-century small-town residents had no choice but to shop locally. They couldn't hop in the car. Critics also point out that Seaside, for all its charm, is still more of a weekend retreat than a fulltime community (although this is not true of most other New Urbanism developments). If developments such as Seaside remain primarily second homes for those able to afford them, the developments will only be homogenous elitist enclaves.

Underlying much of the criticism is the question of how much community design can affect behavior. Can communities be designed to encourage community living? Is Kentlands, for example, just a place that looks like Georgetown but is in actuality no different from other suburban subdivisions built off the Beltway? Is it simply a suburb in disguise, as some charge?[44]

A concern of New Urbanism advocates, as well as critics, is that the new communities with all their traditional charm will become just a niche market for affluent home buyers. If this occurs it will defeat the goal of providing complete and varied New Urbanism communities for all who want to live there.

SUMMARY

Ancient cities were rarely designed places. In Athens and Rome the central public areas were planned, but residential areas were not. Renaissance cities often were planned, sometimes in highly stylized fashion. The rebuilding of Paris in the 1860s is one of the most successful urban redesigns.

While North American cities as diverse as Quebec in the north and Savannah in the south were initially planned settlements, 17th-, 18th-, and 19th-century American cities show minimal urban planning. Washington, D.C., is the most noticeable exception, although Washington did not rediscover planning until the early 20th century.

The "City Beautiful" movement developed out of Chicago's Columbian Exposition in 1893. The fair's use of a neoclassical or beaux arts style captured the spirit of an imperialistic age and set the model for government buildings for half a century. Daniel Burnham created the master plan that Chicago still uses, and City Beautiful planning can be seen in Washington's Mall and federal buildings. Turn-of-the-century social reformers thought that by destroying city slums they would reform social behavior.

City planning from the 1920s to the 1970s emphasized civil engineering and making the city run more efficiently. The major land-use tool was zoning. Master plans created in this era were rarely implemented. Today most planning is more locally based and socially responsive. Equity planners focus on the needs of less-powerful city residents. By increasing natural surveillance and defining boundaries between public and private space, crime prevention through environmental design (CPTED) seems to decrease the opportunity for crime.

Europeans generally favor government urban planning, control of land, housing subsidies, and subsidized public transport. Stockholm controls three-quarters of the land within its boundaries and thus land-appreciation profits go to the municipality rather than speculators. Postwar emphasis on high-rise housing projects has been replaced with an emphasis on using subsidies to revitalize central-city housing. The Netherlands, having the highest population density in Europe, uses local and regional planning policies to stop sprawl and save open spaces near the city.

Ebenezer Howard founded the New Town movement in Britain at the beginning of the 20th century. The new towns would be publicly owned, totally self-contained, residential and manufacturing units surrounded by a permanent greenbelt of open land. In addition to two early "garden city" or "greenbelt" towns initiated by Howard—Letchworth and Welwyn Garden City—the United States government built

Greenbelt, Maryland; Greenfields, Ohio; and Greendale, Wisconsin, as demonstration projects during the Depression. Following World War II the British government built some 34 new towns. European new towns, in contrast to those in Britain, are designed to be primarily residential places along mass transit lines. During the late 1960s Congress voted loan-guarantee funds for 12 private American new towns, but the funds were withdrawn in 1975 and the projects failed. After rough starts in the 1960s, the private new towns of Reston, Virginia, and Columbia, Maryland, are now prospering. Both are organized into neighborhoods of approximately 900 houses each with an elementary school, recreational center, and convenience store.

New Urbanism or Traditional Neighborhood Development communities currently are much discussed. New Urbanism emphasizes keeping the scale of a small town, discouraging auto usage and curvilinear streets, providing open common areas, and encouraging walking. It rejects postwar suburban subdevelopments as nonfunctional for residents. New Urbanism projects such as Seaside, Florida, and Kentlands, Maryland, have narrow streets and small residential lots that seek to reproduce the ethos of a small town. At this point it is uncertain how much design can affect behavior, or whether New Urbanism communities will spread or just be a niche market for affluent home buyers.

REVIEW QUESTIONS

1. What are the major differences between urban planning in Western Europe and the United States?

2. How were new 19th-century American cities laid out and why?

3. What was the focus of the City Beautiful movement, and from what event did it take its inspiration?

4. What was the City Efficient and what was its major planning tool?

5. What are the four conditions that Jane Jacobs says are indispensable to generating city liveliness?

6. How do the Dutch deal with the problem of urban sprawl and control of land?

7. What are the principles and planning practices underlying Howard's New Town movement?

8. What are the major American new towns and how are they spatially organized?

9. What are the basic tenets of "New Urbanism" community design?

10. How are New Urbanism towns designed to create a sense of community, and how does this differ from traditional post–World War II suburbs?

NOTES

1. Aristotle, *Politics, Book VII, ii, 8*, B. Jowett (trans.), 1932 ed.

2. Daniel R. Mendelker, *Green Belts and Urban Growth*, University of Wisconsin Press, Madison, 1962, p. 27.

3. Charles N. Glaab and A. Theodore Brown, *A History of Urban America*, Macmillan, New York, 1967, p. 253.

4. Christopher Tunnard, *The City of Man*, Scribner, New York, 1953, p. 77.

5. Edmund K. Faltermayor, *Redoing America*, Harper & Row, New York, 1968, p. 17.

6. C.M. Robinson, *City Planning*, Putnam, New York, 1916, p. 16.

7. Ibid. p. 122.

8. Stanley Buder, *Pullman*, Oxford University Press, New York, 1967, p. vii.

9. Dolores Hayden, *The Grand Domestic Revolution: A History of Feminist Designs for American Homes, Neighborhoods and Cities*, MIT Press, Cambridge, Mass., 1981.

10. Phil Patton, "Sell the Cookstove if Necessary but Come to the Fair," *Smithsonian*, June 1993, p. 38.

11. Jacob Riis, *The Children of the Poor*, Scribner, New York, 1892.

12. *Model Homes*, City and Suburban Homes Company, New York, 1905, p. 5.

13. F. Baker Newman, *Legal Aspects of Zoning*, University of Chicago Press, Chicago, 1927, p. 24.

14. Christopher Silver and John V. Moeser, *The Separate City: Black Communities in the Urban South, 1940–1968*, University Press of Kentucky, Lexington, 1995.

15. "Ignoring Zoning Laws Helped New York City Succeed in Spite of Itself," *New York Times*, Metro section, April 21, 1996, pp. 1, 42.

16. Herbert J. Gans, "Planning, Social: II, Regional and Urban Planning," in David Sills (ed.), *International Encyclopedia of the Social Sciences*, Crowell Collier and Macmillan, New York, 1968, vol. 2, p. 130.

17. Allan Heskin, "Crisis and Response: A Historical View on Advocacy Planning," *Journal of the American Planning Association* 46:50–63, January 1980.

18. "Perspective: Listening to Equity Planners," *Urban Affairs*, Autumn 1994, p. 4.

19. Oscar Newman, *Defensible Space*, Macmillan, New York, 1972.

20. Timothy D. Crowe and Diane L. Zahm, "Crime Prevention through Environmental Design," *Land Development*, Fall 1994, pp. 22–23.

21. CANeilsen, "Car Ownership and Our Purchase Intentions," www2.caneilsen.com/reports/documents, March 2005.

22. Civitas Trend Setter, "60,000 New Public Transport Customers," www.trendsetter-europe.org, July 2003.

23. Ebenezer Howard, *Garden Cities of Tomorrow*, Faber and Faber, London, 1902

24. Frederick J. Osborn, *Green-Belt Cities*, Schocken, New York, 1969, p. 28.

25. Howard, op. cit., pp. 45–46.

26. For a detailed discussion of the community's organization, see Osborn, op. cit. For a detailed description of the history of new towns, see E. R. Scoffham, *The Shape of British Housing*, George Godwin, London, 1984.

27. Frank Schaffer, *The New Town Story*, MacGibbon and Kee, London, 1970, p. 4.

28. Lloyd Rodwin, *The British New Towns Policy*, Harvard University Press, Cambridge, Mass., 1956, pp. 12–13.

29. Wyndham Thomas, "Implementation: New Towns," in Derek Senior (ed.), *The Regional City*, Aldine, Chicago, 1966, pp. 19–20.

30. Ray Thomas and Peter Cresswell, *The New Town Idea*, Open University Press, London, 1973, p. 24.

31. William Michelson, "Planning and Amelioration of Urban Problems," in Kent P. Schwirian et al. (eds.), *Contemporary Topics in Urban Sociology*, General Learning Press, Morristown, N.J., 1977, pp. 562–640.

32. Christopher Caldwell, "Revolting High Rises," *New York Times Magazine*, Nov. 27, 2005, p. 28–30.

33. Amy Westerfield, "Motor-Age Town Now a Landmark," *Associated Press*, April 9, 2000.

34. Martin J. Schiesl, "Designing the Model Community: The Irving Company and Suburban Development, 1950–1988," in Robert Kling, Spencer Olin, and Mark Posner (eds.), *Posturban California: The Transformation of Orange County Since World War II*, University of California Press, Berkeley, 1991, pp. 55–91.

35. For further details on Reston and Columbia, see J. John Palen, *The Suburbs*, McGraw-Hill, New York, 1995, pp. 110–16.

36. Jim Charlton, "It Takes a Village to Lure Buyers Back to Town," *Wall Street Journal*, March 8, 2006, p.B4.

37. Andrés Duany, Elizabeth Plater-Zyberk, and Jeff Speck, *Suburban Nation: The Rise of Sprawl and the Decline of the American Dream*, North Point Press, Boston, 2000; and Andrés Duany and Elizabeth Plater-Zyberk, "The Second Coming of the American Small Town," *Wilson Quarterly*, Winter 1992, pp. 19–48.

38. Edward J. Blaely and David L. Ames, "Changing Places: American Planning Policy for the 1990s," *Journal of Urban Affairs* 14:433, 1992.

39. Two books have been written about life in Celebration. See Douglas Frantz and Catherine Collins, *Celebration, U.S.A.: Living in Disney's Brave New Town*, Henry Holt & Co., New York, 1999; and Andrew Ross, *The Celebration Chronicles: Life, Liberty, and the Pursuit of Property Value in Disney's New Town*, Ballantine, New York, 1999.

40. Jayson Blair, "Failed Disney Vision: Integrated City," *New York Times*, Sept. 23, 2001, p. A21.

41. For a full discussion of these ideas, see Philip Langdon, *A Better Place to Live: Reshaping the American Suburb*, University of Massachusetts Press, Amherst, 1994.

42. Douglas Blackmon and Thadius Herrick, "The Man With the Plan," *Wall Street Journal*, May 3, 2006, p. B1

43. Clay Risen, "The Cul-de-Sac Ban," *New York Times Magazine*, December 13, 2009, p. 34.

44. Alex Marshal, "Suburb in Disguise," *Metropolis*, July/August 1996, pp. 70–71, 100–103.

Part V

Worldwide Urbanization

CHAPTER 14

Developing Countries

He that will not apply new remedies must expect new evils; for time is the greatest innovator.

Sir Francis Bacon

OUTLINE

Introduction: The Urban Explosion
    Megacities
    Plan of Organization
    Common or Divergent Paths?
Developing-Country Increases
Rich Countries and Poor Countries
Global Cities
Characteristics of Third World Cities
    Youthful Age Structure
    Multinationals
    The Informal Economy
    Squatter Settlements
    Primate Cities
    Overurbanization?
The 21st Century
Summary

INTRODUCTION: THE URBAN EXPLOSION

The first decade of the 21st century marked a major transition to half the world's population living in urban places. Currently, roughly 90 percent of world population growth is taking place in cities. This amounts to adding 165,000 people a day to the world's urban population. As of 2010 the United Nations estimated the world urban population at 3.5 million.[1] Virtually all the current urban growth is taking place in developing countries. Overall, the large cities in developing countries are adding a million people a week. The result is that twice as many people now live in cities in developing countries as in developed nations. And the difference between developed and developing is going to increase dramatically. It now takes the nations of the developed world some 804 years to double. By contrast, the doubling time for less-developed countries (LDCs) is only 42 years. Each year the world's population increases by 83 million persons, and only 1 million of these are born in industrialized countries.

According to the World Bank, one-quarter of the world's urban population lives in poverty, and urban shantytowns are doubling in size every five to seven years. It is estimated that there are one billion urban squatters.[2] According to United Nations estimates, every year some

7.8 million children worldwide die from what they eat, drink, and breathe. Even meeting basic health needs is a challenge in less-developed countries, where only 40 percent of all dwellings are connected to sewers. Even for those who are connected to sewers, more than 90 percent of all sewage and wastewater is untreated.

Rapid economic development is not an unmixed blessing. Globally, air pollution kills nearly 3 million people a year—nearly 6 percent of all deaths. Air pollution with heavy lead and other contaminants is a particular concern in third world cities such as Beijing and Mexico City, where heavily leaded gas is still used and vehicles have no emission controls. Mexico City, one of the world's largest cities, has some of the most polluted air on the globe. It had pollution emergencies half the days in 2009, and schoolchildren are not allowed to go outside to play during much of the winter. The World Health Organization estimates that some 700,000 premature deaths a year could be prevented in developing countries if three pollutants—suspended particulate matter, carbon monoxide, and lead—were brought down to safer levels.[3]

Megacities

The United Nations coined the term *megacities* in the 1970s to designate urban agglomerations with a population of 8 million or more. In the 1990s the threshold was raised to 10 million. There were just eight megacities in 1985. Currently the United Nations lists 21 megacities and projects an additional 13 megacities by 2015. Of these 34 megacities of 10 million or more, only 6 will be in the more-developed world (Los Angeles, Moscow, New York, Osaka, Paris, and Tokyo). As table 14.1 indicates, by 2015 eight of the world's 10 largest cities will be in developing countries. At that time some 400 million people will live in megacities.

The so-called population explosion is in actuality an urban population explosion, and of the 414 million-plus cities, three-quarters are in the developing world. How many of us could name more than 50 of these cities? For the first time in history the world is not only more urban than rural, but most of the growth is taking place in developing world cities.[4] Mumbai (Bombay), for example, is adding 500,000 people a year. Mexico City, which reached 1 million population only in 1930, now has over 20 million in city and suburbs. And it is not alone. Estimates place São Paulo at roughly the same size. The United Nations estimates that by 2015 Mumbai will reach 28 million and Lagos, Nigeria, 23 million.[5] To ignore these major urban developments would be the height of ethnocentrism.

It is difficult to keep up either mentally or emotionally with the spectacular nature of contemporary developing world changes, and while this text devotes more attention than others do to developing countries, we obviously cannot look at every city. What this and the following chapters hope to do is give the reader some feeling and understanding of the changing patterns.

Plan of Organization

The chapters in Part V: Worldwide Urbanization, because of limited space, necessarily focus on what is common to third world cities rather than on their unique differences. Readers should keep in mind, though, that particular cities may differ from the general pattern.

Common or Divergent Paths?

Large-scale urbanization in Europe and North America was a process that spanned the 19th and 20th centuries and involved massive economic and social change. Industrialization and the need for workers encouraged in-migration from rural hinterlands. As documented in Chapter 2: The Emergence of Cities, urban places in Europe, with their high death rates, were able to grow only because of massive inflows of rural population. The question is

Table 14.1   World's Largest Megacities, 1970 and 2015

Population (in millions)			
1970		**2015**	
1. Tokyo, Japan	16.5	1. Mumbai (Bombay), India	28.2
2. New York, United States	16.2	2. Tokyo, Japan	26.4
3. Shanghai, China	11.2	3. Lagos, Nigeria	23.2
4. Osaka, Japan	9.4	4. Dhaka, Bangladesh	23.0
5. Mexico City, Mexico	9.1	5. São Paulo, Brazil	20.4
6. London, England	8.6	6. Karachi, Pakistan	19.8
7. Paris, France	8.5	7. Mexico City, Mexico	19.2
8. Buenos Aires, Argentina	8.4	8. Delhi, India	17.8
9. Los Angeles, United States	8.4	9. New York, United States	17.4
10. Beijing, China	8.1	10. Jakarta, Indonesia	17.3

Source: United Nations, *World Urbanization Prospects: The 1999 Revision,* United Nations Fund for Population Activities, New York, 2000.

whether LDCs today are converging on the western pattern or whether they are following a different path.

The ecology-modernization approach implies that there is a general pattern and that developing world cities will in time follow the western model. As Chapter 4: Ecology and Political Economy Perspectives indicates, those taking a political economy approach see differences among cities reflecting differences between capitalist and socialist economic systems. A world-systems perspective sees LDCs remaining in a "dependent" or "peripheral" position as suppliers of raw material and labor to the developed capitalist states.[6]

Contemporary urbanization in less-developed countries differs from that of North America and western Europe in several respects. The extent and rapidity of the urban increase in LDCs is outpacing anything that occurred in the West. For example between 1975 and 2000 the population of Dhaka, the capital of Bangladesh increased by 8 million people. While western cities grew rapidly during the 19th and early 20th centuries, the absolute numbers of urbanites were not anywhere as large as the numbers found today in Cairo, Manila, or Lagos.

First, the pace of change has accelerated. New York and London were the two largest cities in 1950. It took them each nearly 150 years to reach 8 million residents. By contrast, Mumbai, Lagos and São Paulo will each house more than 20 million people in under 10 years. The developing-world cities of Jakarta (Indonesia), Dhaka (Bangladesh), Karachi (Pakistan), and Shanghai (China) are not far behind.

Second, industrialization, rather than providing a spur for urbanization, often trails *behind* the rate of urban growth. Growth is taking place at comparatively lower levels of economic development. In the 19th century the western, industrializing cities needed workers. Often the jobs were low-paying, physically exhausting, and emotionally unsatisfying, but they were available. The cities of the Industrial Revolution were magnets drawing peasants off the land.

Today, by contrast, people flood into the cities even in spite of high urban unemployment because of a push from overpopulated rural areas. Without employment in rural areas, migration becomes the only mechanism to relieve rural population pressures. In India today, for example, there is only one acre of arable land for each peasant farmer. With 18 million Indians being added each year, it is invariable that surplus population gravitates toward the cities.

Third, cities in LDCs differ from the western model in having continued high rates of growth by *natural increase* (births) as well as in-migration. Until a century and a half ago, western cities lost more inhabitants through disease and illness than they gained through births. By contrast, rural to urban migration accounted for a little over half of LDC city growth between 1975 and 2010. Even if immigration ceased tomorrow, LDC cities would continue to grow. Birth rates may be lower, but they are applied to an ever-expanding population base. Sixty percent of China's urban growth comes from natural increase. Cities in some developing countries may appear unhealthful by contemporary western standards, but they are, nonetheless, comparatively healthy places. The consequence often is dramatic urban growth.

However, lower urban death rates don't necessarily translate into pleasant cities. Developing-world cities suffer from high levels of soil, water, and air pollution. Dirty water claims between 5 and 12 million persons a year, depending on the definition of a water-related disease. The World Health Organization says most city dwellers in developing countries do not have access to proper sanitary facilities, and half lack a regular supply of potable water. Cities generate 80 percent of all carbon dioxide, a major cause of global warming. Developing-world factories rarely have any pollution controls and developing countries still use leaded gas—banned in the United States, Canada, Japan, and Western Europe for decades.

Fourth, LDC cities of today still reflect the *legacy of colonialism*. While colonialism is now history, poorer developing nations remain beholden to trading patterns that exploit their natural resources. As detailed in the next chapters, LDC cities were often founded not as a consequence of internal economic development but rather because of the colonial powers' need for trade and administrative centers. Their industrial and economic bases, or lack of

same, thus reflect colonial patterns of economic exploitation. Today developing nations remain dependent on the international market and economy. They are dependent on multinational corporations. They do not control their own economic futures.

DEVELOPING-COUNTRY INCREASES

Roughly 70 percent of the world's urban population of 3.5 billion live in developing countries. The impact of this urban explosion on cities of the developing world is difficult to overstress. As previously noted, some cities in less-developed countries already top 10 million and are projected to add millions more. (Paris, Berlin, and Tokyo, by contrast, may decline slightly.) While each LDC city is in some ways unique, they generally share problems of unemployment, poverty, crowding, slums and squatter settlements, inadequate transportation systems, and heavy pollution.

Recently publicity has been given to the fact that the worldwide rate of population increase has begun to show declines. Today's (2010) growth rate of 1.2 percent may continue to decrease. This, however, emphatically does not mean that world population will be declining since today's growth rates are being applied to a base population of 6.8 billion. This translates into 225,000 persons being added to the world's population each day or 83 million a year. Even with declines in fertility, some billion people will be added during this decade. The Population Reference Bureau projects that the world population in 2025 will be 8 billion people.[7]

Increases of this magnitude are certain to create tremendous pressures for food, better living conditions, more education, and more employment. Total fertility rates—that is, the number of children born per woman—range from a low of 1.3 children per woman in Germany and Italy, to a high of 7.1 children per woman in Niger. Zero population growth may be the reality in Europe, Japan, and the European-background populations of the United States and Canada; but it is still only a slogan in the developing world, where the combined population of the various developing countries is currently increasing by 73 million a year. This means an additional 73 million persons a year who must be fed, clothed, housed, and otherwise provided for before the countries can even begin to improve the quality of life for those already present. Figure 14.1 shows the differences between more developed and less developed countries.

Much of the developing world population explosion, with its yearly national population increases can be traced to the importation of modern sanitation, public health, and medicine. Following World War II, malaria, for example, was largely eradicated in Sri Lanka (Ceylon) by the decision of a handful of officials in government ministries to spray DDT from airplanes. This achieved a decline in the death rates of 40 percent in two years, a decline

that took half a century in the West. The result was a population explosion. In contrast, the decision to restrict the number of births must be made by millions of individual couples. Even when a society favors small families, there is a time lag in implementation.

The resulting population increases greatly exacerbate already serious problems, including those of economic development. Funds that might be devoted to economic development are instead consumed, providing minimal subsistence to an ever-increasing number of people. Rather than investing capital, some developing nations are forced to spend it in order to meet, even marginally, the needs of their growing populations.

In addition to the economic demands put on developing countries by new mouths to feed, increasing demands also come from those already present. This "revolution of rising expectations" occurs because increasing numbers of people in developing countries—and particularly in the cities—are aware that

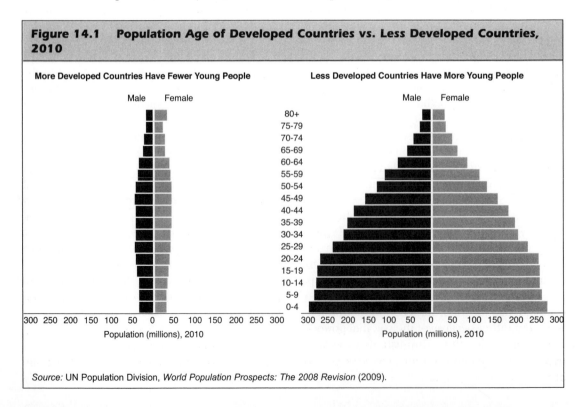

Figure 14.1   Population Age of Developed Countries vs. Less Developed Countries, 2010

Source: UN Population Division, *World Population Prospects: The 2008 Revision* (2009).

Bangkok is renowned for its heavy traffic. The revered Thai elephants, once used in hauling timber, now show up in Bangkok with their handlers seeking tips from locals and tourists. Richard Vogel/AP Images

their condition of poverty is not the immutable natural order of life elsewhere. Developments in communication technology—cell phones, computers, and television—have exposed the urban underclass to the knowledge of others having higher standards of living. The urban populations, with their greater exposure to alternatives and their greater awareness of nontraditional ways of life, have expectations for themselves and their children; and governments that ignore these expectations do so at their own risk.

RICH COUNTRIES AND POOR COUNTRIES

Less-developed countries vary in their rates of development, but they all suffer in varying degrees from common problems such as low manufacturing output, low rates of savings, inadequate housing, poor roads and communication, a high proportion of the labor force engaged in agriculture, insufficient medical services, inadequate school systems, high rates of illiteracy, poor diets, and sometimes malnutrition. The developing countries contain two of every three people in the world, but they ac-

count for only one-sixth of the world's income, one-third of the food production, and one-tenth of the industrial output.

The term *developing country* often is a euphemism. Various other terms, such as *modernizing country, less-developed country,* and *third world country,* sometimes reflect ideological differences, but all essentially are polite ways of saying "poor country." While the differences between the developed and the developing countries may be phrased less harshly, the major distinction is that one category includes the "haves" and the other the "have-nots."

This rich–poor classification cuts across conflicting ideological systems and geographical regions. Developed nations, whether in Europe, Asia, or the Western Hemisphere, all have urban-industrial or postindustrial economies. Less-developed countries are so named because of their relationship to the economic power of the developed countries. Development thus is a relative rather than an absolute state. Developing countries are underdeveloped in the context of an economic comparison with Europe, the United States, or Japan. Whether the indigenous economic organization of a developing country is simple or complex—and in many cases it is extremely complex—it is invariably not a modern industrialized urban economy, much less a postindustrial economy.

The poorest LDCs of Asia, Africa, and Latin America find themselves locked into an economic system where prices for the raw products they produce remain relatively stable while the cost of imported goods increases. Such nations are seeking to achieve economic development while the marketplace in which they must operate is largely controlled by developed nations' multinational corporations.

Those taking a world-systems approach argue that underdevelopment of third world countries, then, is due not to traditionalism or internal problems, but to a worldwide system of structural dependency and unequal exchange. Data indicate that for many of the poorest developing nations the status of "underdevelopment" may become relatively permanent; while the poorest nations are not getting poorer—as a whole—the rich nations are certainly getting richer.

On the other hand data now show that LDC status is not necessarily permanent since some former "developing" nations have moved to the developed category. In the last 20 years countries such as Korea, Taiwan, Thailand, and more recently China and India, have made major strides. A new category, newly industrialized country (NIC), refers to countries that already have made major movement toward economic development. Today many of the NICs are in Asia—countries such as Taiwan, Korea, Malaysia, Thailand, and China are in this category. Newly industrialized countries invariably show not only economic development but also sharply declining birthrates. The demographic reality is that all poor less-developed countries have high birthrates, while all developed countries have low birth rates.

GLOBAL CITIES

Until roughly 50 years ago cities largely operated each within their own national market, rather than an international market. Most of the large cities in the developed world were manufacturing centers. However, during more recent decades many large corporations in the United States, England, Germany, and Japan began moving their production facilities (but not home offices)from developed world cities to economically less developed places such as Mexico and Asia.[8] While the workers in many older manufacturing cities lost jobs, the largest cities in the developed world transformed themselves from manufacturing places into highly concentrated global oriented financial and service centers. Saskia Sassen has effectively argued that it is these financial and service global cites, rather than the nations in which they are found, that are now the core elements in the world economy.[9] Urban based multinational corporations, especially those headquartered in New York, London, and Tokyo, now dominate the world economy. This is the era of global cities; cities that wherever they are located, are oriented more to the needs of multinational corporations than to the needs of the city's inhabitants.

CHARACTERISTICS OF THIRD WORLD CITIES

Youthful Age Structure

While each city, like each person, is distinct and in some ways unique, certain characteristics are more or less generic to cities of the developing world. The first of these is a youthful population age structure. An almost certain comment of tourists upon first encountering third world cities is that "children and young people are everywhere." This is not an illusion but an observation of demographic reality. As of 2010, LDCs had young age structures with between 30 to 40 percent of the population age 15 or younger. By contrast, only 17 percent are dependent young in developed countries. The consequence is that the cities of the developing world are filled with young who must be fed, clothed, housed, educated, and otherwise provided for. Developing countries have an age structure in which much of the population consists of dependents who have yet to make any contribution to the economic well-being of their families or nations. Even if more schools are built and new jobs created, there is no gain if these advances merely keep pace with growing numbers of young people.

Differences by region underline the problem: in Africa 41 percent of the 2010 population was age 15 and under; in Asia it was a lower 27 percent. By comparison, in Europe only 15 percent of its population is age 15 and under. For North America the figure is 20 percent. The consequence of these differences is that the cities of developing countries are getting hit twice. First, they have fewer resources. Second, the lower resource base must be stretched to cover double the proportion of young dependents. Of course, it goes without saying that this leaves less for either personal or national investment purposes. The old saying "The poor get children" is clearly the case for developing countries.

Multinationals

Of all the common problems cities in developing countries face, the problem of providing employment is perhaps the most severe. According to the United Nations, LDCs already have 500 million unemployed or underemployed workers. Moreover, some 30 million new workers enter the job market every year. This situation is quite different from the one economically advanced western countries faced during their earlier periods of urban-industrial expansion. In the era of western industrialization during the 19th century, farmers and peasants were drawn to the city because of the economic opportunities it offered. Entry-level jobs, both in manufacturing and in services, were generally available, and demand for unskilled, if low-paid, workers was solid. This was true both in Europe and in North America.

The experience of the developing countries has been quite different. There is less need today for armies of industrial workers. Instead of being labor intensive, contemporary industrial and post-industrial economies depend on capital and technology. In developing countries workers flood into the cities, not so much because of the availability of jobs, but because of the lack of opportunity in the rural areas and small villages. Stagnating rural economies simply cannot absorb more workers. It has long been recognized that high agricultural density and plantation-type agriculture spur urbanization regardless of the rate of economic development. The consequence is "subsistence urbanization," in which the ordinary citizen has only the bare necessities for urban survival. Urban unemployment rates commonly exceed one-quarter of the workforce.

Multinational corporations, which now account for almost one-third of the gross world economy, commonly take advantage of the excess labor in less-developed countries. They move production facilities from high-wage countries such as the United States to low-wage, nonunion third world nations where they can reduce both labor and natural resource costs. A typical semiskilled worker who makes $19 an hour in wages and benefits in the United States can be replaced for $2.10 an hour in Mexico. Elsewhere labor costs are even lower. The average Nike worker in Indonesia makes under $2.00 a day. Labor costs are especially low in China.

Saskia Sassen points out that multinationals shape international cities to their own high-tech image, while exploiting the low-income others.[10] Despite this, cities still offer more economic hope than rural areas. Cities also offer access to health facilities and schools. For women, the city can also provide some relief from traditional patterns of male domination.

The Informal Economy

The majority of urban workers in less-developed countries are employed in the informal

The informal economy includes the drug trade, which is significant in various Central and Latin American countries and Mexico. Here the Colombian city of Medellin, long known as a haven for drug smugglers, is shown with its shantytowns embedded in the surrounding hillside. Today, the city is working hard to turn its reputation around. © Grigory ubatyan/Dreamstime.com

sector of the economy—that is, small enterprises without access to credit, banks, or formally trained personnel. Often these are family-run businesses. They may involve everything from small manufacturers to street stall vendors.[11] The informal sector commonly provides most of the consumable food products and much of the services, trade, transportation, and construction.[12]

During periods of economic downturn, the informal economy provides a safety net for workers. It isn't ideal, but the informal sector provides a critical backup in much of the world. Informal sector businesses are usually small and operate on minimal capital. Most often they operate outside the law in that they are not registered, don't pay minimum wages, and rarely pay taxes. Government statistics on "economic activity" in third world countries often exclude those not in the wage economy, and thus may grossly understate actual economic activity. Unemployment figures that do not count the informal economy will also be in error.

Within the formal economy, gains in industrial productivity and increases in gross national income do not necessarily reduce the rate of unemployment. Industrialization starting from the low base found in the developing world may have only a limited effect on employment even when the *rate* of industrialization is relatively high. Modern industrialization, unlike the labor intensive industrialization in the United States during the latter part of the 19th century, does not require a tremendous number of laborers. For example, oil production and refining may dramatically increase a nation's wealth, but modern computer-controlled refineries require only a limited number of highly skilled operators. Nor do public works necessarily benefit those most in need. Public funds may be invested in projects such as airports or multi-lane highways for the automobiles of the rich and universities for their offspring, while slums still have mud roads and the poor receive only minimal schooling.

A conservative estimate by the United Nations is that 28 percent of city dwellers in developing countries live in poverty.[13] In sub-Saharan Africa as of 2009 75 percent of the population made less than $2 a day.[14]

Squatter Settlements

The population growth of developing-world cities has outrun the capacity of municipalities to house them. Decaying central-city slums and new squatter settlements often house one-third of the entire urban population. The present squatter population of Mexico City exceeds 4 million, and squatters in Kolcata (Calcutta) number over 2 million. With shantytowns mushrooming at 15 percent a year (doubling their size in six years), the squatter population of poorer cities is certain to increase. By technical definition, squatter housing illegally occupies the land on which it is built.[15] Nonetheless, squatter housing serves a vital function.

Squatter and peripheral settlements are called *barriedas, favelas, bustees, kampongs,* or *bidonvilles* in various countries, but everywhere their function is the same: to house those who have the least resources and nowhere else to go. In squatter settlements, shanties and shacks initially are built in random fashion out of whatever material the builder can salvage. Old packing crates, loose lumber, and odd pieces of metal are somehow patched together to provide a shelter. Shantytowns that are "illegally" occupying the land on which they are built cannot demand city services. Streets, police, and fire protection, and—most importantly—sanitary services are usually nonexistent. Water almost always has to be carried from the nearest public tap. Schools are rare. Electricity, on the other hand, is commonly found since wires can easily be strung illegally from shack to shack.

Public services such as running water and schools are first provided to those with economic clout. Shanty dwellers in Lima, for instance, pay 10 times as much for water carried on private trucks as the middle class pays for plumbing in its homes. Health problems are exacerbated by the crowding, by the lack of proper disposal for sewage and refuse, and by the fact that the settlements are frequently built on the least desirable terrain, such as city dumps, marshlands, or hillsides.

Attempts by the government to remove squatters are invariably unsuccessful: if one slum is destroyed, another is built overnight with the refuse from the earlier settlement. When no other city housing is available, there is little alternative. Developing-world cities do not provide "standard" housing for all, or even most, of the urban poor, no matter how one defines "standard."

Demolishing settlements and relocating the urban poor in new fringe settlements is often disastrous for the poor. It often impoverishes families who not only lose what they have invested in the demolished squatter shack, but also are faced with increased transportation costs. Women in particular tend to become unemployed because of the increased distance to their traditional places of work. Most countries have stopped bulldozing squatter settlements. Even when countries provide outlying resettlement areas they are rarely successful since for the very poor a location near work is much more important than the quality of shelter. The same was true of the 19th-century American poor, who crowded into tenements to be near central-city factories.

Primate Cities

A characteristic common to most developing countries is the so-called primate city. According to the classic definition, a primate city is a principal city overwhelmingly large in comparison with all other cities in the country. In many countries, the primate city is frequently the only city of note. Commonly, developing countries have no hierarchy of cities of various sizes such as that found in developed nations. Ethiopia, for example, is 95 percent rural and has few towns; but its capital city, Addis Ababa, has over 1.5 million inhabitants. Bangkok, with approximately 9 million people, is the most extreme case. Today, Bangkok is over 20 times larger than Thailand's second largest city, Chiang Mai.

Most primate cities owe their development to European colonialism. Cities such as Accra, Nairobi, Saigon, Hanoi, Singapore, and Hong Kong do not have long histories as urban places but rather were created consciously by colonial powers in order to establish bases from which they could exercise administrative and commercial control. They were established as little "Europes in Asia" or "Europes in Africa." Thus, they were usually located along coasts to facilitate communication with, and transportation of, raw material to the mother country. From the very first, the orientation of the primate city was toward other cities in the developed countries rather than toward its own hinterland, and this pattern of commerce and culture coming from the outside has largely endured to this day.

The concentration of population and economic activity in primate cities presents some typical features throughout the developing world:

1. In the earlier stages, the economies of such cities were primarily export oriented, and the cities also specialized in political and administrative activities. Today, manufacturing, government, and services are the primary economic activities.
2. Economic advantages result from the concentration of industry. Thus, income from peripheral areas finds its way to the metropolitan area. The higher rate of return attracts more capital; and this in turn leads to more enterprises, particularly services.
3. The concentration of industrial activities—and above all the accompanying services—increases employment. Skilled workers are attracted from peripheral locations. Thus, the city represents an advantage in terms of quality as well as quantity.
4. Concentration of population and economic activities goes hand in hand with the centralization of administrative activity. The decision-making power of the primate city increases, while that of outlying cities and towns decreases. The center thus receives the lion's share of the available investment funds.
5. The basic infrastructure of the nation is heavily determined by the requirements of the major city. This in turn encourages further concentration.[16]

The rate of growth of large developing-nation primate cities invariably outpaces that of the country as a whole. The largest city grows the fastest. This is often in spite of government policies to encourage more regional growth. The cities of Mexico City, Bogotá, and Santiago continue to grow faster than their national populations even though the governments of Mexico, Colombia, and Chile all seek a more balanced growth. In Latin America one-fifth (21 percent) of the urban population is found in very large cities of over 5 million persons.

A primate city dominates the rest of its nation economically, educationally, politically, and socially. It controls the lion's share of the manufacturing, administrative, investment, and service activities of the country. Government, education, and commerce all are concentrated in the primate city, and skilled workers are attracted from outlying regions. The city thus has a qualitative as well as a quantitative advantage. Growth and concentration, as noted earlier, lead to further concentration of resources, which, in turn, leads to greater growth. The decision-making power of the city increases while that of outlying towns decreases. Urban-bred civil servants, teachers, and employees are, perhaps understandably, most reluctant to give up the activity and excitement of city life for the underdevelopment of the more backward hinterland.

However, given the situation described above, it does not necessarily follow that such places are parasitic on the countryside. While regional balance is a desirable goal of planners, many smaller developing nations simply cannot support more than one major city at this point. In time, intermediate-size cities may emerge, but meanwhile there frequently is no realistic alternative to the primate city. Whatever their faults, primate cities grew in part because the residents were—and still are—open to economic and social change. Most of the movements for independence were nurtured in the cities, and those who currently set policy and govern are invariably urban dwellers. The city remains an incubator of change.

Overurbanization?

Closely related to the concept of primate cities is the concept of overurbanization. The term *overurbanization* is in many ways a loaded one insofar as it suggests that, for the nation's level of economic development, there is too large a proportion of the nation's population residing in cities. Overurbanization is defined as "a level of urbanization higher than that which can 'normally' be attained given the level of industrialization."[17] Given the level of national economic development, there are too many urban residents for the available jobs, housing, schooling, and other services. Some urbanists, for example, refer to Egypt, with 45 percent of its population in cities, as being overurbanized.

While there has been some attempt to keep the term *overurbanization* free of any connotation of values, the concept invariably has negative connotations: it suggests that overurbanization is both artificial and harmful to economic growth. As UN Secretary-General Ban Ki-moon expressed it in 2008, "urban areas consume most of the world's energy and are generating the bulk of our waste."[18]

However, the picture is not as glum as the term *overurbanization* suggests, for the productivity of the rural in-migrants is higher in the city than in the rural areas, and per capita incomes of rural immigrants to cities are almost universally higher than in rural areas. If the concept of overurbanization is meant to suggest the undesirability of rapid urbanization in developing countries, the argument is difficult to prove. Certainly the data do not support the belief that rapid urbanization necessarily slows or impedes economic development.

It can be argued that the rapid growth of cities is a positive sign of the social and economic development of an area.[19] The city not only is the first area to reflect change, but also is a source of change. City growth is correlated with the change from dependence on agricultural to industrialism, with economic rationality, with lower birthrates and death rates, with opportunities for women, with increased literacy and education—in short, with the whole process of modernization. Insofar as urbanization is associated with the development of a modernized mode of life, the problem in much of the developing world, one could argue, is not overurbanization but underurbanization. The continued growth of a metropolis is evidence that, on balance, the positive aspects continue to outweigh the negative. The World Bank says cities are growing so fast precisely because they generate vast economic advantages.[20]

Some see the argument as evidencing an anti-urban bias. It has been argued, for example, that the burden of new urban dwellers on existing urban infrastructures far outweighs the cost of absorbing new persons in rural areas.[21] However, what is good for the nation and what is good for individual immigrants may differ. For the newcomer, life may be difficult in the city, but it is almost always better than life in the countryside. Thus peasants invariably vote with their feet for urban life. In the city there is, at least, always hope of something better.

THE 21ST CENTURY

We can make a number of observations regarding the most likely patterns for the early decades of the 21st century. The reader should keep in mind, though, that what follows are this author's views; the opinions of others may differ.

First, cities in the developing world are going to continue to grow, and to grow at a rapid rate. Growth will occur in spite of government policies to the contrary. For example, to reduce crowding in Jakarta the Indonesian government sent 2 million persons from Java to less-populated islands, and an equal number migrated on their own. Nonetheless, massive Jakarta still continues to grow and is now one of the largest cities in the world. India's policies in the 1990s of directing growth to smaller places were equally unsuccessful. Natural increase as well as in-migration spur city growth.

Second, given urban growth, squatter settlements, which currently hold one-third of the urban population, are unavoidable. Official disapproval will not make them go away. Thus, it is best to accept and legalize them and provide minimal community services. Squatter settlements are going to be a part of LDC cities for the indefinite future. Increasingly the response is to support self-help housing.

Third, although improving, urban infrastructure will remain inadequate. For example, attempts to provide "standard housing" are probably doomed to failure, though countries experiencing economic development or new wealth (as from oil), and highly organized states such as Singapore, are exceptions. Industrialization and the post-industrial service sector will lag behind population growth and thus will not provide necessary urban jobs. Many of the new jobs will be provided by multinational companies seeking cheap labor. A low-paid secondary informal labor market and high unemployment will remain facts of developing nations' urban life.

Fourth, the factors just noted suggest that political instability may be a serious problem in some countries. Rising expectations, widespread needs, and the availability of mass media will enable charismatic leaders (e.g., Chavez in Venezuela) to exploit anger and frustrations. Throughout developing nations, unprecedented urban growth and urban industrialization are transforming traditional societies. Traditional attitudes, beliefs, customs, and behaviors are being upset. Scholars and politicians can debate whether these changes are for the better, but it is certain that urban growth means change—a great deal of change.

SUMMARY

For the first time in history the globe holds more urban than rural people. Roughly 90 percent of the world's population growth is taking place in cities, almost entirely in the developing world. Large cities in the developing world are adding a million people a week. Already there are twice as many people in developing-world cities as in developed-world cities, and the difference will increase during the 21st century.

In Europe and North America, urbanization was a process that spanned the 19th and 20th centuries and involved massive economic and social changes. The rapidity of change in less-developed countries (LDCs) outpaces anything that took place in the West. Population changes that took a century in Europe and North America sometimes only take a decade in cities of the developing world. The question is whether LDC cities today are converging on the Western pattern as ecology or modernization theory would hypothesize, or whether they will remain permanently peripheral as suggested by political economy theory.

Contemporary third world city growth differs from Western urban growth in several ways. First, the extent and rapidity of LDC urbanization outpaces anything that took place in the West. Second, unlike the Western pattern, industrialization lags behind urban population growth. Third, over half of current LDC growth comes from natural increase rather than in-migration.

As of 2010 almost two-thirds of the world's urban population of 3.4 billion lived in the developing world. The current world growth rate is down to 1.2 percent a year, but this still translates into 225,000 persons being added to the globe every day. By 2025 the world population will be 8 billion. Terms such as *developing country, modernizing country, less developed country,* and *third world* country are euphemisms for "poor country." While the terms sometimes have ideological connotations, they are essentially less harsh ways of distinguishing between the "haves" and the "have-nots." All developed nations have low birthrates; all developing countries have high birthrates. Newly industrialized countries (NICs) such as Korea, Malaysia, and Thailand have declining birthrates.

Third world countries are noted for having young age structures—over one-third of their populations are aged 15 and under. In Africa 41 percent of the population is 15 and under, while the figure for Asia has dropped to 27 percent. By contrast, the figure for Europe is 15 percent, and for North America 20 percent. This means that LDCs with fewer resources have to devote a greater percentage of their limited resources to sustaining young dependents rather than to national investment. In the 19th and early 20th centuries, Western rural dwellers were pulled into the cities by available low-skill, low-wage jobs. Third world urban growth is more likely to be pushed by the absence of rural opportunity. Multinational corporations take advantage of the excess labor in developing countries, often paying less than $2 a day. Still the city offers opportunities not found in the countryside. This is particularly true for women. The majority of workers in developing country cities are employed in the informal business sector. Government statistics often overlook these workers.

Squatter settlements commonly house one-third or more of the urban population of third world cities. Attempts by governments to ban or remove squatters are inevitably unsuccessful since "standard" housing for poorer residents simply is not available. Most developing countries are characterized by having one primate city that is overwhelmingly large compared to all other cities in the nation. Most primate cities, such as Accra, Lagos, Hanoi, and Hong Kong, are along coasts and trace their origin to colonialism. Primate cities dominate their nations politically, economically, educationally, and socially. The term *overurbanization* is loaded insofar as it suggests that too large a proportion of the nation's population lives in cities. In spite of problems of growth, city residents have higher per capita incomes than rural residents, and cities encourage not only economic development, but also social changes such as literacy, lower birthrates, and opportunities for women.

The first decades of the 21st century show continued rapid developing world urban growth. Squatter settlements will remain common and urban infrastructure inadequate. The continued rapid transformation of once traditional agrarian societies may lead to political unrest and instability.

REVIEW QUESTIONS

1. In what four ways do patterns of urbanization in developing countries differ from those found in U.S. and European cities of a century ago?

2. What is meant by the *urban explosion*?

3. What are some of the demographic characteristics of cities in the developing world?

4. What is the informal economy, and what role does it play in cities in the developing world?

5. What role do multinational corporations play in contemporary third world development?

6. Where were the largest cities in the world located 50 years ago, where are they now, and what does this suggest about the urban future?

7. What are the characteristics of primate cities, and where are they located?

8. What is meant by the concept of overurbanization, and how serious a problem is it?

9. What is life like in squatter settlements, and what does the text recommend be done regarding squatter settlements?

10. What four factors does the text suggest will impact third world urban growth during the next decade?

NOTES

1. United Nations Population Division, *World Urbanization Prospects: 2009 Revision,* United Nations, New York, 2010.

2. Robert Neuwirth, *Shadow Cities: A Billion Squatters in a New Urban World,* Routledge, New York, 2004.

3. Win Carty, "Greater Dependence on Cars Leads to More Pollution in World's Cities," *Population Today* 27:1, December 1999.

4. J. John Palen, *Cities and the Future: The Urban Explosion,* United Nations Fund for Population Activities Report, New York, 1985.

5. United Nations Population Division, *World Urbanization Prospects The 1999 Revision,* United Nations, New York, 2000.

6. Immanuel Wallerstein, *The Modern World System,* vols. 1–3, Academic Press, New York, 1979, 1980, 1989.

7. Population Reference Bureau, "World Population Data Sheet," Washington, D.C., 2010.

8. Mark Abrahamson, *Global Cities,* Oxford University Press, New York, 2004, p.6.

9. Saskia Sassen, *The Global City,* Princeton University Press, Princeton, N.J., 1991.

10. Saskia Sassen, *Cities in a World Economy.* 2e, Pine Forge, Thousand Oaks, Calif., 2000.

11. Sanjoy Chakravorty, "From Colonial City to Globalizing City?" in P. Marcuse and R. van Kempten (eds.), *Globalizing Cities; A New Spatial Order?* Blackwell, Oxford, 2000, p. 58.

12. S. V. Sethuram, "The Informal Urban Sector in Developing Countries; Some Policy Implications," in Alfred de Souza (ed.), *The Indian City,* South Asia Books, New Delhi, India, 1978, pp. 1–15; and Johannes F. Linn, *Cities in the Developing World,* World Book Publications, Oxford University Press, New York, 1983.

13. United Nations World Population Fund, *The State of World Population 1996, Changing Places: Population Development and the Urban Future,* United Nations, New York, 1996.

14. Population Reference Bureau, "2009 World Population Data Sheet," Washington, D.C., 2009.

15. Edesio Fernandes and Ann Varley, (eds.), *Illegal Cities: Law and Urban Change in Developing Countries,* St. Martin's, New York, 1998.

16. Based on "Some Regional Development Problems in Latin America Linked to Metropolitanization," *Economic Bulletin for Latin America,* United Nations, New York, 17:58–62, 1972.

17. Manuel Castells, *The Urban Question,* Alan Sheridan (trans.) MIT Press, Cambridge, Mass., 1977, pp. 4–43.

18. Quoted in "Cities and Growth: Lump Together and Like It," *The Economist,* November 8, 2008, p. 75.

19. Not all scholars agree that overurbanization and primate cities are not a problem. See, for example, Anthony J. LaGreca, "Urbanization: A Worldwide Perspective," in Kent P. Schwirian (ed.), *Contemporary Topics in Urban Sociology,* General Learning Press, Morristown, N.J., 1977.

20. World Bank, *World Development Report,* http://www.worldbank.org/wdr2009.

21. Joseph Gugler, "Overurbanization Reconsidered," *Economic Development and Cultural Change* 31:173–189, October 1982.

CHAPTER 15

Asian Urban Patterns

The whole city is arranged in squares just like a chessboard,
and disposed in a manner so perfect and masterly that it is impossible
to give a description that should do it justice.

Marco Polo, writing on Beijing in 1298

OUTLINE

Introduction
    Asian Cities
    Indigenous Cities
    Colonial Background Cities
India
    Mumbai (Bombay)
    Kolkata (Calcutta)
    Prognosis
China
    Treaty Ports
    Urbanization Policies
    Forced Movement from Cities
    Rural to Urban Migration
    Economic Boom
    Shanghai
    Beijing
    Hong Kong
Japan
    Extent of Urbanization
    Current Patterns
    Tokyo
    Planning
    Planned New Towns
    Suburbanization

Southeast Asia
    General Patterns
    Singapore
    Other Cities
Summary

INTRODUCTION

This and the following chapter will discuss cities in Asia, Africa, and Latin America. Most, but not all, of these cities are in developing nations. Such a world urbanization perspective helps us both to better understand international urban processes and to place the cities with which we are most familiar into a larger context. With three chapters devoted to worldwide urbanization, this text gives far more attention than others to cities outside North America, but it makes no attempt to detail all the unique regional and national variations. This is by design, for the reader's focus should be more on overall patterns of urbanization than on unique cases. Regional variations and specific cities are discussed in order to illustrate world patterns. To put it in simple terms, pay attention to the

309

trees, but also keep in mind that they are part of a larger forest. As the text title says, we are discussing the urban world.

Asian Cities

Care is required when generalizing about Asian cities. (See figure 15.1.) Patterns of urbanization in China, Japan, India, and Southeast Asia have different historical roots and have developed in dissimilar cultures. These areas do, of course, have many things in common, but generalizations must be applied with some care to individual cities.

Asia has a great tradition of city life and numerous cities whose histories go back many centuries. In fact, until 200 years ago Asia contained more city dwellers than the rest of the world combined.[1] Today Asia again has more city dwellers than any other continent. As of 2010 Asia's population was almost two-thirds of the world population (4 billion of 7 billion), and the continent already contains more large cities and a larger number of people—but not a larger *percentage* of people—in cities than either Europe or America.[2] Some 60 percent of the next decade's urban growth will be in Asia.

Saying Asia has large numbers of urbanites and huge cities does not mean that most Asians are city dwellers. The majority of Asia's population still consists of village-based agrarians; only a minority live in true urban places. Overall, some 43 percent of the population of Asia is urban. This low level of overall urbanization places Asia close to Africa (with 38 percent urban) as regards the percentage of the population that is urbanized. However, Asia does have many of the world's largest cities. Tokyo, for example, has between 9 and 27 million people, depending upon whether one uses the most restrictive definition of the historic 23 wards of the city or the broad definition of the Tokyo agglomeration. The Asian cities of Shanghai, Beijing, Kolkata (Calcutta), Mumbai (Bombay), and Jakarta also number among the world's largest. It has been suggested that less-developed Asian nations find themselves in the position of being "overurbanized." However, as suggested in Chapter 14, *overurbanization* is a loaded term. All over Asia peasants are voting with their feet for city opportunities.

Indigenous Cities

Indigenous pre-industrial Asian cities originally were predominantly political, cultural, and religious centers, and only secondarily economic centers. The function of traditional capital cities was to serve as a symbol of the authority, legitimacy, and power of the national government. Administrative functions were everywhere more important than commercial or economic functions.

Such cities were located inland, near the centers of their empires, except in Japan and parts of Southeast Asia, where this was not practical. Such inland cities were far safer from attack than coastal cities. Beijing, Old Delhi, and Angkor are classic examples: they were designed to serve as symbols of authority and were planned with monumental architecture, such as temples and palaces, that would emphasize this role. Beijing is famous for its Forbidden City Palace, Old Delhi for its magnificent Red Fort, and Angkor for its many fine temples (many unfortunately destroyed during the Pol Pot "Killing Field" era of the 1970s). In China and often in India cities were walled; in Southeast Asia they usually were not; and in medieval Japan walls rarely existed.

Colonial Background Cities

Western-type city organization was imported into Asia, mostly during the 19th century, by Europeans seeking trade. These cities, in contrast to the traditional pre-industrial cities, were primarily oriented toward exportation of goods and commercial activities, and thus were located along seacoasts in order to facilitate trade and communication with the mother

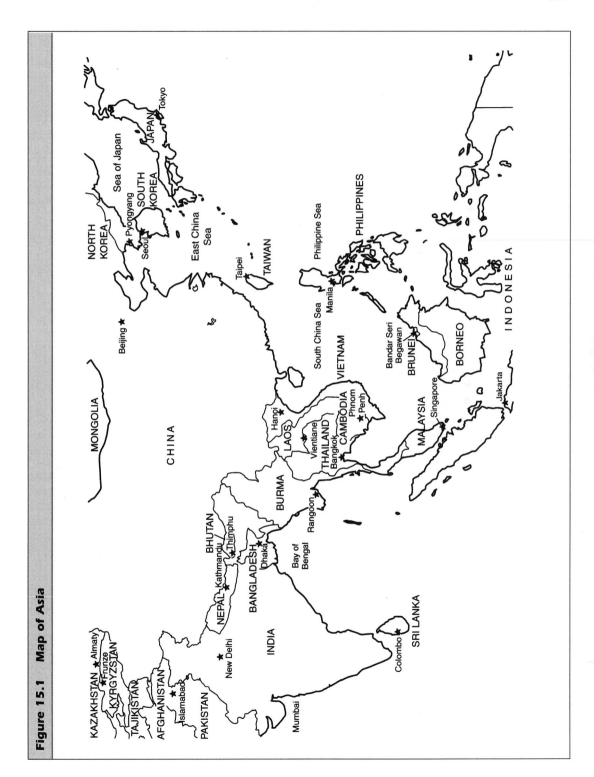

Figure 15.1   Map of Asia

country. Originally established as small trading sites, perhaps with a small fort for protection, these cities are now among the largest in the world. Hong Kong, Singapore, Shanghai, Kolkata (Calcutta), and Mumbai (Bombay) all developed as foreign-dominated port cities.

INDIA

India is only 29 percent urban, but that is 29 percent of 1.2 billion people, or 350 million city dwellers, more city dwellers than the total population of all but the most populous countries.[3] And with one-third of India's population age 15 or under, dramatic urban growth is certain to continue. India has a history of cities going back to 2000 B.C., but the modern period began with British colonial rule during the 18th century. The Indian colonial city was the location of the colonial administration. As such, it not only reflected Western organization and values, but also housed the upper-class "sahibs." Industrialization played only a limited role in the growth of Indian cities.[4] British "civil lines" contained civil administrative headquarters and the homes of the British in the Indian civil service, while "cantonments"—military reservations—graciously housed the British officers.

In contrast to the model typical in the United States, the military reservations occupied central city land rather than being peripherally located. Much of the city of Poona, for instance, is still occupied by military cantonments, reflecting that city's heritage as a headquarters for the British and then the Indian army. Even within New Delhi, military bases continue to occupy much prime land. Attempts to persuade the military to move to outlying areas have been notably unsuccessful.

The spacious houses of the colonial city, graciously separated by large lawns and trees, also reflect the 19th century's lack of knowledge about causes of disease. Malaria was thought to be caused by bad air (*mala aria*),

and so the British constructed their residential areas with ample space for circulation of air between homes. The Indian term for these airy single story homes was *bungalow,* a term that has come into English.

Sometimes the colonial city was built right next to the traditional city. Old Delhi, with its stores and homes right on the edges of its always crowded streets and lanes, is a world apart from New Delhi, with its lawns and boulevards. Delhi has the fifth-highest housing density in the world.[5] The high figure for Old Delhi, moreover, is not for an area of apartment buildings but for an area of one- and two-story buildings. In parts of Old Delhi the density rises to 600 to 700 persons per acre. Density does not, however, necessarily mean despair. Old Delhi is also a remarkably lively and interesting place. It is important to keep in mind that even when indigenous cities lack some modern amenities, this may be more than compensated for in the eyes of residents by the areas' vitality and activity.

In the following pages we will focus on India's two largest cities—the economically dominant city of Mumbai (Bombay) and the more economically stagnant (until recently) city of Kolkata (Calcutta).

Mumbai (Bombay)

The last two decades have seen India take off economically, and Mumbai (Bombay's new name—both are locally used) is the nation's most dynamic city.[6] It is the heart of India's financial and industrial life and the center of the nation's large and colorful film industry. Mumbai houses both the Bombay and the National Stock Exchanges, and "Bollywood" turns out 400 films a year—the world record. India's abandonment of its controlled economy for a free market system in the early 1990s has dramatically accelerated Mumbai's boom. According to the 2001 census the city proper housed 12 million people (15 million in 2010).[7] Greater Mumbai, with 20 million residents as of

Workers at SurePrep office, Bombay, preparing U.S. tax returns. Santosh Verman/
New York Times/Redux

2010, provides a full one-third of India's income taxes and 30 percent of India's gross national product.[8] For over a decade Mumbai has experienced a major building boom accompanied by skyrocketing land prices. The cost of prime commercial property in Mumbai is four times higher than in the heart of New York City.

Mumbai is a great city, but it is a city of contradictions. It has far more growth than it can handle and is showing signs of coming apart at the seams. The city is built on a peninsula and can extend only northward along a narrow corridor of two rail lines, but it contains far more people than it can reasonably service—and the situation is getting worse. Mumbai gains 10,000 residents every day, and few cities anywhere could keep up with such an influx. Most come seeking not better employment, but any employment. The municipal sewage systems, housing, educational systems, and transportation systems are overwhelmed. For example, only one-fifth of the sewage now receives treatment, and the once-beautiful beaches along

the bay are badly polluted. Likewise, the air is seriously polluted.

Daily some 7 million people commute by rail from the suburbs on the once-excellent but now alarmingly overused and overextended commuter railroads. Riders hang on to the exterior of windows and even crowd the roofs. Not surprisingly, there are frequent accidents and approximately a dozen deaths each day on the commuter lines.[9] Overloaded derelict trucks, crowded buses, cars, and bicycles all congest the city's jammed streets. More than half the population lives in slums. "Slumdog Millionaire," which won 8 Academy Awards in 2009, was set in the sprawling Mumbai slum of Dharavi.

Mumbai's social fabric threatens to unravel. Greater Mumbai has perhaps 20 million residents and, like other great cities, has always had its wealthy and its poor. However, the gap between the super rich and the super poor has become sharper and more painful. The rich are becoming very wealthy, and the poor find their wages lagging behind in the growing economy. Half of the Indian population makes less than $2 a day.[10] Mumbai's poverty shocks Western visitors. As noted, half the population lives in slums. Now even the slum neighborhoods are being taken from the poor and gentrified as neighborhoods for the new rich. The poor are being forced out, and they have nowhere to go. There is an immense and growing gap between the rich residing in the high-rise apartments lining the bay and the poor. Some 2 million have no home but the street.[11] These 2 million "pathway dwellers" live, eat, sleep, work, and raise their families while living in hovels along the streets and roadways. For the middle class, Mumbai is a city of opportunity; for Mumbai's pavement people, the city streets are not paved with gold. Rather, they are the last refuge.

To stress the point made earlier, Mumbai is better off than many LDC (less-developed country) cities. Mumbai has an industrial base and a growing computer-based information sector. It is the location of "Bollywood," India's huge film industry. The city is also fortunate to have a trained civil service to administer the city. However, planners and city administrators openly concede they are losing the battle. Given Mumbai's population growth, overall urban stress is likely to continue.

Equally important, the gap between the growing affluent upper and middle classes and the desperately poor is growing greater. Greater Mumbai could possibly even cope with 10 million—but it has 20 million. And the 20 million are straining Greater Mumbai beyond its limits.

Kolkata (Calcutta)

Kolkata (Calcutta), on the eastern side of India, is opposite from Mumbai, both geographically and emotionally. If Mumbai is entrepreneurial, Kolkata is fatalistic. Until 1911 Calcutta was the proud seat of the British Raj and a major financial center, landscaped with Victorian parks and monuments. Today, the very name Calcutta suggests the nadir of urban

life. As of 2006 two-thirds of Kolkata's population lived below the Indian poverty level. However, change is very much in the air in Kolkata.

Kolkata's city population is 6 million and the overall metropolitan-area population is 16 million, but Kolkata is not growing as rapidly as Mumbai or New Delhi. Nor is much of its aging industrial economy. The once-active machine shop industry, for example, is now too antiquated to compete with more advanced operations elsewhere in India. The once-important jute industry is also affected by obsolescence. The Hooghly River running through the city received half of India's imports at the end of World War II; today the port is virtually closed with silt. The computer revolution, which has transformed cities such as Madras and Bengaluru (Bangladore), originally had less impact on Calcutta. However, the last decade has seen major new information technology firms locating in Calcutta's rapidly expanding suburbs.

For decades Kolkata has been run by a Marxist local government that was best known for radical labor laws, constant strikes, and opposition to any change. Nor has the national government been eager to invest in what they considered a basket case. Today Kolkata still has a Marxist government, but one that behaves increasingly like full-blown capitalists. In a successful attempt to lure high-tech companies the local government offers free land and tax breaks. Downtown Kolkata is still filled with dilapidated grimy buildings, but half an hour away the suburban Salt Lake district is another world. The spotless district of tree-lined boulevards is filled with gleaming new buildings housing information technology firms.

Three-quarters of the population of Calcutta is housed in crowded tenements and *bustee* huts. These *bustee* dwellers are in some ways fortunate, for between half a million and 1 million pathway dwellers—no one knows the exact figure—have no housing of any type. They work, eat, sleep, live, and die on the streets without the benefit of any shelter. Attempts by the Municipal Development Authority to upgrade the slums, and by the Municipal Corporation to maintain them (a major problem), are hampered by lack of funds. Meanwhile, people and the sacred cattle coexist in the *bustees*. As a form of recycling, women and children collect cattle dung and form it into circular patties that serve as fuel when dried.

The city of Kolkata's attempts to upgrade itself also are hampered by a unique land-tenure system that promotes non-maintenance of slum properties. In the *bustee* or slum, one person owns the land, another then builds a hut upon it, and a third serves as a tenant, paying a monthly rent without any claim to either the land or the hut. Under this land-tenure system no one has any incentive to maintain the property.

Physically, much of the city of Kolkata is still in a state of decay. Half of the city's buildings are more than 100 years old. Twenty percent of the buildings are classified as unsafe. Development plans to arrest further deterioration have not yet reversed the damage done by decades of infrastructure collapse. For instance, drainage and sewer networks, all of which were laid in the central city prior to 1910, are in a serious state of disrepair. Much of the sewer system is either inoperative or badly clogged. As of 2010 Calcutta had no working sewage treatment plant. All this is of little consequence to the majority of municipal-area residents living in *bustees* or in outlying squatter settlements since most of their dwellings are without private toilets or sewers. Water, electricity, and telephone systems are also overloaded and in need of both major repairs and extensive upgrading. Power blackouts are a regular feature, and telephones often do not work (today everyone relies on cell phones). Kolkata residents periodically go without city-supplied electricity. Water supplies are, however, getting better, with three-quarters of Calcutta's residents now having some access to piped drinking water—frequently from a street standpipe. There is a decent metro system, and in 2008 a major mall opened in the southern part of the city.

Within the city, groups traditionally have occupied geographical wards largely on the basis of religion (Hindu or Muslim), caste, and ethnic region of origin. Occupations are also ethnically segregated. For example, the dominant Bengalis traditionally occupied white-collar jobs, while laborers were mostly Bihari. Taxi drivers used to be largely Punjabi but now also include Bengalis. The city has new luxury condominiums next to the shacks of street people.

Kolkata, even with all its social and physical problems, remains one of the world's more vital cities. It has a vibrant cultural scene. It remains the active center of Bengali poetry, literature, and theatre. Most Bengalis would not trade the city's excitement for all the fine neighborhoods and homes of New Delhi. Kolkata also has low levels of street crime. Residents fatalistically may accept power outages, poor housing, malaria, antiquated transportation, and strikes that close down municipal services, but they do not tolerate street crime against women. Any violator risks the wrath of the ever-present street crowds. Indian women in Kolkata can walk even at night with a degree of safety unknown in New Delhi, London, or New York. Physically the city suffers from decay; socially it retains a vigor, life, and pride that other cities might envy.

Prognosis

India's population is now 1.2 billion and at current growth rates it will top 1.5 billion by 2030. To put it in more understandable terms, each year India is adding 18–20 million persons, or slightly less than the total population of Australia. India's population will soon surpass China's as the world's largest. Some projections are as high as 2 billion people.[12]

The good news is that the prognosis for economic growth is strong. Until 1992 India had a state-managed economy that shut the subcontinent off from economic and technology changes elsewhere. For example, there were virtually no automatic dishwashers in the country since they were not manufactured internally and could not legally be imported. Now all that has changed and India is undergoing a massive technology and consumer revolution.

TV satellite dishes are everywhere, replacing the few dull state-run stations that for decades were all that was available. A serious example of the transformation is that India now trains more computer programmers than any nation on earth. Increasingly, American computer related jobs are being outsourced to India. India feeds itself, and also has very substantial non-agricultural resources. Paradoxically, Indian government figures for 2005–06 showed that the country's share of malnourished children remains among the worst in the world, while many middle-class children suffer from child-hood obesity.[13]

Economic growth thus far benefits the elite and the middle class far more than the masses. (Nationally, half of the urban families must survive on monthly incomes of less than $75.) As a result of continued population growth attention is focused on meeting the basic needs of an ever-larger population. Problems such as improving mass education and providing housing for the poor until very recently have received lower priority. Questions of environmental quality receive far less attention.

CHINA

China is currently the world's economic growth machine. In 2010, it passed Japan to become the world's second largest economy. China's population numbers some 1.3 billion people. To put China's population in terms most westerners would understand, the population of China *alone* is roughly equal to the combined populations of all the 21 nations of western Europe, all the 36 nations of Latin America and the Caribbean, plus the populations of the United States and Canada. Yearly, China adds 17 million persons to its population even though as of 2010 it had dropped its rate of natural increase to 0.5 percent. This is a third of the 1.7 percent of other developing nations.[14]

The U.S. Census Bureau projects that China's population will reach 1.5 billion in 2030 and then level off.[15] Without its one-child family policy, China would now have 300 million more people (the size of the U.S.). The proportion of China's billion-plus population that is urban is calculated a number of ways. For example, figures published by the State Statistical Bureau indicate China's proportion of urban population doubled from 21 percent in 1982 to 41 percent four years later in 1986.[16] This is because the latter figure included counties under municipal jurisdiction even if they were not truly urban. Today the urban figure is 46 percent.[17] The actual figure might be lower. This means that China—although 63 percent rural—still has the world's largest population of urban dwellers. China currently has an urban population of over 500 million. Increasingly, urban population growth has been primarily due to rural-to-urban movement.

Growth is concentrated in specific areas. The People's Republic of China has an area of about 3.8 million square miles, with 96 percent of the population living on 40 percent of the land area. The population of China is concentrated in the southern and eastern sections of the country. The greatest density is found in the Yangtze Valley, where there are 2,000 to 2,500 persons per square mile.

Treaty Ports

The first modern manufacturing and industrial cities of China were the Western-dominated treaty ports. The European powers forced the weak and ineffectual Manchu, or Qing, dynasty to give foreigners substantial control over the economic life of the major Chinese cities. Chinese coastal cities until World War II were physically controlled and occupied by European, and Japanese, administrators and troops. Europeans lived in separate, newer sections of the cities. The foreign concessions of Shanghai were even policed by European troops, and foreigners could not be tried for crimes in Chinese courts. In Shanghai, the largest and most prosperous of the treaty ports, the park along the "Bund," or riverfront, according to legend had signs stating, "No Dogs or Chinese Allowed."

Even the capital of Peking had its "legation quarter" for foreigners, near the central Imperial City.

The Nationalist government, which replaced the Qing dynasty in 1911, was made up of an urban military and upper-class elite that continued the traditional practices of taxing and coercing the peasants to support the urban-based government. Landowners, many of whom lived in the cities, had little sympathy for the declining quality of life in rural China. The government continued ·to serve the landowners and disregard the plight of the peasants; land reform was ignored.

The communists also initially ignored the peasants and attempted to organize in the cities, but having failed at that, Mao Zedong redirected attention to the peasants. After decades of internal struggle and the civil war of 1947–1949, the communists achieved national dominance.

Urbanization Policies

China's policy under Mao was resolutely anti-urban. This was in part a reaction to the treaty port cities being seen (correctly) as the centers of Western thought and influence. "The foreign presence (in China) was almost exclusively urban."[18] Inland cities such as Tsinan were more successful in resisting foreign intervention. The initial failures of the communist cause in the cities further separated the cities from the original communist leadership.

Today the booming cities of China are again dominant. They are the economic engines driving the country's development.

Forced Movement from Cities

Following the economic crisis brought on by the failure of the "great leap forward" campaign in 1963, the government decided to stabilize the urban population at 110 million, which was considered a manageable figure. During the "Cultural Revolution" of 1966–1976, the government therefore forcibly sent surplus urban population, especially young school graduates, into the countryside. A combination of social coercion and ideological conviction was used to persuade 15 to 25 million urban Chinese youths to "volunteer" to resettle permanently in rural villages. Most of these migrants made a poor adjustment to their new rural surroundings.

Following the bloody repressions at Tiananmen Square in 1989, there briefly was some attempt to return to the practice of sending students to the countryside. The job assignment system in which graduates are permanently assigned to jobs also was reasserted. However, neither of these survived for long, and now both have been abandoned under what is clearly a capitalistic economy in practice if not name. Four decades of anti-urban ideology emphasizing the reduction of urban growth have run up against economic reality. China politically remains controlled by the Communist Party, but economically it now essentially is a free-enterprise system. But a system with few worker protections, or environmental controls.

Rural to Urban Migration

China is making a major effort to relocate industries to outlying areas in order to stem the potential flood of rural-to-urban migrants. This is because the Labor Ministry has estimated that some 114 million workers are migrating to the cities to seek employment. Moreover, Chinese government officials estimate that mechanization of farming will displace a total of 300 million peasants by 2020, and eventually 500 million.[19] This is the largest movement in human history.

Planners hope to relocate displaced peasants in small cities and towns scattered across the countryside. Medium and small-sized cities are rapidly expanding. However, contrary to government claims, such cities do not provide a better quality of life than large cities.

In the past, rural-to-urban migration was held in check by a very strictly enforced policy of household registration that did not legally permit those without urban jobs to remain in

Shanghai is changing dramatically. The expressway pictured here goes from Shanghai across the Huangpu River to the new industrial, commercial, and residential Shanghai district of Pudong. Established in 1990, Pudong has grown to a population of 5 million, is the site of Shanghai's international airport, and has become the major business and commercial center of China. © Typhoonski/ Dreamstime.com

the cities. However, while nominally still in force, such regulations are now ignored. Still, life is hard for the unsanctioned so-called "floating population." Unsanctioned migrants and their children do not have access to schools, health care, and necessary social services.[20] An indirect consequence of this policy is the proliferation of marginal jobs outside the formal structure, such as free-enterprise markets and food stalls—places where those not supposed to be in the city can find work. It is estimated that 40 percent of the construction workers in Beijing are unsanctioned migrants. Today, none of the government mobility controls have any force.

Economic Boom

The economic reforms of the last decades occurred first, not in the established cities of Beijing and Shanghai, but in Special Economic Zones set up in the south. Southern Guandong province with its new factories and cities initially catapulted far ahead of the north. In spite of the political hostility between the mainland and Taiwan, many of the factories in the southern zone are actually financed and managed by Taiwanese businessmen who have invested more than $35 billion in the region. (Hong

Kong still provides the majority of investors.) It is an open secret that some of the goods labeled "Made in Taiwan" are actually assembled in mainland factories.

As a result of the economic boom the southern zones now boast a considerable prosperity that is easily seen in the new superhighways and neighborhoods of spacious garden apartments. Southern provinces also tend to ignore decrees from Beijing that interfere with local business or convenience. Thus, for example, bans on satellite dishes are totally ignored. The south tends to follow the ancient Chinese saying that "The mountains are high, and the Emperor is far away."

Shanghai

Shanghai, China's largest city at 16.7 million, grew as a treaty port built by Western commercial enterprise. Within a decade of its opening to foreign trade in 1843, Shanghai's manufacturing sector had become a physical and economic embodiment of 19th-century European colonialism. In 19th-century Shanghai, with its extraterritoriality laws (foreigners had their own laws, police, and courts), foreign concessions, and gunboats, the modern industrial world of European rationality came face to face with the traditional seclusionist ways of the Chinese Empire.

Following the communist takeover in 1949, the city was allowed to deteriorate. Political leaders in Beijing distrusted Shanghai's independence and drained tax monies from the city. Only in the last decade were Shanghai's needs seriously addressed. Shanghai also had to overcome the effects of the previous pattern of mixed foreign domination. Each of the foreign settlements had not only its own administration and police, but also its own pattern and width of streets, water pipes, and sewers. Developing a uniform citywide street pattern has required widening existing streets as well as extending others by tearing down buildings and houses. Today Shanghai has a good system of roads. The once–ever-present bikes have been banned from major city roads.

Old neighborhoods are rapidly being demolished to make way for new high-rise buildings, department stores, offices, and elevated highways. Some 129 acres in the center of the city has been redeveloped from crowded housing to a landscaped corporate office park. Hundreds of thousands of residents of old Shanghai have been moved to cheap public housing in the suburbs—housing that may lack the character of the old neighborhoods but has running water, electricity, and better ventilation.

Hong Kong and Shanghai are competitors as to which city will be the main commercial hub of China. Shanghai as of 2005 became the world's largest cargo port. While for decades Shanghai was punished by officials in Beijing for being a cosmopolitan center of business, vice, and intellectual freedom, it now is encouraged to get rich again. Shanghai took to heart Deng Xiaoping's declaration that "to get rich is glorious." Shanghai is home today to one of the two stock exchanges in China, and getting rich is the new way of life, promoting the emergence of sharp class differences.

Symbolizing the new Shanghai is the New Area project of Pudong across the Huangpu River from the traditional Bund. Totally built since the 1990s, Pudong has replaced Beijing as the financial capital of China. Pudong is a new 21st-century Chinese electronics, commerce, and manufacturing city, mostly built since 1990. It is Shanghai's answer to the New Industrial Zones of south China. The architecture in Pudong is bold, big, rich, and flashy. Volkswagen, Xerox, Pepsico, Coca-Cola, Mitsubishi, and Sony are but a few of the firms with corporate headquarters located in Pudong.[21] In 2000 Coca-Cola, for example, moved its Chinese operations headquarters from Hong Kong to a new 1-million square foot, seven-story building in Pudong.[22] Pudong is also full of factories, high-tech parks, warehouses, workers' housing developments, and expensive new housing estates. A tunnel and a dramatic new bridge now connect the old colonial business district of the riverfront Bund with the east bank of the Huangpu River and Pudong. Towering over Pudong is the Oriental Pearl Television tower, advertised in tourist brochures as the highest edifice in Asia.

With rapid economic growth and the mass of industrial activity still located within the city proper, Shanghai's bad pollution has gotten considerably worse. Many of the city's factories and utilities burn heavily polluting soft coal for energy. Plans call for switching Shanghai's utilities to lower-pollution natural gas. With no real pollution controls on vehicles, and the number of cars and trucks rapidly increasing, the pollution and congestion from automobiles also is growing. However, much of the populace still uses the overcrowded bus system and bicycles. There still are 5 million bicycles in the city.

Shanghai is still paying for the excesses of the Cultural Revolution. Virtually everything in the city stopped for a decade. For example, the prestigious Singapore Conservatory of Music saw, not only its once fine buildings decay, but most of its instruments destroyed and historically invaluable sheet music sold as scrap paper. During the decade of the Cultural Revolution, virtually no new urban building, repairs, or even painting was done anywhere in China. The official policy was "Production first, Livelihood second, Construction where there is room." Housing was considered part of the "nonproductive" sector.

Now old housing is being repaired or torn down, and new high-rise buildings are being constructed at a dramatic rate. Under the Communist "Iron Rice Bowl" system everything was provided. One's place of work usually not only provided a job, but also managed the housing where one lived. Serious crowding was a problem, but the rent was low; the average working family paid only 4 to 8 percent of its income for monthly rent. Now housing is on a market rent system, and new, expensive housing projects are going up everywhere. Booming Shanghai sees itself as China's future.

The local government is now transforming the old industrial area on both sides of the Hangpu River, which became the site of the 2010 Shanghai World Expo into a new 1,305-acre eco-friendly central city zone of parks, convention centers, and pedestrian friendly retail and commercial space. Moreover, it will be constructed with eco-friendly materials, some coming from the demolished giant pavilions of the 2010 World Expo. Renewal energy, mostly from wind and solar, will power the site. Shanghai is seeking to become China's symbol of sustainable growth.

Beijing

Beijing (it translates as northern capital) was first made the capital of China in the Yuan Dynasty in 1292. The old walled city was expanded during the Ming and Qing Dynasties into the political and cultural center of the nation. The Forbidden City, which housed the imperial court and bureaucracy, is now a museum.

Old Beijing is now largely history. Since 2000, Beijing has become a modern city in which virtually everyone lives in high-rise buildings—many constructed in the last decade. Beijing, China's second-largest city, has 12 million residents. This may not be an accurate reflection of the actual metro population, for the Beijing municipality covers a huge, 16,800-square-kilometer territory (roughly

four-fifths the size of New Jersey), and 3.4 million of the inhabitants of the municipality are rural residents. They represent a highly prosperous category of largely independent farmers who help feed the capital city. Independent farmers markets are found throughout the city.

Beijing is booming economically, and its urban residents are the most economically favored in China. The average annual salary of a Beijing worker is more than four times the national average. This reflects Beijing's role as the home of China's political leaders and top bureaucrats. It is also the chief center of political, administrative, educational, and cultural activity.

During the 1950s, when Soviet influence was still important, the city was divided into functional zones for different activities following the Moscow model. Factory sectors were concentrated in the eastern and southern suburbs, while the northwest sector was primarily for higher education and research. Since the prevailing winds are from the northwest, this also helps to keep down pollution levels. Nevertheless, Beijing has very serious pollution problems, particularly in the winter, when businesses and families use 20 million tons of soft coal for heating. Even on cloudless winter days the sun often is not visible until afternoon because of the heavy pollution. Yet shutting down major industrial polluters has proved to be a difficult task, and little environmental reform has been implemented. With 2,000 cars a day being added to the 4 million already on the road both air pollution and traffice are getting worse. In 2010, on the outskirts of Beijing, there was a 60-mile traffic jam that lasted more than a month.[23]

Contributing to the problem of windblown particulate matter is Beijing's location on an almost treeless plain south of the Gobi Desert. During the Cultural Revolution, the government decreed that all cats and dogs be killed for health reasons. This led to a proliferation of nuisance birds, who were then ordered killed. This led to a proliferation of insects, so the municipal government then decreed that all grass be torn up. This was done, with the result of substantially increased dust in the air. This is an interesting example of how social organization policy decisions can negatively impact the environment.

The 2008 Beijing Summer Olympics required severe measures to reduce pollution. All major factories were shut down for the full 17 days, and everyone in Beijing was ordered to turn down their air conditioning. A half-million official cars were ordered off the roads and at least an equal number of other drivers "volunteered" not to use their vehicles. Still, prevailing winds brought dirty air from neighboring provinces, which are among the most polluted regions in the world.

The 1983 plan for the future development of Beijing envisioned placing the entire former central Imperial Forbidden City under special protection to preserve historic buildings and prohibit any more houses taller than two stories in that area.[24] This plan was ignored, and the Forbidden City today is surrounded by high-rise buildings. In 2000, much to the upset of historically minded Chinese, a Starbucks opened inside the Forbidden City.

Dramatic building is going on in Beijing. But, in spite of all the new high-rise flats, crowded housing still remains a major problem. Beijing, tied as it is to the old political order, has shown somewhat less rapid economic change than have the more freewheeling Shanghai and south coastal provinces. Beijing plans within a handful of years to become a world metropolis of the first rank.

Hong Kong

Until 1997, when it reverted to China, Hong Kong was a British Crown Colony. Now Hong Kong, with its 7 million population, has special status, but legally is part of China. Still, Hong Kong remains most noted for its laissez-faire economic structure. Hong Kong's population is heavily concentrated in a narrow ring around the harbor. The hilly environment, plus the strong desire of newcomers to remain in the city proper, means that Hong Kong's population density is the highest in the world. At 14,482 persons per square mile it is double that of Los Angeles.[25] Much of Hong Kong's 402 square miles are kept green because they are so steep and mountainous as to be inaccessible for development, or they are on scattered islands where development would be uneconomical.

In an attempt to provide public housing for all who need it, Hong Kong is developing several new towns. Tsuen Won already holds over 800,000 persons and eventually will have over 1 million. (Obviously the new towns are far larger than Ebenezer Howard's vision of self-contained communities of only 30,000.) Hong Kong's new towns (or cities) are developed as self-sufficient entities, but in fact cannot fully meet their own educational, retail trade, and entertainment needs, nor provide their own employment base.

The Hong Kong economy is the eighth-largest trading entity in the world, and the city is noted for its vitality. What it has not produced is a means of equitably sharing its economic miracle. Nonetheless, for its residents, Hong Kong represents living standards and opportunities less available in mainland China. The city boasts a very substantial middle class. However, the long-term consequences of Chinese control remain uncertain. The Chinese government has promised not to change the economic system in Hong Kong for 50 years. However, the Chinese government has indicated that its guarantees are not absolute but are dependent upon Hong Kong having only limited elected self-government and following the mainland's political line.

JAPAN

Any discussion of Asian urban patterns must include Japan, the region's most urbanized large nation. Japan is not an urban newcomer; it has an urban tradition even longer than that of India as regards the role of the city in regional and national life. Japan's urban tradition goes back at least to the 15th century. The so-called castle towns formed a basic urban stratum upon

Box 15.1   Density and Economic Development

It should be noted that there is no clear relationship between population density per se and the level or rate of economic development. High agricultural density is usually seen as a sign of underdevelopment, but high urban densities may or may not be desirable, depending on the level of economic development.

High densities of rural, and particularly agricultural, labor indicate inefficient agricultural production and a surplus of personnel who are either unemployed or underemployed. In closed extractive economies—such as farming, lumbering, and mining—the employment of a high proportion of the labor force in such pursuits means smaller average holdings. India, for example, employs about 70 percent of its labor force in agriculture, with an average holding of about two acres for every person of working age (15 to 65 years of age). In Asia more than 83 percent of the available acreage is already under cultivation; thus increases in rural population will necessarily mean less land per person. Rural out-migration thus will continue to be a major force into the foreseeable future.

In developed countries, where non-extractive industries dominate and a large volume of trade is possible, density is frequently an advantage rather than a liability. The industrial ring cities of the Netherlands and the Rhine River urban complex of Germany both have extremely high densities and high standards of living. Hong Kong, as noted, provides an even more extreme example. Nonetheless, Hong Kong has for years managed to increase its GNP at a rate much in excess of the rest of the world. Hong Kong has practically no natural resources, but it is blessed with a literate, energetic, and trained labor force. Its extremely high population

density has not prevented Hong Kong from achieving one of the highest levels of per capita income in Asia.

This in no way suggests, of course, that high densities automatically result in high income levels and economic expansion. However, high density can be an advantage to a highly organized and heavily industrialized economy. The city concentrates large numbers of people in one place and thus minimizes what has been called "the friction of space." Production can be concentrated in one place; the city itself is a massive factory. Technological breakthroughs in transportation and communication also are means of overcoming the friction of space, and they allow the city to export both to its rural hinterland and to other urban areas.

In the non-economic sphere, population concentration also permits and encourages specialized educational, cultural, and scientific organizations. Accumulations of personal and capital resources necessary for the emergence of such organizations can be found only in the city. The requirements of urban living also produce new problems, such as housing, sanitation, and the prevention of crime; and the necessity of dealing with these problems can lead to an emphasis on innovation and rational problem solving.

The requirements of contemporary urban life and those of industrialization and post-industrialization complement one another. Both emphasize the importance of adapting to changing conditions. Urbanization and industrialization are not the same thing, but it is not surprising that industrialism in the third world is directly associated with the growth of urban areas and the spread of urban ideas.

---

which later cities were built. Edo, as Tokyo was then called, may have had 1 million people in 1700, while Osaka, the great trade center, and Kyoto, the ancient capital, both had several hundred thousand inhabitants.[26]

Extent of Urbanization

The forced opening of Japan to Western influences in the mid-19th century led to a boom in city building. Cities such as Tokyo, Nagoya, and Osaka grew, first as trading centers and later as

manufacturing and commercial cities. Industrialization and urbanization took place so completely that today Japan equals, and in some cases surpasses Western levels in these two areas. Today Japan is 86 percent urban, a percentage higher than North America.[27] Moreover, the urban population of Japan is remarkably concentrated, with an overall national density of more than 300 persons per square kilometer and 45 percent of the total population occupying only 1 percent of the land area. Unlike the United States, Japan does not have a Jeffersonian tradition of idealizing rural areas and distrusting cities. Everyone wants their activities to be located in Tokyo.

Current Patterns

In discussing contemporary Japanese urbanization, it is important to remember that while Japan is an Asian country, its levels of urbanization and industrialization are more similar to those of Europe and North America than to those of Asia. The strengths and problems of Japanese cities are largely similar to those of developed Western metropolises. Japan, along with the small enclaves of Hong Kong and Singapore, has both a level and a pattern of modern urbanization atypical of Asia in general.

Many current urban problems in Japan are a result of the decision of the Japanese after World War II to concentrate all their efforts on industrial production for export. Only minimal attention and resources were devoted to "social overhead" such as sewage systems, water systems, pollution control, and urban transportation. For years Japan spent less on urban infrastructure than did other industrial nations. Now that has changed radically. In an attempt to spur its economy, Tokyo has been investing largely in public works.

Although Japan's economy essentially remained flat without growth from the mid 1990s to 2010, Japan still possesses great resources. Japan has the technology, the skilled personnel, and the financial resources to rebuild and remake its cities. During the last decade, large public works projects have been initiated, in good part in a vain attempt to jumpstart economic growth. Recently the economy has resumed slow growth.

Tokyo

Tokyo–Yokohama is the world's most populous metro area, with 28 million persons as of 2010.[28] Tokyo is to the Western observer a series of contradictions. The economy is stagnating, but signs of prosperity are everywhere, from the streets clogged with new automobiles to futuristic new office buildings to luxury department stores unmatched in Paris, London, or New York. Until the last two decade's economic downturn, street people were nonexistent. Few would disagree with the statement made to this author by the president of Tokyo University that Japanese women are, as a group, better and more expensively dressed than women anywhere in Europe or the United States.

Yet, in spite of its affluence, Japan has not been able to house its population at a level taken for granted in other developed countries. For example, housing conditions are extremely cramped and excessively expensive by American standards. Even after the 1990s bust in property costs small single-family homes within a 45-minute commute of Tokyo average over $500,000. For this money you get very little dwelling space. The typical Tokyo dwelling has only 172 square feet of space per person. Nationwide, the average Japanese home has only 900 square feet, compared to 2,100 square feet in the United States. Young people, therefore, spend money on consumer goods and holidays since, without parental assistance, they often are unable to purchase homes.

Housing. Unfortunately, within the Tokyo–Yokohama agglomeration, the traditional Japanese gardens exist only in memory or on the estates of the wealthy. Exorbitant land costs have resulted in structures being built wall to wall up to the lot lines. Also there is relatively little open public land. Tokyo has half the parkland of Washington, D.C., and one-tenth that of London. Zoning regulations are minimal, and they are frequently flouted. This absence of control over construction is notable in what is often considered a structured society.

Within the jurisdiction of the Tokyo metropolitan government (the old city of 23 wards and the immediate surrounding suburbs with a population of 12 million), basic services are being upgraded. As recently as the 1990s only 85 percent of the population had flush toilets.[29]

Nationally only half the homes are connected to sewage systems. In spite of their cost, Japanese homes are often cold. Less than one-quarter of Japanese houses had central heating as of 2000. Even new suburban homes do not usually have central heating. At the same time, 97 percent of the homes have color television.

Because central-city housing is prohibitively expensive, most Japanese are forced to commute long distances between their offices and cheaper residential accommodations in satellite towns on the outskirts of Tokyo. Even the homes of well-paid white-collar "salarymen" are small by world standards. Even given the high housing costs, construction quality is not always the best. The devastating 1995 Kobe earthquake demonstrated the danger of putting heavy tile roofs on weakly supported walls. Government housing policies tend to push up rather than decrease real estate prices and thus hamper new housing construction. Therefore, Japanese national savings have been invested in safe postal accounts, or foreign stocks and properties, rather than local housing.

Transportation. Japan's subway and train system are among the world's finest. Trains between communities are frequent and always on time. Tokyo has a remarkably clean and efficient subway system, but during rush hours it (and commuter rail lines) must employ an army of 700 pushers whose job it is to force additional passengers into the crowded cars. The Yamanote Line, which rings central Tokyo, commonly operates at 250 percent of capacity during rush hours.[30] Above ground, the roads are continually packed with wall-to-wall vehicles. Tokyo–Yokohama is not only the world's largest metropolitan area, it is also among the world's most congested. Roadways are vast bottlenecks during rush hours, so most workers take public transport. Because space is at a premium, express roads are usually built above existing roadways, but they also are commonly clogged. The system is simply not adequate for a city half Tokyo's size.

For many Japanese the bicycle, not the auto, is the most efficient means of transportation. The nation has some 55 million bicycles, and at least 5.6 million of these are in Tokyo. Since one-third of all Tokyo office workers spend between two and four hours a day commuting, a bicycle stored during the day at the suburban railway station may help people cut 10 or 15 minutes off commuting time in the morning and evening. It also leads to unbelievable seas of bicycles outside railway stations and stores. Periodically police confiscate illegally parked bicycles (200,000 in Tokyo each year), but it seems to have little impact.

Crime. Tokyo is one of the world's safest cities and Japan has one of the world's lowest crime rates. Comparisons with the United States put Japanese achievements in perspective. The United States has just over twice the population of Japan, but more than 10 times as many murders, 45 times as many rapes, and 270 times as many robberies. During the mid-1990s Japanese newspapers spoke of the country having a crime wave, but by this they meant that the nation of 126 million people had 38 murders in 1994. By 1995 the figure had dropped back to the more normal half that number.

Why the huge differences in crime? Experts cite several factors. First, Japan has a unified culture and racial population with fewer of the sharp differences between wealthy and poor found in the United States. Second, Japanese have a strong sense of the group and the individual's secondary position. Criminal behavior shames one's group. Third, Japan has had strict gun control for 400 years. Only those in law enforcement can possess handguns. Finally, Japan relies on some 15,000 small neighborhood police stations known as *koban*. In suburban and rural areas, the policeman and his family actually live in the *koban*. In the cities, as well as small localities, police make local rounds by foot or bicycle, knocking on doors to inquire about neighborhood concerns. They are an integral part of the neighborhood, spending far more time providing neighborhood services than solving crimes. Thus, even in Tokyo, the *koban* provides the local neighborhood with small-town services and atmosphere.

Planning

During the final years of World War II much of Tokyo was leveled—the city lost 56 percent of its housing stock—and Tokyo had the opportunity to rebuild itself with widened streets, open spaces, parks, and reasonable lot sizes. The fact that this was not even seriously considered is still seen as more of a tragedy by outsiders than by the business elites of Tokyo. Until the 1990s these elites continued Japan's extremely successful emphasis on foreign exports and trade surpluses, while strongly resisting any meaningful national or municipal government spending on infrastructure. Since then infrastructure expenditures have dramatically increased, but Tokyo remains a congested city. Tokyo citizens have only one-eighth the parkland New York City residents have. Thus far, urban planning has taken a distinct backseat to economic growth.

Planned New Towns

There are, of course, some exceptions. For example, Suma New Town, near Kobe, currently with a population exceeding 100,000, was built on reclaimed land. To provide land the tops of hills were literally blasted and bulldozed off, and the rock was then carried underground for miles to the sea on huge conveyer belts. The fill was then used to construct the artificial port and Rokko Islands in Kobe harbor. The inland project, which was officially dedicated in 1980, is estimated to have cost $2.5 billion. The 1995 Kobe earthquake, unfortunately, demonstrated that filled-in land becomes virtually liquid in a major earthquake.

Public housing, in new towns or elsewhere, is built for middle-class rather than low-income groups. The public Japan Housing Corporation, for example, is required by law to break even financially on the projects it constructs, and so rents are usually far more than the poor can afford. Limited public housing for low-income groups is built by the Metropolitan Housing Supply Corporation.

Suburbanization

Suburbanization has been a factor in Japan ever since the massive earthquake of 1923, which first encouraged decentralization. The Japanese have a long tradition of city living, and before World War II, the poor lived outside the municipal boundaries, particularly in marshy areas.

More recently, high land costs have resulted in heavy middle-class and even upper-class suburbanization. Since Japanese commute to and from suburbs largely by rail, the greatest suburban development has been along the very profitable suburban rail lines. The average commuter travels a remarkable 1.5 hours each way. (The U.S. average is under half an hour each way.) It is estimated that the average white-collar "salaryman" commuter spends three and a half years of his life commuting.

As land prices rise, the center of Tokyo is more and more given over to shops and commercial and business activities. The resident central-city population can be expected to decline further while suburban growth—some of it quite distant—accelerates.

SOUTHEAST ASIA

General Patterns

Most major cities of Southeast Asia—except Bangkok in Thailand—are a product of European colonial expansion, Chinese enterprise, or a combination of the two. This is to some extent an exaggeration, but generally the pattern holds true. Cities in Southeast Asia are relatively new. Few date back more than a century or two. Primate cities, particularly ports, are common.

Most of the cities originally were clearly divided into Western and non-Western districts. Ho Chi Minh City (now again popularly called Saigon) provides an example.

Saigon's urban history began in 1859, when the French captured a village of temporary structures. On this site the French built Saigon as an administrative capital, laying out the streets in a grid pattern. The Chinese quarter and marketplace, known as Cholon, developed simultaneously with Saigon. Thus Saigon became the French colonial capital for Vietnam with orderly growth while Cholon grew haphazardly. The two areas were merged by the French in 1932 for administrative purposes.

Before World War II, the largest population group in Saigon–Cholon was Chinese. Roughly 60 percent of Cholon, and 30 percent of the entire city, was Chinese at this time. Following the Vietnam War the government of Vietnam expelled the Chinese, fearing that they would dominate the economy and constitute a potential "fifth column" loyal to China. The majority of the Vietnamese "boat people" fleeing Vietnam were ethnic Chinese. Today Saigon is again a vibrant city filled with an entrepreneurial population and new businesses.

Singapore

The Republic of Singapore, a modern island, is atypical of Southeast Asia. Whether this is good or bad depends on the perspective of the observer. Economically there is no question that, in spite of the total absence of natural resources (Singapore even has to import sand for building), the country is prosperous. Singapore has some 5 million persons in an area of only 225 square miles (584 square kilometers), making it one of the most densely crowded areas on the globe.[31] Singapore has roughly 10 times the density of Holland, which is the most densely populated Western country. Officially, Singapore is 100 percent urban.

One of the things that makes Singapore unique is its strategy for control and development. Since independence in 1965, the government has had an ambitious program to replace virtually all of Singapore's previous housing with high-rise apartment buildings. Slums and squatter settlements have been eradicated, sometimes by the use of draconian measures. The old Chinese neighborhoods of street vendors and dilapidated, overcrowded buildings, so dear to the hearts of tourists, and the Malay *kampongs* (villages) have been replaced by government-sponsored high-rise estates and new office buildings and hotels. Currently, more than four-fifths of the population resides in government-built high-rise housing estates. Singapore has also built several new towns—also of high-rises—the largest of which is Woodlands New Town, with a population of over 300,000.

The rapid transformation of Singapore into an ultramodern city, however, is not without its critics. Some charge that too much of the traditional culture has been sacrificed to the god of efficiency. For example, once government planners decide to rebuild a district, the land is compulsorily acquired; and although compensation is paid, neither litigation by owners nor public protests by residents will stop redevelopment. If an ancient temple sits on land desired for redevelopment, the temple is either moved or rebuilt elsewhere.

Singapore's sharp break with the past has both advantages and disadvantages. While the high-rise structures are not as effective as the old *kampongs* and squatter settlements in fostering community ties and close human relationships, they do provide high quality housing and living facilities for the majority of the population. Compared with high-rise housing projects in the United States, the buildings are well maintained. Perhaps this is because, as a result of government policy, most residents own rather than rent their flats.

Under the government's "home ownership for the people" scheme, residents can draw upon their mandatory social security payments for the down payment and even monthly payments for their flats. Four-fifths of those living in government-built housing estates are purchasing or have purchased their apartments; more than three-quarters of these used their social security payments for down payments and mortgage payments. It is not uncommon for a family to spend a considerable amount upgrading and redecorating its flat. The Housing and Development Board has "thinned out" some of the earlier projects by tearing down every second building; it has phased out one-room flats by converting them to two-room units. Singapore is thus in the unique position of having solved its physical housing problems, insofar as government-built housing of good quality is available to most residents.

Whether the high-rise projects fully meet the social and community needs of the populace remains to be seen. Singaporeans enjoy one of the highest standards of living in the world, with a per capita income slightly higher than that of North America.[32] Economic prosperity has resulted in so many automobiles that to control congestion and pollution, cars not having an expensive entry permit are banned from the center of the city during working hours. The city is also engaged in a major program of beautification by planting trees and bushes along the roadways. (Because Singapore is near the equator, newly planted trees grow rapidly.)

Overall, Singaporeans live in a tightly controlled society where efficiency ranks well ahead of citizen participation in making decisions. Regulations, even on littering (a $225 fine), are enforced. Singapore is a modern, well-regulated commercial city. If it isn't as free-wheeling, colorful, and interesting as in the old days, that is a price most residents seem willing to pay.

Other Cities

Other Southeast Asian cities that merit attention include Jakarta, the booming capital of Indonesia; Bangkok, the capital and principal city of Thailand; Kuala Lumpur, the dominant center of Malaysia; Seoul, capital of South Korea; Manila, the capital of the Philippines; and Taipei, the major city of Taiwan. Sprawling Jakarta already has 10 million people and may well have twice as many by 2015. A priority of the government is to stabilize the economy and attract new industry. Jakarta, which as of 1980 had only a handful of high-rise buildings, now has a skyline filled with high-rises, and some of the world's worst traffic jams. Its excitement has been only somewhat affected by the growing Muslim fundamentalism of the last few years.

Bangkok, officially, has 6 million persons, but actually it has twice that number. It is one of the most dynamic and most chaotic cities in Asia. While crowding and pollution are serious, the city is an economic, educational, and cultural magnet, not only for Thais, but for other Asians. Bangkok is reputed to have the world's worst traffic jams. The new Tanayong elevated railway system is efficient, and new expressways are being built. However, these improvements barely dent traffic congestion.

Kuala Lumpur, once a mining town, now the national capital, has grown with more speed than planning. Kuala Lumpur is a vital city. Two high-rise towers, the Petronas Towers, were the tallest buildings in the world, until surpassed by Taipei 101 in 2003. Surrounding Kuala Lumpur is suburban sprawl that is spreading ever farther over what were once agricultural estates.

Manila is also struggling with sprawl, and the government seems unable to address the issue. Only the good nature of its residents provides some relief. Seoul, a very modern city, was largely destroyed in the Korean War (1950–1953) and is now a city of modern skyscrapers. Little of the historic city remains. As a city, Seoul is efficient rather than comfortable. The big local issue as of this decade is not nearby North Korea, but the economy and housing prices.[33]

In Taiwan the Taipei metropolitan area holds some 6 million persons who do not generally consider it to be either well designed or environmentally satisfactory. Located in a natural basin, air pollution remains a serious problem, but after decades of neglect, environmental problems are now being addressed. Other improvements are also being made. Clogged Taipei now has an elevated transportation system and even a new park on cleared central-city land. It also has the world's second tallest building, the 101-story Taipei 101. What Taipei lacks in beauty it makes up in energy.

SUMMARY

Everywhere in Asia physical urbanization and social urbanism as a way of life are both increasing spectacularly. Even in China, where government policies encourage population control, the cities are inevitably going to grow because industrial development and jobs are attracting migrants into the cities.

Within Asia, individual cities are frequently immense, but the overall level of urbanization, at 42 percent, is still relatively low. This is certain to change. Looking at Asia as a whole, it is clear that dramatic urban growth will be the pattern for the first decades of the 21st century. Increasingly the great cities of the world will be Asian cities.

Generalizing beyond this point for the entire Asian region is impossible since the outstanding characteristic of the area is its diversity. Many of the countries' urban problems may be similar, but the solutions to date have differed widely in both content and degree of success.

Japan is by far the most urbanized of the large nations of Asia and has the greatest resources, both technical and economic, that can be brought to bear on specific problems such as housing, sanitation, and transportation. China has immense human resources and a growing technological base. For decades it managed potential urban problems by controlling urban population growth—something it is not currently able to do. China's major cities show great potential for dramatic growth and upgrading over the next decade.

Indian cities for years came closest to the old "teeming masses of Asia" stereotype, but the introduction of a free market system in the 1990s has brought dramatic changes. Indian cities are booming. However, the economic boom, while benefiting the middle class, has further exacerbated the divisions between the prosperous and the poor. Rapid population growth has severely strained the physical capabilities of cities such as Mumbai and Kolkata to house, educate, and employ their poorer residents. Indian cities, though, possess a vitality and color that other nations might envy.

It is important not to try to transfer American ideas about urban problems to cities elsewhere. In Asia cities are booming, not declining. In Asia the cities, even with all their very real problems, are not places of abandonment and despair but of growth, hope, and optimism. American clichés such as the "decline of the city" have no meaning in the Asian context. In Asia the city is the future.

REVIEW QUESTIONS

1. What are the differences between the colonial and indigenous backgrounds of third world cities?

2. How does the Indian city of Mumbai differ for the rich and the poor?

3. How do the two Indian cities of Mumbai and Kolkata compare?

4. What was the attitude of the Chinese communist party toward its cities until the last 20 years?

5. How has Shanghai changed over the last 20 years?

6. What is the relationship between density and economic development?

7. What is the level of urbanization in Japan and why?

8. What is the housing situation in Japan for middle-class families and why?

9. How do Singapore's housing policies differ from those in the rest of Asia?

10. What are the advantages and the disadvantages of Singapore's housing policies?

NOTES

1. Rhoads Murphey, "Urbanization in Asia," *Ekistics* 21:8, January 1966.

2. Population Reference Bureau, "2010 World Population Data Sheet," Washington, D.C., 2010.

3. Ibid.

4. Hans Nagpaul, "India's Giant Cities," in Mattei Dogan and John D. Kasarda (eds.), *The Metropolis Era*, vol. 1, Sage, Newbury Park, Calif., 1988, p. 254.

5. John T. Martin, Immanuel Ness, and Stephan Collins, *Book of World City Rankings*, Free Press, New York, 1988, p. 371.

6. This section is partially based upon discussions with officials of the Mumbai Metropolitan Region Development Authority and the City of Mumbai Industrial Development Corporation. The opinions are, of course, the author's.

7. S. Carl Haub and O. P. Sharma, "India's Population Reality: Reconciling Change and Tradition," *Population Bulletin*, 61:3, Sept. 2006.

8. *Demographia World Urban Area and Population Projections, Fifth Comprehensive Edition*, http://www.demographia.com, April 2009, Table 1, p. 11.

9. Somini Sengupta, "In Mumbai, Public Indignity Is Poverty's Partner," *New York Times International*, Feb. 10, 2002, p. 3.

10. Population Reference Bureau, "2009 World Population Data Sheet," Washington, D.C., 2009.

11. Boaventura de Sousa Santos, "Mumbai and the Future," *ASA Footnotes*, March, 2004, p. 8.

12. "Is India's Population Heading Toward 2 Billion?" Population Reference Bureau, www.prb.org/2007/IndiaProjections.aspx.

13. B Somini Sengupta, "India Prosperity Creates a Paradox: Many Children are Fat, Even More Are Famished," *New York Times*, Dec. 31, 2006, p. 8.

14. Population Reference Bureau 2010, op. cit.

15. Bingham Kennedy Jr., "For China a Census That Really Counts," *Population Today*, Population Reference Bureau, Washington, D.C., November/December 2000, p. 2.

16. State Statistical Bureau, *Statistical Yearbook of China*, State Publishing House, Beijing, 1982, p. 89.

17. Population Reference Bureau 2006, op. cit.

18. Rhoads Murphey, "The Treaty Ports and China's Modernization," in Mark Eivin and G. William Skinner (eds.), *The Chinese City between Two Worlds*, Stanford University Press, Stanford, Calif., 1974, p. 67.

19. Jim Yardley, "Chinese Migrants Deluge Cities," *New York Times*, Sept. 12, 2004, p. A7.

20. Kam Wing Chan, "International Migration In China: A Dualistic Approach," in Frank Pieke and Hein Malley (eds.), *Internal and International Migration: Chinese Perspectives*, Curzon Press, Richmond, England, 1999, pp. 49–71.

21. Ian Buruma, "The 21st Century Starts Here," *New York Times Magazine*, February 18, 1996, p. 31.

22. Isabella Ng, "A Run for the Money," *Time*, January 22, 2001, p. B14.

23. Shai Oster, "China's Boom Snarls Traffic in 60-Mile Jam," *Wall Street Journal*, August 25, 2010, p. A7.

24. "Beijing to Be Turned into a Metropolis," *Hong Kong Standard*, August 3, 1983.

25. Yushi Li, "Hong Kong," *Population Today*, Population Reference Bureau, Washington, D.C., December 1996, p. 7.

26. Edwin O. Reishauer, *The Japanese*, Belknap Press, Cambridge, Mass., 1978, p. 25.

27. Population Reference Bureau, 2009, op. cit.

28. *Demographia World Urban Area and Population Projections*, 2009, op. cit.

29. T.R. Reid, "Japan's Housing: Pricy, Chilly, and Toilet Poor," *Washington Post*, March 4, 1991, p. A9.

30. James Sterngold, "Life in a Box: Japanese Question Fruits of Success," *New York Times*, January 2, 1994, p. A6.

31. J. John Palen, "Singapore," in Willem van Vliet (ed.), *International Handbook of Housing*, Greenwood Press, Westport, Conn., 1989, chap. 20.

32. Population Reference Bureau 2009, op. cit.

33. Evan Ramstad, "South Korean Home Prices Spiral Higher," *Wall Street Journal*, Dec. 20, 2006, p. B6.

CHAPTER 16

African and Latin American Urbanization

Men come together in cities for security; they stay together for the good life.
Aristotle

OUTLINE

Introduction
Africa
    Challenges
    Responses
    Regional Variations
Urban Development
    Early Cities
    Colonial Period
    Indigenous African Cities
    Contemporary Patterns
    Social Composition of African Cities
    Ethnic and Tribal Bonds
    Status of Women
    Differences from the Western Pattern
Latin America: An Urban Continent
Spanish Colonial Cities
    Colonial Organization
    Physical Structure
Recent Developments
    Urban Growth
    Economic Change
    Urban Characteristics
    Crime
    Shantytowns
    Future of Settlements
    Maquiladoras

Myth of Marginality
A Success Story
Summary

INTRODUCTION

This chapter examines patterns of urbanism, and urbanization in Africa and Latin America. Although geographically and socially different they share rapid rates of urbanization. As globalization increases, their futures and ours become ever more closely linked.

AFRICA

Africa, with a billion inhabitants, is currently the least urbanized of the continents. As of 2010, only 38 percent of its inhabitants lived in urban places. At the same time Africa is the continent with the highest rate of increase in urban population. In 1950 only two African cities had populations greater than a million. By 2000, there were 37 such cities. Lagos, Nigeria, according to estimates, has between 9 and 18 million inhabitants, and one United Nations projection even said it would be the third-largest city in the world by 2010.[1] This clearly is an overstatement, but African cities are dramatically expanding. The number of city dwellers multiplied tenfold between 1950 and 2000, and another doubling is expected by 2020. Two-thirds of today's African urban dwellers live in slums.[2] The Lagos slum, known as "The Jungle," is said to have 6 million inhabitants. Birthrates are collectively the world's highest at 36 per 1,000. As of 2010 the average number of births per woman in sub-Saharan Africa was 5.3. Niger has the world's highest birthrate with 7.4 children per woman.[3] (The North American number of births per woman is 2.) Sub-Saharan cities are growing by an average of almost 6 percent a year—a rate that doubles the cities every 12 years.

Challenges

Everyone acknowledges that Africa faces serious challenges and problems. The most serious of these is AIDS. Life expectancy rates in Africa have actually dropped due to the scourge of AIDS. Life expectancy in sub-Saharan Africa has dropped to 51 years, far below that of any other world area.[4] A decade ago it was 55 years. In the 29 African countries hardest hit by AIDS, life expectancy is now seven years lower than it would be without AIDS.[5] Africa accounts for only 13 percent of the world's population but 69 percent of the cases of HIV infection. Over 30 million Africans are HIV positive and more than 11 million children have lost one or both parents to AIDS.

The effect of AIDS was initially felt most heavily in the cities of sub-Saharan Africa, where in some countries a quarter of the working-age population is infected with HIV. In the cities the death of workers due to AIDS is decreasing productivity, increasing operating costs, and decreasing markets. AIDS is severely disrupting agricultural production as well. The Food and Agriculture Organization (FAO) projects that by 2020 16 million more sub-Saharan agricultural workers will die.[6]

Most HIV infection in Africa is heterosexually transmitted. In Africa, unlike elsewhere, more women than men are infected, perhaps 1.3 women for every man. One reason for this is that women contract the disease younger and are more likely to become infected during any given exposure. Sub-Saharan Africa's population was projected to more than triple by 2030. However, the AIDS epidemic that is ravaging the continent almost certainly will lower these estimates. South Africa gives an example of the effect of the devastation in one country: 17 percent of the adult population is estimated to be HIV positive. As of 1990 life expectancy for a child born in South Africa was age 60. Life expectancy for a child born in South Africa in 2010 is expected to be just 55 years.[7] This is actually an improvement over the last decade.

A second problem facing many sub-Saharan countries has been their economic policies. The U.N. says, "Africa is the only region in the world without a true newly industrializing economy."[8] By a decade ago, government economic policies had driven most African economies below their level of 20 years earlier. The combination of war, government policies, drought, and desert encroachment resulted in per capita food production as of 2000 that was 20 percent lower than it was in 1970. Although nearly self-sufficient in food in 1970, today sub-Saharan Africa has to import one-fifth of its grain requirements. As a consequence, when drought strikes, its effects are far more severe than might otherwise be the case. Today, some 150 million people in 22 countries face hunger and malnourishment.

The third problem facing much of Sub-Saharan Africa other than South Africa is unstable and/or unresponsive governments. Parliaments frequently have little real power and governments frequently change by military coup. Personal rule is common. Corruption in many countries also is endemic. Nigeria and the Democratic Republic of the Congo have long been viewed as prime examples. Although there are notable exceptions, venal government officials

Figure 16.1   Map of Africa

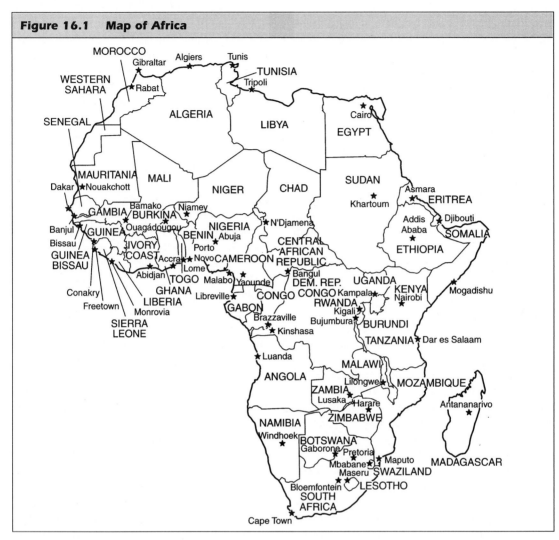

too often have put augmenting their personal wealth ahead of the national good.

Responses

There are signs that the future may be brighter. New, lower-cost AIDS drugs are being introduced and government AIDS programs are becoming more responsive. Politically, South Africa is now a stable multiracial nation. Population control is spreading, and many African nations are undergoing real economic reform. Across the continent governments have taken tough economic steps to make exchange rates

reflect reality, end unenforceable price controls, and tighten monetary policies. Inefficient and corrupt state industries are being sold off, and farmers, who make up 80 percent of most societies, are being permitted to sell at market prices. The countries that instituted the most extensive reform policies are enjoying the strongest resurgence in economic performance. The downside is that freeing up domestic markets is creating major economic disparities within countries. More advanced regions and ethnic groups with education and infrastructure are doing far better than more backward regions. Cities are almost always doing better than the countryside. Still in the continent's largest nation, Nigeria, nine-tenths of the population live on less than $2 per day.[9]

Regional Variations

Africa has some 54 separate nations, and African cities vary greatly, the major regional distinction being between the cities of North Africa and those of sub-Saharan Africa. North Africa is the most urbanized of the African regions. All the countries bordering the Mediterranean Sea have between two-fifths and three-fifths of their populations in places of 20,000 or more inhabitants. This is not surprising when one considers the great civilizations this region has produced and its superior location on the Mediterranean. Away from the coast much of the land of North Africa is either mountainous or arid desert and hardly suited for urban growth (the Nile Valley being the obvious exception). Thus the population is highly concentrated in a limited area.

West and Central Africa lie in the middle range of African urbanization—ranging from 10 percent in Burundi to 84 percent in Gabon.[10] The larger cities are located along, or within easy access to, the coast. Their founding and development can almost always be tied to their role as colonial entrepôt cities. Of the West African countries, oil-rich Nigeria, 158 million inhabitants, is the largest and has by far the most cities. Nigeria's population could double to 307 million by 2050. East Africa has always been the least urbanized part of the continent. It does not have a tradition of cities. Tiny Djibouti is by far the most urban at 76 percent, while Uganda is only 13 percent urban. In Kenya, 18 percent, and in Tanzania, 25 percent of the population lives in cities.

Virtually none of what can be said regarding the rest of sub-Saharan Africa applies to South Africa. The Republic of South Africa is by far the most industrialized nation on the continent, with just over half of its population in urban places. In terms of economic position, South Africa, with its gold reserves and indus-

trial base, is, in spite of recent economic difficulties, the continent's greatest economic power. South Africa now is a multiracial society with its third black president and its former policy of *apartheid,* or forced racial segregation, behind it. Still, within South Africa the economy remains heavily influenced by whites, and neighborhoods remain largely racially segregated.

URBAN DEVELOPMENT

Early Cities

Until recent decades, a reading of the literature on Africa gave the impression that there were few, if any, indigenous African cities south of the Sahara. This was due partially to a biased colonial mentality that did not admit the possibility that "backward natives" were capable of building cities and partially to a lack of serious research on African history. Muslim scholars also have been prone to minimize the contributions of black Africa. For instance, Hamdan suggests that "historic (or ancient) capitals are confined to Arab Africa and that 'Native' (or medieval) capitals are in fact a transition between the historical and colonial capitals. . . . Culturally, they are universally associated in one way or another with intrusive, alien influences, mainly Arab and generally Asian."[11] The reality is that Africa did produce substantial cities, some of which had considerable importance, especially during the Ghana, Mali, and Songhay empires of West Africa (roughly the 11th to late 16th centuries).

Of all African cities, those of North Africa have the longest urban traditions. Alexandria was founded by its namesake, Alexander the Great, in 332 B.C., but settlements on that location go back at least another 1,000 years. The North African city of Carthage, until it was utterly destroyed, was the greatest rival of Rome. During the height of the Roman Empire, North Africa was dotted with many important cities, some of which may have contained as much as 25 percent of the population of their regions.[12]

With the decline of the Roman Empire most of them disappeared—although, again as in Europe, newer cities now sometimes sit over the ancient ruins.

Elsewhere in Africa, many cities were first built during the revival of trade in the 10th century. Trade benefited not only North African cities such as Fez and Algiers but also sub-Saharan towns, including Kano in northern Nigeria. The Yoruba towns of southwest Nigeria also emerged at about this time, as did caravan centers such as Timbuktu. During the following centuries a number of West African kingdoms created capitals, but most of these capitals had short histories. Segou in Mali, Labe in Guinea, Zinder in Niger, and Kumasi in Ghana all rose and fell. These cities served their kingdoms primarily as market and trade centers.

Then, as now, East African cities were less numerous, with the towns found generally along the coast of the Indian Ocean. Present cities such as Mogadishu in Somalia and Mombassa in Kenya prospered as trading centers; trading in goods and slaves from the interior for shipment to Arabia.

Colonial Period

Until the late 19th century, Europeans showed little interest in colonization. Cape Town in the Republic of South Africa, for example, was only established by the Dutch East India Company as a naval supply station to provide meat, fresh produce, and water to the Dutch ships on the way to the Indies. European seizure of land in black Africa rapidly accelerated during the last quarter of the 19th century. Britain, France, Germany, Belgium, and Portugal all rushed in to carve up the continent into colonies.

Most major African cities of the present are the products of this colonialism since each colony had to have an administrative capital. Cities founded during the colonial period, with the dates of their founding, are Accra, Ghana (1876); Abidjan, Ivory Coast (1903); Port Harcourt, Nigeria (1912); Yaoundé, Cameroon

(1889); Kampala, Uganda (1890); Nairobi, Kenya (1899); and Johannesburg, South Africa (1886). Of the major settlements founded during this period, Addis Ababa in Ethiopia (1886) and Omdurman in Sudan (1885) were the only major indigenous rather than colonial creations.

The colonial city was organized around the central district, which in addition to stores and other business offices also included the administrative offices of the colonial government. Streets were usually wide and crossed at right angles in a grid pattern. A description of colonial Stanleyville (now Kisangani) is typical:

> The physical layout of the town could be seen as both an expression and a symbol of the relations between Africans and Europeans. European residential areas were situated close to, and tended to run into, the area of administrative offices, hotels, shops, and other service establishments, while African residential areas were strictly demarcated and well removed from the town centre.[13]

Spatial location thus reflected power within colonial society.[14] Without significant industrialization, central residence was preferred. Africans who worked in the European center were in effect commuters from suburban locations—although in such cases the suburbs were high-density indigenous communities. This is, of course, the reverse of the pattern in American industrial cities, where the poorest lived in the inner city.

Until 50 years ago, most African cities were relatively small. Nairobi, until thirty years ago one of the most pleasant of all African cities, had a population of only 33,000 in 1930. The population jumped to 200,000 in the 1950s, and today it is estimated to be between 3 and 4 million. The pattern is similar, and in many cases even more spectacular, in other African cities. Kinshasa, for example, has tripled its population in the last two decades. In spite of these increases, Africa still remains—as has been noted—the least urbanized of the world's major regions.

Indigenous African Cities

In West Africa the most noted cities of strictly African origin are the Yoruba cities of Nigeria. For years scholars have debated whether historically these were true cities or extremely large agglomerations of basically agricultural villages. The literature refers to them as "rural cities," "city villages," or "agrotowns." In any case, the Yoruba cities had the largest populations in sub-Saharan Africa before the colonial period. Ibadan as of 1850 had roughly 70,000 inhabitants. In East Africa many of the functions of towns, such as markets, took place at permanent sites, although residence was not one of these sites' functions.[15]

Ecologically, indigenous cities were not as sharply differentiated as colonial cities. In the indigenous city the main focus was the central market, which commonly was quite large and frequently out of doors. Nearby were the quarters of the chief or ruling prince. The main mosque is also centrally located in Muslim cities. Historically, the quarters of the lesser chiefs and nobles surrounded this central core. These areas contained not only the nobles but also their retainers, soldiers, followers, and servants. Each quarter was a self-contained area within the larger city. Much of this legacy persists today in cities such as Addis Ababa.

Quarters were divided on the basis of tribal or religious affiliation—not by social class, as in America. Walls and gates sometimes separated the quarters from one another. Within a quarter, there was no overall plan or scheme. Streets wound in an irregular pattern and were for walking or animal traffic, since the lanes were narrow. Structures were rarely more than two stories high and were constructed of local materials. Congestion was common.

As these indigenous towns came under the control of colonial powers, an administrative area on the European style was frequently appended to the periphery of the old city, and a major road or two would be cut through the old city to connect its center with the offices of

Traffic in Lagos, Nigeria, is frequently stalled in massive traffic jams. George Osodi/AP Images

the colonial administrators. Rarely did the indigenous city and the colonial city blend. Though existing side by side, they frequently even followed different laws, with Western legal systems applying only in the European quarters. During the first half of the 20th century the European quarters expanded to include modern commercial and business districts. In a few cases, the modern city came completely to surround the old city. The Casbah in Algiers, for example, has long been completely enclosed by a modern city initially created by the French during their colonial occupation.

Contemporary Patterns

Primate Cities. The term *primate city* fits the pattern of urbanization found in most nations of sub-Saharan Africa. For example, well over half of Kenya's urban population is found in Nairobi; 83 percent of Mozambique's in Maputo; half of Tanzania's in Dar es Salaam; and half of Zimbabwe's in Harare. Moreover, the importance of the primate city is increasing. Cities—and most particularly the capital cities—are the dominant economic force, the seats of government, the cultural centers, and the hubs of transportation and communication networks. The primate city is the manufacturing center, the break-of-bulk transportation node, the major market, and the financial center. Imported capital-intensive technologies often provide only a limited number of jobs.[16]

The importance of the primate cities is heightened by the economic separation of the major city from its surrounding countryside. Africa even today is noted for a break between the modernizing city and the tribal "bush." Urban influences are concentrated in the cities themselves. Going into the bush can take someone not only away from built-up areas but also away from the influence of the city.

In Africa the city is the incubator of social change; it is where the independence movements took root. It was in the urban townships rather than the countryside where Nelson Mandela's ANC (African National Congress) gained its strength. More than on any other continent, the African city not only towers over the countryside; it controls it economically, educationally, politically, and socially.

Squatter Slums. Squatter settlements or shantytowns are a fact of city life of every growing African city, from Casablanca in the north to Lusaka in the south. They house one-third of the total urban population. Most governments simply do not have the resources to engage in massive housing programs. Moreover, improvements are in a sense counterproductive, since improvements act as magnets drawing ever more rural newcomers.

The increasing low-income urban populations cannot pay even the minimal rents that standard built housing would require. Food and clothing generally absorb at least two-thirds of a newcomer's income. That doesn't leave much for extras such as decent housing. Shantytowns thus will be part of the urban scene for years to come.

Social Composition of African Cities

Sociologist Louis Wirth's view of the city as a place where social relations are dominated by the labor market and contacts with others are superficial, impersonal, and transitory is not accurate as a description of African urbanism. There is no question that some of the disorganizing aspects of urbanism posited by Wirth can be found in any large African city. Family life sometimes breaks down, and prostitution, which contributes to the rapid spread of AIDS, is common. Cities have a disproportionate number of males. The situation is reasonable in West African cities, where in the cities there is a ratio of roughly 95 females to every 100 urban males. However, in parts of East Africa there are only 75 females per 100 urban males. Historically, absence of family is associated with drunkenness, gambling, prostitution, and crime. The situation is not unlike that found in the towns of the American West before the arrival of the homesteaders with their families.

Problems of psychological maladjustment to city life appear as a rule to be far rarer than Wirth's thesis would suggest. Since a major proportion of the townspeople were once migrants themselves, almost all newcomers know someone in the city who will take them in and who will help them adjust to urban life. Family ties and wider kinship ties are surprisingly strong and resilient to urban pressures. Relatives are expected to take the newcomers in and provide for their basic needs until they can get on their feet. A migrant who does get a job is then expected to contribute to providing for the family.

The pull of the town is not uniform for all groups. The Masai of Kenya, although pres-

Box 16.1   A Case Study of an Indigenous City

Probably the most notable African indigenous city is Addis Ababa, Ethiopia. Although founded in 1886 at the height of European colonial expansion, the city is an authentically African creation.* Addis Ababa (the name means "New Flower") was not originally intended to be a permanent city. Rather, it was founded by Emperor Menelik II (1844–1913) as a temporary capital. Having no urban tradition, the Ethiopian emperors moved their capital from time to time as military factors, weather, or exhaustion of local resources (food and firewood) dictated. Addis Ababa—which was Menelik's eighth capital—was laid out as an armed camp. The emperor chose for his *guebi,* or palace, a hill above the northern thermal springs and then allotted various surrounding quarters, known as *sefers,* to his leading nobles. Social organization was feudalistic. Each *sefer*—literally, "camp"—included the residence of an important noble plus all the noble's warriors, troops, retainers, and slaves and their families. No distinctly upper- or lower-class areas were initially developed, as was the case in colonial cities.

Early visitors to Addis Ababa universally commented that it resembled a large straggling village more than a city.** Contributing to this impression of a large floating camp were fluctuations in the city's population. The normal population around 1910 was roughly 60,000; during the rainy season, it sometimes dropped to as low as 40,000.† When important chiefs came to the capital, they brought their entire armies and households with them. There are reports of chiefs who brought 100,000 to 150,000 people with them, and even as late as 1915 it was not unusual for a governor to bring 30,000 to 50,000 people along as a personal guarantee of safety.

As the city grew, its eastern side surrounding the palace gradually developed into the administrative center, while the western zone surrounding the old marketplace, or *mercado,* became the commercial center. Because the ruling Amhara tribe despised any type of commercial activity or trade, business activities were relegated to subordinate tribes. Emperor Haile Selassie I ruled the country from 1916 to 1973. (The Italians occupied Ethiopia from 1936 to 1941. They envisioned Addis Ababa as the capital of their sub-Saharan African empire.) From 1973 to 1991 Ethiopia was a totalitarian Marxist state continually at war with its northern province of Eritrea, now a separate nation. Today it has an elected government and it is rebuilding after decades of stagnation.

Although its present population is over 2.5 million, Addis Ababa still retains much of its non-urban character. As of the 1990s only 10 percent of the homes had running water or bathrooms.†† Some housing units are still constructed of *chica*—a mixture of earth, straw, and water plastered around eucalyptus poles. The ever-present and fast-growing eucalyptus trees also serve to give the city a small-town appearance by masking the houses. The trees do a yeoman service, since they provide firewood for heating and cooking, lumber for building, and wood for furniture. Even the leaves are used in baking the Ethiopian bread called *injera.* The rural feeling of the city is also partially due to the fact that Addis Ababa is a city of rural migrants. Three-quarters of the inhabitants were not born in the city. Various famines from the 1980s to the present encouraged movement to the city.

In terms of its functional base, Addis Ababa is still primarily a political and administrative center. All major Ethiopian government agencies, all foreign embassies, African Union headquarters, and the United Nations Economic Commission for Africa are located in the capital. Recently there have been noticeable increases in the transportation, communications, manufacturing, and education sectors. Industrialization is growing but still limited. Transportation to and from the city is still difficult, particularly for goods. A sole narrow gage railroad connects Addis Ababa and the port of Djibouti.

At the beginning of the 21st century Addis Ababa remains both a traditional city and a modern city. It is both an overgrown village and the headquarters of the United Nations Economic Commission for Africa. It has high-rise apartments, but still no sanitary sewers. It is a vibrant place whose contradictions mirror the continent.

* John Palen, "Urbanization and Migration in an Indigenous City: The Case of Addis Ababa," in Anthony Richmond and Daniel Kubat (eds.), *International Migration,* Sage Publications, London, 1976.

** Docteur Merab, *Impressions d'Ethiopie,* vol. 2, Leroux, Paris, 1921–1923, p. 11.

† Richard Pankhurst, "Notes on the Demographic History of Ethiopian Towns and Villages," *The Ethiopian Observer* 9:71, 1965.

†† J. T. Marlin, I. Ness, and S. T. Collins, *Book of World City Rankings,* Free Press, New York, 1986, p. 354.

sured by the Kenyan government to adopt modern ways, have consistently rejected town life in favor of their traditional rural culture. The Ila of Zambia have also rejected urbanization and modernization. Both tribes seem to be an embarrassment to their national governments because they don't want to "modernize." The Kenyan government plans to divide up the Masai communal lands and give each family individual plots. The United States government tried a similar program early in the 20th century to modernize the American Indians, with the result that many Indians lost their lands. The same fate may await the Masai.

Ethnic and Tribal Bonds

Urbanization is supposed to weaken traditional bonds, but it can be argued that urbanization in Africa has strengthened rather than weakened tribal identification.[17] Some immigrants, rather than being "detribalized," are "supertribalized" as a result of coming into contact with people from other cultures. Tribal origin often replaces kinship as a symbol of belonging. This is an expansion of identity from the parochial to the more general. The role tribal subsystems play in modernizing societies is analogous to that played by immigrant enclaves in the American city of several decades ago.

First, the tribal, ethnic, or other group introduces newcomers to others in the city and indoctrinates them in the ways of the city. Information on such matters as where to live and how to get a job is transmitted to migrants in order to aid their adaptation to the city.

Second, the subgroup, being originally itself a part of the rural culture, maintains within the city many rural customs and traditions. While learning the new ways, migrants still have some contact with their past.

Third, because migrants return to rural areas for periods of time, the customs and ways of the city (urbanism) are spread to villages—and thus patterns of urbanism are gradually being diffused throughout rural areas.

Kinship and ethnic-tribal affiliation provide bridges by which the migrant crosses into the urban arena. Being a member of a group gives a newcomer an immediate identification that everyone recognizes. It tells the newcomer how to behave, and it provides a more or less ready-made group of associates, friends, and even drinking partners. While tribalism may have negative effects in a country seeking to develop national loyalties, on the individual level one's tribal membership eases the adjustment of city life. A far less positive use of tribalism is national leaders' deliberate manipulation and exploitation of ethnic differences in order to stay in power. Ex-President Moi of Kenya, for example, was accused of instigating tribal bloodshed as part of a "divide and rule" strategy.[18]

Status of Women

It is difficult to make generalizations about the status of women, since this varies from country to country and from one tribal and cultural group to another. Still, it is generally safe to say that norms, attitudes, and values in Africa have a long history of strongly favoring male dominance. It is also clear that, regardless of other factors, cities are far more egalitarian in practice than the countryside. Urban populations are young, newer to urban life, and more flexible than their rural counterparts.

In rural villages, the position of women is set by custom; but in the city, with its new occupations and skills, the occupational structure is more flexible. New occupations in fields such as information technology are not sex defined. Skills and professional training of all sorts are usually in short supply, so that women who have had the benefit of education can generally use their training. On the other hand, women (or men, for that matter) without specific skills or abilities are likely to remain locked into poverty. While it is true that trained women participate in the social and economic life of the city to an extent unknown in the countryside, it is also true that poorer women without husbands fre-

Women have long played a major role in the market economy of West Africa. This is a micro-enterprise female shop owner in Kaneshie Market in Accra, Ghana. ©Richard Lord/The Image Works

quently have little alternative to prostitution and other marginal economic enterprises.

Women often are part of the informal self-employed sector. For many it is the only viable alternative to marriage.[19] In Ghana "mammy wagons" (small buses) dominate local transportation and 90 percent of the retailing of food and other goods is controlled and operated by women. Even in African Muslim cultures, where the status of females traditionally has been inferior, changes are taking place in the education of women and participation by women in national life. However, while the overall situation is improving, women have yet to attain equal status with men. No African nation at the time of this writing has a female head of government or any women in top policy-making positions. Women are underrepresented in the education system, with roughly two boys at school for every girl in most countries.[20]

Differences from the Western Pattern

The geographer William Hance assembled a number of characteristics differentiating be-

tween urban growth in Africa and urban growth in the West. The points of difference are:

1. The rates of growth, particularly of the major cities, are much more rapid in Africa. Some have achieved their present position in one-fifth to one-tenth the time required in western Europe.

2. There is less correlation—association—between the cities' rate of growth and the measures of economic growth in their countries.

3. The growth of urbanization is often not paralleled by a comparable revolution in the rural areas.

4. A less favorable ratio of population to resources in rural areas means that the push factor is more important than it was in Europe. That is, people pour into the cities not so much because the city needs workers, but because the countryside is overpopulated.

5. The linkage of some cities with their domestic hinterlands is less developed,

while the ties of these cities to the outside world and their dependence on it remains strong.

6. There is relatively less specialization in the African cities. The division of labor is less developed.

7. There are higher rates of unemployment. Here the European cities had the advantage of being able to drain off to the New World large numbers of people who might have become redundant. The African cities have no such convenient safety valve.

8. Differences in outlook and values may slow the adjustment to the city and reduce the tempo of its economic life, as, for example, the reliance on the extended family for support.

9. There is a dual tribal and Western structure in many African cities. Western patterns tend to dominate in the economic sphere, while in the family sphere traditional customs retain force.

10. Migrants to the town differ in several important respects: almost all are unskilled in urban occupations, their level of educational achievement is relatively lower though above average as far as the source areas are concerned, and almost all arrive without capital resources.

11. Heavier responsibility is placed on governments, local and national, to provide for the urban residents. In the West, private enterprise normally met the needs for new housing, while local governments had a tax base adequate to provide the public services. Not so in Africa, where the demands on government are far more onerous, and almost none are capable of meeting them.[21]

Overall, in spite of their problems, African cities are places of hope and enterprise.

LATIN AMERICA: AN URBAN CONTINENT

North Americans are presented a somewhat distorted image of Latin America. News media discussions of Latin America focus almost exclusively on drugs, violence, coups, illegal immigration, and economic problems. Even advertisements, such as those for Colombian coffee, portray an image of a peasant (Juan Valdez) leading a donkey. As a consequence many think of Latin America as an overwhelmingly rural continent. The facts are otherwise. Almost all sources indicate that Latin America (Mexico included) is 77 percent urban—or about as urban as the United States. However, the World Bank, which until 2005 used this figure, now says it overstates the urban population by including remote villages with 2,000 people as urban.[22] The World Bank suggests that 58 percent urban is more realistic.

Of the world's 10 largest urban places, possibly four are in Latin America: Mexico City and São Paulo at about 18 million each, and Rio de Janeiro and Buenos Aires with metro populations of roughly 12 million are just behind. Latin American cities are growing at a remarkable rate of 4 percent a year and suffer from the maladies of such fast growth.[23] Urban problems such as violent crime and infrastructure deterioration are especially severe. Metro São Paulo, for example, has about twice as many people as New York City, but its annual operating budget is one-tenth as large.

SPANISH COLONIAL CITIES

Latin America already had grand cities at the time the Pilgrims were beginning to learn from the Indians how to raise corn. In fact, all the Latin American metropolitan areas that had more than 1 million inhabitants in 1960—except Montevideo—were founded in the 16th century. However, while many of the cities have ancient roots, the bulk of their growth is very recent, a product of the last 40–50 years. The Spanish designed their colonial cities to be remarkably similar in both ecological plan and functional purpose. The purpose of the cities was to serve as administrative centers and garrison posts for the Spanish military forces. Growth and development over the centuries have blunted many of the original similarities, but elements of the first cities still remain.

Colonial Organization

Spanish colonial cities did not enjoy the substantial independence of the early English towns in North America. Socially and commercially, the early cities looked toward Spain rather than toward their own hinterland. Cities were placed on the land; they did not grow out of it. The city was the center from which the mining or agricultural hinterland was to be controlled and the funnel through which wealth was to flow to the mother country. Spanish policies had two objectives: "(1) to make the colonies into producers of gold, silver, and precious stones; and (2) to limit their consumption of manufactured goods strictly to those produced in Spain, shipped in convoys from Spanish ports, and destined for a few strongly fortified seaports, of which the principal ones were Vera Cruz, Cartagena, and Callao."[24] The effect of these policies was to throttle trade and commerce in Latin American cities under Spanish domination.

Unlike the North American colonies, the Latin American cities did not develop into commercial or manufacturing centers. The merchant, who enjoyed such a prominent position in the social structure of New England, did not have influence in the Spanish colonies. Spanish colonies lacked the middle-class base of English colonies. The seaports were heavily fortified entrepôts designed for receiving the manufactures of Spain in the annual convoys

and assembling the treasure that was to be shipped to Spain on the return voyage. The impact of this pattern can be seen today; most metropolitan areas are found on the coastline. The planned city of Brasilia is one exception to this rule.

The Spanish colonial government did everything possible to retain a rigid class system. One edict even reserved all the top administrative, religious, and political positions for *peninsulares,* or those born in Spain. Those born in the colonies, regardless of their wealth or family position, were relegated to secondary status—one factor that directly motivated local leaders to instigate the early 19th-century independence movements against Spain.

Physical Structure

Regulations of Charles V (1516–1556) and Philip II (1556–1598), eventually codified into the famous Laws of the Indies, specified how cities were to be organized. For example, cities were to follow a rectangular plan and be founded near rivers in a manner permitting expansion. However, as Hardoy points out, "Legislation only formalized a situation already perfectly defined in practice."[25] Historical and archaeological evidence suggests that among the pre-Columbian Aztec and Mayan civilizations the elites tended to live in the centers of the great cities. The pattern is confirmed by Bishop Landa's account, first published in 1566:

> Before the Spaniards had conquered that country, the natives lived together in towns in a very civilized fashion. . . . In the middle of the towns were their temples with beautiful plazas, and all around the temples stood the houses of the lords and the priests, and those of the most important people. Thus came the houses of the richest and of those who were held in the highest estimation next to these, and at the outskirts of the town were the houses of the lower class.[26]

Figure 16.2   Map of Latin America

Thus the pattern of spatial distribution by social class was set well before the Spaniards arrived. The pattern conforms to that suggested by Gideon Sjoberg for pre-industrial cities.[27] (See Chapter 2: The Emergence of Cities.)

Most Spanish settlements adhered to the classical model of a central *plaza mayor*. Around the central plaza were the cathedral and major government buildings. The *solares,* or house lots, were of uniform shape, and the city was laid out in a grid with intersections at right angles. Houses and grounds were surrounded by walls, and because of this the early cities frequently appeared to be more heavily inhabited than was actually the case. Fortunately, the grid layout of the cities offered considerable flexibility; the boundaries could be expanded as more room was needed. Additional grids were easily added. The focus on the central plaza meant that there were no markets, walls, or storehouses at the periphery of the city to impede expansion.

The large lots (which the law required be enclosed by walls) initially resulted in a relatively low population density. Later, subdivision of lots occurred, and this—along with cutting new streets midway between existing streets—allowed the city to increase its density with relative ease. Since the cities were to serve as fortified strong points performing administrative functions for the surrounding hinterland, they were not always ideally located from the standpoint of transportation; Mexico City, founded by the Aztecs and conquered by the Spanish in 1521, was located on an island in the middle of a lake.

Brazilian cities differed from the model just described in that they were not built to any standard plan such as that provided by the Laws of the Indies. Cities in Brazil were few and with small influence since the Portuguese, who colonized Brazil, unlike the Spaniards, preferred to live a semi-feudal existence on their estates in the country. Portuguese policy also kept towns such as Santos, Bahia, and Recife relatively small. Their splendid natural ports were open only to ships from Portugal, and this trade was not sufficient to turn these towns into real cities. By the 19th century, Rio de Janeiro was the undisputed political, economic, and cultural center of Brazil.

RECENT DEVELOPMENTS

The ecological complex of *population, organization, environment,* and *technology* (POET) (see Chapter 2) helps us understand urban changes. In pre-industrial Latin American cities, the elite preempted the more central areas for their residences, since these were the most accessible sites in an era of primitive transportation technology. Technological changes—automobiles, good roads, extension of power and sewage lines—have drastically reduced the attractiveness of the central city as a place of residence.

The automobile has permitted a degree of population dispersion that was impossible earlier. Advances in communication technology such as cell phones and the Internet mean that interrelated functions can be spatially separated without loss of contact and control. Upper-class and middle-class suburbanization are now found in Latin America on the North American pattern. Latin American cities have evolved toward elites living either in central-city luxury high-rises or in walled villas at urban edges.

Urban Growth

Urbanization in Latin America is currently proceeding at a phenomenal rate. As recently as 1950 only 39 percent of the population lived in places of 20,000 or more. What some consider the world's second and third largest urban places (Mexico City and São Paulo), plus the 10 million-plus cities of Rio de Janeiro and Greater Buenos Aires are all found in Latin America. Moderately high birthrates and dropping death rates mean Latin America is growing rapidly. As of 1950, the North American and Latin American populations were of equal

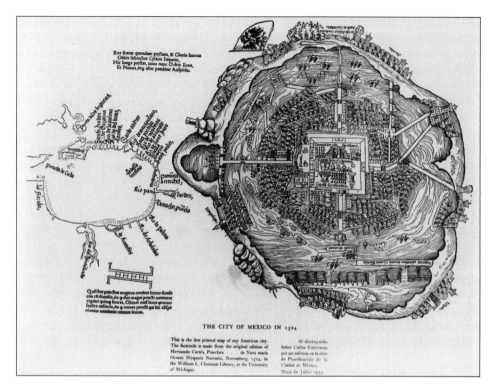

This 1524 map of Mexico City is the first printed map of any American city. Map Division/
New York Public Library

size. As of 2010, Latin America was over half again as large (585 million versus 349 million).[28] By 2025, United Nations projections foresee a Latin American population more than twice as large as that of North America. To put it another way, in 1930 Latin America had only one city of over 1 million persons (Mexico City); in 2000 it had over 50. Greatest growth has been in the very largest cities. Latin America is a continent of primate cities, with over half of its population in cities of more than 100,000 inhabitants.

Within the period of a lifetime, Latin America has been transformed from a rural, agriculturally oriented continent to one that is predominantly urbanized and urban oriented. Its process of urbanization, which took over a century in North America, has been compressed into decades.

Figures for the entire continent, of course, cloud variations among nations. The range of urbanization in Latin American countries is great. As of 2010 only 47 percent of the population in Guatemala was in urban places, while Argentina (91 percent), Chile (87 percent), Venezuela (88 percent), and Uruguay (94 percent) are more urban than the United States.[29] Over half of Uruguay's population lives in the capital city of Montevideo.

Taken as a whole, Latin America, even using the lower World Bank figures, is one of the world's more urbanized regions. It is far more urbanized than Asia or Africa. Latin American cities, and particularly the largest primate cities, are growing at a rate that outpaces their ability to provide urban services and employment. During the 21st century, Latin America's city growth will increasingly come not from rural-to-urban migration but from the natural increase of births over deaths. Fertility rates are declining, but the region's young population profile assures growth for half a century.[30]

Economic Change

The biggest success story in Latin America is Brazil, with its political stability and strong growth rate. Sometime after 2014, Brazil is forecasted to become the world's fifth largest economy, surpassing Britain and France.[31] Rio de Janeiro will host the 2016 Olympics and the 2014 World Cup. On the brink of default in 2002, Brazil now lends money to the International Monetary Fund.

It is sometimes argued that if rural life can be made more attractive, people will be less likely to abandon rural areas for the opportunities of the city. However, while agriculture needs to be made more productive, it makes little economic sense to try to hold the farmers in the country. The costs of modernizing the rural sector are high, particularly when squatter settlements in the cities also need major resources. The same amount of money often can do more for more people if it is spent in the city than if it is spent in the country. Rural electrification is far more expensive than providing electricity for urban slum dwellers. In São Paulo, for instance, 400,000 shanty dwellers' only water source is contaminated with human waste.

Because funds are limited, "community development" often is more effectively directed toward urban populations, who by their very presence in the city have already indicated a willingness to make changes. One of the few rural economic growth sectors has been tourism in coastal areas. In order to increase income from tourism, Mexico (and others) have established resort cities where villages once stood (e.g., Cancún).

For the majority of ruralites, the move to the city is a wise decision. Even low urban standards are likely to represent an improvement in quality of life. On the other hand, what is good for migrants personally is often a problem for the city and nation. The in-migration of ever more peasants simply compounds already severe urban problems. Globalization increasingly links the economies of Latin America to what happens outside the region. For example, the recession beginning in 2007 both severely cut export revenues and decreased the monies sent home by Latin Americans working in the United States.

Urban Characteristics

In Latin America, for years, migration to cities has been more permanent and less seasonal than in other developing regions. The city-bound migrants, like those elsewhere in the world, tend to be mostly young adults. Older people are less prone to leave villages or rural areas for the opportunities and bright lights of the city. Migration of young persons, plus the population explosion—which, of course, adds only young people to the population—means that there are proportionately few people of working age in the urban population. The impression of outsiders that "everyone seems so young" is borne out by the empirical data: some 30 percent of the Latin American population is under fifteen years of age. (The 2010 figure for North America is 20 percent.)

The cities of most developing countries have more males than females; Latin America, on the contrary, has more females than males. In this respect, it is more similar to economically developed Western areas. While there is general agreement that there are more females, there is no agreement about why this is the case. Perhaps the greater degree of urbanization and economic development in Latin America, compared with developing countries elsewhere in the world, accounts for the difference.

Crime

Crime is an unfortunate reality in many Latin American cities. São Paulo, for example, has five times the murder rate of New York. In Mexico drug-related crime is endemic. Police forces are often either ineffectual, corrupt, or both. The wealthy provide security for themselves through private guards, while in slums armed vigilantes and gangs take over entire communities. Mexico City alone has some 1,500 gangs, and in half the cities of Latin America there are whole neighborhoods where police fear to go.[32] Rio de Janeiro has a long-running war between police and drug gangs, and police death squads have been charged with the deaths of hundreds of street children a year. Rio is beautiful, but it is also violent. The national government is pushing to reduce crime before the 2016 Olympics.

Shantytowns

In addition to central-core slums, squatter settlements ring most of the great cities of Latin America. Some observers emphasize the squalor and disorganization of the squatter settlements; some argue that these shantytown settlements are in effect evolving into reasonable low-income suburban housing areas. Frequently, it seems that what a writer describes is not shaped as much by what he or she sees as by the writer's philosophy and political beliefs. There is no unanimity, as the next pages show.

What is agreed upon is that the peripheral slums grow like mushrooms (in Chile they are called *poblaciones callampas,* which means "mushroom towns"). They grow both because of the population explosion and the migration of peasants from the countryside searching for a better life. The number of squatters in São Paulo, Brazil, is estimated to be between 500,000 and 1.5 million. One-quarter of Lima, Peru's population lives in *barriadas* or squatter settlements. In Caracas, the capital of oil rich Venezuela, over 35 percent of the metro area population is living in squatter settlements, while in Bogotá, Colombia, more than half the population lives in neighborhoods considered illegal by officials. (In Bogotá, unlike elsewhere, the illegal occupants are not really squatters since they technically own the land upon which their illegal "pirate developments" have been built.)

Perhaps one-third of Mexico City's inhabitants live in slums and squatter settlements, where it is not uncommon for entire families to live in one room. Many live in the aptly named "lost cities" surrounding Mexico City. Mexico City's "Netz," or Netzahualcoyotl, houses over 3 million persons. Forty years ago it was a dry lake bed; today it is a city of homes made of cinder blocks, crates, corrugated metal, and plastic sheets. Periodically, attempts are made to shut down squatter settlements; they all fail.[33] Half of Mexico's workforce, and most of the shanty dwellers, are in the informal economy. Virtually everyone over the age of 12 contributes to family incomes.[34] Adults work in construction, home manufacturing, vending, domestic service, or one-person businesses such as repairing shoes. The average wage is about $4 a day.[35] Children peddle cigarettes, gum, newspapers, or trinkets on the street. Everyone works because every peso is necessary for survival.

Future of Settlements

It is clear that shantytown squatter settlements will be part of the Latin American urban scene for the foreseeable future. As long as the urban population continues to increase because of high birthrates and migration to the cities, the cities will continue to add more people than they can house. The Peruvian government has been more candid than most in admitting that it is unable to reduce the urban housing deficit because public investment must be directed toward developing national objectives, but the problem is similar elsewhere. Mexico has to pay 60 percent of its income for debt payment.

Already-high levels of drug gang and other violence may become more common in marginal settlements. Clashes between squatters and police often occur in places such as Mexico City when landlords, as land prices escalate, attempt to evict squatters they previously ignored.

Box 16.2   Mexico City

Urban change can be grasped more easily by looking at its impact on an individual city. Mexico City had one-quarter of New York's metro population in 1950 (2.9 million, compared with 12.3 million). Currently, greater Mexico City has 18 million inhabitants. Mexico City receives 1,000 new immigrants every day. Three-quarters of the city's residents earn less than $7 a day.*

The pattern and problems Mexico City represents are, unfortunately, not unique. Even with its high crime rates Mexico City attracts newcomers seeking employment in its 300,000 factories. These factories, plus 4 million motor vehicles without pollution controls and burning leaded gas, result in 6,000 tons of gas and soot pollution falling on the city daily. Since Mexico City is geographically located in a basin, thermal inversions seriously exacerbate an already major smog problem. The thin air is fouled by 5.5 million tons of contaminants a year.** In practical terms this works out to a pound and a half of pollutants a day for every man, woman, and child in the city. Or to put it another way, every resident regardless of age receives the equivalent damage of smoking two packs of cigarettes a day.

One out of every five Mexicans lives in the Mexico City area, making garbage disposal an impossible problem. Each day Mexico City produces 14,000 tons of garbage but can dispose of only 8,000 tons. Another 2,000 to 3,000 tons go into landfills, and the rest sit in open dumps that are the breeding ground of some 115 million rats.† The dumps also are a source of income for poor scavengers who sift the refuse in search of recyclable or salable items.

Whether or not greater Mexico City will eventually reach its projected 26 million persons, or only 20 million, it is a sure bet that the populations of Mexico City and other developing-country metropolitan areas are going to continue to increase for the next several decades. No matter what the eventual figure is, the infrastructure is not up to handling even the present population. Even without natural disasters such as the 1985 earthquake that killed 10,000 people, the city's overloaded transportation systems, sewers, and schools will not be able to cope. Already, 2 million Mexico City children do not have access to a school. Unless a miracle occurs, there is no way that services can adequately be provided for the growing population. Badly overstrained systems simply cannot even handle the present load—not in Mexico City, and not elsewhere.

*. Linda Robinson and Lucy Conger, "The Monster of Mexico," *U.S. News & World Report,* July 27, 1997, p. 45.

**. William Branigan, "Bracing for Pollution Disaster," *Washington Post,* November 28, 1988, p. 14–A.

†. David De Voss, "Mexico City's Limits," in Andrew Maguire and Janel Welsh Brown (eds.), *Bordering on Trouble,* Adler and Adler, Bethesda, Md., 1986, p. 21.

Activist attempts to organize the vast but largely still-silent urban proletariat have had only limited success. Manuel Castells has argued that national governments may sometimes support land invasions by squatters in return for political support from the poor. In effect, the establishment makes a political deal with squatters.[36]

One of the better squatter settlements is Villa El Salvadore, an hour's drive from central Lima. In 1971, a bloody confrontation between landless peasants and police led the Peruvian government to offer the squatters a large tract of desert land then used by the army. Rather than allowing chaotic growth, the government together with squatter leaders laid out a city plan with equal-size lots.

Today, Villa El Salvadore has over 400,000 residents and is the fifth-largest city in Peru. More importantly, residents not only pitched in to build their own homes but also built the city's water and electric systems. They constructed 32 of the 34 schools and five of the nine health clinics.[37] Elected neighborhood residential groups have improved educational opportunities to the extent that 98 percent of school-age children graduate from primary school and 51 percent from high school; both statistics are well above the national average. Women's groups have set up milk and vaccination projects and have helped set up some 250 communal kitchens in which 20 to 30 women pool their money to buy food and take turns cooking.

In generalizing, it has to be remembered that squatter settlements differ markedly not only in their physical appearance and services available but also in the social composition of the groups inhabiting them. Usually, the newest settlements are most disorganized and ramshackle; some others that have existed longer are highly organized "slums of hope." Some squatter settlements even have areas of well-built homes.

Maquiladoras

Fast-growing shantytowns can be seen just south of the United States border where American and other mostly foreign-owned firms have set up *maquiladoras* or assembly plants to cheaply produce goods for the United States market. Some *maquiladoras* work with toxic substances that would require expensive precautions and clean up in the United States. Factories pay higher wages than elsewhere in Mexico, but living costs are also higher. Since *maquiladora* workers cannot live on the average wage of $2 hour, they must moonlight in the informal economy in order to survive.

Mexico now has over 4,000 *maquiladora* plants with more than 1.6 million workers. Most workers live in makeshift shanty housing with water, sewage, and health problems so severe that Mexican health and welfare officials have refused to visit them. The Mexican National Water Commission reports that border towns treat less than 35 percent of the sewage generated daily, and 12 percent of the people have no reliable access to clean water.[38] A third of the homes are not connected to sewers. Drug-related crime is common, but worse is the brutal abduction, rape, and murder of hundreds of female workers known as "las muertas de Juerez." Amnesty International reported in 2005 that as of that date 370 bodies had been found and 400 other women who came to work in the *maquiladoras* were still missing.[39] Still they come because there are jobs. Border cities in recent years have been

wracked by drug gang violence. In 2010 Juarez had over 3,000 murders.

Myth of Marginality

Scholars differ when discussing the way the inhabitants of shantytowns live. The traditional view is that these inhabitants are set apart from the other city residents not only by their poverty but by their marginality and traditional rural orientation.[40] Their rural backgrounds and continued rural ties mean that they remain essentially peasants, but peasants who by force of circumstance live in urban areas. They are in, but not of, the city. The implicit, if not explicit, assumption here is that the problem is how to integrate these non-urban people into a complex modern economic system.

The view of the city as a disorganizing force is part of an intellectual tradition going back to the Chicago School of sociology and its concern with problems of assimilating immigrants into the inner-city slums of North America. Louis Wirth (as discussed in Chapter 7: Urban Lifestyles) defines "urbanism" as the mode of life of people who live in cities and are subject to their influences. These influences, it is said, act to destroy primary groups, weaken family ties, loosen the bonds of kinship, and lessen neighborliness. Disruption of family life, rejection of traditional religion, delinquency and alienation among the young, and a generally fragmented social world were some of the consequences associated with life in the slums of North American industrial cities.

The alternative position is that the rural character of the immigrants is considerably overemphasized, and that problems of adjustment are not severe. What sets squatters apart is not their different values or aspirations, but their lack of opportunity. For example, the largest study of an LDC city—sponsored by the World Bank and called "The City Study"—covered 3,000 householders in Bogotá. It indicated that the behavior of city dwellers in developed and developing countries is much more similar than was once believed.[41] In-migrants to Bogotá, for example, are not worse off than the rest of the population. In fact, they earn higher wages than non-migrants in all income categories. Moreover, informal-sector jobs, such as domestic service, showed wage rates as high as or higher than formal-sector factory worker jobs. The poor, however, were much worse off than the well off, with the lowest 40 percent of the population earning less than 12 percent of the total national income.[42]

The most important finding of the City Study was that even the very poor newcomers to the city showed economic rationality.[43] There was little support for the widely held belief that the poor had a distinctly short-term orientation or culture of poverty that made them unable to defer gratification or plan for the future. The City Study showed that the poor, like others, act to maximize utility. That the poor act rationally does not, however, necessarily mean that they will be economically successful. In spite of their best efforts, they often remain trapped by their poverty.

An unanswered question is how the squatter or slum dweller, after the initial period of adjustment, will respond to his or her relative deprivation, compared with affluent city dwellers. Will the slum dweller accept semi-permanent poverty? News reports from El Salvador, Nicaragua, Brazil, and Mexico suggest not.

A Success Story

Discussions of developing-world cities often have a depressing sameness. Thus, it is useful to look at an out-and-out success. Curitiba, Brazil, a city of 1.6 million, shares many of the problems of the continent: it has increased elevenfold in the past 50 years, and it has an average family income of less than $100 a week. Nonetheless, Curitiba is a green, clean, and very livable city. Its urban success story began 25 years ago when the mayor, rather than building highway overpasses and shopping centers like other Brazilian cities, advocated pedestrian

malls and recycled buildings. Today the center of the city is the *calcadao*, or big sidewalk, which provides 49 blocks of pedestrian streets clogged with shoppers and strollers. A block long arcade opened in 1992 boasts of 80 shops open 24 hours a day.[44] Crime is minimal. People come into the city center on a system of express buses running in separate high-speed bus lanes.

To help rural migrants adjust and learn new trades, old city buses have been converted into mobile vocational classrooms. Street children can enter an apprentice program in which they work half-time in return for schooling, food, and a living stipend. Since garbage trucks can't get to those living in the hilly shantytowns, the poor are encouraged to bring their garbage to the trucks. Twenty-pound bags of garbage can be exchanged for surplus eggs, butter, rice, and beans.[45] Curitiba isn't a miracle, but it does show that even without substantial outside funding ingenuity and common sense can do a great deal to turn around urban problems. There is hope.

What happens in Latin America is important to North Americans for practical as well as moral and ethical reasons. Questions of land reform and urban poverty in Asia or Africa are literally oceans away. Latin America, however, is a neighbor with whom, in the NAFTA era, we share an increasingly open land border. Also, Latinos are now the largest minority population in the United States. By choice or necessity, what occurs in Latin America is increasingly important to North America.

SUMMARY

Africa is the least urbanized of the continents, but has the highest rate of urban population increase. Africa, and especially sub-Saharan Africa, suffers from problems of the world's highest population increases, political corruption, and poor economic policies. However, the most dramatic problem is that of AIDS. Sub-Saharan Africa has two-thirds of the world's

AIDS cases, which translates to 30 million people who are HIV positive—all of whom may die as a result of the infection. Positive actions are being taken to reduce population growth and to move toward more realistic economic policies that recognize market effects, but corruption remains and the AIDS scourge continues.

North Africa is the most urbanized of Africa's regions, while East Africa is the least urbanized. North African cities go back to antiquity and West African kingdoms had urban places during the period of Muslim expansion. The majority of large contemporary sub-Saharan cities are the result of late 19th-century European colonialism. This is true of major cities such as Lagos, Kinshasa, Nairobi, and Johannesburg. During the same period the Yoruba of Nigeria created large urban places and Addis Ababa in Ethiopia developed as an indigenous city. Districts in indigenous cities were not as sharply differentiated by use as were neighborhoods in colonial cities.

Africa is characterized by massive primate capital cities that dominate their countries by being the centers of government, commerce, industry, and education. The size and external orientation of elites in the primary cities often economically and socially separates the primary city from its countryside. Squatter settlements are a standard part of the landscape. Governments lack the resources to provide standard housing to rapidly expanding populations.

Tribal and ethnic bonds, while dysfunctional in producing a unified nation-state, do help in-migrants identify people of similar background who can help them adjust to the city. In the city tribal identification often replaces kinship as a symbol of belonging. The status of women varies from country to country, but everywhere the city provides employment and social opportunities not available in the patriarchal-based villages.

Latin America is an urbanized continent and holds some of the largest cities in the world. Latin American cities (excluding Brazil) share a common Spanish history and heritage.

The Spanish Law of the Indies restricted the development of trade and commerce in colonial Latin American cities. The colonies supplied mineral wealth and Spain provided manufactured goods. Cities were to be laid out with a central *plaza mayor* with a cathedral and government buildings. Residential areas were to follow a grid pattern with right-angle streets. Since there was no industry, elites lived near the central plaza. This is similar to the pattern of pre-Columbian Aztec and Mayan civilizations. Today the influence of technology (cars, cell phones, e-mail) has made patterns of residential dispersion similar to those found in North American cities.

Latin America's urban areas and urban population are rapidly expanding. The second- and third-largest cities in the world—São Paulo and Mexico City—are both located in South America. Argentina, Chile, Venezuela, and Uruguay all have higher proportions of urban dwellers than the United States or Canada. Shantytowns and squatter settlements are a common feature of major South American cities. Over one-third of Mexico City's residents live in slums or squatter settlements, while São Paulo has more than 1 million squatters. Mexico City's Netzahualcoyotl houses over 3 million persons on what was a dry lake bed. No universal statement applies to all squatter settlements. Some are places of squalor and despair, while others are transitional settlements in the process of physically self-improving.

While some Latin American cities are plagued by crime, congestion, pollution, lack of decent jobs, and poor education, others are doing much better. Even with all their problems cities remain locations of hope and expectation for newcomers. The city is the future.

REVIEW QUESTIONS

1. What has been the pattern of urban economic development in sub-Saharan Africa during the last 20 years?

2. What impact has AIDS had on African cities?

3. How did the spatial pattern of colonial African cities differ from indigenous African cities?

4. What was (is) the function, physical appearance, and social role of African primate cities?

5. How do tribal bonds affect life in African cities?

6. How did the colonial social structure of Spanish Latin American cities differ from that of the English colonies of North America?

7. What role do squatter settlements and shantytowns play in the development of contemporary Latin American cities?

8. What is the "myth of marginality" and how does it apply (or not) to Latin American cities?

9. How would the ecological complex of POET (population, organization, environment, and technology) explain recent developments in Latin American urbanization?

10. What is the importance of the "City Study" for understanding the problems of urban newcomers to Latin American cities?

NOTES

1. The 9 million figure comes from *Demographia World Urban Area and Population Projections, Fifth Comprehensive Edition*, http://www.demographia.com, April 2009, Table 1, p. 11. See also: United Nations Centre for Human Settlement, *The State of World Cities Report 2001* United Nations, Nairobi, 2001. For more information see: United Nations, *World Urbanization Prospects: The 1999 Revision*, United Nations, New York, 2000 and Dennis Rondinelli, "Giant and Secondary City Developments in Africa," in M. Dogan and J. D. Kasarda (eds.), *The Metropolis Era: A World of Giant Cities*, Sage, Beverly Hills, Calif., 1988.

2. Foreign Affairs and International Trade Canada, "Urban Planet," *Canada World View*, Issue 30, Summer 2006, p. 10.

3. Population Reference Bureau, "2010 World Population Data Sheet," Washington, D.C., 2010.

4. Ibid.

5. Carl Haub, "UN Projections Assume Fertility Decline, Mortality Increase," *Population Today*, December 1998, p. 2.

6. Peter Lamptey, Merywen Wigley, Daraa Carr, and Yvette Collymore, "Once an Urban Phenomenon, HIV/AIDS Threatens Lives and Livelihoods of Rural Communities," *Population Reference Bureau*, Aug, 2003, www.prob.org.

7. Population Reference Bureau, op. cit., 2010, and Joint United Nations Programme on HIV/AIDS Epidemic Update, United Nations, New York, 2000.

8. United Nations, The State of World Cities Report, 2001, op. cit., p.2.

9. "2008 African Data Sheet," Population Reference Bureau, Washington, D.C., 2008.

10. Population Reference Bureau 2010, op. cit.

11. G. Hamdan, "Capitals of the New Africa," *Economic Geography* 40:239–241, July 1964.

12. William A. Hance, *Population, Migration, and Urbanization in Africa*, Columbia University Press, New York, 1970, p. 211.

13. V. G. Pons, cited by A. L. Epstein, "Urbanization and Social Change in Africa," *Current Anthropology* 8:(4)277, 1967.

14. Geoffrey K. Payne, *Urban Housing in the Third World*, Routledge & Kegan Paul, Boston, 1977, p. 53.

15. D.R.F. Taylor, "The Concept of Invisible Towns and Spatial Organization in East Africa," *Comparative Urban Research* 5:44–70, 1978.

16. Alan G. Gilbert and Josef Gugler, *Cities, Poverty, and Development: Urbanization in the Third World*, 2nd ed, Oxford University Press, New York, 1992, p. 88.

17. J. Clyde Mitchell, *Cities, Society, and Social Perception: A Central African Perspective*, Clarendon Press, Oxford, 1987.

18. Kenneth Richburg, "Kenya's Ethnic Conflict Drives Farmers Off Land," *Washington Post*, March 17, 1994, p. A36.

19. Vici Nelson, "How Women and Men Get By: The Sexual Division of Labor in the Informal Sector of a Nairobi Squatter Settlement," in Joseph Gugler

(ed.), *The Urbanization of the Third World,* Oxford University Press, New York, 1988, p. 201.

20. "United Nations ICPD Programme of Action," 1994 Cairo United Nations World Population Conference, 1994, p. 8.

21. Hance, op. cit., pp. 293–294.

22. "Latin America is Less Urban than is Officially Thought," *The Economist,* Feb. 19, 2005, p. 38.

23. For data on the six largest cities, see Allen Gilbert (ed.), *The Mega-City in Latin America,* United Nations University Press, New York, 1996. For national data, see Population Reference Bureau, "2010 World Population Data Sheet," Washington, D.C., 2010.

24. T. Lynn Smith, "The Changing Functions of Latin American Cities," *The Americas* 25:74, 1968.

25. Jorge E. Hardoy, *Urbanization in Latin America: Approaches and Issues,* Doubleday Anchor, Garden City, N.Y., 1975, p. 30.

26. Quoted in Edwin M. Shook and Tatiana Proskouriakoff, "Settlement Patterns in Meso-America and the Sequency in the Guatemalan Highlands," in Gordon R. Wiley (ed.), *Prehistoric Settlement Patterns in the New World,* Wenner-Gren Foundation for Anthropological Research, New York, 1956, pp. 93–94.

27. Gideon Sjoberg, *The Preindustrial City: Past and Present,* Free Press, New York, 1960, pp. 96–98.

28. Population Reference Bureau 2010, op. cit.

29. Ibid.

30. Jorge A. Brea, "Population Dynamics in Latin America," *Population Bulletin* 58:1, March 2003.

31. "Brazil Takes Off," *The Economist,* Nov. 14, 2009, p. 15.

32. "Foreign Affairs and International Trade. "Urban Planet," *Canada World View,* Issue 30, Spring 2006, p.10.

33. Mark Stevenson, "Mexico City Launches Crackdown on Squatter Settlements," *Los Angeles Times,* May 3, 1998, p. 11.

34. Robert J. Stout, "Making It Day to Day in Netzahualcoyoltl," *Notre Dame Magazine,* Spring 1993, p. 23.

35. Ginger Thompson, "Chasing Mexico's Dream into Squalor," *New York Times,* February 11, 2001, p. 1.

36. Manuel Castells, "Squatters and the State in Latin America," in Joseph Gugler (ed.), *The Urbanization of the Third World,* Oxford University Press, Oxford, 1988, pp. 33–66.

37. Tyler Bridges, "Shanty Dwellers of Peru Turn Desert Tract into Young Town," *Washington Post,* May 21, 1987, pp. E1–2.

38. Ginger Thompson, op. cit.

39. BBC News, "No End to Women Murders In Mexico," Nov. 23, 2005.

40. Oscar Lewis, *The Children of Sanchez,* Random House, New York, 1961; and *La Vida,* Random House, New York, 1966.

41. R. Mohan and N. Hartline, "The Poor of Bogotá: Who They Are, What They Do, and Where They Live," World Bank Staff Working Paper No. 635, 1984.

42. World Bank, "Anatomy of a Third World City," *Urban Edge,* 8(8):4, 1984.

43. Ibid., p. 3.

44. James Brooke, "Brazilian Mayor Built Third World Showplace by Keeping it Simple," *International Herald-Tribune,* May 29, 1992, p. 3.

45. Ibid.

CHAPTER 17

Conclusion: Toward the Urban Future

We will ever strive for the ideals and sacred things of the city, both alone and with many; we will unceasingly seek to quicken the sense of public duty; we will revere and obey the city's laws; we will transmit this city not only not less, but greater, better and more beautiful than it was transmitted to us.

Oath of the Athenian city-state

OUTLINE

Recapitulation
    Urban Concentration
    Deconcentration
Issues and Challenges
    Urban Funding
    People versus Places
    Changing Metropolitan Population
    Suburban Development
Social Planning Approaches
    Three Approaches to
      Social Planning
    Social Planning and Technology
Planning for the Future City
    Planned Utopias
    Las Vegas
    Quality-of-Life Planning
    Smart Cities
    Planning Metropolitan
      Political Systems
    A Working City
Toward a Metropolitan Future
Summary

RECAPITULATION

This text has sought to give you an understanding and appreciation for the scope and challenge of contemporary urbanization. Initial urban places were severely limited in size by environment and limited agricultural technology. As the 19th century began, only 3 percent of the world's population lived in places of 5,000 or more. Limitations in environment, organization, and technology restricted population growth.

Urban Concentration

Spurred by technological inventions in agriculture, manufacturing, and transportation, 19th-century city populations in Europe and North America began to mushroom. A classic example is Chicago. The city that had only 4,100 people when incorporated in 1833 had some 2 million residents only three-quarters of a century later. The development of railway technology in the 19th century made it possible to

353

locate commercial and industrial cities inland. The technology of the railway fostered concentration. Central-city factories clustered along the rail lines on which they were dependent, while factory workers were forced by both limited income and technology to live nearby in densely packed tenements.

From the Civil War (1861–1865) to World War II (1941–1945), population, power, manufacturing, finance, and fashion concentrated in central cities. Technological developments in transportation and communication during the first half of the 20th century both reinforced the importance of the city core and extended its dominance to the end of the paved road and telephone lines. As Part V: Worldwide Urbanization demonstrated, urban economic, political, and population concentration remains the dominant pattern in developing nations.

Deconcentration

Communication and—to a lesser degree—transportation technologies no longer automatically favor centralization. Urban deconcentration and dispersion have increasingly become the western European as well as the American pattern.[1] Technology has overcome spatial barriers. Today, goods as well as information can move from one coast to another with unprecedented speed. Express companies will guarantee overnight delivery of packages, while cell phones, Twitter, and Facebook provide instantaneous communication worldwide.

The degree to which technology has become a substitute for propinquity is still not fully grasped. We are only beginning to understand, for example, that Nissan's newest automobile plant in semirural Mississippi and a Mercedes plant built in Alabama reflect more than a desire to escape Detroit's unions and wage scales. While the early 20th-century industrial city demanded concentration, the 21st-century city does not. Changed transportation and communication technologies have outmoded the necessity to locate factories in urban

centers. Today, the once-proud, industrial-based, railway-built cities of the industrial East and Midwest have totally reoriented themselves to the postindustrial economy. Pittsburgh, once the grimy center of the steel industry, now has no steel mills and has a service-based economy.

Easy accessibility and propinquity are no longer linked. Technological advances have reduced the friction of space. We e-mail and shop at home on the Shopping Channel. The Internet is global. Spatial uncoupling from the metropolitan area by moving out to exurbia no longer means leaving behind urbanism as a way of life. Increasingly we telecommute to our offices.

The different urban and rural behaviors and characteristics that played such an important part in the late-19th- and early-20th-century social and spatial theories discussed in Chapters 1, 2, and 3 have largely lost their explanatory force. At the end of World War II substantive distinctions could still be made between metropolitan and nonmetropolitan ways of life. Today the U.S. has 361 metropolitan areas and Canada has 33. With the boundaries of existing areas progressively expanding, it is increasingly difficult to distinguish between metropolitan and nonmetropolitan areas. Satellite TV dishes, cable hookups, PCs, and cell phones are now an integral part of nonmetropolitan growth. Increasingly, urban–nonurban differences have ceased to make a difference. Nonetheless, personal interaction with neighbors in rural or small-town areas still involves an expectation of permanence that distinguishes such areas from metropolitan areas.[2]

Most Americans are now suburbanites. In terms of business, suburban locations have become the norm. One of the more interesting developments is decentralization to fringe developments on the periphery of metropolitan areas that are neither urban nor suburban (see Chapter 6: The Suburban Era). These new outlying dispersed areas don't easily fit into urban, suburban, or rural classification schemes. It has been suggested that the state of North Car-

Denver, like an increasing number of North American cities, provides energy efficient public transportation. ©Michael Siluk/The Image Works

olina, with its policy of dispersed economic activity, could be a prototype of a more spatially dispersed residential pattern.[3] None of this should be taken as suggesting that existing urban places are in danger of becoming ghost towns. They aren't. The "death of the city" clichés of earlier decades have turned out to be poor prophesy. Within many older cities both central business districts (CBDs) and residential neighborhoods have arrested their pattern of decline and are showing evidence of both stability and economic prosperity. What is clear is that North American urban places and patterns are undergoing profound changes. It appears that the future will be both more complex and more interesting than previously projected.

The Los Angeles School of urban theory (discussed in Chapter 4) argues that Southern California, and especially Orange County, provides the blueprint for further urban development in the 21st century.[4] Just as Chicago provided the model for early 20th-century ecology, immigration, and community relations, they

say Southern California, with its dispersed pattern, represents the future.

ISSUES AND CHALLENGES

Urban Funding

The broad consensus regarding some federal responsibility for urban places that existed for decades now has been shattered. (We often forget that it was President Nixon who initiated the program of federal revenue sharing.) The 1995 Republican "Contract with America" proposed the elimination of virtually all federal aid to cities. Nor did Presidents Clinton or Bush do anything to put urban funding back on the national agenda, and, as of the time of this writing (2010), President Obama had not sent any major urban initiatives to Congress. Cities are off the national radar (except for Homeland Security) and have been increasingly thrown back upon local and state funding. In Congress support for economic stimulus funds for cities has come almost entirely from Democrats.

Some argue that federal policies have been more part of the urban problem than part of the solution.[5] Federal transportation policies support the expansion of ever more expressways on the urban fringe, while tax and regulatory policies encourage people to move farther out. Disinvestment in urban centers further weakens the core, while federal tax subsidies of homeowner interest and property taxes encourage new housing sprawl. Overall, federal tax and transportation policies have further widened, rather than decreased, the gap between the have and have-not localities.

People versus Places

Beyond the issue of amount of funding, there is dispute whether the limited federal urban funds should be spent on people or places. Should the federal government try to revitalize the economies of older central cities? Or should programs encourage people to move to places of employment? The orthodox response since the Housing Act of 1949 has been to funnel funds into the renewal and rebuilding of the economic and housing bases of the neediest older cities. Programs and policies designed during the 1950s, 1960s, and 1970s had the implicit goal of halting or at least slowing the middle-class exodus to the suburbs. In recent decades, some members of Congress from older cities have sought to enlarge this to include arresting the drift of jobs and population away from older industrial cities. In Canada this would mean support for eastern maritime cities.

However, some urban scholars argue that trying to restore older cities is a mistake.[6] They say that such policies place the needs of places ahead of those of people. They maintain that rather than propping up obsolete industries or declining places, urban policies should be redesigned to help the poor and the unemployed

to migrate to places where job opportunities are expanding. The focus on saving the cities, they argue, results simply in warehousing the poor in cities, to no one's advantage. Obsolete areas should be allowed to shrink to a size where they are economically viable.

In practice this would mean, for example, that the declining steel manufacturing city of Gary, Indiana, which over the last four decades has received the nation's highest per capita infusions of federal money, should not have received the urban renewal, redevelopment, and retraining funds it did. Rather than making a futile attempt to save a dying industrial city, the federal government should have encouraged and aided Gary's residents to move to regions where jobs were available.

Not surprisingly, central-city mayors take strong exception to this view. They say that not attempting to save older cities seriously undermines both the places and the people who live in them. They remind us that cities are not simply to be written off, and people are not simply cargo or items of furniture to be moved from place to place.

On the other hand North America's history is one of immigrants who came—and are still coming—far distances from other countries in search of opportunity. Should residents of depressed areas be encouraged by economic incentives to also move toward opportunities?

Changing Metropolitan Population

For almost 200 years after the American Revolution, American cities had a growth rate far in excess of that of the countryside. This was a combination of heavy migration from abroad and internal movement from farm to city. This pattern is now history. In America's 25 largest metropolitan areas from 1980 to 2000, 23 of the 25 central cities grew slower (or lost population) while the outlying suburban areas of the metro areas all grew. Even major sunbelt cities such as Phoenix, Dallas, and Houston since 2000 have grown slower than their suburbs. However, the 2000 and 2010 censuses showed that even older cities had unexpected vitality. The populations of New York and Chicago, which had lost population every census since 1950, grew in 2000 and 2010.

Maintaining the population in the nation's largest cities is now due mostly to immigrants. The combination of immigrant newcomers and middle-class gentrifiers may well keep central-city populations fairly stable for the next decade. The hemorrhaging population losses that weakened older U.S. cities during the last decades of the 20th century appear to have ended. During the first decade of the 21st century, urban populations generally are remaining stable or even showing minor increases.

Some cities in the Southwest are experiencing major population gains. Between 1990 and 2005 Nevada and Arizona were the fastest-growing states, and virtually all their growth was metropolitan. However, the three growth giants remain Texas, California, and Florida. These three accounted for roughly half the total U.S. population growth between 1980 and 2005. All three states experienced both substantial in-movement from other states (most recently this has slowed due to the recession). All three have substantial foreign immigration, most of it Spanish-speaking. California has also experienced substantial Asian immigration.

However, even growing areas often experience selective out-migration. California, for instance, since the early 1990s has experienced out-movement of working-class whites.[7]

The shift of population also means a shift of political power from the older industrial cities and the farmbelt to the growing areas of the South and Southwest. Political reapportionment based on the 1980, 1990, and 2000 censuses has resulted in the Midwest and Northeast losing over 50 seats in the House of Representatives. In both the 1990 and 2000 reapportionments, suburban areas were the big winners. Cities were the losers. Reapportionment based on the 2010 census will continue the suburban power shift.

Migration in North America today is no longer from farm to city, or even from city to city. It is between the suburbs of one metropolitan area and the suburbs of another. The more affluent and the middle class move from the suburbs of one metropolitan area to the suburbs of another without touching the cities themselves. It is poorer migrants that most commonly go from central city to central city. Aggregate movement in the United States is toward the South and the West, particularly the Southwest. As a people we are moving from central to coastal areas. The effects of coastal population concentration are already all too visible in parts of California and Florida. In Canada population is moving west to Alberta and British Columbia.

Suburban Development

Suburbanism is clearly the dominant American way of life in the 21st century. Middle-income and upper-middle-income households continue to flow toward the suburbs. From 1989 to 1996, 7.4 million upper-income and middle-income households left the cities for the suburbs, while only 3.5 million moved the other way from suburb to city.[8] The income difference between suburbs and cities continues to grow and this decentralization trend is unlikely to reverse. As noted in Chapter 6: The Suburban Era, survey after survey indicates that suburban living is a lifestyle that appeals to most Americans.

Also, an immense investment has already been made in existing suburban homes, office parks, shopping centers, and industrial complexes. Since most suburbanites not only live but also work in suburban areas, they have little incentive to move back to the city for reasons of employment. Population dispersal does not necessarily mean movement from important activities. With activities dispersed, moving "closer to the action" may mean moving away from rather than toward the urban center. Moreover, there is a tendency to exaggerate the time most people spend commuting to work. While commutes in Los Angeles, Washington, D.C., and Atlanta have dramatically lengthened, most Americans spend under 25 minutes commuting each way.

If continued suburban sprawl is to be constrained, it probably will be not by government fiat or smart-growth planning, but by escalating costs. Richard Florida argues that the housing crash beginning in 2008 has made suburban sprawl uneconomical.[9] For some new young homebuyers, a housing alternative may be purchasing a home in a revitalizing gentrifying central-city neighborhood. More adult-oriented lifestyles and priorities combined with commuting costs (time and money) have made peripheral locations less attractive for childless young adults. For young urban professionals, and perhaps even the elderly, the option of living in a restored central-city neighborhood appears to be increasingly attractive. However, as indicated in Chapter 12: Housing Patterns, Sprawl, and Smart Growth, such a location does not appeal to all householders. Most internal metro-area movement is still toward the periphery rather than toward the central city.

Suburbs continue to have a popular image as all-white enclaves, but African American suburbanization—particularly middle-class suburbanization—is rapidly accelerating. Currently more than 4 of 10 metro-area African Americans lives in a suburb, and three-quarters of all African American population growth is in the suburbs. Atlanta, for instance, has 1.4 million African American suburbanites. This is well beyond tokenism. Hispanic American suburbanization is also a major trend, with Latinos accounting for one-quarter of all suburban growth. Meanwhile, Asian Americans are already more suburban than the white population. Native Americans increasingly live in urban and suburban places.

However, as long as whites constitute over five-sixths of the population and continue to live in the suburbs, regardless of the amount of minority group migration to suburbs, it is demographically impossible for suburbia as a whole to be anything but predominantly white.

SOCIAL PLANNING APPROACHES

Three Approaches to Social Planning

Theoretical approaches to planning and problem solving range from the use of existing social mechanisms in conventional ways to attempts to radically restructure the entire system. Three general assumptions regarding problem solving and the resulting approaches to planning can be delineated:

(1) conventional approaches, which assume that problems can be solved by existing mechanisms,
(2) reformist approaches, which assume that the system needs some major modification, and
(3) radical approaches, which assume that problems cannot be solved by the existing social system (see table 17.1).

Conventional approaches to planning and problem solving assume that the system itself is not in question. Inadequacies are attributed to the failings of individuals. Reassessment of priorities is also an essentially conventional response. Here the emphasis is upon the allocation of resources and weighing of priorities within the system rather than upon structural modification of the system itself.

Reformist responses, as outlined in Table 17–1, are characterized by ideological commitment to the goals and ideals of the society but not by attempts to achieve them through conventional means. Reformers are more likely to see the system itself as the source of the problem and to have little faith in correcting it by

Table 17.1 **Strategies for Planning and Problem Solving**		
Assumptions Regarding Problem Solving	**General Approach to Planning**	**Resulting Action Taken**
Most, if not all, can be solved by existing mechanisms	Conventional approaches (system needs minor modifications, fine tuning, or both)	New leadership, better administration, shift in priorities, new legislations
Some problems cannot be solved by existing mechanisms	Reformist approaches (system needs some major modification; likely to see system itself as source of problems)	Mobilization of bases outside existing party structures, quasi-legal protests, civil disobedience
Most, if not all, problems cannot be solved by existing mechanisms	Radical approaches (system needs replacement)	Rejection of societal goals, civil uprising, revolution, planned violence

Source: J. John Palen and Karl Fleming

traditional means. They accept quasi-legal methods falling outside the traditional system, as do some members of the civil rights movement and the environmental movement.

Radical approaches differ from the conventional and reformist positions by rejecting, at least implicitly, the traditional goals of the society as well as the means used to implement them. The existing system is judged to be so corrupt and repressive that the response is to destroy it and start over. Radical responses are almost always overtly ideological in their vision of the new utopia.

Social Planning and Technology

One point upon which most urbanists generally agree is that the core problems of the city are social problems. The difficulty is that we are frequently unwilling to admit the existence of social problems until they reach serious proportions, and even then we seek solutions through other than social reforms in the naive belief that "technology saves." Public housing projects and freeways are perhaps the two best-known examples of how we have, with often disastrous results for cities, attempted to provide engineering solutions for social problems.

The technology, for example, exists for building mile-high apartment buildings. The real question should not be "Is it possible?" but rather "Is it desirable?" Since 9/11 there has been a new caution—at least in the United States—in designing ever-taller skyscrapers. New York, Chicago, and other cities with skyscrapers have upgraded engineering structural requirements and quietly seen many existing buildings retrofitted.

Answers to questions about energy usage or pollution are far more social and political than technical. Technical "solutions" often do little more than shift the strain to elsewhere in the system. Keep in mind that America's social orientation toward automobiles, our values concerning the environment, and our political policies toward the oil monopolies determine whether the nation has an "energy crisis" or "environment crisis" far more than does technology. The decision of an oil company not to build a refinery that produces less-polluting products may be an economic or a political decision, or both, but it is not a technological decision. Of course, if one expects technology to solve all problems there really isn't any need to even consider modifying or changing the social, economic, or political system.

PLANNING FOR THE FUTURE CITY

To many people, urban planning almost automatically means physical planning; but physical planning is never free from social implications—the two are always intertwined. Moreover, our view of the future influences our contemporary behavior.

Planned Utopias

Ebenezer Howard's "garden cities" have already been discussed in Chapter 13: Planning, New Towns, and New Urbanism. Howard advocated a system of compact, self-contained cities of limited size that were designed to attract residents away from large cities such as London. Other planners have had different visions of utopia. Frank Lloyd Wright's model (1934) of a decentralized garden city called "Broadacre City" has been praised by some as a vision of the future.[10] However, Wright's proposed model is explicitly antiurban and looks to the rural past. In Broadacre City there are no large buildings or high-rises, and each family would be allotted at least one acre, which they would be expected to farm. Significantly, his book *The*

Living City ends with material excerpted from Ralph Waldo Emerson's "Essay on Farming."[11]

A different type of "city of tomorrow," and one that has had far more influence on postwar American planners, is Le Corbusier's "Radiant City." Le Corbusier's ideal city was to be composed of a center of towering skyscrapers surrounded by parks and open spaces. Residences, similarly, would be tall, thin apartment superblocks surrounded by greenery.[12] Much of the socially disastrous high-rise urban renewal of the postwar period was based on Le Corbusier's monumental vision of the city of the future.

Similarly, the functional, spartan, glass-box design of Mies van der Rohe dominated the downtown architecture of major American cities during the 1960s and 1970s. This modernist architecture has been praised by architects and sharply criticized as unlivable and unlovely by social critics such as Tom Wolfe.[13] Prince Charles of Great Britain enraged British architects by making similar criticisms.

Brasilia, the new-city capital of Brazil, although not designed by Le Corbusier, followed his general plan: it has a unified high-rise center and residential superblocks united by a ra-

Abu Dhabi, the capital of the United Arab Emirates, is a new, planned capital city that combines the traditions of the old Middle East with the verve of contemporary architecture and culture. Without even a single paved road until 1961, Abu Dhabi, thanks to oil, has become a modern gleaming city of steel and glass, as well as a financial superpower. © iStockphoto

dial system of freeways. However, as indicated in box 17.1 Brasilia, while striking in appearance, is too uncomfortable and monumental for many people, who prefer the chaos of a city such as Rio de Janeiro.

Sometimes physical planning for the future takes on a fanciful "Brave New World" character. The science-fiction vision of Buckminster Fuller is an example: it cuts our ties to the physical earth and to mundane things such as water mains and sewers by means of recycling packs that we could wear on our backs like the astronauts' life-support systems. The prescription of visionary and planner Constantinos Doxiadis for planning an organized community likewise is radically removed from the situation in contemporary cities. Doxiadis proposed a city of 2 million, organized into compact communities of 30,000 to 50,000. Services, schools, stores, businesses, and parks would all be organized so that residents could walk to them; public transit and highways would be around the communities. Movement from community to community within the city would be by means of "deepways," underground highways.[14]

Another fanciful model for future cities is architect Paolo Soleri's "arcology," a compact three-dimensional city. Soleri placed heavy emphasis on building a city vertically, or layer on layer, and on using "miniaturization," or a more compact form, which he believed was the rule of evolutionary development.[15] Instead of urban sprawl Soleri would have cities confined to a few square miles, with buildings 300 stories high. Soleri and volunteers planned to build a 3,000-person, 25-story prototype of the future named "Arcosanti" in Arizona. It would draw energy from the sun and food from greenhouses and there would be no need for automobiles.

However, today Arcosanti contains only a few low-rise auxiliary buildings, some in a half-completed state. Arcosanti, at the end of an unpaved road, resembles an interesting couple of buildings more than a visionary city. The 60 or so staff and students work mostly on fashioning

somewhat high-priced ceramic and brass bells for revenue.

Dantzig and Saatz take the idea of vertical compactness a step further and propose a compact vertical city in one building that makes round-the-clock use of all facilities.[16] Such a city, though, would require constant services. Strikes by municipal workers would paralyze such a compact high-rise city, and thus would have to be prohibited. It is possible to foresee such a city turning into a tightly monitored totalitarian state.

Planned utopias, such as those just noted, may challenge the imagination, but they also frequently appear rather sterile and lifeless. They seem better suited to guided tours than day-in, day-out habitation. To theorize about the future is one thing; to want to live in it is another. Cities covered by domes could theoretically be built in otherwise hostile environments such as desert regions or even the smog-filled Los Angeles basin. Inside the domes, artificial light, controlled heating and cooling, and even grass could be provided. The question is whether we really want to live inside bubbles.

On the other hand, viewing the future as a lineal multiplication of the past is not only far less interesting, but over the long run almost certain to be inaccurate. It would be rather depressing if our only dream for the future of the metropolitan area was of an endless growth of subdivisions and shopping malls.

One place where real-life cities of the future are now being built is in the small oil-rich states strung out along the Persian Gulf. From Kuwait in the north to Bahrain, to Qatar, to Abu Dhabi new cities are emerging like mirages where the desert meets the gulf. These rich new cities boast cutting-edge architecture. Dubai even has built a series of man-made islands offshore that are built to look like a map of the earth.

Fifty years ago, the city of Abu Dhabi was a Bedouin encampment subsisting mainly on fishing. Today, Abu Dhabi, capital of the United Arab Emirates (U.A.E.), is a modern

Box 17.1   New Planned Capitals

Twentieth-century planned capital cities have been mixtures of success and failure. Canberra, Australia, which was begun in 1918, is pleasing to the eye; but it is difficult to go anywhere in Canberra without using a car, owing to the strict segregation of the city into governmental, residential, and commercial areas. The economic base of Canberra is almost completely dependent on government, middle-class employment. The population is widely dispersed in single-family homes, which makes it difficult to develop a sense of community. Canberra is sometimes referred to as the world's most inconvenient suburb.

Like Canberra, Brasilia is a planned capital city. Inaugurated as the capital of Brazil in 1957, Brasilia is located 700 miles inland from Rio de Janeiro; it was deliberately located far inland in order to develop the interior economically.

Brasilia was designed from the ground up, primarily by Lucio Costa. The city was designed to reflect contemporary times, and it is characterized by massive superblocks of concrete and glass. While the design is unquestionably bold and creative, it is also somewhat stark and abstract—and the visitor finds it hard to escape the feeling that Brasilia is not really meant to be lived in.

The city was conceived in the shape of an airplane, with government offices, commerce, and recreation occupying the central axis and residences located along the wings (creating monumental twice-daily traffic jams). Brasilia was designed to house 2 million persons by the year 2000 and now has reached that level. Fears are that its population will swell to 4 million in a decade—a population that the current city cannot reasonably support. Without any rivers or springs, Brasilia has a serious water problem, and water is rationed during the dry season.

Brasilia has been rediscovered as a "retro-futuro" dreamland by art critics, but it still has living problems.* The central city has good jobs, a cultural life, and low crime. The 16 satellite cities where most inhabitants live have none of these advantages. The influx of poor workers into the so-called satellite cities and the favelas (unplanned peripheral slums) continues at a rate of 10 percent a year. The superblocks of the central city—known as the "plano piloto" (pilot plan)—house the upper and middle classes, while the huge satellite-city slum settlements where most people live are largely hidden from view miles from the center of the city.

Too much may have been expected of the utopian city. As Brasilia's designer, Costa, replies to critics:

> Things are done differently here. You have to accept the country for what it is. Of course, half the people in Brasilia live in favelas. Brasilia was not designed to solve the problems of Brazil, it was bound to reflect them.**

Although Brasilia encouraged the economic development of the center of the country, much of this development has been an ecological disaster. Nor has Brasilia been successful in generating that perhaps indefinable human response we experience in the great cities of the world. Brasilia lacks Rio's human warmth and livability. The city is a remarkable monument, but monuments are not always comfortable places in which to live. Perhaps the Brazilian spirit will, with the passage of time, convert Brasilia, if not into another Rio, at least into a more comfortable and livable city. Meanwhile, it is becoming a gigantic slum.

* "The Retro-Futuro City," *Wilson Quarterly,* Winter 2000, pp. 10–11.

** "Brazil's Dream City Has Flaws," United Press International, August 19, 1973.

city of air-conditioned high-rises. Over the next decade Abu Dhabi plans to replace Beirut and Cairo by becoming the new cultural capital of the Middle East. Plans call for four museums, a performing arts center, and 19 art pavilions designed by the world's most celebrated architects; and all to be built on a filled-in island.[17] This could be written off as another pipe dream except for one thing: it is being subsidized by Abu Dhabi to the extent of 27 billion dollars. The U.A.E. is the fourth-largest OPEC oil producer, but Abu Dhabi also is looking toward the future and developing alternative renewable energy sources. It is building a state-of-the-art solar power plant to be operational in 2009 and also exploring wind power and hydrogen fuel. Plans for a graduate-level renewable-energy research center in combination with MIT have been announced.[18] Dubai, already a city of glitzy skyscrapers, in 2010 opened Burj Khalifa, by far the tallest building in the world. The once backward Arab Persian Gulf region is now the cutting edge for new cities. Dubai not only has built into the sea artificial archipelagoes shaped like palm trees, it also has the world's largest air terminal, which also happen to be the world's largest building covering 370 acres.

Las Vegas

A fanciful city of the future in the United States that already exists, complete with large dollops of weirdness and kitsch, is Las Vegas, known for $500-a-pull slot machines, a score of wedding ministers dressed as Elvis, and the world's largest hotels, featuring everything from an ersatz Great Pyramid, to King Arthur's Castle, to the Eiffel Tower, to the Statue of Liberty. But Las Vegas is more than the architectural mayhem of a multi-themed, over-the-top fantasy park; it is also a real city where people live.[19] In fact, until 2008 it was the fastest-growing large city in the country—the Las Vegas metro area has 1.4 million residents. Las Vegas was a boomtown before the local housing market collapsed.[20] Las Vegas is a major city in the middle of a desert that has per capita daily water usage of 343 gallons, compared with 200 in Los Angeles.

Contemporary Las Vegas goes way beyond what any of the postwar "city of the future" models ever imagined. It didn't grow organically from its environment, nor is it architecturally authentic, but then neither are most suburban communities built today. Keep in mind that the neo-traditional New Urbanism communities that seek to restore a human scale to suburban life also are artificial creations. Front porches and picket fences may contribute to a sense of community, but we really don't live in the late 19th century. In a sense, none of our physical communities are natural: all are artificial—some just work better for people than others.

Quality-of-Life Planning

The choice for the future is not between planning and no planning—we will plan, even if it is only on the level of individual buildings. The question thus is not whether planning should be done, but rather on what level it should be done. Planners and urban critics often seem caught in all-or-nothing approaches by which we exercise our imaginations either in grand fantasies or not at all. The trick is to find the line between speculative fancy and unimaginative extension of the past. This is far simpler in theory than in practice, for novel and innovative schemes are all too often considered unrealistic and dismissed out of hand. As Machiavelli accurately observed centuries ago, "There is nothing more difficult to carry out, nor more doubtful of success, nor more dangerous to handle than a new order of things."[21]

It is crucial to remember that whatever our formal plans for the city of the future, much of what will actually happen is the result of untold numbers of diverse decisions made by different individuals. As stated by Jane Jacobs:

> Most city diversity is the creation of incredible numbers of different people and different private organizations with vastly differing ideas and purposes, planning and contributing outside the formal framework of public action. The main responsibility of city planning and design should be to develop—insofar as public policy and action can do so—cities that are congenial places for this great range of unofficial plans, ideas and opportunities to flourish, along with the flourishing of the public enterprises.[22]

It can be argued that rather than grand schemes we need more ideas and programs of the middle range. An interesting architectural innovation in housing design, for example, was Moshe Safdie's "Habitat," erected in Montreal. Safdie's design of modular boxes piled irregularly upon one another was originally hailed by some observers as the answer to the urban housing problem. The modular units were prefabricated and shipped to the construction site; the irregular placement of the

Las Vegas was the fastest growing metro area in the United States until the 2008 recession. Currently it has the highest percentage of foreclosures in the nation. Las Vegas photo credit: © iStockphoto; foreclosure sign credit: © iStockphoto

units provided not only for variety but also for balconies and private space. The result was a rare combination of both privacy and a sense of community. Unfortunately, "Habitats" have turned out to be more expensive than was hoped. In addition to the financial difficulties, there is also a less clearly expressed but nevertheless deep reluctance to try anything as different from conventional apartment buildings as Habitat. Forty years after its construction, it still remains a "radical" idea.

Smart Cities

Many cities are beginning to look to solar, wind, and nuclear power to fuel post–fossil fuel "smart cities." In Japan the 2010 Yokohama Smart City Project is a consortium of seven major Japanese companies, including Nissan, Panasonic, and Toshiba, working to drastically cut carbon emissions. The project leaders see selling this technology as Japan's next major export.[23]

A lot can be done with what seem like simple changes. Chicago's Mayor Richard M. Daley turned once-gritty Chicago into a green city. Twenty some years ago the city began planting trees and flowers to beautify the city. Today Chicago is noted for its "green" look. The city has planted more than 400,000 trees and employs more arborists than any city in North America.[24] Chicago also encourages green roofs on office buildings; there are 2.5 million square feet of green roofs in the city. Chicago's City Hall roof is planted with 150 varieties of plants and is 50 degrees cooler in summer than nearby asphalt roofs.

Another example of what can be done is the city of Calgary, where new housing developments must put 10 percent of their land into public parks or pathways. Cities such as Calgary and Seattle have also tried to limit downtown driving by providing free bus service within the downtown area. Also, both cities, and a number of others, have added bike racks to the front of buses so riders can combine bus and bike travel.

Simple ideas are often best. A transportation alternative proposed by this author is the "borrow a bike" plan. This plan actually has been implemented in Copenhagen, Portland, Oregon, and Charlottesville, Virginia, while Paris is trying a modified version. The borrow a bike idea is not restricted to cities. My neighboring University of Richmond now has a "Grab a bike and go" program. (Although the author first proposed this idea in print more than 30 years ago, he makes no claim to having influenced its usage. Good ideas appear independently.) The idea is quite simple: The city puts up numerous clearly marked municipal bicycle racks and fills them with city-owned bicycles. (There are 2,000 solid-tire single-speed bikes in Copenhagen; rather than wheel spokes, the bikes have solid disks carrying advertising.) Anyone can use any bike from any rack, the only requirement being that he or she eventually return it to one of the racks.

All bikes are simple, straightforward, one-speed models painted a distinctive common color (white in Copenhagen, yellow in Portland). There is little point in stealing the bikes, since they are basic models, and are freely available everywhere as transportation to anyone who wants them. Some riders doubtlessly move on to purchase their own more-elaborate models, so that the scheme increases rather than decreases sales by private dealers—just as Henry Ford's cheap Model T spurred the purchase of more elaborate and comfortable automobiles. Bicycles can be manufactured and assembled at little cost by the city itself, employing persons on public assistance who want jobs but have only minimal skills.

Such schemes reduce pollution, reduce gasoline consumption, ease traffic, and increase the physical—and probably emotional—health of the population. Increasing public awareness of the importance of regular exercise should contribute to the plan's success. The concept would have even greater appeal in certain types of communities, such as university towns and sunbelt retirement areas. Major urban bike commuting already exists. In Copenhagen, more than one-third of workers pedal to their offices, while in Amsterdam 40 percent of commuters go to work by bike.[25] The city has constructed a new bike parking facility near the train station that holds 10,000 bikes.

The possible disadvantages of providing public bikes would be the initial cost of the bicycles (although reduced costs of repairing streets would far more than compensate for this) and the fact that in some cities the bikes might not be used much through the winter months. Also, even if the plan saved the city money, some residents would no doubt complain that it was socialistic nonsense, and that government had no business giving people bicycles. In fact in Portland, because of liability concerns, the bikes are not provided by the city but by a nonprofit group that can't effectively be sued because it has no resources. On the other hand, in cities such as Montreal, the city rents bikes at downtown bike racks. Green roofs, free public transit, and the "borrow a bike" plan are just examples of how, without massive rebuilding or expense, we can make our cities more healthy and livable. Planning does not always have to be large scale. Some of the best planning is that which simply focuses on improving people's lives.

Planning Metropolitan Political Systems

Organizationally, metropolitan areas appear in a state of confusion and disorganization. Home rule provides for local control at a substantial price. The political system itself can become a major obstacle to effective planning. A multiplicity of city, suburban, county, township, regional, state, and federal bureaucracies all must intermesh if the metropolitan area is to be serviced effectively and at minimum cost, and this rarely works as well in practice as in theory. The interminable squabbling between city mayors and suburban political officials is one index of the ineffectiveness of the present system. The New York conurbation (admittedly an extreme example) includes people from three different states and some 1,400 different jurisdictions of one sort or another.

One alternative would be to abandon most local jurisdictions and move in the direction of one metropolitan-area government such as those found in Dade County, Florida (Miami); Nashville, Tennessee; or Toronto, Ontario. However, in spite of the generally favorable reports on these consolidations, there is little real agitation or political pressure in major urban areas for adoption of consolidation. Although during the 1990s the book *Cities without Suburbs* stirred up interest among planners in a single metropolitan government, there is little political support for such a move.[26] While in the past cities could offer suburban areas higher levels of services as an inducement to consolidation; today suburbs often offer the higher level of services. Nor do suburban areas want to associate themselves politically with cities in economic or social trouble. Additionally, elected city officials often represent minority populations that were previously excluded from city decision making, and most of these city officials oppose consolidation. They fear that if the city became part of a larger political unit there would be a dilution of their influence and power. Thus, the majority of both suburban and city elected officials overtly or covertly oppose metropolitan consolidation. It is a good idea without a solid political base.

Another approach is a two-level system that would move certain decision-making powers and organization to the level of a county or MSA while other functions would be handled by dividing the entire area—including the central city—into political units the size of suburbs that would deal with local problems. (Toronto, Canada, was a successful example of the two-tiered approach, but it has now abandoned it to create a larger megacity. Critics charge that this was done to dilute the influence of Toronto's effective and activist neighborhood associations.)

Under the larger metropolitan unit are placed functions common to the urban system as a whole, such as water supply, waste disposal, expressways and streets, control of air and water pollution, museums, public hospitals, and major recreational facilities. More local matters, such as education, enforcement of housing codes, and recreation are left to the local community. As for education, there is no reason why local central-city areas should not have their own school boards and school policies, just as suburbs currently do.

Police departments could also be organized on a local basis—with a common radio network and other specialized facilities—while fire protection could move to a metropolitan basis. It makes little sense for suburban fire departments to duplicate expensive equipment; fire services should be determined by the need for fast arrival rather than by political boundaries. Police officers, on the other hand, need day-to-day contact with their community, which firefighters do not. Locally administered departments such as those found in suburbs are most likely to provide a setting in which the police and the community come to know and respect one another. Large bureaucratic departments in which police are shifted from district to district seldom are able to establish rapport with citizens. What would happen if locally controlled police forces replaced the present system? A new system would certainly be worth trying in selected cities as a closely monitored experiment.

Emergency management of disasters such as hurricanes, tornadoes, earthquakes, and terrorism also has to be carried out on a met-

Little things can often make a big difference. After an area is cleared but before new construction takes place, Ann Arbor, Michigan puts in "A Little Park for a Little While." Joseph Palen

ropolitan rather than local basis. The 1989 San Francisco–Oakland earthquake, the 1994 Los Angeles earthquake, the 2001 Seattle earthquake, and the 2005 New Orleans hurricane demonstrate the need for truly regional responses.

A WORKING CITY

Amid all the discussions of urban problems, it is worthwhile to keep in mind that not all urban places are in crisis; some are working quite well. Portland, Oregon, home to over 500,000 people in the city and 2 million in the area, provides an example of what "smart-growth" policies can produce. Thirty years ago Portland had a beautiful location on the Willamette River, but its industries were closing, the bus system was bankrupt, and the downtown showed increasing signs of stores closing and decline. Today the warehouses and

riverfront expressway have been replaced with a waterfront park that opens the city to the river, the downtown gleams with not only a Nordstrom and Saks Fifth Avenue, but also some 1,100 smaller stores. Moreover, the number of people working downtown has risen from 59,000 to 94,000, and nearly 40 percent of them ride downtown on the tri-county transit authority bus system known as Tri-Met or on its MAX light-rail system.[27] Downtown Portland is filled with trees, small parks, and fountains, which along with the heavy use of brick walkways act to soften the downtown and make it people friendly.

To make the city physically more attractive a small percentage (1.33 percent) of the construction costs for state buildings, and a voluntary dedication from state income tax refunds, goes toward supporting public outdoor art. Downtown Portland is pedestrian friendly, so even on weekends one finds people shopping downtown, rummaging in bookstores, or enjoying themselves in coffeehouses and restaurants. Neighborhoods remain active and vital, and Portland really doesn't have zones of industrial or residential abandonment as blight other cities.

All this didn't just happen. Major credit goes both to Portlanders' moral and civic culture, which is deeply concerned with the common good and quality-of-life issues, and the implementation in 1972 of an excellent downtown development plan. Fortunately, 19th-century Portland was designed with small square blocks of the type advocated by Jane Jacobs (see Chapter 13: Planning, New Towns, and New Urbanism). In order to make the area more attractive, new buildings, including garages, must be friendly at ground level. Blank walls are prohibited. This means that even public buildings must have stores or eating places on ground level. It also means that buildings are built so dumpsters are placed inside, rather than outside, buildings. To encourage use of public transit, Portland limited, rather than expanded, the number of parking places in the core. In contrast to what is happening elsewhere, locally adopted planning policy calls for a 20 percent *reduction* in vehicle miles traveled per capita over the next 20 years.[28] To encourage less auto traffic, the 300-block downtown area has free public transit: as long as you travel within the downtown zone, there is no fare. Additionally, bike racks have been installed on the fronts of public buses so you can combine bus and bike travel.

Portlanders are deathly afraid of becoming another sprawl city like Los Angeles and for 20 some years the state has required that growth take place within a 362-square-mile metro area. This growth area has recently been expanded. All the communities in the area must follow plans that require half of new housing to be multifamily or apartment construction. This has the dual purpose of keeping housing costs affordable while preserving open land. Portlanders' fear that their highly civil way of life is going to be swamped by the in-migration of ever more Californians. Oregon residents tend to view southern California as an example of what they do not want to become.

TOWARD A METROPOLITAN FUTURE

What are likely to be the future influences on the North American metropolis? Over the decades the crystal balls of experts have proven to be quite murky. For example, the massive growth of suburbs simply wasn't foreseen at the time of World War II. However, for what it is worth, following are the top-10 influences on the American metropolis during the next 50 years as ranked for the Fannie Mae Foundation by 50 urban planners and urban historians.[29]

1. *Growing disparities of wealth.* The winners will increasingly isolate themselves in gated communities while the poor and struggling working classes increasingly find themselves trapped in deteriorating central cities and deteriorating suburbs.
2. *Suburban political majority.* The suburban political majority will determine policy for the next 50 years.
3. *Aging of the baby boomers.* The 80 million baby boomers (born 1946 to 1964) who represent 30 percent of the population are now approaching retirement, and their needs, such as for suburban assisted living, will determine future metropolitan investments.
4. *Perpetual "underclass" in central cities and inner-ring suburbs.* This is the disturbing implication of the disparity in wealth cited above.
5. *"Smart growth" and environmental and planning initiatives to limit growth.* Smart growth, if it is to be more than just a slogan, must be backed by wide-ranging regional political coalitions.
6. *The Internet.* Will the Internet doom cities as cyberspace communication replaces

the face to face, or will cities bloom as the new centers of art and creativity? We don't know.

7. *Deterioration of first-ring post-1945 suburbs.* Many postwar suburbs have aged badly. Are we destined to see further sprawl as affluent areas move from deteriorating inner suburbs built earlier?

8. *Shrinking household size.* Over the past three decades the proportion of married-couple households with children has decreased from 40 percent of all households to 30 percent.

9. *Expanded superhighway system of "outer beltways" to serve new edge cities.* We are beginning to spend some limited money on improving public transit, but most of the money is being spent the old way, laying more concrete.

10. *Racial integration and increased diversity in cities and suburbs.* This partially goes against several of the items listed above. (But who said all the predictions had to be consistent?)

Whether or not the above projections regarding the metropolitan future will come to pass is unknown. The future is not fixed; it will be determined by what you do—and by what you choose not to do. It is largely in your hands. If the nation adopts an urban agenda— including elements such as smart growth, urban reinvestment in central-city places, and leveling the playing field between older and newer communities and their residents—the above projections will simply be a historic curiosity. However, if we continue on the path of recent decades, the more negative predictions regarding the decline of urban society may come to pass.

Personally, I tend more toward optimism and have doubts whether the above prophesies of the passage of the city, and the decline of inner suburbs will come to be. Both the 2000 and 2010 censuses indicate that cities are doing better than expected. To paraphrase Mark Twain's famous remark on being told that he had been reported dead, the reports of the death of the city have been greatly exaggerated. What is certain is that for the first time in history we live in an urban world, and urbanism has become *the* way of life not only in North America, but around the globe.

SUMMARY

During the 19th century, cities in North America and Europe experienced rapid growth. Transportation technologies such as the railroad fostered manufacturing and worker concentration near city centers along railway lines. Early 20th-century developments in transportation and communication extended the city's dominance to the end of the paved road and the telephone line. Now communication and, to a lesser degree, transportation technologies no longer encourage concentration. Technological advances such as the Internet, e-mail, and cell phones have reduced the friction of space. It is increasingly difficult to distinguish between metropolitan and nonmetropolitan areas.

Broad bipartisan federal support for cities is a thing of the past. There is also dispute whether funds should go to restructure needy areas, or whether those living in economically depressed areas should be encouraged to move elsewhere. Rural-to-urban in-migration into cities is now a thing of the past. Many of the urban newcomers today are immigrants from other countries. Of America's 25 largest central cities, 23 grew slowly (or lost population) while all 25 metro suburban areas grew faster. Growing cities are most common in the Southwest, while half of all national growth is taking place in California, Texas, or Florida.

Most movement in North America today is from the suburbs of one metro area to the suburbs of another. Twice as many upper- and middle-income families continue to leave the city for the suburbs as go from suburb to city. With the majority of employment and shopping now located in the suburbs, moving "closer to the action" may mean moving away from rather than toward the city center. Suburbia is increasingly ethnically and racially diverse, and more than 4 of 10 metro-area African Americans are suburbanites and one-quarter of all suburban growth is Hispanic.

Physical planning is never free of social implications. Conventional approaches to planning assume that the system needs minor modifications or tuning. Reformist approaches see the system itself as the problem. Radical approaches seek to totally replace the system. Planned utopias such as Le Corbusier's "Radiant City" are uncomfortable. Frank Lloyd Wright's "Broadacre City" is expressly anti-urban. Abu Dhabi is building a $27 billion city of culture. A fanciful vision of the future, with a certain weirdness, can be seen in contemporary Las Vegas, the fastest-growing large city in North America. Las Vegas reminds us that all our physical communities are artificial, some just more so than others.

Livable cities often are the result not of grand schemes but of programs and policies of the middle range, such as the ideas of Jane Jacobs. Chicago has planted 400,000 trees. Politically, metropolitan areas often are a collection of scores of different jurisdictions. Nonetheless, however much planners might advocate consolidation or single jurisdictions, it is unlikely to occur since most suburban and city politicians oppose it. Two-tiered systems, though rational, also are unlikely to be adopted. The Portland metro area provides a good real-life example of what smart-growth planning can produce.

Some 50 urban planners and urban historians surveyed by the Fannie Mae Foundation see a problematic urban future for the next 50 years. Along with suburban domination, they suggest there will be growing disparities of wealth, a growing urban underclass, and a deterioration of postwar suburbs. Whether or not this will occur largely depends on the action (or inaction) of people such as yourself. I personally tend toward more optimism. What is for certain is that we now live in what is statistically and socially an urban world.

REVIEW QUESTIONS

1. What will be the major patterns of urban growth and internal immigration in the United States during the next decade?

2. What roles are transportation and communication technologies playing in shaping metropolitan growth?

3. What is the "people versus places" issue in distributing federal urban funding?

4. How has the suburban shift in population affected political power at the national level?

5. What are the assumptions of the conventional, reformist, and radical approaches to urban problem solving?

6. What have been some of the planned utopias of the past 50 years, and how successful have they been?

7. What does planning of the middle range mean, and what are some examples?

8. How did Portland, Oregon, use smart-growth policies to revitalize the city and how successful have the policies been?

9. What are the major future influences on the American metropolis as ranked for the Fannie Mae Foundation?

10. Based on your reading of *The Urban World*, what do you see as the main problem facing North American cities during the next decade?

NOTES

1. Daniel R. Vining et al., "Population Dispersal from Core Regions: A Description and Tentative Explanations of Patterns in 21 Countries," in Don-

ald A. Hicks and Norman J. Glickman (eds.), *Transition to the 21st Century,* JAI Press, Greenwich, Conn., 1983, pp. 81–111.

2. I am indebted to Thomas Drabek of the University of Denver for making this point.

3. John Herbers, *The New Heartland,* Times Books, New York, 1986.

4. Michael Dear, *From Chicago to L.A.: Making Sense of Urban Theory,* Sage, Thousand Oaks, Calif., 2001.

5. Bruce Katz, "Enough of the Small Stuff! Toward a New Urban Agenda," *Brookings Institution,* Summer 2000, p. 9.

6. See John D. Kasarda, "The Implications of Contemporary Redistribution Trends for National Urban Policy," *Social Science Quarterly* 61:373–400, 1980; and Gerald D. Suttles, "Changing Priorities for the Urban Heartland," in J. John Palen (ed.), *City Scenes: Problems and Prospects,* Little, Brown, Boston, 1981.

7. William Frey, "The New White Flight," *American Demographics,* April 1994, pp. 40–88.

8. Bruce Katz, op. cit., p. 8.

9. Richard Florida, "How the Crash Will Reshape America," *The Atlantic,* March 2009, pp. 44–56.

10. For a defense of Wright's Broadacre City, see Robert Fishman, "Megalopolis Unbound," *Wilson Quarterly,* Winter 1990, pp. 25–45.

11. Frank Lloyd Wright, *The Living City,* Mentor-Horizon, New York, 1958.

12. Le Corbusier, *The Radiant City,* Part I, Pamela Knight (trans.); Parts II and VI, Eleanor Levieux (trans.); Parts III, IV, V, VII, and VIII, Derek Coltman (trans.); Grossman-Orion, New York, 1967; this is a translation of the 1933 French version, *La Ville Radieuse.*

13. Tom Wolfe, *From Bauhaus to Our House,* Farrar Straus Giroux, New York, 1981.

14. C.A. Doxiadis, *Ekistics,* Hutchinson, London, 1968.

15. Paolo Soleri, *Arcology, The City in the Image of Man,* M.I.T. Press, Cambridge, Mass., 1969.

16. George B. Dantzig and Thomas L. Saatz, "*Compact City: A Plan for a Liveable Urban Environment,* Freeman, San Francisco, 1973.

17. Nicolai Ouroussoff, "A Vision in the Desert," *New York Times,* Feb. 4, 2007, p AR 1.

18. Hassan Fattah, "Abu Dhabi Explores Energy Alternatives," *New York Times,* March 18, 2007, p. 14.

19. John Hannigan, "Fantasy City: Pleasure and Profit in the Postmodern Metropolis," *Journal of Urban Affairs,* 21:455-458, 1999

20. Catherine Moye, "Real Estate, The New Game in Town," *Financial Times,* May 7, 2005, p. W10.

21. Niccolò Machiavelli, *The Prince,* W. K. Marriot (trans.), J. M. Dent, London, 1958, p. 29.

22. Jane Jacobs, *The Death and Life of Great American Cities,* Vintage/Random House, New York, 1961, p. 241.

23. "Japan Looks to Sell 'Smart Cities.'" Associated Press, October 10, 2010.

24. "Chicago Now a Green Leader," *Washington Post News Service,* Aug. 11, 2006.

25. "Building a Better Bike Lane," *Wall Street Journal,* May 4, 2007, p. W1.

26. David Rusk, *Cities without Suburbs,* Johns Hopkins University Press, Baltimore, Md., 1993.

27. Philip Langdon, "How Portland Does It," *Atlantic,* November 1992, p. 136.

28. Carl Abbott, "Portland: People, Places, and Politics," *Urban Affairs,* Winter 1995, p. 4.

29. Robert Fishman, "The American Metropolis at Century's End: Past and Future Influences," *Housing Policy Debate* 11(1):199–213, 2000.

Name Index

Note: Page references with an italicized *f, t, b,* or *n* indicate a figure, table, box, or note on the designated page.

Abbot, Carl, 368*n*
Abbott, Walter F., 78*n*
Abrams, Charles, 251*n*
Abrahamson, Mark, 86n, 300n
Adams, John, 195
Adams, Robert, 27*n*, 28*n*
Adelman, Robert M., 242*n*
Alba, Richard, 139*n*, 181*n*, 202*n*, 212*n*
Alihan, Milla R., 76*n*
Allard, Scott, W. 116*n*
Allen, Walter R., 192*n*
Anderson, Elijah, 153, 162*n*, 172*n*, 182*b*, 182*n*, 205*n*
Andre, Carolyn D., 137*n*
Aristotle, 31,32, 330
Augustus, 33

Bacchus, J., 172*n*
Bahr, Howard, 171*n*
Baldassare, Mark, 173*n*, 257*n*
Baltzell, E. Digby, 117*n*
Barringer, Herbert, 223*n*
Baum, Alice S., 177*n*
Baum, L. Frank, 271
Beauregard, Robert, 20*n*, 82, 149*n*, 230*n*
Beecher, Catherine, 189, 190*n*
Bellair, Paul, 181*n*
Bensman, Joseph, 10
Berger, Bennett, 131
Bernard, Richard M., 109*n*
Berry, Brian J. L., 9*n*, 240
Berube, Alan, 100*n*, 134*n*
Bianchi, Suzanne, 193
Biderman, A. D., 172*n*
Bielski, Zosia, 191*n*
Blais, Andre, 156*n*
Blakely, J. Edward, 130*n*
Bogue, Donald J., 176*n*
Boulding, Kenneth E., 149*n*
Bourne, Larry, 95*n*

Bradford, William, 51
Braidwood, Robin, 24*n*
Braudel, Fernand, 37*n*
Brea, Jorge A., 345
Bridenbaugh, Carl, 50, 51*n*
Brockerhoff, Martin P., 7*n*
Brooks, David, 157*n*
Brown, A. Theodore, 51*n*, 269*n*
Brown, Dee Alexander, 224*n*
Brown-Saracino, Japonica, 158*n*
Buckout, Robert, 173*n*
Buder, Stanley, 270*n*
Bullock, Charles, 193*n*
Burgers, E. W., 16*n*
Burgess, Ernest, 18*n*, 73, 73*f,* 75–79, 80, 85, 99, 111, 127*n*
Burnes, Donald W., 177*n*
Burnham, Daniel, 271, 272
Burr, Aaron, 56*f*
Burr, Theodosia, 56*f*
Bush, George W., 116, 135, 255, 355

Caldwell, Christopher, 284*n*
Calhoun, John B., 173
Campbell, Paul, 105*n*
Caplow, Theodore, 171
Carcopino, Jerome, 34*n*
Carr, Daraa, 331*n*
Carrey, Jim, 287
Carson, Daniel H., 173*n*
Carty, Win, 295*n*
Cassedy, James H., 54*n*
Castells, Manuel, 20*n*, 83, 305*n*, 347*n*
Castillo, Bernal Diaz del, 24*b*
Cayton, Horace, 202*n*
Chadwick, Bruce, 171*n*
Chakravorty, Sanjoy, 302*n*
Chan, Kam Wing, 318*n*
Chandler, Mittie Olion, 254*n*

Chandler, Tertius, 4*n*
Changon, Stanley A., 79*n*
Chant, Collin, 43*n*
Chaplin, Charlie, 149
Charlemagne, 36
Charles, Prince, 360
Charles V, 323
Chen, Donald D. T., 260*n*, 261*n*
Chen, Hsiang-Shui, 222*n*
Childe, V. Gordon, 26*n*, 29
Choldin, Harvey M., 173*n*, 277*n*
Chudacoff, Howard, 52*n*, 53*n*, 56*n*
Churchill, Winston, 247
Claudius, 33
Clegg, I. E., 38*n*
Clinton, DeWitt, 57
Clinton, William J., 97, 135, 238*b*
Cohen, Carl I., 176*n*
Collins, Catherine, 287*n*
Collins, Stephan, 312*n*
Collymore, Yvette, 331*n*
Cooke, Robert, 23*n*
Coolidge, Calvin, 193
Coulanges, Numa Denis Fustel de, 31*n*
Creel, Herrlee Glessner, 28*n*
Cressey, Paul, 61*n*
Cresswell, Peter, 282*n*
Crowe, Timothy D., 258*n*, 277*n*
Cummings, Scott, 109*n*, 232*n*
Curtis, Lynn A., 231
Curwen, E. Cecil, 22*n*
Cutsinger, Jackie, 157*n*, 243*n*

Daley, Richard J., 116, 364
Danielsen, Karen A., 2618*n*
Daniere, Amrita, 277*b*
Dantzig, George B., 361
Darley, J. M., 173*n*
Darwin, Charles, 73
da Vinci, Leonardo, 32, 39

Davis, Kingsley, 26n, 38n
Davis, Michael, 82, 230n
Davis, William T., 50
Dear, Michael, 82, 176n, 355n
Deauz, George, 39n
D'Emilio, John, 154n
Denton, Nancy, 142n, 202, 203n
de Tocqueville, Alexis, 66
Detwyler, Thomas, 79n
De Voss, David, 347b
de Vries, Jan, 39n
Dickens, Charles, 44, 44b, 172, 173n
Dougherty, Conor, 231n
Douglass, Frederick, 199
Doxiadis, Constantinos, 361
Drabeck, Thomas, 354n
Drake, St. Clair, 202n
Dreiser, Theodore, 12
Duany, Andres, 286, 288
DuBois, W. E. B., 200
Duncan, Beverly, 96n
Duncan, O. D., 9n, 20n, 106
Duneier, Mitchell, 163n
Durkheim, Émile, 14, 17n, 42b, 149, 158
Durrett, Charles, 191n

Eachman, Donald, 79n
Edmonston, Barry, 126n, 219n, 221n
Eisenhower, Dwight D., 96
Eisenstadt, S. N., 36n
Eisler, Kim Isaac, 224n
Eldridge, Hope Tisdale, 17n
Ellison, William, 200
Elmore, Cindy, 252n
Emerson, Ralph Waldo, 360
Engels, Friedrich, 18n, 44b, 45
Epstein, A. L., 334n

Faltermayor, Edmund K., 269n
Farley, Reynolds, 127n, 213
Fava, Sylvia F., 192n, 193n
Feagin, Joe, 17n, 22n, 82n, 84, 106n,
    110n, 125n
Fernandes, Edesio, 302n
Firey, Walter, 12, 18n, 75
Fischer, Claude, 153n, 154, 155n, 169,
    173n, 192n, 234n
Fisher, Robert Moor, 29n
Fishman, Robert, 116n, 360n, 368n
Flaming, Karl, 153n, 359b
Flanagan, William G., 80n
Flannery, Kent J., 22n
Florida, Richard, 158, 261n, 358
Fogelson, R. M., 230n
Fong, Timothy P., 142n, 222n
Ford, Henry, 96, 118
Ford, P. L., 54n
Fox, Gerald, 17n
Fox, James A., 182n
Frantz, Douglas, 287n
Freedman, Jonathan, 173n, 175n
Freudenburg, William R., 153n
Frey, William, 105n, 138n, 142n, 199n,
    201n, 202, 248n, 357n
Frieden, Bernard, 98n,
Friedman, Samantha, 102n, 202n
Frisbie, Parker, 106n
Fromm, Dorit, 191n
Fulton, William, 261n

Galaster, George , 157n, 242n
Galle, O. R., 173n
Gans, Herbert J., 136b, 153–154, 157,
    160, 161n, 173n, 192, 275
Gardner, Robert, 218n, 223n
Garland, Hamlin, 271
Garreau, Joel, 99
Gates, Henry Louis, Jr., 203
Gerth, H. H., 18n
Gettys, Warner E., 75n
Gibbon, Edward, 33
Gilbert, Allen, 340n
Glaab, Charles N., 51n, 54n, 117n, 269n
Glaeser, Edward L., 139n, 202n
Glazer, Nathan, 236n
Glotz, Gustave, 30n
Goffman, Erving, 169
Gottdiener, Mark, 17n, 22n, 75n, 82n
Graham, Dawn, 103n
Graham, Lawrence Otis, 203n
Grant, Madison, 198n
Graunt, John, 40
Green, Constance McLaughlin, 52n, 53n
Greer, Scott, 172, 213, 359
Grier, George, 140n
Grove, Walter R., 173n
Gruen, Victor, 103
Guest, Avery M., 153
Gugler, Joseph, 305n, 336n
Guterbock, Thomas, 98n, 126n
Gyouroko, Joseph E., 261n

Haggerty, Lee J., 79n
Hall, Stephen S., 175n
Halsey, Frank D., 36n
Hamdan, G., 333
Hamilton, Alexander, 56f
Hammel, Daniel J., 240, 256n
Hammond, Mason, 35n
Hance, William, 333n, 339
Hannaford, Ivan, 198n
Hannigan, John, 363n
Hanson, Susan, 193n
Hardoy Jorge E., 321n, 323
Harris, Chauncy, 79
Harris, Fred R., 231
Hartley, Shirley Foster, 168n
Hartline, N., 349n
Harvey, David, 85, 231n
Hatt, Paul K., 106n
Haub, Carl, 23n, 312n
Hauser, Philip, 3n,
Haussmann, Baron, 268
Hawley, Amos, 26, 80
Hayden, Dolores, 191n, 270n
Hays, Allen, 254n
Hemmings, Sally, 199
Herbers, John, 105n, 134n, 355n
Herandez, Leon, Rubin, 214n
Herenblat, Alan, 236n
Heskin, Allan, 275n
Hicks, Louis, 171n
Higham, John, 195n, 197n
Hill, Reuben, 171n
Hiller, Harry A., 156n
Hiorns, Frederick, 37n
Hippodamus of Miletus, 267
Hochschild, Arlie, 193n
Hohenberg, Paul M., 39n

Hollingsworth, Leslie J., Jr., 202n
Hoover, J. Edgar, 222
Howard, Ebenezer, 31, 280–282, 274, 360
Howe, Lord, 53
Hoyt, Homer, 79, 85
Huang, Ray, 23n
Hunter, Albert J., 171n
Hutchinson, Ray, 17n
Huttman, Elizabeth, 254n

Iceland, John, 202n

Jackson, Kenneth T., 51n, 117n
Jacobs, Jane, 23n, 276b–277b, 273, 273,
    363
Jankowski, Martin Sanchez, 183
Janowitz, Morris, 169n, 172
Jaret, Charles, 213
Jayson, Sharon, 249n
Jefferson, Thomas, 56, 66, 199
Jencks, Charles, 82n
Jencks, Christopher, 176, 176n
Jogues, Isaac, 51
Johnson, Daniel, 12, 18n
Johnson, Kenneth, 90n
Johnson, Lyndon, 116
Johnson, Michael P., 200n
Jones, K. O., 79n

Karmen, Andrew, 179n
Kasarda, John, 106n, 169n, 235n, 240,
    356n
Katz, Bruce, 137n, 141n, 356n, 357n
Keating, Larry, 243n, 255n
Keller, Suzanne, 171n
Kelling, George L., 179
Kellogg, Alex, 140n
Kelly, Barbara, 136b
Kennedy, Bingham, Jr., 316n
Kennedy, John F., 116, 129
Kenyon, Kathleen Mary, 22n
Khaldun, Ibn, 26
Kitano, Harry, 222
Kitsuse, Alicia, 261n
Kiviat, Barbara, 251n
Kling, Robert, 298n
Knapp, Gerrit-Jan, 262n
Kneebone, Elizabeth, 134n
Kokin, Joel, 231
Kowinski, William, 102
Kraut, Richard, 32n
Krech, Shepard, 51n
Kurte, Josh, 109n

LaGory, Mark, 96n, 160n
LaGreca, Anthony J., 305n
Lake, Robert W., 137n
Lampara, Eric, 46n
Lamptey, Peter, 331n
Landa, Bishop, 343
Lang, Robert E., 23n, 100n, 137n, 141n,
    261n
Langdon, Philip, 287n, 367n
Langer, William L., 38n, 39n
Laska, Shirley, 240n
Latane, B., 173n
Le Corbusier, 360
Lee, Barrett A., 141n
Lee, Chang-ray, 133n

Lee, Sharon M., 220*n*, 221*n*
Lees, Lynn Hollen, 39*n*
LeFaivre, Michele, 221*n*
Lemann, Nicholas, 137*n*
LeMasters, E. E., 161*n*
L'Enfant, Pierre, 269
Lenski, Gerhard, 27*n*
Lenski, Jean, 27*n*
Levin, Michael J., 223*n*
Levine, Robert, 151, 153
Levy, Frank, 248*n*
Lewis, Oscar, 348*n*
Lewis, Rebecca, 262*n*
Li, Yushi, 321*n*
Lieberson, Stanley, 198*n*
Lincoln, Abraham, 254, 269
Lippmann ,Walter, 211
Lobo, Susan, 225*n*
Lofland, Lyn, 18*n*, 75*n*, 168, 193*n*
Logan, John, 21*n*, 85, 87, 127–128*n*,
    139*n*, 181*n*, 221*n*, 233*n*, 258*n*
London, Bruce, 88*n*, 233*n*
Loo, Chalsa M., 222*n*
Loomis, Charles P., 14*n*
Lorimer, E. O., 34*n*
Louisa, M., 167*n*
Low, Seth, 130*n*
Luconi, Stefano, 197*n*
Lynd, Helen Merrell, 171
Lynd, Robert S., 171

Machiavelli, Niccolò, 363
Mao Tse-tung, 317
Marcuse, Peter, 240, 302*n*
Marshal, Alex, 288*n*
Martain, Philip, 194*n*
Martin, John, 312*n*
Martindale, Don, 31*n*
Marx, Karl, 13–14, 44*b*, 70, 149,150
Masotti, Louis H., 80*n*
Matre, Marc C., 79*n*
McGahan, Peter, 52*n*
McKay, Henry D., 183*n*
McKenzie, Roderick, 7*n*, 16*n*, 73, 93,
    127*n*
McManus, Susan, 193*n*
Mendelker, Daniel R., 268*n*
Menelik II, 337*b*
Merab, Docteur, 337*b*
Merry, Sally, 258*n*
Merton, Robert, 64*n*
Michelangelo, 39
Michelson, William, 192*n*, 283*n*
Milgram, Stanley, 151
Mills, C. Wright, 14*n*
Miranne, Kristine B., 189*n*
Mitchell, J. Clyde, 338*n*
Moeser, John V., 274*n*
Mohan, R., 349*n*
Moi, President, 338
Mollenkopf, John H., 108
Molotch, Harvey, 85, 87, 233*n*
Montgomery, R., 277*n*
Monti, Daniel, 75*n*
Moore, Joan W., 218*n*
Mumford, Lewis, 22, 23, 33, 37*n*, 40, 51*n*
Mundy, John H., 38*n*
Munro, William B., 149*n*

Murphey, Rhoads, 310*n*, 318*n*
Myers, Albert Cook, 52*n*
Myers, Dowell, 212*n*, 261*n*
Myrdal, Gunnar, 199

Nachmias, Chava, 230n, 240*n*,
    242*n*
Nadeau, Richard, 156*n*
Nagourney, Adam, 219*n*
Nagpaul, Hans, 312*n*, 314*n*,
Nelson, Arthur C., 133
Nelson, James, 96*n*
Nelson, Vici, 339*n*
Nero, 33
Neuwirth, Gertrud, 31*n*
Neuwirth, Robert, 294*n*
Newman, F. Baker, 274*n*
Newman, Katherine S., 163*n*
Newman, Oscar, 257, 275
Nixon, Richard M., 210,355

Obama, Barack, 236, 355
Ofshe, Richard, 173*n*
Oglethorpe, James, 269
O'Hare, William P., 142*n*, 217*n*, *224n*
Oldenburg, Ray, 169
Olin, Spencer, 98*n*, 285*n*
Oliver, Melvin L., 204*n*
Olmsted, Frederick Law, 195*n*, 270
Ong, Bill, 213*n*
Orum, Anthony, 82*n*
Osborn, Frederick, 280–281
Oster, Shai, 320*n*

Palen, J. John, 18*n*, 62*n*, 77*n*, 79, 95*n*,
    104*b*, 96*n*, 100*b*, 123*n*, 125*n*, 153*n*,
    157*n*, 183*n*, 202*n*, 233*n*, 240*n*,
    242*n*, 285, 326*n*, 317*n*, 337*b*, 359*b*
Pankhurst, Richard, 337*b*
Park, Robert, 7*n*, 15–16, 18*n*, 73, 127*n*
Parker, Robert, 22*n*, 125*n*,
Parker, William, 106*n*
Pascal, R., 14*n*
Patillo-McCoy, Mary, 204, 204*n*, 238*b*
Penn, William, 50, 53, 269
Perlman, Jannice, 59*n*
Petersen, William, 32*n*
Pettigrew, Thomas F., 201*n*
Philip II, 341
Piggot, Stuart, 29*n*
Pinlott, Daniel, 132*n*
Pirenne, Henri, 36*n*, 37, 39*n*
Plater-Zyberk, Elizabeth, 286, 287
Plato, 32, 266
Pliny, 33
Pollard, Kelvin M., 217*n*, 224*n*
Pons, V. G., 334*n*
Popenoe, David, 136*b*
Poplin, Dennis E., 171*n*
Portes, Alejandro, 212*n*
Poster, Mark, 95*n*, 285*n*
Pratt, Geraldine, 193*n*
Proskouriakoff, Tatiana, 341*n*
Pullman, George, 270
Putnam, Robert, 170

Rainwater, Lee, 163*n*
Redfield, Robert, 15
Reed, Henry, 57*n*

Reid, Lesley Williams, 242*n*
Reishauer, Edwin O., 322*n*
Reitzes, Donald C., 213
Reutter, Mark, 124*n*
Reynolds, Malvina, 135*b*, 135
Reynolds, Sian, 37*n*
Rice, Bradley R., 110*n*
Riesenberg, Peter, 38*n*
Riis, Jacob, 273
Ritzer, George, 150*n*
Roark, James L., 200*n*
Robey, Bryant, 220*n*
Robinson, C. M., 270*n*
Roncek, Dennis, 173*n*
Rondinelli, Dennis, 331*n*
Roof, Wade Clark, 202*n*
Roosevelt, Franklin D., 194, 222, 250
Rörig, Fritz, 36*n*
Rose, Arnold, 135*n*
Rosenbaum, Emile, 202*n*
Ross, Andrew, 287*n*
Ross, E. A., 198
Ross, John, 23*n*, 79*n*
Rossi, Peter H., 176, 176*n*, 177*n*
Roth, Benjamin, 116*n*
Rusk, David, 260*n*, 366*n*
Russell, J. C., 37*n*
Rybcynski, Witold, 58*n*, 261*n*

Saalman, Howard, 36*n*
Saatz, Thomas L., 361
Safdie, Moshe, 363
Sagalyn, Lynne B., 98*n*
Salama, Jerry J., 256*n*
Sale, Kirkpatrick, 109*n*
Salins, Peter D., 213*n*
Sanchez, Loretta, 218, 208*f*
Sanchez, Thomas W., 133
Sanchez-Jankowski, Martin, 217*n*
Sancton, Andrew, 277*n*
Santos, Boaventura, de Sousa, 314*n*
Sanz, Rogelio, 214*n*
Sassen, Saskia, 86*n*, 192–193, 300–301
Sawers, Larry, 109*n*
Scamozzi, Vicenzo, 267
Schaffer, Frank, 282*n*
Schiesl, Martin J., 285*n*
Schneider, Mark, 127–128*n*
Schneider, William, 116*n*, 135*n*, 231*n*
Schnore, Leo, 3*n*, 17*n*, 75, 79*n*, 137*n*
Schuller, Phillip, 54*f*
Schutty, Stanley K., 51*n*
Schwartz, Barry, 137*n*
Schwarz, Phillip, 200*n*
Schwirian, Kent P., 79*n*, 283*n*, 305*n*
Scoffham, E. R., 282*n*
Schulte, Bret, 191*n*
Seeger, Pete, 135
Selassie, Haile, I, 337*b*
Selleck, Tom, 132
Sengupta, Somini, 313*n*
Sethuram, S. V., 302*n*
Shachar, A., 36*n*
Shapiro, Thomas M., 204*n*
Sharma, D. P., 312*n*
Sharp, Harry, 137*n*
Shaw, Clifford R., 18*n*, 183*n*
Sheridan, Alan, 19*n*
Shook, Edwin M., 341*n*

Silver, Christopher, 274n
Silverman, Carol J., 169n
Silverman, Eli B., 179n
Simmel, Georg, 14, 17n, 149, 151
Simpson, George, 14n
Sinclair, Upton, 12
Singer, Audrey, 141n
Sjoberg, Gideon, 42b, 80n, 343
Sjoquist, David, 243n, 255n
Sloane, John J., III, 183n
Smelser, Neil, 106n
Smith, David A., 17n, 82n, 83–84, 86n
Smith, Joel, 79n
Smith, John, 51n
Smith, Judith E., 53n
Smith, Michael P., 18n
Smith, Neil, 233n
Smith, Peter, 220n
Smith, T. Lynn, 341n
Snipp, C. Mathew, 224n
Snyder, Mary Gail, 130n
Socrates, 31
Sohn, Jungyul, 262n
Soja, Edward, 82
Sokolovsky, Jay, 176n
Soleri, Paolo, 361
Sowell, Thomas, 199n
Spain, Daphne, 192, 193, 240n
Speare, Alden, 142n
Spectorsky, A. C., 133n
Spengler, J. J., 9n
Squires, Gregory D., 259n
Srole, Leo, 12n, 153n
Stahura, John M., 128, 141n, 183n
Stegman, Michael, 254n
Stengel, Casey, 72
Stepick, Alex, 212n
Sternlieb, George, 137n, 231
Stevenson, Mary Huff, 97n
Stoll, Michael, 204n
Stout, Robert J., 348n
Strong, Josiah, 59, 66, 196, 197n
Sullivan, Louis, 272
Suro, Robert, 141n
Sutter, Ruth E., 52n
Suttles, Gerald, 159n, 160, 173n, 168n, 356n
Swan, James A., 173n

Tabb, William K., 109n
Taeuber, Alma F., 202n
Taeuber, Karl E., 137n, 202n
Taub, Richard, 204
Taylor, D. R. F., 335n
Teaford, Jon C., 252n
Terkel, Studs, 159, 160n
Thomas, Ray, 282n
Thomas, Wyndham, 282n
Timberlake, Michael, 82n, 83–84, 86n
Titus, 34
Toffler, Alvin, 151
Tönnies, Ferdinand, 13, 14,18n, 149
Trigger, Bruce, 21n
Tringham, Ruth, 21n
Truman, Harry S, 198
Tuan, Mia, 221n
Tucker, William, 237n
Tull, Jethro, 41, 43
Tunnard, Christopher, 57n, 269n
Twain, Mark, 369

Ucko, Peter, 21n
Ullman, Edward, 79–80
Updike, John, 137

Valey, Thomas Van, 202n
van der Rohe, Mies, 360
van Kempten, R., 302n
van Vliet, Willem, 125n, 254n, 326n
Varley, Ann, 302n
Vidich, Arthur J., 10, 17n
Vigdor, Jacob L., 139n, 202n
Vining, Daniel R., 354n
Voss, David De, 347b

Wacquant, Loic J. D., 162n, 204n
Wade, Richard, 199n
Wagner, David, 178n
Wallerstein, Immanuel, 86, 296n
Ward, Sally, 109, 126n
Warner, Sam B., Jr., 55n, 58n, 118n
Warner, W. Lloyd, 171
Warren, Earl, 223
Warren, Roland, 171
Washington, Booker T., 16, 200
Washington, George, 195
Watt, James, 43, 252

Wattenberg, Ben J., 171n
Webber, Melvin M., 159n
Weber, Adna, 17n, 116n
Weber, Max, 13, 15, 17, 31, 36n, 38n, 149
Weihner, Gregory R., 231n
Weinberg, Daniel, 202n
Weiss, Michael, 132n
Wellman, Barry, 171n
Wheeler, David L., 198n
White, Katherine J. Curtis, 153
White, Michael J., 202n
White, Morton, 66n
Whyte ,William, 137, 152, 175, 193, 197
Wiese, Andrew, 141n
Wigley, Merywen, 331n
Wiley, Gordon R., 341n
Williams, Peter, 233n
Willmott, Peter, 173n
Wilson, James Q., 167n, 172
Wilson, Thomas C., 147n
Wilson ,William J., 162n, 182n, 204, 256n
Windsberg, Morton D., 141n
Winthrop, John, 52
Wirth, Louis, 10, 17, 18n, 41b–42b, 72–74, 150–152, 155, 348
Witcox, Jerome E., 202n
Wohlwill, Joachim F., 172n
Wolch, Jennifer R., 172n
Wolfe, Michael, 40n
Wolfe, Tom, 360n
Wood, Peter B., 141n
Woods Tiger, 213
Woodward, C. Van, 200n
Wren, Christopher, 268
Wright, Frank Lloyd, 360
Wright, James D., 176n, 177n
Wright-Isak, Christine, 193n
Wyly, Elvin K., 240, 256n

Young, Alma H., 189n
Young, Brigham, 270
Young, Michael, 173n

Zhou, Min, 221n, 257n
Zlatic, Mila, 86n
Znaniecki, Florian, 18n
Zorbaugh, Harvey W., 18n, 74, 151
Zuniga, Victor, 216n

Subject Index

Note: Page references in **bold** indicate a definition or main discussion; page references with an italicized *f, t, b,* or *n* indicate a figure, table, box, or note on the designated page.

Abu Dhabi, 361–363
"Acrosanti," 361
Addis Ababa, Ethiopia, 304, 334, 337*b*, 331
Africa, 330–340. *See also* North Africa; South Africa; sub-Saharan Africa
  birthrates, 331
  challenges, 331–332
  colonial era, 334
  early empires and cities of, 333–334, 337*b*
  economic policies in, 331–332
  family and kinship ties in societies, 338
  HIV/AIDS in populations of, 331–332
  indigenous cities in, 335, 337*b*
  life expectancy rates in, 311–313
  primate cities in, **335–336**
  regional variations of, 333
  social composition of cities in, 336–337
  squatter slums in, **336**
  status of women, 338–339
  tribal bonds, 338
African Americans, 198–205
  and black flight, 140–141
  crime rates, 181–183
  driving while black (DWB), 182
  economically disadvantaged, 204–205
  economically successful, 203–204
  free persons of color, 200
  Great Migration to the North of, 200–201
  historical patterns, 198–199
  housing discrimination, 202–203
  Jim Crow laws, 200
  moving South, 201
  population and growth of, 198–199
  segregation patterns, 201, 202

  slavery in cities,199
  suburbanization, 138*t*, 137–141
agriculture
  agricultural revolution of, 22–25, 37, 41–42
  changes during the Renaissance period, 39–40
  development of grain cultivation, 22–24
  effects of erosion, deforestation, and war on, 24
  sedentary agriculture and social organization with, 25–26
  slash-and-burn method of, 23
AIDS in Africa, 331–332
air pollution, 61*b*, 81*b*, 295, 347*b*
Albany, New York, 57
Albuquerque, New Mexico, 110
American Dream, 133
American Indians. *See* Native Americans/American Indians
American Revolution, settlement and city growth before and after, 54, 55*t*
Amish, urban influences on, 10
annexation, 118
Annual Housing Survey, 192
"Arcology," 361
Asia, 309–328. *See also specific country*
  cities and urban patterns of, 295–307
  colonial trading cities in, 310, 312
  development of agriculture in, 23
  indigenous and traditional cities in, 310
  new towns in, 325
  urban growth in, 4*f*, 6, 6*t*, 310
Asian American population, 219–224
  education, 220

  ethnic origins of, 221
  model minority, 220–221
  immigration, 210–212
  income and economic status of, 220–221, 223
  projected population in the U.S. of, 219
  residential segregation in, 221–222
  suburban populations of, 142, 222
Athens, Greece, 30–32
Atlanta, Georgia
  amount of sprawl in, 259, 262*b*
  average commuting time in, 123
  black suburban populations of, 138*t*, 137–141
  as brain-gain city, 158*b*
  Hispanic/Latino populations in, 139*t*, 142
Australia
  planned city of Canberra, 362*b*
  urban growth in, 6*t*
Austria, 5
automobile
  and dispersion, 118–120
  in European cities, 279
  impact of the Model T, 118–119
  and pollution, 83
  role in emergence of suburbs, 118–120
  and sprawl, 257
Aztecs, civilization and cities of, 25, 341, 343, 350

"baby boom," 125
baby boomers, 368
Babylon, city site of, 21, 25
Baltimore, Maryland, 55*t*, 85, 158*b*
Baltimore Study, 85
Bangkok, Thailand, 327
Barbary coast, 78*b*

Barcelona, Spain, 37*t*
barriadas, 78
Bath, England, 33
bedroom suburbs, 93, 97
behavior codes, 169
Beijing, China, 295, 320–321
Bible, the
  descriptions of survival of early cities
    in, 29
  Old Testament family systems in, 25
  story of Joseph in, 27
"black death," 38–39, 46. *See* plague
Blue-Blood Estates, suburbs as, 132
Blue-Chip Blues, suburbs as, 132
"BO-BOs," **151**
Bogotá, Columbia, 348
"Bollywood," 294, 295
Bombay. *See* Mumbai
Boomburgs, **100**
"Borrow a bike" plan, 365
Boston, Massachusetts, 52, 54, 55*t*, 75,
  117–118, 158*b*
Boston Common, 72
Bourg, **14**
Bourgeois, **14**
bourgeois utopias, 116
BP oil spill, 111
brain-gain cities, 152*b*
Brasilia, Brazil, 362*b*
Brazil, 5, 86, 343, 349, 362*b*,
"Brownfields," **237, 261**
Brown v. Board of Education of Topeka, 200
burg, **14**
Burkina Faso, 333
Bury My Heart at Wounded Knee (Brown),
  224
Bustees, 314
Byzantine Empire, 36

Cahokia Indians, 49
Calcutta, India. *See* Kolkata
California, 210–211
Canada
  auto use, 279
  Census Metropolitan Areas (CSAs) in,
    94*b*
  crime rates in, 180
  early settlements and growth of, 54
  planning of Mont Royal, 271
  planning of Ottawa in, 272
  "Quiet Revolution " of Montreal in,
    156*b*
  West Edmonton Mall in Alberta, 103,
    104*b*
  "white Canada" immigration policy of,
    198
  and zonal theory, 79
Canberra, Australia, 362*b*
Cape Town, South Africa, 334
capitalism
  Marx and, 13
  political economy approach of, 82–86
Carthage (Tunisia)
  Neolithic population in, 25
  Roman Empire defeat of, 34
Catholic Church and impact of the black
  death, 39
cattle, development of selective breeding
  of, 41–42

Celebration, Florida, New Urbanism
  project of, 287
Central America. *See* Latin America
central business district (CBD), 72, 76*f*,
  77, 80, 234–235
Charleston, South Carolina, 53, 54
Charlottesville, Virginia, 285
Chicago, Illinois, 58, 61,79*b*, 117–118,
  269, 353, 364
Chicago Plan, 272
Chicago School, **15–16,** 74–79, 150–152,
  167
China
  antiurban policies of, 317
  colonial control of treaty ports in, 316
  Communist rule of, 317
  contemporary rural-to-urban forced
    migration in, 317–318
  economic boom in southern rural to
    urban migration in, 317–318
  Nationalist government of, 317
  New Area project of Pudong in, 319
  repression at Tienanmen Square by,
    317
  Special Economic Zones in, 318
Christ, birth of, 34
Cincinnati, Ohio, 57
Cities
  in Africa, 330, 340
  ancient, 25–49
  in Asia, 309–328
  Canadian, 54, 97
  colonial American 54–57
  colonial Asian, 310, 312
  concepts of, 12–17
  crime in, 178–184
  definition of, 7–9
  downtown housing, 235–236
  early American, 50–58
  efficient, 273–274
  and environment, 81*b*
  "Episcopal," 36–37
  ethnics in, 194–197
  evolution in social organization,
    26–29
  and fiscal health, 236–237
  and gender, 193
  global, 299
  and grid patterns, 267
  Hellenic, 31–33
  homelessness in, 175–178
  and immigrants, 194–197
  indigenous African, 335
  indigenous Asian, 310
  and infrastructure, 237
  industrial, 41–42, 58–59
  in Latin America, 340–349
  life-styles in, 148–165
  Mayan, 24–25
  medieval, 36
  and Native Americans, 225–226
  and neighborhood revival, 237
  pollution, in, 61*b*
  and political economy, 231–233
  and population, 26–27
  preindustrial and industrial, 41, 42*b*
  primate, 335–336
  and race, 194–201
  and religion, 155

Renaissance, 39–40
  revival during medieval, 36–37
  Roman, 32–35
  and slavery, 199
  social psychology and culture of,
    11–16, 149–154
  Spanish colonial, 340–343
  and strangers, 167–169
  and Sunbelt, 106–110
  survival of, 30–31
  and technology, 29
  and twenty-first century, 233–234
  and urban crisis, 230–231
  and urban renewal, 251–253
  and urban revival, 231
  and urban revolution, 29
  utopian, 360–365
  world systems theory, 86
City Beautiful movement, 271–273
city efficient, 273–274
city planning. *See* urban planning
"City Study, The" (World Bank), 348–349
Civil Rights Movement, 201–202
Civil War, 55–58
Civitas, **3**
Claritas, commercial definitions of
  suburbs by, 132–133
Clinton, William, 98, 238
coastal living, population shifts to,
  110–111
cohousing and downsizing, **191**
colonialism
  in Africa, 334–345
  in Asia, 310, 312
  Eco Village, 191
  in Latin America, 340–341
  legacy of, 297
Columbia, Maryland, 285–286
Columbian World Exhibition, 271–273,
  272*f*
Combined Statistical Areas (CSAs), 94*b*
common-interest developments (CIDs),
  130–131, 131
communities
  categories of local communities in,
    171–172
  community of limited liability in,
    171–172
  contrived or conscious community in,
    171–172
  defended neighborhoods in, **171–172**
  defined, **171**
  expanded community of limited
    liability in, **171–172**
  gated, 130
  and New Urbanism, 287–288
  and zip codes, 132
Community Development Corporations
  (CDCs), 255
Community for Creative Non-Violence,
  175
commuting, 95–96, 105–106. 123, 205,
  260*f*, 262*b*
compositional theory, **153–154**
concentric-zone hypothesis (also *see* zonal
  hypothesis), 75, 76*b*, 77–79
Consolidated Metropolitan Statistical
  Areas (CMSAs),
  94*b*

contrived or conscious community,
171–172
cosmopolite urban lifestyle, **157**
Country Club Plaza, Kansas City, 103
Copenhagen, Denmark, 365
Corruption
and American cities, 63–64
and political bosses, 63–64
and reform movement, 65
and urban services, 63–65
crime/crime rates
and age, 181
in the Barbary Coast in San Francisco,
78*b*
black on black, 181
"broken window theory" of, **179–180**
city size and, 180–181
crime prevention though
environmental design (CPTED)
and, **275–276**
ethnic and racial composition of,
181–182
juvenile offenders in, 181
lack of street crime in Calcutta, 315
low crime rates in Japan, 324–325
as a male activity, 181
National Crime Victimization Survey
of, **180**
perceptions of, 178–179r
rates of, 178–179
and race, 181–183
and racial profiling, 181–182
street conduct/street etiquette and,
182*b*
in the suburbs, 183–184
Uniform Crime Report (UCR) of, **179**
and youth, 181
crowding, effects of, 172–175
crusaders, impact on populations in
Middle Ages, 37
cultural pluralism model, **212–213**
Curitiba, Brazil, 349

Dallas, Texas, 110
Darwinian struggle, in urban ecology
studies, 71, 85
Daughters of the American Revolution
(DAR), 194
Death and Life of Great American Cities, The
(Jacobs), 267*b*
deconcentration of urban areas, impact
of technology on, 354–355
defended neighborhoods, **171–172**
Defensible Space (Newman), 262
Democratic Republic of the Congo,
331–332
demographic transition, **40–41**, 46
Denmark, urban definition, 7
Density
and crowding, 172–175
and economic development, 322*b*
and New Urbanism, 287–288
Desperate Housewives, 182
determinist theory of urbanism, **152–153**
Detroit, Michigan, 201, 354
developing versus developed countries,
281, 288
Dhaka, Bangladesh, 5, 278*t*
Dick and Jane, 190

DINKS, **157**
disadvantaged, 204–205
dispersion, 60–63
Djibouti, 333
downtown housing, 235–236
drug abuse, 162–163, 238*b*
Dubrovnik, medieval city of, 35*f*
Dutch East India Company, 334
Dutch planning, 280

East Africa, urbanized areas of,
333
ecological complex model in urban
change, **20–21**
ecological perspective, 73–84
and Burgess model, 75–79
criticisms of, 74–75
development of, 73–74
economy
in Africa, 331
in China, 318–319
and cities, 233–239
and density, 322*b*
and gentrification, 241
in Hong Kong, 321
and informal sector, 301
in Japan, 323
in Kolkatta, 313–314
in Latin America, 345, 348–349
in Mumbai, 313
in Singapore, 327
ecosystem, **20**
edge cities, 99–100
Edmonton, 104
education
and African Americans, 203–205
and Asian Americans, 220
in the Hispanic/Latino populations,
217
and Native Americans, 224–225
and Puerto Ricans, 219
and women, 191
Egypt, 27–28,
electric streetcar era, 117–118
Embargo Acts, 54
Emerald City, Oz, 271
emergency management, 366–367
eminent domain, 252
employment
of women, 193
in LDCs, 301–302
in suburbia, 131
Enclosure Acts, 42
England. *See* Britain
environment
and brownfields, 237
and Canadian settlement, 54
and early American settlements, 51,
56–59
and early American transportation, 55
and crime prevention, 275–276
and ecological complex, 20–21
and Jane Jacobs, 276*b*
and nineteenth century cities, 44–45
in POET, 20
"Episcopal cities," 36
equity planning, **275**
Erie Canal, 57
Ethiopian city development, 337*b*

ethnics
and ethnic enclaves, 221
family norms, 161
neighborhood housing, 161
peer group orientation, 160–161
and racial inferiority, 197–198
restrictions on inmovement, 118,
128–129
territoriality of neighborhoods, 160
vulnerability, 161–162, 274
white ethnic immigrants, 194–198
ethnic villagers, **158–162**
ethnicity
in Africa, 338
and immigration, 194–198
and urban populations, 158–162
European and American planning
compared, 277
European planning, 277–280
European social theories of urbanization,
12–15
expanded community of limited liability,
171
Exurbanites, The (Spectorsky), 133
exurbia, 133
exurbs, **133**

Fairfax County, VA, 102, 129
Fair Housing Act of 1968, 202
families
African American variations, 203–205
Asian American supportive family
households of, 221
changes in preindustrial cities of, 41*b*
ethnic life in, 161
faubourgs, 36
favelas, **303**
Federal Housing Administration (FHA),
120–121, 123, 250–251
federal housing programs, 249–252, 255,
257
female domesticity, **189–190**
feminist housing preferences, 191
feudal system, 36–38
fire department organization, 366
First Peoples, 224
first settlements 21–25
Florida housing, 248
"Folk society," 7, 15
Ford plant, Milpitas suburb near, 131
free persons of color, 200
French Canada, 194
funding for urban programs, 355–356
future of cities, 368–369

Gabon, 333
gangs, 162, 182*b*
"garden cities," 280–283, 281*b*
"Gated communities," 130
Gay households, 157–158
Gecekondulas, 78
Gemeinschaft, **14**
gender
and crime, 181
and domesticity, 189–190
gendered housing preferences of,
191–193
gendered public spheres of women,
193

gendered residential space, 190–192
and work place, 193
gentrification
demographic changes in, 240–241
and displacement of the poor, 242
economic factors in, 241
factors contributing to, 228–230, 232
of the Harlem neighborhood, 238b
lifestyle choices with, 241–242
process of, 78, 239–244
as "urban stayers," 244
Gesellschaft, 7
global cities, 219–230
globalization, 86, 230
government
and American new towns, 284–285
and British new towns, 280–283
and downtown housing, 236
and European new towns, 283–284
and European planning, 277–280
and gentrification, 240
great leap forward, China, 317
great migration, 200–201
Great Recession, 90, 98, 108, 123, 156,
163, 233
Greece. *See* Hellenic city
Green Hills, Ohio, 284
greenbelt cities, **280–282**
Greenbelt, MD, 284
Greendale, WI, 284
gridiron plan, 267
growth control, 258
growth models, 75–79, 76b
growth policies, 279–280

"Habitat" (Safdie), 363–364
handguns, 172
Harlem
and gentrification, 98, 238b
and night life, 126
health
in Africa, 331
in eighteenth-century cities, 44–45, 61
and homelessness, 176–177
and urbanization, 12
Hellenic cities, 30–32, 255, 267
Hispanics. *See* Latinos
HIV/AIDS, 331–332
homelessness
amount of, 175–176
characteristics of, 176–178
decreasing tolerance of, 177
housing for, 178
politicized issue of, 178
social disabilities in, 176–177
social problems of, 177–178
Homestead Act, 254
homesteading, 254–255
Hong Kong, China, 321, 322b
HOPE VI projects, 255–257
households, 247, 249
housing
and African Americans, 202–203
in China, 320
costs of, 248–249
downtown, 235
European housing priorities, 278–279
federal policies, 247,
249–251

gendered housing preferences of,
190–191
and gentrification, 237–240
and Hispanics, 141–142
and homelessness, 175–177
in Hong Kong, 321
in India, 313–315
in Japan, 323–324
in Latin America, 346–348
in Levittown 122b
and middle income neighborhoods,
242–243
and New Urbanism, 287–288
and poor, 115
and post WWII, 123–125
price boom, 90
problems, 163
in Roman cities, 34–35
and segregation, 201–203
in Singapore, 326–327
in squatter settlements, 303
subsidies, 251
in suburbs, 119, 123–133
in twenty-first century, 305–306
and women, 191–192
Housing Act of 1937, 250
Housing Act of 1949, 249, 252
Housing and Community Development
Act, 254
Houston, Texas, 20, 106, 110
human ecological approach in urban
studies, 11
human ecology, 11, 73
hunting and gathering societies, 22

Indians. *See* Native Americans
ideal type, 13
ideology of female domesticity, 189–190
immigrants/immigration
arrival of first-wave in America,
194–195
Asian populations, 137, 138, 140t,
219–220
in Burgess's zonal hypothesis, 76f,
77
and early American cities, 64–65
fourth wave, 211–212
Great Migration, 200–201
and growing cities, 357
Hispanic/Latino, 214–216
and immigrant problems, 64–68
and racial inferiority, 197–198
second wave, 195
third wave, 195–198
India, 312–316
Indians. *See* Native Americans
indigenous cities
in Africa, 335, 337b
in Asia, 310
Industrial Revolution, 6–7, 43–44
industrial slums, 44b
industrialization
in Japan, 322
in LDCs, 300
industry
in American cities, 58–63
in China, 310
informal economy, 301–303
infrastructure of American cities, 237

integration
African Americans, 200–203
Asian, 220–221
Hispanic, 217–219
of suburbs, 141
Internet, 95, 102, 368–369
interstate system, 96
invasion and succession, **74**
Iraq, Neolithic farming sites in, 23
Irish, 64, 195
Irving, CA, 285
Islam, advances in the 7th century by, 35

J. C. Penney, 101
Jack Roller, The (Shaw), 16
Jakarta, Indonesia, 5, 327
Jamestown, English settlement of, 51
Japan, 321–325
Japanese American population
assimilation of, 224
financial losses during World War II
of, 212
442nd Regimental Combat Team of,
223
internment camps, 222–223
Nisei, second generation of, 223
racist hysteria against, 211–212, 215
upward mobility of, 223–224
Jarmo, Iraq, 23–24
Jericho, "city" site of, 29–30
Jewish population, 51, 128–129
Jim Crow laws, **200**
Jungle, The (Sinclair), 12

Kampongs, 326
Katrina, hurricane, 234b
Kentlands, MD, 287
Kenya, 338
kingships and dynasties, 27–28, 46
Kisangani, Congo, 334
Know-Nothing Party, 193
Korean War, 308
Kuala Lumpur, Malaysia, 327
Kuwait, 361

Ladies Home Journal, The, 190
Lagos, Nigeria, 5, 330
Lakewood Villages, CA, 120
Las Vegas, NV, 86, 109, 363
Latin America
colonial organization, 341
crime rates in, 345–346
economic change, 345
future of, 346–348
Law of Indies, 350
physical layout of colonial cities in,
341–343
Portuguese colonial cities in, 334, 343
primate cities in, 325
rural migration to cities in, 344–345,
348
shantytowns and squatter settlements
in, 346–348
Spanish colonial cities in, 340–343
urban growth in, 4f, 6t, 343–345
Latino/Latina population diversity,
215–216
growth of population, 214–215
illegal immigrants, 211

income, 215–216
and metropolitan areas, 214–215
and smaller metro areas, 215
suburbanization, 139*t* 141–142
women, 216
less-developed countries
    (LDCs)
age structure, 200
changes, 4–6
and dependency, 296
economy, 301
characteristics of, 300–305
developing versus developed
    countries, 296–297
growth of population, 294–295,
    296–297
informal sector economy in cities of,
    301–303
and multinationals, 300–301
and overurbanization in, **305**
primate cities in, **303–304**
squatter settlements in, **284,** 285, 289
urban growth in, 6, 6*t*
Letchworth, England, 282
Levittown, U.S.A, suburbs as, 121, 122*b,*
    136*b*
life styles in cities
characteristics of, 148–163
and Chicago School, 151–152
and compositional theory, 153–154
and deprived, 163
and determinist theory, 152–153
and ethnicity, 155
and ethnic villagers, 158–162
and gender, 155
and socioeconomic status, 155–156
Lima, Peru, 347
Links, 203
Little Boxes (Reynolds), 135*b,* 135
Llano del Rio, California, 270
limited liability, community of,
    172
London, England, 40, 44, 181, 279, 300
Los Angeles, California, 20, 90, 108, 119,
    159, 368
Los Angeles School of Urban Theory, 82,
    355
Louisiana, out-migration of blacks from,
    192
Louisville, Kentucky, 56

Mali Empire, 333
"malling" of the land, 102–103
Mall of America, 104*b*
malls
characteristics of, 102–104
number of, 116
and safety, 103
Manchester, England, 44*b*
Manhattan. *See* New York
Manila, Philippines, 327
Maquiladoras, 348
marginality, myth of, 348–349
Marxism
conflict-based model of, 82–85
ecological models in, 74
and theory, 13–14
and urban crisis, 231–233
master plans for cities, 275

Mayan cities, 25, 29
McCarran-Walter Act of 1952, 198
"mechanical solidarity," **14**
Medieval cities, 36–38
Medieval feudal system, 36–37
megacities, **5,** 295
"melting pot" model, **212–213**
mental health
    of homeless, 176–177
    in rural and urban populations, 12
Mesa, Arizona, 125
Mesa Verde, cliff dwellings of, 51
Mesoamerica, 24–25, 29
Mesopotamia, 23, 26
"Metropolis and Mental Life, The"
    (Simmel), 14
metropolitan areas
characteristics, 91–97
combined statistical areas, **94***b*
emergence and shifts to the sunbelt,
    106–108
future influences on, 368–369
Metropolitan Statistical Areas (MSAs),
    94*b*
national metropolitan system of,
    105–106
planning for, 365–366
police and fire departments in, 66
political systems in future, 365–366
urbanized areas in, **94***b*
Mexican Americans
characteristics of, 216–219
diversity of, 216–217
education of, 217
housing, 218
political involvement, 218–219
urbanization of, 217
Mexico City, 5, 24*b,* 159, 295, 340–344,
    347*b*
Miami, Florida, 159
Micropolitan Statistical Area (Micro SAs),
    94*b*
Middle Ages. *See* Medieval feudal system
Middle Colonies, 53
middle-income neighborhoods, 242, 243
Middletown (Lynd and Lynd), 171
Middletown in Transition (Lynd and
    Lynd), 171
Middletown study, 171
migration
    and African Americans, 200–201
    and Asians, 219–220
    in China, 317–318
    Great Migration, 200–201
    and Hispanics, 217
    and Native Americans 225
    to U.S. coasts, 110–112
    and white ethnics, 194–198
Milpitas, California, 131
mismatch hypothesis, 235
model minority, 220–221
Model T auto, 118–119
Monterey Park, California, 222
Montreal, Quebec
early settlement and growth of, 52, 54
Parti Quebecois of, 156*b*
"Quiet Revolution" in, 156*b*
"moral density," in preindustrial cities,
    41*b*

moral hazard problem, 111
mortgage crises, 100
Moscow, Russia, 6
muckrakers, 65
multinationals, 300–301
Multi-Nuclei theory, 79–80
Mumbai (Bombay) India, 2, 8, 295,
    312–314
Muncie, Indiana, (Middletown), 171
myth of marginality, 348–349
myth of rural virtue, 69
myth of suburbia, 134–135

Nairobi, Kenya, 325
National Association of Colored People
    (NACP), 258
National Association of Home Builders
    (NAHB), 258
National Crime Victimization Survey, 179
National Flood Insurance Act, 111
national metropolitan society, 105–106
National Origins Act of 1929, 198
national urban policies, 249–252
Nationalists in China, 317
Native Americans/American Indians
assimilation of, 225
census estimates of, 224
economic status and living
    conditions of, 224
education levels in, 224–225
government reservations for, 225
impact of colonial urban growth, 51
movement to the cities of, 225
non-urban orientation of, 225
population growth, 224
profits from reservation casinos of,
    224
non-urban orientation, 225
neighborhoods
characteristics of, 170–172
ethnic suburban, 128
ethnic villagers, 158–160
gentrification of, 238*b,* 239–240
middle-income decline, 242–243
revival of, 237–239
revival of working class, 243
neo-Marxist. *See* political economy
Netherlands
medieval populations in, 38*t*
new towns built in, 280
urban growth policies of, 2280
Nevada
Las Vegas as city of the future in,
    363
New Amsterdam, 53
Newburyport, Massachusetts,
    55*t*
New England, Puritan colonies in, 52
New Orleans, 243*b*
newly industrialized countries (NICs),
    300
New Mexico
Newport, Rhode Island, 53, 55*t*
New towns
American, 284–286
British, 280–283
Dutch, 280
European, 283–284
Hong Kong, 321

Japan, 325
  Singapore, 326–327
New Town Act of 1946, 282
new urbanism
  creating communities with, 286–287
  handling traffic in, 286
  limitations of, 288
  "old-fashioned" style homes in, 287
  rear garage requirements in, 287
  "smart growth" practice in, **286–288**
  as walking small towns, 286
new urban sociology, 83
New York, 5, 55, 57, 59, 64, 82, 90, 96, 101, 108, 181, 260, 300
Newport, Rhode Island, 53, 55t
New Zealand, urban growth in, 6t
Nigeria
  colonial cities in, 314, 331
  indigenous cities in, 315–316
  urbanized areas of, 277, 331
Nile River
  Aswan Dam on, 265
  early cities in, 29
  farming communities along, 23, 26f
  Neolithic farming sites in, 25
Nigeria, 333, 334
Nineveh, urban site of, 21
Nippur, urban site of, 21
Nissei, 223
nonmetropolitan growth areas, 105
Norma Rae–Ville, suburbs as, 133
North American Free Trade Agreement (NAFTA), 349
North Carolina
  Hispanic/Latino population in, 215
  Research Triangle community in, 286
  year-round seaside populations of, 111
Northgate, Seattle, 103
North Shore, Chicago, 4

Oceania, urban growth in, 6t
occupations and gender, 203–204
office space, 109
Old Delhi, India, 312
Oliver Twist (Dickens), 44, 172–173
Olympics, 200b, 321
"organic solidarity," **14, 150**
Oslo, Norway, 279
Ottawa, 272
overurbanization, **305**

pagan, 31
Palma Nova, Italy, 267, 268f
Paris, France, 6, 38t, 80, 268
parks, 270–271
patriarchal family systems, 25
peer-group society, **160–162**
Peking. *See* Beijing
Peoria, 107
Peru, 23, 347
Philadelphia, Pennsylvania, 53, 55, 59
  CMSA in, 93t, 94b
  population growth of, 53, 53t
  urban renewal projects in, 239
Phoenix, Arizona, 107, 110, 123, 259
phratries, 30
Piraeus, Greece, 31, 267
Pittsburgh, Pennsylvania, 61b, 97

plague
  impact on the feudal social structure, 39
  outbreaks in the Middle Ages, 38–39
planning
  of American cities, 268–277
  in ancient Greece and Rome, 267
  approaches, 358–359
  British new towns, 280–283
  City Beautiful, 271–273
  for city dwellers, 363–365
  creating parks systems in, 256, 257
  Dutch, 280
  early planned communities, 270
  equity, 275
  European, 277–280
  of "garden cities," 280, 283
  gridiron pattern in, 267
  and growth policies, 279–280
  in the Hellenic city, 31
  and housing priorities, 278–279
  and Jane Jacobs, 276–277b
  of metropolitan political systems, 365–367
  parks, 270–271
  priorities in European planning, 262–265, 274
  providing security in public housing, 244
  quality of life, 363–365
  in Renaissance cities, 39–41, 46, 267–268
  "smart growth" policies in, 261–263
  transportation, 279
  urban planning in Biblical times, 266–267
  in U.S. cities, 273–274
  utopian communities, 360–363
Plano, Texas, 101
Plessy v. *Ferguson,* 200
plow, invention of, 23
Plymouth Colony, 52
Plymouth Rock, 52
"POET"(population, organization, environment, technology), **20,** 25, 52, 343
police department organization, 366
polis, **30,** 46
Polish Peasant in Europe and America, The (Thomas and Znaniecki), 16, 151
political economy models
  as approach to urban studies, **11,** 20–21
  assumptions, 84–85
  Baltimore study of, 85
  challenges for models of, 86–87
  and urban crisis, 231–233
  urban growth machine theory of, 85–86
  world systems theory of, 86
politics
  in American cities, 6 3–64, 67–68
  and Hispanics, 218–219
  and sunbelt cities, 108–109
  and women, 193
pollution and autos, 119
  in Beijing, 320–321
  in early American cities, 61b
  in Mexico City, 347b

and sunbelt cities, 109–11
and sprawl, 260–261
polygamy, emergence with sedentary agriculture, 25
Pools and Patios, suburbs as, 132
population
  in Africa, 330
  African American, 198
  age structure in developing world, 298f, 300–301
  Asian American, 219–220
  agricultural revolution in growth of, 23–24
  as concept/variable in ecological complex studies, 20
  demographic transition, 40–41
  densities and economic levels in, 322b
  "Population Density and Social Pathology" (Calhoun), 173
  explosion in early settlements, 23–25
  growth in early cities of, 22–23
  growth by region, 6f
  in Hellenic cities, 31–32
  Hispanic, in U.S., 213–215
  in Indian cities, 312, 315
  in Japan, 322–323
  in Latin America, 340
  of Mexico City, 347b
  of medieval cities, 38–39
  in Mesoamerica, 24–25
  movement to the coasts, 110–111
  into metro areas, 91–93, 95
  and Native Americans, 224
  out-movment to periphery in U.S., 95
  and plague, 38–39
  in Roman cities, 32–33
  rural, 105
  shifts in U.S., 92f, 112
  and sunbelt cities, 106–110
  urban percentage of, 6t
  urban percentage U.S. of, 54, 55t
  world population growth of, 44f, 279
Portland, Oregon
  "borrow a bike" plan of, 365
  example of a working city, 367–368
  New Urbanism project in, 287
  "smart growth" policies of, 287, 368
postindustrial city, 97–99
postmodern city, 82
poverty
  in Africa, 336–338
  African American, 199, 201, 204–205
  Hispanic, 216–217
  in India, 314, 324–325
  in Latin America 348–349
  and metropolitan future, 368
  and native Americans, 224–225
  and Puerto Ricans, 219
  suburban poverty, 134–135
Prairie Stone, Illinois, 101f, 102
primate cities
  in Africa, 335–336
  definition and description, **303–305**
  in preindustrial cities, 41–42
  in Latin America, 344
private edge cities, 99–100
projections of urban growth, 306
Providence, Rhode Island, 55t

psychological approach to urban studies,
    11
public housing
    and HOPE VI projects, 255–257
    in U.S. 253–254
Pudong, Shanghai, 319
Puerto Rican population, 215–219
Puritans, in North American colonies, 51,
    52

Qatar, 361
Quebec, Canada, 52, 54, 269
"Quiet Revolution," 156b
Qing dynasty, China, 317

race
    and crime rates, 181–183
    and gentrification, 238b
    and Hispanics, 215–219
    and immigration, 197–198
    and "racial inferiority" of immigrants,
        197
    and restrictive covenants, 202
    and segregation, 201–203
    and suburbs, 137–142
Radburn, New Jersey, 284
railroads, 59, 117, 353
Radstand, 280
redlining, 202
reform movements in cities, 65
religion
    and early cities, 27, 29
    in Hellenic cities, 31
    Mayans and, 24
Renaissance cities, 39–40
Research Triangle, 286
Reston, VA, 285
restrictive covenants, 202
rent vouchers, 255
Rio de Janeiro, Brazil, 343, 346
River Place, OR, 287
Roman Empire, 26, 32–35
Rouse Company, 103
rural image, 68–69
rural vs urban values, 12–16
"rural renaissance" and "rural rebound"
    in, 105
rural simplicity, 12
rurban areas, 133–134
Rustbelt, **107**

safety
    and environmental design, 257–258
    in malls, 103–104
Saigon (Ho Chi Min City), Vietnam,
    326
Saint Petersburg, 6
Salem, MA, 53t
Salt Lake City, UT, 270
San Diego, 110
San Francisco, CA, 78b, 269
San Jose, CA, 130
São Paulo, Brazil, 5, 295
Sears, suburban relocation to "Prairie
    Stone" locations, 101f, 102, 116
Seaside, FL, 287
second wave immigration, 195
Section 8 program, 255
sector theory of urban growth, 79

segmentation in ethnic areas, 160,
    201–203
segregation
    of African-American populations,
        201–203
    and Asian Americans 221–223
    government housing policies of,
        250–251
    of Hispanic/Latino populations,
        217–218
Seoul, Korea, 327
September 11, 2001, urban life after, 2,
    359
serfdom, **36**
settled agriculture and urban
    populations, 22–23, 46
Sex in the City, 155
Shanghai, China, 318–320
shantytowns. *See* squatter settlements
Shelly v. *Kraemer*, 202
shopping malls, 102–104
Silicone Valley, 211
Singapore, 326–327
Sister Carrie (Dreiser), 12
slash-and-burn agriculture, **23**
slaves/slavery, 51, 198–199
Small House Society, 191
Small Town in Mass Society (Vidich and
    Bensman), 10
"smart growth" policies
    advantages, 261–262
    legislation, 262–263
    policies, 368
social class
    and African Americans, 203–205
    and clothing, 168–169
    development of, 28
    and kinship, 28
    in Medieval towns, 37
    in suburbs, 128–130, 131–133
social media
    Facebook, 10, 153, 170
    Twitter, 10, 98
social organization
    in African cities, 330–336, 338–240
    in early cities, 12
    in Hellenic cities, 31–33
    in Latin American cities, 345–349
    in Levittown, 136b
    in medieval towns, 36–37
    in the Renaissance, 39–40
    in Roman Empire, 33–34
social evolution, in early cities, 26–28, 46
social integration, in preindustrial cities,
    42b
"Socialist City," 255
social planning approaches
    assumptions of problem solving in,
        358, 359t
    conventional approaches to, 358, 359t
    radical approaches to, 359, 359t
    reformist approaches to, 358, 359t
social psychology of urban life, 9–12, 14,
    149–154
social theories of change, 12–16
sociocultural approach, 11, 75
socioeconomic status
    and African Americans, 199–200,
        203–205

and Asian Americans, 220–221
    emergence of, 25–27
    and Hispanics, 215–217
    indicators of, 168–169
    and Native Americans, 224–225
    and suburbs, 117–121, 134–136
social psychology of urban life, 9–12, 14,
    149–154
Songhay empire, 333
South Africa, 331, 333
Southdale Center MN, 103
Southeast Asia, 325–328
southern colonies, 53–54
South Korea, 84
Spain
    arrival of conquistadors in Mexico
        City, 24b, 25
    colonization in Central America by, 49
    early cities of, 33
Spanish Law of the Indies, 350
Special Economic Zones
    in China, 318
spillover in suburbs, 128, 141
sprawl
    amount of, 259–260
    auto driven, 259
    costs and consequences, 260–261
    in developing world, 303
    Dutch solutions, 280
    and growth control, 258
    and smart growth, 261–262
    and suburbs, 262
    and voters, 123
SRO (single room occupancy) housing,
    178
St. Petersburg, Russia, 5
"Stadtluft macht frei" ("City air makes one
    free"), 38
Standard State Zoning Enabling Act,
    274
Stockholm, Sweden, 279
Storyville district of New Orleans, 75b
strangers in the city, 168–169
streetcars, 61, 117–118
street etiquette, 182b
Streetwise (Anderson), 182b
"subcultural theory," **154**
Sub-Saharan Africa
    early cities, 333–334
    epidemic of HIV/AIDS in, 331–332
    indigenous cities, 335, 337b
    primate cities in, **336**
    social composition of, 336–338
squatter slums, 336
    women in, 338–339
suburbanites, 358
suburbs
    affluent neighborhoods in, 128–129
    and African Americans, 137–141
    annexation of, 118
    and Asian Americans, 130b, 142
    and automobiles, 118–120
    as "bourgeois utopias," 116
    as "boxes in a row," 135b
    business growth, 100–102
    categories of, 127–133
    causes of growth, 123–125
    characteristics of suburbanites, 134
    commercial definitions of, 132

common-interest developments,
130–131
CIDs in, **130–131,** 143, 259
dominance of, 116
emergence of, 116–117
ethnicity and religion in, 128
exodus to, 123–126
exurbs, 133
and FHA and VA loans, 123
and future, 368–369
gated communities, 130
and integration, 141
in Japan, 325
Levittowns, *120f,* 122*b*
and mass suburbanization, 120–121
and minorities, 137–142
myth of, 135–137
non-reasons for, 125–126
persistence of characteristics, 127–128
rurban, 133–134
sprawl, 121–123, 262*b*
in the twenty-first century, 357–358
and white flight, 140
and zoning, 369
subcultural theory, 154
sunbelt
advantages of, 106–108
consequences, 109
problems, 109–110
Sweden
control and ownership of land, 278
new towns, 283–284
public transportation, 279

Taipei, Taiwan, 327–328
Tammany Hall, 63–64
tax credits, 257
technology
and American cities, 58–63
and dispersion, 60–63, 354–355
and early cities, 25–26, 28–29
and ecological complex, 20–21, 73–74
and deconcentration, 106
and first urban revolution, 29
and Hellenic city, 31
in industrial revolution, 43–45
and medieval cities, 37
and Renaissance cities, 39–40
in Roman empire, 34
and social planning, 359
and sunbelt, 110, 112
tenement reform, 273
Teotihuacan, Mexico, 24, 46
terriorality, 160
theorists of social life, 12–16, 149–151
Third World. *See also* LDCs, 299, 300–305
Tiananmen Square, 317
Title VIII, 203
Tokyo-Yokohama, Japan
bicycle use, 324
castle-town of Edo in, 321–322
commuting time, 324
crime rates, 324–325
housing conditions in, 323–324
infrastructure spending and planning,
325
planned new towns, 325
Toronto, Ontario, 130, 220, 276
towns in colonial America, 50–54

"Traditional society," **14,** 150
transportation
automobile and suburbs, 118–119
"borrow a bike" plans for, 365
commuting, 95, 325
electric streetcar era of, 117–118
federally funded expressways for, 96,
123–124
federal policies for, 337
interstate system for, 96
metropolitan growth with advances in,
95
and New Urbanism, 286–288
public transit policies in, 279, 368
railroad systems in, 59, 117
Roman Empire routes of, 34, 46
shipping by air in, 93
suburban emergence with, 116–119
systems in Tokyo-Yokohama, 324
trucking of intercity goods in, 96
Treatise on Domestic Economy
(Beecher), 189
treaty ports in China, 316–317
tribal subsystems, in Africa
twenty-first century patterns, 233–235
Two More Rungs, suburbs as, 131
typologies, 13–15

underclass, 2–4, 205, 368
Uniform Crime Report (UCR), 179
United Arab Emirates, (UAE), 361–363
United Nations, 5f, 5n, 6n, 7n, 277, 282,
287, 294–295, 311, 325, 331
United Nations Centre for Human
Settlement, 311n
University of Chicago (See Chicago
School)
unmarried or childless, 157
urban
behavior codes, 169
bosses, 63–64
change, theories of, 12–17, 149–154
characteristics of population,
154–157
concentration, 59–60
corruption, 63–64
crime,178–183
crisis, 230–233
definition of, **94***b*
dispersion, 60–63
ecology, 20–21, 73–79
explosion, 6–7, 294–297
fiscal crisis, 230–231
funding, 355–356
growth, 3, 90–93
growth machine, 85–86
growth policies, 279–280, 283–284
homesteading, 254–255
imagery,65–69
life styles, 157–158
political economy models, 82–87
predictions, 368–369
reform, 65
renewal, critique of 252–253
revival, 231
revolution, 3, 29, 45
theories, 12–16, 149–154
urban planning. *See* planning, Urban
Renewal Act

urbanism
as a way of life, 41*b*–42*b,* 151–152, 348
defined, **9–10**
"Urbanism as a Way of Life" (Wirth),
17, 41*b*–42*b* 145–146, 158
urbanization
in Africa, 333–340
and African Americans, 200–203
in American cities, 54–63
and Asian Americans, 225–226
in China, 316–321
definition of, **8–9**
and division of labor, 27–28
and environment, 81
and Hispanics, 217
in industrial cities, 43–46
in Japan, 322–323
in Latin America, 340–345
in LDCs, 294–305
and Native Americans, 225
percentage of world, 4*t,* 6*t*
process of, 43
and social theories, 12–16
and women, 190–193
and world system, 86
urbanized areas, defined by census, **94***b*
urban renewal policies, 251–254
Utopian cities, 360–363

Vancouver, British Columbia, 19, 82, 236
Van Dyke housing, New York, 257–258
Veterans Administration (VA), 121, 122*b,*
123
vandals, 34
Versailles, planning of, 267
Vienna, Austria, 5, 33, 38*t*
Vietnam War, 326
Villa El Salvadore, Peru, 347

Walt Disney Company, 287
War of 1812, 54
Washington, D.C.
Asian American suburban populations
of, 140*t,* 142
black suburban populations of, 138*t,*
139–141
as a "brain gain" city, 158*b*
"city beautiful" projects in, 272
city planning of, 269
urban housing revival in, 252
Welwyn Garden City, 282
West Africa, 333
West Edmonton Mall, 104*b*
"While the City Sleeps," 12
women
in Africa, 338–339
and female domesticity, 189–190
and Hispanics, 216
and housing, 191–192
in metropolitan life, 189
in planned communities, 191
and public spaces, 193
and residential space, 190–191
in suburbs, 191–192
in the workplace, 193
working-class suburbs, 131–132
World Bank, 294
World Columbian Exhibition. *See*
Columbian World Exhibition

world systems theory, 86–87
World War I, prewar suburb patterns of, 118
World War II, 78, 93, 119–120, 251, 282, 354

Yangtze river valley, 316
Yankee City (Warner), 171
youthful age of LDC cities, 298*f*, 300–301

yuppies, **157**

Zip codes, market research of, 132
zonal hypothesis
    Burgess growth hypothesis, 75, 76*b*, 77–79
    in Canada, 79
    limitations of, 79

outside North America, 80, 82
    and role of culture, 75
zone of transition, 76*f*, 77
zoning
    in early suburbs, 119
    as a control device,
    history of zoning in U.S., **274**
    and Jane Jacobs, 276

About the Author

J. John Palen is professor emeritus at Virginia Commonwealth University. He is the author of over a dozen books, is listed in *Who's Who in America*, has received the Virginia Commonwealth University Distinguished Scholar Award, was a Distinguished Fulbright Chair, and has held the Fulbright Chair in North American Studies at the University of Calgary. He has received research grants from NSF, NIMH, the Population Council, and the Ford and Rockefeller Foundations. Dr. Palen is a Civil War buff who enjoys progressive jazz, hiking in Virginia's Blue Ridge Mountains, and observing the street life of urban places.